READINGS

CRIMINAL JUSTICE

Volume 3 of *Crime and Society*

The Sociology of Work: Concepts and Cases by Carol Auster

Adventures in Social Research: Data Analysis Using SPSS by Earl Babbie and Fred Halley (available in *DOS* or *WINDOWS* version)

Crime and Everyday Life: Insights and Implications for Society by Marcus Felson

Race, Ethnicity, Gender, and Class: The Sociology of Group Conflict and Change by Joseph F. Healey

Sociological Snapshots: Seeing Social Structure and Change in Everyday Life, 2nd ed., by Jack Levin

Expressing America: A Critique of the Global Credit Card Society by George Ritzer

The McDonaldization of Society, rev. ed., by George Ritzer

Shifts in the Social Contract: Understanding Change in American Society by Beth Rubin

The Pine Forge Press Series in Crime and Society

VOLUME 1 *Crime*
edited by Robert D. Crutchfield, George S. Bridges, and Joseph G. Weis

VOLUME 2 *Juvenile Delinquency*
edited by Joseph G. Weis, Robert D. Crutchfield, and George S. Bridges

VOLUME 3 *Criminal Justice*
edited by George S. Bridges, Joseph G. Weis, and Robert D. Crutchfield

The Pine Forge Press Series in Research Methods and Statistics,
edited by Richard T. Campbell and Kathleen S. Crittenden

Investigating the Social World: The Process and Practice of Research by Russell K. Schutt

A Guide to Field Research by Carol A. Bailey

Designing Surveys: A Guide to Decisions and Procedures by Ronald Czaja and Johnny Blair

How Sampling Works by Richard Maisel and Caroline Hodges Persell

Sociology for a New Century
A Pine Forge Press Series edited by Charles Ragin, Wendy Griswold, and Larry Griffin

Global Inequalities by York Bradshaw and Michael Wallace

How Societies Change by Daniel Chirot

Cultures and Societies in a Changing World by Wendy Griswold

Crime and Disrepute by John Hagan

Gods in the Global Village by Lester R. Kurtz

Waves of Democracy: Social Movements and Political Change by John Markoff

Development and Social Change: A Global Perspective by Philip McMichael

Constructing Social Research by Charles C. Ragin

Women and Men at Work by Barbara Reskin and Irene Padavic

Cities in a World Economy by Saskia Sassen

READINGS

CRIMINAL JUSTICE

Volume 3 of *Crime and Society*

EDITORS

George S. Bridges

Joseph G. Weis

Robert D. Crutchfield

University of Washington, Seattle

PINE FORGE PRESS

Thousand Oaks, California   London   New Delhi

For information address:

 Pine Forge Press
A Sage Publications Company
2455 Teller Road
Thousand Oaks, California 91320
(805) 499-4224
E-mail: sales@pfpsagepub.com

Sage Publications Ltd.
6 Bonhill Street
London EC2A 4PU
United Kingdom

Sage Publications India Pvt. Ltd.
M-32 Market
Greater Kailash I
New Delhi 110 048 India

Printed in the United States of America

Library of Congress Cataloging-in-Publication Data

Criminal justice / editors, George S. Bridges, Joseph G. Weis, Robert D. Crutchfield.
p. cm. — (Crime and society; v. 3)
Includes bibliographical references and index.
ISBN 0-8039-9080-4 (p: alk. paper)
1. Criminal justice, Administration of—United States
I. Bridges, George S. II. Weis, Joseph G. III. Crutchfield, Robert D.
IV. Series.
HV9950.R42 1996
964.973—dc20   95-43517

96 97 98 99 10 9 8 7 6 5 4 3 2 1

Production Manager: Rebecca Holland
Special Editor: Gillian Dickens
Typesetter: Janelle LeMaster
Design: Susan Hood
Cover: Lee Fukui and Mauna Eichner

About the Editors

The editors of **Crime and Society** are criminologists in the Department of Sociology at the University of Washington. Each has been actively involved for many years in studying crime and teaching courses in criminology, juvenile delinquency, and criminal justice. They have worked together on a number of major research projects, developed a coordinated curriculum in the area of deviance and social control, and share a strong commitment to teaching, especially at the undergraduate level. Their courses are among the largest on campus, with enrollments of hundreds of students. Their many years of teaching experience are reflected in the organization and content of each of the three volumes, as is their editorial experience, which they drew upon to edit the papers in each reader.

George S. Bridges is Associate Professor of Sociology and Director of Faculty Fellows, a program for faculty teaching effectiveness. He has served as a staff member of the policy office of the Attorney General of the United States as well as Deputy Editor of *Criminology*. Among his publications is *Crime, Inequality, and Social Control,* with Martha Myers.

Robert D. Crutchfield is Associate Professor of Sociology and Director of the Institute for Ethnic Studies. He served on the Washington State Juvenile Sentencing Commission and is also a former juvenile probation officer and adult parole officer. He was a Deputy Editor of *Criminology* and has published a number of papers on labor markets, crime, and racial and ethnic disparities in the administration of justice, including "Labor Stratification and Violent Crime."

Joseph G. Weis is Professor of Sociology and the Director of the Center for Law and Justice. He served for a number of years as the Director of the National Center for the Assessment of Delinquent Behavior and Its Prevention, funded by the U.S. Department of Justice, as well as a member of the Washington State Governor's Juvenile Justice Advisory Committee. He is a past Editor of the journal *Criminology* and a co-author, with Michael J. Hindelang and Travis Hirschi, of *Measuring Delinquency.*

About the Publisher

Pine Forge Press is a new educational publisher, dedicated to publishing innovative books and software throughout the social sciences. On this and any other of our publications, we welcome your comments and suggestions. Please call or write to:

Pine Forge Press
A Sage Publications Company
2455 Teller Road
Thousand Oaks, California 91320
(805) 499-4224
Fax (805) 499-7881
E-mail: sales@pfp.sagepub.com

Crime and Society

is dedicated to

Clarence C. Schrag,

colleague and friend

Brief Contents

Detailed Contents

Foreword

WHEN I was a graduate student studying the best works in criminology, my equally striving graduate student colleagues and I knew every work worth reading in the field. I mean *every work*. I could quote volumes, numbers, pages of *Journal of Criminal Law and Criminology*. I could cite chapters from Barnes and Teeters, Kinsey, Gillin. Nothing escaped us.

As we have shown in *Evaluating Criminology* (New York: Elsevier [with Robert M. Figlio and Terence P. Thornberry] 1979), there was an explosion of criminological literature in the 28 years from 1945 to 1972. Since then, there has been an even greater increase in publication of books and articles in this field. Not even the most ardent reader can keep abreast of everything. Selections have to be made.

Having made selections for publications in the past, I know the difficulties of making choices, of screening among the enormous numbers of publications for inclusion in a series. I have carefully read the table of contents and many of the articles in these three volumes and am prepared to defend them as the best in the field.

These three editors have shown that age of publication is less important than substance. Some pieces are from 1938, 1958, and the early 1960s. Why? Because they are nearly timeless in the significance of their observations, theory, or empirical research. There are also very recent articles of excellence.

Within the three volumes is the essence of the best we know in causation, theory, delinquency, and criminal justice. Anyone who reads and absorbs the readings of these volumes will have a full degree of knowledge to match anyone in the field of criminology. We cannot read everything, but we can read the cream of the crop. This is what is contained in these three volumes—works that cut across time and ideologies.

–MARVIN E. WOLFGANG

Preface

AS we near the end of the twentieth century, few social problems arouse the visceral public response as does crime. Seemingly, every politician wants to get tough on crime, the popular media continue to show great interest in it as news or entertainment, and at colleges and universities students and teachers alike spend considerable time and energy studying, thinking, and talking about crime, juvenile delinquency, and criminal justice. When it comes to crime and its control, things have not changed much. Twenty-five years ago, in *Crime and Justice,* Leon Radzinowicz and Marvin E. Wolfgang wrote, "There can be no doubt that optimism has gone, platitudes have proven empty. We are living through a time when, more than ever before, there can be no consensus on how to tackle crime. We do not feel it our business to try to resolve the current conflicts, but we feel it our duty to try to reflect them." Today, criminologists, politicians, and the general public are no closer to consensus on how to confront the problem of crime. In the three volumes of **Crime and Society** (*Volume 1: Crime, Volume 2: Juvenile Delinquency,* and *Volume 3: Criminal Justice*) we too do not attempt to settle the continuing controversies about crime, but we do try to represent the range of debate about the causes of crime and the variety of approaches to its control.

The idea for an integrated set of readings on a comprehensive range of criminological topics came out of our experiences as both students and teachers. When we were students, each of us took a variety of courses in criminology (at the University of California at Berkeley, the University of Pennsylvania, and Vanderbilt University, respectively) that used one or more of the volumes in the classic set of readings in criminology that Wolfgang, Savitz, and Johnston initiated, the first edition being published in 1962 (*The Sociology of Crime and Delinquency* and *The Sociology of Punishment and Corrections*) and the last in 1970. The concept of coordinated anthologies on crime was continued in 1971 by Radzinowicz and Wolfgang, with the publication of a set (*Crime and Justice*) of three edited volumes entitled *The Criminal in Society, The Criminal in the Arms of the Law,* and *The Criminal in Confinement.*

When we became professors, we used these three readers in courses we taught on criminology, juvenile delinquency, criminal justice, and corrections. It seemed like everyone in the field had a set of these volumes on their bookshelf, using them in their undergraduate and graduate classes, as well as for reference and research purposes. With the publication of the last editions in 1977, a void in the field was created that we certainly noticed (and we suspect that many others in the field did as well). That was almost twenty years ago, and nothing quite like those comprehensive, integrated sets of readers on crime has come along to fill that void. So, we decided to resurrect that legacy with **Crime and Society.**

The organizing principle behind **Crime and Society** is that the scholarly literature, both the old and the new, provides an important basis for thinking about crime, for professionals, students, and the general public. As a result, we have included some of the classic works of criminology along with contemporary empirical research. We have included theoretical statements and pieces that reflect how those theories have developed since their initial statements. It is our belief that students will be better educated if they have the opportunity to study the diversity of the criminological literature.

In compiling these three volumes we have had to make two kinds of choices. The first was simply what to include, or more accurately, what to exclude. There is a great deal of good work written by our colleagues that could have been included, but we had to make some difficult choices. Second, a number of selections could have been placed in more than one of the volumes, but we decided that the books would better serve readers if they did not duplicate selections. In fact, we intentionally selected a number of papers because they complement pieces in another volume. As a result, you will find that **Crime and Society,** as a series, covers most of the important issues in contemporary criminology.

The three volumes began in our conversations about teaching our classes at the University of Washington. We believe that students should read the actual work of scholars who study crime, juvenile delinquency, and criminal justice. Reading the original literature is an important part of a liberal education. The public debate about crime and what to do about it will be better informed if the public is exposed to what we know, how we have come to know it, as well as to what we do not know.

Nearly all of the selections in **Crime and Society** have been used in one or more of our courses. We have included, and even emphasized, a number of theoretical pieces because they form the basis of scholarship in criminology and also because most common-sense explanations of the causes of crime and delinquency have actually been captured in those theories. When we explain this to students we can help them see why theory is important to criminologists and also why it can be of interest to them. The empirical pieces in these volumes frequently reflect modifications and refinements in classic theories. The books also contain some work that can be characterized as basic, and some as applied, research. In the *Juvenile Delinquency* and *Criminal Justice* volumes, readers will find literature on societal responses to crime, as well as on its prevention.

We have attempted to edit the pieces to make them more accessible to students who are not yet familiar with the subject matter of criminology or with the research procedures and statistical methods used by criminologists while maintaining the critical substance and message of each paper. Study questions and suggested readings for students are included for every section in each of the three volumes of **Crime and Society.** There is also an accompanying *Instructor's Manual* for the set of readers, which includes multiple choice and essay questions for every reading, a synopsis of each paper, and suggestions for using the books, independently or together, in courses on crime, juvenile delinquency, and criminal justice.

The Foreword to the series, **Crime and Society,** was written by Marvin E. Wolfgang, and an Introduction to *Crime* by James F. Short, Jr., to *Juvenile Delinquency* by Travis Hirschi, and to *Criminal Justice* by Jerome H. Skolnick. Their essays set the stage, we hope, for a broad exposure to some of the best thinking and research on crime and its control produced by criminologists over the years, in different academic disciplines, with different theoretical and ideological orientations, and diverse ideas on the best ways to prevent and control crime in our society.

Acknowledgments

Assembling the readings that comprise the three volumes of **Crime and Society** has been particularly challenging. Many persons, beyond those whose work is included in the volumes, assisted in the completion of the series. Although we alone are responsible for the editing, we are indebted to each of these individuals for their efforts. We could not have completed the series without their dedication and help.

Among the most important has been graduate student Eddie Pate in the Department of Sociology, who worked with us in locating and assembling the readings for the books. He worked tirelessly in obtaining the readings and deserves much credit in assisting us in meeting important deadlines. Dee Boersma assisted in the preparation of the draft manuscripts. She was a source of encouragement *and* organization. Without her persistence and determination in getting through the manuscripts, we might all have decided that the effort of assembling and editing the work was impossible. Janet Wilt in the Department of Sociology also assisted our efforts. Her last-minute work in editing and revising many of the manuscripts was extremely helpful. Finally, the editorial staff at Pine Forge Press—Rebecca Holland, Sherith Pankratz, and Gillian Dickens— were encouraging throughout the production process in a way that kept us on-task. We much appreciate their competence and their friendly approach to a difficult job.

Steve Rutter, the president of Pine Forge Press, deserves enormous credit for his tireless commitment to this project and to the vision of developing books that have value in the classroom. Throughout the course of this project, Steve's encouragement and enthusiasm for this series never diminished. And when the three of us were overwhelmed with the details of editing manuscripts and could not capture the forest from the trees, Steve routinely offered insights and advice that enabled us to complete this work successfully. We are deeply indebted to him for his support and excellent ideas.

Many graduate students in the department of sociology assisted our efforts less directly but in no less important ways: Kristin Bates, Rod Engen, Randy Gainey, Charis Kubrin, and Sara Steen—many collaborators on ongoing research projects—exhibited enormous tolerance of the time this project took away from our other responsibilities at the university and in our research. In their own ways, each carried some of the weight of editing this series by helping out in these other areas. We are extremely indebted to each of them.

We are particularly grateful for the helpful comments supplied by reviewers of earlier drafts of three manuscripts, including:

Barbara Costello, *Mississippi State University*
Michael Israel, *Kean College*
Jim Kanan, *Pennsylvania State University*
A. L. Marsteller, *Drury College*
Bruce MacMurray, *Anderson University*
Jon'A Meyer, *University of New Mexico*
Carrie Uihlien Niles, *Marshall University*
Dwayne Smith, *University of North Carolina, Charlotte*

Finally, our families supported us through this project. In their own ways, George's family (Kari, Lauren, Seth, Anna, and James), Bob's family (Susan and Danielle), and Joe's family (Karen, Braia, and Brett) deserve enormous credit for putting up with the long evenings and weekends, in addition to the moments of frustration and difficulty, associated with completing a project of this magnitude in a timely and effective way.

–THE EDITORS

Introduction

WHEN we envision the idea of a liberal education, what comes to mind is surely not studies in criminal justice. Aristotle and Plato, Shakespeare and Milton are the sorts of names that resonate to the concept of an educated person, as well they should.

I would argue, however, that familiarity with theories and research in criminal justice are part of what is means to be one who can richly fulfill a classical notion of citizenship based on knowledge and understanding. Just as an undergraduate education is incomplete without a knowledge of American and world history, so too, I suggest, is an undergraduate education lacking knowledge of the best writings in criminal justice.

The principal question of Plato's *Republic* and of the political philosophers who followed him—Hobbes, Locke, Mill, and Bentham—was "What does it mean for a state to be just?" If that is the question, part of the answer must be found in the theories, the organization, and the practices of criminal justice. And the readings in this volume attest this is no simple matter.

Consider the richness and complexity of the topics covered in this volume. First, we learn that criminal justice is basically about a system for the implementation of punishment. The law of crimes, the substantive criminal law, is a demanding moral code. The procedural criminal law embodies some of our most prized ideas of criminal justice, such as that a person accused of crime shall be presumed to be innocent, and the state bears the burden of proving guilt beyond a reasonable doubt. These ideas are moral at their core and reflect our abhorrence at imprisoning an innocent person.

And what could be more important to contemplate when weighing the justice of a state than the rationale for that system? One of those, retribution, presumably satisfies our feelings for what is equitable. The capital punishment of a murderer does nothing to bring the victim to life, but it may bring a feeling of vindication and closure, of justice served, to those closest to her or him. The other rationales for punishment are more practical. An incapacitated criminal cannot commit crimes beyond the walls of prison. When released, the painful experience of prison may deter the criminal from committing further crimes. Others, who might consider committing criminal acts, may be dissuaded by the threat of imprisonment. So goes the theory of deterrence, discussed in the articles in this volume, as is the question of whether criminals can be rehabilitated.

Criminal justice does not happen automatically. Criminals must be apprehended, prosecuted and tried. But to say that we assign police to apprehend criminals is altogether too simple. As the articles in this volume discuss, discretion is inseparable from the act of policing. Police interpret behavior and they share a culture, a way of looking at the world that influences their decision to arrest and charge. And they are the criminal justice actors who are closest to the people. Every adult has had some experience with a cop, positive or negative or both. And since the capacity to use force is central to the role of the police, the punishment they mete out may happen on the street as well as in the courtroom, where prosecutors, defense attorneys, and judges are the key players.

Criminologists who have studied these players have addressed the realities of the criminal justice system, along with its ideals. Most criminal cases are settled outside of court, through guilty pleas settlements negotiated between defense attorneys and prosecutors. Judges exercise more or less control over these, depending upon the jurisdiction. Besides, the role of the judge in sentencing has become increasingly restricted, as more states and the federal government have adopted sentencing guidelines mandated by legislatures and the Congress. When guideline sentencing prevails, the prosecutor's decision to charge the defendant with a more or less serious offense determines severity of penalty more than the sentencing decision of a judge.

In a just state, every citizen would be treated equally by the criminal justice system, regardless of color, race, gender, or other social attributes. Is American criminal justice unbiased? In some ways, yes; in others, no. The articles in Part V discuss this important and increasingly controversial issue.

Finally, when someone is convicted of a crime, what will they experience when sentenced to serve time in an American prison? What are alternatives to imprisonment and how effective are they in achieving the rationales for punishment that are discussed in the beginning of the volume? The readings in the final part discuss these issues, and so the readings come full circle. Students who examine them carefully will have been informed of the many realities and complexities of American criminal justice practices and policies. They consequently will be better able to consider and perhaps even answer the classical question of political theory, that is, whether the nation in which they reside fulfills the qualities of a just state.

–JEROME H. SKOLNICK

I

WHAT IS CRIMINAL JUSTICE? PERSPECTIVES ON THE STUDY OF PUNISHMENT

I N recent years, increased concern about crime has prompted public and political leaders across the country to pursue changes in the administration of criminal justice that seek to improve our society's response to criminal behavior. Citizen initiatives have launched new measures that increase the severity of penalties for crime. Police departments have initiated new approaches to policing in an effort to increase their effectiveness in controlling crime. State and federal governments have undertaken major capital construction programs to expand the capacity of our communities' prisons and correctional facilities.

Despite the salience of public concern and the prominence of some of these measures, there is little agreement about what criminal justice is and ought to be in our society. Whereas some groups want the legal process to be more efficient in handling criminal cases and less concerned about protecting the rights of persons accused of crimes, other groups are acutely concerned that any attempts to enhance the effectiveness of law enforcement or the courts in combating crime will either eliminate or seriously weaken important legal protections that safeguard defendants in criminal cases. Similarly, although some members of our society believe that our current legal process is soft on crime and that harsher prison sentences are needed for convicted felons, others point to the large number of persons already in our state and federal prisons and argue that the United States currently has one of the most punitive legal systems in the world.

Scholars who study criminal justice—sociologists, political scientists, and criminologists—recognize that it is not necessarily possible or desirable to reconcile such differing views on crime and punishment. Rather, most believe that issues in criminal justice are extremely complex and that multiple perspectives offer different vantage points for studying and explaining these issues. Furthermore, most would argue that understanding different perspectives on criminal justice is an important beginning point for identifying the specific problems encountered in the administration of criminal justice and for developing more effective remedies to crime in our society.

This first section of our book explores different perspectives on the study of criminal punishment. The essays included in this section examine the question, What is criminal justice? They identify different approaches to the study of criminal justice and different factors that may influence the operation of the criminal justice system.

David Garland's essay, "The Study of Punishment," lays a groundwork for this book and our approach to the study of criminal justice. Garland argues that justice—the study of penalty or punishment—begins with an assumption that law and legal processes involve human and social forces that are often misunderstood. At the heart of his argument is the idea that punishment—the workings of law enforcement, courts, and correctional systems—cannot be understood apart from other institutions in society. Furthermore, there exists no single valid explanation or theory of how punishment operates. Rather, there are multiple theories, and each offers an important perspective on the role and workings of criminal justice in a modern society. Persons who study criminal justice need each theory to understand better the different aspects and functions of criminal justice. Finally, Garland notes that our institutions of punishment are much more than "instruments" of crime control—that is, agencies that only respond to crime problems in our communities. Although they are "oriented toward the control of crime," they are heavily influenced by the social, cultural, and historical contexts in which they operate. Thus, to understand how our legal institutions operate, we must first understand the nature and importance of these contexts.

Controversies in criminal justice do not occur in a political vacuum. Francis Cullen and Lawrence Travis argue in their essay "Criminal Justice Theories and Ideologies" that contemporary debates in crime and criminal justice often are shaped and influenced by political ideologies in the American political system. This essay offers an overview of those ideologies —conservative, liberal, and radical—describing how they translate into different strategies for public policy on crime and punishment. At the heart of the Cullen and Travis essay is the assertion that ideological differences among government officials and policymakers foster conflict in the society over contemporary criminal justice policy. Thus, the political context of criminal justice must be an ingredient in studies of crime and punishment.

The third essay in Part I examines two models that represent two separate value systems that compete for priority in the operation of the criminal process. In his classic essay "Two Models of the Criminal Process," Herbert Packer gives the reader two convenient and opposing perspectives for viewing the operation of criminal justice and the norms that operate within criminal justice agencies. The models are ideal-typical—the reader would never find an agency operating in accordance with only one of the models nor would he or she find any agency or organization of criminal justice in which all aspects of one model were represented. The essay's real value is in Packer's description of the models and the corresponding normative contexts of criminal justice they represent. These contexts are extremely useful in understanding the working policies of criminal justice agencies and in explaining how normative pressures on agencies influence the outcomes of criminal cases.

The final essay in this section argues that there currently exists a theoretical vacuum in research on the administration of criminal justice. John Hagan's chapter, "Why Is There Little Criminal Justice Theory? Neglected Micro- and Macro-Level Links Between Organization and Power," contends that the two main theoretical perspectives that have dominated scholarly writing over the past few decades—consensus and conflict theories—have found only limited support in empirical research. Hagan reasons that these perspectives are too general to explain adequately how criminal justice agencies and personnel operate. He believes, as do other scholars, that explanations of criminal justice must more effectively incorporate information on the social and political contexts in which justice is administered. According to Hagan, theories of criminal justice must specify the relationships between the macro-level characteristics of communities (for example, the distribution of political power in communities) and the micro-level characteristics of individual participants in criminal justice agencies (for example, the types of persons prosecuted for crimes). He also argues that North American criminal justice, unlike other justice systems in the world, often comprises a "loosely coupled" set of organizations—agencies that are responsive to one another but that operate more or less independently. The loosely coupled nature of criminal justice seriously complicates development of theory. Hagan's essay develops the foundation for a new theory of criminal justice, one that stresses the structural contexts of criminal justice organizations.

The Study of Punishment

DAVID GARLAND

THE present study is a work in the sociology of punishment or, more precisely, in the sociology of criminal law, criminal justice, and penal sanctioning. Moving from the premise that penal phenomena in modern society are problematic and badly understood, it seeks to explore the penal realm in all its different aspects, reopening basic questions about punishment's social foundations, seeking to chart its functions and its effects. Its ultimate aim is to uncover the structures of social action and the webs of cultural meaning within which modern punishment actually operates, thereby providing a proper descriptive basis for normative judgments about penal policy.

I take the sociology of punishment, broadly conceived, to be that body of thought which explores the relations between punishment and society, its purpose being to understand punishment as a social phenomenon and thus trace its role in social life. Being concerned with punishment and penal institutions, it shares its central subject matter with "penology," but is distinguishable from the latter by virtue of its wider parameters of study. Whereas penology situates itself within penal institutions and seeks to attain a knowledge of their internal "penological" functioning (throughout the nineteenth century "penology" was a synonym for "penitentiary science"), the sociology of punishment views the institutions from the outside, as it were, and seeks to understand their role as one distinctive set of social processes situated within a wider social network.

It is, at present, possible to point to at least four distinctive theoretical perspectives within the sociology of punishment, three of them already established, and a fourth which is in the process of emerging. The Durkheimian tradition stresses punishment's moral and social-psychological roots as well as its putative solidarity-producing effects. Marxist studies highlight punishment's role in what it takes to be class-based processes of social and economic regulation. Michel Foucault's work has argued that disciplinary punishments operate as power-knowledge mechanisms within wider strategies of domination and subjectification, while the work of Norbert Elias has prompted writers such as Spierenburg to situate punishment within an analysis of changing sensibilities and cultural mentalities. None of these interpretative perspectives is absurd or without merit. Each makes serious claims for our attention because each has something important to say about its object of study. Moreover, as even this brief characterization suggests, each is concerned to bring into view different aspects of what turns out to be a rather complex set of penal phenomena. Each of them has a capacity to make visible particular aspects of a possibly complicated and many-sided reality and to connect these aspects to wider social processes. Each mode of enquiry sets up a particular image of punishment, defining it in a particular way, highlighting some of the aspects, while inevitably obscuring or neglecting others.

If we treat these interpretations as representing a variety of perspectives—each one employing a different angle of approach and a shifting focus of attention—then there is no in-principle reason why they should not be brought together to help us understand a complex object in its various aspects and relations. However, it is all too common for questions of interpretation which are capable of multiple answers to be understood as questions of ontology or of causal priority, in which case only a singular response will suffice. Once this occurs, and we assume that all theories are attempts to answer the questions "what is the essential nature of punishment?" or "what is *the* cause of punishment?" then we are always forced to choose between one or the other theoretical account. The result is an approach which tends to be needlessly one dimensional in its understanding.

The point I wish to make about levels of analysis is rather similar. It is certainly the case that grand social theories such as those developed by Marx, Durkheim, or Elias give incompatible accounts of the central dynamics of social life. (Foucault's work is incompatible for the different reason that it denies the validity of theories pitched at this global level.) If it were the case that the analyses of punishment which derive from these various traditions were no more than miniaturizations of the larger global theories, then all the incompatibilities would be reproduced at this more detailed level. But this, in fact, is not the case. Specific analyses which are launched from within a certain set of axioms will tend to ask distinctive questions and focus on particular aspects of the phenomenon under study, in accordance with the dictates of the general theory. But the findings produced in this way will not be mere reproductions of the global social theory—unless, of course, we are dealing with deductive dogmatics, in which case the theory is not being "applied" but merely repeated.

Concrete spheres of social life, such as punishment, are never exact microcosms of the social structures depicted by general theory. Each particular sector of society can be assumed to display its own peculiar mechanisms and dynamics. And so, in any process of theoretical interpretation which is open to empirical information, the concrete character of the phenomenon should help determine the analytical results as much as the set of axioms which launched the enquiry. This being the case, the specific findings of any theory brought to bear on punishment may or may not be compatible with others produced from within a different interpretative

perspective. The question of their relationship is always an empirical one and is not settled in advance. Thus, for example, Marxist analyses may discover ways in which penal practice reinforces class divisions and ruling-class dominance, and Durkheimian studies may point to other elements of the penal process which appear to express sentiments or reinforce solidarities which are not class based. Unless one assumes that penal practice is all of a piece, with a single, unitary meaning—that it is all a matter of class or all a matter of cross-class solidarity—there is no reason to reject either analysis out of hand. Instead, what is required is a more subtle, in-depth analysis which examines how these two aspects seem to coexist within the complex set of practices which make up the penal realm.

If, then, we are committed to a comprehensive examination of the structures and meanings of punishment in modern society, there appears to be no ready-to-hand general framework within the sociology of punishment which will allow us to pursue this enquiry. Instead, we find a range of interpretative traditions, each one projecting a slightly different image of punishment and its connection with the rest of the social world and each one bearing an as-yet-indeterminate relationship to the others. Given this situation, the best strategy appears to be one which is inclusive and open to synthesis, at least in the first instance. The sociological accounts of punishment that we currently possess have each isolated and abstracted a particular aspect or facet of punishment and have provided powerful analyses based on this. But although such interpretations can often be brilliantly illuminating and insightful, they are also prone to be partial and somewhat one sided. One symptom of this is the tendency of historians of punishment, seeking to convey a rounded sense of the institution as it is operated at a particular time and place, to write *against* such theories, showing their monolithic interpretations to be incomplete at best and completely untenable at worst. But the real point of their complaint is not that historians do not need theory. It is that theories which are too narrow in compass simply act as an obstacle to understanding and need to be replaced by better theories which will be more adequate to their task.

Having discussed the various interpretative stances adopted toward punishment, it is perhaps time to say something about punishment itself. The first point to note here is that *punishment,* despite this singular generic noun, is not a singular kind of entity. Indeed, it seems likely that some of the variation of interpretative results which one finds in the sociology of punishment has to do with the nature of the thing analyzed, rather than with the analytical process brought to bear on it. We need to remind ourselves, again and again, that the phenomenon which we refer to, too simply, as punishment is in fact a complex set of interlinked processes and institutions, rather than a uniform object or event. On close inspection, it becomes apparent that the different interpretative perspectives have tended to focus in on quite different aspects or stages of this process. Thus, when Pashukanis discusses the ideological forms of the criminal law, Durkheim focuses on condemnatory rituals, Foucault shifts attention to institutional routines, and Spierenburg points to the sensibilities involved, each of them is, in effect, moving back and forth between different phases of the penal process, rather than producing different interpretations of the same thing. Unfortunately, though, such differences of focus have often been disguised by a lack of analytical specificity and by the failure of individual theorists to place their own work in the context of other interpretations. It is important that discussions of punishment begin by discussing this question in some detail and that in subsequent analyses they avoid the tendency to treat punishment as if it were all of a piece.

An observation made by Friedrich Nietzsche can serve to orient our discussion.

I would say that in a very late culture such as our present-day European culture the notion "punishment" has not one but a great many meanings. The whole history of punishment and of its adaptation to the most various uses has finally crystallized into a kind of complex which it is difficult to break down and quite impossible to define.

Punishment is taken here to be the legal process whereby violators of the criminal law are condemned and sanctioned in accordance with specified legal categories and procedures. This process is itself complex and differentiated, being composed of the interlinked processes of lawmaking, conviction, sentencing, and the administration of penalties. It involves discursive frameworks of authority and condemnation; ritual procedures of imposing punishment; a repertoire of penal sanctions; institutions and agencies for the enforcement of sanctions; and a rhetoric of symbols, figures, and images by means of which the penal process is represented to its various audiences. Two things should follow from this fact of internal differentiation. The first is that discussions of punishment can have a whole range of possible referents which are all properly part of this institutional complex. The second is that the penal process is likely to exhibit internal conflicts and ambiguities, stemming from its fragmented character. I have tried to capture this sense of internal complexity by proposing the generic term *penality* to refer to the network of laws, processes, discourses, representations, and institutions which make up the penal realm, and I will use this term as a more precise synonym for punishment in its wider sense.

This focus on the legal punishment of criminal law offenders means that although punishment also takes place outside the legal system—in schools, families, workplaces, military establishments, and so on—these forms of punitive practice will largely be left out of the present study. Punishment in some form or other is probably an intrinsic property of all settled forms of association, and there is much to be learned from viewing punishment in these various social settings. Despite being derivative in a certain sense—in that all penal domains in modern society depend on the delegation of authority from the sovereign legal order—these forms have their own specificity and are not mere imitations of state punishments. They will, however, be considered here only where their discussion can further our understanding of the legal order of punishment and not as a topic in themselves. Nor will this study concentrate on the nonlegal but often routine forms of punishment which occur in modern criminal justice—for example, the informal rituals of humiliation involved in some police work or the implicit penalties involved in the prosecution process—since my primary concern will be those punishments which are authorized by law. This may appear to be a serious exclusion, since the informal actions of police, prosecutors, and state officials clearly play a large role in crime control and constitute an important aspect of state power. However, my concern here is to understand legal punishment and its social foundations, not to chart the repertoire of deterrents that are in use or to trace all of the forms in which state power is exercised through the criminal justice apparatus.

The location of state punishment within a specifically legal order gives punishment certain distinctive characteristics which are not a feature of punishments in other social settings. For example, the sovereign claims of the law give legal punishments an obligatory, imperative, and ultimate nature which are unmet with elsewhere. Similarly, the forms of law, its categories, and principles are important in shaping penal discourses and procedures, although it should be stressed that penal institutions such as the prison are sometimes legally authorized to adopt procedures which fall far short of the normal juridical standards, for example, on due process in disciplinary hearings. Location within a legal order, then, is one determinant of punishment's forms and functions, but is by no means the only determinant involved.

Although legal punishment is understood to have a variety of aims, its primary purpose is usually represented as being the instrumental one of reducing or containing rates of criminal behavior. It is thus possible to conceive of punishment as being simply a means to a given end—to think of it as a legally approved method designed to facilitate the task of crime control. Nor is this an uncommon or particularly inadequate perception of punishment.

Crime control is indeed a determinant of penal practice and this ends-means conception is widely adopted both by penologists and by philosophers of punishment. This instrumental, punishment-as-crime-control conception has, however, been unattractive to sociologists of punishment. These sociologists have usually perceived a sense in which punishment's significance or social function runs beyond the narrow realm of crime control, and they consider such an instrumentalist conception to be an unjustified narrowing of the field of study. Indeed, in some instances, certain theorists have gone so far as to deny punishment's crime control function altogether, arguing that penality is not well adapted to this particular end and that therefore some other end must be posited to explain its character. The most celebrated instance of this is Emile Durkheim's declaration that "if crime is not pathological then the purpose of punishment cannot be to cure it," but similar positions are adopted by writers such as Mead, Rusche and Kirchheimer, and, more recently, Michel Foucault. Each of these writers points to the "failure" of punishment as a method of crime control and argues that it is badly adapted to this end, before going on to discuss alternative ways of understanding the phenomenon.

In a sense, this kind of approach is liberating for anyone who wishes to think about punishment, since it frees us from the need to think of punishment in penological terms and opens up the question of penality's other social functions. There are, however, serious problems with such a position, despite its obvious attractions. For one thing, it continues to think of punishment as a means to an end: if not now the end of crime control, then some alternative telos, such as social solidarity (Durkheim) or political domination (Foucault). But this "purposive" or teleological conception of a social institution makes for bad sociology. Not only is it quite possible, as Nietzsche points out, for a single, historically developed institution to condense a whole series of separate ends and purposes within its sphere of operation, it is also the case that institutions are never fully explicable purely in terms of their "purposes." Institutions like the prison or the fine or the guillotine are social artifacts, embodying and regenerating wider cultural categories as well as being means to serve particular penological ends. Punishment is not wholly explicable in terms of its purposes because no social artifact can be explained in this way. Like architecture or diet or clothing or table manners, punishment has an instrumental purpose, but also a cultural style and a historical tradition, and a dependence on "institutional, technical, and discursive conditions." If we are to understand such artifacts, we have to think of them as social and cultural entities whose meanings can only be unraveled by careful analysis and detailed examination. As in all spheres of life, a specific need may call forth a technical response, but a whole process of historical and cultural production goes into the shaping of that "technique."

The need to control crime in its various forms, and to respond to the depredations of lawbreakers, is thus only one of the factors which helps shape the institutions of penality. It is, no doubt, an important one, and it would make little sense, for example, to analyze U.S. penal policy without bearing in mind the levels of crime experienced in the United States and the social and political consequences which follow from this. But even if one could disentangle "real" crime rates from the processes of policing, criminalizing, and punishing (through which we generate most of our knowledge of crime—and at least some of its actuality), it is clear enough that criminal conduct does not determine the kind of penal action that a society adopts. For one thing, it is not "crime" or even criminological knowledge about crime which most affects policy decisions, but rather the ways in which "the crime problem" is officially perceived and the political positions to which these perceptions give rise. For another, the specific forms of policing, trial, and punishment, the severity of sanctions and the frequency of their use, institutional regimes, and frameworks of condemnation are all fixed by social convention and tradition rather than by the contours of criminality. Thus, to the extent that penal systems adapt their practices to the problems of crime control, they do so in ways which are heavily mediated by independent considerations such as cultural conventions, economic resources, institutional dynamics, and political arguments.

Thinking of punishment as a social artifact serving a variety of purposes and premised on an ensemble of social forces thus allows us to consider punishment in sociological terms without dismissing its penological purposes and effects. It avoids the absurdity of thinking about punishment as if it had nothing to do with

crime, without falling into the trap of thinking of it solely in crime control terms. We can thus accept that punishment is indeed oriented toward the control of crime—and so partly determined by that orientation—but insist that it has other determinants and other dynamics which have to be considered if punishment is to be fully understood.

Punishment, then, is a delimited legal process, but its existence and operation are dependent on a wide array of other social forces and conditions. These conditioning circumstances take a variety of forms—some of which have been explicated by historical and sociological work in this field. Thus, for example, modern prisons presuppose definite architectural forms, security devices, disciplinary technologies, and developed regimes which organize time and space—as well as the social means to finance, construct, and administer such complex organizations. And as recent work has shown, specific forms of punishment are also dependent for their support on less obvious social and historical circumstances including political discourses and specific forms of knowledge; legal, oral, and cultural categories; and specific patterns of psychic organization or sensibility. Punishment may be a legal institution, administered by state functionaries, but it is necessarily grounded in wider patterns of knowing, feeling, and acting, and it depends on these social roots and supports for its continuing legitimacy and operation. It is also grounded in history, for, like all social institutions, modern punishment is a historical outcome which is only imperfectly adapted to its current situation. It is a product of tradition as much as present policy: hence, the need for a developmental as well as a functional perspective in the understanding of penal institutions. It is only by viewing punishment against the background of these wider forms of life and their history that we can begin to understand the informal logic which underpins penal practice. In consequence, we should be prepared to find that this "logic" is the social logic of a complex institution built on an ensemble of conflicting and coordinating forces, rather than the purely instrumental logic of a technical means adapted to a given end.

Criminal Justice Theories and Ideologies

FRANCIS T. CULLEN
LAWRENCE TRAVIS

CURRENT controversy over the appropriate direction for American criminal justice policy does not exist in an ahistorical or apolitical vacuum. Contemporary debates concerning the causes of crime, the proper purpose of the criminal sanction, and the pragmatics of criminal justice reform are outgrowths of the prescriptions and policies of past students of criminal justice. Hence, to facilitate our understanding of the issues which surround the current dispute over crime and punishment in America, we will examine two schools of criminology which have dominated thinking about crime and criminal justice for the past two hundred years. The classical and positivist schools are based on distinct sets of underlying ideological assumptions, posit differing rationales for punishment, and suggest unique social policies to deal with crime. Their disparate assumptions, as we shall see throughout this chapter, lie at the heart of the debate between supporters of rehabilitation and supporters of punishment.

In this chapter, we will delineate three modern political ideologies which reflect vastly differing assumptions and value stances concerning crime and criminal justice. It should be noted that ideologies are unprovable sets of assumptions about the proper state of things. They are generally "unexamined presumptions" which shape an individual's stance on given issues and are often highly emotionally charged.

It is important to be able to recognize one's own ideological stance as well as those of others with respect to issues of crime and punishment. As Walter Miller has observed, "Ideology and its consequences exert a powerful influence on the policies and procedures of those who conduct the enterprise of criminal justice, and . . . the degree and kinds of influence go largely unrecognized. Ideology is the permanent hidden agenda of criminal justice." In a similar vein, ideological concerns can have an impact on social scientists studying crime and social policy. One's ideological stance can affect the type of problems selected for study, the process of theory construction, interpretation of research findings, and recommended social policies. One must thus be on guard against "statements forwarded as established conclusions [which] are based on ideological doctrine rather than empirically supportable evidence."

Before discussing the conservative, liberal, and radical positions in more detail, however, we will first set out the central features of the classical and positivist schools of criminology.

SCHOOLS OF CRIMINOLOGICAL THOUGHT

The Classical School

The classical school, represented most prominently by Cesare Beccaria and Jeremy Bentham, was at its core a movement to bring about the reform of the criminal justice systems of Europe in the eighteenth century. Legal and judicial institutions of that period were characterized by such abuses as trial by torture, secret accusations, presumptions of guilt before trial, and arbitrary court procedures. Further, judges possessed virtually unrestrained discretion in setting penalties, and many of the penalties were barbarous indeed: death by burning, by the gibbet, or by breaking on the wheel and punishment by such means as branding or amputation.

The reformers of the classical school were influenced in their own views by such social contract theorists of the Enlightenment as Montesquieu, Rousseau, and Hobbes. Along these lines, Beccaria argued that in order to gain the security and liberty of an organized society, humans freely and willingly gave up part of their liberty to the state. Laws exist to ensure the maintenance of society, and when laws are broken and the state or its citizens thereby endangered, punishment is both necessary and justified. In this regard, "the true measure of crimes is . . . the harm done to society." Laws that are not necessary for the welfare of the state and its citizens are unjust restrictions on individual liberty, however.

Equality was another theme central to Enlightenment thinkers which was adopted by the classical school. Since all men were created equal (in the state of nature) and are equally possessed of reason and free will, equality before the law (if not in property or rank) should be a fundamental principle of society.

In light of these social and intellectual influences on Beccaria and Bentham, the central assumptions of the classical school included the following:

1. Only the legislator has the authority to make laws. Only laws, in turn, can set the punishment for crimes. Therefore, it is the legislature, not the judge, which should fix the precise punishments for violations of the law. Prohibited acts and their attendant penalties should be matters of public knowledge. The role of the judge should be limited to the determination of guilt or innocence of the accused; thus, the judge is allowed little or no role in the determination of penalties for given offenses/offenders.

2. Human beings are both rational and possessed of free will and can thus be held responsible for their actions. Humans are governed by the principle of *utility;* that is, they seek pleasure or happiness and avoid pain or unhappiness.

3. Punishment should be based on the social harm of the act and not on the "intention" of the offender. Therefore, like offenses should receive like punishment; punishment should "fit the crime" and not the criminal.

4. The goal of punishment is primarily the prevention of crime and only secondarily to exact retribution for the harm an offender has caused. To prevent crime, punishments should be just severe enough for the pain or unhappiness created by the punishment to outweigh the pleasure or happiness obtainable from the crime. This is all that is required for an offender to decide that "crime does not pay" and thus to be deterred from violating the law once again in the future ("specific deterrence"). Similarly, if the costs are higher than the benefits that can be derived from illegal behavior, those in the public contemplating criminal acts will also decide against pursuing such activities ("general deterrence").

Notably, Beccaria believed that any punishment beyond the minimum level needed to deter people from breaking the law unjustly restricts individual liberty, is nonutilitarian, and thus must be viewed as illegitimate.

5. Certainty and swiftness of punishment are more crucial to the prevention of crime than is severity; hence, "the certainty of a punishment, even if it be moderate, will always make a stronger impression than the fear of another which is more terrible but combined with the hope of impunity."

6. The rights of accused persons should be protected against abuse. In particular, the accused should be presumed innocent until sufficient proof of guilt is introduced. Moreover, court hearings should be governed by clear and fair procedures.

In sum, Beccaria contended that "for punishment not to be, in every instance, an act of violence of one or of many against a private citizen, it must be essentially public, prompt, necessary, the least possible in the given circumstances, proportionate to the crimes, dictated by the laws."

The proposals of the classical school met with some success in the years after their introduction. Beccaria's *Essay on Crimes and Punishments,* originally published in 1764, was translated into several languages shortly thereafter, including a French-language edition for which the introduction was written by Voltaire. Classical ideas also became an integral part of the French Code of 1791.

Practical problems of implementing pure classical principles into the French Code provided the impetus for a modification of these principles. These modifications came to be embodied in a movement called the neoclassical school.

It must be remembered that in his desire to avoid the possibility of capricious and arbitrary punishments by judges, Beccaria argued that penalties should be set ahead of time by the legislatures. Equally "harmful" offenses were to receive equally "painful" penalties without regard to the characteristics of individual offenders. As these tenets were embodied in the French Code of 1791, circumstances of individuals were ignored to the extent that all offenders— whether first offenders or recidivists, children, insane, or incompetent—were dealt with only on the basis of the act committed. Proponents of the neoclassical school, while in the main accepting basic classical assumptions, modified these principles to allow for the consideration of certain individual circumstances as a pragmatic response to the exigencies of criminal sentencing. Thus, mitigated penalties and partial responsibility became possible for youth, the insane, the feebleminded, and for other offenders under certain environmental or mental circumstances.

It has been suggested that this neoclassical model has formed the philosophical underpinnings of the agencies of social control in modern industrial societies. Certainly, this is true in that the classical school provided a *rationale* for punishment, although punishment as a feature of criminal justice systems antedated classical pronouncements. A legalistic definition of crime is another characteristic common to the classical school and to modern criminal justice. And clearly, the neoclassical concept that criminals should be held responsible for (i.e., subject to punishment for) their actions, although less so in certain circumstances or for particular categories of individuals, is firmly embedded in our legal system.

Their accommodation of classical principles notwithstanding, the criminal justice and correctional systems of the industrialized Western world have also been influenced by a school of thought that arose to challenge classical assumptions: positivism.

The Positivist School

The guiding concept of the positivist school of criminology has been the application of the scientific method to the study of the criminal. During the period between Beccaria's *Essay* (1764) and the publication of the positivists' first treatise, Lombroso's *The Criminal Man* in 1876, science rather than reason alone had become the dominant means of understanding the world. Thus, it became the task of the early positivists of the Italian school—Lombroso, Garofalo, and Ferri—to extend the assumptions and methodology of science to the problem of criminal behavior.

Cesare Lombroso, often referred to today as the father of criminology, adopted a largely biological theory of crime causation. His early work emphasized the notion of the "born criminal," an individual more primitive and atavistic than the noncriminal and who could be identified by means of certain visible "stigmata." While never totally abandoning the idea of the born criminal and the biological basis for crime, his later work also cited the importance of social and environmental factors in the causation of crime. He is remembered today less for the specific content of his theories than for his insistence on the gathering of empirical data, emphasis on objectivity and the use of the scientific method, stress on determinism rather than free will as the primary impetus to human action, and recognition of environmental factors as contributory to criminality.

It is also important to note that positivism can take (and has taken) other forms than the biological variety. For example, psychological positivism, instead of locating the cause of criminal behavior within the biological makeup of an individual, might instead look for the cause in faulty personality development of the offender. Sociological positivism, conversely, might point to aspects of the social structure or the social environment as primary causal factors. Indeed, it has been concluded that "most contemporary scientific criminology is positivistic in method and in basic formulations."

In order to understand more fully the impact of the positivist school on criminology and criminal justice in America, it is important to explicate the central features of this approach. First, positivists, in seeking the source of criminal behavior, tend to assume that crime is *determined* by factors largely outside the control of the individual. Although they may differ as to whether the factors are primarily biological, psychological, or sociological in nature, they generally accept the idea of multiple-factor causation —that is, that crime is caused by the interaction of a number of complex variables. Consequently, free-will explanations of crime are rejected in this model, and the differences between criminals and noncriminals are emphasized.

Second, since criminals did not freely choose their criminal behavior, it is inappropriate to punish them for their crimes. Early positivists argued that the small proportion of offenders whose behavior cannot be altered and who represent a danger to the community should be held in lifelong confinement. For most others, individualized treatment of the offender is appropriate so that the underlying causes of criminal behavior may be eliminated. In this regard, the "medical model" provides a vocabulary with which positivists can talk about and understand crime:

And as medicine teaches us that to discover the remedies for a disease we must first seek and discover the causes, so criminal science in the new form which it is beginning to assume, seeks the natural causes of the phenomenon of social pathology which we call crime: it thus puts itself in the way to discover effective remedies.

Since the individual cannot be cured of his criminal tendencies through his own efforts, it is for the good of society as well as for the offender's own good that the state undertake to *rehabilitate* him. Allen has described the *rehabilitative ideal* as "the notion that a primary purpose of penal treatment is to effect changes in the characters, attitudes, and behavior of convicted offenders, so as to strengthen the social defense against unwanted behavior, but also to contribute to the welfare and satisfaction of offenders."

Third, in the positivist scheme, more emphasis is placed on the offender than on the offense. Penalties are to be tailored to the unique and varied circumstances of each individual rather than to be based on considerations of social harm and deterrence. It is possible and even desirable that two persons committing similar offenses may receive varying dispositions if their individual conditions vary. In order that the goal of individualized treatment may be achieved, judges and correctional officials must be free to fit the type and duration of penalty to offender needs; in other words, punishments should not be immutably preset by legislatures. One important means for achieving this goal of particularized treatment is the indeterminate sentence: offenders remain in prison for as long as it takes to effect a "cure."

It is clear that the core assumptions and goals of the classical and positivist schools are frequently in conflict with one another.

Ostensibly, the positivist rehabilitative ideal has dominated criminal justice policy throughout the past century. The legacy of the positivists includes the indeterminate sentence, probation and parole, the reformatory, and the juvenile justice system. It is perhaps more correct to say, however, that our criminal justice and correctional apparatus represents a combination of classical and positivist principles. And most recently, as we shall see later in the chapter, positivist assumptions and policies have been giving way to a resurgence of classical thought in the United States.

POLITICAL IDEOLOGIES AND CRIMINAL JUSTICE POLICY

We have seen that the unique sets of assumptions of two predominant schools of criminological thought give rise to vastly different explanations of and prescriptions for the problem of crime. Likewise, both "expert" and "public" viewpoints about preferred criminal justice policy are frequently grounded in the political ideologies which are held by individuals. These ideologies tend to rest on sets of unexamined assumptions rather than on solid empirical data, tend to have an emotional component, and are relatively resistant to change. Thus, an understanding of criminal justice trends cannot rest on an examination of research results alone; the role of political viewpoints in the advocacy of particular policies toward crime also must be assessed.

In the course of this discussion, three varieties of political perspectives will be examined: conservative, liberal, and radical. Each will be defined with respect to its guiding principles and the implications of those principles for the control of crime. Then, current classical and positivist perspectives on crime will be analyzed in relation to their ideological bases.

Conservative Ideology

Conservative thought places primary emphasis on the importance of maintaining social order; thus, the concerns of conservatism are more directed toward protecting society than toward aiding the offender. At the same time, the conservative assumes that existing social arrangements are basically sound and reflect widespread consensus among the members of society. The offender, then, is viewed as one who is "out of step" with the rest of the society."

Conservatives tend to eschew rapid social change. They are likely to decry the breakdown of traditional values and to seek to preserve traditional institutions. From their perspective, the sources of crime are often to be found in the erosion of discipline and respect for authority, coupled with an increase in permissive attitudes and practices throughout society.

Individuals are seen as being responsible for their own actions—good or bad—in the conservative view. In this regard, self-reliance and individual achievement are to be encouraged. Conversely, a lack of faith in the ability of the government to solve individual and social problems abides in conservative thought. As a result of the foregoing premises, conservatives focus on punishment rather than rehabilitation as the proper goal of the criminal justice system.

In keeping with their emphasis on social order, system goals which focus on the protection of innocent citizens—that is, deterrence and incapacitation—are of primary importance. Sympathy is also directed toward the victim of crime. On the other hand, the criminal justice system is seen as being too lenient toward the offender. "Technicalities" which allow the guilty to go free should be minimized, and punishments should become both more certain and more severe in order to help reduce crime.

Liberal Ideology

According to proponents of liberalism, the central goals of society should be individual rights and equal opportunity for all. Liberals see current social arrangements as imperfect in that certain economic and social inequities persist in society. Although the social structure is probably not ultimately perfectible, improvements in the direction of greater equality are possible. Further, the state, through its programs, can provide the means to improve the condition of its citizens.

Moreover, there is a fundamental assumption in liberalism that crime is caused by the structural conditions of society rather than by the individual's calculation that crime pays. The long-term remedy for the crime problem, then, is fundamental social change. Short-term programs, favored by liberals, tend to focus on improving the situation of the offender as well as on reducing crime, and tend to be piecemeal in nature.

Traditionally, liberals have placed their faith in rehabilitation as a central goal of criminal justice. However, the ebbing belief in the efficacy of rehabilitative programs among a number of liberals has served to divide the liberal camp. On the one hand, there are those who might be called the "traditional liberals," who argue that the goal of treatment of offenders is being prematurely jettisoned. Their contention is that the resources of the criminal justice system have never yet been fully committed to rehabilitation as a *real* goal of corrections. In addition, they argue, there are rehabilitative programs which have been shown to be effective with some offenders, but these successes have been glossed over by critics of treatment goals. On a philosophical level, rehabilitative programs represent a means of "doing good" for offenders; they also embody a rationale for humane treatment which opposes the conservative pressure to "get tough on crime."

Conversely, "justice model liberals" contend that the rehabilitative ideal is bankrupt as a strategy for reducing crime. Moreover, the structural concomitants of the philosophy of treatment—discretion and the indeterminate sentence—have brought about long penalties as well as real inequities in the penalties for similar offenses, thus undermining the "justice" of the system. As a remedy, liberals should thus abandon rehabilitation and instead embrace the more realistic and limited goal of just deserts, together with reductions in system discretion, short sentences commensurate with offense gravity, and determinate sentencing.

Finally, both liberal camps tend to agree in their support of decriminalization of victimless offenses and of deinstitutionalization and expanded use of alternatives to incarceration.

Radical Ideology

Radicals assume that their primary goals of true economic, social, and political equality for all cannot be achieved under the present capitalist system. The currently dominant pattern of relations of production is designed to keep those who own the means of production in power and to keep those who do not without power. Consequently, crime in capitalist society is due to the efforts of the powerful to maintain their power at all costs, as well as to the brutalization of the working class under capitalism or to their conscious resistance to exploitation by the powerful.

Thus, the causes of crime are intimately connected to the fundamental flaws in the capitalist system. Programs of piecemeal reform which leave the relations of production unaltered are unlikely to achieve positive objectives. In fact, criminal justice and correctional reforms may have the effect of actually extending the domination of the powerful over the powerless in that these reforms may deflect attention away from the fundamental problems underlying capitalist systems. That is, improvements that make current conditions more tolerable may, in the long run, reduce the likelihood that the disadvantaged will push for revolutionary change in their material position. Notably, in the radical view, true social justice and a fundamental resolution of the problem of crime must await the demise of capitalism and the rise of the socialist state.

CLASSICISM, POSITIVISM, AND POLITICAL IDEOLOGY

It is important to note that a bifurcation of the liberal camp was brought about by the justice model liberals' rejection of the rehabilitative ideal. For liberal-justice-model supporters, their defection represents a basic shift away from positivist and toward classical principles. Thus, as in the classical paradigm, punishment and the assumption of criminal responsibility are embraced as the guiding tenets of the criminal justice system. Similarly, in both models punishment is to be based on the social harm of the offense, not the characteristics of the offender. Legislatures are to set penalties, punishment is not to be severe, judicial discretion is to be reduced, and sentences are to be determinate in both plans. Justice model proponents, however, assign a lesser role to deterrence in the determination of penalties than does the classical school.

Interestingly, conservative ideology also shares several common elements with the classical school. Each strongly emphasizes deterrence as a central goal of punishment, and each allows considerations of deterrence to influence the magnitude of penalties. Conservative ideology shares with classicism a view of crime as a willful act against the social order by an essentially rational individual. Conservative thinkers, however, tend to favor escalating criminal penalties to ensure maximum deterrent and incapacitative effects, while classical thinkers tended to downplay severity in favor of certainty and swiftness of punishment.

Given the close relationship of each to classical doctrine, it appears that the conservative and the liberal justice models share a number of common assumptions about the rationale for punishment. The most important area of disagreement between the two, it would seem, lies in the role of deterrence—which, in turn, is linked to the issue of magnitude of punishment. Given that these liberal justice model advocates now share an ideological base with conservatives, a fundamental problem arises for this group: how will these liberals now be able to effectively oppose the conservatives' call for more severe punishments? How will they avoid having their programs for criminal justice reform co-opted and penalties escalated by conservative interests in the name of "justice," amid cries of "get tough on crime?" What will happen to the needs of offenders now that liberals ask nothing of the correctional systems other than to punish the offenders therein? It is obvious that this liberal ideological shift will have profound effects on the structure and function of the criminal justice system in the years to come.

CONCLUSION

The ideologies represented in the classical and positive schools, as well as the political ideologies of conservatism, liberalism, and radicalism, are at the center of current crises in criminal justice policy. Classical, conservative, and liberal justice models center around punishment and retribution as dominant criminal justice goals; traditional liberal and positivist models stress rehabilitation; and radical models call for the elimination of capitalism as the only effective means of system reform.

Two Models of the Criminal Process

HERBERT L. PACKER

PEOPLE who commit crimes appear to share the prevalent impression that punishment is an unpleasantness that is best avoided. They ordinarily take care to avoid being caught. If arrested, they ordinarily deny their guilt and otherwise try not to cooperate with the police. If brought to trial, they do whatever their resources permit to resist being convicted. And even after they have been convicted and sent to prison, their efforts to secure their freedom do not cease. It is a struggle from start to finish. This struggle is often referred to as the criminal process, a compendious term that stands for all the complexes of activity that operate to bring the substantive law of crime to bear (or to keep it from coming to bear) on persons who are suspected of having committed crimes. It can be described, but only partially and inadequately, by referring to the rules of law that govern the apprehension, screening, and trial of persons suspected of crime. It consists at least as importantly of patterns of official activity that correspond only in the roughest kind of way to the prescriptions of procedural rules. As a result of recent emphasis on empirical research into the administration of criminal justice, we are just beginning to be aware how very rough the correspondence is.

At the same time, and perhaps in part as a result of this new accretion of knowledge, some of our lawmaking institutions—particularly the Supreme Court of the United States—have begun to add measurably to the prescriptions of law that are meant to govern the operation of the criminal process. This accretion has become, in the past few years, exponential in extent and velocity. We are faced with an interesting paradox: the more we learn about the "Is" of the criminal process, the more we are instructed about its "Ought" and the greater the gulf between Is and Ought appears to become. We learn that very few people get adequate legal representation in the criminal process; we are simultaneously told that the Constitution requires people to be afforded adequate legal representation in the criminal process. We learn that coercion is often used to extract confessions from suspected criminals; we are then told that convictions based on coerced confessions may not be permitted to stand. We discover that the police often use methods in gathering evidence that violate the norms of privacy protected by the Fourth Amendment; we are told that evidence obtained in this way must be excluded from the criminal trial. But these prescriptions about how the process ought to operate do not automatically become part of the patterns of official behavior in the criminal process. Is and Ought share an increasingly uneasy coexistence. Doubts are stirred about the kind of criminal process we want to have.

The kind of criminal process we have is an important determinant of the kind of behavior content that the criminal law ought rationally to comprise. Logically, the substantive question may appear to be prior: decide what kinds of conduct one wants to reach through the criminal process, and then decide what kind of process is best calculated to deal with those kinds of conduct. It has not worked that way. On the whole, the process has been at least as much a given as the content of the criminal law. But it is far from being a given in any rigid sense.

The shape of the criminal process affects the substance of the criminal law in two general ways. First, one would want to know, before adding a new category of behavior to the list of crimes and therefore placing an additional burden on the process, whether it is easy or hard to employ the criminal process. The more expeditious the process, the greater the number of people with whom it can deal and, therefore, the greater the variety of antisocial conduct that can be confided in whole or in part to the criminal law for inhibition. On the other hand, the harder the process is to use, the smaller the number of people who can be handled by it at any given level of resources for staffing and operating it. The harder it is to put a suspected criminal in jail, the fewer the number of cases that can be handled in a year by a given number of policemen, prosecutors, defense lawyers, judges and juries, probation officers, and so on. A second and subtler relationship exists between the characteristic functioning of the process and the kinds of conduct with which it can efficiently deal. Perhaps the clearest example, but by no means the only one, is in the area of what have been referred to as victimless crimes, that is, offenses that do not result in anyone's feeling that he has been injured so as to impel him to bring the offense to the attention of the authorities. The offense of fornication is an example. In a jurisdiction where it is illegal for two persons not married to each other to have sexual intercourse, there is a substantial enforcement problem (or would be, if the law were taken seriously) because people who voluntarily have sexual intercourse with each other often do not feel that they have been victimized and therefore often do not complain to the police. Consensual transactions in gambling and narcotics present the same problem, somewhat exacerbated by the fact that we take these forms of conduct rather more seriously than fornication. To the difficulties of apprehending a criminal when it is known that he has committed a crime are added the difficulties of knowing that a crime has been committed. In this sense, the victimless crime always presents a greater problem to the criminal process than does the crime with an ascertainable victim. But this problem may be minimized if the criminal process has at its disposal measures designed to increase the probability that the commission of such offenses will become known. If suspects may be entrapped into

committing offenses, if the police may arrest and search a suspect without evidence that he has committed an offense, if wiretaps and other forms of electronic surveillance are permitted, it becomes easier to detect the commission of offenses of this sort. But if these measures are prohibited and if the prohibitions are observed in practice, it becomes more difficult, and eventually there may come a point at which the capacity of the criminal process to deal with victimless offenses becomes so attenuated that a failure of enforcement occurs.

Thus, a pragmatic approach to the central question of what the criminal law is good for would require both a general assessment of whether the criminal process is a high-speed or a low-speed instrument of social control, and a series of specific assessments of its fitness for handling particular kinds of antisocial behavior. Such assessments are necessary if we are to have a basis for elaborating the criteria that ought to affect legislative invocation of the criminal sanction. How can we provide ourselves with an understanding of the criminal process that pays due regard to its static and dynamic elements? There are, to be sure, aspects of the criminal process that vary only inconsequentially from place to place and from time to time. But its dynamism is clear—clearer today, perhaps, than ever before. We need to have an idea of the potentialities for change in the system and the probable direction that change is taking and may be expected to take in the future. We need to detach ourselves from the welter of more or less connected details that describe the myriad ways in which the criminal process does operate or may be likely to operate in mid-twentieth-century America, so that we can begin to see how the system as a whole might be able to deal with the variety of missions we confide to it.

One way to do this kind of job is to abstract from reality, to build a model. In a sense, a model is just what an examination of the constitutional and statutory provisions that govern the operation of the criminal process would produce. This in effect is the way analysis of the legal system has traditionally proceeded. It has considerable utility as an index of current value choices, but it produces a model that will not tell us very much about some important problems that the system encounters and that will only fortuitously tell us anything useful about how the system actually operates. On the other hand, the kind of model that might emerge from an attempt to cut loose from the law on the books and to describe, as accurately as possible, what actually goes on in the real-life world of the criminal process would so subordinate the inquiry to the tyranny of the actual that the existence of competing value choices would be obscured. The kind of criminal process we have depends importantly on certain value choices that are reflected, explicitly or implicitly, in its habitual functioning. The kind of model we need is one that permits us to recognize explicitly the value choices that underlie the details of the criminal process. In a word, what we need is a *normative* model or models. It will take more than one model, but it will not take more than two.

Two models of the criminal process will let us perceive the normative antinomy at the heart of the criminal law. These models are not labeled Is and Ought, nor are they to be taken in that sense. Rather, they represent an attempt to abstract two separate value systems that compete for priority in the operation of the criminal process. Neither is presented as either corresponding to reality or representing the ideal to the exclusion of the other. The two models merely afford a convenient way to talk about the operation of a process whose day-to-day functioning involves a constant series of minute adjustments between the competing demands of two value systems and whose normative future likewise involves a series of resolutions of the tensions between competing claims.

I call these two models the Due Process Model and the Crime Control Model. In the rest of this chapter, I shall sketch their animating presuppositions. As we examine the way the models operate in each successive stage, we will raise two further inquiries: first, where on a spectrum between the extremes represented by the two models do our present practices seem approximately to fall; second, what appears to be the direction and thrust of current and foreseeable trends along each such spectrum?

There is a risk in an enterprise of this sort that is latent in any attempt to polarize. It is, simply,

that values are too various to be pinned down to yes-or-no answers. The models are distortions of reality. And, since they are normative in character, there is a danger of seeing one or the other as good or bad. The weighty questions of public policy that inhere in any attempt to discern where on the spectrum of normative choice the "right" answer lies are beyond the scope of the present inquiry. The attempt here is primarily to clarify the terms of discussion by isolating the assumptions that underlie competing policy claims and examining the conclusions that those claims, if fully accepted, would lead to.

VALUES UNDERLYING THE MODELS

Each of the two models we are about to examine is an attempt to give operational content to a complex of values underlying the criminal law. As I have suggested earlier, it is possible to identify two competing systems of values, the tension between which accounts for the intense activity now observable in the development of the criminal process. The actors in this development—lawmakers, judges, police, prosecutors, defense lawyers—do not often pause to articulate the values that underlie the positions that they take on any given issue. Indeed, it would be a gross oversimplification to ascribe a coherent and consistent set of values to any of these actors. Each of the two competing schemes of values we will be developing in this section contains components that are demonstrably present some of the time in some of the actors' preferences regarding the criminal process. No one person has ever identified himself as holding all of the values that underlie these two models. The models are polarities, and so are the schemes of value that underlie them. A person who subscribed to all of the values underlying one model to the exclusion of all of the values underlying the other would be rightly viewed as a fanatic.

. . . . .

Crime Control Values

The value system that underlies the Crime Control Model is based on the proposition that the repression of criminal conduct is by far the most important function to be performed by the criminal process. The failure of law enforcement to bring criminal conduct under tight control is viewed as leading to the breakdown of public order and thence to the disappearance of an important condition of human freedom. If the laws go unenforced, which is to say, if it is perceived that there is a high percentage of failure to apprehend—and convict in the criminal process—a general disregard for legal controls tends to develop. The law-abiding citizen then becomes the victim of all sorts of unjustifiable invasions of his interests. His security of person and property is sharply diminished, and, therefore, so is his liberty to function as a member of society. The claim ultimately is that the criminal process is a positive guarantor of social freedom. In order to achieve this high purpose, the Crime Control Model requires that primary attention be paid to the efficiency with which the criminal process operates to screen suspects, determine guilt, and secure appropriate dispositions of persons convicted of crime.

Efficiency of operation is not, of course, a criterion that can be applied in a vacuum. By "efficiency" we mean the system's capacity to apprehend, try, convict, and dispose of a high proportion of criminal offenders whose offenses become known. In a society in which only the grossest forms of antisocial behavior were made criminal and in which the crime rate was exceedingly low, the criminal process might require the devotion of many more man-hours of police, prosecutorial, and judicial time per case than ours does and still operate with tolerable efficiency. A society that was prepared to increase even further the resources devoted to the suppression of crime might cope with a rising crime rate without sacrifice of efficiency while continuing to maintain an elaborate and time-consuming set of criminal processes. However, neither of these possible characteristics corresponds with social reality in this country. We use the criminal sanction to cover an increasingly wide spectrum of behavior thought to be antisocial, and the amount of crime is very high indeed, although both level and trend are hard to assess. At the same time, although precise measures are not available, it does not appear that we are disposed in the public sector of the economy to increase very drastically the quantity, much less the quality, of the resources devoted to the suppression of criminal activity through the operation of the criminal process. These factors have an important bearing on the criteria of efficiency, and therefore on the nature of the Crime Control Model.

The model, in order to operate successfully, must produce a high rate of apprehension and conviction, and must do so in a context where the magnitudes being dealt with are very large and the resources for dealing with them are very limited. There must then be a premium on speed and finality. Speed, in turn, depends on informality and on uniformity; finality depends on minimizing the occasions for challenge. The process must not be cluttered up with ceremonious rituals that do not advance the progress of a case. Facts can be established more quickly through interrogation in a police station than through the formal process of examination and cross-examination in a court. It follows that extrajudicial processes should be preferred to judicial processes, informal operations to formal ones. But informality is not enough; there must also be uniformity. Routine, stereotyped procedures are essential if large numbers are being handled. The model that will operate successfully on these presuppositions must be an administrative, almost a managerial, model.

. . . . .

The criminal process, in this model, is seen as a screening process in which each successive stage—prearrest investigation, arrest, postarrest investigation, preparation for trial, trial or entry of plea, conviction, disposition—involves a series of routinized operations whose success is gauged primarily by their tendency to pass the case along to a successful conclusion.

What is a successful conclusion? One that throws off at an early stage those cases in which it appears unlikely that the person apprehended is an offender and then secures, as expeditiously as possible, the conviction of the rest, with a minimum of occasions for challenge, let alone postaudit. By the application of administrative expertness, primarily that of the police and prosecutors, an early determination of probable innocence or guilt emerges. Those who are probably innocent are screened out. Those who are probably guilty are passed quickly through the remaining stages of the process. The key to the operation of the model regarding those who are not screened out is what I shall call a presumption of guilt. The concept requires some explanation, since it may appear startling to assert that what appears to be the precise converse of our generally accepted ideology of a presumption of innocence can be an essential element of a model that does correspond in some respects to the actual operation of the criminal process.

The presumption of guilt is what makes it possible for the system to deal efficiently with large numbers, as the Crime Control Model demands. The supposition is that the screening processes operated by police and prosecutors are reliable indicators of probable guilt. Once a man has been arrested and investigated without being found to be probably innocent, or, to put it differently, once a determination has been made that there is enough evidence of guilt to permit holding him for further action, then all subsequent activity directed toward him is based on the view that he is probably guilty. The precise point at which this occurs will vary from case to case; in many cases it will occur as soon as the suspect is arrested, or even before, if the evidence of probable guilt that has come to the attention of the authorities is sufficiently strong. But in any case the presumption of guilt will begin to operate well before the "suspect" becomes a "defendant."

The presumption of guilt is not, of course, a thing. Nor is it even a rule of law in the usual sense. It simply is the consequence of a complex of attitudes, a mood. If there is confidence in the reliability of informal administrative fact-finding activities that take place in the early stages of the criminal process, the remaining stages of the process can be relatively perfunctory without any loss in operating efficiency. The presumption of guilt, as it operates in the Crime Control Model, is the operational expression of that confidence.

It would be a mistake to think of the presumption of guilt as the opposite of the presumption of innocence that we are so used to thinking of as the polestar of the criminal process and that, as we shall see, occupies an important position in the Due Process Model. The presumption of innocence is not its opposite; it is irrelevant to the presumption of guilt; the two concepts are different rather than opposite ideas. The difference can perhaps be epitomized by an example. A murderer, for reasons best known to himself, chooses to shoot his victim in plain view of a large number of people. When the police arrive, he hands them his gun and says, "I did it and I'm glad." His account of what happened is corroborated by several eyewitnesses. He is placed under arrest and led off to jail. Under these circumstances, which may seem extreme but which in fact characterize with rough accuracy the evidentiary situation in a large proportion of criminal cases, it would be plainly absurd to maintain that more probably than not the suspect did not commit the killing. But that is not what the presumption of innocence means. It means that until there has been an adjudication of guilt by an authority legally competent to make such an adjudication, the suspect is to be treated, for reasons that have nothing whatever to do with the probable outcome of the case, as if his guilt is an open question.

The presumption of innocence is a direction to officials about how they are to proceed, not a prediction of outcome. The presumption of guilt, however, is purely and simply a prediction of outcome. The presumption of innocence is, then, a direction to the authorities to ignore the presumption of guilt in their treatment of the suspect. It tells them, in effect, to close their eyes to what will frequently seem to be factual probabilities. The reasons why it tells them this are among the animating presuppositions of the Due Process Model, and we will come to them shortly. It is enough to note at this point that the presumption of guilt is descriptive and factual; the presumption of innocence is normative and legal. The pure Crime Control Model has no truck with the presumption of innocence, although its real-life emanations are, as we shall see, brought into uneasy compromise with the dictates of this dominant ideological position. In the presumption of guilt, this model finds a factual predicate for the position that the dominant goal of repressing crime can be achieved through highly summary processes without any great loss of efficiency (as previously defined), because of the probability that, in the run of cases, the preliminary screening processes operated by the police and the prosecuting officials contain adequate guarantees of reliable fact-finding. Indeed, the model takes an even stronger position. It is that subsequent processes, particularly those of a formal adjudicatory nature, are unlikely to produce as reliable fact-finding as the expert administrative process that precedes them is capable of. The criminal process thus must put special weight on the quality of administrative fact-finding. It becomes important, then, to place as few restrictions as possible on the character of the administrative fact-finding processes and to limit restrictions to such as enhance reliability, excluding those designed for other purposes. As we shall see, this view of restrictions on administrative fact-finding is a consistent theme in the development of the Crime Control Model.

In this model, as I have suggested, the center of gravity for the process lies in the early, administrative fact-finding stages. The complementary proposition is that the subsequent stages are relatively unimportant and should be truncated as much as possible. This, too, produces tensions with presently dominant ideology. The pure Crime Control Model has very little use for many conspicuous features of the adjudicative process, and in real life works out a number of ingenious compromises with them. Even in the pure model, however, there have to be devices for dealing with the suspect after the preliminary screening process has resulted in a determination of probable guilt. The focal device, as we shall see, is the plea of guilty; through its use, adjudicative fact-finding is reduced to a minimum. It might be said of the Crime Control Model that, when reduced to its barest essentials and operating at its most successful pitch, it offers two possibilities: an administrative fact-finding process leading (1) to exoneration of the suspect or (2) to the entry of a plea of guilty.

Due Process Values

If the Crime Control Model resembles an assembly line, the Due Process Model looks very much like an obstacle course. Each of its successive stages is designed to present formidable impediments to carrying the accused further along in the process. Its ideology is not the converse of that underlying the Crime Control Model. It does not rest on the idea that it is not socially desirable to repress crime, although critics of its application have been known to claim so. Its ideology is composed of a complex of ideas, some of them based on judgments about the efficacy of crime control devices, others having to do with quite different considerations. The ideology of due process is far more deeply impressed on the formal structure of the law than is the ideology of crime control, yet an accurate tracing of the strands that make it up is strangely difficult. What follows is only an attempt at an approximation.

The Due Process Model encounters its rival on the Crime Control Model's own ground in respect to the reliability of fact-finding processes. The Crime Control Model, as we have suggested, places heavy reliance on the ability of investigative and prosecutorial officers, acting in an informal setting in which their distinctive skills are given full sway, to elicit and reconstruct a tolerably accurate account of what actually took place in an alleged criminal event. The Due Process Model rejects this premise and substitutes for it a view of informal, nonadjudicative fact-finding that stresses the possibility of error. People are notoriously poor observers of disturbing events—the more emotion arousing the context, the greater the possibility that recollection will be incorrect; confessions and admissions by persons in police custody may be induced by physical or psychological coercion so that the police end up hearing what the suspect thinks they want to hear rather than the truth; witnesses may be animated by a bias or interest that no one would trouble to discover except one specially charged with protecting the interests of the accused (as the police are not). Considerations of this kind all lead to a rejection of informal fact-finding processes as definitive of factual guilt and to an insistence on formal, adjudicative, adversary fact-finding processes in which the factual case against the accused is publicly heard by an impartial tribunal and is evaluated only after the accused has had a full opportunity to discredit the case against him. Even then, the distrust of fact-finding processes that animates the Due Process Model is not dissipated. The possibilities of human error being what they are, further scrutiny is necessary, or at least must be available, in case facts have been overlooked or suppressed in the heat of battle. How far this subsequent scrutiny must be available is a hotly controverted issue today. In the pure Due Process Model the answer would be at least as long as there is an allegation of factual error that has not received an adjudicative hearing in a fact-finding context. The demand for finality is thus very low in the Due Process Model.

This strand of due process ideology is not enough to sustain the model. If all that were at issue between the two models was a series of questions about the reliability of fact-finding processes, we would have but one model of the criminal process, the nature of whose constituent elements would pose questions of fact not of value. Even if the discussion is confined, for the moment, to the question of reliability, it is apparent that more is at stake than simply an evaluation of what kinds of fact-finding processes, alone or in combination, are likely to produce the most nearly reliable results. The stumbling block is this: how much reliability is compatible with efficiency? Granted that informal fact-finding will make some mistakes that can be remedied if backed up by adjudicative fact-finding, the desirability of providing this backup is not affirmed or negated by factual demonstrations or predictions that the increase in reliability will be x percent or x plus n percent. It still remains to ask how much weight is to be given to the competing demands of reliability (a high degree of probability in each case that factual guilt has been accurately determined) and efficiency (expeditious handling of the large numbers of cases that the process ingests). The Crime Control Model is more optimistic about

the improbability of error in a significant number of cases, but it is also, although only in part therefore, more tolerant about the amount of error that it will put up with.

The Due Process Model insists on the prevention and elimination of mistakes to the extent possible; the Crime Control Model accepts the probability of mistakes up to the level at which they interfere with the goal of repressing crime, either because too many guilty people are escaping or, more subtly, because general awareness of the unreliability of the process leads to a decrease in the deterrent efficacy of the criminal law. In this view, reliability and efficiency are not polar opposites but rather complementary characteristics. The system is reliable *because* it is efficient; reliability becomes a matter of independent concern only when it becomes so attenuated as to impair efficiency. All of this the Due Process Model rejects. If efficiency demands shortcuts around reliability, then absolute efficiency must be rejected. The aim of the process is at least as much to protect the factually innocent as it is to convict the factually guilty. It is a little like quality control in industrial technology: tolerable deviation from standard varies with the importance of conformity to standard in the destined uses of the product. The Due Process Model resembles a factory that has to devote a substantial part of its input to quality control. This necessarily cuts down on quantitative output.

All of this is only the beginning of the ideological difference between the two models. The Due Process Model could disclaim any attempt to provide enhanced reliability for the fact-finding process and still produce a set of institutions and processes that would differ sharply from those demanded by the Crime Control Model. Indeed, it may not be too great an oversimplification to assert that in point of historical development the doctrinal pressures emanating from the demands of the Due Process Model have tended to evolve from an original matrix of concern for the maximization of reliability into values quite different and more far-reaching. These values can be expressed in, although not adequately described by, the concept of the primacy of the individual and the complementary concept of limitation on official power.

The combination of stigma and loss of liberty that is embodied in the end result of the criminal process is viewed as being the heaviest deprivation that government can inflict on the individual. Furthermore, the processes that culminate in these highly afflictive sanctions are seen as in themselves coercive, restricting, and demeaning. Power is always subject to abuse—sometimes subtle, other times, as in the criminal process, open and ugly. Precisely because of its potency in subjecting the individual to the coercive power of the state, the criminal process must, in this model, be subjected to controls that prevent it from operating with maximal efficiency. According to this ideology, maximal efficiency means maximal tyranny. And, although no one would assert that minimal efficiency means minimal tyranny, the proponents of the Due Process Model would accept with considerable equanimity a substantial diminution in the efficiency with which the criminal process operates in the interest of preventing official oppression of the individual.

The most modest-seeming but potentially far-reaching mechanism by which the Due Process Model implements these antiauthoritarian values is the doctrine of legal guilt. According to this doctrine, a person is not to be held guilty of crime merely on a showing that in all probability, based upon reliable evidence, he did factually what he is said to have done. Instead, he is to be held guilty if and only if these factual determinations are made in procedurally regular fashion and by authorities acting within competences duly allocated to them. Furthermore, he is not to be held guilty, even though the factual determination is or might be adverse to him, if various rules designed to protect him and to safeguard the integrity of the process are not given effect: the tribunal that convicts him must have the power to deal with his kind of case ("jurisdiction") and must be geographically appropriate ("venue"); too long a time must not have elapsed since the offense was committed ("statute of limitations"); he must not have been previously convicted or acquitted of the same or a substantially similar offense ("double jeopardy"); he must not fall within a category of persons, such as children or the insane, who are legally immune to conviction ("criminal re-

sponsibility"); and so on. None of these requirements has anything to do with the factual question of whether the person did or did not engage in the conduct that is charged as the offense against him, yet favorable answers to any of them will mean that he is legally innocent. Wherever the competence to make adequate factual determinations lies, it is apparent that only a tribunal that is aware of these guilt-defeating doctrines and is willing to apply them can be viewed as competent to make determinations of legal guilt. The police and the prosecutors are ruled out by lack of competence, in the first instance, and by lack of assurance of willingness, in the second. Only an impartial tribunal can be trusted to make determinations of legal as opposed to factual guilt.

In this concept of legal guilt lies the explanation for the apparently quixotic presumption of innocence of which we spoke earlier. A man who, after police investigation, is charged with having committed a crime can hardly be said to be presumptively innocent, if what we mean is factual innocence. But if what we mean is that it has yet to be determined if any of the myriad legal doctrines that serve in one way or another the end of limiting official power through the observance of certain substantive and procedural regularities may be appropriately invoked to exculpate the accused man, it is apparent that as a matter of prediction it cannot be said with confidence that more probably than not he will be found guilty.

Beyond the question of predictability this model posits a functional reason for observing the presumption of innocence: by forcing the state to prove its case against the accused in an adjudicative context, the presumption of innocence serves to force into play all the qualifying and disabling doctrines that limit the use of the criminal sanction against the individual, thereby enhancing his opportunity to secure a favorable outcome. In this sense, the presumption of innocence may be seen to operate as a kind of self-fulfilling prophecy. By opening up a procedural situation that permits the successful assertion of defenses having nothing to do with factual guilt, it vindicates the proposition that the factually guilty may nonetheless be legally innocent and should therefore be given a chance to qualify for that kind of treatment.

The possibility of legal innocence is expanded enormously when the criminal process is viewed as the appropriate forum for correcting its own abuses. This notion may well account for a greater amount of the distance between the two models than any other. In theory, the Crime Control Model can tolerate rules that forbid illegal arrests, unreasonable searches, coercive interrogations, and the like. What it cannot tolerate is the vindication of those rules in the criminal process itself through the exclusion of evidence illegally obtained or through the reversal of convictions in cases where the criminal process has breached the rules laid down for its observance. And the Due Process Model, although it may in the first instance be addressed to the maintenance of reliable fact-finding techniques, comes eventually to incorporate prophylactic and deterrent rules that result in the release of the factually guilty even in cases in which blotting out the illegality would still leave an adjudicative fact-finder convinced of the accused person's guilt. Only by penalizing errant police and prosecutors within the criminal process itself can adequate pressure be maintained, so the argument runs, to induce conformity with the Due Process Model.

Another strand in the complex of attitudes underlying the Due Process Model is the idea—itself a shorthand statement for a complex of attitudes—of equality. This notion has only recent basis for pressing the demands of the Due Process Model, but it appears to represent, at least in its potential, a most powerful norm for influencing official conduct. Stated most starkly, the ideal of equality holds that "there can be no equal justice where the kind of trial a man gets depends on the amount of money he has." The factual predicate underlying this assertion is that there are gross inequalities in the financial means of criminal defendants as a class, that in an adversary system of criminal justice an effective defense is largely a function of the resources that can be mustered on behalf of the accused, and that the very large proportion of criminal defendants who are, operationally speaking, "indigent" will thus be denied an effective defense. This factual premise has been strongly reinforced by recent studies that in turn have been both a cause and an effect of an increasing emphasis upon norms for the criminal process based on the premise.

The norms derived from the premise do not take the form of an insistence upon governmental responsibility to provide literally equal opportunities for all criminal defendants to challenge the process. Rather, they take as their point of departure the notion that the criminal process, initiated as it is by government and containing as it does the likelihood of severe deprivations at the hands of government, imposes some kind of public obligation to ensure that financial inability does not destroy the capacity of an accused to assert what may be meritorious challenges to the processes being invoked against him. At its most gross, the norm of equality would act to prevent situations in which financial inability forms an absolute barrier to the assertion of a right that is in theory generally available, as where there is a right to appeal that is, however, effectively conditional upon the filing of a trial transcript obtained at the defendant's expense. Beyond this, it may provide the basis for a claim whenever the system theoretically makes some kind of challenge available to an accused who has the means to press it. If, for example, a defendant who is adequately represented has the opportunity to prevent the case against him from coming to the trial stage by forcing the state to its proof in a preliminary hearing, the norm of equality may be invoked to assert that the same kind of opportunity must be available to others as well. In a sense, the system as it functions for the small minority whose resources permit them to exploit all its defensive possibilities provides a benchmark by which its functioning in all other cases is to be tested: not, perhaps, to guarantee literal identity but rather to provide a measure of whether the process as a whole is recognizably of the same general order. The demands made by a norm of this kind are likely by their very nature to be quite sweeping. Although the norm's imperatives may be initially limited to determining whether in a particular case the accused was injured or prejudiced by his relative inability to make an appropriate challenge, the norm of equality very quickly moves to another level on which the demand is that the process in general be adapted to minimize discriminations rather than that a mere series of post hoc determinations of discrimination be made or makable.

It should be observed that the impact of the equality norm will vary greatly depending upon the point in time at which it is introduced into a model of the criminal process. If one were starting from scratch to decide how the process ought to work, the norm of equality would have nothing very important to say on such questions as, for example, whether an accused should have the effective assistance of counsel in deciding whether to enter a plea of guilty. One could decide, on quite independent considerations, that it is or is not a good thing to afford that facility to the generality of persons accused of crime. But the impact of the equality norm becomes far greater when it is brought to bear on a process whose contours have already been shaped. If our model of the criminal process affords defendants who are in a financial position to do so the right to consult a lawyer before entering a plea, then the equality norm exerts powerful pressure to provide such an opportunity to all defendants and to regard the failure to do so as a malfunctioning of the process of whose consequences the accused is entitled to be relieved. In a sense, this has been the role of the equality norm in affecting the real-world criminal process. It has made its appearance on the scene comparatively late, and has therefore encountered a system in which the relative financial inability of most persons accused of crime results in treatment very different from that accorded the small minority of the financially capable. For this reason, its impact has already been substantial and may be expected to be even more so in the future.

. . . . .

There are two kinds of problems that need to be dealt with in any model of the criminal process. One is what the rules shall be. The other is how the rules shall be implemented. The second is at least as important as the first. As we shall see time and again in our detailed development of the models, the distinctive difference between the two models is not only in the rules of conduct that they lay down but also in the sanctions that are to be invoked when a claim is presented that the rules have been breached and, no less important, in the timing that is permitted or required for the invocation of those sanctions.

As I have already suggested, the Due Process Model locates at least some of the sanctions for breach of the operative rules in the criminal process itself. The relation between these two aspects of the process—the rules and the sanctions for their breach—is a purely formal one unless there is some mechanism for bringing them into play with each other. The hinge between them in the Due Process Model is the availability of legal counsel. This has a double aspect. Many of the rules that the model requires are couched in terms of the availability of counsel to do various things at various stages of the process—this is the conventionally recognized aspect; beyond it, there is a pervasive assumption that counsel is necessary in order to invoke sanctions for breach of any of the rules. The more freely available these sanctions are, the more important is the role of counsel in seeing to it that the sanctions are appropriately invoked. If the process is seen as a series of occasions for checking its own operation, the role of counsel is a much more nearly central one than is the case in a process that is seen as primarily concerned with expeditious determination of factual guilt. And if equality of operation is a governing norm, the availability of counsel to some is seen as requiring it for all. Of all the controverted aspects of the criminal process, the right to counsel, including the role of government in its provision, is the most dependent on what one's model of the process looks like, and the least susceptible of resolution unless one has confronted the antinomies of the two models.

I do not mean to suggest that questions about the right to counsel disappear if one adopts a model of the process that conforms more or less closely to the Crime Control Model, but only that such questions become absolutely central if one's model moves very far down the spectrum of possibilities toward the pure Due Process Model. The reason for this centrality is to be found in the assumption underlying both models that the process is an adversary one in which the initiative in invoking relevant rules rests primarily on the parties concerned, the state, and the accused. One could construct models that placed central responsibility on adjudicative agents such as committing magistrates and trial judges. And there are, as we shall see, marginal but nonetheless important adjustments in the role of the adjudicative agents that enter into the models with which we are concerned. For present purposes, it is enough to say that these adjustments are marginal, that the animating presuppositions that underlie both models in the context of the American criminal system relegate the adjudicative agents to a relatively passive role, and therefore place central importance on the role of counsel.

What assumptions do we make about the sources of authority to shape the real-world operations of the criminal process? Recognizing that our models are only models, what agencies of government have the power to pick and choose between their competing demands? Once again, the limiting features of the American context come into play. Ours is not a system of legislative supremacy. The distinctively American institution of judicial review exercises a limiting and ultimately a shaping influence on the criminal process. Because the Crime Control Model is basically an affirmative model, emphasizing at every turn the existence and exercise of official power, its validating authority is ultimately legislative (although proximately administrative). Because the Due Process Model is basically a negative model, asserting limits on the nature of official power and on the modes of its exercise, its validating authority is judicial and requires an appeal to supralegislative law, to the law of the Constitution. To the extent that tensions between the two models are resolved by deference to the Due Process Model, the authoritative force at work is the judicial power, working in the distinctively judicial mode of invoking the sanction of nullity. That is at once the strength and the weakness of the Due Process Model: its strength because in our system the appeal to the Constitution provides the last and the overriding word; its weakness because saying no in specific cases is an exercise in futility unless there is a general willingness on the part of the officials who operate the process to apply negative prescriptions across the board. It is no accident that statements reinforcing the Due Process Model come from the courts, while at the same time facts denying it are established by the police and prosecutors.

Why Is There So Little Criminal Justice Theory? Neglected Macro- and Micro-Level Links Between Organization and Power

JOHN HAGAN

CRIMINAL justice research lacks theoretical initiative. Much criminal justice research in the 1970s and 1980s was derivative in the sense of drawing its theoretical initiative from consensus and conflict theories of society. These broadly framed theories of social relations were useful in stimulating work that was concerned with the influence of legal and extralegal variables on criminal justice outcomes. A consensus theory of social relations predicted a powerful role for legal variables, reflecting the influence of broadly shared societal values in the punishment of criminal norm violations. A conflict theory of social relations predicted a substan- tial role for extralegal variables, reflecting the influence of power imbalances in the punishment of crimes that posed threats to existing power relationships.

While the large debate that organized discussions of consensus and conflict theories in the social sciences proved useful in stimulating and framing much of the early research on criminal justice operations, the results of this research did not offer much support for either theory. Where consensus theory led researchers to expect the influence of legal variables, such as offense seriousness and prior record, to be strong and persistent, the results of this research found the

From "Why Is There So Little Criminal Justice Theory?" by J. Hagan, 1989, *Journal of Research in Crime and Delinquency, 26,* pp. 116-135. Copyright 1989 by Sage Publications, Inc. Reprinted by permission.

influence of these variables to be moderate and inconsistent. Where conflict theory led researchers to expect the influence of extralegal variables, such as class and race, to be substantial and pervasive, the results of this research found the influence of these variables to be modest and uncertain. Literature reviews vary somewhat with regard to these summary statements, but the larger point nonetheless holds: Neither consensus nor conflict theory generated large-scale empirical support.

Meanwhile, no other theory of criminal justice has emerged to fill the void. This is remarkable in that there is so much research in this field. The thesis of this article is that broadly framed consensus and conflict theories fail to accommodate unique aspects of criminal justice processes and outcomes and that new theoretical developments are necessary to stimulate more meaningful research. More specifically, consensus and conflict theories do not provide sufficient attention to the structural relationships that emerge from a joining of organizational and political forces in the direction of criminal justice operations. Below we review studies that illustrate regularities observed in the joint influence of organizational and political factors in criminal justice operations. However, before turning to these illustrations we outline a theoretical framework within which these studies are considered. This framework is the base for a "structural-contextual theory of criminal justice."

THE STRUCTURE AND CONTEXT OF A LOOSELY COUPLED SYSTEM

There is important variation in the degree to which criminal justice systems and subsystems are connected or coupled internally. Criminal justice operations are not unique in this respect. This is true of schools, churches, hospitals, and many other kinds of formal organizations. Nonetheless, many commentators in particular have called attention to a looseness that characterizes American criminal justice policies and operations. Gibbs writes that "American penal policy is a mishmash." Eisentein and Jacob observe that even at the highest levels of decision making in this system "the judge does not rule or govern, at most, he manages, and often he is managed by others." The same impression is conveyed by Reiss when he speaks of the American criminal justice system as a "loosely articulated hierarchy of subsystems." Reiss suggests that this hierarchy is so loosely articulated that "the major means of control among the subsystems is internal to each," with the result that "each subsystem creates its own system of justice." It has been argued that this degree of looseness in criminal justice policies and operations is necessary to provide "individualized" treatment for suspects and offenders, but Jerome Skolnick implied something more when he titled his classic study of the police, *Justice Without Trial*. In any case, our interest is in the consequences of this loose form of organization for our theoretical understanding of criminal justice operations.

A key point in our argument is that in the absence of political power that is directed toward particular crime-linked goals, American criminal justice systems and subsystems tend to be loosely coupled. This is a common condition in the U.S. federal, state, and local systems of criminal justice we know best, but this condition may not characterize many or most criminal justice systems of the world. For example, totalitarian regimes of the right and the left are often characterized by tightly coupled criminal justice systems and subsystems linked to specific crime-related goals. The loose coupling that is characteristic of American systems of criminal justice

may be our way of accommodating diverse societal interests, while at the same time preserving autonomy, and in this sense impartiality, for the judicial branch of government. By these means, a loosely coupled criminal justice system can sometimes serve powerful legitimation needs in a democratic society.

However, our more immediate concern is with another appearance this loose coupling sometimes gives to day-to-day American criminal justice operations. This appearance is one of randomness that is conveyed, for example, in media portrayals of the justice system as chaotic, in Gibbs's description of this system as a "mishmash," and most important, for our immediate purposes, in empirical results of studies of the justice system that leave great amounts of unexplained variance in decisions about arrest, prosecution, and sentencing. For example, the single finding that is consistent throughout the large research literature on judicial sentencing is that whether legal or extralegal factors are the focus of analysis, the unexplained variance in sentencing looms large. This observation holds even in studies where the two types of variables are combined.

This situation is characteristic of what organizational theorists call a loosely coupled system. In connotative terms, loose coupling is meant to evoke the image of entities (e.g., court subsystems) that are responsive to one another, while still maintaining independent identities and some evidence of physical or logical separateness. Meyer and Rowan add to this conception a denotation of characteristics associated with loosely coupled formal organizations—structural elements are only loosely linked to one another and to activities, rules are often violated, decisions often go unimplemented, or if implemented have uncertain consequences, and techniques are often subverted or rendered so vague as to provide little coordination. Many of these characteristics are manifest in the criminal justice system, so that, for example, as the literature on sentencing reviewed above suggests, many of the consequences of this loose coupling can be recognized at the level of individual sentencing decisions. At this level of analysis, Glassman suggests that entities may be considered loosely coupled to the extent that (a) they share few variables in common, (b) the variables shared in common differ substantially in their degree of influence, or (c) the variables shared in common are weak in comparison to other variables considered. The interesting and neglected questions of criminal justice research are why these loosely coupled micro-level patterns of individual decision making are characteristics of American criminal justice operations, and how and when we might look for these patterns to vary. To find answers to these kinds of questions we need to consider neglected macro- and micro-level links that can occur between organizational and political forces, often involving shifts in political power in criminal justice operations.

First, however, we should emphasize that loosely coupled organizations have a unique capacity to absorb changes in the surrounding political environment. For example, when challenged to change, such organizations can take on new appendages, while at the same time selectively ignoring the activities of these new appendages. An example of this pattern from the first half of this century involved the introduction of probation officers into the presentencing process. In response to many of the macro-level political changes associated with the Progressive era in North American politics, probation departments and probation officers were added to juvenile and adult courts throughout the United States and Canada. A major innovation accompanying this change was that probation officers were to prepare presentencing reports that were intended to individualize disposition through their impact on judicial sentencing decisions. However, there is little evidence that sentencing patterns in North America changed much as a result of this innovation. The loosely coupled structure of North American systems of criminal justice absorbed this innovation with little threat to the established judicial and prosecutorial roles in sentencing.

Yet it is also the case that loosely coupled criminal justice organizations do sometimes change, with important consequences for their operations. This brings us to the first of the case studies we consider as developing a structural-contextual theory of criminal justice.

GHETTO REVOLTS AND THE ABANDONMENT OF "NORMAL" COURT OPERATIONS

When a political change or challenge comes swiftly or unexpectedly even a loosely coupled organization will have difficulty absorbing those effects with no more than ritual or ceremonial consequences. Such a situation is described by Balbus in his study of court responses to black ghetto revolts in the mid-1960s in Los Angeles, Detroit, and Chicago. Balbus is explicit in noting that these events were exceptional in the sense of posing a substantial threat to "normal" court operations.

The threat derived from the need of the courts to strike a balance among three interests that Balbus identifies as constituting the core functions of courts and their authorities in the liberal state: order, formal rationality, and organizational maintenance. Normally, these functions can be served jointly with the loosely structured kinds of operations apparent, for example, in studies of sentencing referenced above. In these studies a mixture of predominantly legal variables exercises a modest and variable influence on sentencing decisions. However, the nature and volume of the cases involved in the American ghetto riots challenged the normal mode of court operation, with results that Balbus suggests were predictable given system needs.

These results were most apparent at the bail stage, where prior appearances of individualization that we have associated with loosely coupled court operations apparently gave way to more tightly coupled procedures necessary to achieve a massive and uniform processing of cases. Some of the micro-level processes involved must be inferred from the accounts Balbus offers, since the analysis Balbus provides is concentrated at the macro level of the political events, with only summary use of micro-level data.

Nonetheless, some very important patterns are observed as well as suggested by this analysis. In the aftermath of uprisings in each of the cities, bail releases were far less frequent during the first few days following arrest than normal, while releases subsequent to this initial period were dramatically *more* frequent. The explanation of this sequence is that during the revolts an interest in achieving *order* by "clearing the streets" was paramount, while subsequently an interest in *formal rationality* and *organizational maintenance* (created by the earlier priority given to order) combined to produce a major effort aimed at "clearing the jails." Balbus notes that this pattern was particularly striking in Los Angeles and Detroit, in part because it represented a reversal of normal criminal justice operations.

Thus we found in both cities a striking reversal of the standard model of the criminal process which posits a series of screens whose holes progressively diminish in size and from which the defendants thus find it increasingly difficult to escape; following the Los Angeles and Detroit major revolts, in contrast, the "holes" became progressively larger, and it was much easier to "escape" at the preliminary hearing and trial stages than it was at the earlier prosecution stage.

Although Balbus does not present micro-level data to make the following points, the implications of his analysis are that this shift from "normal" court operations could not have occurred without (a) a tightening of the coupling between the police, prosecutorial, and judicial subsystems, so that bail decisions became less variable; and (b) systematic changes in the "normal" sanctioning of black suspects and defendants, first resulting in unusual restrictiveness, and later in uncharacteristic lenience. The combined result should markedly increase over most prior research the variation that could be explained in bail outcomes through consideration of organizational (e.g., prosecutorial recommendations), legal (e.g., offense specific), and extralegal (e.g., race) variables.

For reasons explained above, we have here needed to infer results at the micro level from the largely macro-level account provided by Balbus. This will not be necessary in case studies we consider later. However, regardless of the speculative nature of some of this discussion, the point nonetheless is made that there is a need to link the study of micro- and macro-level organizational and political forces to account more

fully for criminal justice operations and to understand the important kinds of variations that can occur in these operations across contexts. To better establish this point we turn now from this case study of unexpected social and political events and their impacts on court operations to two classic studies of policing that together highlight the consequences that more crescive and purposive undertakings in law enforcement can produce, again through context-specific variation in the organization of justice system operations.

PROACTIVE POLICING AND THE COURTS

Black and Reiss and Skolnick provide two classic analyses of policing in different parts of the United States. These studies emphasize very different aspects of police work, but taken together they have a unique importance for our understanding of justice system operations. Early in their work, Black and Reiss drew a now well-known distinction between reactive and proactive police work, with reactive police work organizing enforcement activity around responses to citizen complaints about crime, and proactive police work organizing enforcement activity around initiatives taken by the police in seeking out crime. The two kinds of police work are quite different in organization and results, and while Reiss and Black focus their research on the nature of the more numerous reactive responses to crime, Skolnick focuses his research on the consequences of the most provocative, proactive responses to crime.

As a result, Reiss and Black reach different conclusions about modern policing than Skolnick. Where Black and Reiss tend to see police work as having a more democratic cast that is often highly regularized and routine, Skolnick tends to see police work as more selective and biased. The key point for our purposes is that reactive policing seems to fit with the "normal" mode of North American police operations based on loosely coupled processes and outcomes, while proactive policing requires more tightly coupled practices.

Proactive policing requires a more tightly coupled organizational response because of the absence of complainants that is the distinguishing difference between these two modes of modern police work. In the absence of complainants, it is necessary for the police to develop other sources of information and assistance in developing cases. Skolnick established this point primarily through his observations and analysis of narcotics law enforcement. Like Reiss and Black, Skolnick sees narcotics enforcement, and the work of what he more generally calls law offices, as being much different from the work of more conventional patrol officers.

Skolnick notes that to acquire information and cooperation in narcotics work it is necessary to adopt one or more of three kinds of tactics involving going undercover, using entrapment, or developing informants. The results of doing so are often important not only for narcotics work, but also as sources of information about other kinds of underworld activities, which make narcotics officers powerful actors in the justice system more generally. In particular, prosecutors must often rely on narcotics officers for the information they need in developing cases, and they therefore are often willing to give these officers extra consideration. The key forms this consideration takes involve charging decisions and plea and sentence bargaining, which both narcotics officers and prosecutors depend on to develop cooperation and assistance from otherwise unwilling informants and codefendants. Of course, judges too must ultimately be brought into these arrangements, since judges must implement and ratify the forms that plea sentence bargains and charge reductions finally take.

Proactive police work therefore involves a tightening of the coupling among the police, prosecutorial, and judicial subsystems. Reactive police work can thrive in a more loosely coupled organizational environment, through its access to and reliance on complainants, whom it is often useful to keep *decoupled* from the criminal justice process. Were victim-complainants more closely coupled into a more tightly linked criminal justice system, it would be difficult if not impossible to maintain the autonomy of law from victim demands. In the "normal" course of

North American criminal justice, loose coupling serves as a brake on the potential vindictiveness of citizen input.

However, insofar as a political environment demands a more proactive response to particular kinds of crime in specific times and places, a tightening of subsystem operations will often if not always be necessary. Skolnick's work articulates how and why proactive policing operates as it does, but like Balbus, Skolnick's purpose is not to provide the micro-level detail necessary to establish what the consequences of this tightening of justice system operations looks like in correlational terms. We turn next to an analysis of changes over time in the politics of drug law enforcement, in the federal district court in Manhattan. This analysis provides the mixture of micro- and macro-level detail that is necessary to reveal what the consequences of this kind of political change are for the processing of crime in changing contexts of enforcement.

THE CHANGING POLITICS OF DRUG LAW ENFORCEMENT

A concern with drug law enforcement has been a recurrent theme in American politics, dating at least to the turn of the century and the emergence of drug law legislation to deal with narcotic and other kinds of drugs. A contemporary example of the ebb and flow of the political environment that surrounds drug law enforcement is provided in Peterson and Hagan's analysis of the rise and decline in justice system activity surrounding drugs that occurred during the Nixon administration in the United States.

This study divides its attention to the prosecution and sentencing of drug offenders into three periods: from 1963 to 1969, a period of relative calm in the pursuit of drug law violations; from 1969 to 1973, a period of great political activity and public concern in relation to drug use and abuse; and 1974 to 1976, a period of consolidation in which politicians and the public were less preoccupied with drug issues. The middle period in this study is characterized as an antidrug crusade in which well-developed relational distinctions between "victims" and "villains" with the drug trade were embedded in law and enforcement efforts. The key to the political discourse of this period was a compromise between conservative and liberal impulses in which "big dealers" were identified as villains, while middle-class youth and blacks (but only insofar as the latter were not, of course, big dealers in what was then, and still largely remains, a racially stratified drug trade) were preconceived as victims. Peterson points out that this compromise, involving the assignment of a victim status, was made possible by the relative power of middle-class parents. The resulting leniency was then generalized to more ordinary drug offenders.

In any case, the intriguing consequences of this shifting political environment included an increased punitiveness in the sentencing of big dealers in the period from 1969 to 1973, combined with lenient treatment of ordinary black drug offenders, and the very severe sentencing of black big dealers. But perhaps most important for our purposes is the apparent role played by plea bargaining during this period. Peterson and Hagan's analysis reveals that the plea variable became uniquely important in the sentencing of big dealers, and that levels of explained variance in sentencing outcomes increased substantially during the period of this antidrug crusade. These effects are consistent with the point we have been making about the coupling of subsystem operations in periods that involve changes in the political environment and the imposition of political power. To accomplish the political goal of singling out the villainous big dealers in this antidrug crusade, it was necessary to reward cooperating players in the development of major cases, while also imposing especially severe sanctions on those who did not cooperate and/or who were the primary targets of major drug prosecutions. This combination of rewards and punishments, which is characteristic of the kind of proactive narcotics enforcement identified by Skolnick, involves a tightening of police, prosecutorial, and judicial subsystems that is ultimately reflected in the allocation of penal sanctions. The plea effects identified in this case study, the especially severe treatment of black big dealers, the lenient treatment of most others, and the overall increases in explained variance in outcomes, are suggestive of the kinds of de-

partures from "normal" court operations that can accompany important shifts in the political environment, and newly proactive criminal justice operations.

THE PROSECUTION AND SENTENCING OF WHITE-COLLAR CRIME

Thus far we have considered an area of proactive law enforcement, narcotics, that is focused disproportionately on the poor and minorities. While proactive law enforcement may most often be imposed on such defendant populations, this need not always be the case. A counter instance involves the prosecution of white-collar crime, which during the post-Nixon era in North America briefly became an area of proactive prosecution in some jurisdictions.

Hagan, Nagel, and Albonetti analyze sentencing decisions in one such American federal jurisdiction that pursued a proactive prosecutorial policy toward white-collar crime. They compare individual-level data from this jurisdiction with nine other federal district courts. It is crucial to note here that while narcotics and white-collar crime may involve somewhat different offender populations, they share in common the absence of complainants who can knowledgeably inform and assist enforcement efforts. The thesis of the Hagan et al. study is that the proactive prosecution of white-collar defendants and their white-collar crimes therefore comes down to the problem of how to get the leverage required to "turn witnesses," and the key to obtaining this leverage, it is argued, is to forge a connection between negotiations, and concessions and coercion in sentencing. In other words, prosecutors must overcome the tendency toward loose coupling that we have identified as the norm in most criminal justice systems, and establish instead a direct connection between plea negotiations and sentencing decisions in white-collar cases. Hagan et al. suggest that this is accomplished in two ways: by carefully managing the severity of the charges in these cases, so that judges can use statutory guidelines in arriving at lenient sentences, and by getting judges to reward negotiated pleas directly.

The results of this study reveal both of these processes at work in a district that is uniquely proactive. First, the seriousness of the charges placed against white-collar offenders in this proactive district is much more influential for college-educated, white-collar offenders than in the more reactive districts; and, second, the plea variable that we saw above was so important during the Nixon administration crusade against drugs is now again important in the sentencing of college-educated, white-collar offenders in the proactive district, but of negligible importance elsewhere. Overall, Hagan et al. find that the explained variance in sentencing in the proactive district is much higher than in the other districts. They also find that while the proactive prosecutorial policies result in increased convictions for white-collar crime, the net result for college-educated, white-collar offenders is more lenient sentencing. Together, these findings again suggest a tightening of links between the prosecutorial and judicial subsystems that we have argued is characteristic of criminal justice operations in proactive political environments.

The crucial role of charging practices is further revealed in a subsequent Canadian study by Hagan and Parker of the proactive prosecution of a specific form of white-collar crime, securities violations, consequent to Watergate and related scandals in Canada. This study focuses on a choice between quasi-criminal securities acts and criminal code charges in the prosecution of securities violators. Like the earlier American study, this analysis also reveals a variation in charging practices that accompanies proactivity in relation to white-collar crime, and that again results in increased convictions and reduced sentences. The overall implication is that proactive prosecution results in selective patterns of enforcement and sanctioning, involving increased levels of intersystem coordination and exchanges that can combine increased enforcement with reduced sanctions.

A PROSECUTORIAL EXPERIMENT

The last several case studies we have considered have involved political initiatives aimed at increasing the prosecution of selected crimes that characteristically are pursued most actively through a tightening of connections between prosecutorial and judicial subsystems. The last of the case studies we consider consists of a quasi experiment in which, for different political purposes, this kind of prosecutorial activity effectively is reversed. This study involves an analysis by Rubenstein and White of a period during the mid-1970s in which plea bargaining was banned by the attorney general of Alaska.

In this instance the political initiative bore no direct or intended relationship to the prosecution of crimes without complainants. The initiative instead was aimed at changing the public and justice system perception of the place of plea bargaining in the courts of Alaska. Rubenstein and White note that until the mid-1970s, Alaskan judges and lawyers took plea bargaining for granted. However, in December of 1984 a new attorney general, Avrum Gross, was appointed to office and established the following policy:

District Attorneys and assistant District Attorneys will refrain from engaging in plea negotiations with defendants designed to arrive at an agreement for entry of a plea of guilty in return for a particular sentence. . . . While there continues to be nothing wrong with reducing a charge, reductions should not occur to obtain a plea of guilty. . . . Like any general rule, there are going to be exceptions to this policy which must be approved by the Chief prosecutor or myself.

Our interest is not in whether this was a good or bad policy initiative or in whether or not it worked, but rather in its consequences for the criminal justice process more generally, and specifically in relation to proactive areas of prosecutorial activity. Rubenstein and White point out that an explicit purpose of the ban on plea bargaining in Alaska was to "return the sentencing function to the judges." This meant that a further provision of the ban was that while prosecutors were expected to go to an open sentencing hearing and to present to the judge "factors relevant to a consideration for sentence," they were not to offer agreed upon recommendations for a specific sentence.

Rubenstein and White argue that the overall effect of the ban on plea bargaining was to reduce dramatically, if not eliminate, the occurrence of plea negotiations in the Alaskan courts. Apart from whether this was the case or whether this experiment could be replicated in larger more urbanized jurisdictions, however, Rubenstein and White also report several more specific findings that are important for our purposes. First, they found that prosecutors after the ban gave far fewer recommendations for sentencing: There was a reduction of recommendations from about 50% of cases to fewer than 20%. Second, they found that sentences for several groups of offenders increased significantly: The length of prison sentences for *drug* felony cases increased 233%, while sentences in check fraud and related *white-collar* offenses increased 117%. These are, of course, the two areas of proactive prosecutorial activity that we have focused on in the preceding case studies. In each area there was clear evidence of sentence reductions that were a key part of the tightened/proactive prosecutorial efforts.

Overall, the picture that emerges from the ban on plea bargaining in the Alaskan courts is one in which the tightening of connections between prosecutors and judges, involving plea bargaining and charge reductions that are ratified with sentence reductions, was substantially reduced. With regard to the specific issue of sentence recommendations and their impact, Rubenstein and White cite one Alaskan prosecutor as explaining, "We're just sulking—why bother saying anything if we can't be specific?" The implication of such a pattern is a radically decoupled system in which subsystems become highly self-contained and in which political initiatives aimed at the proactive pursuit of targeted kinds of criminal enterprise become more difficult to organize, and consequently less likely to occur.

Between the Alaskan experiment in banning plea bargaining, and the similarly atypical American and Canadian efforts at specific kinds of proactive prosecution, probably are found the more characteristic loosely coupled systems that are most frequently encountered in North American criminal justice research.

TOWARD A STRUCTURAL-CONTEXTUAL THEORY OF CRIMINAL JUSTICE

We began this article with a question: Why is there so little criminal justice theory? We are now in a position to offer some speculative answers to this question that are linked to an effort to suggest new possibilities in the development of criminal justice theory. One answer may be that criminal justice researchers are bewildered by the results their studies have produced. As we have noted, these studies are characterized by unexpected evidence of randomness and inconsistency in the influence of legal and extralegal variables. Our premise is that these results should not be ignored. They form an important starting point for a theory that posits that the normal mode for North American, and perhaps most Western democratic systems of criminal justice, is a loosely coupled form of organization. Our structural-contextual theory therefore begins with the following premises.

Orienting Premises

(1) North American criminal justice systems tend to be loosely coupled, with low levels of explained variance in outcomes across subsystems.

(2) To the extent these outcomes can be explained, they are explained by different variables within different subsystems.

From these premises follow some preliminary propositions.

Preliminary Propositions

(1) The flow of crimes with complainants is more resistant to control by political forces, so political initiatives to increase levels of law enforcement activity most often increase the prosecution of crimes without complainants.

(2) The prosecution of crimes without complainants increases the use of proactive prosecutorial techniques, including plea negotiations, charge bargaining, and sentence reductions.

(3) Increases in the use of proactive prosecutorial techniques lead to increases in levels of explained variance within and across subsys-

tems, as the connections between these subsystems are tightened.

(4) These increased levels of explained variance are reflected in the increased influence of organizational (i.e., plea and prosecutorial recommendations), legal (i.e., offense and prior record), and extralegal (i.e., race, class, and status) variables.

These premises and propositions obviously provide no more than a provisional base for the development of a theory of criminal justice. Beyond this, however, their importance may lie as much in their implications for research methodology as for the purposes of theory construction. This is because the implication of the structural-contextual approach proposed is that we should move away in this field of research from so frequently focusing on normal or conventional criminal justice operations, while giving more attention to contexts that depart from the norm, particularly in terms of political environment.

The case studies we have considered all are atypical in that they involve contexts where the surrounding political environment has man-dated departures from normal criminal justice operations. Characteristically, these departures involve the imposition of political power sometimes targeting the prosecution of a particular form of crime and criminal, often involving morals offenses and sometimes white-collar crimes, or less frequently targeting some feature of system operations, such as plea bargaining. We learn a great deal about system operations in these circumstances. Most significant, research of this kind suggests the means by which criminal justice operations can be tightened for the purpose of focusing attention on political goals.

In the end, of course, the purpose of criminal justice research is not simply to increase explained variance in criminal justice outcomes, but rather to increase our understanding of criminal justice operations. The thesis of this article is that neglected connections between the imposition of political power and organizational forms in the criminal justice system hold a key to understanding the operations of this system, in typical as well as atypical situations. Attention to structure and context can increase our understanding of what too often seems to be a system in random disarray.

SUGGESTED READINGS

Austin, James and Barry Krisberg. 1991. "Wider, Stronger and Different Nets: The Dialectics of Criminal Justice Reform." *Journal of Research in Crime and Delinquency* 19:165-96.

Blumberg, Abraham. 1967. *Criminal Justice.* Chicago: Quadrangle.

Cicourel, Aaron. 1968. *The Social Organization of Juvenile Justice.* New York: John Wiley.

Davis, Kenneth Culp. 1969. *Discretionary Justice.* Chicago: University of Chicago Press.

Garland, David. 1990. *Punishment in Modern Society: A Study in Social Theory.* Chicago: University of Chicago Press.

———. 1985. *Punishment and Welfare: A History of Penal Strategies.* Brookfield, VT: Gower.

Morris, Norval and Gordon Hawkins. 1970. *The Honest Politician's Guide to Crime Control.* Chicago: University of Chicago Press.

Packer, Herbert. 1968. *The Limits of Criminal Sanction.* Palo Alto, CA: Stanford University Press.

Scheingold, Stuart A. 1992. *The Politics of Street Crime.* Philadelphia: Temple University Press.

QUESTIONS FOR DISCUSSION AND WRITING

1. Garland argues that social and historical contexts play an important role in explaining "penality." What does he mean? Explain with illustrations.

2. Contrast Cullen and Travis's ideas about political ideology and Packer's two models of criminal justice. Do Packer's ideas correspond to different political ideologies? Explain why or why not.

3. If you were asked to describe the current direction of American criminal justice in terms of Packer's models, which model would you argue most accurately characterizes recent proposals (e.g., "three strikes and you're out")? Be specific and explain your answer.

4. John Hagan's essay argues that North American criminal justice is a loosely coupled system. Do you agree with his assessment that, in many instances, criminal justice agencies such as the police, courts, or correctional systems operate independently of one another? Explain why or why not.

5. Contrast Hagan's assessment of how criminal justice should be studied with the approach Packer uses. How would studying the norms of criminal justice agencies (i.e., Packer's models) inform our understanding of the structural contexts Hagan believes are so important to theory in criminal justice?

II

WHY PUNISH? RATIONALES FOR PUNISHMENT

JUST as there are different perspectives on what criminal justice is and how it should be studied, there are different views on the purposes of criminal punishment and what it should accomplish. Whereas some people believe that our system of punishments, as embodied in criminal law and justice, should primarily protect society from crime by incapacitating criminal offenders for long periods from the rest of the population, others argue that punishments should instead be tailored to the reformative needs of offenders, thereby reducing the likelihood that offenders will re-offend. Others are less concerned about protecting society or reforming criminal offenders. Some desire a system of punishments that deters criminal offenders and the general public from committing crimes by heightening the threat of criminal punishment. Others simply seek a retributive system of punishment, one that inflicts pain on those who commit crimes commensurate with the seriousness of the crimes committed.

Part II of our book examines these different purposes for punishments, offering a selection of essays on the major purposes: deterrence, incapacitation, rehabilitation, and retribution. Typically, there are two types of essay in each section. The first offers an overview of philosophical or policy issues related to a particular rationale for punishment. The second reviews the results of research on the effects of criminal punishment from the perspective of a particular rationale. Thus, some of the essays review evidence on the deterrent effects of criminal punishments, others review measures designed to rehabilitate criminal offenders, and others describe the effects of programs designed to incapacitate chronic criminal offenders.

DETERRENCE

The first set of essays examines the doctrine of deterrence. Franklin Zimring and Gordon Hawkins's essay, "Deterrence: The Legal Threat in Crime Control," describes the deterrence doctrine in terms of the moral claims or prescriptions the doctrine's advocates make about the preventive effects of criminal punishments on the public and on criminal offenders. This essay stresses some of the difficulties associated with establishing whether punishments in fact deter. Zimring and Hawkins have serious concerns about how the deterrent effects of punishment are demonstrated in statistical research. The essay offers three clever examples of common errors that officials and legislators make in inferring deterrent effects of punishment from statistics on crime, when in fact no deterrent effects may actually be present.

One of the most controversial areas of research on the deterrence has examined the effects of capital punishment. In the second essay, titled "Deterrence or Brutalization: What Is the Effect of Executions?" William Bowers and Glenn Pierce examine whether executions decrease or increase rates of criminal homicide. This essay contrasts two views on capital punishment. The first is the view that the death penalty protects society by deterring would-be murderers from future crimes. In contrast is the view that capital punishment has a brutalization effect. Rather than deterring crimes, this perspective argues that executions increase crime and brutality in society by showing that lethal violence is an appropriate response to criminal offenders. Bowers and Pierce offer empirical evidence from a study of over 5,000 executions that lends more support to the hypothesis that executions brutalize than to the hypothesis that they deter.

A second area in which research has examined deterrent effects of punishment is police intervention in crimes involving domestic assaults. The remaining three essays on deterrence examine whether arrests for domestic assault deter subsequent assaultive behavior. In 1984, Lawrence Sherman and Richard Berk published their research, an excerpt of which is included as our third essay in this section, "The Specific Deterrent Effects of Arrest for Domestic Assault." Their work provoked national interest in whether police arrest practices deter assaults by showing that the rate of repeat assaults among those arrested for assault in Minneapolis was 50 percent less than among those involved in assaults but not arrested. The importance of this research must be underscored. Following release of the study findings, numerous police departments across the country developed and adopted mandatory arrest policies in domestic assault cases.

Given the importance of the Sherman and Berk results, other scholars sought to replicate the findings in other locales. One of these studies is reported in the essay by Franklyn Dunford, David Huizinga, and Delbert Elliott, titled "The Role of Arrest in Domestic Assault." In marked contrast to the earlier research, Dunford and his colleagues found no differences in rates of subsequent assaultive behavior in Omaha between those involved in domestic assaults who were arrested and those who were not. Differences between the two studies in research design suggest that the Dunford et al. study may have involved a more carefully controlled experiment than Sherman and Berks' and that their findings may offer a more accurate assessment of the deterrent effects of arrest.

The final essay in this section, "From Initial Deterrence to Long-Term Escalation in Domestic Violence," assists in reconciling some of the differences between the Omaha and Minneapolis experiments. The essay reports the results of a follow-up experiment in Milwaukee in which only some of the findings of the Minneapolis experiment were substantiated. Sherman and his colleagues conclude that the consequences of arrest are anything but standard across cities, at least for domestic violence. Furthermore, they conclude that the results raise major policy questions about the possible deterrent effects of arrest and other forms of custody.

INCAPACITATION

The second set of essays in this section explores the incapacitation effects of criminal punishment. Interest in incapacitation strategies heightened in the early 1970s in part because of public concern about increases in crime, disillusionment with efforts to rehabilitate offenders, and research findings by Wolfgang and his colleagues showing that a small subset of the population was responsible for a very large share of crimes committed. Jacqueline Cohen's essay, "Incapacitation as a Strategy for Crime Control: Possibilities and Pitfalls," offers an excellent overview of the issues involved in incapacitation research. A pivotal concept in the literature on incapacitation is the criminal career and the extent to which periods of imprisonment can interrupt an offender's criminal career. Advocates of incapacitation, Cohen argues, maintain that in general, the higher the individual's personal crime rate and the longer the career, the more crimes can be averted through incapacitation. Peter Greenwood's essay, "The Concept of Selective Incapacitation," continues this line of reasoning, describing a prediction and classification scheme for identifying and incapacitating career criminals. Greenwood also describes the survey research on inmates that became, for at least a decade, the empirical basis for much of the writing on incapacitation. His research, along with that of others, suggested that some offenders had extremely high rates of offending in the years prior to their incarceration. This essay summarizes his research findings and their implications for developing a method to identify high-rate offenders before their criminal careers actually develop.

The third essay in this section describes the possible effects of incapacitation on the crime rates in individual states and regions of the country. Alfred Blumstein and his colleagues extend the reasoning of the first two essays to a discussion of what the implications of incapacitation may be for criminal justice agencies. This essay is important because it shows how, according to the leading proponents of incapacitation, direct reductions in crime can be achieved by selectively incarcerating chronic criminal offenders. Furthermore, this essay offers an empirical method for estimating incapacitation effects on crime, using information on the length and amount of crime committed over criminal careers and on expansion of capacity in state prisons.

In response to the research by Cohen, Greenwood, Blumstein, and others, numerous critics of incapacitation emerged in the 1980s, vociferously attacking its proponents' logic and reasoning. The final essay in this section is one of the more intriguing attacks, directly challenging a report on incapacitation prepared for the National Institute of Justice (NIJ), the primary research division of the U.S. Department of Justice. The NIJ report argued that major reductions in crime could be achieved through effective implementation of selective incapacitation at the state level. Franklin Zimring and Gordon Hawkins's essay, "The New Mathematics of Imprisonment," disputes the validity of the claim, pointing to some of the errors inherent in much of the reasoning on incapacitation and its effects.

REHABILITATION

At least since the beginning of the nineteenth century, some criminologists and correctional experts have argued that punishments, if coupled with measures designed to remedy the problems causing criminal behavior, can rehabilitate individual offenders. This approach received renewed and extensive attention in the 1960s and 1970s, with important theoretical and empirical work on the rehabilitative effects of treatment programs for convicted criminals. Karl Menninger's essay, "The Crime of Punishment," represents the classic statement of the rehabilitative ideal, stressing that criminal offenders should be treated not punished and that any punishment without treatment was a mistake of criminal proportion. Menninger argues from a medical perspective, reasoning that criminal behavior, although it is not a disease, should be treated as though it were. He reasons that the treatment should consist of education, medication, counseling, and training, all tailored to meet the specific rehabilitative needs of the individual offender.

Since Menninger's statement nearly thirty years ago, research on rehabilitation has fueled controversy over the actual effects of treatment programs on the behavior of offenders. Perhaps the most prominent of these studies is summarized in Robert Martinson's essay, "What Works? Questions and Answers About Prison Reform." Martinson reviews the results of a study he coauthored showing that very few programs have any significant effects on the subsequent criminal behavior of treated offenders. His study sparked enormous controversy when it was released, prompting the National Academy of Sciences to empanel a group of scholars to review the research on rehabilitation programs for criminal offenders. The essay by Lee Sechrest and his colleagues, titled "The Rehabilitation of Criminal Offenders: Problems and Prospects," is an excerpt of the panel's report, and it supports many of Martinson's claims.

More recently, D. A. Andrews and his colleagues have conducted reviews of research of treatment and rehabilitation programs that challenge the Martinson claims. In response to the earlier work of Martinson and more recent work by Steven Lab and John Whitehead, Andrews et al.'s essay, "Does Correctional Treatment Work?" offers a summary of this research, showing that effects of rehabilitation programs vary in direct relation to the risk, need, and responsivity of treated offenders. The essay maintains that appropriate correctional treatment yields lower levels of posttreatment recidivism than criminal penalties involving no rehabilitative services.

The final essay in this section is a critical response to the Andrews et al. essay prepared by Steven Lab and John Whitehead. In the essay, titled "From 'Nothing Works' to 'the Appropriate Works,'" Lab and Whitehead argue that the research of Andrews and his associates has serious flaws and that the struggle to identify programs that actually reduce the likelihood of recidivism is far more challenging than most proponents of rehabilitation portray.

RETRIBUTION

The final essays in this part of our book examine the philosophy of punishment known as retribution or "just deserts." In the first essay, Andrew von Hirsch examines the idea of retribution and its implications for the sentencing policies and practices of criminal justice agencies. The von Hirsch essay is important because it offers a very clear statement about the retributive rationale for punishment. The second essay, titled "Is Punishment Necessary?" by Jackson Toby, reviews some of the problems associated with adopting a retributive approach to punishment. Toby argues that the necessity of its use depends, among other factors, on whether society identifies with the victim and whether punishment actually restores the moral balance in society upset by criminal acts.

DETERRENCE

Deterrence: The Legal Threat in Crime Control

FRANKLIN E. ZIMRING
GORDON J. HAWKINS

BELIEF in the deterrent efficacy of penal sanctions is as old as the criminal law itself. It has informed and does inform political, administrative, and judicial policy to so great a degree that deterrence has been described as a "primary and essential postulate" of almost all criminal law systems.

The nature of that postulate as traditionally conceived is succinctly stated in earlier editions of C. S. Kenny's classic *Outlines of Criminal Law*. Kenny, who cites as authorities "the most generally accepted writers—as for instance Beccaria, Blackstone, Romilly, Paley, Feuerbach—defines "deterrence by punishment" as a "method of retrospective interference; by holding out threats that, whenever a wrong has been actually committed, the wrongdoer shall incur punishment." The object is "to check an offence by thus associating with the idea of it a deterrent sense of terror. . . . The restraint of terror . . . is supplied by the criminal law very efficiently."

Until quite recently, discussion of punishment in general and deterrence in particular has been in the main quite unscientific in character. The bulk of the literature consists of deductive argument. The level of dialectic subtlety is often high; the factual content is minimal. Matters of fact are passed over with candid confessions of ignorance, occasionally supplemented by random speculation. Discussion of what we are justified in doing not only takes precedence over, but even precludes consideration of, what in practice we can do.

Indeed, the theory of punishment as traditionally conceived is largely made up of recommendations or prescriptions; of rhetorical statements rather than propositions which could be evaluated on the basis of fact. As Professor H. L. A. Hart says:

Theories of punishment are not theories in any normal sense. They are not, as scientific theories are, assertions or contentions as to what is or what is not the case; the atomic theory or the kinetic theory of gases is a theory of this sort. On the contrary, those major positions concerning punishment which are called deterrent or retributive or reformative "theories" of punishment are moral *claims* as to what justifies the practice of punishment—claims as to why, morally, it *should or may* be used.

And clearly, insofar as this is true, such theories cannot be subjected to empirical investigation.

It is true that in recent years the need for empirical research has been emphasized even in philosophical literature. And deterrence has received an increasing amount of attention from scholars in a variety of fields. The volume of empirical studies of crime control policies has increased. Research relevant to deterrence in social psychology and other fields has grown impressively since World War II.

From *Deterrence: The Legal Threat in Crime Control* (pp. 1-31) by F. E. Zimring and G. J. Hawkins, 1973, Chicago: University of Chicago Press. Copyright 1973 by the University of Chicago Press. Reprinted by permission.

Nevertheless, the net effect of increasing attention and study is something less than a knowledge explosion. There are doubts about both the reliability and the relevance of much of the psychological experimentation that has been done. Lack of methodological rigor combined with extrapolative extravagance have in many studies produced counterfeit conclusions. There have been modest increments in understanding, but most results have been suggestive rather than definitive. Many questions remain unanswered, among them inevitably those as yet unformulated.

FOUNDATIONS OF OFFICIAL BELIEFS

Official Ideologies

"English judges," says Professor R. M. Jackson in *Enforcing the Law,* "have a great belief in the general deterrent effect of sentences." This belief is not confined to English judges. As Norval Morris has pointed out: "Every criminal law system in the world, except one, has deterrence as its primary and essential postulate. It figures most prominently throughout our punishing and sentencing decisions legislative, judicial and administrative."

And although it would be foolish to regard all those with legislative, judicial, and administrative power in our society as being unquestioning adherents of an established faith in deterrence, it is undeniable that some community of attitude exists. Different groups of officials do appear to share attitudes about deterrence to the extent that generalization does not seem unfair. This is not to say that there is an official dogma which has been formally stated or authoritatively proclaimed. Yet there is an official ideology of deterrence which, although not a system of integrated assertions or an organized body of concepts, does have sufficient definable content to make analytical discussion possible.

When confronted with a crime problem, legislators often agree that the best hope of control lies in "getting tough" with criminals by increasing penalties. Police subscribe to the notion of getting tough, but are apt to put more emphasis on what is termed "strict law enforcement," a concept that accords the major role to policing. Even correctional officers who are publicly committed to a rehabilitative ideal will sometimes privately confess allegiance to a more punitive approach with deterrent purposes in mind. There are of course significant exceptions to these patterns. Many legislators, but far from a majority, now doubt the efficacy of the death penalty as a marginal deterrent when compared with the threat of protracted imprisonment. Many police express less than total faith in the ability of strict law enforcement alone to make a very positive contribution in such areas as the control of prostitution and illegal gaming.

But the exceptions are relatively few, and people more often seem to think in a straight line about the deterrent effect of sanctions: if penalties have a deterrent effect in one situation, they will have a deterrent effect in all; if some people are deterred by threats, then all will be deterred; if doubling a penalty produces an extra measure of deterrence, then trebling the penalty will do still better. Carried to what may be an unfair extreme, this style of thinking imagines a world in which armed robbery is in the same category as illegal parking, burglars think like district attorneys, and the threat of punishment will result in an orderly process of elimination in which the crime rate will diminish as the penalty scale increases by degrees from small fines to capital punishment, with each step upward as effective as its predecessor. Other officials, however—frequently those engaged in correctional work, the discouraging end of deterrence—will sometimes take a different but equally unitary view: since human behavior is unpredictable and crime is determined by a variety of causes, deterrence is a myth.

Commonly, both those who assert the necessary and universal effectiveness of punishment threats and those who deny their relevance to human behavior do not provide more than alternative slogans or catchwords. So it is impossible to determine what evidential bases their views rest on. The truth is (and it is a cheap point) that deterrence is far too complicated a matter to be contained within either of these procrustean views. Such beliefs have no truth value. Nevertheless, it is of considerable importance to examine the bases upon which they rest. The discussion which follows represents an attempt to provide the necessary analysis.

When crime rates rise, law enforcement officials are frequently held—and many hold themselves—in some degree responsible. Some of them, it is true, may feel either that the problem is insoluble or that the solution lies beyond their sphere of influence. But for the most part, law enforcement officials and society at large find themselves in agreement that fluctuations in the crime rate are subject to political control—and responsive to crime control policy.

The law enforcement official, however, soon finds that he has a limited range of crime control options. He is not in a position—nor will he always feel the need—to introduce millennial measures to end poverty or eradicate social and economic inequity. He can make crime physically more difficult in only a limited number of situations—by urging citizens to lock their cars; fostering the use of automatic locks on bank vaults; raising the height of fire alarm boxes to secure them from the whims of 5-year-old children; doubling and trebling the number of police on the street to hamper the mugger, the purse thief, and the random attacker.

Many prevention strategies are expensive, and the administrator is the first to feel the brunt of this type of expense. To double the police force, we must more than double our budget for police. If citizens are required to take expensive precautions, they will object. If precautions are not made mandatory, many will not heed warnings. Beyond this, many of the most serious of crimes—homicide, aggravated assault, rape, indoor robbery, larceny, and crimes against trust—are committed where police cannot prevent them.

Thus, a belief in the efficacy of deterrent measures is attractive, because it offers crime control measures where alternatives appear to be unavailable and does so without great apparent cost. It is not surprising that deterrence through threat and punishment is among the most valued official weapons in the war against crime. Nor is this merely a matter of political expedience. For it is difficult to deny that, as Professor Packer puts it, "People who commit crimes appear to share the prevalent impression that punishment is an unpleasantness that is best avoided." To threaten with punishment is therefore a very promising strategy for influencing behavior. And deterrence is a strategy that shows promise of working in areas of behavior where the official has no other technique for crime reduction at hand.

Yet it is one thing to believe that deterrent measures may be a promising strategy in some situations and quite another to espouse a monolithic theory of deterrent efficacy. And it is not immediately apparent why so many people do hold monolithic attitudes about deterrence—whether affirming or denying the effectiveness of legal threats. It seems that they allow themselves to hold only one idea about the nature of deterrence. Once the complex of issues about deterrence is transformed into a yes-or-no question, the results are of course predictable. If the only question at issue is whether deterrence is possible or not, those who believe that it is possible will achieve a substantial majority as a matter of common sense. But when a complex series of different issues is bent into the form of a yes-or-no question, the margin of error obtained from answering that question either way approaches 50 percent.

The tendency to have only one idea about deterrence is not peculiar to officials, nor is it confined to those who deal with the subject of deterrence. The "single idea" phenomenon is a characteristic of prescientific speculation in most areas of human knowledge. One factor is no less basic than human nature; we all would prefer to have simple rather than complicated explanations for the questions that perplex us. Complicated explanations evolve from the pressure that experience exerts on our simple initial constructs by a process of trial and error. Since so little evaluative research has yet been done in the area of deterrence, there is little pressure toward rethinking unitary positions. Thus, there are few inconsistent results to sensitize officials to the differences in situation which may, in turn, condition differences in threat effectiveness. Moreover, the limited amount of data available can be comfortably fitted into the official's initial opinion—it can be either accepted at face value or rejected as inconclusive. The absence of reliable research in deterrence does not mean that officials are without any basis for their opinions. In most cases, they will have personal and administrative experience in the light of which to test their views of deterrent effectiveness.

The official's personal experience is in most cases likely to lend support to his belief in deterrence. Having worked hard to achieve the regard of his fellows, he is more sensitive than most to the threat of social stigma. He likes to regard himself as a rational man and will be anxious to give himself credit for responding in the only rational manner to threats. The official is also a law-abiding man and attributes some of his obedience to the threat of sanctions. He remembers slowing down when seeing a police car on the highway, remembers considering the possibility of audit when filling out his income tax return. He is less likely to recall deviations.

It is probable that another source of information is the official's own experience with crime control policies. In his official capacity, the legislator "tries out" deterrent threats; the results of these trials are integrated into his attitudes about deterrence. In the absence of controlled research, the apparent results of ongoing crime control policy are the most important data available about deterrence, and these results will inevitably have a profound effect on official attitudes. Unhappily, as we shall see, the unquestioning acceptance of the unanalyzed results of experience with crime control policy is not a satisfactory substitute for careful evaluative research.

The Lessons of Experience

We cannot demonstrate the truth of our assertion that an important source of those shared beliefs about deterrence which influence penal policy is to be found in the experience of our lawmakers and law enforcers. Nor can we show conclusively that their beliefs are derived from their experience in the manner which we suggest. We can only adduce argument in support of our view, mainly by showing that officials rationalize their beliefs by pointing to that experience. Moreover, the study of such rationalization is itself important.

We do not claim to be, in T. S. Eliot's phrase, "expert beyond experience." But experience as a teacher has defects other than the commonly observed characteristic that it seems to inspire reminiscential garrulity. The truth is that there are different types of experience from which knowledge may be derived, and it is necessary to distinguish from one another at least two meanings of the word *experience*.

First, by experience we may mean the experiences which men accumulate as a result of direct participation in events and being engaged in a particular activity, without making any special effort to explore, investigate, or test hypotheses. Second, we may refer to the special data of experience which men collect by undertaking methodical research and making systematic observations.

Our contention is that the experience of lawmakers and law enforcement officials is usually of the first kind and that it is subject to serious limitations as a source of knowledge. It is particularly defective when used as a basis for generalization or inductive inference. In order to emphasize some of the common pitfalls that officials encounter in trying to read the significance of the results of crime control policies, we may start with three examples of common errors made in inferring more from statistics than the statistics will support.

AUNT JANE'S COLD REMEDY   One common inferential error, or failure to satisfy the conditions of valid or correct inference, can be illustrated by an example drawn from the field of folk medicine. Aunt Jane's Cold Remedy is a mixture of whiskey, sugar, and hot water. It is widely recommended as a treatment for the common cold which can be guaranteed to be effective as a cure within ten days. In a great many cases, moreover, it does appear to be effective. The great majority of those who take the remedy are likely to be quite satisfied with it because every time they take it their cold disappears within the nominated period.

However, apart from some possible temporary, symptomatic relief, Aunt Jane's Cold Remedy has no known effect on the common cold. The cold goes away within ten days because most colds run a course of from three to ten days whether treated or not—that is the nature of the malady. Yet if the adherents of Aunt Jane's Cold Remedy are faithful, they will have no way of knowing that the remedy did not effect a cure. And if, as is quite possible, they have some kind of emotional investment in believing in the cure, they may staunchly resist the suggestion that the remedy is useless, even when their colds go away without being treated with it. Such untreated colds, when recovered from, can be explained away as milder infections.

Legislators and law enforcement officials treat crime, not colds, but they are prone to adopt similar modes of inference. When life is proceeding normally, no great pressure is put on the legislator to increase penalties or on the police official to double or triple patrols. Pressure for strong new countermeasures comes when the crime rate suddenly spurts. Often the scenario then follows this course: (1) spurt in crime rate, (2) countermeasure, (3) return of crime rate to more normal historical level.

Did the countermeasure reduce crime? If so, by how much? The headlines read, "Police dogs reduce ghetto crime by 65%," or "Computer reduces false alarms by 35%," and enforcement officials are reluctant to avoid credit for the change. But if we remember that an unusual spurt in the crime rate was responsible for the countermeasure, another possible explanation of the reduction exists: the crime rate simply returned to its usual level, which would have been the case whether or not the computer or police dogs or new patrols had been introduced.

It is sometimes impossible to tell what the crime rate would have been if a particular program had not been introduced. So it is not always possible to determine how much of the reduction can be attributed to natural causes and how much can be credited to the program. But in most cases, knowledge that the program was introduced in a peak period should at least make observers sensitive to the possibility that a good part of the decrease might have been unrelated to the new program. Detailed study of historical trends in the crime rate, or comparisons with untreated areas, could show that the decrease was not solely attributable to Aunt Jane.

Still, if officials desire to maintain a unitary faith in deterrent countermeasures, they can easily do so. Because new programs are normally tried during periods when the rate of the particular crime is high, the official can take credit for any decreases in rate that follow the introduction of the new measures. If the crime rate stays high, who can say that it would not have climbed higher were it not for the new program? Indeed, the rise in crime shows conclusively that we need more of the new countermeasures.

Subjecting our crime prevention strategies to evaluative research will prove less comforting but, in the long run, more valuable. In some situations, close analysis will show that the crime rate could have been expected to decrease even if no new treatment had been administered; in others, a steady rise in crime over a long period of time that can be attributed to factors such as an increase in the population at risk will indicate that, in the absence of a new treatment, the crime rate would probably have continued to increase. Evaluative research may be able to provide rough estimates of how much the rate would have increased or decreased in the absence of treatment and thus give us a baseline for testing the value of new treatments.

Providing a baseline, so that reliable determinations can be made about the degree of crime reduction attributable to particular countermeasures, is an absolute necessity in any but the most wasteful of crime control policies. Without such a baseline, it may be assumed that some strategies reduce crime when in fact they do not. The preventive effects of other programs may be underestimated because we fail to account for expected increases in crime. When countermeasures do have some effect on crime, overestimating that effect by neglecting the possibility of natural decrease may provoke the use of programs that are not worth their cost—and, worse still, postpone the development of new and more effective strategies.

TIGER PREVENTION Alexander King prefaces his *May This House Be Safe From Tigers*—the second volume of his memoirs—with an anecdote about a Buddhist prayer which provides him with his title and will provide us with an illustration.

There are many versions of the story King tells, but that which we favor seems more closely analogous to the way in which what we call the tiger prevention fallacy may both vitiate official thinking and set up a formidable barrier to the revision of crime control strategies. In our version, a man is running about the streets of mid-Manhattan, snapping his fingers and moaning loudly, when he is intercepted by a police officer. Their conversation follows:

Police officer: What are you doing?
Gentleman: Keeping tigers away.
Police officer: Why, that's crazy. There isn't a wild tiger within five thousand miles of New York City!
Gentleman: Well then, I must have a pretty effective technique!

Other factors than the Buddhist's benediction are responsible for Alexander King's immunity from tigers, just as other factors account for the absence of tigers in New York City. But as long as those who practice such preventive methods continue to do so they will not find that out.

In crime control, the tiger prevention problem is subtle and difficult to resolve. Officials who administer very high penalties acquire the firm conviction that only those penalties stand between them and huge increases in the crime rate. Having assumed that the penalty is the only reason for the absence of a crime wave, the official has "proved" that high penalties deter crime more effectively than less severe penalties.

One of the most celebrated examples of the tiger prevention approach to crime control is British Chief Justice Lord Ellenborough's now classic response to a nineteenth-century proposal that, while the death penalty for shoplifting should remain, the value of the goods stolen which incurred that penalty be raised from five to ten shillings. Speaking in the House of Lords, Ellenborough said:

I trust your lordships will pause before you assent to an experiment pregnant with danger to the security of property. . . . Such will be the consequence of the repeal of this statute that I am certain depredations to an unlimited extent would immediately be committed. . . . Repeal this law and . . . no man can trust himself for an hour out of doors without the most alarming apprehension that on his return, every vestige of his property will be swept off by the hardened robber.

The proof is the same as that offered by the tiger preventers except in one respect: because penalties may well influence crime rates, it cannot be assumed, as in the tiger example, that the countermeasure bears no relation to the rate of crime. Being unable to assume that there is no relation between penalty level and crime rate, we can only determine whether and how much the two are related by varying the penalty. But since that would involve risk taking, the status quo and the "proof" of deterrence built into it persist. The tiger prevention argument is not refutable when posed as a barrier to experimental decreases in punishment; it is, however, patently absurd to present high penalties combined with low crime rates as proof of deterrence.

Studies of different areas with different penalties, and studies focusing on the same jurisdiction before and after a change in punishment level takes place, show rather clearly that level of punishment is not the major reason why crime rates vary. In regard to particular penalties, such as capital punishment as a marginal deterrent to homicide, the studies go further and suggest no discernible relationship between the presence of the death penalty and homicide rates. Although imperfect, these studies certainly use the best methods available of testing whether more severe sanctions have extra deterrent force in particular situations.

But even in comparative and retrospective studies, the tiger prevention fallacy may crop up in a more sophisticated form. Consider a study that shows homicide to be both the most severely punished and the least often committed crime in a particular jurisdiction. Proof of deterrence? Or tiger prevention? It is quite possible that the rate of homicide would remain low even if the penalty for homicide were less severe, because of the strong social feelings against homicide. Indeed, one reason why the penalty for homicide is so high may be that citizens view this crime as so terrible. Both the low rate and the high penalty may be effects of the same cause: strong social feelings against homicide. Thus, showing that crimes which are punished more severely are committed less often may only be one way of showing how accurately a penalty scale reflects general feeling about the seriousness of crimes.

This problem can also arise in connection with some forms of comparative research. Assume we find out that homicide is punished more severely in one state than in another, and that the homicide rate is much lower in the severe penalty state. Does the higher penalty cause the lower rate? It may be that the higher penalty shows that people in that state have stronger social feelings about homicide, and these feelings, rather than the extra penalty, may explain the difference in homicide rate. In order to test the effect of penalties alone, areas that are similar to each other in all respects except penalties should be sought out and compared. This would be a strategy far more cumbersome than assuming that harsh criminal sanctions are keeping the tigers away but, again, far more reliable and rewarding.

THE WARDEN'S SURVEY   A third type of faulty inference is found most frequently among those who work at what we have called "the discouraging end of deterrence." Once again the argument is based on experience, but this time the conclusion drawn is diametrically opposite to that exemplified above.

The earliest example we have come across of the type of argument we have in mind occurs in a 1931 article by Warden George W. Kirchwey of Sing Sing. Writing as one "*that has known the convict*" (our italics), Kirchwey maintains that "it argues a curious ignorance of human psychology to attach much importance to the doctrine of deterrence." He goes on to say that belief in "the deterrent effect of exemplary punishments or in their moralizing effect on the community at large is" a blind faith.

The same sort of inference is drawn much more explicitly in a book by another celebrated warden of Sing Sing, Lewis E. Lawes, published in 1940. In his *Meet the Murderer,* Lawes states that "the threat of capital punishment lacks the deterrent force most people believe it possesses." On the basis of "*many years' acquaintance with all types of murderers*" (our italics again), he avers that "a person who commits murder gives no thought to the chair." Last, and even more explicitly, we find Warden Clinton T. Duffy of San Quentin giving his views on the effectiveness of the death penalty as a deterrent in his *88 Men and Women.* "But the prison man knows this threat is no deterrent," says Duffy, "*for convicts have told him so again and again*" (our italics).

The warden's survey is unpersuasive for two reasons. First, in none of the instances cited is it at all clear that the prisoners would have told the warden even if they *had* been deterred by penalties at some time in their lives. It could hardly be in their interests to do so. But more significantly, in each case the warden's sample of people to ask about deterrence and base his inference upon is hopelessly biased. For he has based his conclusion on experience with groups of men who have evidently not been deterred or they would not be in prison.

Our tiger preventers and our wardens make contradictory assumptions about the relation between those criminals in jail and the potential crime problem. The tiger prevention advocate assumes that large numbers of law-abiding citizens are held in check by the threat of penalties; indeed, that only severe penalties can perform this job. The warden seems to assume that, when he interviews prisoners, he is talking to the totality of the potential crime problem, or at least to a representative sample. Consequently, because these assumptions are unsupported, both the "proof" and "disproof" of deterrence must fail.

But the fact that these patterns of thinking fail to prove or disprove deterrence does not mean they are unimportant and can be ignored. Officials will continue to act on severe convictions, whether or not these convictions are well founded. Thus, a significant step toward more rigorous research in deterrence, and ultimately toward a more rational crime control policy, would be to make officials more sensitive to new insights and more understanding of the complexities that undermine monolithic attitudes about deterrence. For this reason, the careful study of "cold remedy . . . tiger prevention," and "warden's survey" patterns of inference are an important part of a program for progress in crime control.

Deterrence or Brutalization:
What Is the Effect of Executions?

WILLIAM J. BOWERS
GLENN L. PIERCE

A critical feature of the debate over capital punishment has been the impact of executions on society. Advocates of the death penalty say that it protects society by dramatically demonstrating to would-be murderers that such crime does not pay. Opponents argue that capital punishment brutalizes society because executions show that lethal violence is an appropriate response to those who offend.

Historically, these arguments came into bold relief in the debate over public executions in America in the 1830s and 1840s. Advocates argued that removing executions from public view would deprive them of their unique power as a deterrent. Opponents said that public executions stimulate the kinds of violence for which they are imposed. These opposing arguments also figured in the controversy over press coverage of executions in the 1890s and later. Indeed, they surfaced again recently in response to a proposal to televise executions in Texas. Some, including once presidential hopeful John Connally, see this as the best way to "harness the deterrent power" of the death penalty. Others are afraid that televising executions would incite imitative execution-like behavior in society. They cite Gary Gilmore's execution as a case in point, saying it was followed by a rash of bizarre acts of violence by mentally unstable persons apparently seeking public attention. What are

the assumptions and implications of these two opposing positions?

DETERRENCE

The deterrence argument assumes a rationalistic perspective in which human behavior is seen as a function of individually perceived costs and benefits of alternative choices or actions. The individually perceived costs and benefits are further assumed to reflect directly, if imperfectly, objectively ascertainable variations in these costs and benefits to the individual. Thus, in the case of murder, not unlike other less violent and more instrumental crimes, deterrence theory assumes that potential offenders exercise rational judgment in deciding whether or not to kill and that they are predictably sensitive to the actual range of variation in certainty and severity of legal punishment for murder at the time of the decision to act. This rationalistic view is familiar in economics, and has served as the basis for a theory of legal punishment, at least since Jeremy Bentham.

From what we know about murder, however, there is reason to doubt these assumptions. Most murders are acts of passion between angry or frustrated people who know one another. Indeed, many murders are the result of assaults occurring under the influence of alcohol, and many of the murderers are persons who have previously and repeatedly assaulted the victim. Encounters that result in murder typically involve "face saving" or the maintenance of favorable "situational identities" in the presence of

From "Deterrence or Brutalization? What Is the Effect of Executions?" by W. J. Bowers and G. L. Pierce, 1980, *Crime and Delinquency*, *26*, pp. 453-484. Copyright 1980 by Sage Publications, Inc. Reprinted by permission.

threats, insults, and demands for compliance. In a recent study, having intoxicated and unarmed victims is what best distinguished imprisoned killers from those incarcerated for aggravated assault. We know further that extreme brutality or cruelty toward the victim or killing in the act of another crime is the circumstance most likely to bring down a death sentence. In effect, most murderers, and particularly those who reach death row, do not fit the model of the calculating killer.

Moreover, it is doubtful that the calculating potential offender, even if he wanted to do so, could make a rational decision that takes execution risk into account. Police statistics reported to the Federal Bureau of Investigation and execution records from the National Bureau of Prisons indicate that only a small fraction of criminal homicides have resulted in executions—no more than 2 percent per year since 1930. It has been virtually impossible for the public to know the proportion of first-degree or capital murders for which executions were carried out in a given jurisdiction over a given period of time. Even experts have found it difficult to estimate the number of capital murders. About the only way potential offenders can develop some vague impression that committing murder has become more or less risky is from the number and pacing of executions as reported in the press.

Beyond these misgivings about the rational model of the murder decision, there is further reason to doubt that potential offenders actually get the deterrence message executions are presumed to convey. An execution can be viewed from various vantage points. If one could put himself in the shoes of the offender who gets executed, he might see that the same could be in store for him were he to follow in that offender's footsteps. That is, the person who identifies with an executed offender may get the deterrence message. But the psychology of identification tells us that people identify personally with those they admire or envy. What we know about those murderers who are eventually executed makes it seem quite unlikely that any sane or rational person will identify with them. They are characteristically uneducated, impoverished misfits who have committed cruel or cowardly acts without provocation or remorse. They may have strangled small children, killed whole families, dismembered their victims, and the like. Will calculating potential murderers identify with them, or will they not, instead, contrast themselves with these wretches? Might they not infer that the death penalty is reserved as punishment only for people unlike themselves?

BRUTALIZATION

The argument that executions have a brutalizing effect draws on different assumptions about the message that executions convey. The first serious critic of capital punishment in modern times, Cesare di Beccaria, in 1764 attacked the death penalty for the "savage example" it presents to men:

Laws designed to temper human conduct should not embrace a savage example which is all the more baneful when the legally sanctioned death is inflicted deliberately and ceremoniously. To me it is an absurdity that the law which expresses the common will and detests and punishes homicide should itself commit one.

A similar argument was advanced in 1846 by Robert Rantoul, Jr., who was among the first to present statistical evidence on the brutalizing effect of execution: "After every instance in which the law violates the sanctity of human life, that life is held less sacred by the community among whom the outrage is perpetrated."

The lesson of the execution, then, may be to devalue life by the example of human sacrifice. Executions demonstrate that it is correct and appropriate to kill those who have gravely offended us. The fact that such killings are to be performed only by duly appointed officials on duly convicted offenders is a detail that may get obscured by the message that such offenders deserve to die. If the typical murderer is someone who feels that he has been betrayed, dishonored, or disgraced by another person—and we suggest that such feelings are far more characteristic of those who commit murder than a rational evaluation of costs and benefits—then it is not hard to imagine that the example executions provide may inspire a potential murderer to kill the person who has greatly offended him. In effect, the message of the execution may be lethal vengeance, not deterrence.

Implicit in the brutalization argument is an alternative identification process, different from the one implied by deterrence theory. The potential murderer will not identify personally with the criminal who is executed, but will instead identify someone who has greatly offended him—someone he hates, fears, or both—with the executed criminal. We might call this the psychology of "villain identification." By associating the person who has wronged him with the victim of an execution, he sees that death is what his despised offender deserves. Indeed, he himself may identify with the state as executioner and thus justify and reinforce his desire for lethal vengeance.

Granted, it is uncommon to think of potential murderers as self-righteous avengers who identify with the executioner, but the more common view that they will think of themselves as criminals and identify with those who are executed may be wishful thinking. We have already observed that those who get executed are a wretched lot with whom few would identify—the kinds with whom one might identify his worst enemies. Perhaps the reason people are inclined to believe that potential murderers will recognize their criminal tendencies and be deterred by the executions of other murderers is that this distinguishes "them" from the rest of "us" and provides a justification for executions that masks the desire for lethal vengeance. Also, by imagining that potential murderers will get the deterrence message, the "law-abiding" have the satisfaction of believing that they are taking effective steps to combat society's most heinous and feared crimes.

Executions might stimulate homicides in other ways. For some people, the psychology of suggestion or imitation may be activated by an execution. In this connection, research on the aftermath of the John F. Kennedy assassination and two highly publicized mass murders has shown that they were succeeded by significantly increased rates of violent crime in the months immediately following. The investigators offer the following three-point interpretation of imitative violence:

One, aggressive ideas and images arise. Most of these thoughts are probably quite similar to the observed event, but generalization processes also lead to other kinds of violent ideas and images as well. Two, if inhibitions against aggression are not evoked by the witnessed violence or by the observers' anticipation of negative consequences of aggressive behavior, and if the observers are ready to act violently, the event can also evoke open aggression. And again, these aggressive responses need not resemble the instigating violence too closely. Three, these aggressive reactions probably subside fairly quickly but may reappear if the observers encounter other environmental stimuli associated with aggression—and especially stimuli associated with the depicted violence.

Furthermore, there is evidence that such a process of suggestion or stimulation may also include an element of identification with the victim. Thus, research on highly publicized suicides has shown that they are followed in the succeeding month by a significantly higher than expected number of suicides in the population. It is estimated, for example, that Marilyn Monroe's suicide provoked some 363 suicides in the United States and Britain.

As an escape from life, execution may be preferable to suicide to some troubled individuals. Although most people find it hard to imagine, there are many cases of persons who have killed others for self-destructive motives. In these cases, the individuals typically have a deep-seated antipathy toward themselves and others, a need to express and act on their feelings, and a guilt-inspired desire to be punished for their feelings and actions. For those burdened with self-hatred, death by execution is punishment as well as escape. With the crime that leads to execution, the offender also strikes back at society or particular individuals. The execution itself may provide an opportunity to be seen and heard, to express resentment, alienation, and defiance. Thus, even for the troubled few who may find it possible to identify with the executed criminal, or at least with his situation, the message of an execution may be imitation rather than deterrence.

In the era of public executions, such imitative behavior was noted in the press and commented on by prominent social critics. The *Times* of London on January 25, 1864, contained the following observation:

It has often been remarked that in this country a public execution is generally followed closely by instances of death by hanging, either suicidal or accidental, in consequence of the powerful effect which the execution of a noted criminal produces upon a morbid and unmatured mind.

Writing in the New York *Daily Tribune* of February 18, 1853, no less a social critic than Karl Marx elaborated specifically on this observation. Citing data on executions, suicides, and murders for forty-three days in 1849, he commented as follows: "This table . . . shows not only suicides but also murders of the most atrocious kind following closely upon the execution of criminals."

Even after executions had been largely removed from public view, it was argued that they still had a brutalizing impact in stimulating imitation of the crimes of the condemned through their coverage in the press: "This morbid press publicity has a most demoralizing effect upon the community and many weak-minded persons of inadequate self-control are thus enabled to dwell on the details of horrible crimes with the real danger of repeating them."

The suggestion is that publicizing an execution, let alone allowing people to witness one, may cause some people—perhaps those on the fringe of sanity—to become fascinated or obsessed with the condemned person's crime, even to the point of imitating it.

Nor is the suggestive or imitative impact of an execution necessarily limited to the condemned person's crime. Thus, some have suggested that the execution itself may be imitated:

Lynchings are the sequel of the imposition of the death penalty by the state, which, setting the example of sending criminals to the gallows, leads mobs to adopt similar methods of punishment

when aroused. This is not unlike the argument . . . that the public executions of old, instead of deterring criminals from crime, lead them into it by brutalizing their feelings and cheapening the value of human life.

Notably, the fact that lynching was itself a capital offense in most states where it prevailed did not deter thousands of otherwise "law-abiding" citizens; there have been roughly 3,500 documented lynchings since 1890.

Indeed, death-risking behavior is sometimes a way of affirming one's commitments and winning favor in society. It is a sign of courage and bravery in wartime, a source of recognition and admiration among sportsmen and adventurers, an affirmation of honor in the face of insults, and a demonstration of allegiance with others who share a common cause or fear. The very existence of the death penalty may provide some fanatical or troubled people with an unparalleled opportunity to "prove a point" or draw attention to themselves.

EXISTING EVIDENCE

Most studies have examined variations in the availability or use of executions over extended periods of time with officially recorded statistics on murder or homicide for evidence of whether death as punishment prevented or provoked the kinds of crimes for which it was imposed. A few studies have focused on the more immediate impact of executions by examining homicides in the days, weeks, and months surrounding executions. In our review of this empirical literature, it will be convenient to distinguish between studies of the longer-term effects of executions conducted with data on homicides for years or longer periods of time and studies of their more immediate impact done with data on homicides nearer to the time of execution.

Long-Term Effects

Well over a century ago, when capital punishment was under attack and public executions in the United States were coming to an end, the impact of executions on homicides was being studied with statistics from various countries covering extended periods of time. Perhaps America's most prominent compiler and interpreter of these data was Massachusetts legislator and man of letters Robert Rantoul, Jr. In 1846, he addressed a series of six letters containing detailed tabulations and interpretations of these data to the legislature and governor of Massachusetts. Rantoul's analyses of these data were broadly comparative across jurisdictions and time periods:

In England, France, Prussia, Belgium, and Saxony, as well as many other nations that might be mentioned, where the proportion of executions to convictions is much smaller than in Massachusetts, and much smaller than fifty years ago in the same countries, murders have rapidly diminished in those countries in which executions are scarcely known; slightly in France where the change of policy was not so great; while in England, down to about 1835, murders and attempts to murder increased, since which, under a milder administration of the law, there has been a change for the better.

Rantoul was also sensitive to short-term fluctuations in executions as they might affect the incidence of homicides. Thus, for the period 1796-1833 in Belgium, he observed,

Not only does this result follow from the table taken as a whole, but each period in which a change in the degree of severity occurs, teaches the same lesson.

The three years in which more than fifty executions occurred in each year, were followed respectively by the three years of most numerous murders.

Rantoul's analysis is remarkable even by modern standards for its scope, logic, and attention to detail. If he did not convincingly rule out the possibility that declining homicide rates or other associated factors might have relaxed the public's desire for executions—as an alternative to the brutalizing hypothesis—he did at least address the issue of causal priority with selected data on the temporal sequence of movements in executions and homicides. Certainly, the deterrence argument finds no support in these data; they are, instead, consistent with the argument that executions, at least public executions, have a brutalizing effect on society.

In a second reform era when capital punishment was again under attack and public executions had virtually disappeared, the focus of research shifted from the actual use to the legal availability of executions. The development of Census Bureau registration of mortality statistics around the turn of the century provided a new, more reliable measure of homicide—one more strictly comparable across states and over time. In 1919, using these data, Raymond Bye compared abolitionist states with neighboring death penalty states, and periods of abolition with periods of retention in states that had abolished or reinstated the death penalty. This work marked the beginning of a series of such investigations based initially on the willful homicide data of the Census Bureau and later on the criminal homicide statistics of the FBI. Best known in this tradition of research is the work of Thorsten Sellin.

Each of these investigations concluded that the study provided no consistent or reliable evidence that the de jure availability of executions had a deterrent effect on homicides. Yet as a group, these investigations suggest a different conclusion: the balance of evidence is consistent with a brutalizing effect of executions. Thus, every study comparing abolitionist and neighboring retentionist states has shown that the former tend to have lower homicide rates than the latter. Studies of the killing of policemen, prison guards, and prison inmates have found that the rates tend to be lower in abolitionist than in death penalty states. And, in studies comparing abolition and retention periods in a given state with contiguous states to control for trends, the differences tend to be more consistent with the brutalization than with the deterrence argument.

At the critical juncture in the history of capital punishment in the United States, after executions had ceased and the Supreme Court had declared previous capital statutes unconstitutional, a new brand of research on the effects of executions appeared using annual execution and homicide data—as Rantoul had done well over a century earlier. Instead of comparing matched abolition and retention jurisdictions as Sellin and others had done, this econometric modeling approach attempted to adjust statistically, by multiple regression techniques, for differences across states or over time which could be expected to produce differences in homicide rates that otherwise might mistakenly be attributed to the imposition of executions.

In 1975, Isaac Ehrlich published the first econometric study of execution risk and homicide rates, based on data for the nation as a whole over the period 1933-1969. This study purported to show—contrary to all previous investigations—that each execution saved seven or eight innocent lives by deterring murders that would otherwise occur. This work is noteworthy not for the validity of its claims, which have now been discredited by a number of reanalyses of these data, but for its impact in promoting the cause of capital punishment and for the series of further studies it provoked. These latter studies have, on balance, yielded more empirical support for the brutalizing than for the deterrent effect of executions.

What did careful reanalyses of these data show? First, execution risk tended to be positively associated with homicide rates from the mid-1930s through the early 1960s, using Ehrlich's data and analytic approach. Second, the relationship also tended to be positive in the 1960s when this period was examined independently of the earlier years. Third, the relationship tended to be even more positive, approaching statistical significance, when less flawed homicide data were used in the analyses.

Studies have gone on to show with Ehrlich's data and with other time series and cross-sectional data sets that positive execution effects occur with the addition of explanatory variables omitted from Ehrlich's analysis. Thus, positive execution effects have emerged in time series analyses with measures of handgun ownership and noncapital violent crime rates and in cross-sectional analyses with variables reflecting certainty and severity of imprisonment for criminal

homicide—despite the negative bias that error in measuring homicides may introduce. In the only analysis we know of that is not subject to the negative bias introduced by the common term problem (execution risk is a conditional measure computed by dividing the number of persons executed in 1960 by the number of murderers imprisoned in that year), William Bailey found statistically significant positive effects of execution risk on homicide rates consistent with a brutalizing effect of executions.

Short-Term Impact

At the high point of executions in America in the mid-1930s, research began to deal with the more immediate impact of executions—in the spirit of Marx's commentary on forty-three days of executions and homicides in London in 1849 but more systematic in its approach. In 1935, Robert Dann examined five executions in Philadelphia (occurring in 1927, 1929, 1930, 1931, and 1932), which had in common the fact that no other execution had been imposed within sixty days. Dann then tallied the homicides occurring in sixty-day periods before and after each of these executions and reported a total of 91 homicides before and 113 homicides after these five executions—an average increase of 4.4 homicides in the sixty days after each execution. As it happens, Dann's results are not independent of seasonal fluctuations in homicides. A crude adjustment for seasonal variations in homicides in Philadelphia indicates that a total of 105 homicides might have been expected in the postexecution period. Thus, a more reliable estimate of the impact of these five executions would be eight additional homicides—an average of 1.6 more homicides in the sixty days following each execution.

In summary, studies of the long-term effect and short-term impact of executions give ample indication that executions may have—contrary to prevailing belief—not a deterrent but a brutalizing effect on society by promoting rather than preventing homicides. The earliest research in the period of public executions was fully and strongly consistent with such a brutalizing effect. Later studies comparing periods of abolition and retention between and within jurisdictions consistently show lower homicide rates at times and places of abolition, suggesting that the availability, and by implication the use, of the death penalty stimulates homicide. And recent studies using econometric modeling and regression estimation techniques have begun to reveal more positive than negative estimates of the effects of execution risk on homicide rates—notwithstanding analytic problems which have tended to bias results in favor of deterrence.

DATA AND ANALYSIS

With the publication of the Teeters-Zibulka inventory of *Executions Under State Authority: 1864-1967,* systematic information has become available on some 5,706 executions imposed over the past century. For most states, this represents a complete listing of executions since they were moved from local jurisdictions to the central authority of the state. The inventory includes information on type of offense, county of prosecution, race and age of offender, appeals before execution, and, for present purposes, date of execution.

With the development of the Vital Statistics program of the U.S. Bureau of the Census, systematic information became available by states on the numbers of deaths from various causes, including "willful homicide." A willful homicide is defined in the International Classification of the Causes of Death as "a death resulting from an injury purposely inflicted by another person." Notably, the definition of willful homicide has remained relatively unchanged (with one critical but tractable exception throughout successive revisions of the classification scheme):

Since 1900 the causes of death have been classified according to seven different versions of the International Classification of Diseases. Each revision has produced some breaks in the comparability in the causes-of-death statistics. However, homicide is among the causes for which the classifications are essentially comparable for all revisions.

Of all states, New York has imposed the most executions under state authority, some 695 since 1890, when it became the first state to use the electric chair. New York has also had more homicides than any other state for most of this period. Moreover, New York has had an active Vital Statistics program at the state level since 1907. The numbers of homicides recorded monthly for New York State since 1907 are available from the Department of Health. The comparatively high incidence of homicides and executions in New York and the relatively long period of time over which data are available on a monthly basis make New York the state best suited to the purposes of our analysis.

The analysis to be presented here is a simple one. It asks how the number of homicides in a given month is affected by the occurrence of executions throughout the preceding year. The data are homicides and executions occurring monthly. The monthly homicide figures run from their starting point in January 1907 through August 1964, a year after the last execution in New York State. The monthly execution data for this analysis cover the period from January 1906 through the date of New York's last execution, in August 1963. For purposes of statistical analysis, this is a time series of 57 years and 8 months, or some 692 monthly observations.

These figures say that, on the average, the presence of one or more executions in a given month adds two homicides to the number committed in the next month. A similar but weaker effect appears for the presence of executions two months earlier. This suggests that, on the average, executions imposed in a given month add one homicide to the number committed two months later. We say "suggest" here because the observed pattern in the data is not sufficiently strong under any of the time trend controls in this sample of 692 observations to be statistically significant at the .05 probability level.

Further Controls for
Temporal Variation

Abrupt and temporary departures from steady temporal trends may, for example, be the product of discrete historical events. To the extent shifts in the level of homicides, for example, are not traced by the time trend controls in our analyses, they will add error. Furthermore, to the extent that executions are affected by periodic historical events, perhaps increased or diminished in number, biases will be introduced into our estimates of execution effects. It is important, therefore, that our temporal controls incorporate the effects of such events.

War is one of the most disruptive events societies experience. Those who go to war are disproportionately from the groups in society that contribute most to the homicide rate. It is reported, for example, that New York City shrank by three-quarters of a million persons, mostly young males, during World War II. Studies have shown that domestic homicide rates tend to drop off during wartime and that they tend to climb precipitously immediately after war. Although not fully understood, these systematic temporal fluctuations are certainly affected by the movement of more homicide-prone individuals out of civilian society during wartime and by the impact of war on those who return from combat to face problems of adjusting to civilian life. War may also foster an acceptance of lethal violence in the broader society—as some say executions do.

This raises the possibility that our analysis of the impact of executions on homicides is missing an important component that would improve its explanatory power and strength and thus increase the reliability of our results. On the assumption that major wars and their aftermaths tend to produce significant departures from secular trends in domestic homicides, we have extended the analysis to include factors representing the period of U.S. involvement in World War II and a two-year postwar adjustment period.

The war years obviously dropped well below the trend line; from 1941 to 1944 there were on the average six fewer homicides per month than would otherwise be expected. In the year the war ended and the troops returned home in massive numbers, homicides increased substantially, to a monthly average four homicides above the trend line. In the two years after the war, homicides rose further, to ten per month above the trend line. Perhaps those who went to war came back more violent, maybe they returned to a more violent society, or possibly problems of reintegration and adjustment were the cause. In any case, the war evidently had a brutalizing effect on postwar society.

CONCLUSIONS

There is room to quarrel about whether these data show a brutalizing effect of two or three homicides, on the average, occurring after a month in which an execution is carried out. It is certainly consistent with the notion of a brutalizing effect of two homicides in the first month immediately after an execution to have some "temporal spillover" into the second month after an execution. Indeed, if, on the average, executions tend to fall in the middle of a month, then the fact of two homicides in the following month suggests a six-week brutalizing effect. For executions imposed at the end of a month, this would naturally extend the duration of effect into the second month after the execution. The point is that such a distributive effect—two homicides one month later and one homicide two months later—is thoroughly consistent with a commonly observed pattern of dissipating effects over time.

The fact that we see a consistently negative effect of executions at least suggests that some of those who were stimulated to kill by the occurrence of an execution would have done so anyway, but did so *sooner* because of the execution. That is, just as these data suggest a third additional homicide in the second month after an execution, they also suggest (although less strongly) that one of the three might have occurred a month or so later anyway. In any case, the data definitely show an addition of at least two to the incidence of homicides, not simply a change in the timing of homicides.

It should be noted that in this analysis we have probably underestimated the brutalizing effect of executions. We have ignored those instances in which a brutalizing effect may have occurred in the same month as an execution. The analysis of this issue is complicated, however, by the possibility of a "repressive response" effect. That is, whether or not an execution occurs may, in some measure, be affected by the incidence of homicides in that month (and/or the preceding one). Thus, for example, the decision to grant a stay of execution may be more difficult to make in the presence of an exceptionally high level of homicides in the days and weeks immediately preceding the scheduled execution date. Hence, a greater than expected number of homicides in a month with an execution might reflect the impact of homicides on the occurrence of executions instead of executions on the occurrence of homicides. This matter, to be addressed in subsequent research, requires the use of a more complicated analytic model than we have dealt with here.

Of course, in states with smaller populations and/or fewer executions the brutalizing effect will yield fewer homicides (unless it extends beyond jurisdictional boundaries). Parenthetically, this may, in part, account for the failure of previous studies based on state-level aggregate annual homicide data to detect brutalizing effects. Notably, the studies that have suggested a brutalizing effect of executions have worked with data on homicides occurring days, weeks, and months before and after executions. Indeed, the only other study to examine monthly homicide data found borderline statistical support for a brutalizing effect in the month after the occurrence of an execution story in South Carolina. In fact, the magnitude of the brutalization effect relative to the incidence of homicides was roughly similar in South Carolina and New York; South Carolina had about half the homicides in an average month (20.4 vs. 40.4) and

about half the brutalizing effect (1 as opposed to 2 additional homicides), despite the fact that its population was approximately one-sixth that of New York for the respective periods of analysis.

This suggests that the brutalization occurs among the pool of potential killers (as this may be reflected in the actual number of homicides) and not the population at large. This tends to confirm the notion that the brutalizing effect is specific to the person who has reached a state of "readiness to kill," in which the potential killer has a justification, a plan, a weapon, and above all a specific intended victim in mind. It is precisely for such people with a victim in mind that an execution may convey the message of lethal vengeance. They need only place the intended victim in the shoes of the executed criminal, the process we have called "villain identification." Of course, some guilt-laden, self-destructive persons in a state of readiness of kill might be prompted by the execution to imitate the crime for which it was imposed.

The implications of this research, given the present status of capital punishment in the United States, are ominous. At this writing, there are some 642 persons under sentence of death. If the execution of each one produced two or three homicides, the cost in innocent lives would be outstanding. Moreover, the audience for executions in this era may not be jurisdictionally specific—it may be nationwide, suggesting that the increase in homicides experienced by New York State represents only a fraction of what might be expected for the nation as a whole.

The Specific Deterrent Effects of Arrest for Domestic Assault

LAWRENCE W. SHERMAN
RICHARD A. BERK

with 42 patrol officers of the Minneapolis Police Department, Nancy Wester, Donileen Loseke, David Rauma, Debra Morrow, Amy Curtis, Kay Gamble, Roy Roberts, Phyllis Newton, and Gayle Gubman

SOCIOLOGISTS since Durkheim have speculated about how the punishment of individuals affects their behavior. Two bodies of literature, specific deterrence and labeling, have developed competing predictions. Durkheim, for example, implicitly assumed with Bentham that the pains of punishment deter people from repeating the crimes for which they are punished, especially when punishment is certain, swift, and severe. More recent work has fostered the ironic view that punishment often makes individuals more likely to commit crimes because of altered interactional structures, foreclosed legal opportunities, and secondary deviance.

Neither prediction can muster consistent empirical support. The few studies that allege effects generally employ weak designs in which it is difficult, if not impossible, to control plausibly for all important factors confounded with criminal justice sanctions and the rule-breaking behavior that may follow. Thus, some claim to show that punishment deters individuals punished, while others claim to show that punish-

ment increases their deviance. Yet all of these studies suffer either methodological or conceptual flaws as tests of the effects of punishment, especially the confounding of incarceration with attempts to rehabilitate and the frequent failure to differentiate effects for different types of offenders and offenses.

Perhaps the strongest evidence to date comes from a randomized experiment conducted by Lincoln and associates. The experiment randomly assigned juveniles who had already been apprehended to four different treatments ranked in their formality: release, two types of diversion, and formal charging. The more formal and official the processing, the more frequent the repeat criminality over a two-year follow-up period. This study supports labeling theory for arrested juveniles, although it cannot isolate the labeling or deterrent effects of arrest per se.

In all likelihood, of course, punishment has not one effect, but many, varying across types of people and situations. As Lempert argues, "It is only by attending to a range of such offenses that we will be able to develop a general theory of deterrence." The variables affecting the deterrability of juvenile delinquency, white-collar crime, armed robbery, and domestic violence may be quite different. Careful accumulation of findings from different settings will help us differentiate the variables which are crime- or situation-specific and those which apply across settings.

In this spirit, we report here a study of the impact of punishment in a particular setting, for a particular offense, and for particular kinds of individuals. Over an eighteen-month period, police in Minneapolis applied one of three intervention strategies in incidents of misdemeanor domestic assault: arrest, ordering the offender from the premises, or some form of advice which could include mediation. The three interventions were assigned randomly to households, and a critical outcome was the rate of repeat incidents. The relative effect of arrest should hold special interest for the specific deterrence-labeling controversy.

POLICING DOMESTIC ASSAULTS

Police have been typically reluctant to make arrests for domestic violence, as well as for a wide range of other kinds of offenses, unless victims demand an arrest, the suspect insults the officer, or other factors are present. Parnas's qualitative observations of the Chicago police found four categories of police action in these situations: negotiating or otherwise "talking out" the dispute, threatening the disputants and then leaving, asking one of the parties to leave the premises, or (very rarely) making an arrest. Similar patterns are found in many of the cities. Surveys of battered women who tried to have their domestic assailants arrested report that arrest occurred in 10 percent or 3 percent of the cases. Surveys of police agencies in Illinois and New York found explicit policies against arrest in the majority of agencies surveyed. Despite the fact that violence is reported to be present in one-third to two-thirds of all domestic disturbances police respond to, police department data show arrests in only 5 percent of those disturbances in Oakland, 6 percent of those disturbances in a Colorado city, and 6 percent in Los Angeles County.

The best available evidence on the frequency of arrest is the observations from the Black and Reiss study of Boston, Washington, and Chicago police in 1966. Police responding to disputes in those cities made arrests in 27 percent of violent felonies and 17 percent of the violent misdemeanors. Among married couples, they made arrests in 26 percent of the cases, but tried to remove one of the parties in 38 percent of the cases.

An apparent preference of many police for separating the parties rather than arresting the offender has been attacked from two directions over the past fifteen years. The original critique came from clinical psychologists, who agreed that police should rarely make arrests in domestic assault cases and argued that police should mediate the disputes responsible for the violence. A highly publicized demonstration project teaching police special counseling skills for family crisis intervention failed to show a reduction in violence, but was interpreted as a success nonetheless. By 1977, a national survey of police agencies with 100 or more officers found that over 70 percent reported a family crisis intervention training program in operation. While it is not clear whether these programs reduced separation and increased mediation, a decline in arrests was noted for some. Indeed, many sought explicitly to reduce the number of arrests.

By the mid-1970s, police practices were criticized from the opposite direction by feminist groups. Just as psychologists succeeded in having many police agencies respond to domestic violence as "half social work and half police work," feminists began to argue that police put "too much emphasis on the social work aspect and not enough on the criminal." Widely publicized lawsuits in New York and Oakland sought to compel police to make arrests in every case of domestic assault, and state legislatures were lobbied successfully to reduce the evidentiary requirements needed for police to make arrests for misdemeanor domestic assaults. Some legislatures are now considering statutes requiring police to make arrests in these cases.

The feminist critique was bolstered by a study showing that for 85 percent of a sample of spousal homicides, police had intervened at least once in the preceding two years. For 54 percent of the homicides, police had intervened five or more times. But it was impossible to determine from the cross-sectional data whether making more or fewer arrests would have reduced the homicide rate.

In sum, police officers confronting a domestic assault suspect face at least three conflicting options, urged on them by different groups with different theories. The officers' colleagues might recommend forced separation as a means of achieving short-term peace. Alternatively, the officers' trainers might recommend mediation as a means of getting to the underlying cause of the "dispute" (in which both parties are implicitly assumed to be at fault). Finally, the local women's organizations may recommend that the officer protect the victim (whose "fault," if any, is legally irrelevant) and enforce the law to deter such acts in the future.

RESEARCH DESIGN

In response to these conflicting recommendations, the Police Foundation and the Minneapolis Police Department agreed to conduct a randomized experiment. The design called for random assignment of arrest, separation, and some form of advice which could include mediation at the officer's discretion. In addition, there was to be a six-month follow-up period to measure the frequency and seriousness of domestic violence after each police intervention. The advantages of randomized experiments are well known and need not be reviewed here.

The design only applied to simple (misdemeanor) domestic assaults, where both the suspect and the victim were present when the police arrived. Thus, the experiment included only those cases in which police were empowered (but not required) to make arrests under a recently liberalized Minnesota state law; the police officer must have probable cause to believe that a cohabitant or spouse had assaulted the victim within the last four hours (but police need not have witnessed the assault). Cases of life-threatening or severe injury, usually labeled as a felony (aggravated assault), were excluded from the design for ethical reasons.

The design called for each officer to carry a pad of report forms, color coded for the three different police actions. Each time the officers encountered a situation that fit the experiment's criteria, they were to take whatever action was indicated by the report form on the top of the pad. We numbered the forms and arranged them in random order for each officer. The integrity of the random assignment was to be monitored by research staff observers riding on patrol for a sample of evenings.

After police action was taken, the officer was to fill out a brief report and give it to the research staff for follow-up. As a further check on the randomization process, the staff logged in the reports in the order in which they were received and made sure that the sequence corresponded to the original assignment of treatments.

Anticipating something of the victims' background, a predominantly minority, female research staff was employed to contact the victims for a detailed face-to-face interview, to be followed by telephone follow-up interviews every two weeks for twenty-four weeks. The interviews were designed primarily to measure the frequency and seriousness of victimization caused by the suspect after the police intervention. The research staff also collected criminal justice reports that mentioned the suspect's name during the six-month follow-up period.

RESULTS

The 205 completed initial interviews provide some sense of who the subjects are, although the data may not properly represent the characteristics of the full sample of 314. They show the now familiar pattern of domestic violence cases coming to police attention being disproportionately unmarried couples with lower than average educational levels, disproportionately minority and mixed race (black male, white female), and who were very likely to have had prior violent incidents with police intervention. The 60 percent suspect unemployment rate is strikingly high in a community with only about 5 percent of the workforce unemployed. The 59 percent prior arrest rate is also strikingly high,

TABLE 1

Victim and suspect characteristics: Initial interview data and police sheets (in percentages).

A. Unemployment		
Victims	61	
Suspects	60	
B. Relationship of suspect to victim		
Divorced or separated husband	3	
Unmarried male lover	45	
Current husband	35	
Wife or girlfriend	2	
Son, brother, roommate, other	15	
C. Prior assaults and police involvement		
Victims assaulted by suspect, last six months	80	
Police intervention in domestic dispute, last six months	60	
Couple in counseling program	27	
D. Prior arrests of male suspects		
Ever arrested for any offense	59	
Ever arrested for crime against person	31	
Ever arrested on domestic violence statute	5	
Ever arrested on alcohol offense	29	
E. Mean age		
Victims	30 years	
Suspects	32 years	

F. Education	Victims	Suspects
< high school	43	42
high school only	33	36
> high school	24	22
G. Race		
White	57	45
Black	23	36
Native American	18	16
Other	2	3

Note: N = 205 (those cases for which initial interviews were obtained).

suggesting (with the 80 percent prior domestic assault rate) that the suspects generally are experienced lawbreakers who are accustomed to police interventions. But with the exception of the heavy representation of Native Americans (due to Minneapolis' unique proximity to many Indian reservations), the characteristics in Table 1 are probably close to those of domestic vio-

TABLE 2

Speed of reunion and recidivism by police action.

	Time of Reunion (in percentages)				New Quarrel Within	New Violence Within
Police Action	Within 1 Day	More Than 1 Day but Less Than 1 Week	Longer or No Return	(N)	a Day (n)	a Day (n)
Arrested (and released)	38	30	32	76	2	1
Separated	57	31	10	54	6	3
Advised	—	—	—	72	4	1

Note: N = 202 (down from the 205 in Table 7.1 due to missing data).

lence cases coming to police attention in other large U.S. cities.

Twenty-six percent of those separated committed a repeat assault, compared to 13 percent of those arrested. The mediation treatment was statistically indistinguishable from the other two. To help put this in perspective, 18.2 percent of the households failed overall.

Thus, the police data indicate that the separation treatment produces the highest recidivism, arrest produces the lowest, with the impact of "advise" (from doing nothing to mediation) indistinguishable from the other two effects.

The analysis also examined patterns of crime from the interview reports of victims. A "failure" is defined as a new assault, property destruction, or a threatened assault. (Almost identical results follow from a definition including only a new assault.) These results suggest a different ordering of the effects, with arrest still producing the lowest recidivism rate (at 19 percent), but with advice producing the highest (37 percent). Overall, 28.9 percent of the suspects "failed." Still, the results are much the same as found for the official failure measure.

An obvious rival hypothesis to the deterrent effect of arrest is that arrest incapacitates. If the arrested suspects spend a large portion of the next six months in jail, they would be expected

to have lower recidivism rates. But the initial interview data show this is not the case: of those arrested, 43 percent were released within one day, 86 percent were released within one week, and only 14 percent were released after one week or had not yet been released at the time of the *initial* victim interview. Clearly, there was very little incapacitation, especially in the context of a six-month follow-up. Indeed, virtually all those arrested were released before the first follow-up interview. Nevertheless, we introduced the length of the initial stay in jail as a control variable. Consistent with expectations, the story was virtually unchanged.

Another perspective on the incapacitation issue can be obtained by looking at repeat violence which occurred shortly after the police intervened. If incapacitation were at work, a dramatic effect should be found in households experiencing arrest, especially compared to the households experiencing advice. Table 2 shows how quickly the couples were reunited, and of those reunited in one day, how many of them, according to the victim, began to argue or had physical violence again. It is apparent that all of the police interventions effectively stopped the violence for a 24-hour period after the couples were reunited. Even the renewed quarrels were few, at least with our relatively small sample size.

Hence, there is again evidence for an incapacitation effect. There is also no evidence for the reverse: that arrested offenders would take it out on the victim when the offender returned home.

DISCUSSION AND CONCLUSIONS

It is apparent that we have found no support for the deviance amplification point of view. The arrest intervention certainly did not make things worse and may well have made things better. There are, of course, many rejoinders. In particular, over 80 percent of offenders had assaulted the victims in the previous six months, and in over 60 percent of the households the police had intervened during that interval. Almost 60 percent of the suspects had previously been arrested for something. Thus, the counterproductive consequences of police sanction, if any, may for many offenders have already been felt. In labeling theory terms, secondary deviation may already have been established, producing a ceiling for the amplification effects of formal sanctioning. However, were this the case, the arrest treatment probably should be less effective in households experiencing recent police interventions. No such interaction effects were found. In future analyses of these data, however, we will inductively explore interactions with more sensitive measures of police sanctioning and prior criminal histories of the suspects.

There are, of course, many versions of labeling theory. For those who theorize that a metamorphosis of self occurs in response to official sanctions over a long period of time, our six-month follow-up is not a relevant test. For those who argue that the development of a criminal self-concept is particularly likely to occur during a lengthy prison stay or extensive contact with criminal justice officials, the dosage of labeling employed in this experiment is not sufficient to falsify that hypothesis. What this experiment does seem to falsify for this particular offense is the broader conception of labeling implicit in the prior research by Lincoln et al., Farrington, and others: that for every possible increment of criminal justice response to deviance, the more increments (or the greater the formality) applied to the labeled deviant, the greater the likelihood of subsequent deviation. The absolute strength of the dosage is irrelevant to this hypothesis, as long as some variation in dosage is present. While the experiment does not falsify all possible "labeling theory" hypotheses, it does at least seem to falsify this one.

The apparent support for deterrence is perhaps more clear. While we certainly have no evidence that deterrence will work in general, we do have findings that swift imposition of a sanction of temporary incarceration may deter male offenders in domestic assault cases. And we have produced this evidence from an unusually strong research design based on random assignment to treatments. In short, criminal justice sanctions seem to matter for this offense in this setting with this group of experienced offenders.

A number of police implications follow. Perhaps most important, police have historically been reluctant to make arrests in domestic assault cases, in part fearing that an arrest could make the violence worse. Criminal justice sanctions weakly applied might be insufficient to deter and set the offender on a course of retribution. Our data indicate that such concerns are by and large groundless.

Police have also felt that making an arrest was a waste of their time: without the application of swift and severe sanctions by the courts, arrest and booking had no bite. Our results indicate that only 3 of the 136 arrested offenders were formally punished by fines or subsequent incarceration. This suggests that arrest and initial incarceration alone may produce a deterrent effect, regardless of how the courts treat such cases, and that arrest makes an independent contribution to the deterrence potential of the criminal justice system. Therefore, in jurisdictions that process domestic assault offenders in a manner similar to that employed in Minneapolis, we favor a *presumption* of arrest; an arrest should be made unless there are good, clear reasons why an arrest would be counterproductive. We do not, however, favor *requiring* arrests in all misdemeanor domestic assault cases. Even if our findings were replicated in a number of jurisdictions, there is a good chance that arrest works far better for some kinds of offenders than others and in some kinds of situations better than others. We feel it best to leave police a loophole to capitalize on that variation. Equally important, it is widely recognized that discretion is inherent in police work. Simply to impose a requirement of arrest, irrespective of the features of the immediate situation, is to invite circumvention.

The Role of Arrest in Domestic Assault

FRANKLYN W. DUNFORD
DAVID HUIZINGA
DELBERT S. ELLIOTT

IN what has come to be known as a landmark study, the Minneapolis Domestic Violence Experiment by Sherman and Berk assessed the effects of different police responses on the future violence of individuals apprehended for domestic assault. The authors reported:

Arrest was the most effective of three standard methods police use to reduce domestic violence. The other police methods—attempting to counsel both parties or sending assailants away—were found to be considerably less effective in deterring future violence in the cases examined.

Sherman and Berk specified arrest and initial incarceration, "alone," as deterring continued domestic assault and recommended that the police adopt arrest as the favored response to domestic assault *on the basis* of its deterrent power. These findings and recommendations came at a time when advocacy for increased sensitivity to women's rights was strong and pressure was mounting to change the social service approach to domestic violence that had dominated law enforcement and court policy over the preceding two decades. Sherman and Berk's recommendations were uniquely appealing for the times and were received by many women's advocates and law enforcement administrators as justification for change.

The overwhelming reaction of the research community to the Minneapolis experiment, with its recommendation for presumptory arrests in cases of misdemeanor domestic assault, was a call for additional studies to corroborate its conclusions. The Omaha Domestic Violence Police Experiment, funded by the National Institute of Justice, was conceived and designed to determine if the findings reported for the Minneapolis experiment could be replicated elsewhere.

THE OMAHA RESEARCH DESIGN

Omaha is a city of approximately 400,000 inhabitants, 10 percent of whom are black and 2 percent of Hispanic origin. The city is split into three sectors (south, west, north) for police purposes. In concert with Chief Robert Wadman of the Omaha Police Division and after surveying 9-1-1 dispatch records, it was determined that approximately 60 percent of all disturbance calls were reported during the hours of C shift (4 p.m. to midnight). On this basis, the decision was made to limit the replication experiment in Omaha to eligible domestic assaults coming to the attention of the police throughout the city (all three sectors) during the hours of C shift. In this way, no segment of the city (e.g., socioeconomic status [SES] or ethnic group) would be excluded from participation in the experiment by the research design, and the majority of domestic violence calls would be included in the study.

Following the design of the Minneapolis experiment, police calls for domestic violence found to be eligible for the study were randomly assigned to "arrest," "separation," or "mediation" for all instances in which both victims and suspects were present when the police arrived. A case was eligible for the experiment if (1) probable cause for an arrest for misdemeanor assault existed, (2) the case involved a clearly identifiable victim and suspect, (3) both parties to the assault were of age (18 or older), (4) both parties had lived together sometime during the year preceding the assault, and (5) neither party to the offense had an arrest warrant on file. Cases for which the police had no legal authority to make an arrest (i.e., no probable cause to believe that an assault had occurred) were excluded from the experiment, as were more serious cases (i.e., felony cases).

DESCRIPTION OF THE EXPERIMENT

In February 1986, all of the command and patrol officers assigned to C (and D) shift were trained during a succession of three-day training sessions. Training focused on the rationale, content, and mechanics of the experiment. At each shift change thereafter, officers new to C shift were similarly trained. A total of 194 officers were ultimately assigned to the participating shifts and received training on the methods and procedures of the experiment. Of that number, 31 (16 percent) did not refer any cases to the study, and 61 (31 percent) accounted for approximately 75 percent of the referrals.

Because random assignment to treatment was sometimes violated, there were four different ways to analyze the data: treatment as assigned, treatment as officially recorded, treatment immediately delivered, and treatment ultimately delivered. The first measure, treatment as assigned, was the treatment that was randomly assigned by computer and communicated to officers in the field by the Information Unit: arrest, separate, or mediate. The second measure, treatment as officially recorded, was treatment as recorded by responding officers on the Domestic Violence Report form. After re-

ceiving a randomized treatment from the Information Unit, officers recorded the disposition on the Domestic Violence Report form, along with other relevant information, and forwarded the report to headquarters. When the 330 treatments as assigned were compared with the treatments as officially recorded on the Domestic Violence Report forms, one discrepancy was found. The third measure, treatment as immediately delivered, reflects estimates of the initial treatment that was actually delivered at the scene of an eligible case. This measure was determined by asking victims about treatments delivered to suspects and by reviewing what police officers wrote on the Domestic Violence Report form about the treatment delivered and comparing the two. Some of the discrepancies between treatment as assigned and treatment as immediately delivered appear to have involved differences in perceptions of what happened rather than any real differences, while others were clear misdeliveries of treatments.

The final treatment category consisted of treatment as ultimately delivered. This classification was determined by comparing treatments as assigned with what victims reported as ultimately happening and what police officers recorded on the Domestic Violence Report forms as ultimately happening and by comparing arrests with official records of police, prosecuting attorney, and court actions. If, for example, in the course of delivering mediation a suspect assaulted an officer and was arrested, the case was defined as follows: treatment as assigned = mediation; treatment as immediately delivered = mediation; treatment as ultimately delivered = arrest. Also, if the assigned treatment was arrest and no official record could be found that an arrest was made, the case was classified on the treatment as ultimately delivered measure as mediation. Treatment as ultimately delivered is problematic in that the absence of an officially recorded arrest is not foolproof evidence that an arrest was not made. In several cases, for example, no record of arrest was found in the police record bureau even though the case had been officially recorded as "booked" into the jail. Conversely, cases were found in the police record bureau that were not found in the "jail" booking records.

Two types of outcome measures were included in the research design. The first was official recidivism as measured by new arrests and complaints for any crimes committed by suspects against victims, as found in official police records. The second was a victim report of three forms of repeated violence: (1) fear of injury, (2) pushing-hitting, and (3) physical injury. Both types of outcome measures permit assessment of the effects of differential treatment on preventing subsequent conflict. The design called for interviewing victims twice over a six-month follow-up period; the initial interview was held at the end of the first week after the presenting offense and the second six months later.

FINDINGS

Omaha-Minneapolis Comparisons

The Minneapolis and Omaha experiments differ on a few key points. Differences in the penalties resulting from court appearances associated with random assignment to arrest, differences in the areas of the cities covered by the experiments, differences in interview completion rates, and differences in outcome measures and the way they were aggregated may affect the relevance of the two experiments for one another.

Treatment Effects

The effects of treatments/dispositions as randomly assigned were examined using each of the five outcome measures (official arrest and complaints and three victim reports of repeated violence) obtained during the six-month period following the date of entry into the experiment. The findings are as follows. Arresting suspects had no more effect on deterring future arrests or complaints (involving the same suspects and victims) than did separating or counseling them. The overall statistical comparisons revealed no significant differences in the prevalence or frequency of offending between treatment groups.

When the crimes associated with the repeat arrests were tabulated by offense, 27 of the charges (68 percent) were for assault, 8 (20 percent) were for disorderly conduct, 2 (5 percent) were for criminal mischief, and one each (2.5 percent) were for trespassing, failing to leave on request, and destruction of property. When statistical tests for differences in arrest outcome were limited to the 27 repeat assault cases, no differences by treatment were found.

Comparisons of victim reports of repeated violence also resulted in no statistically significant differences between treatment groups, although the interpretation of the findings was complicated somewhat by the presentation of missing data. Thus, it was concluded that victims whose partners were arrested were no less likely to experience repeated violence from that partner than were victims whose partners received a randomized "separate" or "mediate" disposition from the police.

It is important to note that the data do not favor any specific type of treatment. Repeated domestic violence did not appear to be related to police decisions to arrest suspects, to separate them from victims, or to mediate disputes in which they were involved. Further, the same outcome was observed when similar analyses were conducted to control for (1) prior arrests, (2) ethnicity, or (3) time spent in jail; or to cases limited to (4) couples in conjugal relationships at the time of the presenting offense, (5) cohabitants who had lived together for the entire six-month follow-up period, or (6) persons who had lived together for at least some time during the follow-up period.

Time-to-Failure Analysis

Notwithstanding an inability to find differences in repeat offending between treatment groups six months after the presenting offense, it is still possible that one treatment may delay repeated instances of conflict longer than other treatments. If, for example, the Minneapolis experiment's finding that arrest delayed recidivism for significantly longer periods of time than other treatments could be replicated, it would have policy implications quite independent of the failure to replicate the Minneapolis prevalence outcomes in Omaha. However, there were no real differences between the treatments in the delay of recidivism. At most the results were inconsistent across treatment groups.

DISCUSSION

Conclusions based on the results of the research conducted in Omaha must be considered together with the outcomes of the five other research efforts currently funded by the National Institute of Justice to replicate the Minneapolis experiment. Since the results from all of these studies are not yet available, what follows must be considered tentative. It must also be remembered that the results of the Omaha experiment cannot be generalized beyond Omaha or beyond the types of cases defined as eligible during the hours of the experiment. Finally, although a serious attempt was made to replicate the Minneapolis experiment in Omaha, comparisons of the details of the two experiments reveal a number of significant differences. Whether these differences account for the differences in the findings of the two experiments is uncertain.

Given the strength of the experimental design used in Omaha and the absence of any evidence that the design was manipulated in any significant way, the inability to replicate findings associated with the Minneapolis experiment calls into question any generalization of the Minneapolis findings to other sites. First, arrest in Omaha, by itself, did not appear to deter subsequent domestic conflict any more than did separating or mediating those in conflict. Arrest, and the immediate period of custody associated with arrest, was not the deterrent to continued domestic conflict that was expected. If the Omaha findings should be replicated in the other five sites conducting experiments on this issue, policy based on the presumptory arrest recommendation coming out of the Minneapolis experiment may have to be reconsidered. Second, although arrest, by itself, did not act as a deterrent to continued domestic conflict for the misdemeanor domestic assault cases coming to the attention of the Omaha police, neither did it increase continued domestic conflict between parties to an arrest for assault. That is, victim-reported measures of repeated conflict, which are measures of behavior (as opposed to arrest and complaint data, which are measures of official police reaction to known violations of the law), clearly did not indicate that victims whose partners were arrested were at greater risk of subsequent conflict than were those whose partners were handled informally (mediated or separated) by the police. Arrest did not appear to place victims in greater danger of increased conflict than did separation or mediation. It would appear that what the police did in Omaha after responding to cases of misdemeanor domestic assault (arrest, separate, mediate) neither helped nor hurt victims in terms of subsequent conflict.

The failure to replicate the Minneapolis findings will undoubtedly cast some doubt on the deterrent power of a mandatory or even a presumptory arrest policy for cases of misdemeanor domestic assault. At this point, researchers and policymakers are in the awkward position of having conflicting results from two experiments and no clear, unambiguous direction from the research on this issue. Nevertheless, the data from the Omaha police experiment clearly suggest that the adoption of an arrest policy for cases of misdemeanor domestic assault may not, by itself, have any impact on the likelihood of repeated violent acts. For those who are directly involved in responding to domestic assaults, it might be profitable to begin thinking about new or additional strategies for dealing with this problem.

From Initial Deterrence to Long-Term Escalation in Domestic Violence

LAWRENCE W. SHERMAN
JANELL D. SCHMIDT
DENNIS P. ROGAN
PATRICK R. GARTIN
ELLEN G. COHN
DEAN J. COLLINS
ANTHONY R. BACICH
and 35 officers of the Milwaukee Police Department

DOES the length of time in custody affect the odds of future criminality? This question is central to public policy and criminological theory, yet it remains virtually unanswered. Little enough is known about the individual effects of incarceration for any length of time, let alone for varying times in custody. Yet at every step of the criminal justice process, there is enormous variation in the length of time each offender is held captive. Given the modern reliance on incarceration as a primary criminal sanction, the ignorance about its dosage-response effects is bewildering. If incarceration were a drug, the Food and Drug Administration would long ago have required animal tests for its toxicity, large-scale randomized trials to demonstrate its benefits, and large-scale user surveillance for allergic reactions.

The question of varying time in custody is especially important at the point of arrest, for several reasons. One is the fact that arrest is the aspirin of criminal justice—the most widely dispensed incarceration "drug" in the United States. Each year, about 56 times more people are arrested than are committed to prison. Another reason is that the range of variation of time in custody is proportionately far greater for arrest than for prison. Although prison terms generally range from about 1 to 25 years, custody associated with arrest often ranges from one day to one week (168 hours). For serious offenses with suspects who cannot make bail, pretrial incarceration can last for months.

Wide variation in arrest time has become an especially important issue for misdemeanor domestic violence. The growth of mandatory arrest laws and policies may be associated with the 70 percent growth in national per capita arrest rates for simple assault from the 1984 publication of the Minneapolis domestic violence experiment to 1989. These laws appear to be premised on a conception of arrest as a homogeneous treatment, a standard pill that has virtually the same effects on everyone. But there is increasing evidence that neither domestic violence arrests nor their effects are homogeneous.

The Minneapolis experiment itself reported a range of time in custody of from under one day to over one week. Since the publication of the

Minneapolis results, the National Institute of Justice has funded six replication experiments, of which results from three (Omaha, Nebraska; Charlotte, North Carolina; and Milwaukee, Wisconsin) are available at this writing. Those experiments also showed wide variation in time in custody both across and within cities. One of them, in fact, made such variation an explicit part of the research design. The Milwaukee domestic violence experiment randomly assigned *short* (under three hours) and full arrests (about 12 hours), as well as no arrest (warning only), to persons eligible to be arrested. This chapter reports the varying effects of time in custody found in that experiment.

In other publications, we report the Milwaukee interaction-effect results showing the varying effects of the same dosage of custody on different kinds of people. Full arrest had no deterrent effect on employed persons, but a criminogenic effect on unemployed persons. Similar effects have been found for other indicators of "social bonds." Taken together, these findings suggest that both the content and the consequences of arrest are anything but standard, at least for domestic violence. The results raise major policy questions, not just about domestic violence but about arrests and other forms of custody in general.

TIME IN CUSTODY
AND RECIDIVISM

The effects of time in custody on recidivism are not at all clear from the previous literature, which has been largely confined to nonexperimental studies of prison and jail time. In 1970, the Hood and Sparks review of several English and American studies of juvenile and adult offenders found little difference in recidivism, despite substantial variations in length of sentences. Other research suggests longer terms in prison may increase criminality or recidivism for certain types of offenders. These and other studies have been hard to interpret given third factors (such as prior record) affecting both time in custody and recidivism. Attempts to control for such factors can suffer unknown specification error.

DOMESTIC VIOLENCE ARRESTS

The domestic violence research has prompted new scrutiny of the variation in arrest times for misdemeanors across communities. Our experiment in Wisconsin, for example, led us to research the variation in that state when a mandatory arrest law went into effect after our experiment was completed but before its results were announced. In a mail survey of 39 smaller police departments throughout the state conducted in 1990, over half (8 of 15) respondents said they released suspects arrested for misdemeanor domestic violence within three hours. In Milwaukee, by contrast, the average time in custody for a full arrest is almost 12 hours.

Although communities may differ in the average length of time misdemeanor arrestees are held in custody, there is also substantial variation within communities. Sherman and Berk, for example, reported victim interview data showing that 43 percent of domestic violence arrestees were released within one day, another 43 percent were released within one week, and 14 percent were released after more than one week in jail. Dunford and his colleagues reported that official records on total time in custody data were unavailable, although police interviews showed a minimum of one hour in custody would be associated with each arrest. Under 20 percent of the domestic violence arrestees in the Omaha experiment were released from *custody* within two hours after booking. The mean time to release to another floor for *posting bond* (but not release from custody until bonding was completed) was 15 hours and 46 minutes. Only about half of those released to post bond actually did so; the rest were held until a court appearance.

The Charlotte domestic violence arrest experiment fell between the long and short custody periods for arrest. The median time in custody was nine hours with 10 percent of all suspects released within one hour.

Goldstein suggested that time in custody for domestic violence arrest poses a risk to victims when it is very short, as in Charlotte. He hypothesized that in jurisdictions where the suspect is released within an hour or two of arrest (unlike the minimum overnight custody in the Minneapolis experiment), the likelihood of intoxication or anger persisting from the original event would be very high. Under such conditions, he suggested, the odds of immediate recidivism would be very high: the suspect could return to the victim and perhaps commit even more serious violence.

Sherman and Berk reported that introducing the natural variation in time in custody had no impact as a control variable in a model of the deterrent effect of arrest. But two factors limit the reliability of that conclusion. One is that the variation was natural, rather than assigned experimentally at random. Even more important is the small sample size and low response rate from the victims that formed the basis for their time in custody data, rather than observations or official records.

Theoretically, we posited that punishment causes both *anger* at the punishers and *fear* of repeat punishment. Under conditions of low dosage of custody, the fear may be too weak to overcome the anger—anger against the same victim whose evidence gave rise to the arrest, against any victim symbolically representing that victim, or against society in general. Thus, we expected that a low custody dosage could backfire, causing more crime than no custody, in both the short and the long run.

EXPERIMENTAL DESIGN

From April 7, 1987, to August 8, 1988, we conducted a randomized experiment in arrest in collaboration with the Milwaukee Police Department. The experimental design had been given the unanimous approval of the Milwaukee Common Council (the local legislature) and was subject to a contract with the Crime Control Institute approved by the Milwaukee City Attorney.

Sample Population

The sample consisted of all eligible cases of probable cause to arrest for misdemeanor domestic battery encountered by a special team of 35 Milwaukee patrol officers. The team was selected from the four districts with the greatest number of domestic violence reports. The reports were generated under a citywide mandatory-arrest and offense-reporting policy for domestic violence for about one year prior to the experiment. The experimental team members all worked the "power shift" of 7 p.m. to 3 a.m., seven days a week (8 p.m. to 4 a.m. on some Saturdays). The four districts were all racially mixed, but they featured the greatest concentration of poor minority areas in the city. Areas within each district were highly segregated in terms of class and race, and each district included vast tracts with ghetto poverty characteristics.

Random Assignment

Experimenting officers complied extraordinarily well with the random assignment procedure, which remained entirely in the control of research staff. Once the officers declared the cases eligible, they telephoned or radioed our office at police headquarters, where civilian research staff logged the cases in. Once the case identifiers were recorded, the researchers opened a sealed, sequentially numbered envelope containing the number 1, 2, or 3, corresponding to the three experimental treatments and determined by a random numbers formula. Researchers told the officers the code number and entered it in the case log. This system entailed far less threat to internal validity than the Minneapolis system, in which the research officers knew what the randomly assigned treatment was while they were assessing cases for eligibility.

Almost all of the treatments (98.25 percent) were delivered as assigned. Only 20 cases were found to have been treated differently from the random assignment, usually for reasons beyond the officers' control. By design, we counted any repeat couples or individuals as new cases, for a total of 1,112 unique couples across the 1,200 randomized cases.

The main difference between the two arrest groups was the time in custody. The mean times of 2.8 and 11.1 hours were computed partly through direct measurement and partly through estimations. The difference was very close to our objective of testing how arrest might work in cities which process misdemeanor battery suspects much more quickly. But in the process, we created some additional differences that may not be typical of normal arrest processing in such cities.

Consistent with the deterrence hypotheses, the short-custody suspects clearly took the arrest experience more "lightly" than the long-custody ones. They were twice as likely to say they were not bothered by the arrest or did not care (25 vs. 13 percent). They were less likely to say they were afraid of what would happen next (31 vs. 39 percent). They were less likely (29 vs. 42 percent) to expect the arrest to hurt their future ability to get a job or a loan to buy a car. And they were twice as likely (21 vs. 11 percent) to expect their friends to be angry with their *partners* for the arrest, not angry with them.

These differences in perception were probably magnified after the jail interview, when the officers personally escorted the suspects through the expedited booking process, often passing other prisoners and going to the front of the line. This procedure was adopted early in the experiment after the booking unit was unable to get the short-custody suspects out much faster than the long-custody suspects. To be released in two hours, the suspects had to be processed immediately at each step in the booking process: fingerprinting, photographing, property identification, and warrant checking. To what extent this experience magnified the suspect's perception of the arrest as a "light" treatment, we can only speculate.

As in Minneapolis, but not Omaha and Charlotte, the arrest treatments in Milwaukee involved virtually no prosecution. Only 37 of the 802 arrests made in our experiment (5 percent) had initial charges filed, and only 11 convictions resulted (1 percent)—despite the fact that victims went downtown to meet with prosecutors in half the arrest cases. Sherman and Berk reported that only 3 out of 136 arrests in Minneapolis received any court-ordered sanction. In contrast, Dunford and his colleagues reported a court sanction rate of 64 percent of all arrests, including jail, probation, and fines, in Omaha; and Hirschel and his colleagues reported a 17 percent conviction rate in the Charlotte experiment.

Unlike Omaha and Charlotte but like Minneapolis, then, in Milwaukee we can attribute any treatment effects to the time in custody for *arrest,* rather than to any additional custody or sanctions produced by prosecution and conviction.

RESULTS

Initial Deterrence

There is good evidence of an initial deterrent effect from short-custody arrest and some evidence of an initial deterrent effect from full arrest. The analyses examined the *prevalence* of repeat violence (up to the date the interview was conducted) on all measures for the 705 cases with initial victim interviews. Interview measures show that both short and full arrest reduced the risk of *any* repeat violence—comparable to what was found in Minneapolis—by about two-thirds. The results do not support the Goldstein hypothesis that short arrests increase risk to the same victim in the short run. The prevalence of repeat violence on first reunion (data not displayed) was virtually identical for short (2.2 percent) and full (1.7 percent) arrest, and both favorably compared with the 7 percent of warning group victims who reported being battered again immediately upon the departure of the police.

Official measures fail to show initial effects of arrest on the prevalence of repeat violence, but the story is different for its frequency (data not displayed). The frequency rate of hotline reports per suspect for the first 30 days after the presenting incident in all 1,200 cases was .09 for the warning group, .07 for full arrest, and .05 for short arrest. Only the short-arrest difference is significant, but full arrest also had lower hotline frequency than warning. Although the other overlapping official measures revealed no significant differences (data not displayed), they all detected fewer cases than the hotline reports, the most comprehensive and statistically most powerful of the official measures.

The magnitude of short arrest's initial deterrent effect was substantial, about a 50 percent reduction in same-victim-reported prevalence and in the rate of any-victim official recidivism per day. This is especially important for the same victim, because total hotline recidivism per day peaked during the initial 30-day period (data not displayed). The continuous official hotline measure, however, showed that short arrest's initial deterrent effect disappeared by the second 30-day period and that a significant criminogenic effect in the third 30-day period was followed by insignificant 30-day differences until the second year.

Longer-Term Criminogenic Effects

By the time of the follow-up interviews, none of the measures showed a deterrent effect of either type of arrest, including same- and any-victim tests of prevalence and frequency. Follow-up victim interviews, for example, showed prevalence of any repeat violence for 35 percent of the full-arrest group, 30 percent of the short-arrest group, and 31 percent of the warning group. Hotline prevalence was virtually identical (at 27, 27, and 26 percent), as were other official measures. However, the period after the first year was marked by short arrest showing a significant criminogenic effect in increasing the mean number of any-victim hotline reports per subject per day. And although the sample size in the final period is reduced from the full experiment, there was no case attrition in the sense that the long-term sample constitutes 100 percent of the cohort of earliest cases to enter the experiment. Thus, although there might have been a mid-1987 "period" effect, there is no danger of sample selection bias in these analyses. Data on the first and second six-month periods for the only group with an 18-month follow-up are included in the analyses to demonstrate the lack of a period effect; they show the same results in each follow-up window as the full sample.

Long-Term Before-After Criminogenic Effects

The most powerful analytic design we employed was the pairwise comparison of before-after changes in official measures of violence in both arrest groups compared with changes in the warning group. This design produced strong evidence of a long-term criminogenic effect of short arrest, but no such evidence for full arrest. Four of eight possible tests of short arrest were significant, two at $p = .10$ and two at .05 (the standard established in advance). None of the tests for full arrest was significant. Moreover, if we limit the official data analysis to the hotline reports as the most comprehensive measure, all four of the possible before-after comparisons of short arrests reveal a criminogenic effect (.10) compared with warnings, but full arrests had no effect. (Recall that no before-after frequency rate comparisons are possible with the victim interview data.)

The raw data for the before-after any-victim hotline frequency test show that although the total frequency of hotline reports per days at risk increased over time in all three groups, it increased about twice as much in the short-arrest group as in the warning group. A similar difference between short arrest and warning, although not as large (46 percent more), occurred with the frequency of arrests. In contrast, the before-after data for the full-arrest group show no consistent criminogenic or deterrent effects compared with warnings. The relative rate of increase is about one-third greater for the full-arrest group than for the warning group in the hotline measure data, but it is about 25 percent lower in the arrest measure data.

The reason for the increase in hotline and arrest rates in all three groups must be noted. Like many police crackdowns, the mandatory arrest and reporting policy for domestic violence gained momentum over time in Milwaukee. In 1986, there were only 4,653 hotline reports from the beginning of the policy on May 1 to December 31, for an annualized estimate of 6,980. In 1987, there were 7,835 hotline reports, and in 1988 there were 8,671, a 24 percent citywide increase over the 1986 rate. Although this does not fully account for the 60 percent overall increase in hotline reports per day in the after period compared with the before period, it seems likely that most of the citywide increase in hotline reports was concentrated on the population in our sample areas, which were purposely selected for their high number of hotline reports in the first year. Such a pattern of concentration could easily explain a 60 percent increase in the sample's rate, as well as the overall increase in the rate of interest.

A conclusion that only short arrest was criminogenic is strengthened by the analysis of before-after changes in prevalence of any-victim hotline reports. The any-victim hotline participation rate for short arrest ($N = 398$) rose from 30 percent before to 38 percent after, but it rose from only 34 to 36 percent for full arrest ($N = 404$) and from 33 to 35 percent for the warning group ($N = 398$). This difference of differences of proportions was borderline significant ($p = .10$) for short arrest versus warning, but not for full arrest versus warning. The same results were found for same-victim prevalence of hotline reports ($p = .056$), but not for same-victim offense reports or any-victim prevalence of arrest reports. These prevalence comparisons would be even stronger without the bias against short arrest in the differing numbers of days at risk.

DISCUSSION

How persuasive is this evidence for a long-term reversal of an early deterrent effect? Should the findings be written off because so many other influences can intercede in a year's time that an effect of one arrest on a suspect seems implausible? Or should the power of the randomized design, combined with its near-perfect implementation by the police, be allowed to speak for itself?

Our findings were not, after all, completely consistent with our theoretically derived predictions. Nor is it obvious how to explain them from any existing theoretical perspective. The findings are, however, consistent with portions of the evidence from the three other available domestic violence experiments and from a review of 18 quasi-experiments in the general deterrent effects of policing. If the empirical regularities do not fit current theory, it seems better to discard the theories than the data. Few would pretend, in any case, that theories of sanctioning effects—as distinct from the causes of crime—have been well developed.

Assuming that there is a long-term, and definitely not a short-term, criminogenic effect of short arrest, we can draw two conclusions about our hypotheses. One is that the Goldstein hypothesis of short-term danger from short arrest is clearly contradicted by these data. The other is that short arrest, over the longer term, apparently did something that full arrest did not do to provoke more violence against intimates. Goldstein's concern about the use of short arrest, then, appears to be warranted, but for very different empirical reasons than he suggested.

The policy implications of these findings are highly debatable, because they produce a moral dilemma between short-term victim interests and long-term control of domestic violence. For the victim who wishes to avoid the 7 percent risk of a repeat attack as soon as police leave, short arrest is clearly preferable to no arrest. Even with a 2 percent risk of repeat violence upon the suspect's return home, short arrest nets the same victim two-thirds lower odds of repeat violence in the short run. Yet the long-term cost of that choice is to increase the total violence committed by that suspect against all potential intimate victims. This long-term effect does not clearly develop with full arrest, which may justify its continued use as a policy. But in order to avoid the long-term escalation of recidivism from short arrest, such policies or laws would have to specify 12-hour minimum times in custody.

Moreover, many would argue that a proper policy analysis of arrest would include other effects, such as unemployment by the suspect and the impact of arrest on the domestic relationship. Others might argue that the criminal justice model of "victim" and "suspect" used in this experiment is inappropriate for what are arguably situations of mutual conflict more properly labeled "disputes." Still others would argue that arrest is appropriate as a just desert, regardless of its effects on recidivism.

An additional policy consideration not discussed here, but also raised by Sherman and Berk, is the varying effects of arrest on different types of offenders. No discussion of either policy or theory should ignore the finding that some arrest has very strong, early-on, and persistent criminogenic effects on certain types of offenders, which we report elsewhere. Indeed, full interpretation of the differences and consistencies of findings across sites must also take these interactions into account in examining the long-term criminogenic effect of arrest.

To the extent that mandatory arrest policies are founded on a premise of long-term specific deterrence, then, the current experiment clearly refutes that premise, at least in ghetto poverty areas like Milwaukee's. As the third experiment to reach that conclusion out of four reported to date, the current analysis is the first to conclude (although not to show evidence) that arrest can actually increase domestic violence. This should give considerable pause to advocates of mandatory arrest who flatly assert a deterrent effect from arrest no matter what the time in custody, no matter what the population arrested.

Two other findings tend to call into question the deterrent value of mandatory arrest. One is the relatively low percentage of the victims (24 percent) and suspects (19 percent) interviewed who were aware of the city's mandatory arrest policy, which was over one year and 5,000 arrests old for most of the experiment. This finding suggests, but does not demonstrate, a lack of general deterrence from a mandatory arrest policy. The second finding is the very rare occurrence of any serious injury in the recidivism against the same victims. The total of 28 serious injuries reported in 921 follow-up interviews suggests that mandatory arrest is hard to justify on the grounds of a high probability of serious violence in the near future.

We find no reason in these data to challenge Sherman and Berk's recommendation against mandatory arrest laws, but good reason to challenge their recommendations of presumptive arrest policies regardless of time in custody. This paper suggests that such laws or policies may be harmful when they are implemented through short arrest, at least with urban underclass populations. Other kinds of legal innovation may be far more useful, such as nonarrest strategies to forestall violence immediately after police leave. The initial deterrence period may also offer a window of opportunity for new approaches to intervention, either by police or others.

Perhaps the most important theoretical and policy implication of these findings is the difference that dosage apparently makes. The results are consistent with, but do not directly test, the hypothesis that short arrest increases suspect anger at society without increasing fear of rearrest. The less criminogenic effects of full arrest could be explained by its higher cost to suspects in custody time. What this hypothesis does not explain is why short arrest should provide stronger evidence of an initial deterrent effect than full arrest. Nor does it explain why the escalation effect should take so long to appear.

Yet, if the number of hours in custody affects underclass recidivism for this offense, what about for other offenses? Dosage might even make even more or less difference for suspect populations with lower prevalence of prior arrests. Given the recent growth of arrests for drug possession and other charges routinely dropped, U.S. police now make over 14 million nontraffic arrests each year, many with short-custody dosage. Policymakers and criminologists should therefore consider the possibility that a little jail time can be worse than none.

INCAPACITATION

Incapacitation as a Strategy for Crime Control: Possibilities and Pitfalls

JACQUELINE COHEN

INCAPACITATION involves denying an offender the opportunity or ability to commit future crimes. In recent years, there has been growing interest in incapacitation as a strategy for controlling crime. The logic is simple: an offender who is locked up cannot commit crimes in the community.

Interest in incapacitative strategies heightened in the early 1970s because of public concern about continuing increases in crime and widespread disillusionment with efforts to rehabilitate offenders or otherwise meaningfully affect their future criminal behavior. Martinson's widely influential article on the general failure of correctional evaluations to document the rehabilitative effects of treatment programs appeared in 1974. At about the same time, arguments for an incapacitative strategy appeared in the academic press, while James Q. Wilson argued for incapacitation to a broader public audience.

Support for incapacitation policies, especially for high-rate offenders, has gained momentum in the 1980s, partly as a result of the increasing strains on existing prison resources experienced throughout U.S. jurisdictions. State and federal prison populations have been growing steadily since 1974; by the end of 1982 there were 412,303 prisoners under state or federal jurisdiction. The national incarceration rate rose from 139 per 100,000 resident population in 1980 to 170 in

1982. In 1982, the annual growth rate in prison population set a new record of 12.2 percent. Prison capacity has not kept pace. In 1981, thirty-one states were under court orders to reduce prison overcrowding, and thirty-seven states were involved in litigation about some aspect of prison conditions.

For both fiscal and policy reasons, prison capacity is not likely to increase rapidly. State governments face growing citizen resistance to taxes and increased demands for state support for other public services for which federal support has declined. These fiscal concerns have combined to limit support for increased prison expenditures out of states' annual operating budgets and contributed to the defeat by voters of proposed bond issues to cover the costs of new prison construction in New York and Rhode Island.

Demographic projections of prison populations provide another basis for limiting the growth of prison capacity. Projections in Pennsylvania suggest that when individuals born during the postwar baby boom, from 1947 to 1962, move out of the most crime-prone ages of the late teens by 1980, crime rates will begin to decline. The baby boom population, however, will reach the ages most vulnerable to imprisonment—the middle and late twenties—and so commitments to prison can be expected to increase through 1985. These projections for Pennsylvania, where the population is stable but aging, are likely to be representative of many states in the United States, especially in the Northeast and Midwest. In states with growing young populations, particularly in the south and

From *Crime and Justice: An Annual Review of Research* (pp. 1-48), M. Tonry and N. Morris, editors, 1983, Chicago: University of Chicago Press. Copyright 1983 by the University of Chicago Press. Reprinted by permission.

West, the growth in prison populations is likely to continue beyond 1990.

The most recent data on reported crimes for 1981 and 1982 are fully consistent with these projections. Between 1980 and 1981, there was essentially no change in the reported number of index crimes (excluding arson) in the United States. Over this same period, index crimes decreased by about 1 percent in the northeast and north central regions of the country and increased slightly in the south and west. As expected from the demographic projections, index crimes then decreased a full 5 percent in the first six months of 1982 from the same period in 1981. In the northeast and north central regions with their older populations, the decrease was larger at 9 percent; the decline was less at 2-3 percent in the south and west. This contrasts with national average annual increases of 4.4 percent between 1974 and 1980. A continuation of the recent declines in reported crimes in coming years would provide additional support for the expected turnaround in prison populations to begin in the early 1990s.

Nevertheless, we will continue to confront a prospect of rapidly increasing prison populations in the 1980s, and there is a growing interest in finding ways to use the limited available prison space in the most effective manner for achieving crime control. The problem of *allocation*—deciding which offenders are to be incarcerated—has emerged as an important consideration in developing imprisonment policies. From an incapacitation perspective, incarceration should be used primarily for those offenders who are likeliest to continue to commit serious crimes at reasonably high rates. Conversely, offenders who do not present a significant social threat could be released from prison early or not imprisoned at all. Such a policy has the potential of directly preventing the most crimes for a given level of prison resources, but it requires reasonably accurate bases for distinguishing among offenders and faces a variety of challenges to the legitimacy of differential sanctions.

Two different types of incapacitation policy are often distinguished: *selective* incapacitation and *collective* incapacitation. Selective incapacitation involves *individually based* sentences, in which sentencing decisions are tailored to the particular individual. Such sentences would be individualized to vary with differences in predictions of the individual's propensity to commit future crimes. Selective incapacitation permits quite different sentences for the same offense in order to accommodate the differences in crime control potential among offenders convicted of the same crime. The effectiveness of a selective incapacitation policy in preventing crime rests on the predictive capability to identify the worst offenders—those who commit crimes at high rates.

Collective incapacitation refers to *aggregate-offense-based* sentencing policies. Unlike a selective incapacitation policy, under an aggregate policy, individuals are sentenced solely on the basis of their present offense and perhaps their prior criminal record. Aggregate policies do not invoke any predictions about the expected future behavior of a particular individual. Within certain bounds (reflecting, e.g., a concern that sentences be commensurate with the seriousness of the offense), aggregate policies may vary in the types of offense that are subject to imprisonment and in the average length of prison terms applied to different offenses. But within an offense and prior record class, all convicted offenders would be sentenced uniformly. To the extent that individual offending patterns vary with the nature of the present offense and prior record, the choices among different aggregate policies have the potential for differential impact in preventing crimes. In estimating these effects, the variations across particular individuals are ignored, and only the average consequences of a collective incapacitation policy are considered.

THE CRIMINAL CAREERS FRAMEWORK

A key consideration in evaluating the merit of incapacitative strategies is the estimated crime control effects of those policies in the free community. When studying incapacitative effects, it is useful to characterize the nature of an individual's criminal activity as a "criminal career."

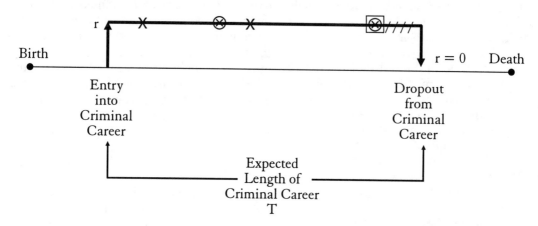

FIGURE 1 *An individual criminal career.* x: *crimes (committed at rate* r); *circle: arrest for a crime (with probability* q_A); *box: conviction after arrest (with probability* q_c); *hatching: time served after conviction (with probability* J *and mean length* S).

Criminal Careers

The period during an individual's lifetime when crimes are likely to be committed can be viewed as a criminal career. During a criminal career, there is some chance that the individual will commit crimes; before and after a career the individual is crime free. The likelihood of committing crimes during a career is represented by the individual crime rate, lambda. An individual with a crime rate of ten crimes per year, for example, has a .027 likelihood (10/365) of committing a crime on any day in a year. Whether a crime is actually committed will depend on the circumstances of the offender and the opportunities for crime on that day.

It is unlikely that an individual will commit exactly the same number of crimes each year. In the example above, the offender with a rate of ten crimes per year will actually commit less than ten crimes in some years and more than ten crimes in others; there may even be years when no crimes are committed, even though the rate remains at ten that year. If it were possible, however, to observe this same individual over many years during a career, or to observe the careers of many different individuals who each commit crimes at a rate of ten per year, we would expect that in the long run the average number of crimes per year per individual would be ten.

Careers begin when the chance of committing crimes equals the value of lambda. This may be at or before the first crime committed. Likewise, careers end when there is no longer any chance of committing crimes, which may occur at or after the last crime committed. The period during lifetimes when there is some chance of committing crimes is the observed length of an individual's career.

The actual beginning and end points of a career will vary with chance for an individual. If it were possible to let the same individual repeat his career over many different lifetimes, the observed length of the career would likely vary across these different lifetimes. In the long run, the expected length of an individual's career would be the average length found over all those hypothetical careers.

In this formulation of a criminal career, the criminal activities of an individual are not deterministic, fixed events. Instead, they are the result of a chance process. With such a chance process, it is important to distinguish between the particular realization of a career that is actually observed and the underlying rates and chance processes that give rise to that realization. In the case of coin flipping, this distinction is between the outcome on any particular flip (say a head) and the underlying stable process for a fair coin where the chance of a head is one-half. With enough coin flips, we expect the underlying process to be revealed, with about one-half of the outcomes being heads.

A similar distinction applies to criminal careers. The number and timing of crimes committed and the responses of the criminal justice system (e.g., arrests) vary according to a chance process. It is this chance process that characterizes criminal careers. For each individual, we can observe only one particular realization of that process. If it were possible to replicate an individual's lifetime repeatedly, or if we have many different individuals all subject to the same chance process, the particular course of the criminal career observed would undoubtedly be different each time. The long-run average pattern of career realizations, however, would accurately reflect the underlying chance process that characterizes criminal careers.

In general, the higher the individual crime rate and the longer the career, the more crimes can be averted through incapacitation. Larger individual crime rates mean more crimes averted for each unit of time incarcerated. Longer careers, on the other hand, decrease the likelihood of wasting incapacitation on offenders who end their careers while incarcerated and who would thus not be committing any further crimes whether incarcerated or not. The incapacitative effect actually achieved will depend on the effectiveness of the criminal justice system in identifying and ultimately incarcerating offenders. The less likely offenders are to be incarcerated, the smaller the incapacitative effect.

Critical Assumptions

All existing estimates of incapacitative effects share certain basic assumptions. To begin with, all offenders are assumed to be vulnerable to arrest and incarceration; there is no subpopulation of offenders who will—with certainty—never be caught and incarcerated and who are responsible for a substantial portion of unsolved crimes. If there were such an invulnerable group, incapacitative effects would be reduced and would only affect the smaller number of crimes committed by offenders who do have some chance of arrest and incarceration. The likelihood that such a group of invulnerable

offenders exists is not great. The more unsolved crimes are attributed to invulnerable offenders, the fewer unsolved crimes remain to be committed by the offenders who do get caught. This would greatly increase the chance of arrest after a crime for the offenders who do get caught. In the extreme case, all unsolved crimes would be committed by invulnerable offenders, and the vulnerable population would be arrested for every crime they commit—a very unlikely scenario.

It is also assumed that the crimes of offenders who are taken off the streets are not replaced by those of other offenders. This could happen if, for example, the offender were part of an organized illegal economic activity like drug sales or burglaries organized by a fence; in this event a replacement might simply be recruited from an available "labor market" to continue the crimes that would otherwise be committed by the incarcerated offender. Alternately, if the offender were part of a crime-committing group, the remaining members of the group might continue their criminal activity, with or without recruiting a replacement. The social networks capable of sustaining the crimes of an incarcerated offender are more likely to be found among juveniles; they are less of a problem in estimates of incapacitative effects for adults.

A final assumption generally invoked in estimates of incapacitative effects is that periods of incarceration do not alter criminal careers by changing the expected length of criminal careers or the individual crime rate. More specifically, it is assumed that there are no rehabilitative or criminogenic effects of prison terms on the careers of incarcerated offenders, and no general deterrent effects that curtail the criminal careers of nonincarcerated offenders. To the extent that these effects, when they exist, are not immediate, but rather affect the future course of careers after release, the short-run estimates of incapacitative effects would be unaffected.

At a minimum, the accuracy of estimates of incapacitative effects will depend on the accuracy of these assumptions. Failure of any of the assumptions will result in over- or underestimates of incapacitative effects. For the most part, the available estimates of incapacitative effects are similarly vulnerable to these various sources of error. So while the absolute magnitudes of the different estimates might be subject to errors, the relative magnitudes in comparisons across estimates are less likely to be affected.

These three assumptions appear, in general, to be well founded. Except for offenses, like retail drug trafficking, in which imprisoned offenders are likely to be replaced by other offenders, weakness in these assumptions should not vitiate the general credibility of the findings of incapacitation research.

CONCLUSION

This review of research on incapacitation has highlighted a number of problems in pursuing incapacitative strategies. Most important is the recognition that the crime reduction benefits of any incapacitative strategy are inherently limited by the large number of offenders who have no prior convictions. The crimes of these offenders could not have been prevented by any incapacitation policy that requires a conviction before imposing prison terms. Collective incapacitation policies that involve uniform increases in the use of prison for a wide range of offense types were found to have only modest impacts on crime while requiring enormous increases in prison populations. By targeting incapacitation more narrowly on career criminals or habitual offenders with their higher rates of offending, selective incapacitation strategies offer the possibility of achieving greater reductions in crime at considerably smaller costs in terms of prison resources. The success of a selective incapacitation strategy, however, depends critically on our ability to identify the career criminals reasonably early in their careers.

For the purposes of incapacitation, career criminals are individuals who can be expected to continue as high-rate offenders, to engage in reasonably serious offenses, and to do so over a number of years into the future. Under this definition, career criminals are characterized by the intensity of their offending, the crime types they engage in and the length of their criminal careers. Until recently, these aspects of criminal careers were measured only poorly, if at all. As a result, most attempts to identify career criminals have used a wide variety of more immediately accessible offender attributes in addition to official criminal record variables. These other prediction variables include personal demographics (especially age), psychological profiles, employment histories, and history of drug or alcohol abuse. These past prediction efforts, however, have been hampered by a number of ethical and empirical problems that seriously limit their ability to identify career criminals with a reasonable degree of accuracy.

Recent research examining criminal careers directly has suggested the possibility of developing an alternative strategy to individual-level predictions for pursuing incapacitation. In particular, the emerging estimates for aspects of criminal careers such as individual crime rates and the length of criminal careers suggest that offense-related variables (i.e., the crime type of the current charge and prior criminal record) can be used to distinguish offenders who on average have high crime rates and long careers. The observed variations in criminal career patterns opens up the opportunity to develop sentencing policies that take advantage of the differential reductions in crime associated with different offenses. Such policies have the distinct advantage of relying only on offense-related variables in distinguishing sentences. These policies take a collective incapacitation strategy of aggregate sentences that are uniformly applied but focus it more narrowly on just those offenses with the greatest incapacitative potential.

The Concept of Selective Incapacitation

PETER GREENWOOD

IN this report, we introduce the term *selective incapacitation* to refer to sentencing policies that attempt to distinguish between higher-rate and lower-rate criminal offenders in determining who will be incarcerated and for how long. For instance, if convicted robbers who have a prior conviction for robbery or use particular types of drugs are found to have the highest average offense rates for robbery, then under selective incapacitation sentencing they might be given longer terms than other convicted robbers.

One obvious argument against selective incapacitation rests on moral and ethical grounds. This involves the classic problem of "false positives"—that is, our ability to discriminate high-rate from low-rate offenders. Under a policy of selective incapacitation, some of the offenders who would be categorized as high-rate offenders and sentenced to longer terms would not actually have high offense rates. This possibility may offend some who would apply the same standards required for conviction—proof beyond a reasonable doubt—to the identification of high-rate offenders. Nevertheless, for a number of reasons, the concept of selective incapacitation should not be immediately judged categorically unacceptable on ethical grounds.

Most states now use highly subjective criteria to single out particular types of offenders for more severe sentences. In some instances, deterrence is used as the theoretical justification for these longer terms (e.g., longer terms for offenders who use guns, for those whose victims are elderly or infirm, or for those who rob transit employees) even though there is no clear evidence of their deterrent effect. In other instances, the longer terms are clearly designed to incapacitate those thought to represent high risks to society (e.g., offenders with serious prior records). Habitual offender statutes and career criminal prosecution programs obviously fall in this category. Since legislators are likely to continue distinguishing particular groups of offenders for harsher sentencing, it may make more sense to base these distinctions on valid predictors of risk rather than on emotional responses to particular crimes or on mere hunches.

As a moral or ethical issue, the problem of false positives is not exclusive to selective incapacitation. At this time in the development of criminal justice, both research evidence and conventional wisdom support incapacitation as the most direct means of reducing street crime. In response to the continuing high rate of crime, citizens are demanding tougher sentences to reduce crime.

Suppose we adopt the Blumstein and Cohen position that society will adjust its laws and sentencing practices to incarcerate a fixed proportion of the population, which is roughly the same as assuming that the current pressure for tougher sentences will result in the available prison space being filled to capacity. In either case, a given number of offenders will be incarcerated. The limiting factor on sentence severity, then, is capacity, not society's view of appropriate sentences. On the average, offenders will be serving shorter terms than society believes is just. The issue becomes whether all offenders should be granted equal leniency or whether the leniency required by strained prison capacity should be granted selectively to those who sta-

From *Selective Incapacitation* (pp. 15-50) by P. Greenwood, 1982, Santa Monica, CA: RAND Corporation. Copyright 1982 by The RAND Corporation. Reprinted by permission.

tistically pose the least risk. Currently, it is on similar grounds that probation is often granted.

As an alternative, we might assume that society can and will continue to increase overall sentence severity until the crime rate falls below an acceptable level. As will be discussed in a later section, it can be shown that selective incapacitation can achieve the same reduction in crime as a general incapacitation approach, but at a considerably lower level of incarceration. More important, by using selective incapacitation to achieve a given crime level we can reduce the number of false positives within the category of those low-rate offenders (or offenders not likely to recidivate) who are incarcerated.

In summary, incapacitation offers the only objective or functional basis for distinguishing among different offenders as to their appropriate sentence length. The severity of the offense (robbery is more serious than theft) can be used to order punishment severity among different crime types, but not to establish a scale of severity within the crime types. The concept of selective incapacitation suggests which offenders should serve longer terms. Whether one believes that the prison population is constrained by capacity or driven by the prevailing crime rate, selective incapacitation provides a means of minimizing unnecessary incarceration.

For those who are troubled by the idea that two people who commit the same crime may receive different sentences, we point out that this has always been the case. For instance, men serve longer terms than women; defendants with prior records are more likely to be incarcerated than those without. We are simply offering a more rational method for distinguishing among offenders. Every offender would be on notice as to what sentence he would face in the future. The different prescribed terms for different categories of offenders would be published in the form of sentencing guidelines or legislatively prescribed sanctions. An offender would know exactly what risks he faced. In this way, selective incapacitation is no different than the selective career criminal prosecution programs adopted by many prosecutors across the country, with the one exception that under selective incapacitation, those identified for longer terms would be distinguished on a scientific or objec-

tive basis. Under career criminal prosecution, the process of identifying the career criminal is more subjective.

The above discussion of selective incapacitation should not be interpreted as uncritical endorsement. The decision to adopt such policies would involve difficult choices among conflicting values, and such choices are not the purpose of this report. Our discussion is intended to present a controversial concept in a reasoned context so that it can be weighed against the other feasible alternatives.

DEFINITION OF THE CONCEPT

As we define it, the concept of selective incapacitation involves three elements:

1. A prediction or classification scheme that divides offenders into groups with substantially different average offense rates.
2. A perception of the sentencing framework as a device for allocating the available incarceration (prison and jail) capacity.
3. A procedure for developing sentencing criteria that improve or optimize the incapacitation effects achieved for any given level of incarceration.

A sentencing policy has an "incapacitation effect" to the extent that crimes are prevented by the incarceration of offenders who would otherwise be active. The amount of crime prevented is a function of the rate at which offenders commit crimes and the amount of time they are restrained. For instance, if at any given time a state has 40,000 offenders and 10,000 of them are incarcerated, the actual crime rate would be only 75 percent of what it would be without incarceration. If an identifiable group of 5,000 offenders accounted for half the crimes of the total group, then incarcerating these offenders for half of their careers would reduce the crime rate by 25 percent even if no one else were locked up. In the second case, a 25 percent reduction in crime would be achieved by an incarceration level of only 2,500 instead of 10,000.

A MODEL FOR ESTIMATING INCAPACITATION EFFECTS

The basic concepts for the model used in this study to estimate the effects of incapacitation were developed by Shinnar and Shinnar. They assumed that there is only one type of crime and that all offenders committed crimes at random intervals at the same average rate. They further assumed that all offenders are subject to the same probability of arrest and conviction for any one crime and have the same probability of being incarcerated upon conviction. Among those incarcerated, they assumed sentence lengths to be exponentially distributed.

If we were able to identify the high-rate offenders and we wanted to maximize the incapacitation effect achieved by the incarcerated population, we would increase the terms of the high-rate offenders or increase their probability of going to prison and decrease the terms of low-rate offenders until we approached a situation where we had all high-rate offenders and some low-rate offenders in prison. This would achieve a major reduction in the amount of crime that would result from a policy of sentencing all offenders equally.

Of course, we cannot identify all of the high-rate offenders with certainty. The best that we can do, as we demonstrate in the following section, is identify a number of characteristics associated with high-rate offenders. If we interviewed the incarcerated offenders, we would learn that a high percentage of the high-rate offenders were drug users compared with a low percentage of the low-rate offenders. Therefore, we might choose drug use as an important factor on which to base selective incapacitation. What about those offenders who are predicted to be high-rate offenders because of their drug use, but are not? The obvious answer is that they will be penalized and serve longer terms. But overall, the number of low-rate offenders held in prison will decline.

This shift in the nature and size of the prison population is a critical characteristic of what we are calling "selective incapacitation" policies. If a jurisdiction is attempting to reduce its crime rate through selective incapacitation and its ability to differentiate high-rate from low-rate offenders is not perfect, as it can never be, then some low-rate offenders will serve longer terms. However, the average term served by all low-rate offenders will be lower and the number of offenders incarcerated will be smaller than if the same crime reduction were achieved by a generalized incapacitation strategy.

Thus far we have described selective incapacitation policies as if all sentencing were done by a machine, as if information on the defendant's characteristics and his current offense goes in and out comes his sentence—"5.2 years, next defendant please." This is obviously not the way the system currently works, nor the way it is likely to work in the future. The sentencing policies used as examples here are simplifications adopted for analytical and expositional purposes. In reality, the concept of selective incapacitation could enter into the felony disposition process in a variety of ways, just as the concepts of rehabilitation or deserts enter into the current process. There are a number of distinct phases of the process in which the concept could be relevant.

Many police departments are not able to conduct complete investigations for every reported felony or even for every felony suspect in custody. They need to ration their resources. Moreover, the chances of successful prosecution depend almost exclusively on the quality and thoroughness of the police investigation efforts—the availability of physical evidence, the testimony of several witnesses, and amount of detail conveyed to the prosecutor in written reports or recorded testimony. The police might want to use the concept of selective incapacitation to help develop priorities concerning which cases they will investigate most thoroughly.

Similarly, the prosecutor must dispose of more cases than he can ever bring to trial or even completely prepare. Most cases are now disposed of through informal negotiations between the prosecution and defense. Career criminal prosecution was developed as a method of providing greater attention to cases involving serious repetitive defendants. The concept of selective incapacitation is consistent with that of career criminal prosecution and would provide a more systematic means of identifying who should be the target of such programs.

In sentencing decisions, selective incapacitation concepts could be written into explicit guidelines concerning choices between probation or incarceration or in setting term lengths. These guidelines could range from simply advising to mandating specific terms.

Similarly, in those states where a parole board still retains the power to set release dates, selective incapacitation concepts could be incorporated into their decisions. The great diversity in sentencing practices that currently exists across states and the limited amount of research on the effects of changes in sentencing practices on case outcomes make it impossible to be more specific about how selective incapacitation concepts could best be incorporated into practice. A lot will depend on which agency—legislative, prosecutor, parole board, and so on—is motivated to adopt them.

INDIVIDUAL OFFENSE RATES

In preceding sections, we have summarized recent research findings on the pattern of criminal careers and introduced the concept of selective incapacitation as a method of incorporating this information into sentencing policies to increase the impact of incarceration on crime reduction. We have also shown that the effectiveness of selective incapacitation policies depends critically on the distribution of individual offense rates and on the ability of the system to identify high-rate offenders.

In this section, we use self-reported data provided by RAND's second inmate survey to describe the distribution of individual rates and to develop and evaluate a simple scale for identifying high-rate offenders.

The Second Inmate Survey

The primary objective of RAND's second inmate survey was to obtain accurate estimates of individual crime rates and their variation across sites. The survey instrument used a complex series of questions about each crime type in order to elicit accurate responses. Specifically, each respondent filled in a calendar that showed whether he was incarcerated, hospitalized, or

out on the street during each month of a one- to two-year period. All of the questions about his recent criminal behavior referred to periods in this calendar.

Prevalence of Various Crime Types

Previous studies of criminal career patterns have shown that there is little specialization among offenders. Studies of arrest histories also show that there is little correlation among offense types in subsequent arrests. In other words, the probability that an offender's next arrest will be for burglary is virtually independent of what the last arrest was for.

In the first RAND survey, Peterson and Braiker found that more than half of the sample engaged in at least four different types of crime during the three-year period before their current term. The results from the second RAND survey are basically consistent with these prior findings. However, there was some evidence that offenders could be classified in terms of the maximum degree of violence or force they were likely to use.

For example, out of the 178 convicted robbers in the California sample, 76 percent reported committing robberies during the two-year window preceding their current term, 58 percent reported committing burglaries, and 57 percent sold drugs. Among the 24 percent of the convicted robbers who did not report committing any robberies, some denied committing any crime, while others reported committing other related types of crime, such as kidnapping or assault.

Three findings from the survey are particularly noteworthy. First, convicted robbers are more likely to be engaged in any given type of crime than any type of offender other than the type convicted of the given crime. For instance, the only type of offender who is more likely to be selling drugs than convicted robbers is a convicted drug dealer. Second, in Texas all of the offenders other than convicted robbers tend to be active in fewer types of crime than offenders in California or Michigan. Third, Chaiken and Chaiken found that the 20 percent of the sample who reported committing only one type of crime were primarily drug dealers, assaulters, and burglars.

Individual Offense Rates

Six years ago, there was virtually no available information on individual rates of criminal activity. Estimates of average offense rates, which were based on various methods of estimation from aggregate crime and arrest data, ranged from less than one felony per year to five or more. Petersilia's study of 49 robbers estimated that this group averaged about 20 crimes per year. Subsequently, Peterson and Braiker and Blumstein and Cohen developed estimates for specific offense types based on self-reports and arrest histories, respectively.

The study analyzed the average annual individual offense rates among active offenders in the three sample states, broken down by conviction offense type. From these data, several patterns emerge. Among California and Michigan inmates, the offense rates within any conviction crime category are considerably higher than those previously reported. In California, convicted robbers reported committing, on the average, 53 robberies per year. Those who were active in burglary (58 percent) reported 90 per year. The offense rates reported by Texas offenders were considerably lower than those in the other two states for the same period of time. The difficulty lies in identifying those with high rates.

Methods of Identifying High-Rate Offenders

The impact of incarceration on street crime is a direct function of the rate at which incarcerated offenders would have committed crime if they had not been confined. If the average offense rate of the incarcerated population can be increased by more careful selection of who goes to prison or by adjusting sentence lengths, the amount of crime on the street can be reduced.

There are two basic methods for attempting to identify dangerous or high-rate offenders. One is subjective and relies on expert evaluations of an offender's background, behavior, and psychological characteristics. The other relies on actuarial data.

The subjective approach has been the traditional method used in sentencing. A convicted defendant may be referred to a panel of court-appointed psychologists or psychiatrists or to a reception clinic within the correctional system. The evaluations of the panel or clinic are then considered by the court in determining the sentence. If a defendant is sentenced to an indeterminate term, periodic evaluations will be made to determine when he is suitable for release. Recent evaluations of these procedures have shown that they have very little predictive accuracy.

The second method of prediction, based on actuarial data, has been used most frequently in the form of parole experience tables to guide release decisions. These tables, which use a variety of factors to predict an offender's chances of success on parole, have been shown to be more accurate than diagnostic studies.

The method of identifying high-rate offenders that we propose in this study is also based on actuarial data, rather than subjective judgments about individual offenders. Basically, the approach involves analyzing data from a large sample of offenders to determine which of many individual characteristics are associated with high offense rates.

From a scientific viewpoint, the most appropriate method of conducting this analysis to develop information for selective incapacitation would be roughly as follows. First, within some specified geographic area and time period, we would randomly select a large sample of offenders convicted for crimes for which selective incapacitation is to be considered. Second, for each offender, we would gather and code information on characteristics that could conceivably be made available to the court for sentencing purposes. These would obviously include such factors as prior convictions and age, and might also include such factors as juvenile record, drug use, and employment history. They would clearly not include such factors as race, income, or mental attitudes. Third, at some point in the future, when the defendants had each had an opportunity to accumulate a significant amount of street time (at least two years), we would estimate their individual offense rates through self-reports or from their recorded arrests. And finally, having assembled these data, we could then use a variety of multivariate statistical procedures to estimate the relationships among the possible predictive factors and offense rates. In order to test the accuracy of these estimates, it would be necessary to test them against a set of data separate from that from which they were derived.

The approach described above was not feasible for this study, given the nature of our sample. In our analysis, we proceeded as follows. First, using the self-reported data from the second inmate survey, we estimated the offense rates and characteristics of the respondents during the two-year period preceding their current arrest and confinement. Then, starting with a list of all characteristics measured in the survey, we identified a set of candidate predictive factors that satisfied both of the following criteria: (1) possible legal relevance and appropriateness for the court's consideration and (2) relevance on the basis of prior research or theory. Limiting our analysis to defendants convicted of either robbery or burglary, we then categorized the respondents within each of the six combinations of state and conviction offense type (three states and two crimes) according to their self-reported offense rate for their conviction crimes as follows:

Low rate = below the medium rate reported for their offense type and state.
Medium rate = between the 50th and 75th percentile for their offense type and state.
High rate = above the 75th percentile for their offense type and state.

Next, we cross-tabulated each of the candidate predictors against these three self-report offense rate groups. We then selected the following seven variables to comprise a simple additive prediction scale:

1. Prior conviction for the instant offense type.
2. Incarcerated more than 50 percent of preceding two years.
3. Conviction before age 16.
4. Served time in a state juvenile facility.
5. Drug use in preceding two years.
6. Drug use as a juvenile.
7. Employed less than 50 percent of the preceding two years.

The selection of these variables was based on the strength of their association with individual crime rates and their suitability for sentencing purposes.

This scale can be used to assign any individual offender a score ranging from 0 to 7. Offenders with a high score should have higher offense rates.

From these figures on how offenders at each level of the scale are distributed across the three offense rate groups alone we can see that the scale discriminates fairly well. Although 50 percent of the respondents are by definition low-rate offenders (below the median offense rate in their state), only 18 percent of those who score 5 or more are low rate. Conversely, while 25 percent of the full sample are by definition high rate (above 75th percentile), only 9 percent of those who score 0 or 1 are high rate.

THE EFFECTIVENESS OF
THE PREDICTION SCALE

There are a variety of ways to test how well the prediction scale described above discriminates between low-rate and high-rate offenders. Perhaps the clearest evidence is provided by a comparison of the predicted offense rate groups within each state. By definition, within each scale category, half the respondents reported offense rates lower than the median. In four out of six groups, the median of the predicted high group is more than ten times larger than the median for the predicted low group. In the other two cases, the difference is greater than a factor of 5.

According to other tests, the prediction scale works best for California and least well for Michigan. In California, our predicted high-rate burglars commit 33 times as many burglaries per year as the predicted low-rate burglars. High-rate and low-rate robbers differ by a factor of 15. In Michigan, the predicted low-rate burglars actually commit more crimes than the predicted median-rate burglars. This is due to two respondents who reported very high rates but had no prior records.

Offenders predicted to be high rate for their conviction crimes are also higher rate for other crimes. Among inmates in California convicted of robbery, those predicted to be high-rate robbers also commit burglary at 30 times the rate of predicted low-rate offenders and sell drugs eight times as frequently.

One final basis of evaluating the accuracy of the prediction scale involves the sentences being served by respondents. If we categorize each group convicted of either robbery or burglary within each state as high-, medium-, or low-rate offenders on the basis of their sentence length, we can evaluate the accuracy of the predictions implicit in the sentences in the same way we evaluated our prediction scale.

On the scale implied by their sentences, only 42 percent of the respondents were correctly categorized. Seven percent who were among the lowest in offense rate were among the highest in sentence length, and 5 percent who were among the highest in offense rate were among the lowest in sentence length. According to these data, our scale increases the fraction of respondents who are accurately labeled by about 20 percent and decreases the percentage who are grossly mislabeled by almost half. This pattern is generally found across each combination of offense type and state.

Clearly, our prediction scale does discriminate between low-rate and high-rate offenders. Better scales can probably be developed. Simpler scales will work almost as well.

Incapacitation

ALFRED BLUMSTEIN
JACQUELINE COHEN
DANIEL NAGIN

INCAPACITATION involves removing an offender from general society and thereby reducing crime by physically preventing the offender from committing crimes in that society. The incapacitative effect of a sanction refers exclusively to that preventive effect and does not include any additional reduction in crime due to deterrence or rehabilitation.

Decisions on whether or not to send individuals to prison are based on the offenses for which the individuals were convicted and their prior criminal records. Once imprisoned, they are prevented from committing further crimes in general society. Under sentencing policies more stringent than current ones, more convicted offenders might be sent to prison or they might be sentenced to longer average terms. Presumably, such policy changes will prevent some crimes; in order to assess this increment of crime reduction, some means for estimating the incapacitative effect of imprisonment is needed.

ESTIMATES OF THE MAGNITUDE OF THE INCAPACITATIVE EFFECT

There are fewer problems in inferring the existence of effects from incapacitation than in establishing the deterrent effects of criminal sanctions. As long as the offenders who are imprisoned would have continued to commit crimes if they had remained free, there is a direct incapacitative effect: that is, the number of crimes at any time is reduced by the crimes avoided through the imprisonment of some criminals. The magnitude of that incapacitative effect is directly related to the rate at which an individual offender commits crime, K crimes per year. If an individual would have remained criminally active in society during a period of incarceration of S years, the potential number of crimes averted by this offender's incapacitation is $K \times S$ crimes.

There are factors that may operate to reduce the incapacitative effect to less than $K \times S$ crimes. If a criminal would have reduced his rate of committing crimes or stopped committing crimes entirely during the period of imprisonment, then the number of crimes averted would be correspondingly less than $K \times S$. It is also possible that for some offenses, especially certain organized crimes involving vice or burglary managed by fences, the incarcerated offender would be replaced through an illegitimate labor market, and the incapacitative effect would be less than $K \times S$ crimes.

A pattern of multiple offenders per crime, and especially gang activities, will similarly reduce the incapacitative effect if only one or a few of the participants are incarcerated and the collective criminal activity persists. This phenomenon is likely to vary with age, being most common among juvenile offenders. Unfortunately, there is very little empirical evidence about the magnitude of these diminishing effects. If these effects are large, ignoring them could result in an

From *Deterrence and Incapacitation: Estimating the Effects of Criminal Sanctions on Crime Rates* (pp. 12-28, 109-143) by A. Blumstein, J. Cohen, and D. Nagin, 1978, Washington, DC: National Academy Press. Copyright 1978 by the National Academy of Sciences. Reprinted courtesy of the National Academy Press.

appreciable overestimate of the incapacitative effect.

The net long-term benefits from incapacitation might also be affected by any possible rehabilitative or "criminogenic" effects of prison. To the extent that prisons rehabilitate criminals, resulting in lower individual crime rates or earlier terminations of criminal activity after release, there is an additional reduction in crime. If, on the other hand, prisons have a criminogenic effect, increasing an individual's propensity to commit crimes or extending the duration of criminal careers, the benefits in reduced crime from incapacitation may be offset by the additional crimes a criminal commits once released.

The available research on the impact of various treatment strategies both in and out of prison seems to indicate that, after controlling for initial selection differences, there are generally no statistically significant differences between the subsequent recidivism of offenders, regardless of the form of "treatment." This suggests that neither rehabilitative nor criminogenic effects operate very strongly. Therefore, at an aggregate level, these confounding effects are probably safely ignored.

The literature on incapacitation contains a number of studies offering widely divergent estimates of the incapacitative effect of imprisonment. Some argue that these incapacitative effects are negligible, while others claim that a major impact on crime is possible through increases in the use of imprisonment. In reviewing these studies, we conclude that there is more consistency among the analyses than their opposite policy conclusions would suggest; they are in general agreement about basic assumptions, but differ in the particular parameter values used. The principal disagreement is over the value of the individual crime rate, an issue that can only be resolved empirically. This is a task that should be given high priority.

All of the available models for estimating the incapacitative effect rest on a number of important, but as yet untested, assumptions that characterize individual criminal careers. A criminal career is considered to begin at the first crime committed by an individual and to end at the last crime. During a career, an individual commits crimes, accumulates arrests and convictions for some crimes, and may be imprisoned for some time.

Most analysts model a criminal career as a stochastic process and incapacitation as a disruption to that process. In calculating the incapacitative effect, the models implicitly deal with offenders who operate alone and are not part of a larger criminal network. While free during a career, these criminals commit crimes at the rate of K crimes per year. During a period of imprisonment of length S, the potential exists to prevent $K \times S$ crimes.

Estimating the incapacitative effect of an imprisonment policy, however, also depends on the probability of being sentenced to prison if a crime is committed. This probability consists of the conditional probabilities of arrest given a crime, of conviction given arrest, and of a prison sentence given conviction. These probabilities are measures of criminal justice system performance, and they contribute directly to the level of incapacitation by determining the chance that a criminal is caught and convicted and so available for imprisonment.

Estimates of the crimes averted by incapacitation should also be adjusted for the possibility that a career ends while an individual is imprisoned. Once a career ends, no further crimes are prevented and any time served after that does not contribute to the incapacitative effect. Characterizing this end of a criminal career requires information on the distribution of career lengths in the criminal population (e.g., desistance probabilities by age).

Under the assumptions of models designed to predict criminal careers, an additional man-year in prison (e.g., one more individual serving one year in prison or two more individuals each serving six months) will prevent X crimes, since X is the number of crimes that each imprisoned individual would commit in a year if not imprisoned. However, the *relative* impact of X crimes prevented per man-year in prison will vary with the crime rate current prison population.

The principal imprisonment variables of concern are the probability of a prison sentence given a crime (P) and the average time served (S). The product of the two ($P \times S$) is the expected number of man-years in prison given the commission of a crime. Thus, $P \times S$ is equivalent to the average number of man-years in prison per crime.

The sensitivity of the incapacitative effect to the particular values of the imprisonment variables has important implications in considering incapacitation policies to reduce rime. It has already been shown that the percentage reduction in crime from a given increase in incapacitation is least when the imprisonment sanction levels are already low. Jurisdictions with lower imprisonment probabilities and with lower expected times served in prison per crime also tend to be the ones with the highest crime rates. Thus, the high-crime-rate jurisdictions that are most likely to be looking to incapacitation as an important solution to their crime problem are likely to have to pay the highest price for it in terms of increased prison populations.

For example, California and Massachusetts must increase their index prison populations by over 150 percent and 310 percent, respectively—given their crime rates—in order to achieve a 10 percent reduction in index crimes through incapacitation; for violent crimes, the prison population increases are 23 percent and 27 percent, respectively.

Further, the cost of an incapacitative strategy varies considerably with the crime types that are chosen as targets; the values of $P \times S$ for all index crimes are generally much lower than the same values for violent crimes. Thus, incapacitation is a more viable alternative when targeted at violent crimes. Under the assumptions of the available models, such a strategy could reduce violent crimes with reasonable increases in the population of violent offenders in prison. This is in sharp contrast to the much larger increases in the index prison populations required to achieve the same percentage reductions in the level of index crimes.

Even though the percentage of crimes averted through incapacitation is not very large in high-crime-rate jurisdictions, the number of these crimes averted may be substantial. From a national perspective, there could well be an interest in the reduction of a given number of crimes, with little concern for where that reduction occurs. From that perspective, the high-crime-rate jurisdictions do look attractive.

As an example, the objective might be to reduce the index crime rate by 100 crimes per 100,000 population. Since crime rates vary among jurisdictions, 100 crimes in the index rate represents a different percentage reduction in different jurisdictions. For example, in 1970 a reduction of 100 in the index crime rate represented 19,766 fewer crimes in California (2.3 percent less) and 2,220 fewer crimes in Mississippi (an 11.6 percent decrease). While the percentage change in California is quite low when compared to Mississippi, the absolute number of crimes involved is considerably larger.

At a rate of five crimes prevented for each additional man-year in prison, the crime reduction in California will increase the prison population by 3,953, or 36.1 percent, while the reduction in Mississippi requires 444 additional prisoner years (a 39.1 percent increase). Thus, a uniform change in the absolute crime rate in each jurisdiction has a more homogeneous effect on the relative increase in prison populations in each state.

PREDICTION OF INDIVIDUAL CRIMINALITY

There is a long tradition in sentencing of selectively imprisoning some individuals because of their prior criminal records. This is reflected in laws that prescribe mandatory sentences for habitual offenders. This differential treatment of convicted persons is typically justified by appeals to retributive rationales that encourage harsher penalties for persons who have clearly demonstrated their commitment to crime through repeated criminal activities. While selective imprisonment does not now involve explicit prediction of future criminality, a policy of selectively imprisoning the worst offenders (those who commit the more serious crimes and have a higher rate of committing crimes) has the potential of increasing the incapacitative effect.

If those persons whose individual crime rates are higher than the group average could be identified and selectively imprisoned, the incapacitative effect would be increased. Such a selective incapacitation policy, however, introduces both the technical problem of predicting individuals' future crime rates and the ethical and legal problems of explicitly imprisoning people to avoid crimes they may commit in the future.

The ethical questions derive from legal and philosophical positions on the appropriate functions of imprisonment. One position is that the principal basis for determining sentence should be retribution. An extreme expression of this position is that prison sentences should be based only on "just deserts" for the current crime and that any utilitarian use of imprisonment, and especially selective incapacitation, is inherently unjust. On the other hand, most people believe imprisonment should have a more utilitarian purpose, with crime reduction as an appropriate function of imprisonment.

Selective incapacitation of offenders with higher crime rates as a means of enhancing the incapacitative effect inherently requires prediction of criminal propensity in order to identify such offenders. Use of such predictions, however, raises concern for the errors in them. Poor prediction not only undermines the utilitarian justification for selectively incapacitating some convicted offenders, but it also introduces concern for the injustice suffered by those who are imprisoned because their future crime propensity is erroneously predicted to be higher than it is.

The available research on predicting individual criminality is largely limited to attempts to distinguish between recidivists and nonrecidivists, where recidivism is variously defined as subsequent arrest, conviction, or imprisonment for specified crimes, often limited to violent offenses. These predictions attempt to discriminate among individuals on the basis of the average criminal propensities of the groups in which they fit (e.g., based on attributes such as age, sex, marital status, or military record). A review of various predictive studies of this sort reveals considerable variability in the estimated prediction error.

A principal component of prediction error is the "false positive" problem, that is, imprisoning persons because of prediction that they will commit crimes in the future when in fact they would not commit any. This problem is particularly severe when predicting behavior that has an inherently low probability; even good predic-tion procedures would suffer very high false-positive rates.

The false-positive rate observed is sensitive to the threshold used for the criterion event. A review of the literature on prediction technology reveals that estimates of false positives cover an extremely broad range of between 50 percent and 99 percent among the predicted positives. This range results largely from variations in the breadth of activities considered as "future criminality," the duration of the follow-up period in which a criminal act might be observed, and the level of proof required to conclude that a subsequent criminal act in fact occurred (e.g., whether one relies on self-reports, arrests, or convictions). Furthermore, many of those considered to be false positives may indeed be true positives who committed a criterion event, but who successfully evaded detection or conviction for that offense.

Estimating the individual crime rates of recidivists is even more difficult than predicting whether an individual will recidivate or not. In view of the considerable uncertainty about the accuracy of such estimation, it would be inappropriate at this point to consider using explicit predictions of individual crime rates as the basis for selectively incapacitating high-crime-rate offenders.

Nevertheless, certain schemes of differential sentencing of offenders may still be justified. The information to distinguish among offenders could be based on the individual's criminal record (including the current crime type and the number of previous convictions and incarcerations, also by crime type). The use of information other than prior criminal record in determining sentences may be unjust because of the discriminatory or capricious quality of such variables. Information on hair color, for example, would be totally inappropriate to use in determining sentence, even if it were a good predictor. On the other hand, there is a long tradition that fully accepts taking account of the prior criminal record in determining a just sentence.

This practice could also achieve the benefits of selective incapacitation effects if persons with more extensive criminal records also have a higher propensity to commit future crimes.

Some evidence is available indicating that an individual's prior criminal record is a reliable indicator of future criminality. In a four-year follow-up of the subsequent criminal activity of persons released from the federal criminal justice system in 1965, the FBI reports that the likelihood of a subsequent arrest for a new offense varied by the crime type of record in 1965, with reasonably high repeat rates for the predatory crimes of burglary, assault, and robbery.

Similarly, a study of recidivism in England and Wales reports that the likelihood of reconviction for a new offense increases with the number of prior convictions in a person's criminal record. However, these results do not control for other factors that might be contributing to the observed difference, such as age and prior record in the United States data and type of disposition on the original charge in both the United States and English data.

The New Mathematics of Imprisonment

FRANKLIN E. ZIMRING
GORDON HAWKINS

S TUDENTS of correctional policy have recently been given a view of the bright side of prison overcrowding. In "Making Confinement Decision," Dr. Edwin Zedlewski, an economist on the staff of the federal government's National Institute of Justice, presents an assessment of the costs and benefits of increasing levels of imprisonment that might come as a surprise to many observers who are concerned about the increasing number in our nation's prisons.

Introducing this publication, James K. Stewart, Director of the National Institute of Justice, makes reference to the difficult choices confronting policymakers faced with a prison population of 500,000 that is growing at a rate of 1,000 a week and says:

Dr. Zedlewski's findings suggest that arguments that confinement is too expensive may not be valid when weighed against the value of crimes prevented through incapacitation and crimes deterred by the threat of imprisonment.

In fact, that description understates the claims for cost-effectiveness that the study makes. The bottom-line estimates presented in this analysis are arresting. One year's imprisonment is said to involve total social costs of $25,000, whereas the social costs averted by that imprisonment through incapacitation alone, at $430,000, are over seventeen times as great—a cost-benefit ratio rare indeed in the annals of public administration.

From "The New Mathematics of Imprisonment" by F. E. Zimring and G. Hawkins, 1988, *Crime and Delinquency, 34,* pp. 425-436. Copyright 1988 Sage Publications, Inc. Reprinted by permission.

While Dr. Zedlewski acknowledges that the dollar estimates used in reaching this conclusion are only "approximated crudely," he argues that variations in the cost estimates due to imprecision are of little consequence. "The conclusion holds even if there are large errors in the estimates." What difference should it make after all if a marginal investment in prison space of one dollar will generate only a $10 saving in social costs rather than $17?

This and other questions we propose to discuss at some length, indeed at greater length than that of the research publication that is the focus of our attention. We think that a careful review of this document can teach us about the difficulties encountered with uncritical use of statistics, about the intractable problems we confront when trying to calculate the social costs of both crime and imprisonment, and about a debate in which the same arguments for and against prison expansion can be and are made at almost any level of current imprisonment. After setting out the methods used to generate these National Institute of Justice report numbers in Part I, we turn our attention to some statistical implications of these estimates. Part II contains a critique of the study and reflections on the current prison policy debate.

I

Dr. Zedlewski's conclusion that communities are paying far more by releasing offenders than by expanding prison capacity is derived from an estimate of the cost of crime based on "every published expenditure on crime that could be found." He contrasts this with an estimate of confinement costs arrived at by adding to custodial costs (according to the American Correctional Association), the amortized costs of constructing a prison facility (according to a 1984 General Accounting Office report), and his estimate of the indirect costs incurred by removing an offender from the community, such as welfare payments to offenders' families.

Direct expenditures due to crime and crime prevention are given as approximately $100 billion in 1983. These expenditures were divided among victim losses ($35 billion); private security goods and services ($31 billion); and the operation of the criminal justice system, including prisons, jails, police, and the courts ($42.6 billion). It is noted that prison and jail operations consume only $8.6 billion, less than 10 percent of the total, and that a year in prison implies "total social costs of about $25,000."

The next step in the analysis is to weigh the social cost of an imprisonment decision—about $25,000 per year—against the social costs incurred by releasing offenders. What are called "release costs" are approximated by estimating the number of crimes per year an offender is likely to commit if released and multiplying that number by an estimate of the average social cost of a crime.

The first of these two figures is derived from a National Institute of Justice-sponsored survey by the RAND Corporation of inmates confined in jails and prisons in California, Michigan, and Texas. The survey found that inmates said they were committing crimes at what would be an annual rate of between 187 and 287, exclusive of drug deals, just prior to their most recent incarceration.

To compute the cost of an average offense, total expenditures on crime in the United States, estimated at $99.8 billion in 1983, were then divided by the total number of crimes (as reported in Bureau of Justice statistics and estimated in the last reported National Crime Survey), estimated as totaling 42.5 million. Dollars spent divided by crimes resulted in a figure of $2,300 per crime.

By combining crime costs and offense rates (at 187 crimes per year), it was calculated that a typical inmate was responsible for $430,000 in crime costs ($187 \times 2,300 = \$430,100$). The conclusion derived from this analysis is that sentencing 1,000 more offenders to prison would cost an additional $25 million per year. By contrast, about 187,000 felonies would be averted through the incapacitation of these offenders, representing about $430 million in social costs. Ten thousand extra prisoners would save slightly over $4 billion and 100,000 extra prisoners would generate $40 billion in additional savings.

Some Implications

One insight into the significance and validity of these cost-benefit calculations is to study some of the statistical relations implied by this analysis and to see how closely our recent history conforms to predictions that this confinement study produces.

The first such set of predictions concerns crimes saved through incapacitation. If the rate per offender is stable, as the study estimates, at 187 per offender, the total crime rate of 42.5 million is attributable to just 227,800 street criminals (42.5 m/187) of the kind we imprison. Thus a 35 percent decrease in the population behind bars should double the crime rate by releasing about 225,000 of the 700,000 persons in U.S. prisons and jails. And a 33 percent increase in the prison and jail population from 700,000 to about 930,000 should reduce crime to zero in the United States ($230,000 \times 187 = 43,010,000$). Since 230,000 persons is about one-eighth of the number of adults on probation in the United States, such a shift could be achieved by changes in sentencing policy without changes in apprehensions, and would cost less than $6 billion in total social cost as the study estimates ($230,000 \times \$25,000 = \$5,750,000,000$). In short, about 6 percent more than our current criminal justice and crime expenditures would cure the crime problem.

But there are indications that these estimates are far from accurate. First, the normal turnover in the prison and jail population provides one natural test of the criminal propensities of the incarcerated population. Almost all of the U.S.

jail population of more than 200,000 are released during each year and more than 200,000 of the 500,000 in the prison population. Even if all of these persons were back behind bars after one year, at an annual rate of 187 crimes per subject, the 221,768 offenders released from prison in 1984 should have been responsible for just under 100 percent of all crime in the United States in 1985. One problem with this estimate is that it leaves no room for juveniles, new recruits, a dark figure of adult offenders, the almost two million on probation, or even ex-inmates who were released from confinement the year before that. Even then, the hundreds of thousands of jail releases who should, at 187 crimes per person, account for almost 100 percent of crime themselves must instead be assumed to be crime free in 1985, or we have explained almost 200 percent of the crime rate with jail and prison releases alone. So these estimates seem not merely wrong, but ludicrously wrong.

There is another straightforward test of these crime-imprisonment ratios, a natural experiment we have been running in the United States since the early 1970s. Since the U.S. prison population has been rising substantially, we can use the methods of analysis put forward in "Making Confinement Decisions" to test the study's conclusions against our recent history.

We start with 1977, needing two numbers to match the analysis in "Making Confinement Decisions," an estimated number of crimes per criminal and a total volume of crime. The estimated number of crimes per criminal can be taken at 187. Indeed, this figure was derived from inmate self-reports of their offenses during the late 1970s rather than later dates. The total volume of crime estimated by the methods used by "Making Confinement Decisions" was about forty million in 1977. At 187 crimes per criminal, the incarceration of about 230,000 extra offenders should reduce crime to zero on incapacitation effects alone. The problem is that on this account, crime disappeared some time ago because the U.S. prison population expanded by a total of 237,000 from 1977 through mid-1986.

A similar point can be made about the costs of crime saved by imprisonment. In the reported calculus, each crime prevented by incapacitation saved $2,300 in social costs, and 34 percent of those savings are in public expenditures on criminal justice. This criminal justice saving of $782 per crime adds up to just over $146,000 that each year an offender spends in prison will reduce the criminal justice budget.

These estimates yield predictions about patterns of public expenditures that can be tested on the recent experiment in prison population expansion. Between 1977 and 1987, the prison population in the United States grew by 237,000. At 146,000 1983 dollars per prison year, this growth should have reduced criminal justice expenditures by a net figure of about 34.6 billion per year by the end of the ten-year period 1977-1987. But, in fact, the criminal justice budget increased from about 15 billion current dollars in fiscal 1975 to 45 billion current dollars in 1985, with no sign of any savings attributable to prison-based incapacitation reducing police, court, or correctional budgets.

One final statistical grace note relates to the negative marginal cost of imprisonment in this study. According to this calculus, each person sent to prison for a year saves almost $37,000 in prison and jail expenditure during that year ($.086 \times \$2,300 = \$197.80 \times 187 = \$36,988.60$), or more than the estimated cost of imprisoning the inmate ($15,000). Taken literally, this predicts that aggregate expenditures for prisons should decrease as the number of inmates increases.

Estimates of this type raise procedural as well as substantive questions. When a set of estimates reduces crime to zero for $6 billion, shouldn't this lead to skeptical questions being asked at the agency that funds and reviews criminal justice research for the federal government? When a study argues that locking up 230,000 additional offenders should reduce nondrug crime by forty million units, shouldn't someone in the National Institute of Justice or in the scholarly community point out that we have just finished running that experiment with no such results? As we turn in Part II to the substantive explanation of these kinds of mistakes, we remain puzzled by the processes that leave this work substantially unexamined.

II

The foregoing analysis suggests that the conclusions advanced in "Making Confinement Decisions" are not simply wrong, but rather that they are case studies in compound catastrophic error. How did this happen?

Six features of the study that contribute to the magnitude of error deserve mention: the high estimate of incapacitation effects; disregard of the diminishing marginal returns of predictive imprisonment; the problematic allocation of public expenditures such as police budgets as costs of crime; the "average cost" treatment of all offenses (other than drug crimes) as representing equal social costs; the assumption that the costs of crime prevention and law enforcement are marginally proportional to crime rates; and the imprecision and vagary associated with the concept of the social cost of crime and thus of any cost-benefit comparison. Each problem raises issues of importance of serious students of criminal justice.

The study takes its 187 crimes per offender from a 1982 RAND Corporation survey of inmates sponsored by the National Institute of Justice. There are a variety of different ways of estimating the average number of crimes that would have been committed by a group of individuals had they not been incarcerated. The estimate cited by Dr. Zedlewski is the highest that he could have found in National Institute of Justice-sponsored research on which to base assessment of the extent of incapacitative effects.

Much well-regarded research would place crime prevention volume at less than one-tenth of the 187 crimes per offender figure. Indeed, some of the studies that are cited in "Making Confinement Decisions" give much more modest levels of crime potentially preventable by imprisonment. Yet this is not mentioned in the study and neither the controversy over the correct levels of criminal incapacitation effects nor the 1986 National Academy of Sciences panel study on this issue is referred to.

Not only are the criminal propensities of those currently incarcerated overestimated but the problem of diminishing marginal returns in crime prevention as a larger number of individuals are sent to prison is ignored in the computations. Yet that problem is clearly evident in

the RAND Corporation study principally relied on in "Making Confinement Decisions." It is graphically illustrated in the Table of Inmate Annual Offense Rates from the RAND Corporation study, reproduced at page 3 of "Making Confinement Decisions." The table shows that robbers and burglars in California prisons report robbery rates four times as high and of burglary more than twice as high as robbers and burglars in Texas prisons. The reason for this difference is that Texas has a much higher rate of imprisonment so that high-rate offenders make up a larger proportion of the California prison population than of the Texas prison population. This relatively large proportion of high-rate offenders (as of 1982) is the reason why the overall estimates in the RAND Corporation study are so high in California. It is a function of a relatively low level of imprisonment. Texas had already watered down its prison stock when the survey was taken by mixing in a greater number of low-rate offenders. This explains why whereas the California prisoners report a robbery rate of fifty, the corresponding number for Texas prison inmates is only twelve. But this does not mean that the incarceration of the next Texas prisoner at the margin will prevent as many as twelve robberies that would otherwise have been committed. As long as most high-rate offenders are already in prison, then offenders at the margin of imprisonment will have much lower average crime rates than those already in prison. Thus, the phenomenon of diminishing marginal returns.

The author of "Making Confinement Decisions" seems to be schizophrenic about this feature of the research results. On one hand, he acknowledges the highly skewed distribution of individual offense rates in the RAND Corporation study (half of the inmates surveyed reporting individual crime rates that were less than one-tenth of the 187 crimes figure). Moreover, in relation to current sentencing practice, he acknowledges that "on average, we would expect those released to be somewhat less criminal than those incarcerated." On the other hand, the 187 annual crimes estimate is used without amendment and without explanation.

The problems associated with estimating the number of crimes prevented by incapacitation are compounded by the difficulties involved in calculating the cost of crime. The method employed of measuring the cost of crime is artless in its simplicity. In the case of public expenditure on crime and crime prevention, the entire budget of all of the agencies of criminal justice is assumed to be part of the cost of crime. Yet with regard to the police, by far the largest public expenditure item, that allocation is ludicrous. Less than one-tenth of all police budgets is devoted to the investigation of crime and the apprehension of criminals. And crime prevention is one of many general police functions. The police also maintain public order, control traffic, provide a range of citizen services, and respond to a wide variety of public needs not related to the FBI "part one" crime rate or to the size of the prison population. Most police expenditures would continue even if crime rates decreased. They are not in this sense costs of crime.

Not only are all the costs of law enforcement assumed to be costs of crime in this analysis, but it is also assumed that the correct way to express the cost of a crime is by dividing total costs by the total number of crimes committed. Allocating this average figure to each crime seems wrong both in theory and in practice, obscuring the need for priority decisions and also inconsistent with any known economic theory of crime. If both a single robbery and a single theft have cost estimates of $2,300, we should be indifferent as to which offense our policies would prevent. This $2,300 estimate in the text is unobjectionable only if it is meaningless. Since no rationale for this procedure can be found in "Making Confinement Decisions," it is impossible to determine what justification for the practice the author of the study may have had in mind.

The study's guess about how much money would be saved if the crime rate dropped is based on the assumption that the cost of an individual crime is that act's proportional share of the total cost of all crime. Thus, if the total number of robberies is one hundred and the total police budget for robbery is $200,000, the report assumes that reducing the volume of robbery from one hundred to ninety will reduce police expenditure for robbery by $20,000—from $200,000 down to $180,000. Yet there is no reason to suppose that reducing the volume of robbery from one hundred to ninety will reduce police expenditure in the same proportion, nor is any reason given to support this assumption of marginal proportionality.

In fact, there is good reason to suppose that reductions in crime rates of this magnitude would generate cost savings at a considerably lower level. If $200,000 of police resources are invested in the prevention of robbery when the robbery rate is one hundred, it may well be thought prudent not to disturb that investment at all if the rate drops to ninety. The productivity of prevention programs is based on the number of potential robberies, not the actual crime rate.

As to the resources devoted to the apprehension of robbery offenders, it is unlikely that any of those engaged in that task will be reassigned simply because of a 10 percent drop in the offense rate. It is more likely that the police establishment will view the decline as providing an opportunity to do a more effective job with a stable level of police resources.

With regard to some other public sector costs of crime, a reduction in the crime rate achieved by increasing the number of offenders sent to prison or by increasing the length of sentences imposed could actually increase rather than decrease total criminal justice system costs. By raising the stakes in so many criminal prosecutions, the total costs of prosecution, defense, trial, and appeal will increase for the "get tough" group of cases. Even a smaller number of cases could lead to a greater aggregate expenditure of resources if the penal stakes of the average criminal prosecution increase.

With respect to private expenditures for crime prevention, there is also no evidence to suggest that reductions in crime rates will lead to proportional reductions in crime prevention expenditure. If the chances of being burglarized fall from ten in one hundred to nine in one hundred in a particular neighborhood, is it plausible to assume that the number of dogs purchased and fed on account of the fear of burglary will decline by 10 percent? Why? Yet that is precisely the assumption made in this study's estimates of the costs of crime and the benefits of imprisonment.

There has been experience in recent years of the consequences for public expenditure on criminal justice during periods of decline in the rates of some types of crime. Yet the study marshals no evidence from this experience to support its claims. And we are aware of no jurisdiction in which a decline in the incidence of a particular category of crime has led to a proportional drop in private or public expenditure.

One reason why crime prevention expenditures are not responsive to crime rates on a strictly proportional basis is that the fear and anxiety generated by crime is unlikely to be reduced by a corresponding degree when a crime rate falls. If robbery rates are reduced by 25 percent, there is little likelihood that the fear of robbery will undergo an equivalent reduction. It seems more probable that fear and anxiety are responsive only to sustained shifts in perceived personal risk. So that even if the total abolition of robbery would yield public savings of $50 million, it does not follow that cutting robbery by 50 percent would reduce the cost of that crime to the community by $25 million.

The foregoing analysis suggests that "Making Confinement Decisions" contains a number of specific errors in the computation of the costs of crime and the costs and benefits of prison as crime prevention, and the list compiled here could be considerably lengthened. But an emphasis on the avoidable errors in such an exercise may leave the mistaken impression that it is feasible to perform an analysis of the social costs of crime on which a reliable and precise cost-benefit estimate could be based in dollar terms.

Yet the history of efforts to quantify the social costs of crime counsels against the assumption that this can be achieved. Over half a century ago, the Wickersham Commission demonstrated that it was possible to measure levels of public expenditure by the institutions of criminal justice, but stopped short of relating those expenditures to particular crimes and was unable to make any estimate of the total cost of crime. Thirty-five years later, another Presidential Commission invested substantial resources in trying to assess the cost of crime but abstained from analysis under that rubric in favor of simply investigating what it called "the economic impact of crime."

One difference between the concepts of the "cost" and "the economic impact" of crime is that a study restricted to economic impact does not attempt to monetarize such essentially non-pecuniary losses as pain, fear, shock, or diminished social interaction and sense of security. Nor does the economic impact approach provide a direct guide to action—for example, gambling has a much larger economic impact than homicide ($7 billion as opposed to $750 million, according to the 1967 commission)—but it avoids the inherent difficulties that confront attempts to assess comprehensively the social cost of crime.

The Imprisonment Debate

There may be many different ways to measure the harm attributable to crime. But even if we confine ourselves to trying to estimate costs in dollars, the attempt to aggregate guard-dog food expenditures with victim dollar losses with variations in police pension levels into a single monetary total seems misconceived. Those who invest resources in pursuing this goal may be barking up the wrong tree, and in relation to "Making Confinement Decisions," the level of error in the exercise suggests that it was a case of the wrong dog barking up the wrong tree.

There is one final aspect in which both the argument and the context of "Making Confinement Decisions" are instructive. One of the most significant features of the study is the fact of its appearance in 1987. It appeared at a time when prison populations in the United States had increased by almost 150 percent in fifteen years. Even after this degree of expansion, what Dr. Zedlewski calls "a popular sentiment for more prison space" persists. This publication is not alone. There are many who argue with conviction that substantial further expansion in prison population will produce benefits far exceeding its costs, that lenient treatment of offenders is a central problem.

This suggests that there is no natural level of prison accommodation or rate of imprisonment that would significantly reduce the need felt by many citizens for more prisons. Moreover, the arguments made for expanding prison capacity do not change much as statistics change. The same arguments are propounded with the same force with a prison population of 500,000 as were made when it was 217,000 and will probably also be made when it reaches 750,000.

As long as levels of crime are high enough to generate substantial anxiety, those who view increased imprisonment as a solution will continue to demand more prisons and will do so in terms that do not change markedly at any level of incarceration. Indeed, the more attenuated the link between the malady and the proposed remedy, the more insatiable will be the demand for more of the remedial measure.

REHABILITATION

The Crime of Punishment

KARL MENNINGER

THE word *treatment* has many meanings. Applied to human beings, it may mean kindness or it may mean cruelty. "Alcoholics should be treated like sick people, not like criminals," someone exclaimed in my hearing recently; two different meanings of treatment were obviously implied.

The medical use of the word treatment implies a program of presumably beneficial action prescribed for and administered to one who seeks it. The purpose of treatment is to relieve pain, correct disability, or combat an illness. Treatment may be painful or disagreeable but, if so, these qualities are incidental, not purposive. Once upon a time, we must admit, we doctors with the best of intentions did treat some patients with torture. That, thank God, was long ago.

But the treatment of human failure or dereliction by the infliction of pain is still used and believed in by many nonmedical people. "Spare the rod and spoil the child" is still considered wise warning by many.

Whipping is still used by many secondary schoolmasters in England, I am informed, to stimulate study, attention, and the love of learning. Whipping was long a traditional treatment for the "crime" of disobedience on the part of children, pupils, servants, apprentices, employees. And slaves were treated for centuries by flogging for such offenses as weariness, confusion, stupidity, exhaustion, fear, grief, and even

overcheerfulness. It was assumed and stoutly defended that these "treatments" cured conditions for which they were administered.

Meanwhile, scientific medicine was acquiring many new healing methods and devices. Doctors can now transplant organs and limbs; they can remove brain tumors and cure incipient cancers; they can halt pneumonia, meningitis, and other infections; they can correct deformities and repair breaks and tears and scars. But these wonderful achievements are accomplished on willing subjects, people who voluntarily ask for help by even heroic measures. And the reader will be wondering, no doubt, whether doctors can do anything with or for people who do not want to be treated at all, anyway. Can doctors cure willful aberrant behavior? Are we to believe that crime is a disease that can be reached by scientific measures? Is it not merely "natural meanness" that makes all of us do wrong things at times even when we "know better"? And are not self-control, moral stamina, and willpower the things needed? Surely, there is no medical treatment for the lack of those!

Let me answer this carefully, for much misunderstanding accumulates here. I would say that according to the prevalent understanding of the words, crime is not a disease. Neither is it an illness, although I think it should be! It should be treated, and it could be; but it mostly is not.

Illness is what we call those unpleasant states of being for the relief and alteration of which the medical profession exists and is consulted. We have admitted that most criminal behavior is not a disease, nor even—for the most part—a commonly recognized illness. Crime is still a willful and avowed breaking of the rules, a flagrant disobedience, a flaunted infraction. The pain experienced by the subject is negligible compared to the pain suffered by society. Most recognized illnesses, however disagreeable for society, involve some conspicuous suffering or disability for the subject. The propensity for committing crime does not *look* like suffering; nor does it cause any obvious disability. It rarely arouses pity except in those very close to the offender. It does not correspond to the commonly held notion or general course of illness or sickness or disease.

Nevertheless, many a parent today secretly takes his son to doctors for just exactly this kind of illness—insufficiently controlled aggression. To the parent, the son's behavior is not normal, not comprehensible, not consonant with health. It *must* be a symptom of illness. He wants to believe it is something the doctor can cure. It is a horrid, alien thing afflicting and deforming his otherwise lovable and promising child. His neighbors and friends may not concur in this view. With the aid of a lawyer, he might persuade a judge to agree with it. But even his family physician may give the theory little support. For there is no such disease described in the textbooks of medicine and surgery.

When the community begins to look upon the expression of aggressive violence as the symptom of an illness or as indicative of illness, it will be because it believes doctors can do something to correct such a condition. At present, some better-informed individuals do believe and expect this. However angry at or sorry for the offender, they want him "treated" in an effective way so that he will cease to be a danger to them. And they know that the traditional punishment, "treatment-punishment," will not effect this.

What will? What effective treatment is there for such violence? It will surely have to begin with motivating or stimulating or arousing in a cornered individual the wish and hope and intention to change his methods of dealing with the realities of life. Can this be done by education, medication, counseling, training? I would answer yes. It can be done successfully in a majority of cases, if undertaken in time.

The present penal system and the existing legal philosophy do not stimulate or even expect such a change to take place in the criminal. Yet change is what medical science always aims for. The prisoner, like the doctor's other patients, should emerge from his treatment experience a different person, differently equipped, differently functioning, and headed in a different direction from when he began the treatment.

It is natural for the public to doubt that this can be accomplished with criminals. But remember that the public used to doubt that change could be effected in the mentally ill. Like criminals, the mentally ill were only a few decades ago regarded as definitely unchangeable—"incurable." No one a hundred years ago believed mental illness to be curable. Today, all people know (or should know) that mental illness is curable in the great majority of instances and that the prospects and rapidity of cure are directly related to the availability and intensity of proper treatment.

In the city in which I live, there had been for many years a gloomy, overcrowded, understaffed place of horror called "the insane asylum." In its dark wards and bar-windowed halls, as late as 1948, one psychiatrist and one nurse were on duty for nearly two thousand sick people. There was no treatment for them worthy of the name. There was no hope. There were few recoveries.

Today, this old asylum is a beautiful medical complex of forty one- and two-story buildings, with clinics and laboratories and workshops and lecture halls surrounded by parks and trees and recreational areas. Some patients are under intensive treatment; others are convalescent; many are engaged in various activities in the buildings or about the grounds. Some leave their quiet rooms each morning to go to work in the city for the entire day, returning for the evening and their night's rest at the hospital. The average length of time required for restoring a mentally ill patient to health in this hospital has been reduced from years, to months, to weeks. Four-fifths of the patients living there today will be back in their homes by the end of the year. There are many empty beds, and the daily census is continually dropping.

WHAT IS THIS
EFFECTIVE TREATMENT?

If these "incurable" patients are now being returned to their homes and their work in such numbers and with such celerity, why not something similar for offenders? Just what are the treatments used to effect these rapid changes? Are they available for use with offenders?

The forms and techniques of psychiatric treatment used today number in the hundreds. Psychoanalysis; electroshock therapy; psychotherapy; occupational and industrial therapy; family group therapy; milieu therapy; the use of music, art, and horticultural activities; and various drug therapies—these are some of the techniques and modalities of treatment used to stimulate or assist the restoration of a vital balance of impulse control and life satisfaction. No one patient requires or receives all forms, but each patient is studied with respect to his particular needs, his basic assets, his interests, and his special difficulties. In addition to the treatment modalities mentioned, there are many facilitations and events which contribute to total treatment effect: a new job opportunity (perhaps located by a social worker) or a vacation trip, a course of reducing exercises, a cosmetic surgical operation or a herniotomy, some night school courses, a wedding in the family (even one for the patient), an inspiring sermon. Some of these require merely prescription or suggestion; others require guidance, tutelage, or assistance by trained therapists or by willing volunteers. A therapeutic team may embrace a dozen workers—as in a hospital setting—or it may narrow down to the doctor and the spouse. Clergymen, teachers, relatives, friends, and even fellow patients often participate informally but helpfully in the process of readaptation.

All of the participants in this effort to bring about a favorable change in the patient, that is, in his vital balance and life program, are imbued with what we may call a *therapeutic attitude.* This is one in direct antithesis to attitudes of avoidance, ridicule, scorn, or punitiveness. Hostile feelings toward the subject, however justified by his unpleasant and even destructive behavior, are not in the curriculum of therapy or in the therapist. This does not mean that therapists approve of the offensive and obnoxious

behavior of the patient; they distinctly disapprove of it. But they recognize it as symptomatic of continued imbalance and disorganization, which is what they are seeking to change. They distinguish between disapproval, penalty, price, and punishment.

This is the deepest meaning of the therapeutic attitude. Every doctor knows this; every worker in a hospital or clinic knows it (or should). I once put this principle in a paragraph of directions for the workers in our psychiatric hospital:

If we can love: this is the touchstone. This is the key to all the therapeutic programs of the modern psychiatric hospital; it dominates the behavior of its staff from director down to gardener. To our patient who cannot love, we must say by our actions that we do love him.

You can be angry here if you must be; we know you have had cause. We know you have been wronged. We know you are afraid of your own anger, your own self-punishment—afraid, too, that your anger will arouse our anger and that you will be wronged again and disappointed again and rejected again and driven mad once more. But we are not angry—and you won't be either, after a while. We are your friends; those about you are all friends; you can relax your defenses and your tensions. As you—and we—come to understand your life better, the warmth of love will begin to replace your present anguish—and you will find yourself getting well.

RIGHT YOU ARE IF
YOU THINK YOU ARE

Do I believe there is effective treatment for offenders, and that they can be changed? Most certainly and definitely I do. Not all cases, to be sure; there are also some physical afflictions which we cannot cure at the moment. Some provision has to be made for incurables—pending new knowledge—and these will include some offenders. But I believe the majority of them would prove to be curable. The willfulness and the viciousness of offenders are part of the thing for which they have to be treated. These must not thwart the therapeutic attitude.

It is simply not true that most of them are "fully aware" of what they are doing, nor is it true that they want no help from anyone, although some of them say so. Prisoners are individuals: some want treatment, some do not. Some do not know what treatment is. Many are utterly despairing and hopeless. Where treatment is made available in institutions, many prisoners seek it even with the full knowledge that doing so will not lessen their sentences. In some prisons, seeking treatment by prisoners is frowned upon by the officials.

Various forms of treatment are even now being tried in some progressive courts and prisons over the country—educational, social, industrial, religious, recreational, and psychological treatments. Socially acceptable behavior, new work-play opportunities, new identity and companion patterns all help toward community reacceptance. Some parole officers and some wardens have been extremely ingenious in developing these modalities of rehabilitation and reconstruction—more than I could list here even if I knew them all. But some are trying. The secret of success in all programs, however, is the replacement of the punitive attitude with a therapeutic attitude.

A therapeutic attitude is essential regardless of the particular form of treatment or help. Howard Gill of the American University's Institute of Correctional Administration believes that 30 percent of offenders are overwhelmed with situational difficulties, and for such individuals crisis intervention often works wonders. Case work, economic relief, or other social assistance often will induce a favorable behavior pattern change in these offenders. In another 30 percent, he estimates, personal psychological problems exist in the offender which require technical treatment efforts. For these, the help of psychiatrists, physicians, and psychologists are needed. Still another 30 percent of prisoners are essentially immature individuals whose antisocial tendencies have never found the proper paths of distribution and transformation in socially acceptable ways. These men are usually amenable to redirection, education, and guidance. They can achieve development of self-control and social conformity by the various programs which we call milieu treatment. In

other words, one can think of the categories of treatment as falling largely into the three modalities of sociological, psychological (medical), and educational.

TREATMENT FOR THE MANY

In thinking of ways to provide truly corrective therapy for large numbers of offenders at minimal expense, penologists might take a leaf from the book of modern psychiatry. It was long assumed that only under detention, that is, in the hospital, was it possible to effectively control and treat and change severely disturbed individuals. Early in the twentieth century, an experiment of "out patient" psychiatric treatment was made in Boston by Ernest Southard of Harvard. Today, half a century later, the majority of all psychiatric patients are in outpatient status. Furthermore, there is a steadily rising preponderance of outpatients over inpatients. "Day hospitals," where patients spend some daylight hours in scheduled activities with other patients but go home in the evening for sleep, privacy, and family adaptation, have also proved useful. Similarly, "night hospitals" came into use for patients who could adapt themselves well enough to a work situation or a school setting but who did better by spending their nights under the protective care of the friendly hospital.

Thus, there has developed the outpatient principle, which holds that it is optimal for the patient to continue living and working in his ordinary, everyday-life ways as much as possible, seeing his psychiatrist, psychologist, social worker, therapist, teacher, or clergyman in successive sessions at intervals in their offices. Obviously, this is a great saving of time and money for everyone. And, curiously, it has proved to be just as effective, statistically measured, in nurturing favorable change in patients as were our carefully planned and elaborated inpatient hospital programs. Not the least advantage was the diminished stigmatization of the nonconfined patient.

All this the correctional system might emulate—and in some progressive jurisdictions it does. Some individuals have to be protected against themselves, some have to be protected from other prisoners, some even from the community. Some mental patients must be detained for a time even against their wishes, and the same is true of offenders. Offenders with propensities for impulsive and predatory aggression should not be permitted to live among us unrestrained by some kind of social control. But the great majority of offenders, even "criminals," should never become prisoners if we want to "cure" them.

What we want to accomplish is the reintegration of the temporarily suspended individual back into the mainstream of social life, preferably a life at a higher level than before, just as soon as possible. Many, many precariously constituted individuals are trying to make it on the outside right now, with little help from us. We all have to keep reminding ourselves that most offenders are never even apprehended. Most of those who are caught and convicted, we must remember, are released either free or on probation. But they rarely have the benefit of treatment.

What Works? Questions and Answers About Prison Reform

ROBERT MARTINSON

ONE of the problems in the constant debate over "prison reform" is that we have been able to draw very little on any systematic empirical knowledge about the success or failure that we have met when we have tried to rehabilitate offenders, with various treatments and in various institutional and noninstitutional settings. The field of penology has produced a voluminous research literature on this subject, but until recently there has been no comprehensive review of this literature and no attempt to bring its findings to bear, in a useful way, on the general question of "What works?" My purpose in this essay is to sketch an answer to that question.

THE TRAVAILS OF A STUDY

What we set out to do in this study was fairly simple, although it turned into a massive task. First, we undertook a six-month search of the literature for any available reports published in the English language on attempts at rehabilitation that had been made in our corrections systems and those of other countries from 1945 through 1967. We then picked from that literature all those studies whose findings were interpretable—that is, whose design and execution met the conventional standards of social science research. Our criteria were rigorous but hardly esoteric: a study had to be an evaluation of a treatment method; it had to employ an independent measure of the improvement secured

From "What Works? Questions and Answers About Prison Reform" by R. Martinson, 1974, *Public Interest*, 35, pp. 22-54. Copyright 1974 by National Affairs, Inc. Reprinted by permission.

by that method; and it had to use some control group, some untreated individuals with whom the treated ones could be compared. We excluded studies only for methodological reasons: they presented insufficient data, they were only preliminary, they presented only a summary of findings and did not allow a reader to evaluate those findings, their results were confounded by extraneous factors, they used unreliable measures, one could not understand their descriptions of the treatment in question, they drew spurious conclusions from their data, their samples were undescribed or too small or provided no true comparability between treated and untreated groups, or they had used inappropriate statistical tests and did not provide enough information for the reader to recompute the data. Using these standards, we drew from the total number of studies 231 acceptable ones, which we not only analyzed ourselves but summarized in detail so that a reader of our analysis would be able to compare it with his independent conclusions.

These treatment studies use various measures of offender improvement: recidivism rates (i.e., the rates at which offenders return to crime), adjustment to prison life, vocational success, educational achievement, personality and attitude change, and general adjustment to the outside community. We included all of these in our study, but in these pages I will deal only with the effects of rehabilitative treatment on recidivism, the phenomenon which reflects most directly how well our present treatment programs are performing the task of rehabilitation. The use of even this one measure brings with it enough methodological complications to make a clear reporting of the findings most difficult. The groups that are studied, for instance, are exceedingly disparate, so that it is hard to tell whether what "works" for one kind of offender also works for others. In addition, there has been little attempt to replicate studies; therefore, one cannot be certain how stable and reliable the various findings are. Just as important, when the various studies use the term *recidivism rate,* they may in fact be talking about somewhat different measures of offender behavior—that is, "failure" measures such as arrest rates or parole violation rates, or "success" measures such as favorable discharge from parole or probation. And not all of these measures correlate very highly with one another. These difficulties will become apparent again and again in the course of this discussion.

With these caveats, it is possible to give a rather bald summary of our findings: with few and isolated exceptions, the rehabilitative efforts that have been reported so far have had no appreciable effect on recidivism. Studies that have been done since our survey was completed do not present any major grounds for altering that original conclusion. What follows is an attempt to answer the questions and challenges that might be posed to such an unqualified statement.

EDUCATION AND VOCATIONAL TRAINING

1. *Isn't it true that a correctional facility running a truly rehabilitative program—one that prepares inmates for life on the outside through education and vocational training—will turn out more successful individuals than will a prison which merely leaves its inmates to rot?*

If this is true, the fact remains that there is very little empirical evidence to support it. Skill development and education programs are in fact quite common in correctional facilities, and one might begin by examining their effects on young males, those who might be thought most amenable to such efforts. A study by New York State found that for young males as a whole, the degree of success achieved in the regular prison

academic education program, as measured by changes in grade achievement levels, made no significant difference in recidivism rates. The only exception was the relative improvement, compared with the sample as a whole, that greater progress made in the top 7 percent of the participating population—those who had high IQs, had made good records in previous schooling, and who also made good records of academic progress in the institution. And a study by Glaser found that while it was true that when one controlled for sentence length, more attendance in regular prison academic programs slightly decreased the subsequent chances of parole violation, this improvement was not large enough to outweigh the associated disadvantage for the "long attenders": those who attended prison school the longest also turned out to be those who were in prison the longest. Presumably, those getting the most education were also the worst parole risks in the first place.

In sum, many of these studies of young males are extremely hard to interpret because of flaws in research design. But it can safely be said that they provide us with no clear evidence that education or skill development programs have been successful.

When one turns to adult male inmates, as opposed to young ones, the results are even more discouraging. There have been six studies of this type; three of them report that their programs, which ranged from academic to prison work experience, produced no significant differences in recidivism rates, and one—by Glaser—is almost impossible to interpret because of the risk differentials of the prisoners participating in the various programs.

Two things should be noted about these studies. One is the difficulty of interpreting them as a whole. The disparity in the programs that were tried, in the populations that were affected, and in the institutional settings that surrounded these projects make it hard to be sure that one is observing the same category of treatment in each case. But the second point is that despite this difficulty, one can be reasonably sure that, so far, educational and vocational programs have not worked. We do not know why they have failed. We do not know whether the programs themselves are flawed or whether they are incapable of overcoming the effects of prison life in general. The difficulty may be that they lack applicability to the world the inmate will face outside of prison. Or perhaps the type of educational and skill improvement they produce simply does not have very much to do with an individual's propensity to commit a crime. What we do know is that, to date, education and skill development have not reduced recidivism by rehabilitating criminals.

THE EFFECTS OF INDIVIDUAL COUNSELING

2. *But when we speak of a rehabilitative prison, aren't we referring to more than education and skill development alone? Isn't what's needed some way of counseling inmates, or helping them with the deeper problems that have caused their maladjustment?*

This, too, is a reasonable hypothesis, but when one examines the programs of this type that have been tried, it is hard to find any more grounds for enthusiasm than we found with skill development and education. One method that has been tried—although so far, there have been acceptable reports only of its application to young offenders—has been individual psychotherapy. For young males, we found seven such reported studies. One study, by Guttman at the Nelles School, found such treatment to be ineffective in reducing recidivism rates; another, by Rudoff, found it unrelated to institutional violation rates, which were themselves related to parole success. It must be pointed out that Rudoff used only this indirect measure of association, and the study therefore cannot rule out the possibility of a treatment effect. A third, also by Guttman but at another institution, found that such treatment was actually related to a slightly higher parole violation rate, and a study by Adams also found a lack of improvement in parole revocation and first suspension rates.

There have been two studies of the effects of individual psychotherapy on young incarcerated female offenders, and both of them report no significant effects from the therapy. But one of the Adams studies does contain a suggestive, although not clearly interpretable, finding: if this individual therapy was administered by a psychiatrist or a psychologist, the resulting parole suspension rate was almost two and a half times higher than if it was administered by a social worker without this specialized training.

There has also been a much smaller number of studies of two other types of individual therapy: counseling, which is directed towards a prisoner's gaining new insight into his own problems, and casework, which aims at helping a prisoner cope with his more pragmatic immediate needs. These types of therapy both rely heavily on the empathetic relationship that is to be developed between the professional and the client. It was noted above that the Adams study of therapy administered to girls, referred to in the discussion of individual psychotherapy, found that social workers seemed better at the job than psychologists or psychiatrists. This difference seems to suggest a favorable outlook for these alternative forms of individual therapy. But other studies of such therapy have produced ambiguous results. Bemsten reported a Danish experiment that showed that sociopsychological counseling combined with comprehensive welfare measures—job and residence placement, clothing, union and health insurance membership, and financial aid—produced an improvement among some short-term male offenders, although not those in either the highest-risk or the lowest-risk categories. On the other hand, Hood, in Britain, reported generally nonsignificant results with a program of counseling for young males. (Interestingly enough, this experiment did point to a mechanism capable of changing recidivism rates. When boys were released from institutional care and entered the army directly, "poor risk" boys among both experimentals and controls did better than expected. "Good risks" did worse.)

So these foreign data are sparse and not in agreement; the American data are just as sparse. The only American study which provides a direct measure of the effects of individual counseling—a study of California's Intensive Treatment Program, which was "psychodynamically" oriented—found no improvement in recidivism rates.

GROUP COUNSELING

Group counseling has indeed been tried in correctional institutions, both with and without a specifically psychotherapeutic orientation. There has been one study of "pragmatic," problem-oriented counseling on young institutionalized males, by Seckel. This type of counseling had no significant effect. For adult males, there have been three such studies of the "pragmatic" and "insight" methods. Two report no long-lasting significant effects. (One of these two did report a real but short-term effect that wore off as the program became institutionalized and as offenders were at liberty longer.) The third study of adults, by Shelley, dealt with a "pragmatic" casework program, directed toward the educational and vocational needs of institutionalized young adult males in a Michigan prison camp. The treatment lasted for six months, and at the end of that time Shelley found an improvement in attitudes; the possession of "good" attitudes was independently found by Shelley to correlate with parole success. Unfortunately, though, Shelley was not able to measure the *direct* impact of the counseling on recidivism rates. His two separate correlations are suggestive, but they fall short of being able to tell us that it really is the counseling that has a direct effect on recidivism.

With regard to more professional group *psychotherapy,* the reports are also conflicting. We have two studies of group psychotherapy on young males. One, by Persons, says that this treatment did in fact reduce recidivism. The improved recidivism rate stems from the improved performance only of those who were clinically judged to have been "successfully" treated; still, the overall result of the treatment was to improve recidivism rates for the experimental group as a whole. On the other hand, a study by Craft of young males designated "psychopaths," comparing "self-government" group psychotherapy with "authoritarian" individual counseling, found that the "group therapy" boys afterward committed *twice* as many new offenses as the individually treated ones. Perhaps some forms of group psychotherapy work for some types of offenders but not others; a reader must draw his own conclusions, on the basis of sparse evidence.

With regard to young females, the results are just as equivocal. Adams, in his study of females, found that there was no improvement to be gained from treating girls by group rather than individual methods. A study by Taylor of borstal (reformatory) girls in New Zealand found a similar lack of any great improvement for group therapy as opposed to individual therapy or even to no therapy at all. But the Taylor study does offer one real, positive finding: when the "group therapy" girls did commit new offenses, these offenses were less serious than the ones for which they had originally been incarcerated.

As with the question of skill development, it is hard to summarize these results. The programs administered were various; the groups to which they were administered varied not only by sex but by age as well; there were also variations in the length of time for which the programs were carried on, the frequency of contact during that time, and the period for which the subjects were followed up. Still, one must say that the burden of the evidence is not encouraging. These programs seem to work best when they are new, when their subjects are amenable to treatment in the first place, and when the counselors are not only trained people but "good" people as well. Such findings, which would not be much of a surprise to a student of organization or personality, are hardly encouraging for a policy planner, who must adopt measures that are generally applicable, that are capable of being successfully institutionalized, and that must rely for personnel on something other than the exceptional individual.

TRANSFORMING THE INSTITUTIONAL ENVIRONMENT

3. *But maybe the reason these counseling programs don't seem to work is not that they are ineffective per se, but that the institutional environment outside the program is unwholesome enough to undo any good work that the counseling does. Isn't a truly successful rehabilitative institution the one where the inmate's whole environment is directed toward true cor rection rather than toward custody or punishment?*

This argument has not only been made, it has been embodied in several institutional programs that go by the name of "milieu therapy." They are designed to make every element of the inmate's environment a part of his treatment, to reduce the distinctions between the custodial staff and the treatment staff, to create a supportive, nonauthoritarian, and nonregimented atmosphere, and to enlist peer influence in the formation of constructive values. These programs are especially hard to summarize because of their variety; they differ, for example, in how "supportive" or "permissive" they are designed to be, in the extent to which they are combined with other treatment methods such as individual therapy, group counseling, or skill development, and in how completely the program is able to control all the relevant aspects of the institutional environment.

One might well begin with two studies that have been done of institutionalized adults, in regular prisons, who have been subjected to such treatment; this is the category whose results are the most clearly discouraging. One study of such a program, by Robison, found that the therapy did seem to reduce recidivism after one year. After two years, however, this effect disappeared, and the treated convicts did no better than the untreated. Another study, by Kassebaum, Ward, and Wilner, dealt with a program which had been able to effect an exceptionally extensive and experimentally rigorous transformation of the institutional environment. This sophisticated study had a follow-up period of 36 months, and it found that the program had no significant effect on parole failure or success rates.

The results of the studies of youths are more equivocal. As for young females, one study by Adams of such a program found that it had no significant effect on recidivism; another study, by Goldberg and Adams, found that such a program did have a positive effect. This effect declined when the program began to deal with girls who were judged beforehand to be worse risks.

As for young males, the studies may conveniently be divided into those dealing with juveniles (under age 16) and those dealing with youths. There have been five studies of milieu therapy administered to juveniles. Two of them —by Laulicht and by Jesness—report clearly that the program in question either had no significant effect or had a short-term effect that wore off with passing time. Jesness does report that when his experimental juveniles did commit new offenses, the offenses were less serious than those committed by controls. A third study of juveniles, by McCord at the Wiltwyck School, reports mixed results. Using two measures of performance, a "success" rate and a "failure" rate, McCord found that his experimental group achieved both less failure and less success than the controls did. There have been two positive reports on milieu therapy programs for male juveniles; both of them have come out of the Highfields program, the milieu therapy experiment which has become the most famous and widely quoted example of "success" via this method. A group of boys was confined for a relatively short time to the unrestrictive, supportive environment of Highfields, and at a follow-up of six months, Freeman found that the group did indeed show a lower recidivism rate (as measured by parole revocation) than a similar group spending a longer time in the regular reformatory. McCorkle also reported positive findings from Highfields. But, in fact, the McCorkle data show this improvement was not so clear: the Highfields boys had lower recidivism rates at 12 and 36 months in the follow-up period, but not at 24 and 60 months. The length of follow-up, these data remind us, may have large implications for a study's conclusions. But more important were other flaws in the Highfields experiment: the populations were not fully comparable (they differed according to risk level and time of admission); different organizations—the probation agency for the Highfields boys, the parole agency for the others— were making the revocation decisions for each group; more of the Highfields boys were discharged early from supervision and thus removed from any risk of revocation. In short, not even from the celebrated Highfields case may we take clear assurance that milieu therapy works.

In the case of male youths, as opposed to male juveniles, the findings are just as equivocal and hardly more encouraging. One such study by

Empey in a residential context did not produce significant results. A study by Seckel described California's Fremont Program, in which institutionalized youths participated in a combination of therapy, work projects, field trips, and community meetings. Seckel found that the youths subjected to this treatment committed more violations of law than did their nontreated counterparts.

So the youths in these milieu therapy programs at least do no worse than their counterparts in regular institutions and the special programs may cost less. One may therefore be encouraged—not on grounds of rehabilitation but on grounds of cost-effectiveness.

WHAT ABOUT MEDICAL TREATMENT?

4. *Isn't there anything you can do in an institutional setting that will reduce recidivism, for instance, through strictly medical treatment?*

A number of studies deal with the results of efforts to change the behavior of offenders through drugs and surgery. As for surgery, the one experimental study of a plastic surgery program—by Mandell—had negative results. For nonaddicts who received plastic surgery, Mandell purported to find improvement in performance on parole, but when one reanalyzes his data, it appears that surgery alone did not in fact make a significant difference.

One type of surgery does seem to be highly successful in reducing recidivism. A 20-year Danish study of sex offenders, by Stuerup, found that while those who had been treated with hormones and therapy continued to commit both sex crimes (29.6 percent of them did so) and non-sex crimes (21.0 percent), those who had been castrated had rates of only 3.5 percent (not, interestingly enough, a rate of zero; where there's a will, apparently, there's a way) and 9.2 percent. One hopes that the policy implications of this study will be found to be distinctly limited.

As for drugs, the major report on such a program—involving tranquilization—was made by Adams. The tranquilizers were administered to male and female institutionalized youths. With boys, there was only a slight improvement in their subsequent behavior; this improvement disappeared within a year. With girls, the tranquilization produced worse results than when the girls were given no treatment at all.

THE EFFECTS OF SENTENCING

5. *Well, at least it may be possible to manipulate certain gross features of the existing, conventional prison system—such as length of sentence and degree of security—in order to affect these recidivism rates. Isn't this the case?*

At this point, it's still impossible to say that this is the case. As for the degree of security in an institution, Glaser's work reported that for both youths and adults, a less restrictive "custody grading" in American federal prisons was related to success on parole, but this is hardly surprising, since those assigned to more restrictive custody are likely to be worse risks in the first place. More to the point, an American study by Fox discovered that for "older youths" who were deemed to be good risks for the future, a minimum-security institution produced better results than a maximum-security one. On the other hand, the data we have on youths under age 16—from a study by McClintock done in Great Britain—indicate that so-called borstals, in which boys are totally confined, are more effective than a less restrictive regime of partial physical custody. In short, we know very little about the recidivism effects of various degrees of security in existing institutions, and our problems in finding out will be compounded by the probability that these effects will vary widely according to the particular type of offender that we are dealing with.

The same problems of mixed results and lack of comparable populations have plagued attempts to study the effects of sentence length. The implication here is quite clear and important: even if early releases and short sentences produce no improvement in recidivism rates, one could at least maintain the same rates while lowering the cost of maintaining the offender and lessening his own burden of imprisonment. Of course, this implication carries with it its concomitant danger: the danger that although shorter sentences cause no worsening of the recidivism rate, they may increase the total amount of crime in the community by increasing the absolute number of potential recidivists at large.

More important, the effect of sentence length seems to vary widely according to type of offender. In a British study, for instance, Hammond found that for a group of "hard-core recidivists," shortening the sentence caused no improvement in the recidivism rate. In Denmark, Bemsten discovered a similar phenomenon: that the beneficial effect of three-month sentences as against eight-month ones disappeared in the case of these "hard-core recidivists." Garrity found another such distinction in his 1956 study. He divided his offenders into three categories: "pro-social," "anti-social," and "manipulative." Prosocial offenders he found to have low recidivism rates regardless of the length of their sentence; antisocial offenders did better with short sentences; the manipulative did better with long ones. Two studies from Britain made yet another division of the offender population and found yet other variations. One (in Great Britain in 1964) found that previous offenders—but not first offenders—did better with longer sentences, while the other found the *reverse* to be true with juveniles.

To add to the problem of interpretation, these studies deal not only with different types and categorizations of offenders but with different types of institutions as well. No more than in the case of institution type can we say that length of sentence has a clear relationship to recidivism.

DECARCERATING THE CONVICT

6. *All of this seems to suggest that there's not much we know how to do to rehabilitate an offender when he's in an institution. Doesn't this lead to the clear possibility that the way to rehabilitate offenders is to deal with them outside an institutional setting?*

This is indeed an important possibility, and it is suggested by other pieces of information as well. For instance, Miner reported on a milieu

therapy program in Massachusetts called Outward Bound. It took youths age 15 1/2 and over; it was oriented toward the development of skills in the out-of-doors and conducted in a wilderness atmosphere very different from that of most existing institutions. The culmination of the 26-day program was a final 24 hours in which each youth had to survive alone in the wilderness. And Miner found that the program did indeed work in reducing recidivism rates.

But by and large, when one takes the programs that have been administered in institutions and applies them in a noninstitutional setting, the results do not grow to encouraging proportions. With casework and individual counseling in the community, for instance, there have been three studies; they dealt with counseling methods from psychosocial and vocational counseling to "operant conditioning," in which an offender was rewarded first simply for coming to counseling sessions and then, gradually, for performing other types of approved acts. Two of them report that the community-counseled offenders did no better than their institutional controls, while the third notes that although community counseling produced fewer arrests per person, it did not ultimately reduce the offender's chance of returning to a reformatory.

PSYCHOTHERAPY IN COMMUNITY SETTINGS

There is some indication that individual psychotherapy may "work" in a community setting. Massimo reported on one such program, using what might be termed a "pragmatic" psychotherapeutic approach, including "insight" therapy and a focus on vocational problems. The program was marked by its small size and by its use of therapists who were personally enthusiastic about the project; Massimo found that there was indeed a decline in recidivism rates. Adamson, on the other hand, found no significant difference produced by another program of individual therapy (although he did note that arrest rates among the experimental boys declined with what he called "intensity of treatment"). And Schwitzgebel, studying other, different kinds of therapy programs, found that the programs did produce improvements in the attitudes of his boys—but, unfortunately, not in their rates of recidivism.

And with group therapy administered in the community, we find yet another set of equivocal results. The results from studies of pragmatic group counseling are only mildly optimistic. Adams did report that a form of group therapy, "guided group interaction," when administered to juvenile gangs, did somewhat reduce the percentage that were to be found in custody six years later. On the other hand, in a study of juveniles, Adams found that while such a program did reduce the number of contacts that an experimental youth had with police, it made no ultimate difference in the detention rate. And the attitudes of the counseled youths showed no improvement. Finally, when O'Brien examined a community-based program of group psychotherapy, he found not only that the program produced no improvement in the recidivism rate but that the experimental boys actually did worse than their controls on a series of psychological tests.

PROBATION OR PAROLE VERSUS PRISON

By far the most extensive and important work that has been done on the effect of community-based treatments has been done in the areas of probation and parole. This work sets out to answer the question of whether it makes any difference how you supervise and treat an offender once he has been released from prison or has come under state surveillance in lieu of prison. This is the work that has provided the main basis to date for the claim that we do indeed have the means at our disposal for rehabilitating the offender or at least decarcerating him safely.

One group of these studies has compared the use of probation with other dispositions for offenders; these provide some slight evidence that at least under some circumstances, probation may make an offender's future chances better than if he had been sent to prison. Or, at least, probation may not worsen those chances. A

British study by Wilkins reported that when probation was granted more frequently, recidivism rates among probationers did not increase significantly. And another such study by the state of Michigan in 1963 reported that an expansion in the use of probation actually improved recidivism rates—although there are serious problems of comparability in the groups and systems that were studied.

Quite a large group of studies deals not with probation as compared to other dispositions, but instead with the type of treatment that an offender receives once he is on probation or parole. These are the studies that have provided the most encouraging reports on rehabilitative treatment and that have also raised the most serious questions about the nature of the research that has been going on in the corrections field.

Five of these studies have dealt with youthful probationers from age 13 to 18 who were assigned to probation officers with small caseloads or provided with other ways of receiving more intensive supervision. These studies report that, by and large, intensive supervision does work—that the specially treated youngsters do better according to some measure of recidivism. Yet these studies left some important questions unanswered. For instance, was this improved performance a function merely of the number of contacts a youngster had with his probation officer? Did it also depend on the length of time in treatment? Or was it the quality of supervision that was making the difference, rather than the quantity?

INTENSIVE SUPERVISION: THE WARREN STUDIES

The widely reported Warren studies in California constitute an extremely ambitious attempt to answer these questions. In this project, a control group of youths, drawn from a pool of candidates ready for first admission to a California Youth Authority institution, was assigned to regular detention, usually for eight to nine months, and then released to regular supervision. The experimental group received considerably more elaborate treatment. They were released directly to probation status and assigned to 12-man caseloads. To decide what special treatment was appropriate within these caseloads, the youths were divided according to their "interpersonal maturity level classification," by use of a scale developed by Grant and Grant. And each level dictated its own special type of therapy.

"Success" in this experiment was defined as favorable discharge by the Youth Authority; "failure" was unfavorable discharge, revocation, or recommitment by a court. Warren reported an encouraging finding: among all but one of the "subtypes," the experimentals had a significantly lower failure rate than the controls. The experiment did have certain problems: the experimentals might have been performing better because of the enthusiasm of the staff and the attention lavished on them; none of the controls had been directly released to their regular supervision programs instead of being detained first; and it was impossible to separate the effects of the experimentals' small caseloads from their specially designed treatments, since no experimental youths had been assigned to a small caseload with "inappropriate" treatment, or with no treatment at all. Still, none of these problems were serious enough to vitiate the encouraging prospect that this finding presented for successful treatment of probationers.

This encouraging finding was, however, accompanied by a rather more disturbing clue. As has been mentioned before, the experimental subjects, when measured, had a lower failure rate than the controls. But the experimentals also had a lower *success* rate. That is, fewer of the experimentals as compared with the controls had been judged to have successfully completed their program of supervision and to be suitable for favorable release. When my colleagues and I undertook a rather laborious reanalysis of the Warren data, it became clear why this discrepancy had appeared. It turned out that fewer experimentals were "successful" because the experimentals were actually committing more offenses than their controls. The reason that the experimentals' relatively large number of offenses was not being reflected in their failure

rates was simply that the experimentals' probation officers were using a more lenient revocation policy. In other words, the controls had a higher failure rate because the controls were being revoked for less serious offenses.

So it seems that what Warren was reporting in her "failure" rates was not merely the treatment effect of her small caseloads and special programs. Instead, what Warren was finding was not so much a change in the behavior of the experimental youths as a change in the behavior of the experimental *probation officers,* who knew the "special" status of their charges and who had evidently decided to revoke probation status at a lower than normal rate. The experimentals continued to commit offenses; what was different was that when they committed these offenses, they were permitted to remain on probation.

One must conclude that the "benefits" of intensive supervision for youthful offenders may stem not so much from a "treatment" effect as from a "policy" effect—that such supervision, so far as we now know, results not in rehabilitation but in a decision to look the other way when an offense is committed. But there is one major modification to be added to this conclusion. Johnson performed a further measurement in his parole experiment: he rated all the supervising agents according to the "adequacy" of the supervision they gave. And he found that an adequate agent, whether he was working in a small or a large caseload, produced a relative improvement in his charges. The converse was not true: an inadequate agent was more likely to produce youthful "failures" when he was given a small caseload to supervise. One cannot much help a "good" agent, it seems, by reducing his caseload size; such reduction can only do further harm to those youths who fall into the hands of "bad" agents.

So with youthful offenders, Johnson found, intensive supervision does not seem to provide the rehabilitative benefits claimed for it; the only such benefits may flow not from intensive supervision itself but from contact with one of the "good people" who are frequently in such short supply.

INTENSIVE SUPERVISION OF ADULTS

The results are similarly ambiguous when one applies this intensive supervision to adult offenders. There have been several studies of the effects of intensive supervision on adult parolees. Some of these are hard to interpret because of problems of comparability between experimental and control groups (e.g., general risk ratings or distribution of narcotics offenders or policy changes that took place between various phases of the experiments), but two of them do not seem to give evidence of the benefits of intensive supervision. By far the most extensive work, though, on the effects of intensive supervision of adult parolees has been a series of studies of California's Special Intensive Parole Unit (SIPU), a 10-year-long experiment designed to test the treatment possibilities of various special parole programs. Three of the four phases of this experiment produced "negative results." The first phase tested the effect of a reduced caseload size; no lasting effect was found. The second phase slightly increased the size of the small caseloads and provided for a longer time in treatment; again there was no evidence of a treatment effect. In the fourth phase, caseload sizes and time in treatment were again varied, and treatments were simultaneously varied in a sophisticated way according to personality characteristics of the parolees; once again, significant results did not appear.

The only phase of this experiment for which positive results were reported was Phase 3. Here, it was indeed found that a smaller caseload improved one's chances of parole success. There is, however, an important caveat that attaches to this finding: when my colleagues and I divided the whole population of subjects into two groups—those receiving supervision in the north of the state and those in the south—we found that the "improvement" of the experimentals' success rates was taking place primarily in the north. The north differed from the south in one important aspect: its agents practiced a policy of returning both "experimental" and "control" violators to prison at relatively high rates. And it was the north that produced the higher success rate among its experimentals. So this improvement in experimentals' performance was taking place only when accompanied by a "realistic threat" of severe sanctions.

THE EFFECTS OF COMMUNITY TREATMENT

In sum, even in the case of treatment programs administered outside penal institutions, we simply cannot say that this treatment in itself has an appreciable effect on offender behavior. On the other hand, there is one encouraging set of findings that emerges from these studies. For from many of them there flows the strong suggestion that even if we cannot treat offenders so as to make them do better, a great many of the programs designed to rehabilitate them at least did not make them do worse. And if these programs did not show the advantages of actually rehabilitating, some of them did have the advantage of being less onerous to the offender himself without seeming to pose increased danger to the community. And some of these programs, especially those involving less restrictive custody, minimal supervision, and early release, simply cost fewer dollars to administer. The information on the dollar costs of these programs is just beginning to be developed, but the implication is clear: if we cannot do more for (and to) offenders, at least we can safely do less.

There is, however, one important caveat even to this note of optimism: in order to calculate the true costs of these programs, one must in each case include not only their administrative cost but also the cost of maintaining in the community an offender population increased in size. This population might well not be committing new offenses at any greater rate, but the offender population might, under some of these plans, be larger in absolute numbers. So the total number of offenses committed might rise, and our chances of victimization might therefore rise too. We need to be able to make a judgment about the size and probable duration of this effect; as of now, we simply do not know.

DOES NOTHING WORK?

7. *Do all of these studies lead us irrevocably to the conclusion that nothing works, that we haven't the faintest clue about how to rehabilitate offenders and reduce recidivism? And if so, what shall we do?*

We tried to exclude from our survey those studies which were so poorly done that they simply could not be interpreted. But despite our efforts, a pattern has run through much of this discussion—of studies which "found" effects without making any truly rigorous attempt to exclude competing hypotheses, of extraneous factors permitted to intrude upon the measurements, of recidivism measures which are not all measuring the same thing, of "follow-up" periods which vary enormously and rarely extend beyond the period of legal supervision, of experiments never replicated, of "system effects" not taken into account, of categories drawn up without any theory to guide the enterprise. It is just possible that some of our treatment programs are working to some extent, but that our research is so bad that it is incapable of telling.

Having entered this very serious caveat, I am bound to say that these data, involving over two hundred studies and hundreds of thousands of individuals as they do, are the best available and give us very little reason to hope that we have in fact found a sure way of reducing recidivism through rehabilitation. This is not to say that we found no instances of success or partial success; it is only to say that these instances have been isolated, producing no clear pattern to indicate the efficacy of any particular method of treatment. And neither is this to say that factors *outside* the realm of rehabilitation may not be working to reduce recidivism, such as the tendency for recidivism to be lower in offenders over the age of 30; it is only to say that such factors seem to have little connection with any of the treatment methods now at our disposal.

From this probability, one may draw any of several conclusions. It may be simply that our programs are not yet good enough—that the education we provide to inmates is still poor education, that the therapy we administer is not administered skillfully enough, that our intensive supervision and counseling do not yet provide enough personal support for the offenders who are subjected to them. If one wishes to believe this, then what our correctional system needs is simply a more full-hearted commitment to the strategy of treatment.

It may be, on the other hand, that there is a more radical flaw in our present strategies—that education at its best, or that psychotherapy at its best, cannot overcome, or even appreciably reduce, the powerful tendency for offenders to continue in criminal behavior. Our present treatment programs are based on a theory of crime as a "disease"—that is to say, as something foreign and abnormal in the individual which can presumably be cured. This theory may well be flawed, in that it overlooks—indeed, denies—both the normality of crime in society and the personal normality of a very large proportion of offenders, criminals who are merely responding to the facts and conditions of our society.

This opposing theory of "crime as a social phenomenon" directs our attention away from a "rehabilitative" strategy, away from the notion that we may best ensure public safety through a series of "treatments" to be imposed forcibly on convicted offenders. These treatments have on occasion become, and have the potential for becoming, so draconian as to offend the moral order of a democratic society, and the theory of crime as a social phenomenon suggests that such treatments may be not only offensive but ineffective as well. This theory points, instead, to decarceration for low-risk offenders—and, presumably, to keeping high-risk offenders in prisons which are nothing more (and aim to be nothing more) than custodial institutions.

The Rehabilitation of Criminal Offenders: Problems and Prospects

LEE B. SECHREST
SUSAN O. WHITE
ELIZABETH BROWN

THE promise of the rehabilitative ideal—that criminal offenders can be reformed or their behavior changed in such a way that they can live socially productive lives in the larger community without engaging in more criminal activity than most of their fellow citizens—makes the debate about rehabilitation one of the most important of our time.

The appropriate handling of criminal offenders has never been a settled issue in American society. Over the years, the dominant purposes of criminal justice have shifted from a strictly punitive goal toward a rehabilitative ideal. In the eighteenth century, felony justice meant corporal or capital punishment; prisons, as places for punishment, did not exist. Prisons were introduced as a more humane way of punishing convicted criminals as well as a way of providing a means of incapacitation. The rehabilitative ideal is a relatively recent addition to these goals. The notion of rehabilitating offenders was initially intended to counter the punitiveness of correctional institutions by introducing a positive "reform the offender" orientation. The growth of the idea of rehabilitation, however, was paralleled by the development of the behavioral sciences, and eventually the rehabilitative ideal became virtually synonymous with

the so-called medical model of corrections. According to the medical model, criminal behavior is like a disease that can be cured if the right sort of therapy is applied. This combination of a hopeful outlook toward solving a major social problem with a claim of expertise within the scientific/clinical community dominated the corrections field for many years. More recently, however, widespread perceptions that crime rates are rising and little persuasive evidence that recidivism rates are falling have led to the focusing of critical attention on the effectiveness of correctional institutions and, now, to doubts about the concept of correctional rehabilitation itself. Even though there is no evidence that successful rehabilitation would have a detectable impact on crime rates—and perhaps even in the absence of any reason to believe that there should be an impact—the concept of rehabilitation is under attack.

Part of the disenchantment with rehabilitation stems from ideological or philosophical concerns: some people simply prefer a punitive approach to deviant behavior. This traditionally conservative position has been buttressed by a libertarian argument that the therapeutic approach can be more coercive and dehumanizing than the "just deserts" of punishment. But the disillusionment stems also from the fact that high recidivism rates seem to give lie to claims for expertise or for behavioral technologies that can indeed reform the criminal offenders receiving the "treatments." Consequently, the medical model itself is criticized because it has not

From *The Rehabilitation of Criminal Offenders: Problems and Prospects* (pp. 11-99) by L. B. Sechrest, S. O. White, and E. Brown, 1979, Washington DC: National Academy Press. Copyright 1979 by the National Academy of Science. Reprinted courtesy of the National Academy Press.

proved capable of accomplishing its own stated goals. Instead of reforming the criminal offender, so the criticism goes, correctional rehabilitation merely masks the reality of a strictly punitive system of control under the guise of doing good.

This critique of the rehabilitative ideal is persuasive for many reasons and particularly because crime and recidivism rates strongly suggest to the public that in general offenders are not being rehabilitated by current programs. Rehabilitation, it is commonly said, is simply not working. But what if it did work? Would the philosophical arguments against rehabilitation be persuasive if recidivism rates were really decreasing as a consequence of rehabilitative efforts? The social benefit to be derived from reforming criminal offenders would be great indeed, provided that the methods used were morally and politically acceptable. Surely, the promise of the rehabilitative ideal remains attractive even though it may have been corrupted in actual practice.

Part of the motivation for our study, therefore, is a commitment to determine whether the promise of rehabilitation can ever be realized. This is a very complex question. And on the surface, at least, the evidence for the effectiveness of rehabilitation appears to be weak or nonexistent. But the significance of the goal mandates that the strongest possible effort be made before the rehabilitative ideal is abandoned. We turn, then, to consideration of what we know, and what we can know, about the effectiveness of rehabilitation.

THE KNOWLEDGE PROBLEM

The immediate occasion for this research on the effectiveness of rehabilitation was a widely discussed controversy over whether existing evaluation studies of rehabilitative programs necessitate the conclusion that "nothing works." Unlike the largely philosophical debates, the controversy over the proper inferences to be drawn from evaluation studies raises technical issues about the validity of evidence, about how one measures effectiveness, and ultimately

about what can be known in this complex area of human behavior.

A variety of complex, possibly intractable, problems have made it difficult to obtain knowledge about the effectiveness of rehabilitative techniques in corrections. This report is largely concerned with identifying these problems and making clear how they have subverted the validity of prior studies and could contaminate the results of future research. Basically, the problems are of two kinds: those having to do with maintaining the integrity of both treatments and experimental research designs within institutions that are dominated by other concerns and those that stem more from methodological problems. We have labeled the first kind problems of implementation and the second kind problems of evaluation. Overcoming both types of problems is essential if reliable information about the effectiveness of rehabilitative techniques is to be developed.

We find little in the review of existing studies, and of the problems involved in implementing and evaluating treatment programs, to allay the current pessimism about the effectiveness of institutional rehabilitation programs as they now exist. Our emphasis is not on the impossibility of rehabilitating criminal offenders, but rather on the difficulty of successful rehabilitation in an institutional setting. This is not to say that well-conceived and properly implemented treatment programs have no effects, for they may well provide helpful therapy and training and generally preserve the sanity of prison inmates. But we should continue to treat as problematic the assumption that long-term behavior in a nonprison environment can be significantly affected by institutional programs.

It should be understood that it is not impossible, nor even very difficult, to change someone's behavior when there is no limit as to what may be done to effect the change. An individual can be rendered physically or mentally incapable of certain acts. The possibilities for modifying both short- and long-term behavior are numerous. But extreme interventions are ethically and legally unacceptable in this society. The real question, therefore, is not whether behavior can be changed, but whether it can be done successfully within the moral and legal limits that the society imposes on the task.

PROSPECTS FOR
EFFECTIVE REHABILITATION

If rehabilitation is understood as an attempt to change behavior instead of as a set of programs for reforming the institutionalized criminal offender, a perspective different from that traditionally believed in the field emerges. Rehabilitation is simply a term used to label attempts to "correct" undesirable behavior. It involves problems of inducing behavior change that are similar in critical respects to all problems of behavior change. To put the issue in these terms is not to shift away from a humanistic perspective, for it is certainly no more manipulative than the "coerced cure" that is the goal of correctional rehabilitation today. Our concern is to move away from a programmatic definition of problems toward a perspective grounded in scientific theories of behavior and a sound understanding of the nature of behavior change.

The first consequence of this approach is the realization that correctional rehabilitation as it is currently practiced (and to the extent that it is practiced at all) seems to have developed out of trends in clinical treatment that happen to be current, regardless of the often tenuous relationship between the particular behaviors involved and the premises of those treatments. And because programs are generally designed for an institutional setting, the connection between the treatment and the individual's life outside the institution that is presumably the target for change is never systematically made.

Conceptually, a number of dimensions are ignored in varying degree in the use of rehabilitative techniques for correctional purposes. Among these are the different effects of the timing of interventions across different stages of an individual's life, the intensity (both frequency and strength) of treatment, the inevitably inhibiting effects of social and institutional constraints on the integrity of treatment, the relative weight of environmental as opposed to dispositional or individual trait factors, and variations in the personality and experiential characteristics of individual subjects.

A sound theoretical approach can both broaden and deepen one's perspective on the effectiveness of rehabilitation. We believe that the prospects for rehabilitation, although pessimistic or at least limited from an institutional point of view, remain an open question.

NATURE AND THEORY
OF REHABILITATION

Rehabilitation is a complex concept, embodying a number of quite different aspects: its social purpose, its various programmatic interpretations, the behavioral assumptions that underlie it, and the many methodological problems that have plagued all attempts to determine whether it "works." Some of the problems of analysis, therefore, are definitional. Others require a delineation of the various approaches that have been or might be taken in order to identify a particular problem in the more general theoretical context of such problems. Such analytical mapping is the purpose of this section. Its three parts cover questions of definition, a brief discussion of the theoretical bases for correctional rehabilitation, and a description of different types of rehabilitative techniques.

Definition

The term *rehabilitation* can be defined in various ways, which causes confusion in the scientific literature and among those who seek to evaluate the effectiveness of rehabilitation programs. In order to arrive at a definition that will be most helpful for the purposes of this report, it is necessary, first, to clarify the function of rehabilitation as compared to other societal responses to crime and, second, to distinguish the effects of rehabilitative techniques from the effects of other forces that also act to modify criminal behavior.

Seven reasons are commonly given to explain why society sanctions a person who has violated its laws:

1. to deter the offender from offending again by punishment or fear of punishment (without necessarily changing him or her in any other way);
2. to deter others from behaving as the offender has;
3. to incapacitate the offender and thus deprive him or her of the opportunity to offend again for a given period of time;
4. to forestall personal vengeance, by those hurt by the offender;
5. to exact retribution from the offender and so set right the scales of moral justice;
6. to educate people morally or socially;
7. to rehabilitate or reform the offender.

We initially defined rehabilitation as the result of any planned intervention that reduces an offender's further criminal activity, whether that reduction is mediated by personality, behavior, abilities, attitudes, values, or other factors. Because precise definition of our subject is a prerequisite to the specification of methodological improvements in research on rehabilitation, however, it was clear that some additional distinctions were necessary. In particular, rehabilitation must be carefully distinguished from what is called specific deterrence (Reason 1, above) and from the developmental effects of the passage of time on behavior (i.e., maturation).

Definitions of rehabilitation found in writings on the topic appear to differ on at least three dimensions: outcome, intervening variables, and intervention.

OUTCOME   While most definitions take a reduction in recidivism as their dependent measure, others allude to the parens patriae notion of making the offender "better and happier" as an alternative or at least an auxiliary goal.

INTERVENING VARIABLE   The appropriate targets of rehabilitative efforts are given variously as the offender's "intent," "motivation," "character," "wish," "person," "habit," "behavior patterns," "personality," "dynamics," "value system," "needs," or "attitudes."

INTERVENTION   The definitions also vary in how inclusive they are with respect to the mechanisms by which rehabilitation is achieved. Some include as rehabilitation anything done that reduces the probability of an offender's recidivism. Others specifically distinguish "intimidation" or specific deterrence from rehabilitation as two separate processes that can result in a decreased rate of future crime in an offender.

Not too much should be expected of definitions in resolving areas of theoretical controversy, since any definition will involve an element of arbitrariness in setting conceptual boundaries. Different definitions may be required for different purposes. For the methodological purposes of this study, the definition adopted takes a narrow view of what will be measured as the outcome of rehabilitation and of what will count as interventions, while allowing flexibility in the choice of intervening variables by which change is to be achieved.

Enough has been written in the past few years on the pitfalls of making people "better" against their will that to adopt offender well-being as the purpose of rehabilitation (outcome to be measured)—or even as a purpose of rehabilitation—appears a hazardous course, one likely to be opposed not only by civil libertarians, but also by offenders, the supposed beneficiaries of the betterment. Reduction in crime, moderated by considerations of justice or moral desert, appears the more appropriate contemporary goal. It should be added that excluding "beneficial" treatment—that is, treatment that is intended to change an individual in ways other than to reduce his or her offense rate—from the definition of rehabilitation in no sense implies that such treatment, on humanitarian grounds, should not be an integral part of the penal system.

To distinguish rehabilitation from specific deterrence is particularly important. The conceptual distinction is sometimes difficult to maintain in practice, and it may be that some forms of "punishment" will turn out to be appropriately rehabilitative as well as effective in modifying behavior. But failure to distinguish, at least conceptually, between specific deterrence and rehabilitation may lead to anomalous conclusions—for example, identifying as rehabilitative an offender's fear of returning to a prison in which he was repeatedly homosexually raped. Similarly, one must separate rehabilitative effects from those achieved by the simple ticking of the clock. The fact that a young man convicted of robbery at age 19 who serves twenty years in prison does not return to prison after his release at age 39 cannot, in itself, be taken as an index of rehabilitation. To do so necessarily would lead to the conclusion that lengthy sentences are per se rehabilitative.

Although a narrow construction of the purpose and scope of rehabilitative techniques appears most appropriate, broad latitude should be granted in defining the intervening variables that become the targets of rehabilitation efforts. There is sufficient disagreement within the research community as to whether behavior change is best achieved by altering personal or attitudinal variables, by focusing directly on extinguishing the problematic behavior, by constructing alternative behavioral skills (e.g., vocational skills), or by altering the individual's social or economic circumstances so that any attempt to resolve the issue by definitional fiat is premature.

In light of these considerations, we evolved the following definition of rehabilitation as a guide to our study: rehabilitation is the result of any planned intervention that reduced an offender's further criminal activity, whether that reduction is mediated by personality, behavior, abilities, attitudes, values, or other factors. The effects of maturation and the effects associated with "fear" or "intimidation" are excluded, the result of the latter having traditionally been labeled as specific deterrence.

In fact, the effects of rehabilitation, maturation, and specific deterrence are intimately intertwined. Almost none of the attempts to measure the effects of rehabilitation have tried to separate or control for the effects of specific deterrence or its interaction with rehabilitation. This definition has three features:

1. *Planned intervention.* Excluded is spontaneous reformation such as may occur with an isolated offender in the absence of any organized program.
2. *Eclecticism.* The definition is free of any prior conception of the processes by which rehabilitation may occur or of any specification of

physiological, psychological, social, or moral hypotheses.
3. *Future criminal activity.* Criminal behavior, rather than offender growth, insight, or happiness, is the sole criterion against which rehabilitation ultimately must be measured. A favorable effect of rehabilitation may be reflected in a selective reduction in certain types of serious crimes as well as by an overall reduction in criminal activity. Psychological or economic outcomes may serve as intervening variables in pursuit of the goal of reducing criminal activity. Although the definition of rehabilitation excludes treatment in prison that does not have a reduction in future criminal activity as its goal, there is no intent to disparage such treatment since it certainly may be justified on other grounds.

MODELS OF CRIME AND STRATEGIES OF REHABILITATION

The empirical relation (if any) between the nature of rehabilitative efforts and ideas about the origins of crime is not yet clear. Still, ideas about the causes and origins of crime should reasonably have some impact on thinking about what rehabilitative techniques should be tried. Current theories of criminal behavior are diverse, some seeking to explain why people become delinquent and taking nondelinquent behavior for granted. Other theories assume that people would naturally engage in crime if not restrained by society and seek to explain why many people do not become delinquent. Some theories seek to explain the behavior of individuals, and others appear directed to the explanation of differences in rates of delinquency among different social groups (defined, e.g., by social class or by location of residence).

These diverse theories sometimes employ concepts such as learning, thinking errors, moral development, attempts to alleviate feelings of oppression, or the absence of shared meanings in groups. Other theories invoke social disorganization, social stress, or anomie as explanatory concepts. Other theorists use labeling as an explanation, or regard economic gain as an incentive to engage in crime. One group of theorists seeks to explain delinquency by reference to the conformity to the norms of deviant subcultures. In contrast, Hirschi has articulated a social-psychological theory of social control in which the weakening of a person's ties to society may result in delinquency. Finally, a number of theorists have discussed the role of human biology in crime and delinquency.

These and other views of the origins of crime, diverse as they are, are not necessarily mutually incompatible. We have not attempted to evaluate any of these views, but each may be tenable in varying degree, perhaps in different degree for different cases. Or some may be useful at one level of explanation or aggregation but not at another. If so, there are important implications for rehabilitative efforts, for it will be necessary to match rehabilitative efforts with the characteristics of individual cases. If the diverse theories are all at least partially tenable, as seems likely, and especially if two or more processes are involved in any person's delinquency, rehabilitative efforts should, to be optimal, be multifaceted. No one rehabilitative effort could be expected to be more than marginally effective, and the task of rehabilitating many offenders might require truly massive interventions.

Most rehabilitative efforts that have been tested have been narrow in scope and have involved weak or relatively minor forms of interventions. It is possible that most offenders who are imprisoned for the first time are never imprisoned again, and issues of rehabilitation do not arise with those offenders. Other data indicate rather clearly that a relatively small number of criminals account for a large proportion of crimes. This being the case, it should be evident that the problem of rehabilitating criminal offenders is formidable since it often involves repeated patterns of behavior and ways of life that are deeply ingrained. It is the judgment of the panel that the rehabilitative techniques and programs that have been tested thus far have generally been inappropriate to the difficulty of the task. Work on rehabilitation appears for the most part to have been theoretical altogether and to have been based on a rather narrow range of views about crime. For the most part, it seems correct to say that the medical model is dominant: that is, present treatment programs assume that crime is a "disease," an individual defect, that can be cured or ameliorated. Even some interventions directed toward improvement of the economic prospects of criminal offenders are based on notions about individual shortcomings such as educational or skill deficiencies. Drawing on a broader theoretical understanding of the origins and nature of criminal activity should provide useful hypotheses for the development of more promising strategies for rehabilitation.

TYPES OF REHABILITATIVE EFFORTS

If one is to make sense of the whole field of rehabilitation, it is necessary to be able to make distinctions within the myriad of rehabilitative techniques that have been tried. No ready taxonomy of rehabilitative efforts has been developed and accepted, but Lipton and his colleagues provide a list of 10 types of treatment whose impact on recidivism has been studied. Most of these methods stem from a view of crime as involving either a specific individual defect or as a set of pathological behavior patterns. Extrainstitutional methods include probation and parole, both of which are ways of managing offenders outside institutions and have aims in addition to (or perhaps instead of) rehabilitation, for example, reduction in costs of corrections and surveillance and early detection of violation. Imprisonment is also listed by Lipton et al. as a correctional treatment.

Methods usually employed within an institutional setting include individual and group psychotherapy, both directed usually to alleviation of personal problems, although group therapy may also be employed to improve social skills. Skill development is another technique for reducing some personal deficit, usually concerned with work habits and skills. Finally, milieu therapy is a rather ill-defined approach that assumes that a generally good and constructive environment can produce behavior change.

It is of more than passing interest that none of these methods of intervention involves a moral view of crime, but neither does any of them stem in any very direct way from a social structural view of crime. Moral views of crime have been reflected to some degree in the treatment described by Yochelson and Samenow, and the Japanese, among other cultures, have also employed a form of moral therapy with criminal offenders.

Nearly all the methods that have been tested to date involve either treatments within institutions or some version of probation or parole. Furthermore, nearly all the methods tested to date have been tested singly. There have been few, if any, comprehensive, multiple-treatment attempts to alter criminal behavior.

As noted earlier, to some extent the effects of specific deterrence must be distinguished from those of rehabilitation. Although the distinction is only conceptual, it is needed as a reminder that the horrors of prison life should not be regarded as inherently rehabilitative even if they do deter further criminal activity. Nonetheless, to the extent that punishment does result in a decrease in frequency or seriousness of criminal activity, it could be considered to have a rehabilitative effect.

Even though punishment is sometimes thought of as a technique for rehabilitation, however, we have only a rough idea of its specific behavioral consequences. If it is to be used effectively, a much better understanding of just what can be considered to be punishment will be required, and a closer inquiry into the specific effects it has will also be necessary. For example, it may not be the case that prison is invariably viewed as punishment or at least that it may not be responded to in the same way as punishment. As unpleasant as prison might seem to most of us, it may be regarded as no more than a normal occupational hazard by many career criminals. When one considers that people regularly and voluntarily join such organizations as the U.S. Marine Corps and the French Foreign Legion, both of which entail occupational hazards often as bad as or worse than prison, it may be that prison can be regarded as a mere hazard to be endured like many others. Perhaps the occupational hazards of prison, like those of the Marine Corps and the Foreign Legion, are more likely to deter initial entry into the occupation rather than performance once recruited. If so, punishment would deserve a larger role in programs designed for the youthful offender who is part of the population most at risk for further crime involvement. Punishment may be less important in programs for more seasoned offenders who may be inured to punitive methods. This kind of speculation could turn out to be empirically false. In any case, the issue is important and merits careful empirical testing.

The mechanism by which punishment may work to change undesirable behavior is also poorly understood. It may be that the commonly accepted notion that punishment works only because individuals will try to avoid it may not be true for all offenders. As an illustrative analogy, pain is often said to have important survival value as a signal that all is not well with one's body. Similarly, punishment may have an important value as a signal to an individual that his or her relationship to society needs changing. From that standpoint, punishment might have a rehabilitative effect through the information it carries rather than through arousing anxiety about behavior. Punishment may be effective in part because it commands attention and ensures that the message is attended to. If that is the case, then punishment would be expected to have maximal effects at early points of deviation, but it would not necessarily have to be severe; it should, on the other hand, occur in close temporal proximity to the deviation, and its connection to the deviation should be made obvious.

Although the very idea of punishment is repugnant to many and although there are reasons to suspect limitations on its effectiveness in controlling criminal behavior, punishment as a control technique has always been with us and always will be. Our task as a society is to achieve a better theoretical and empirical grasp of the nature and effects of punishment and then to use that knowledge in humane ways to maximize the probability that punishment, whether inflicted out of a sense of outrage or of justice, will have whatever constructive effect might be achieved. We do not want to end up repeatedly punishing those who transgress and in return, and at least as often, suffering the counterblows of those persons who feel themselves irretrievably and morally at odds with the rest of us.

THE CURRENT STATE OF KNOWLEDGE: WHAT WORKS?

Although concern about the efficacy of rehabilitation goes back many years, the formation and work of the panel received a strong instigation from the publication of what has come to be known as "The Martinson Report." This was based on work by Lipton, Martinson, and Wilks (hereafter cited as LMW) reviewing a large body of research on the outcomes of various rehabilitative efforts as applied to criminal offenders. Martinson's shorter review was published and widely read, while the larger review volume was not published until the following year. Martinson made use of the materials collected for the book to prepare his lengthy and comprehensive article assessing rehabilitative efforts. There had, however, been previous reviews of a less comprehensive nature that presaged the conclusions ultimately reached by Martinson. The review by Bailey of 100 outcome studies has been widely cited, but Adams lists several other smaller or more specialized review studies.

None of these reviews provided very much cause for optimism about rehabilitation, and Martinson's conclusion was also substantially negative: "With few and isolated experiences, the rehabilitative efforts that have been reported so far have had no appreciable effect on recidivism." In a more cautious form, Martinson's conclusion might be stated: it appears that nothing works or at least that there have not been any consistent and persuasive demonstrations of anything that works. The range of interventions dealt with by Lipton and his colleagues is quite wide, and it cannot reasonably be claimed that they omitted important categories of intervention efforts from their study. Their report dealt with interventions as diverse as cosmetic plastic surgery, psychotherapy, vocational training, work release, and parole supervision. Therefore, while acknowledging that individual studies may have produced the effect they were designed to show, Martinson noted that no one intervention consistently worked when applied to the problem of offender rehabilitation: the problem of crime and the costs incurred by the public as a result of crime were not being reduced.

Martinson's report, published in *The Public Interest* in the spring of 1974, produced considerable reaction in the corrections field, both positive and negative. Rebuttals began to appear as soon as publication lags permitted. A volume compiled by the National Council on Crime and Delinquency to satisfy the demand for a forum on the efficacy of rehabilitation contained a reprint of Martinson's article along with critiques by Palmer and Adams and two rebuttals by Martinson. Palmer in particular insisted that Martinson's conclusions were not justified and were probably quite wrong. The basis for Palmer's criticism was that Martinson's focus was inappropriate: instead of asking what one treatment could work for the offender population, the question should have been "which methods work best for *which* types of offenders and under what conditions or in what types of settings?" Yet Martinson's conclusions were seemingly widely accepted and even welcomed, bolstered by the views of those who already believed that rehabilitation was ineffective, and they meshed well with other emerging views about appropriate ways of dealing with criminals, for example, that they should experience the natural consequences of their acts and receive their just deserts. Nonetheless, an important segment of the corrections community found it difficult to accept a conclusion that efforts at rehabilitation were futile, and its members insisted that Martinson was wrong.

In light of this controversy, we undertook a review of the evidence on the effectiveness of rehabilitation. We have considered a great deal of evidence in deciding whether Martinson's overall conclusions are supportable. As part of our work, we also undertook to review Martinson's work specifically. That task involved an examination of the database from which he operated, that is, the annotations and summaries provided by Lipton and his colleagues; also required was an examination of Martinson's use of that database. To accomplish the first task, Fienberg (a member of the National Academy of Sciences panel) and his colleague Patricia Grambsch drew a random sample of the studies reviewed by Lipton and his colleagues and did an independent analysis of the data to determine the accuracy and fairness with which the original review was done.

An Evaluation of the Work of
Lipton, Martinson, and Wilks

Because of the pivotal role that the LMW book has already played in arguments regarding the efficacy of rehabilitation, it was important that the accuracy of LMW be examined with care. The summaries and annotations of prior studies made by LMW had to be assessed for accuracy, placing special emphasis on the research design of the studies and on the statistical analyses reported. The LMW volume contains both a database (summaries and annotations of selected studies) and a set of conclusions derived from an integration of the components of that database. A sample of the database was reexamined to determine (1) whether the conclusions in the source articles are based on reasonable statistical analyses and tests, (2) whether there are important errors or omissions in the LMW summaries and annotations, and (3) if so, whether the errors and omissions affect the conclusions that might reasonably be drawn from the studies.

The selection procedure to identify studies used by LMW resulted in 231 "acceptable" studies. Our evaluation of LMW focuses only on those acceptable studies. Some have argued that the LMW criteria for inclusion are too stringent. We disagree. Others studying innovations and treatments in different contexts have come to similar conclusions. For example, the biostatistician Muensch has a set of "statistical laws," one of which says, essentially, that nothing improves the performance of an innovation as much as the lack of controls. After examining several studies included by LMW, we concluded that their criteria for methodological acceptability were, if anything, not stringent enough. Many of the 231 studies reported are badly flawed and they contribute little to a proper assessment of the efficacy of rehabilitative programs.

A further issue concerns the criteria to be used for judging whether a particular treatment is successful as a rehabilitative technique. In discussing Martinson's article, Halleck and Witte argue that he used extremely rigorous criteria for the success of a treatment program, and that considering the type of programs evaluated, the failure to achieve dramatic alterations in behavior is certainly not surprising. Palmer suggests

that almost half of the studies described in Martinson show positive or partly positive results; thus, in our review we tried to determine whether LMW downplay such positive findings in their overall summaries. We find little support for the charge that positive findings were overlooked. In fact, as our review of a sample of studies reported by LMW suggests, by ignoring the problems associated with multiple comparisons and simultaneous inference, LMW and the original authors often make claims for partially positive results that cannot be substantiated by the data they report.

Note should be taken of the contention of one of Martinson's major critics, Palmer, that nearly half of the studies cited by Martinson show an effect favorable to rehabilitation. Palmer's optimistic view cannot be supported, in large part because his assessment accepts at face value the claims of the original authors about effects they detected, and in too many instances those claims were wrong or were overinterpretations of data, such as ignoring the risks of picking one significant finding from among a large set of comparisons.

Thus, the work of Fienberg and Grambsch indicates that LMW were reasonably accurate and fair in the appraisal of the rehabilitation literature. Where LMW erred, it was almost invariably by an overly lenient assessment of the methodology of a study or by a failure to maintain an appropriately critical set in evaluating statistical analyses. The net result was that Lipton and his colleagues were, if anything, more likely to accept evidence in favor of rehabilitation than was justified.

Were the conclusions of LMW warranted? Within the limits noted below, we conclude that Martinson and his associates were essentially correct. There is no body of evidence for any treatment or intervention with criminal offenders that can be relied upon to produce a decrease in recidivism. Where there are suggestions of efficacy, they are just that—suggestions. They prove to be elusive, not replicable, not quite statistically significant, working now only with one group, then only with another. We do not believe that it would be possible on the basis of the literature available to Martinson—and if he missed something important, no one has stepped forward to reveal it—to put together an intervention that could be counted on to reduce recidivism rates in any group of offenders.

If the LMW review were the only work available, Martinson's pessimistic view might still be discounted. For one thing, the LMW database extended only to 1968, and a number of important studies have appeared since then. The more recent studies have received a thorough review by Greenberg. His conclusions are essentially the same as those of LMW, and his methodological critique accords closely with that of Fienberg and Grambsch: nothing has been shown to work. Moreover, Brody has recently reviewed the British and American work on institutional treatment of juvenile offenders and has reached similar conclusions about the ineffectiveness of a variety of rehabilitative efforts. The other reports that are available from foreign countries seldom report actual research results, but those that do indicate that no magic answer is to be found in some far-off place.

To conclude, we believe that there is not now in the scientific literature any basis for any policy or recommendations regarding rehabilitation of criminal offenders. The data available do not present any consistent evidence of efficacy that would lead to such recommendations, but the quality of the work that has been done and the narrow range of options explored militate against any policy reflecting a final pessimism. On the basis of its review, the panel believes that the magnitude of the task of reforming criminal offenders has been consistently underestimated. It is clear that far more intensive and extensive interventions will be required if rehabilitation is to be possible; even then, there is no guarantee of success.

Does Correctional Treatment Work?

D. A. ANDREWS
IVAN ZINGER
ROBERT D. HOGE
JAMES BONTA
PAUL GENDREAU
FRANCIS T. CULLEN

DURING the 1970s, the ideological hegemony of the individualized treatment ideal suffered a swift and devastating collapse. Previously a code word for "doing good," rehabilitation came to be seen by liberals as a euphemism for coercing offenders and by conservatives as one for letting hardened criminals off easily. Although the public's belief in rehabilitation was never eroded completely, defenders of treatment were branded scientifically and politically naive apologists for the socially powerful, self-serving human service professionals, or curious relics of a positivistic past. Thus, a number of jurisdictions in the United States and Canada embarked on sentencing reforms that undercut the role of rehabilitation in justice and corrections.

The decline of the rehabilitative ideal cannot be attributed to a careful reading of evidence regarding the effectiveness of rehabilitative treatment. As will be shown, reviews of the effectiveness literature routinely found that a substantial proportion of the better-controlled studies of rehabilitative service reported positive effects and did so for programs that operated within a variety of conditions established by criminal sanctions, such as probation or incarceration. We will also show that criminal sanc-

tions themselves were typically found to be only minimally related to recidivism. Thus, rather than a rational appreciation of evidence, the attack on rehabilitation was a reflection of broader social and intellectual trends. This is evident upon consideration of the particular historical timing and intensity of the attack on rehabilitation.

First, the rapidly changing sociopolitical context of the decade preceding the mid-1970s propelled conservatives to seek "law and order," while liberals attached to class-based perspectives on crime became discouraged about the benevolence of the state and the promise of direct intervention. Second, an emerging social science, informed by labeling and critical Marxist approaches, embraced antipsychological and often antiempirical themes. These emergent perspectives played an important role in legitimating the decision of many academic criminologists and juridical policymakers to declare rehabilitation fully bankrupt. Most noteworthy was Robert Martinson's conclusion that "the rehabilitative efforts that have been reported so far have had no appreciable effect on recidivism." In short order, with the blessing of a major academy of science, the notion that "nothing works" became accepted doctrine. "Nothing works" satisfied conservative political reactions to the apparent disorder of the 1960s, liberal sorrow over perceived failures of the Great Society, and the ideological persuasions of those academicians whose truly social visions of deviance asserted that only radical social change could have an impact on crime.

Perhaps as a result, criticisms of rehabilitation are not in short supply. As Walker comments: "It is wishful thinking to believe that additional research is going to uncover a magic key that has somehow been overlooked for 150 years." Other scholars—as exemplified most notably and recently by Whitehead and Lab's analysis of previous research studies—continue to participate in the scientific exchange on intervention and to present evidence ostensibly bolstering the "nothing works" message.

Our analysis includes, but is not confined to, the Whitehead and Lab sample of studies. Challenging sweeping conclusions regarding program ineffectiveness, we reaffirm a line of analysis for developing meaningful conclusions on the conditions under which programs will work. Our challenge is informed by considerations of research and theory on the causes of crime and by research and theory on behavioral influence processes.

CLINICALLY RELEVANT AND PSYCHOLOGICALLY INFORMED PROGRAMMING, EVALUATION, AND META-ANALYSIS

The psychology of criminal conduct recognizes multiple sources of variation in criminal recidivism. These major sources of variation are found through analyses of the main and interactive effects of (a) preservice characteristics of offenders, (b) characteristics of correctional workers, (c) specifics of the content and process of services planned and delivered, and (d) intermediate changes in the person and circumstances of individual offenders. Logically, these major sources of variation in outcome reside within the conditions established by the specifics of a judicial disposition or criminal sanction. Thus, there is little reason to expect that variation among settings or sanctions will have an impact on recidivism except in interaction with offender characteristics and through the mediators of intervention process and intermediate change. We develop this "criminal sanction"

hypothesis first and then compare it with hypotheses regarding the effectiveness of a correctional service approach that attends to preservice case characteristics, to the process and content of intervention, and to intermediate change within particular sanctions.

A focus upon variation in official disposition is a reflection of one or more of the three sets of theoretical perspectives known as *just deserts, labeling,* and *deterrence.* The just deserts or justice set is not overly concerned with recidivism, but on occasion the assumption surfaces that unjust processing may motivate additional criminal activity. It appears, however, that the devaluation of rehabilitation—in the interest of increasing "just" processing—has been associated with increased punishment and decreased treatment but not with reduced recidivism. The labeling and deterrence perspectives actually yield conflicting predictions regarding the outcomes of different dispositions. Labeling theory suggests that less involvement in the criminal justice system is better than more (because the stigma is less), while deterrence theory suggests the op- posite (because fear of punishment is greater). The assumptions of both labeling and deterrence have been subjected to logical and empirical review, and neither perspective is yet able to offer a well-developed psychology of criminal conduct. Basic differentiations among and within levels and types of sanctions have yet to be worked out, type of offender is likely a crucial moderating variable, and the social psychology of "processing" is only now being explored.

To our knowledge, not a single review of the effects of judicial sanctioning on criminal recidivism has reached positive conclusions except when the extremes of incapacitation are tested or when additional reference is made to moderators (e.g., type of offender) or mediators (e.g., the specifics of intervention). Reading Kirby, Bailey, Logan, and Martinson reveals the obvious but unstated fact that their negative conclusions regarding "treatment" reflected primarily the negligible impact of variation in sanctions, such as probation and incarceration. Thus, we agree with Palmer: the main effects of criminal sanctions on recidivism have been slight and inconsistent.

This hypothesis is extended to judicial "alternatives," because there are no solid reasons for expecting alternative punishments, such as community service or restitution, to have an impact on recidivism. Any anticipated rehabilitative benefit of "alternatives" is based on the hope that offenders will learn that crime has negative consequences, and yet the enhancement of cognitive and interpersonal skills (e.g., future-orientation and perspective-taking) are dependent upon systematic modeling, reinforcement, and graduated practice. Given little reason to expect much from the incidental learning opportunities provided by such sanctions as restitution, correctional treatment service is a crucial supplement to a criminal justice approach that is preoccupied with avoiding stigma while delivering "just" and "innovative alternative" punishment.

Reviewers of the literature have routinely found that at least 40 percent of the better-controlled evaluations of correctional treatment services reported positive effects. For example, considering only the better-controlled studies, the proportion of studies reporting positive evidence was 75 percent (3/4) in Kirby, 59 percent (13/22) in Bailey, 50 percent (9/18) in Logan, 78 percent (14/18) in Logan when Type of Treatment × Type of Client interactions are considered, 48 percent (39/82) in Palmer's retabulation of studies reviewed by Martinson, 86 percent (82/95) in Gendreau and Robs, and 47 percent (40/85) in Lab and Whitehead. This pattern of results strongly supports exploration of the idea that some service programs are working with at least some offenders under some circumstances, and we think that helpful linkages among case, service, and outcome are suggested by three principles known as risk, need, and responsivity.

The Risk Principle and Selection of Level of Service

The risk principle suggests that higher levels of service are best reserved for higher-risk cases and that low-risk cases are best assigned to minimal service. In the literature at least since the Gluecks in 1950, the risk principle has been restated on many occasions. Although the parameters remain to be established, evidence fa-

voring the risk principle continues to grow. In brief, when actually explored, the effects of treatment typically are found to be greater among higher-risk cases than among lower-risk cases. This is expected unless the need and/or responsivity principles are violated.

The Need Principle and Selection of Appropriate Intermediate Targets

Risk factors may be static or dynamic in nature, and psychology is particularly interested in those dynamic risk factors that, when changed, are associated with *subsequent* variation in the chances of criminal conduct. Clinically, dynamic risk factors are called *criminogenic needs,* and guidelines for their assessment are described elsewhere. The most promising intermediate targets include changing antisocial attitudes, feelings, and peer associations; promoting familial affection in combination with enhanced parental monitoring and supervision; promoting identification with anticriminal role models; increasing self-control and self-management skills; replacing the skills of lying, stealing, and aggression with other, more prosocial, skills; reducing chemical dependencies; and generally shifting the density of rewards and costs for criminal and noncriminal activities in familial, academic, vocational, and other behavioral settings. Theoretically, modifying contingencies within the home, school, and work by way of an increased density of reward for noncriminal activity may reduce motivation for crime and increase the costs of criminal activity through having more to lose.

Less-promising targets include increasing self-esteem without touching antisocial propensity, increasing the cohesiveness of antisocial peer groups, improving neighborhood-wide living conditions without reaching high-risk families, and attempts to focus on vague personal/emotional problems that have not been linked with recidivism.

The Responsivity Principle and Selection of Type of Service

The responsivity principle has to do with the selection of styles and modes of service that are

(a) capable of influencing the specific types of intermediate targets that are set with offenders and (b) appropriately matched to the learning styles of offenders. We begin with the general literature on the treatment of offenders and then turn to specific Responsivity × Service interactions.

RESPONSIVITY—GENERAL PRINCIPLES OF EFFECTIVE SERVICE   Drawing upon our earlier review, appropriate types of service typically, but not exclusively, involve the use of behavioral and social learning principles of interpersonal influence, skill enhancement, and cognitive change. Specifically, they include modeling, graduated practice, rehearsal, role playing, reinforcement, resource provision, and detailed verbal guidance and explanations (making suggestions, giving reasons, cognitive restructuring). Elsewhere, we describe the applications of these practices as (a) use of authority (a "firm but fair" approach and definitely not interpersonal domination or abuse), (b) anticriminal modeling and reinforcement (explicit reinforcement and modeling of alternatives to procriminal styles of thinking, feeling, and acting), and (c) concrete problem solving and systematic skill training for purposes of increasing reward levels in anticriminal settings. High levels of advocacy and brokerage are also indicated as long as the receiving agency actually offers appropriate service. Finally, Andrews and Kiessling recommended that service deliverers relate to offenders in interpersonally warm, flexible, and enthusiastic ways while also being clearly supportive of anticriminal attitudinal and behavioral patterns. Interestingly, social learning approaches receive strong, albeit indirect, support from the prediction literature on the causal modeling of delinquency.

RESPONSIVITY—INEFFECTIVE SERVICE   Some types and styles of services should be avoided under most circumstances. Generally, programming for groups is to be approached very cautiously because the opening up of communication within offender groups may well be criminogenic. In group and residential programming, clinicians must gain control over the contingencies of interaction so that anticriminal, rather than procriminal, patterns are exposed and reinforced. For example, Agee's programmatic structures supporting positive change may be contrasted with the failure of unstructured, peer-oriented group counseling and permissive, relationship-oriented milieu approaches. The failure of these unstructured approaches is well documented in open community settings, in group homes operating according to the essentially nondirective guidelines of "guided group interaction." There are also no convincing theoretical grounds for believing that young people will be "scared straight." Fear of official punishment is not one of the more important correlates of delinquency, and yelling at people is counter to the relationship principle of effective service.

Finally, traditional psychodynamic and nondirective client-centered therapies are to be avoided within general samples of offenders. These therapies are designed to free people from the personally inhibiting controls of "superego" and "society," but neurotic misery and overcontrol are not criminogenic problems for a majority of offenders. Authorities such as Freud and the Gluecks (in their classic *Unraveling Delinquency)* warned us about evocative and relationship-dependent psychodynamic approaches with antisocial cases.

SPECIFIC RESPONSIVITY CONSIDERATIONS   The success of highly verbal, evocative, and relationship-dependent services seems to be limited to clients with high levels of interpersonal, self-reflective, and verbal skill. The "I-level" and "conceptual-level" systems provide guidance regarding the types of offenders who may respond in positive ways to services that are less structured than those we have been describing as appropriate for antisocial samples in general.

Summary

Our clinically relevant and psychologically informed principles of treatment predict that criminal sanctioning without attention to the delivery of correctional service will relate to recidivism minimally. Additionally, we suggest that the delivery of services, regardless of criminal sanction or setting, is unproductive if those services are inconsistent with the principles of risk, need, and responsivity. Positively, we predict that appropriate treatment—treatment that is delivered to higher-risk cases, that targets criminogenic need, and that is matched with the learning styles of offenders—will reduce recidivism.

RESULTS AND DISCUSSION

A preliminary comparison of the two samples of studies was conducted on various control variables. The comparisons reflected an obvious concern that any systematic differences between the Whitehead and Lab sample and Sample 2 be documented. Overall, apart from the inclusion of studies of adult treatment in Sample 2, the two samples of studies were found to be reasonably comparable across the various potential predictors of treatment effect size explored in this chapter.

Hypothesis 1: Relative Predictive Potential of Type of Treatment

Across the studies, the correlation between type of treatment and phi coefficients was strong (.60) and, with the introduction of simultaneous control for other variables, the correlation increased (.72). Comparisons from Sample 2, recency of publication and community-based treatment, were each associated with relatively positive effects of treatment. In summary, our first hypothesis was strongly supported: type of treatment was clearly the strongest of the correlates of study findings analyzed.

Hypothesis 2: The Importance of Appropriate Correctional Service

The results of the analyses supported Hypothesis 2 to a stronger degree than was initially anticipated: both appropriate and unspecified correctional services were significantly more effective in reducing recidivism than were criminal sanctions and inappropriate service.

The only factor to interact significantly with type of treatment was year of publication. It appears that criminal sanctions yielded more negative findings on program effects in the earlier literature than in the more recent literature. This reflects a greater representation of studies in the earlier years (the negative implications of residential programs will be discussed below). More interestingly, studies of appropriate correctional treatment in the 1980s yielded a much stronger program effect than did earlier studies of appropriate treatment. Most likely, this reflects three trends. First, the earlier studies included what are now recognized to be unsophisticated applications of token economy systems. Second, studies of the 1980s paid greater attention to cognitive variables. Third, the positive effects of short-term behavioral family counseling have been replicated in the 1980s.

CONCLUSIONS

The meta-analysis has revealed considerable order in estimates of the magnitude of the impact of treatment upon recidivism. As predicted, the major source of variation in effects on recidivism was the extent to which service was appropriate according to the principles of risk, need, and responsivity. Appropriate correctional service appears to work better than criminal sanctions not involving rehabilitative service and better than services less consistent with our a priori principles of effective rehabilitation. This review has convinced us that the positive trends that we and others detected in the literature of the 1960s and early 1970s were indeed worthy of serious application and evaluation. There is a reasonably solid clinical and research basis for the political reaffirmation of rehabilitation.

The importance of clinical and theoretical relevance in programming and in meta-analysis has been demonstrated—the sanction and treatment services should be differentiated and the action in regard to recidivism appears to reside in appropriate treatment. Much, however, remains to be done. We look forward to critiques and revisions of the principles of risk, need, and responsivity as stated and applied herein. What comparisons were assigned to what analytic categories is described in our report and is thereby easily and appropriately the focus of critical review. Reserved for future reports are the many issues surrounding therapeutic integrity, the measurement of recidivism, and methodological issues such as sample size. Gender effects and the treatment of sex offenders, substance abusers, and inmates of long-term institutions require detailed analyses. Toward these ends, our meta-analytic database is being extended. Our focus here, however, remains on type of service and effect size.

Of immediate concern is the meaning of the average phi coefficient of .30 observed across studies for comparisons involving appropriate correctional service. First, until convinced otherwise, we will assume that an average phi of .30 is more positive, clinically and socially, than the mean effects of the alternatives of sanctioning without regard for service or servicing without regard to the principles of effective correctional service. Casual review of recidivism rates will reveal that, on average, appropriate treatment cuts recidivism rates by about 50 percent (in fact, the mean reduction was 53.06 percent). Thus, we do not think that the positive effects are "minimal." Second, the correlation between effect size estimates and type of treatment approached .70. Correlations of this magnitude are unlikely to reflect "lucky outliers," although more systematic sources of error may indeed inflate correlation coefficients. Third, issues surrounding the assessment of the clinical and social significance of diverse measures of effect size are indeed worthy of ongoing research. Future reports on our expanding data bank will compare various estimates of effect size, including some direct estimates of clinical/social significance. For now, we are interested in discovering ethical routes to strengthened treatment effects, but we are not talking about magical cures.

Critics of rehabilitation are correct when they note that the average correlation between treatment and recidivism is not 1.00. At the same time, critics might be asked to report on the variation that their "preferred" variable shares with recidivism. For example, if their preferred variable is social class, they may be reminded that some reviewers have estimated that the average correlation between class and crime is about −.09. If their preferred approach is incapacitation or community crime prevention, they may be reminded of the minimal effects so far

reported for these strategies. Critics, be they supporters of social class or incapacitation, likely will respond with examples of particular studies that yielded high correlations with indicators of crime. We remind them that the largest correlations are no better estimates of the average effect than are the least favorable estimates. We also remind them that the positive evidence regarding appropriate rehabilitative service comes not from cross-sectional research—the typical research strategy of critics of rehabilitation—but from deliberate and socially sanctioned approximations of truly experimental ideals. Finally, we remind the critics that one can be interested in the effects of class, punishment, and prevention programs on individual and aggregated crime rates while maintaining multiple interests and without letting one interest justify dismissal of the value of another.

This meta-analysis has done more than uncover evidence that supported our a priori biases regarding the importance of appropriate correctional service. The finding that the effects of inappropriate service appeared to be particularly negative in residential settings while the positive effects of appropriate service were attenuated was something of a surprise. While sensitive to the difficulties of working with antisocial groups, we did not predict this incidental affirmation of a widely shared preference for community over residential programming. Institutions and group homes, however, remain important components of correctional systems and hence active but thoughtful service is indicated. The literature should be carefully scrutinized in order to avoid inappropriate service, and follow-up services in the community may be necessary in order to maximize effectiveness. Finally, the suppressive impact of residential programming suggests that the negative effects of custody are better established than we anticipated.

The effect of the quality of the research design on estimates of effect size was relatively minor. Even if some design problems do inflate effect size estimates, the interesting finding was that comparisons involving more and less rigorous research designs agreed as to what types of treatment were most effective. Program managers and frontline clinicians who find truly randomized groups to be practically or ethically impossible may consider conducting an evaluation that approximates the ideals of a true experiment. In particular, we strongly endorse the use of designs that introduce controls for the preservice risk levels of clients and that actually report on Risk × Service interactions. In addition, even evaluations that rely upon comparisons of clients who complete or do not complete treatment may be valuable.

Finally, the number of evaluative studies of correctional service should increase dramatically over the next decade. Although millions of young people were processed by juvenile justice systems during the past decade, the total number of papers in the Whitehead and Lab set that involved systematic study of appropriate service was 21. Were it not for behavioral psychologists, the number of papers involving appropriate service would have been nine. From a positive perspective, there is renewed interest, vigor, and sensitivity in the study of the psychology of criminal conduct. There are solid reasons to focus in ethical and humane ways on the client and the quality of service delivered within just dispositions.

From "Nothing Works" to "the Appropriate Works"

STEVEN P. LAB
JOHN T. WHITEHEAD

IN "Does Correctional Treatment Work?" Andrews and his colleagues present evidence that "appropriate" psychological interventions are effective in reducing recidivism. Since Andrews et al. paid particular attention to our reports on the effectiveness of juvenile correctional treatment, we prepared a response to the study, for two primary reasons. First, we felt that the original article unfairly categorized us as "critics of rehabilitation" who "endorse a very firm version of 'nothing works.'" We wanted to set the record straight on this and related criticisms. Second, we felt that there were some substantive problems with the article that merited a response.

Of concern in the work of Andrews and his colleagues are several substantive matters, including the claims that appropriate correctional service reflects three psychological principles of risk, need, and responsivity and that such appropriate correctional service works. The proper application of treatment in accordance with these three factors is the crucial factor in the success of treatment. Before discussing the application of these factors by Andrews and associates, it is enlightening to review their concerns over the inappropriate categorization of treatments found in our earlier analyses.

A major criticism of our analyses is the categorization of studies according to type of criminal justice setting or sanction. The Andrews research maintains that "there is little reason to expect that variation among [criminal justice] settings or sanctions will have an impact on recidivism except in interaction with offender characteristics and through the mediators of intervention process and intermediate change." In effect, the authors are claiming that we (and others) have mixed apples and oranges, including some rotten apples and some rotten oranges. Such "rotten fruit" would be interventions not following their prescribed criteria. In place of our categorization, they call for categorizing studies as sound (i.e., according to risk, need, and responsivity) or unsound.

In response, we chose to categorize the studies we examined according to criminal justice setting/sanction because those are the accepted categories in criminal justice practice and research. Diversion, probation, and so forth are accurate descriptions of actual practice, and the categories represent assessments by criminal justice professionals of differing levels of risk of criminal behavior and/or crime severity. Prison is reserved for the most serious/highest risk offenders, probation is for offenders not meriting incarceration, and diversion is used for first-offender/least serious offenders. We do not see the disappearance of these categories in the near future. Judges, prosecutors, and even offenders will think of these categories as sensible. Even rehabilitation supporters such as Gendreau (one of Andrews's coauthors) and Robs have "reviewed the treatment literature as defined by program structure, such as diversion." Perhaps in some distant future, judges, prosecutors, and correctional policymakers and administrators will assign offenders to programs based on the psychological criteria that Andrews and associates propose. At present, however, practice distinguishes such categories.

The second major criticism of our research is linked to the first. Andrews and associates claim that our categorizing of studies led us to lump together apples and oranges and good fruit with bad fruit. They claim that when one separates out the bad, the average correlation of the good remnant is .30. Further, they attempt to show with statistical tests that this phi is significantly different from zero and that it is more robust than many other correlations in the criminal justice literature. While both of the claims may be correct, the relevance is somewhat questionable. A correlation of .30 may indeed be significantly different from zero but it is much more significantly different from 1.00, and we would argue that it is this criterion which should be desired and not simply a marginal difference from mediocrity.

The fact that their grouping of studies according to their principles resulted in an average correlation of .30 is interesting and certainly calls for further research along the lines suggested by the authors. Nevertheless, the fact remains that our analysis simply did not uncover such grounds for optimism. If one averages the correlation coefficients in our article, the result is .12. Further, our specific examination of the behavioral versus the nonbehavioral interventions did find that 7 of the 16 behavioral interventions exceeded .20 but that 7 also were negative. In other words, previous research showing success for behavioral interventions led us to examine the effectiveness of such interventions versus nonbehavioral interventions. Unfortunately, our reading of the behavioral-nonbehavioral results was not rosy.

Assuming for the sake of argument that Andrews et al. are right in their assertion, the interventions should be considered in light of their psychological soundness rather than according to criminal justice sanction/setting, such a categorization is utopian. Consider just probation. Recent reports from California indicate that caseloads have exceeded 300 offenders in some counties and that funding in real dollars has plummeted dramatically. To call for the implementation of the authors' principles with such excessively high caseloads is chimerical. Even apart from caseload considerations, probation officers spend so much time on presentence investigations and other duties that it is pure fantasy to expect them to follow the psychological principles of the authors. It is our sober assessment that probation and other criminal justice sanctions will continue to be deficient in regard to funding, personnel, and other areas such that it is simply unrealistic to expect dramatic change.

Turning to the actual application of the principles of risk, need, and responsivity in the Andrews et al. study, there appear to be a number of serious shortcomings in the analysis. First, the authors fail to specifically define their terms. While they give general definitions, such as "the risk principle suggests that higher levels of service are best reserved for higher risk cases, and that low-risk cases are best assigned to minimal service," nowhere do they provide explicit information on what criteria are used to determine risk, need, and responsivity. The reader is asked to take their word that the categorization of studies in their analysis is appropriate. A specific example of this type of flaw involves the failure to define what constitutes high- and low-risk clients.

We assume that high versus low risk corresponds to the possibility of future deviant acts. Making such determinations entails the problem of prediction. While space limitations do not allow an extensive review of the literature on prediction, a brief presentation is necessary. There is little debate in criminology that predicting future behavior is, at best, difficult. Various studies show that false predictions exceed correct predictions in many analyses. Indeed, when false predictions exceed the 50 percent mark (and some go as high as 99 percent), one is further ahead by simply flipping a coin. More telling for the present endeavor is the fact that clinical prediction (the one we assume would be preferred in the proposed treatment assignments) performs worse than empirically based actuarial predictions. Interestingly, Cullen (one of Andrews's coauthors) and Gilbert have expressed serious reservations about the ability to ever make accurate predictions: "The technology for accurately predicting conformity simply has not been developed to the point where it can be employed with even minimal confidence. Indeed, given the complexity of the causal forces that underlie the criminal choices of any one offender, evolving such technology may constitute an insurmountable task." The inability, therefore, to accurately assess risk seriously undermines the possibility of using the "psychologically informed" treatment methods proposed by the authors. It could be argued that current judicial decisions on disposition of cases and assignment of treatment may be as good as a psychologist's predictions of future behavior and the resultant expectations of treatment outcomes.

Aside from the problems of prediction, an inspection of the categorization of studies by Andrews and his colleagues reveals what appears to be an uncertainty on their part about specifying what constitutes high and low risk. For example, in some instances low risk is assigned to first offenders and high risk designates all other clients. In the Byles and Maurice study, however, low risk refers to those with one prior offense, while the presence of two or more priors indicates high risk. Other times the authors define risk by type of offense, number of referrals, attitude of the client, or other factors. In some instances, the aforementioned criteria, and other possible factors, are ignored when they appear to be present in the data. Among these are age at first offense, type of offense, the existence of behavioral problems, and number of past offenses. They also make distinctions between males and females in some studies but fail to indicate whether this is due to differential risk (it is assumed that the need is not at issue since both groups receive the same intervention and are listed under the same headings of "appropriate," "inappropriate," etc.). It is interesting to note that the above examples are based solely on a review of the studies taken from our earlier analysis. We infer that similar discrepancies exist in the studies provided by Andrews and associates. The claim that "the effects of treatment typically are found to be greater among higher risk cases than among lower risk cases" is not surprising when risk can apparently be defined and altered to the advantage of the researcher.

The determination of "need" is similarly questionable in the study. The authors note that need refers to targeting various problems and needs for the client. Among these targets are "changing antisocial attitudes . . . ; promoting familial affection . . . ; promoting . . . anticriminal role models;" and others. Each of these assumes a diagnosis of need for each individual client and the subsequent placement of the client into the proper intervention. An examination of most of the evaluation studies which appear in our earlier review does not provide adequate information upon which to assess the need of the individuals. Most of the information in the articles refers to the offense, the demographic characteristics of the clients, and the program into which the clients are placed. Little if any information is provided on the background, psychological makeup, family relations, attitudes, or other factors crucial in assessing need. This suggests that Andrews and colleagues' assessments of need are based on the type of intervention under question and the approach used in the interventions and not the actual need of the clients. That is, if the program is consistent with what constitutes good intervention, according to the authors, the need criterion is met. This is illustrated by the fact that "appropriate service included . . . all behavioral programs . . . and . . . nonbehavioral programs, that clearly stated that criminogenic need was targeted." This seems to indicate that behavioral interventions are needed by all clients. It also suggests that there are treatment interventions in the criminal justice system that do not target criminogenic need. We seriously doubt that this is the case. Rather, we construe the authors' statement as an indication that there are some interventions which *they do not consider* to be targeted to criminogenic need.

The authors also tie the idea of appropriate intervention to "service delivery to higher risk cases" and "behavioral programs (except those involving delivery of service to lower risk cases)." At no point in their analysis does it appear that low-risk cases are ever in need, and therefore, they are always exclusive of "appropriate" interventions. Are they suggesting that low-risk cases (however they define them) should be simply funneled out of the system?

Given their earlier comments on labeling, we seriously doubt this is the case. There must be some form of intervention, such as diversion or police cautioning, which is "appropriate" for low-risk offenders.

We are also surprised by the authors' implication that previous researchers have not addressed any of the issues raised. The authors seem to be unaware, for example, that over a decade ago accountants, without the benefit of graduate training in psychology, reported that an audit of probation records indicated that probationer needs were both obvious and ignored. Specifically, only 23 percent of the probationers studied had completed programs to address their needs and "written [treatment] plans were prepared for only 38% of the probationers under their supervision." The point is that both correctional practitioners and scholars have known the importance of addressing needs for some time. Actually addressing such needs, however, is another matter.

APPLYING THE MODEL

Having presented the ideas of risk, need, and responsivity, Andrews and associates set out to prove that their assumptions are correct and that the treatments do work. In so doing, they make a variety of decisions concerning the classification of studies and the comparison of "treatment" with "control" which are questionable. In many instances, the authors look at only a portion of the sample of clients and ignore many other clients for no apparent reason. There is no reason given for excluding what may often be a large portion of the clients from the analysis.

The authors also list a number of studies as "appropriate" when the only indication of the treatment is that it entails family counseling. This is interesting when "inappropriate" service includes "nondirective relationship-dependent . . . counseling" and "group approaches with an emphasis on within-group communication and without a clear plan for gaining control over procriminal modeling and reinforcement." Most of the family intervention programs do not provide enough information for placing them in the appropriate category. As a result, they should

be classified as either inappropriate or unspecified. Similarly, "appropriate" appears to reflect a simple measurement of the amount of treatment and not the quality of the treatment offered. Conversely, inappropriate studies seem to be determined more by the type of treatment than the need of the client.

Andrews and associates present another confusing point of view in relation to group treatment approaches. The authors note that the "failure of these unstructured approaches is well documented in open community settings [and] in group homes operating according to the essentially nondirective guidelines of 'guided group interaction.'" It is intriguing that rehabilitation supporters would make such a blanket condemnation of guided group interaction when both the Provo and Silverlake studies and later commentators on guided group interaction concluded otherwise. Similarly, their criticism of psychodynamic approaches is contrary to Aichhom, Redl and Wineman, and Bettelheim.

The authors also place the same treatments into different categories of appropriateness and use controls and treatments interchangeably at times. While the authors clearly base their placement of the same treatment into different categories on their assessment of matching risk and need for different clients, our earlier arguments that the studies do not provide adequate information for determining need and that the authors do not use a consistent measure of risk negate their contention. It appears that the authors make the determinations more out of convenience for their argument than based on hard proof that the distinctions reflect "objective" decisions. The use of treatments as controls and controls as treatments in various computations is unclear to us. The authors attempt to reconcile this in a footnote, but the fact remains that they are mixing the apples and oranges which they accuse others of mixing. An inspection of instances in which this occurs seems to yield two possible results. First, some of these computations yield high phi values. Second, many of these yield multiple phi coefficients in support of the authors' hypotheses. Indeed, a number of these instances reflect using a group specified as the control *by the original researchers* in a treatment capacity by Andrews and associates.

We are also concerned about the extreme faith of the authors in psychological interventions. Even if they are accurate in their claims of an average correlation of .30 for the "appropriate" interventions, that still would only explain about 9 percent of the variance. We suspect that one explanation for this is that their criteria for "appropriate" leave little or no room for changing societal conditions conducive to delinquency and pay no attention to more fundamental considerations of personal transformation. The peacemaking perspective, for example, goes beyond behavioral interventions and family therapy to inner reformation for all prisoners, including those who will never see the outside of prison walls. The perspective recognizes that even those offenders have to examine the ultimate meaning of their lives. Thus, we postulate that psychological variables are only part of the crime/delinquency picture and that psychological interventions are only part of the treatment agenda.

Another major flaw in the authors' analysis lies in their failure to demonstrate a critical step in the treatment process. The authors state that "there is little reason to expect that variation among settings or sanctions will have an impact on recidivism except in interaction with offender characteristics and through the mediators of intervention process and intermediate change." We have already shown the questionable basis for identifying offender characteristics, particularly risk and need, used by the authors. We have not addressed the crucial issue of "intermediate change." It is clear that this intermediate change refers to changes in interpersonal skills, cognitive development, self-management skills, and similar factors. The flaw in the analysis is in the lack of evidence that the appropriate or other successful interventions actually brought about any of these intermediate changes. By definition, these things must be altered in order to show that the intervention was the cause of any change in the end product, recidivism.

At no point do the authors address whether the intermediate changes have occurred. It is plausible that the changes in recidivism are a reflection of something other than the introduction of an "appropriate" intervention. The authors simply *hope* this is the case. Indeed, forced treatment or intervention could be serving as a deterrent and not actual rehabilitation. Alternatively, the placement of the clients in a treatment program may be less stigmatizing (a labeling argument), and thus the clients recidivate less. The authors assume that the intermediate changes are occurring since the end product, recidivism, is altered. It is hard to accept the results when the key to the entire argument is nowhere to be found.

A final problem we have involves the authors' development of the criteria of risk, need, and responsivity. It appears to us that the authors' assertions are tautological. They rely on reviews of the research literature to assert that attention to risk, need, and responsivity marks "appropriate" studies. They then criticize other researchers for including both appropriate and inappropriate studies in their samples of studies. Andrews and associates, however, are using the same studies to generate appropriateness criteria and to test the criteria. Under such an approach, there is only one finding which can emerge, that being an affirmation of the approach. Using the same rationale, we too could now delineate appropriate studies and inappropriate ones and prove ourselves correct. It seems more correct, however, to derive the criteria from the past studies and use them the next time around, say in 1995, to check on the validity of the argument.

CONCLUSION

Criminal justice has always been a choice between conscience and convenience. We may have cast a cynical tone to our reports on the effectiveness of correctional interventions, but we fear that Rothman's insight about the history of criminal justice practice will continue to ring true. We join Andrews and his colleagues in the hope that the search for effective correctional treatment will not be a never-ending search for a secular grail, but we fear that the journey will be more arduous than they contend and will require more than a psychological armamentarium.

RETRIBUTION

Desert

ANDREW VON HIRSCH

IN everyday thinking about punishment, the idea of desert figures prominently. Ask the person on the street why a wrongdoer should be punished, and he is likely to say that he *deserves* it. Yet the literature of penology seldom mentions the word. Instead, there is usually listed—along with the three traditional utilitarian aims of deterrence, incapacitation, and rehabilitation—a fourth aim of *retribution*. We do not find retribution a helpful term. It has no regular use except in relation to punishment, so that one is precluded from learning about the concept from the word's use in other contexts. It also seems somewhat narrow. The *Oxford English Dictionary,* for example, defines retribution as "recompense for, or requital of evil done; return of evil"; this suggests a particular view of why punishment is deserved, namely, that the offender should somehow be "paid back" for his wrong. Yet, as we will see presently, there are other explanations of deserved punishment which do not rely on this notion of requital-of-evil. Finally, the word is, perhaps through historical accident, burdened with pejorative associations.

We prefer the term "desert." Its cognate, "to deserve," is widely used: rewards, prizes, and grades, as well as punishments, are said to be deserved or undeserved. And the word desert is somewhat less emotionally loaded.

To say someone "deserves" to be rewarded or punished is to refer to his *past* conduct and assert that its merit or demerit is reason for according him pleasant or unpleasant treatment. The focus on the past is critical. That a student has

From *Doing Justice: The Choice of Punishments* (pp. 161-165) by A. Von Hirsch, 1976, New York: Hill & Wang. Copyright 1976 by Andrew von Hirsch. Reprinted by permission of Hill & Wang, a division of Farrar, Straus, & Giroux, Inc.

written an outstanding paper is grounds for asserting that he deserves an award, but that the award will yield him or others future benefits (however desirable those might be) cannot be grounds for claiming he deserves it. The same holds for punishment: to assert that someone deserves to be punished is to look to his past wrongdoing as reason for having him penalized. This orientation to the past distinguishes desert from the other purported aims of punishment—deterrence, incapacitation, rehabilitation—which seek to justify the criminal sanction by its prospective usefulness in preventing crime.

It is important here to distinguish between the rationale for punishing and the rationale for the underlying legal prohibitions. Concededly, the latter—the criminal law's substantive prohibitions—are forward looking in their aim: murder is prohibited so that citizens will not kill one another. But the question is whether, once a violation has occurred, the basis for punishing the violator is still forward looking, or is retrospective. Once a murder has taken place, is the only reason for penalizing the murderer to prevent subsequent violations by him or others? Or is there, at that point, a retrospective reason for punishing—that the murderer deserves to be punished? And if so, how is the notion of deserved punishment to be explained?

A useful place to begin is with Kant's explanation of deserved punishment, which he based on the idea of fair dealing among free individuals. To realize their own freedom, he contended, members of society have the reciprocal obligation to limit their behavior so as not to interfere with the freedom of others. When someone infringes another's rights, he gains an unfair advantage over all others in the society—since he has failed to constrain his own behavior while benefiting from other persons' forbearance from interfering with his rights. The punishment—by imposing a counterbalancing disadvantage on the violator—restores the equilibrium: after having undergone the punishment, the violator ceases to be at advantage over his nonviolating fellows. (This righting-of-the-balance is not a matter of preventing future crimes. Aside from any concern with prospective criminality, it is the violator's *past* crime that placed him in a position of advantage over others, and it is that advantage which the punishment would eliminate.) As Herbert Morris puts it in a recent restatement of the Kantian argument:

A person who violates the rules has something others have—the benefits of the system [of mutual noninterference with others' rights]—but by renouncing what others have assumed, the burdens of self-restraint, he has acquired an unfair advantage. Matters are not even until this advantage is in some way erased. . . . Justice—that is punishing such individuals—restores the equilibrium of benefits and burdens.

Kant's theory, however, accounts only for the imposition of *some* kind of deprivation on the offender to offset the "advantage" he obtained in violating others' rights. It does not explain why that deprivation should take the peculiar form of punishment. Punishment differs from other purposefully inflicted deprivations in the moral disapproval it expresses: punishing someone conveys in dramatic fashion that his conduct was wrong and that he is blameworthy for having committed it. Why, then, does the violator deserve to be *punished,* instead of being made to suffer another kind of deprivation that connotes no special moral stigma?

To answer this question, it becomes necessary, we think, to focus specifically on the reprobation implicit in punishment and argue that *it* is deserved. Someone who infringes the rights of others, the argument runs, does wrong and deserves blame for his conduct. It is because he deserves blame that the sanctioning authority is entitled to choose a response that expresses moral disapproval: namely, punishment. In other words, the sanction ought not only to deprive the offender of the "advantage" obtained by his disregard of the rules (the Kantian explanation); but do so in a manner that ascribes blame (the reprobative explanation).

This raises the question of what purpose the reprobation itself serves. Blaming persons who commit wrongful acts is, arguably, a way of reaffirming the moral values that were infringed. But to speak of reaffirming such values prompts the further question: Why should the violator be singled out for blame to achieve that end? The answer must ultimately be that the censure is itself deserved: that someone who is responsible for wrongdoing is blame*worthy* and hence may justly be blamed.

With this much preliminary explanation of the idea of deserved punishment, we turn to the main question: whether desert is necessary to justify the criminal sanction.

FROM DETERRENCE TO DESERT

We have already suggested one reason for punishing: deterrence. The criminal sanction is called for to prevent certain kinds of injurious conduct. Why is it not sufficient to rely on that simple argument—and get on with deciding how punishment should rationally be allocated? Why bring in desert, with all its philosophical perplexities?

On utilitarian assumptions, deterrence would indeed suffice. The main utilitarian premise is (roughly) that a society is rightly ordered if its major institutions are arranged to achieve the maximum aggregate satisfaction and the minimum aggregate suffering. On this premise, punishment would be justified if it deterred sufficiently—because, in sum, more suffering would be prevented through the resulting reduction in crime than is caused by making those punished suffer. Our difficulty is, however, that we doubt the utilitarian premise: that the suffering of a few persons is made good by the benefits accruing to the many. A free society, we believe, should recognize that an individual's rights—or at least his most important rights—are prima facie entitled to priority over collective interests. This idea has been best expressed, perhaps, by the philosopher John Rawls in the opening pages of his *Theory of Justice*. "Each person," he writes, "possesses an inviolability founded on justice that even the welfare of society as a whole cannot override . . . justice denies that the loss of freedom for some is made right by a greater good shared by others. It does not allow that the sacrifices imposed on a few are outweighed by the larger sum of advantages enjoyed by many."

Given this assumption of the primacy of the individual's fundamental rights, no utilitarian account of punishment, deterrence included, can stand alone. While deterrence explains why most people benefit from the existence of punishment, the benefit to the many is not by itself a just basis for depriving the offender of his liberty and reputation. Some other reason, then, is needed to explain the suffering inflicted on the offender: that reason is desert. The offender may justly be subjected to certain deprivations because he deserves it, and he deserves it because he has engaged in wrongful conduct—conduct that does or threatens injury and that is prohibited by law. The penalty is thus not just a means of crime prevention but a merited response to the actor's deed, "rectifying the balance" in the Kantian sense and expressing moral reprobation of the actor for the wrong. In other words: while deterrence accounts for why punishment is socially useful, desert is necessary to explain why that utility may justly be pursued at the offender's expense.

In speaking thus of desert as necessary to the justification of punishment, we are not referring to channeling theories such as Oliver Wendell Holmes's: that ordinary citizens believe wrongdoers should suffer, and would resort to private vengeance were the law not to punish. Perhaps the restraint of vengeance is an important function of the criminal sanction, but this is another utilitarian claim: that there will be less social disruption if offenders are punished by the state rather than left to private retaliation. What still must be explained is why, in thus benefiting society, it is just to deprive offenders of *their* rights by penalizing them. To answer that question, a moral claim must be made: not that the public thinks punishment is deserved and will do harm if its opinion is disregarded, but that punishment is deserved.

THE CONVERSE: FROM DESERT TO DETERRENCE

The route of argument just taken is the more familiar in current philosophical literature on punishment: begin with deterrence as a reason for punishing, then consider whether it must be supplemented by desert. However, the logic can be reversed: one can start by relying on the idea of desert. But again, the interdependence of the two concepts—desert and deterrence—will quickly become apparent.

Desert may be reviewed as reason in itself for creating a social institution. This is evident in the case of rewards. Most societies, including our own, reward those who have done deeds of special merit. Rewards may serve utilitarian ends (e.g., as an incentive for desired conduct), but even disregarding such utility, a case for rewarding merit can be made simply on the grounds that it is deserved. Good work and good acts ought to be acknowledged for their own sake, and rewards express that acknowledgment. A parallel argument might be made for punishment: those who violate others' rights deserve to be punished, on the Kantian and reprobative grounds just discussed. A system of punishment is justified, the argument runs, simply because it is deserved.

However, there are countervailing moral considerations. An important counterconsideration is the principle of not deliberately causing human suffering where it can possibly be avoided. With rewards, this principle does not stand in the way: for rewards per se do not inflict pain (other than the possible discomfort of envy). It is otherwise with punishment: while wrongdoers deserve punishment, it is necessarily painful. Arguably, the principle against inflicting suffering should, in the absence of other considerations, override the case for punishing based on wrongdoers' deserts.

It is at this point in the argument that the idea of deterrence becomes critical—for it can supply an answer to the countervailing concern about the infliction of suffering. When punishment's deterrent effect is taken into account, it may cause less misery than not punishing would. Moreover, not only might total misery be reduced, but its distribution would be more acceptable: fewer innocent persons will be victimized by crimes, while those less deserving—the victimizers—will be made to suffer instead. Deterrence thus tips the scales back in favor of the penal sanction. To state the argument schematically:

Step 1: Those who violate others' rights deserve punishment. That, of itself, constitutes a prima facie justification for maintaining a system of criminal sanctions.

Step 2: There is, however, a countervailing moral obligation of not deliberately adding to the amount of human suffering. Punishment necessarily makes those punished suffer. In the absence of additional argument, that overrides the case for punishment in Step 1.

Step 3: The notion of deterrence, at this point, suggests that punishment may prevent more misery than it inflicts—thus disposing of the countervailing argument in Step 2. With it out of the way, the prima facie case for punishment described in Step 1—based on desert—stands again.

The case for punishing differs, then, from the case for rewards. With rewards, it is sufficient to argue that they are deserved: since rewards are not painful, there is no need to point to their collateral social usefulness to excuse the misery they cause. Punishments, likewise, are deserved, but given the overriding concern with the infliction of pain, the notion of deterrence has to be relied upon as well.

The foregoing shows the interdependence of the twin concepts of deterrence and desert. When one seeks to justify the criminal sanction by reference to its deterrent utility, desert is called for to explain why that utility may justly be pursued at offenders' expense. When one seeks to justify punishment as deserved, deterrence is needed to deal with the countervailing concern about the suffering inflicted. The interdependence of these two concepts suggests that the criminal sanction rests, ultimately, on *both*.

THE PRINCIPLE OF COMMENSURATE DESERTS

If one asks how severely a wrongdoer deserves to be punished, a familiar principle comes to mind: severity of punishment should be commensurate with the seriousness of the wrong. Only grave wrongs merit severe penalties; minor misdeeds deserve lenient punishments. Disproportionate penalties are undeserved—severe sanctions for minor wrongs or vice versa. This principle has variously been called a principle of "proportionality" or "just deserts"; we prefer to call it *commensurate deserts,* a phrase that better suggests the concepts involved. In the most obvious cases, the principle seems a truism (who would wish to imprison shoplifters for life, or let murderers off with small fines?). Yet whether and how it should be applied in allocating punishments has been in dispute.

In an earlier era, the principle of commensurate deserts had a firmly established place in criminal jurisprudence. Cesare Beccaria's *Of Crimes and Punishments,* written in 1764, gives it much emphasis. Punishments, he stated, should be carefully graded to correspond with the gravity of offenses. To Beccaria and his followers, the principle was grounded on commonsense notions of fairness—and on utilitarian considerations as well: if penalties were not scaled commensurately with offenses, criminals, it was feared, would as soon commit grave crimes as minor ones. Criminal codes of the era—such as the French Code of 1791 and the Bavarian Code of 1813—reflected this conception. The framers of the original New Hampshire Constitution considered the principle so central to a fair and workable system of criminal justice that they embodied it in the state's Bill of Rights.

Yet, with the rise of the rehabilitative ideology in the nineteenth century, the principle of commensurate deserts went into eclipse.

One school of thought dismissed the principle entirely. Desert was seen as relevant only before conviction—when it was being decided whether the violator had acted with the requisite degree of culpability to be held criminally liable. After conviction, the seriousness of his offense was not to be considered at all; his punishment was instead to be determined by his need for treatment and his likelihood of returning to crime. The Model Sentencing Act (in both its 1963 and its 1972 versions) takes this view. The act does not provide scaled maximum penalties for different categories of offenses. Instead, it gives the judge discretion to impose up to a five-year sentence on an offender convicted of any felony: within this limit, irrespective of the character of the offense, the judge is supposed to fix a sentence on the basis of the risk the offender poses to society.

Others have not been quite so uncompromising, conceding a residual significance to the seriousness of the offense. Most criminal codes provide maximum penalties for different offenses, ranked according to some approximate scale of gravity. But these legislative maxima are set so much higher than the sentences ordinarily expected that they have not much influence on actual dispositions. The American Law Institute's Model Penal Code recommends also that the judge should not set the sentence so low as to "depreciate the seriousness of the offense": the code fails, however, to clarify how much weight should be given this factor of "depreciating the seriousness" as contrasted with other possible goals of sentencing. Although H. L. A. Hart comments briefly in his "Prolegomenon" on how the principle serves as a constraint of fairness, his thoughts on this subject (unlike so much else in his influential essay) did not stimulate much further interest. The justification for the principle; the weight to be assigned it as contrasted with other possible aims of punishing; the meaning of "seriousness"; and the relevance of the principle to the knotty question of sentencing discretion—all these have remained largely unexplored until quite recently.

The principle looks retrospectively to the seriousness of the offender's past crime or crimes. "Seriousness" depends both on the harm done (or risked) by the act and on the degree of the actor's culpability. (When we speak of the seriousness of "the crime," we wish to stress that we are not looking exclusively to the act but also to how much the actor can be held to blame for the act and its consequences.) If the offender had a prior criminal record at the time of conviction, the number and gravity of those prior crimes should be taken into account in assessing seriousness. (The meaning of seriousness and the significance of a prior criminal record will be explored more fully later.)

The principle of commensurate deserts, in our opinion, is a requirement of justice; thus

- The principle has its counterpart in commonsense notions of equity which people apply in their everyday lives. Sanctions disproportionate to the wrong are seen as manifestly unfair—whether it be an employee being fired for a minor rule infraction to make an example of him or a school inflicting unequal punishments on two children for the same misdeed.

- The principle ensures, as no utilitarian criterion of allocation can, that the rights of the person punished not be unduly sacrificed for the good of others. When speaking earlier of the general justification of punishment, we argued that the social benefits of punishing do not alone justify depriving the convicted offender of his rights: it is also necessary that the deprivation be deserved. A similar argument holds for allocation. When the offender is punished commensurately with his offense, the state is entitled to sacrifice his rights to that degree because that is what he deserves. A utilitarian theory of allocation (e.g., one based on deterrence) could lead to punishing the offender more severely than he deserves if the net benefits of so doing were to outweigh the costs. The excess in severity may be useful for society, but that alone should not justify the added intrusion into the rights of the person punished.

- The principle ensures that offenders are not treated as more (or less) blameworthy than is warranted by the character of the offense. Punishment, as we noted earlier, imparts blame. A criminal penalty is not merely unpleasant (so are taxes and conscription): it also connotes that the offender acted wrongfully and is reprehensible for having done so. The offender, in other words, is being treated *as though he deserves* the unpleasantness that is being inflicted on him. That being the case, it should be inflicted only to the degree that it is deserved.

Where standards of criminal liability are concerned, this is a familiar point—for Henry M. Hart made it nearly two decades ago in his defense of the criminal laws *mens rea* requirements. Since punishment characteristically ascribed blame, he contended, accidental violations should not be punished—because they are not blameworthy.

What is often overlooked, however, is that the same holds true after conviction. By then, it has been decided that the offender deserves punishment—but the question *how much* he deserves remains. The severity of the penalty carries implications of the degree of reprobation. The sterner the punishment, the greater the implicit blame: sending someone away for several years connotes that he is more to be condemned than does jailing him for a few months or putting him on probation. In the allocation of penalties, therefore, the crime should be sufficiently serious to merit the implicit reprobation. The principle of commensurate deserts ensures this. If the principle is not observed, the degree of reprobation becomes inappropriate. Where an offender convicted of a minor offense is punished severely, the blame which so drastic a penalty ordinarily carries will attach to him—and unjustly so, in view of the not-so-very-wrongful character of the offense. (This last argument, it should be noted, does not presuppose the general justification of punishment which we urged earlier. Whatever the ultimate aim of the criminal sanction—even if one were to defend its existence on purely utilitarian grounds—punishment still *in fact* ascribes blame to the person. Hence, the severity of the penalty—connoting as it does the degree of blame ascribed—ought to comport with the gravity of the infraction.)

Equity is sacrificed when the principle is disregarded, even when done for the sake of crime prevention. Suppose there are two kinds of offenses, *A* and *B,* that are of approximately equal seriousness but that offense *B* can more effectively be deterred through the use of a severe penalty. Notwithstanding the deterrent utility of punishing offense *B* more severely, the objection remains that the perpetrators of that offense are being treated as though they are more blameworthy than the perpetrators of offense *A*—and that is not so if the crimes are of equivalent gravity.

It is sometimes suggested that the principle of commensurate deserts sets only an upper limit on severity—*no more* than so much punishment. We disagree. Imposing only a slight penalty for a serious offense treats the offender as *less* blameworthy than he deserves. Understating the blame depreciates the values that are involved: disproportionately lenient punishment for murder implies that human life—the victim's life—is not worthy of much concern; excessively mild penalties for official corruption denigrate the importance of an equitable political process. The commensurateness principle, in our view, bars disproportionate leniency as well as disproportionate severity.

Norval Morris has recently suggested that the principle sets only broad upper and lower limits—and that, within those limits, the sentences should be determined on utilitarian grounds (e.g., deterrents). Again, we do not agree. Concededly, it is easier to discern gross excess in lenience or severity than to decide on a specific proportion between a crime and its punishment. But, as we have seen, the principle is infringed when disparate penalties are imposed on equally deserving offenders. If *A* and *B* commit a burglary under circumstances suggesting similar culpability, they deserve similar punishments; imposing unequal sanctions on them for utilitarian ends—even within the outer bounds of proportionality, Morris proposed—still unjustly treats one as though he were more to blame than the other. Our view of the principle as requiring equal treatment for the equally deserving has important implications for the structure of a penalty system, as we will see.

It has also been objected (by the drafters of the Model Sentencing Act, for instance) that applying the principle in sentencing decisions would aggravate disparities, given judges' divergent views of the seriousness of offenses. But that holds true only if, as in current practice, the assessment of seriousness is left to the discretion of the individual judge. The principle has to be consistently applied, and consistent application requires (as we will elaborate later) the articulation of standards in the placing of limits on individual decision makers' discretion.

The commensurate-deserts principle may sometimes conflict with other objectives: for example, if an offense is not serious but can better be deterred by a severe penalty, commensurate deserts and deterrence may suggest divergent sentences. To deal with such conflicts, it becomes necessary to decide what priority should be given the principle.

We think that the commensurate-deserts principle should have priority over other objectives in decisions about how much to punish. The disposition of convicted offenders should be commensurate with the seriousness of their offenses, even if greater or less severity would promote other goals. For the principle, we have argued, is a requirement of justice, whereas deterrence, incapacitation, and rehabilitation are essentially strategies for controlling crime. The priority of the principle follows from the assumption we stated at the outset: the requirements of justice ought to constrain the pursuit of crime prevention.

In giving the principle this priority, we need not claim the priority to be absolute: perhaps there are some unusual cases where it will be necessary to vary from the deserved sentence. But the principle derives its force from the fact that it applies *unless* special reasons for departing from it are shown: the burden rests on him who would deviate from the commensurate sentence.

Giving commensurate deserts this prominence will have practical usefulness in sorting out decisions about punishment. An often-repeated theme in the literature has been that the offender's disposition should be decided by "balancing" the different aims of punishment: the diverse considerations—rehabilitation, predictive restraint, deterrence, possibly desert as well—are to be weighed against each other, to yield an optimum penalty in the offender's particular case. When the different objectives are in conflict, however, saying they should be "balanced" against each other does not offer a principled way of resolving the issue. One escapes this difficulty by giving the commensurate-deserts principle prima facie controlling effect. No longer would it be necessary to weigh these conflicting objectives in each case. Rather, the disposition would be presumed to be—unless there are overriding grounds for deciding otherwise—the one which satisfies the principle of commensurate deserts. Instead of juggling competing rationales to reach a decision, one has a workable starting point.

Is Punishment Necessary?

JACKSON TOBY

OF eleven contemporary textbooks in criminology written by sociologists, ten have one or more chapters devoted to the punishment of offenders. All ten include a history of methods of punishment in Western society and, more specifically, a discussion of capital punishment. Seven discuss punishment in preliterate societies. Seven include theoretical or philosophical discussions of the "justification" of punishment—usually in terms of "retribution," "deterrence," and "reformation." These theoretical analyses are at least as much indebted to law and philosophy as to sociology. Thus, in considering the basis for punishment, three textbooks refer both to Jeremy Bentham and to Emile Durkheim; three textbooks refer to Bentham but not to Durkheim; and one textbook refers to Durkheim but not to Bentham. Several textbook writers express their opposition to punishment, especially to cruel punishment. This opposition is alleged to be based on an incompatibility of punishment with scientific considerations. The following quotation is a case in point:

We still punish primarily for vengeance, or to deter, or in the interest of a "just" balance of accounts between "deliberate" evildoers on the one hand and an injured and enraged society on the other. We do not yet generally punish or treat as scientific criminology would imply, namely, in order to change antisocial attitudes into social attitudes.

Most of the textbook writers note with satisfaction that "the trend in modern countries has been

From "Is Punishment Necessary?" by J. Toby, 1964, *Journal of Criminal Law, Criminology, and Police Science, 55*, pp. 332-337. Copyright 1964 by Jackson Toby. Originally published by Northwestern University School of Law. Reprinted by permission.

toward humanizing punishment and toward the reduction of brutalities." They point to the decreased use of capital punishment, the introduction of amenities into the modern prison by enlightened penology, and the increasing emphasis on nonpunitive and individualized methods of dealing with offenders, for example, probation, parole, or psychotherapy. In short, students reading these textbooks might infer that punishment is a vestigial carryover of a barbaric past and will disappear as humanitarianism and rationality spread. Let us examine this inference in terms of the motives underlying punishment and the necessities of social control.

THE URGE TO PUNISH

Many crimes have identifiable victims. In the case of crimes against the person, physical or psychic injuries have been visited upon the victim. In the case of crimes against property, someone's property has been stolen or destroyed. In pressing charges against the offender, the victim may express hostility against the person who injured him in a socially acceptable way. Those who identify with the victim—not only his friends and family but those who can imagine the same injury being done to them—may join with him in clamoring for the punishment of the offender. If, as has been argued, the norm of reciprocity is fundamental to human interaction, this hostility of the victim constituency toward offenders is an obstacle to the elimination of punishment from social life. Of course, the size of the group constituted by victims and those who identify with victims may be small. Empirical study would probably show that it varies by offense. Thus, it is possible that nearly everyone identifies with the victim of a murderer but relatively few people with the victim of a blackmailer. The greater the size of the victim constituency, the greater the opposition to a nonpunitive reaction to the offender.

It would be interesting indeed to measure the size and the composition of the victim constituencies for various crimes. Take rape as an illustration. Since the victims of rape are females, we might hypothesize that women would express greater punitiveness toward rapists than men and that degrees of hostility would correspond to real or imaginary exposure to rape. Thus, pretty young girls might express more punitiveness toward rapists than homely women. Among males, we might predict that greater punitiveness would be expressed by those with more reason to identify with the victims. Thus, males having sisters or daughters in the late teens or early 20s might express more punitiveness toward rapists than males lacking vulnerable "hostages to fortune."

Such a study might throw considerable light on the wellsprings of punitive motivation, particularly if victimization reactions were distinguished from other reasons for punitiveness. One way to explore such motivation would be to ask the same respondents to express their punitive predispositions toward offenses which do not involve victims at all, for example, gambling, or which involve victims of a quite different kind. Thus, rape might be balanced by an offense the victims of which are largely male. Survey research of this type is capable of ascertaining the opposition to milder penalties for various offenses. It would incidentally throw light on the comparatively gentle societal reaction to white-collar crime. Perhaps the explanation lies in the difficulty of identifying with the victims of patent infringement or watered hams.

THE SOCIAL CONTROL FUNCTIONS OF PUNISHMENT

Conformists who did identify with the *victim* are motivated to punish the offender out of some combination of rage and fear. Conformists who identify with the *offender*, albeit unconsciously, may wish to punish him for quite different reasons. Whatever the basis for the motivation to punish, the existence of punitive reactions to deviance is an obstacle to the abolition of punishment. However, it is by no means the sole obstacle. Even though a negligible segment of society felt punitive toward offenders, it might still not be feasible to eliminate punishment if the social control of deviance depended on it. Let us consider, therefore, the consequences of punishing offenders for (a) preventing crime, (b) sustaining the morale of conformists, and (c) rehabilitating offenders.

Punishment as a Means of Crime Prevention

Durkheim defined punishment as an act of vengeance. "What we avenge, what the criminal expiates, is the outrage to morality." But why is vengeance necessary? Not because of the need to deter the bulk of the population from doing likewise. The socialization process prevents most deviant behavior. Those who have introjected the moral norms of their society cannot commit crimes because their self-concepts will not permit them to do so. Only the unsocialized (and therefore amoral) individual fits the model of classical criminology and is deterred from expressing deviant impulses by a nice calculation of pleasures and punishments. Other things being equal, the anticipation of punishment would seem to have more deterrent value for inadequately socialized members of the group. It is difficult to investigate this proposition empirically because other motivationally relevant factors are usually varying simultaneously, for example, the situational temptations confronting various individuals, their optimism about the chances of escaping detection, and the differential impact of the same punishment on individuals of different status. Clearly, though, the deterrent effect of anticipated punishments is a complex empirical problem, and Durkheim was not interested in it. Feeling as he did that *some* crime is normal in every society, he apparently decided that the crime prevention function of punishment is not crucial. He pointed out that minute gradation in punishment would not be necessary if punishment were simply a means of deterring the potential offender (crime prevention). "Robbers are as strongly inclined to rob as murderers are to murder; the resistance offered by the former is not less than that of the latter, and consequently, to control it, we would have recourse to the same means." Durkheim was factually correct; the offenses punished most severely are not necessarily the one which present the greatest problem of social defense. Thus, quantitatively speaking, murder is an unimportant cause of death; in the United States it claims only half as many lives annually as does suicide and only one-fifth the toll of automobile accidents. Furthermore, criminologists have been unable to demonstrate a relationship between the murder rate of a community and its use or lack of use of capital punishment.

Most contemporary sociologists would agree with Durkheim that the anticipation of punishment is not the first line of defense against crime. The socialization process keeps most people law abiding, not the police—if for no other reason than the police are not able to catch every offender. This does not mean, however, that the police could be disbanded. During World War II, the Nazis deported all of Denmark's police force, thus providing a natural experiment testing the deterrent efficacy of formal sanctions. Crime increased greatly. Even though punishment is uncertain, especially under contemporary urban conditions, the possibility of punishment keeps some conformists law abiding. The empirical question is: *How many* conformists would become deviants if they did not fear punishment?

Punishment as a Means of Sustaining the Morale of Conformists

Durkheim considered punishment indispensable as a means of containing the demoralizing consequences of the crimes that could not be prevented. Punishment was not for Durkheim mere vindictiveness. Without punishment, Durkheim anticipated the demoralization of "upright people" in the face of defiance of the collective conscience. He believed that unpunished deviance tends to demoralize the conformist, and therefore he talked about punishment as a means of repairing "the wounds made upon collective sentiments." Durkheim was not

entirely clear; he expressed his ideas in metaphorical language. Nonetheless, we can identify the hypothesis that the punishment of offenders promotes the solidarity of conformists.

Durkheim anticipated psychoanalytic thinking as the following reformulation of his argument shows: one who resists the temptation to do what the group prohibits, to drive his car at 80 miles per hour, to beat up an enemy, to take what he wants without paying for it, would like to feel that these self-imposed abnegations have some meaning. When he sees others defy rules without untoward consequences, he needs some reassurance that his sacrifices were made in a good cause. If "the good die young and the wicked flourish as the green bay tree," the moral scruples which enable conformists to restrain their own deviant inclinations lack social validation. The social significance of punishing offenders is thereby defined as unsuccessful in the eyes of conformists, thus making the inhibition or repression of their own deviant impulses seem worthwhile. Righteous indignation is collectively sanctioned reaction formation. The law-abiding person who unconsciously resents restraining his desire to steal and murder has an opportunity, by identifying the police and the courts, to affect the precarious balance within his own personality between internal controls and the temptation to deviate. A bizarre example of this psychological mechanism is the man who seeks out homosexuals and beats them up mercilessly. Such pathological hostility toward homosexuals is due to the sadist's anxiety over his own sex-role identification. By "punishing" the homosexual, he denies the latent homosexuality in his own psyche. No doubt, some of the persons involved in the administration of punishment are sadistically motivated. But Durkheim hypothesized that the psychic equilibrium of the *ordinary* member of the group may be threatened by violation of norms; Durkheim was not concerned about psychopathological punitiveness.

Whatever the practical difficulties, Durkheim's hypothesis is, in principle, testable. It should be possible to estimate the demoralizing impact of nonconformity on conformists. Clearly, though, this is no simple matter. The extent of demoralization resulting from the failure to punish may vary with type of crime. The unpunished traffic violator may cause more demoralization than the unpunished exhibitionist —depending on whether or not outwardly conforming members of society are more tempted to exceed the speed limit than to expose themselves. The extent of demoralization may also vary with position in the social structure occupied by the conformist. Thus, Ranulf suggested that the middle class was especially vulnerable:

The disinterested tendency to inflict punishment is a distinctive characteristic of the lower middle class, that is, of a social class living under conditions which force its members to an extraordinarily high degree of self-restraint and subject them to much frustration of natural desires. If a psychological interpretation is to be put on this correlation of facts, it can hardly be to any other effect than that moral indignation is a kind of resentment caused by the repression of instincts.

Once the facts on the rate and the incidence of moral indignation are known, it will become possible to determine whether something must be done to the offender in order to prevent the demoralization of conformists. Suppose that research revealed that a very large proportion of conformists react with moral indignation to *most* violations of the criminal laws. Does this imply that punishment is a functional necessity? Durkheim apparently thought so, but he might have been less dogmatic in his approach to punishment had he specified the functional problem more clearly: making the nonconformist unattractive as a role model. If the norm violation can be defined as unenviable through some other process than by inflicting suffering upon him, punishment is not required by the exigencies of social control.

Punishment can be discussed on three distinct levels: (a) in terms of the motivations of the societal agents administering it, (b) in terms of the definition of the situation on the part of the person being punished, and (c) in terms of its impact on conformists. At this point, I am chiefly concerned with the third level, the impact on conformists. Note that punishment of

offenders sustains the morale of conformists only under certain conditions. The first has already been discussed, namely, that conformists unconsciously wish to violate the rules themselves. The second is that conformists implicitly assume that the nonconformity is a result of *deliberate defiance* of society's norms. For some conformists, this second condition is not met. Under the guidance of psychiatric thinking, some conformists assume that norm violation is the result of illness rather than wickedness. For such conformists, punishment of the offender does not contribute to their morale. Since they assume that the nonconformity is an involuntary symptom of a disordered personality, the offender is automatically unenviable because illness is (by definition) undesirable. Of course, it is an empirical question as to the relative proportions of the conforming members of society who make the "wicked" or the "sick" assumption about the motivation of the offender, but this can be discovered by investigation.

In Western industrial societies, there is increasing tendency to call contemporary methods of dealing with offenders "treatment" rather than "punishment." Perhaps this means that increasing proportions of the population are willing to accept the "sick" theory of nonconformity. Note, however, that the emphasis on "treatment" may be more a matter of symbolism than of substance. Although the definition of the situation as treatment rather than punishment tends to be humanizing—both to the offender and to the persons who must deal with him—there are still kind guards and cruel nurses. Furthermore, it would be an error to suppose that punishment is invariably experienced as painful by the criminal whereas treatment is always experienced as pleasant by the psychopathological offender. Some gang delinquents consider a reformatory sentence an opportunity to renew old acquaintances and to learn new delinquent skills; they resist fiercely the degrading suggestion that they need the services of the "nut doctor." Some mental patients are terrified by shock treatment and embarrassed by group therapy.

What then is the significance of the increasing emphasis on "treatment"? Why call an institution for the criminally insane a "hospital" although it bears a closer resemblance to a prison than to a hospital for the physically ill? In my opinion, the increased emphasis on treatment in penological thinking and practice reflects the existence of a large group of conformists who are undecided as between the "wicked" and the "sick" theories of nonconformity. When they observe that the offender is placed in "treatment," their provisional diagnosis of illness is confirmed, and therefore they do not feel that he has "gotten away with it." Note that "treatment" has the capacity to make the offender unenviable to conformists whether or not it is effective in rehabilitating him and whether or not he experiences it as pleasant. Those old-fashioned conformists who are not persuaded by official diagnoses of illness will not be satisfied by "treatment"; they will prefer to see an attempt made to visit physical suffering or mental anguish on the offender. For them, punishment is necessary to prevent demoralization.

Punishment as a Means of Reforming the Offender

Rehabilitation of offenders swells the number of conformists and therefore is regarded both by humanitarians and by scientifically minded penologists as more constructive than punishment. Most of the arguments against imprisonment and other forms of punishment in the correctional literature boil down to the assertion that punishment is incompatible with rehabilitation. The high rate of recidivism for prisons and reformatories is cited as evidence of the irrationality of punishment. What sense is there in subjecting offenders to the frustrations of incarceration? If rehabilitative programs are designed to help the offender cope with frustrations in his life situation, which presumably were responsible for this nonconformity, imprisoning him hardly seems a good way to begin. To generalize the argument, the status degradation inherent in punishment makes it more difficult to induce the offender to play a legitimate role instead of a nonconforming one. Whatever the offender's original motivations for nonconformity, punishment adds to them by neutraliz-

ing his fear of losing the respect of the community; he has already lost it.

Plausible though this argument is, empirical research has not yet verified it. The superior rehabilitative efficacy of "enlightened" prisons is a humanitarian assumption, but brutal correctional systems have, so far as is known, comparable recidivism rates to "enlightened" systems. True, the recidivism rate of offenders who are fined or placed on probation is less than the recidivism rate of offenders who are incarcerated, but this comparison is not merely one of varying degrees of punishment. Presumably, more severe punishment is meted out to criminals who are more deeply committed to a deviant way of life. Until it is demonstrated that the recidivism rates of strictly comparable populations of deviants differ depending on the degree of punitiveness with which they are treated, the empirical incompatibility of punishment and rehabilitation will remain an open question.

Even on theoretical grounds, however, the incompatibility of punishment and rehabilitation can be questioned once it is recognized that one may precede the other. Perhaps, as Lloyd McCorkle and Richard Korn think, some types of deviants become willing to change only if the bankruptcy of their way of life is conclusively demonstrated to them. On this assumption, punishment may be a necessary preliminary to a rehabilitative program in much the same way that shock treatment makes certain types of psychotics accessible to psychotherapy.

It seems to me that the compatibility of punishment and rehabilitation could be clarified (although not settled) if it were considered from the point of view of the *meaning* of punishment to the offender. Those offenders who regard punishment as a deserved deprivation resulting from their own misbehavior are qualitatively different from offenders who regard punishment as a misfortune bearing no relationship to morality. Thus, a child who is spanked by his father and the member of a bopping gang who is jailed for carrying concealed weapons are both "punished." But one accepts the deprivation as legitimate, and the other bows before superior force. I would hypothesize that punishment has rehabilitative significance only for the former. If this is so, correctional officials must convince the prisoner that his punishment is just before they can motivate him to change. This is no simple task. It is difficult for several reasons:

1. It is obvious to convicted offenders, if not to correctional officials, that *some* so-called criminals are being punished disproportionately for trifling offenses, whereas *some* predatory businessmen and politicians enjoy prosperity and freedom. To deny that injustices occur confirms the cynical in their belief that "legitimate" people are not only as predatory as criminals but hypocritical to boot. When correctional officials act as though there were no intermediate position between asserting that perfect justice characterizes our society and that it is a jungle, they make it more difficult to persuade persons undergoing punishment that the best approximation of justice is available that imperfect human beings can manage.

2. Of course, the more cases of injustice known to offenders, the harder it is to argue that the contemporary approximation of justice is the best that can be managed. It is difficult to persuade Negro inmates that their incarceration has moral significance if their life experience has demonstrated to them that the police and the courts are less scrupulous of *their* rights than of the rights of white persons. It is difficult to persuade an indigent inmate that his incarceration has moral significance if his poverty resulted in inadequate legal representation.

3. Finally, the major form of punishment for serious offenders (imprisonment) tends to generate a contraculture which denies that justice has anything to do with legal penalties. That is to say, it is too costly to confine large numbers of people in isolation from one another, yet congregate confinement results in the mutual reinforcement of self-justifications. Even those who enter prison feeling contrite are influenced by the self-righteous inmate climate; this may be part of the reason recidivism rates rise with each successive commitment.

In view of the foregoing consideration, I hypothesize that punishment—as it is now practiced in Western societies—is usually an obstacle to rehabilitation. Some exceptions to this generalization should be noted. A few small treatment institutions have not only prevented the development of a self-righteous contraculture but have managed to establish an inmate climate supportive of changed values. In such institutions, punishment has rehabilitative significance for the same reason it has educational significance in the normal family: it is legitimate.

To sum up: the social control functions of punishment include crime prevention, sustaining the morale of conformists, and the rehabilitation of offenders. All of the empirical evidence is not in, but it is quite possible that punishment contributes to some of these and interferes with others. Suppose, for example, that punishment is necessary for crime prevention and to maintain the morale of conformists but is generally an obstacle to the rehabilitation of offenders. Since the proportion of deviants is small in any viable system as compared with the proportion of conformists, the failure to rehabilitate them will not jeopardize the social order. Therefore, under these assumptions, sociological counsel would favor the continued employment of punishment.

CONCLUSION

A member of a social system who violates its cherished rules threatens the stability of that system. Conformists who identify with the victim are motivated to punish the criminal in order to feel safe. Conformists who unconsciously identify with the criminal fear their own ambivalence. If norm violation is defined by conformists as willful, visiting upon the offender some injury or degradation will make him unenviable. If his behavior is defined by conformists as a symptom of pathology they are delighted not to share, putting him into treatment validates their diagnosis of undesirable illness. Whether he is "punished" or "treated," however, the disruptive consequence of his deviance is contained. Thus, from the viewpoint of social control, the alternative outcomes of the punishment or treatment processes, rehabilitation or recidivism, are less important than the deviant's neutralization as a possible role model. Whether punishment is or is not necessary rests ultimately on empirical questions: (1) the extent to which identification with the victim occurs, (2) the extent to which nonconformity is pre-vented by the anticipation of punishment, (3) what the consequences are for the morale of conformists of punishing the deviant or of treating his imputed pathology, and (4) the compatibility between punishment and rehabilitation.

SUGGESTED READINGS

Becker, Gary S. 1968. "Crime and Punishment: An Economic Approach." *Journal of Political Economy* 76:169-217.

Black, Donald. 1976. *The Behavior of Law.* New York: Academic Press.

Blumstein, Alfred, Jacqueline Cohen, and David Nagin. 1978. *Deterrence and Incapacitation: Estimating the Effects of Criminal Sanctions on Crime Rates.* Washington, DC: National Academy of Science.

Cook, Philip J. 1977. "Punishment and Crime: A Critique of Current Findings Concerning the Preventive Effect of Criminal Sanctions." *Law and Contemporary Problems* 41:164-204.

Ehrlich, Isaac. 1973. "Participation in Illegitimate Activities: A Theoretical and Empirical Investigation." *Journal of Political Economy* 81:521-64.

Hawkins, Gordon. 1969. "Punishment and Deterrence: The Educative, Moralizing and Habituative Effects." *Wisconsin Law Review* 2:550-65.

Morris, Norval. 1981. "Punishment, Desert, and Rehabilitation." Pp. 257-71 in *Sentencing,* edited by Hyman Gross and Andrew von Hirsch. New York: Oxford University Press.

Spelman, William. 1994. *Criminal Incapacitation.* New York: Plenum.

van den Haag, Ernest. 1975. *Punishing Criminals: Concerning a Very Old and Painful Question.* New York: Basic Books.

von Hirsch, Andrew. 1985. *Past or Future Crimes.* New Brunswick, NJ: Rutgers University Press.

QUESTIONS FOR DISCUSSION AND WRITING

1. Describe the types of inferential errors that Zimring and Hawkins argue many policymakers, judges, and legislators make in concluding from statistical data that punishments deter.

2. What evidence do Bowers and Pierce present supporting the idea that executions have a brutalizing effect on the American public? How compelling is their evidence and argument?

3. Contrast the findings of Sherman and Berk with those reported by Dunford and his colleagues. What are the differences? What are the similarities?

4. What is the hypothetical value of incapacitation as a strategy for controlling crime and criminal behavior?

5. What are some of the major problems associated with implementing selective incapacitation as a sentencing or punitive policy?

6. Zimring and Hawkins argue that estimates of crime reductions that might be achieved using selective incapacitation are seriously flawed. Do their criticisms undermine the incapacitation argument? Explain why or why not.

7. Menninger argues that we should treat crime as though it were a disease. Do you believe crime is treatable—and thus, curable—with education, counseling, and employment training? Explain why or why not.

8. Contrast the conclusions of Martinson and Sechrest and his associates about rehabilitation with the conclusions of Andrews and his colleagues. Is it possible to reconcile the conflicting perspectives?

9. What future directions for research on rehabilitation are suggested by Lab and Whitehead?

10. Proponents of retribution argue that the primary purpose for punishment is to inflict pain on offenders commensurate with the pain their actions have inflicted on society. What implications does this approach to punishment have for judicial sentencing practices and the development of sentencing policies by state and federal legislators?

III

WHAT ROLE DO POLICE PLAY IN CRIMINAL JUSTICE?

THE administration of criminal justice begins with the police. Police officers are the gatekeepers of the legal process—their arrests direct the flow of criminal cases to prosecutors for the filing of criminal charges. In this capacity, police have enormous power. Their decisions to arrest initiate a process by which the state asserts its coercive control over individuals accused of crime. Because the law is never fully enforced—police learn about only a small subset of all crimes and act on an even smaller subset—police exercise great discretion in determining which offenders and which criminal acts are ultimately punished by the state. They have the discretion to be lenient and to ignore entire classes of law violations and violators. They also have the discretion to be punitive and to ensure that even the most petty offense is punished.

Among criminologists and others studying law enforcement and the police, there are many areas of controversy and concern. One of these areas is the exercise of discretion in decisions to arrest individuals accused of crime. Whereas some studies suggest that police action is often capricious and directed as much by the status characteristics (e.g., race, age, gender, and social class) of the accused as by the offense they allegedly committed, others suggest that police more often than not exercise discretion judiciously, typically arresting only those individuals for whom there exists probable cause that they committed a crime. A related area of controversy involves those aspects of policing that influence how discretion is exercised. Numerous studies suggest that there exist unique aspects to police work that assist in explaining how and why police officers make decisions to arrest. Of concern is whether the exercise of discretion is an inherent part of police work that is extremely difficult to monitor and control.

A third area of controversy is police use of deadly force. Unlike any other agency of the state except the military, police are authorized to kill persons who represent serious threats to public safety. Numerous scholars have examined when and under what circumstances police exercise deadly force. Finally, many researchers have examined the actual effects of police practices on community levels and patterns of crime. At the heart of this concern is whether police patrol practices or special crime reduction programs actually influence area levels of criminal behavior, with some practices or programs reducing crime more than others. In recent years, police departments across the country have adopted new patrolling strategies in response to increased concern about fear of crime and actual levels of criminal behavior. An important issue is whether these strategies have yielded significant reductions in levels of fear or in rates of crime.

Part III of our book is divided into two sections. The first section focuses on the general exercise of police discretion. Donald Black's essay, "The Social Organization of Arrest," establishes the context for the remaining essays in this section. Black reports the results of an observational study of policing that shows that the likelihood of arrest is influenced by the social context in which the arrest occurs. He observes that although the police are typically lenient in their routine arrest practices, the probability of arrest is higher in legally serious crime situations than in those of a minor nature. The probability of arrest is also high, however, when a suspect is disrespectful toward the police or when the relational distance between the complainant and suspect is great. Black concludes that police exercise discretion according to these and other characteristics of the context in which arrest decisions are made.

The second and third essays in the section are excerpts from two important studies of policing: Jerome Skolnick's seminal work *Justice Without Trial* and James Q. Wilson's landmark research, titled *Varieties of Police Behavior.* Skolnick's essay, "The Police Officer's 'Working Personality,' " examines aspects of police work that shape the exercise of discretion. Skolnick refers to the conflicting pressures of danger and authority in police work that complicate how officers respond to calls and situations they encounter. In contrast, Wilson's essay, "Police Discretion," reveals that discretion is exercised according to characteristics of the situation (i.e., does it involve law enforcement or order maintenance?) and nature of the police response (i.e., is the action initiated by a citizen or by the police?). Wilson introduces the reader to a scheme classifying police action into four different combinations of situational characteristics and types of responses, with each combination suggesting a different approach to the exercise of discretion.

The fourth essay in the section examines violence in police/citizen encounters. The essay by James Fyfe, titled "Police Use of Deadly Force," reviews research on the factors influencing when and under what circumstances police discharge firearms in encounters with citizens. Fyfe concludes that an extremely important factor affecting the use of deadly force is the organizational context of policing—specifically, departmental policies, informal norms, and the training afforded individual officers.

The final essay in this section of Part III reexamines the work of Black and others, focusing on the social context of arrest. David Klinger's essay, "Demeanor or Crime? Why 'Hostile' Citizens Are More Likely to Be Arrested," reports the results of an observational study of police arrest practices. In contrast to many previous studies, Klinger's research adjusts for the presence of crimes committed in front of the police in analyzing whether hostile or disrespectful behavior increases the likelihood of arrest. Challenging the results of previous studies, Klinger's results show that once adjustments are made for the types of crime committed, particularly those committed in the presence of police officers, hostility or disrespect for the police has no substantial effect on the likelihood of arrest.

The second section of Part III examines different approaches to policing and their relationship to community levels of crime. The first essay is James Q. Wilson and George Kelling's "Broken Windows: The Police and Neighborhood Safety." Wilson and Kelling maintain that traditional conceptions of policing may not be very useful in combating urban crime. Their essay points to the complex problems of some urban areas and suggests that police must work closely in conjunction with community members to address the crime problem effectively. They argue that police work must be tailored to the unique problems of each community.

One approach police use to reduce or displace levels of crime in areas within cities or communities is the police crackdown. Lawrence Sherman's essay, "Police Crackdowns," offers an extensive review of the results of different crackdowns and some of the problems associated with this approach to policing. Sherman provides evidence that some crackdowns initially deter, or at least displace, crime. However, Sherman found that crackdowns have been difficult to sustain over long periods, with decaying deterrence being a frequent problem. The major obstacle to broader police use of crackdowns is one of resources—the limited number of personnel sets firm limits on the feasibility of sustained crackdowns in most departments.

One of the most important experiments in policing is reported by George Kelling and his colleagues in their essay "The Kansas City Preventive Patrol Experiment: A Summary Report," an excerpt from their report with the same title. The essay reviews the results of an experiment conducted in Kansas City, Missouri, examining whether increased preventive patrol by police officers in neighborhoods substantially reduces crime and fear of crime. The experiment yielded surprising results. Increased routine patrols by police in the experimental neighborhoods yielded no substantial changes in levels of crime, arrests, or fear of crime among neighborhood residents or businesses. The essay summarizes these and other study findings, concluding that police are seriously limited in their ability to both prevent crime and apprehend offenders once they have committed crimes.

The final essay, "Problem-Oriented Policing" by Herman Goldstein, reviews new approaches to policing. As described in the essay, problem-oriented or community policing stresses the importance of targeting substantive and frequently occurring problems in neighborhoods and communities. Unlike more traditional police patrol, the problem-oriented approach described by Goldstein stresses coordinated work with other agencies and groups in communities and neighborhoods. At the heart of this approach is the assumption that officers must play an active role in assisting communities to solve their local crime problems.

POLICE DISCRETION

The Social Organization of Arrest

DONALD J. BLACK

THIS essay offers a set of descriptive materials on the social conditions under which policemen make arrests in routine encounters. At this level, it is a modest increment in the expanding literature on the law's empirical face. Scholarship on law-in-action has concentrated upon criminal law in general and the world of the police in particular. Just what, beyond the hoarding of facts, these empirical studies will yield, however, is still unclear. Perhaps a degree of planned change in the criminal justice system will follow, be it in legal doctrine or in legal administration. In any event, evaluation certainly appears to be the purpose, and reform the expected outcome, of much empirical research. This chapter pursues a different sort of yield from its empirical study: a sociological theory of law. The analysis is self-consciously inattentive to policy reform or evaluation of the police; it is intentionally bloodless in tone. It examines arrest in order to infer patterns relevant to an understanding of all instances of legal control. The inquiry seeks to discover general principles according to which policemen routinely use or withhold their power to arrest, and thus to reveal a part of the social organization of arrest.

FIELD METHOD

The data were collected during the summer of 1966 by systematic observation of police-citizen transactions in Boston, Chicago, and Washington, D.C. Thirty-six observers—persons

with law, social science, and police administration backgrounds—recorded observations of encounters between uniformed patrolmen and citizens. Observers recorded the data in "incident booklets," forms structurally similar to interview schedules. One booklet was used for each incident. A field situation involving police action was classified as an "incident" if it was brought to the officer's attention by the police radio system, or by a citizen on the street or in the police station, or if the officer himself noticed a situation and decided that it required police attention. Also included as incidents were a handful of situations which the police noticed themselves but which they chose to ignore.

ROUTINE POLICE WORK

In some respects, selecting arrest as a subject of study implicitly misrepresents routine police work. Too commonly, the routine is equated with the exercise of the arrest power, not only by members of the general public but by lawyers and even many policemen as well. In fact, the daily round of the patrol officer infrequently involves arrest of or even encounters with a criminal suspect. The most cursory observation of the policeman on the job overturns the imagery of a man who makes his living parceling citizens into jail.

Somewhat less than half of the encounters arising from a citizen phone call have to do with a crime—a felony or a misdemeanor other than juvenile trouble. Yet even criminal incidents are so constituted situational as to preclude arrest in the majority of cases, because no suspect is present when the police arrive at the scene. In

From "The Social Organization of Arrest" by D. J. Black, 1971, *Stanford Law Review, 23,* 1087-1111. Copyright by the Board of Trustees of the Leland Stanford Junior University. Reprinted by permission.

77 percent of the felony situations and in 51 percent of the misdemeanor situations, the only major citizen participant is a complainant. In a handful of other cases, the only citizen present is an informant or bystander. When no suspect is available in the field setting, the typical official outcome is a crime report, the basic document from which official crime statistics are constructed and the operational prerequisite of further investigation by the detective division.

The minority of citizen-initiated crime encounters where a suspect is present when the police arrive is the appropriate base for a study of arrests. In the great majority of these suspect encounters, a citizen complainant also takes part in the situational interaction, so any study of routine arrest must consider the complainant's role as well as those of the police officer and the suspect.

Through their own discretionary authority, policemen occasionally initiate encounters that may be called *proactive* police work, as opposed to the *reactive,* citizen-initiated work that consumes the greater part of the average patrol officer's day. On an evening shift (traditionally, 4 p.m. to midnight), a typical workload for a patrol car is six radio-dispatched encounters and one proactive encounter. The ratio of proactive encounters varies enormously by shift, day of week, patrol beat or territory, and number of cars on duty. An extremely busy weekend night could involve 20 dispatches to a single car. Under these rushed conditions, the officers might not initiate any encounters on their own. At another time in another area, a patrol car might receive no dispatches, but the officers might initiate as many as 8 or 10 encounters on the street. During the observation study, only 13 percent of incidents came to police attention without the assistance of citizens. Still, most officers as well as citizens probably think of proactive policing as the form that epitomizes the police function.

The police-initiated encounter is a bald confrontation between state and citizen. Hardly ever does a citizen complainant take part in a proactive field encounter and then only if a policeman were to discover an incident of personal victimization or if a complainant were to step forth subsequent to the officer's initial encounter with a suspect. Moreover, the array of incidents policemen handle—their operational jurisdiction—is quite different when they have the discretion to select situations for attention compared to what it is when that discretion is lodged in citizens. In reactive police work, they are servants of the public, with one consequence being that the social troubles they oversee often have little if anything to do with the criminal law. Arrest is usually a situational impossibility. In proactive policing, the officer is more a public guardian and the operational jurisdiction is a police choice; the only limits are in law and in department policy. In proactive police work, arrest is totally a matter of the officer's own making. Yet the reality of proactive police work has an ironic quality about it. The organization of crime in time and space deprives policemen on free patrol of legally serious arrests. Most felonies occur in off-street settings and must be detected by citizens. Even those that occur in a visible public place usually escape the policemen's ken. When the police have an opportunity to initiate an encounter, the occasion is more likely than not a traffic violation. Traffic violations comprise the majority of proactive encounters, and most of the remainder concern minor "disturbances of the peace." In short, where the police role is most starkly aggressive in form, the substance is drably trivial, and legally trivial incidents provide practically all of the grist for arrest in proactive police operations.

Perhaps a study of arrest flatters the legal significance of the everyday police encounter. Still, even though arrest situations are uncommon in routine policing, invocation of the criminal process accounts for more formal legal cases, more court trials and sanctions, and more public controversies and conflicts than any other mechanism in the legal system. As a major occasion of legal control, then, arrest cries out for empirical study.

COMPLAINANT AND SUSPECT

The police encounter involving both a suspect and a complainant is a microcosm of a total legal control system. In it are personified the state, the alleged threat to social order, and the citizenry. The complainant is to a police encounter what an interest group is to a legislature or a plaintiff to a civil lawsuit. His presence makes a dramatic difference in police encounters, particularly if he assumes the role of situational lobbyist. This section will show, inter alia, that the fate of suspects rests nearly as much with complainants as it does with police officers themselves.

Of the 176 encounters involving both a complainant and a suspect, a little over one-third were alleged to be felonies; the remainder were misdemeanors of one or another variety. Not surprisingly, the police make arrests more often in felony than in misdemeanor situations, but the difference is not as wide as might be expected. An arrest occurs in 58 percent of the felony encounters and in 44 percent of the misdemeanor encounters. The police, then, release roughly half of the persons they suspect of crimes. This strikingly low arrest rate requires explanation.

Evidence

Factors other than the kind of evidence available to an officer in the field setting affect the probability of arrests, for even exceptionally clear situational evidence of criminal liability does not guarantee that arrest will follow a police encounter.

One of two major forms of evidence ordinarily is present when the police confront a suspect in the presence of a complainant: either the police arrive at the setting in time to witness the offense, or a citizen—usually the complainant himself—gives testimony against the suspect. Only rarely is some other kind of evidence available, such as a physical clue on the premises or on the suspect's person. On the other hand, in only three of the complainant-suspect encounters was situational evidence entirely absent. In these few cases, the police acted upon what they knew from the original complaint as it was relayed to them by radio dispatch and upon what they heard about the crime from the complainant, but they had no other information apparent in the field situation linking the suspect to the alleged crime.

In a great majority of felony situations, the best evidence accessible to the police is citizen testimony, whereas in misdemeanor situations the police generally witness the offense themselves. These evidentiary circumstances are roughly equivalent as far as the law of arrest is concerned, since the requirements for a misdemeanor arrest without a formal warrant are more stringent than are those for a felony arrest. In most jurisdictions, the police must observe the offense or acquire a signed complaint before they may arrest a misdemeanor suspect in the field. In felony situations, however, they need only have "probable cause" or "reasonable grounds" to believe the suspect is guilty. Thus, although the evidence usually is stronger in misdemeanor than in felony situations, the law in effect compensates the police by giving them more power in the felony situations where they would otherwise be at a disadvantage. Correspondingly, the law of arrest undermines the advantage felons in the aggregate would otherwise enjoy.

The Complainant's Preference

While complainants frequently are present when policemen fail to invoke the law against suspects who are highly vulnerable to arrest, the complainants do not necessarily resent police leniency. In 24 percent of the misdemeanor situations and in 21 percent of the felony situations, the complainant expresses to the police a preference for clemency toward the suspect. The complainant manifests a preference for an arrest in 34 percent of the misdemeanors and in 48 percent of the felonies. In the remainder of encounters, the complainant's preference is unclear; frequently, the complainant's outward behavior is passive, especially in misdemeanor situations.

In felony situations where a citizen's testimony links a suspect to the crime, arrest results in about three-fourths of the cases in which the complainant specifies a preference for that outcome. When the complainant prefers no arrest, the police go against his wishes in only about one-tenth of the cases. Passive or unexpressive complainants see the police arrest suspects in a little under two-thirds of the situations where the police have a complainant's testimonial evidence. Thus, when the complainant leaves the decision to arrest wholly in police hands, the

TABLE 1

Arrest rates in citizen-initiated encounters, according to type of crime and race of suspect.

Crime	Race	Total Number of Incidents	Arrest Rate (in percentages)
Felony	Black	48	60
	White	11	45
Misdemeanor	Black	75	47
	White	42	38
All crimes	Black	123	52
	White	53	39

police are by no means reluctant to arrest the felony suspect. They become strikingly reluctant only when a complainant exerts pressure on the suspect's behalf.

Relational Distance

When police enter into an encounter involving both a complainant and a suspect, they find themselves not only in a narrow legal conflict but also in a conflict between citizen adversaries within a social relationship—one between family members, acquaintances, neighbors, friends, business associates, or total strangers. The data suggest that police arrest practices vary with the relational nature of complainant-suspect conflicts. The probability of arrest is highest when the citizen adversaries have the most distant social relation to one another, that is, when they are strangers. The felony cases especially reveal that arrest becomes more probable as the relational distance increases. Forty-five percent of suspects are arrested in a family member relationship; 77 percent in a friends, neighbors, acquaintances relationship; and 7 out of 8 or 88 percent in a stranger relationship. In the misdemeanor cases, the pattern is not so consistent. Although the likelihood of arrest is still highest in conflicts between strangers, the lowest likelihood is in situations involving friends, neighbors, or acquaintances. When the complainant's preference is unclear, or when he pre-

fers no arrest, no difference of any significance is discernible across the categories of relational distance; the type of social conflict embodied in the police encounter visibly affects arrest probability only when the complainant presses the police to make an arrest.

Race, Respect, and the Complainant

Police arrest blacks at a higher rate than whites. But no evidence supports the view that the police discriminate against blacks. Rather, the race differential seems to be a function of the relatively higher rate at which black suspects display disrespect toward the police. When the arrest rate for respectful black suspects is compared to that for respectful whites, no difference is apparent. Before examining this last finding in detail, however, the importance of citizen respect in itself should be established.

Considering felony and misdemeanor situations together, the arrest rate for very deferential suspects is 40 percent of 10 cases. For civil suspects, it is effectively the same at 42 percent of 71 cases, but it is 70 percent of 37 cases for antagonistic or disrespectful suspects. Unquestionably, the suspect who refuses to defer to police authority takes a gamble with his freedom. This pattern persists in felony and misdemeanor situations when they are examined separately, but the small samples that result from dividing the data by type of crime prevent any more refined comparison than between civil and disrespectful levels of deference. In the aggregate of cases, the police are more likely to arrest a misdemeanor suspect who is disrespectful toward them than a felony suspect who is civil. In this sense, the police enforce their authority more severely than they enforce the law.

GENERALIZATIONS

Mobilization

Most arrest situations arise through citizen rather than police initiative. In this sense, the criminal law is invoked in a manner not unlike that of private-law systems that are mobilized through a reactive process, depending upon the enterprise of citizen claimants in pursuit of their own interests. In criminal law as in other areas of public law, although the state has formal proactive authority to bring legal actions, the average criminal matter is the product of a citizen complaint.

One implication of this pattern is that most criminal cases pass through a moral filter in the citizen population before the state assumes its enforcement role. A major portion of the responsibility for criminal-law enforcement is kept out of police hands. In this sense, all legal systems rely to a great extent upon private citizens.

Complainants

Arrest practices sharply reflect the preferences of citizen complainants, particularly when the desire is for leniency and also, although less frequently, when the complainant demands arrest. The police are an instrument of the complainant, then, in two ways: generally, they handle what the complainant wants them to handle and they handle the matter in the way the complainant prescribes.

The pattern of police compliance with complainants gives police work a radically democratic character. The result is not, however, uniform standards of justice, since the moral standards of complainants doubtlessly vary to some extent across the population. Indeed, by complying with complainants the police in effect perpetuate the moral diversity they encounter in the citizen mass. In this respect again, a public-law system bears similarity to systems of private law. Both types seem organized, visibly and invisibly, so as to give priority to the demands of their disposed citizens.

Leniency

The police are lenient in their routine arrest practices; they use their arrest power less often than the law would allow. Legal leniency, however, is hardly peculiar to the police. Especially in the private-law sector, and also in other areas of public law, the official process for redress of grievances is invoked less often than illegality is detected. Citizens and public officials display reluctance to wield legal power in immediate response to illegality, and a sociology of law must treat as problematic the fact that legal cases arise at all.

Evidence

Evidence is an important factor in arrest. The stronger the evidence in the field situation, the more likely is an arrest. When the police themselves witness a criminal offense, they are more likely to arrest the suspect than when they only hear about the offense from a third party. Rarely do the police confront persons as suspects without some evidence; even more rarely are arrests unsupported by evidence. The importance of situational evidence hardly constitutes a major advance in knowledge. Evidence has a role in every legal process. It is the definition of evidence, not whether evidence is required, that differs across legal systems. It should be emphasized that even when the evidence against a suspect is very strong, the police frequently take action short of arrest. Evidence alone, then, is a necessary but not a sufficient basis for predicting invocation of the law.

Seriousness

The probability of arrest is higher in legally serious crime situations than in those of a relatively minor nature. This finding certainly is not unexpected, but it has theoretical significance. The police levy arrest as a sanction to correspond with the defined seriousness of the criminal event in much the same fashion as legislators and judges allocate punishments. The formal legal conception of arrest contrasts sharply with this practice by holding that arrest follows upon detection of any criminal act without distinguishing among levels of legal seriousness. Assuming the offender population is aware that arrest represents legislation and adjudication by police officers, arrest practices should contribute to deterrence of serious crime, for the perpetrator whose act is detected risks a greater likelihood of arrest as well as more severe punishment. The higher risk of arrest, once the suspect confronts the police, may help to offset the low probability of detection for some of the more serious crimes.

Intimacy

The greater the relational distance between a complainant and a suspect, the greater is the likelihood of arrest. When a complainant demands the arrest of a suspect, the police are most apt to comply if the adversaries are strangers. Arrest is less likely if they are friends, neighbors, or acquaintances, and it is least likely if they are family members. Policemen also write official crime reports according to the same differential. Relational distance likewise appears to be a major factor in the probability of litigation in contract disputes and other private-law contexts. One may generalize that in all legal affairs relational distance between the adversaries affects the ability of formal litigation. If the generalization is true, it teaches that control may have comparatively little to do with the maintenance of order between and among intimates.

Yet the findings on relational distance in police arrest practices may merely reflect the fact that legal control operates only when sublegal control is unavailable. The greater the relational distance, the less is the likelihood that sublegal mechanisms of control will operate. This proposition even seems a useful principle for understanding the increasing salience of legal control in social evolution. Over time, the drift of history delivers proportionately more and more strangers who need the law to hold them together and apart. Law seems to bespeak an absence of community, and law grows ever more prominent as the dissolution of community proceeds.

Disrespect

The probability of arrest increases when a suspect is disrespectful toward the police. The same pattern appears in youth officer behavior, patrol officer encounters with juveniles, and in the use of illegal violence by the police. Even disrespectful complainants receive a penalty of sorts from the police, as their complaints are less likely to receive official recognition. In form, disrespect in a police encounter is much the same as "contempt" in a courtroom hearing. It is a rebellion against the processing system. Unlike the judge, however, the policeman has no special legal weapons in his arsenal for dealing with citizens who refuse to defer to his authority at a verbal or otherwise symbolic level. Perhaps as the legal system further differentiates, a crime of "contempt of police" will emerge. From a radically behavioral standpoint, indeed, this crime has already emerged; the question is when it will be formalized in the written law.

All legal control systems, not only the police and the judiciary, defend their own authority with energy and dispatch. To question or assault the legitimacy of a legal control process is to invite legal invocation, a sanction, or a more serious sanction, whatever is at issue in a given confrontation. Law seems to lash out at every revolt against its own integrity. Accordingly, it might be useful to consider disrespect toward a policeman to be a minor form of civil disorder, or revolution the highest form of disrespect.

Discrimination

No evidence exists to show that the police discriminate on the basis of race. The police arrest blacks at a comparatively high rate, but the difference between the races appears to result primarily from the greater rate at which blacks show disrespect for the police. The behavioral difference thus lies with the citizen participants, not the police. This finding conflicts with some ideological conceptions of police work, but it is supported by the findings of several studies based upon direct observation of the police. These findings should be taken as a caveat that, in general, improper or illegal behavior toward blacks does not in itself constitute evidence of discrimination toward blacks. A finding of discrimination or of nondiscrimination requires a comparative analysis of behavior toward each race with other variables such as level of respect held constant. No study of citizen opinions or perceptions or of official statistics can hold these variables constant.

The findings on racial discrimination by the police should not remotely suggest that law is oblivious to social rank. On the contrary, broader patterns in the form and substance of legal control seem at any one time to reflect and to perpetuate existing systems of social stratification. That the degradation of arrest is reserved primarily for the kinds of illegality committed by lower-status citizens exemplifies this broader tendency of the law in action.

The Police Officer's "Working Personality"

JEROME SKOLNICK

A recurrent theme of the sociology of occupations is the effect of a man's work on his outlook on the world. Doctors, janitors, lawyers, and industrial workers develop distinctive ways of perceiving and responding to their environment. Here we shall concentrate on analyzing certain outstanding elements in the police milieu, danger, authority, and efficiency, as they combine to generate distinctive cognitive and behavioral responses in police: a "working personality." Such an analysis does not suggest that all police are alike in working personality but that there are distinctive cognitive tendencies in police as an occupational grouping. Some of these may be found in other occupations sharing similar problems. So far as exposure to danger is concerned, the policeman may be likened to the soldier. His problems as an authority bear a certain similarity to those of the schoolteacher, and the pressures he feels to prove himself efficient are not unlike those felt by the industrial worker. The combination of these elements, however, is unique to the policeman. Thus, the police, as a result of combined features of their social situation, tend to develop ways of looking at the world distinctive to themselves, cognitive lenses through which to see situations and events. The strength of the lenses may be weaker or stronger depending on certain conditions, but they are ground on a similar axis.

Analysis of the policeman's cognitive propensities is necessary to understand the practical dilemma faced by police required to maintain order under a democratic rule of law. A conception of order is essential to the resolution of this dilemma. The paramilitary character of police organization naturally leads to a high evaluation of similarity, routine, and predictability. Our intention is to emphasize features of the policeman's environment interacting with the paramilitary police organization to generate a working personality. Such an intervening concept should aid in explaining how the social environment of police affects their capacity to respond to the rule of law.

This essay places emphasis on the division of labor in the police department; "operational law enforcement" cannot be understood outside these special work assignments. It is therefore important to explain how the hypothesis emphasizing the generalizability of the policeman's working personality is compatible with the idea that police division of labor is an important analytical dimension for understanding operational law enforcement. Compatibility is evident when one considers the different levels of analysis at which the hypotheses are being developed. Janowitz states, for example, that the military profession is more than an occupation; it is a "style of life" because the occupational claims over one's daily existence extend well beyond official duties. He is quick to point out that any profession performing a crucial "life and death" task, such as medicine, the ministry, or the police, develops such claims. A conception like working personality of police should be understood to suggest an analytic breadth similar to that of style of life. That is, just as the professional behavior of military officers with

From *Justice Without Trial: Law Enforcement in a Democratic Society* (pp. 41-58) by J. Skolnick, 1966, New York: John Wiley and Sons. Copyright 1994 Prentice Hall, Upper Saddle River, New Jersey. Adapted by permission.

similar styles of life may differ drastically depending upon whether they command an infantry battalion or participate in the work of an intelligence unit, so too does the professional behavior of police officers with similar working personalities vary with their assignments.

The process by which this personality is developed may be summarized: the policeman's role contains two principal variables, danger and authority, which should be interpreted in the light of a "constant" pressure to appear efficient. The element of danger seems to make the policeman especially attentive to signs indicating a potential for violence and lawbreaking. As a result, the policeman is generally a "suspicious" person. Furthermore, the character of the policeman's work makes him less desirable as a friend, since norms of friendship implicate others in his work. Accordingly, the element of danger isolates the policeman socially from that segment of the citizenry which he regards as symbolically dangerous and also from the conventional citizenry with whom he identifies.

The element of authority reinforces the element of danger in isolating the policeman. Typically, the policeman is required to enforce laws representing puritanical morality, such as those prohibiting drunkenness, and also laws regulating the flow of public activity, such as traffic laws. In these situations, the policeman directs the citizenry, whose typical response denies recognition of his authority, and stresses his obligation to respond to danger. The kind of man who responds well to danger, however, does not normally subscribe to codes of puritanical morality. As a result, the policeman is unusually liable to the charge of hypocrisy. That the whole civilian world is an audience for the policeman further promotes police isolation and, in consequence, solidarity. Finally, danger undermines the judicious use of authority. Where danger, as in Britain, is relatively less, the judicious application of authority is facilitated. Hence, British police may appear to be somewhat more attached to the rule of law, when, in fact, they may appear so because they face less danger, and they are as a rule better skilled than American police in creating the appearance of conformity to procedural regulations.

THE SYMBOLIC ASSAILANT AND POLICE CULTURE

In attempting to understand the policeman's view of the world, it is useful to raise a more general question: what are the conditions under which police, as authorities, may be threatened? The policeman, because his work requires him to be occupied continually with potential violence, develops a perceptual shorthand to identify certain kinds of people as symbolic assailants, that is, as persons who use gesture, language, and attire that the policeman has come to recognize as a prelude to violence. This does not mean that violence by the symbolic assailant is necessarily predictable. On the contrary, the policeman responds to the vague indication of danger suggested by appearance. Like the animals of the experimental psychologist, the policeman finds the threat of random damage more compelling than a predetermined and inevitable punishment.

Nor, to qualify for the status of symbolic assailant, need an individual ever have used violence. A man backing out of a jewelry store with a gun in one hand and jewelry in the other would qualify even if the gun were a toy and he had never in his life fired a real pistol. To the policeman in the situation, the man's personal history is momentarily immaterial. There is only one relevant sign: a gun, signifying danger. Similarly, a young man may suggest the threat of violence to the policeman by his manner of walking or "strutting," the insolence in the demeanor being registered by the policeman as a possible preamble to later attack. Signs vary from area to area, but a youth dressed in a black leather jacket and motorcycle boots is sure to draw at least a suspicious glance from a policeman.

Policemen themselves do not necessarily emphasize the peril associated with their work when questioned directly and may even have well-developed strategies of denial. The element of danger is so integral to the policeman's work that explicit recognition might induce emotional barriers to work performance. Thus, one patrol officer observed that more police have been killed and injured in automobile accidents in the past ten years than from gunfire. Although his assertion is true, he neglected to mention that the police are the only peacetime occupational group with a systematic record of death and injury from gunfire and other weaponry. Along these lines, it is interesting that of the 224 working Westville policemen (not including the 16 juvenile policemen) responding to a question about which assignment they would like most to have in the police departments, 50 percent selected the job of detective, an assignment combining elements of apparent danger and initiative. The next category was adult street work, that is, patrol and traffic (37 percent). Eight percent selected the juvenile squad, and only 4 percent selected administrative work. Not a single policeman chose the job of jail guard. Although these findings do not control for such factors as prestige, they suggest that confining and routine jobs are rated low on the hierarchy of police preferences, even though such jobs are least dangerous. Thus, the policeman may well, as a personality, enjoy the possibility of danger, especially its associated excitement even though he may at the same time be fearful of it. Such "inconsistency" is easily understood. Freud has by now made it an axiom of personality theory that logical and emotional consistency are by no means the same phenomenon.

However complex the motives aroused by the element of danger, its consequences for sustaining police culture are unambiguous. It is, therefore, a conception shaped by persistent suspicion. The English "copper," often portrayed as a courteous, easygoing, rather jolly sort of chap, on the one hand, or as a devil-may-care adventurer, on the other, is differently described by Colin MacInnes:

The true copper's dominant characteristic, if the truth be known, is neither those daring nor vicious qualities that are sometimes attributed to him by friend or enemy, but an ingrained conservatism, and almost desperate love of the conventional. It is untidiness, disorder, the unusual, that a copper disapproves of most of all: far more, even than of crime which is merely a professional matter. Hence his profound dislike of people loitering in streets, dressing extravagantly, speaking with exotic accents, being strange, weak, eccentric, or simply any rare minority—of their doing, in fact, anything that cannot be safely predicted.

Policemen are indeed specifically *trained* to be suspicious, to perceive events or changes in the physical surroundings that indicate the occurrence or probability of disorder. A former student who worked as a patrolman in a suburban New York police department describes this aspect of the policeman's assessment of the unusual:

The time spent cruising one's sector or walking one's beat is not wasted time, though it can become quite routine. During this time, the most important thing for the officer to do is notice the normal. He must come to know the people in his area, their habits, their automobiles and their friends. He must learn what time the various shops close, how much money is kept on hand on different nights, what lights are usually left on, which houses are vacant . . . only then can he decide what persons or cars under what circumstances warrant the appellation "suspicious."

The individual policeman's "suspiciousness" does not hang on whether he has personally undergone an experience that could objectively be described as hazardous. Personal experience of this sort is not the key to the psychological importance of exceptionality. Each, as he routinely carries out his work, will experience situations that threaten to become dangerous. Like the American Jew who contributes to "defense" organizations such as the Anti-Defamation League in response to Nazi brutalities he has never experienced personally, the policeman identifies with his fellow cop who has been beaten, perhaps fatally, by a gang of young thugs.

SOCIAL ISOLATION

The patrolman in Westville, and probably in most communities, has come to identify the black man with danger. James Baldwin vividly expresses the isolation of the ghetto policeman:

The only way to police a ghetto is to be oppressive. None of the Police Commissioner's men, even with the best will in the world, have any way of understanding the lives led by the people they swagger about in twos and threes controlling.

Their very presence is an insult, and it would be, even if they spent their entire day feeding gumdrops to children. They present the force of the white world, and that world's criminal profit and ease, to keep the black man corralled up here, in his place. The badge, the gun in the holster, and the swinging club make vivid what will happen should his rebellion become overt. . . .

It is hard, on the other hand, to blame the policeman, blank, good-natured, thoughtless, and insuperably innocent, for being such a perfect representative of the people he serves. He, too, believes in good intentions and is astounded and offended when they are not taken for the deed. He has never, himself, done anything for which to be hated—which of us has?—and yet he is facing, daily and nightly, people who would gladly see him dead, and he knows it. There is no way for him not to know it: there are few things under heaven more unnerving than the silent, accumulating contempt and hatred of a people. He moves through Harlem, therefore, like an occupying soldier in a bitterly hostile country; which is precisely what, and where he is, and is the reason he walks in twos and threes.

While Baldwin's observations on police-Negro relations cannot be disputed seriously, there is greater social distance between police and "civilians" in general regardless of their color than Baldwin considers. Thus, Clinton MacInnes has his English hero, Mr. Justice, explaining:

The story is all coppers are just civilians like anyone else, living among them not in barracks like on the Continent, but you and I know that's just a legend for mugs. We are cut off: we're not like everyone else. Some civilians fear us and play up to us, some dislike us and keep out of our way but no one—well, very few indeed—accepts us as just ordinary like them. In one sense, dear, we're just like hostile troops occupying an enemy country. And say what you like, at times that makes us lonely.

Of the 282 Westville policemen who rated the prestige police work receives from others, 70 percent ranked it as only "fair" or "poor," while less than 2 percent ranked it as "excellent" and another 29 percent as "good." Similarly, in Brit-

ain, two-thirds of a sample of policemen interviewed by a Royal Commission stated difficulties in making friends outside the force; of those interviewed, 58 percent thought members of the public to be reserved, suspicious, and constrained in conversation, and 12 percent attributed such difficulties to the requirement that policemen be selective in associations and behave circumspectly. A Westville policeman related the following incident:

Several months after I joined the force, my wife and I used to be socially active with a crowd of young people, mostly married, who gave a lot of parties where there was drinking and dancing, and we enjoyed it. I've never forgotten, though, an incident that happened on one Fourth of July party. Everybody had been drinking, there was a lot of talking, people were feeling boisterous, and some kid there—he must have been 20 or 22— threw a firecracker that hit my wife in the leg and burned her. I didn't know exactly what to do— punch the guy in the nose, bawl him out, just forget it. Anyway, I couldn't let it pass, so I walked over to him and told him he ought to be careful. He began to rise up at me, and when he did, somebody yelled, "Better watch out, he's a cop." I saw everybody standing there, and I could feel they were against me and for the kid, even though he had thrown the firecracker at my wife. I went over to the host and said it was probably better if my wife and I left because a fight would put a damper on the party. Actually, I'd hoped he would ask the kid to leave, since the kid had thrown the firecracker. But he didn't so we left. After that incident, my wife and I stopped going around with that crowd, and decided that if we were going to go to parties where there was to be drinking and boisterousness, we weren't going to be the only police people there.

Another reported that he seeks to overcome his feelings of isolation by concealing his police identity:

I try not to bring my work home with me, and that includes my social life. I like the men I work with, but I think it's better that my family doesn't become a police family. I try to put my police work into the background, and try not to let people know I'm a policeman. Once you do, you can't have normal relations with them.

Although the policeman serves a people who are, as Baldwin says, the established society, the white society, these people do not make him feel accepted. As a result, he develops resources within his own world to combat social rejection.

POLICE SOLIDARITY

All occupational groups share a measure of inclusiveness and identification. People are brought together simply by doing the same work and having similar career and salary problems. As several writers have noted, however, police show an unusually high degree of occupational solidarity. It is true that the police have a common employer and wear a uniform at work, but so do doctors, milkmen, and bus drivers. Yet it is doubtful that these workers have so close knit an occupation or so similar an outlook on the world as do police. Set apart from the conventional world, the policeman experiences an exceptionally strong tendency to find his social identity within his occupational milieu.

Among the Westville police, of 700 friends listed by 250 respondents, 35 percent were policemen. Further, only 16 percent had failed to attend a single police banquet or dinner in the past year, and of the 234 men answering this question, 54 percent had attended three or more such affairs during the past year. These findings are striking and consistent with the idea that police officers have a strong social identity within their occupation—police are an exceptionally socially active occupational group.

POLICE SOLIDARITY AND DANGER

There is still a question, however, as to the process through which danger and authority influence police solidarity. The effect of danger on police solidarity is revealed when we examine a chief complaint of police: lack of public support and public apathy. The complaint may have several referents including police pay, police prestige, and support from the legislature. But the repeatedly voiced broader meaning of the complaint is resentment at being taken for granted. The policeman does not believe that his status as civil servant should relieve the public of responsibility for law enforcement. He feels, however, that payment out of public coffers somehow obscures his humanity and, therefore, his need for help. As one put it:

Jerry, a cop, can get into a fight with three or four tough kids, and there will be citizens passing by, and maybe they'll look, but they'll never lend a hand. It's their country too, but you'd never know it the way some of them act. They forget that we're made of flesh and blood too. They don't care what happens to the cop so long as they don't get a little dirty.

Although the policeman sees himself as a specialist in dealing with violence, he does not want to fight alone. He does not believe that his specialization relieves the general public of citizenship duties. Indeed, if possible, he would prefer to be the foreman rather than the workingman in the battle against criminals.

The general public, of course, does withdraw from the workaday world of the policeman. The policeman's responsibility for controlling dangerous and sometimes violent persons alienates the average citizen perhaps as much as does his authority over the average citizen. If the policeman's job is to ensure that public order is maintained, the citizen's inclination is to shrink from the dangers of maintaining it. The citizen prefers to see the policeman as an automaton, because once the policeman's humanity is recognized, the citizen necessarily becomes implicated in the policeman's work, which is, after all, sometimes dirty and dangerous. What the policeman typically fails to realize is the extent he becomes tainted by the character of the work he performs. The dangers of their work not only draw policemen together as a group but separate them from the rest of the population. Banton, for instance, comments:

Patrolmen may support their fellows over what they regard as minor infractions in order to demonstrate to them that they will be loyal in situations that make the greatest demands upon their fidelity. In the American departments I visited it seemed as if the supervisors shared many of the patrolmen's sentiments about solidarity. They too wanted their colleagues to back them up in an emergency, and they shared similar frustrations with the public.

Thus, the element of danger contains seeds of isolation which may grow in two directions. In one, a stereotyping perceptual shorthand is formed through which the police come to see certain signs as symbols of potential violence. The police probably differ in this respect from the general middle-class white population only in degree. This difference, however, may take on enormous significance in practice. Thus, the policeman works at identifying and possibly apprehending the symbolic assailant; the ordinary citizen does not. As a result, the ordinary citizen does not assume the responsibility to implicate himself in the policeman's required response to danger. The element of danger in the policeman's role alienates him not only from populations with a potential for crime but also from the conventionally respectable (white) citizenry, in short, from that segment of the population from which friends would ordinarily be drawn. As Janowitz has noted in a paragraph suggesting similarities between the police and the military, "Any profession which is continually preoccupied with the threat of danger requires a strong sense of solidarity if it is to operate effectively. Detailed regulation of the military style of life is expected to enhance group cohesion, professional loyalty, and maintain the martial spirit."

SOCIAL ISOLATION AND AUTHORITY

The element of authority also helps to account for the policeman's social isolation. Policemen themselves are aware of their isolation from the community and are apt to weigh authority heavily as a causal factor. When considering how authority influences rejection, the policeman typically singles out his responsibility for enforcement of traffic violations. Resentment, even hostility, is generated in those receiving citations, in part because such contact is often the only one citizens have with police, and in part because municipal administrations and courts have been known to use police authority primarily to meet budgetary requirements, rather than those of public order. Thus, when a municipality engages in "speed trapping" by changing limits so quickly that drivers cannot realistically slow down to the prescribed speed or, while keeping the limits reasonable, charging high fines primarily to generate revenue, the policeman carries the brunt of public resentment.

That the policeman dislikes writing traffic tickets is suggested by the quota system police departments typically employ. In Westville, each traffic policeman has what is euphemistically described as a working "norm." A motorcyclist is supposed to write two tickets an hour for moving violations. It is doubtful that norms are needed because policemen are lazy. Rather, employment of quotas most likely springs from the reluctance of policemen to expose themselves to what they know to be public hostility.

When meeting "production" pressures, the policeman inadvertently gives a false impression of patrolling ability to the average citizen. The traffic cyclist waits in hiding for moving violators near a tricky intersection and is reasonably sure that such violations will occur with regularity. The violator believes he has observed a policeman displaying exceptional detection capacities and may have two thoughts, each apt to generate hostility toward the policeman: "I have been trapped," or "They can catch me; why can't they catch crooks as easily?" The answer, of course, lies in the different behavior patterns of motorists and "crooks."

The latter do not act with either the frequency or predictability of motorists at poorly engineered intersections. While traffic patrol plays a major role in separating the policemen from the respectable community, other of his tasks also have this consequence. Traffic patrol is only the most obvious illustration of the policeman's general responsibility for maintaining public order, which includes keeping order at public accidents, sporting events, and political rallies. These activities share one feature: the policeman is called upon to *direct* ordinary citizens and therefore to restrain their freedom of action. Resenting the restraint, the average citizen in such a situation typically thinks something along the lines of "He is supposed to catch crooks; why is he bothering me?" Thus, the citizen stresses the "dangerous" portion of the policeman's role while belittling his authority.

Closely related to the policeman's authority-based problems as *director* of the citizenry are difficulties associated with his injunction to *regulate* public morality. For instance, the policeman is obliged to investigate "lovers' lanes" and to enforce laws pertaining to gambling, prostitution, and drunkenness. His responsibility in these matters allows him much administrative discretion since he may not actually enforce the law by making an arrest, but instead merely interfere with continuation of the objectionable activity. Thus, he may put the drunk in a taxi, tell the lovers to remove themselves from the backseat, and advise a man soliciting a prostitute to leave the area.

Such admonitions are in the interest of maintaining the proprieties of public order. At the same time, the policeman invites the hostility of the citizen so directed in two respects: he is likely to encourage the sort of response mentioned earlier (i.e., an antagonistic reformulation of the policeman's role), and the policeman is apt to cause resentment because of the suspicion that policemen do not themselves strictly conform to the moral norms they are enforcing. Thus, the policeman, faced with enforcing a law against fornication, drunkenness, or gambling, is easily liable to a charge of hypocrisy. Even when the policeman is called on to enforce the laws relating to overt homosexuality, a form of sexual activity for which police are not especially noted, he may encounter the charge of hypocrisy on grounds that he does not adhere strictly to prescribed heterosexual codes.

It is difficult to develop qualities enabling him to stand up to danger and to conform to standards of puritanical morality. The element of danger demands that the policeman be able to carry out efforts that are in their nature overtly masculine. Police work, like soldiering, requires an exceptional caliber of physical fitness, agility, toughness, and the like. The man who ranks high on these masculine characteristics is, again like the soldier, not usually disposed to be puritanical about sex, drinking, and gambling. On

the basis of observations, policemen do not subscribe to moralistic standards for conduct. For example, the morals squad of the police department, when questioned, was unanimously against the statutory rape age limit, on grounds that as late teenagers they themselves might not have refused an attractive offer from a 17-year-old girl. Neither, from observations, are policemen by any means total abstainers from the use of alcoholic beverages. The policeman who is arresting a drunk has probably been drunk himself; he knows it and the drunk knows it.

More than that, a portion of the social isolation of the policeman can be attributed to the discrepancy between moral regulation and the norms and behavior of policemen in these areas. We have presented data indicating that police engage in a comparatively active occupational social life. One interpretation might attribute this attendance to a basic interest in such affairs; another might explain the policeman's occupational social activity as a measure of restraint in publicly violating norms he enforces. The interest in attending police affairs may grow as much out of security in "letting oneself go" in the presence of police, and a corresponding feeling of insecurity with civilians, as an authentic preference for police social affairs. Much alcohol is usually consumed at police banquets with all the melancholy and boisterousness accompanying such occasions. As Horace Cayton reports on his experience as a policeman:

Deputy sheriffs and policemen don't know much about organized recreation; all they usually do when celebrating is get drunk and pound each other on the back, exchanging loud insults which under ordinary circumstances would result in a fight.

To some degree the reason for the behavior exhibited on these occasions is the company, since the policeman would feel uncomfortable exhibiting insobriety before civilians. The policeman may be likened to other authorities who prefer to violate moralistic norms away from onlookers for whom they are routinely supposed to appear as normative models. College professors, for instance, also get drunk on occasion, but prefer to do so where students are not present. Unfortunately for the policeman, such settings are harder for him to come by than they are for the college professor. The whole civilian world watches the policeman. As a result, he tends to be limited to the company of other policemen for whom his police identity is not a stimulus to carping normative criticism.

CORRELATES OF SOCIAL ISOLATION

The element of authority, like the element of danger, is thus seen to contribute to the solidarity of policemen. To the extent that policemen share the experience of receiving hostility from the public, they are also drawn together and become dependent upon one another. Trends in the degree to which police may exercise authority are also important considerations in understanding the dynamics of the relation between authority and solidarity. It is not simply a question of how much absolute authority police are given, but how much authority they have relative to what they had, or think they had, before. If, as Westley concludes, police violence is frequently a response to a challenge to the policeman's authority, so too may a perceived reduction in authority result in greater solidarity. Whitaker comments on the British police as follows:

As they feel their authority decline, internal solidarity has become increasingly important to the police. Despite the individual responsibility of each police officer to pursue justice, there is sometimes a tendency to close ranks and to form a square when they themselves are concerned.

These inclinations may have positive consequences for the effectiveness of police work, since notions of professional courtesy or colleagueship seem unusually high among police. When the nature of the policing enterprise requires much joint activity, as in robbery and narcotics enforcement, the impression is received that cooperation is high and genuine. Policemen do not appear to cooperate with one another merely because such is the policy of the chief, but because they sincerely attach a high value to teamwork. For instance, there is a norm among detectives who work together that they will protect each other when a dangerous situation arises. During one investigation, a detective stepped out of the car to question a suspect who became belligerent. The second detective, who had remained overly long in the backseat of the police car, apologized indirectly to his partner by explaining how wrong it had been of him to permit his partner to encounter a suspect alone on the street. He later repeated this explanation privately, in genuine consternation at having committed the breach (and possibly at having been culpable in the presence of an observer). Strong feelings of empathy and cooperation, indeed almost of "clannishness," a term several policemen themselves used to describe the attitude of police toward one another, may be seen in the daily activities of police. Analytically, these feelings can be traced to the elements of danger and shared experiences of hostility in the policeman's role.

Finally, to round out the sketch, policemen are notably conservative, emotionally and politically. If the element of danger in the policeman's role tends to make the policeman suspicious, and therefore emotionally attached to the status quo, a similar consequence may be attributed to the element of authority. The fact that a man is engaged in enforcing a set of rules implies that he also becomes implicated in *affirming* them. Labor disputes provide the commonest example of conditions inclining the policeman to support the status quo. In these situations, the police are necessarily pushed on the side of the defense of property. Their responsibilities thus lead them to see the striking and sometimes angry workers as their enemy and, therefore, to be cool, if not antagonistic, toward the whole conception of labor militancy. If a policeman did not believe in the system of laws he was responsible for enforcing, he would have to go on living in a state of conflicting cognitions, a condition which a number of social psychologists agree is painful.

Police Discretion

JAMES Q. WILSON

ALTHOUGH the legal and organizational constraints under which the police work are everywhere the same or nearly so, police behavior differs from community to community. First, the conduct with which the police must cope varies from place to place. Both crime and disorder are more common in low-income areas than in high-income ones. How frequently the police intervene in a situation, and whether they intervene by making an arrest, will depend in part on the number and seriousness of the demands the city places on them. Second, some police behavior will be affected by the tastes, interests, and style of the police administrator. Finally, the administrator's views of both particular problems and the general level and vigor of enforcement may be influenced, intentionally or unintentionally, by local politics.

In this chapter, the extent to which police behavior varies among eight American communities will be considered, especially the degree to which that variation is in accord with the intentions of the administrator.

DETERMINANTS OF DISCRETION

The patrolman's decision whether and how to intervene in a situation depends on his evaluation of the costs and benefits of various kinds of action. Although the substantive criminal law seems to imply a mandate, based on duty or morality, that the law be applied wherever and whenever its injunctions have been violated, in fact for most officers there are considerations of

utility that equal or exceed in importance those of duty or morality, especially for the more common and less serious laws. Although the officer may tell a person he is arresting that he is "only doing his duty," such a statement is intended mostly to reduce any personal antagonism (i.e., psychic costs to the officer incurred by being thought a bad fellow). Whatever he may say, however, his actual decision whether and how to intervene involves such questions as these: Has anyone been hurt or deprived? Will anyone be hurt or deprived if I do nothing? Will an arrest improve the situation or only make matters worse? Is complaint more likely if there is no arrest, or if there is an arrest? What does the sergeant expect of me? Am I getting near the end of my tour of duty? Will I have to go to court on my day off? If I do appear in court, will the charge stand up or will it be withdrawn or dismissed by the prosecutor? Will my partner think that an arrest shows I can handle things or that I can't handle things? What will the guy do if I let him go?

The decision to arrest, or to intervene in any other way, results from a comparison, different perhaps for each officer, of the net gain and loss to the suspect, the neighborhood, and the officer himself of various courses of action. Under certain circumstances, the policy of his department may set the terms of trade among these various considerations or alter the scales on which these values are measured. Such policies may in some cases make arrest (or no arrest) so desirable that, for all practical purposes, the patrolman has no discretion: he is doing what the department wants done. In other cases, departmental policies may have little or no effect, and thus such discretion as is exercised is almost entirely the officer's and not the department's.

To explain fully the uses of discretion many factors would have to be considered. For simplicity, two major determinants (major in the sense that they explain "enough" of the variation) suffice: whether the situation is primarily one of *law enforcement* or one of *order maintenance* and whether the police response is *police-invoked* or *citizen-invoked*. To repeat the difference between law enforcement and order maintenance, the former involves a violation of a law in which only guilt need be assessed; the latter, although it often entails a legal infraction, involves in addition a dispute in which the law must be interpreted, standards of right conduct determined, and blame assigned. A police-invoked response is one in which the officer acts on his own authority, rather than as the agent of a citizen who has made a specific verbal or sworn complaint (although citizens "in general" may have complained about "the situation"); a citizen-invoked response is one in which the officer acts on the particular complaint or warrant of the citizen. Although some situations cannot be neatly placed in any category, enough can, I hope, so that we can imagine four kinds of situations in which discretion is exercised.

CASE 1: POLICE-INVOKED LAW ENFORCEMENT

In this situation, the police themselves initiate the action in the specific instance, although sometimes in response to a general public concern over the problem, and whatever action they take is on their own authority. If there is an arrest, the officer is the complaining witness. Many crimes handled in this way are "crimes without victims"—that is, no citizen has been deprived and thus no citizen has called the police. Such calls as the police may get are from "busybodies"—persons who dislike "what is going on" but who themselves are not participants. Enforcement of laws dealing with vice, gambling, and traffic offenses are of this character. The rate and form of police interventions in these situations can be strongly influenced by the policy of the administrator. He can apply a performance measure to his subordinates, al-though (to introduce a further distinction) that measure differs with the particular offense. With respect to certain forms of vice and gambling, his measure will be whether a brothel or a bookie operates; if they do, his men are "not performing" and the administrator, if he is so inclined, will urge them to greater efforts. His performance measure is *goal oriented*, that is, it is based on his observation of whether the substantive law enforcement goal has been attained. Accordingly, not only does the administrator have substantial control over his officers, but the community (the mayor, the city council, the newspapers), being able to make the same observations, has substantial opportunity to control the administrator. With regard to traffic enforcement, however, the administrator's measure will be how many traffic tickets the officers have written, not how safe the streets are or how smoothly traffic flows. He cannot judge his men, except perhaps in the extreme case, on these substantive grounds because he knows that writing traffic tickets has only a small effect on actual traffic conditions. Accordingly, his performance measure will be means oriented, and as a result, the community will be less able to hold him responsible for traffic conditions. Should they accuse him, which is unlikely, of letting the accident rate rise, he can reply reasonably that unlike police attitudes toward brothels, police attitudes toward traffic law enforcement are not the sole or even the major determinant of whether there will be accidents.

CASE 2: CITIZEN-INVOKED LAW ENFORCEMENT

Here a citizen is the victim of a crime and he or she complains to the police. The vast majority of crimes with victims are those against property—larceny, auto theft, and burglary—and the vast majority of these are crimes of stealth for which the suspect is unknown. As a result, only a small percentage are solved by an arrest. The patrolman in these circumstances functions primarily as a report taker and information gatherer except when the suspect is still on the scene or has been caught by the victim or an onlooker. This is often the case, for example, with shoplifting. Here the patrolman must decide whether to make an arrest, to tell the citizen that it is up to him to handle the matter by getting a complaint and taking the suspect to court himself, or to encourage him to effect a citizen's arrest on the spot. The police department in turn may insist that prosecutions once started, either by an officer or a citizen, may not be dropped; conversely, it may make it easy for the arresting party to change his mind and forget the whole thing. The patrolman's attitude and departmental policy are amenable to some control by the administrator, especially since a majority of the suspects are likely to be juveniles. The police are formally and legally vested with considerable discretion over juveniles (any person in New York under the age of 16 and in California and Illinois under the age of 18). They can decide, if not whether to intervene (that is decided for them by the citizen who invokes the law), at least how to intervene (to arrest, take into temporary custody, warn and release, and so forth). The police administrator can influence the use of that discretion significantly, not, as with Case 1, by observing substantive outcomes or by measuring the output of individual officers, but by setting guidelines on how such cases will be handled and by devoting, or failing to devote, specialized resources (e.g., in the form of juvenile officers) to these matters.

CASE 3: POLICE-INVOKED ORDER MAINTENANCE

In this instance, the police on their own authority and initiative intervene in situations of actual or potential disorder. The most common charges are drunkenness, disorderly conduct, or breach of the peace. Not all drunk or disorderly arrests, of course, result from a police-invoked response—some, to be discussed below, are police ways of handling disorderly situations to which the police have been called by the citizen. Because the police invoke the law, the administrator has some control over patrolmen's discretion. He can urge them to "keep things quiet" but he cannot, as in traffic enforcement, judge each officer's "production" by how many arrests he makes on the assumption that there is an

almost inexhaustible supply of disturbances to go around. Nor can he insist, as he might with cases of shoplifting, that an arrest is always the best way to handle the situation. In short, discretion in these cases is more under the control of the patrolman and can be modified only by general incentives to be "more vigorous" or to "take it easy." The administrator can boost drunk arrests but only by ordering his officers to treat drunks as problems of law enforcement rather than order maintenance: arrest on sight a man intoxicated in a public place even if he is bothering no one. In this case, a drunk arrest falls under Case 1 and accordingly is subject to the same relatively high degree of control.

CASE 4: CITIZEN-INVOKED ORDER MAINTENANCE

In this last case, a citizen calls for police assistance because of a public or private disorder. But being of assistance is often not an easy matter. In almost every department, such a citizen call must be followed by a police response to avoid the charge of "doing nothing"; however, the way the patrolman handles these situations will depend on his assessment of them and on the extent to which the participants are inclined to be tractable and victims prepared to sign a formal complaint. Thus, although the handling of these situations will vary considerably, that variation will depend more on the personal characteristics of the officer and the citizen participants than on departmental policies. Young college-educated patrolmen in a pleasant suburb may handle these matters in one way; older, working-class officers in a racially mixed central city may handle them in another.

In sum, in Cases 1 and 4 the patrolman has great discretion, but in the former instance it can be brought under departmental control and in the latter it cannot. In Case 2, the patrolman has the least discretion except when the suspects are juveniles and then the discretion is substantial and can be affected by general departmental policies and organization. Case 3 is intermediate in both the degree of discretion and the possibility of departmental control.

Police Use of Deadly Force

JAMES J. FYFE

POLICE use of deadly force first became a major public issue in the 1960s, when many urban riots were precipitated immediately by police killings of citizens. Since that time, scholars have studied deadly force extensively, police practitioners have made significant reforms in their policies and practices regarding deadly force, and the U.S. Supreme Court has voided a centuries-old legal principle that authorized police in about one-half the states to use deadly force to apprehend unarmed, nonviolent, fleeing felony suspects. This essay reviews and interprets these developments.

Because this is a review essay and a reexamination of existing data rather than a report on new research, it provides only limited opportunity for breast-beating about scholarly indifference: one cannot agree to write a review essay without a sizable body of literature to review. Still, *sizable* is a relative term; the existing research on the only unilateral life-or-death decision available to any American criminal justice official is the work of only a few individuals and is dwarfed by the volume of studies on most other (and less critical) decision points in the criminal justice process. My dining-room table could accommodate easily the number of contemporary social scientists who have devoted any serious attention to police deadly force.

THE EMERGENCE OF A PROBLEM

Although Robin's 1963 study was the first systematic look at the use of deadly force, it had little apparent effect on either scholars or offi-

From "Police Use of Deadly Force" by J. J. Fyfe, 1988, *Justice Quarterly*, 5, pp. 165-205. Copyright 1988 by Academy of Criminal Justice Sciences. Reprinted by permission.

cials. The subject did draw attention a year later, when the first of the major urban disorders of the 1960s, in Harlem and in Bedford-Stuyvesant, followed immediately upon the fatal shooting of a 15-year-old black boy who reportedly attacked an off-duty police lieutenant with a knife. Soon it became apparent, as the National Advisory Commission on Civil Disorders (the "Kerner Commission") reported four years later, that this pattern would not remain unique to New York. In May 1966, a year after Los Angeles had suffered its Watts riot, the commission reported that the accidental shooting death of a young black man led to renewed demonstrations and increased tensions in that city. In 1967, the National Guard was called in to restore order at Jackson State College in Mississippi after police attempts to disperse a crowd resulted in the shootings of three blacks, one of whom was killed. The 1967 Tampa riots were triggered by the fatal police shooting of a black youth who was fleeing from the scene of a burglary. The commission also wrote that "only the dramatic ghetto appearance of Mayor Ivan Allen, Jr., had averted a riot" in Atlanta in 1966.

Legal and Administrative Controls on Deadly Force

President Johnson's other major blue-ribbon panel, the President's Commission on Law Enforcement and Administration of Justice, looked carefully at police-community relations. In the report of its Task Force on the Police—which, in my view, remains the single most significant and most influential contribution to American police policy and practice to date—the commission made clear its dismay at the virtual absence of administrative policies to guide police officers' decisions to use deadly force.

The consequence is that while officers know how to care for and use their firearms, many have little or no understanding of when the weapon may be employed. This paradox is similar to teaching an employee how to maintain and drive an automobile while neglecting to instruct him on the subject of motor vehicle regulations. It might be argued, as it often is in the case of firearms regulations, that the driver's "common sense," coupled with a warning not to crash into anybody unless absolutely necessary, would suffice to enable the driver to operate his vehicle at large on the highways. This argument conveniently ignores the fact that driving regulations, like firearms regulations, are not based entirely on common sense or personal safety.

THE BREADTH OF LAW   In the absence of such policies, police shooting discretion generally was limited only by state criminal statutes or by case law defining justifiable homicide. These laws have several inadequacies. First, even the most restrictive state laws permit police to use their weapons in an extremely broad range of situations. Every state historically has permitted police officers to use deadly force to defend themselves or others against imminent death or serious physical harm, a provision that cannot be debated seriously. Indeed, except that generally they are obliged to attempt to retreat to safety before resorting to deadly force, American citizens enjoy the same justification for homicide (see, e.g., the New York Penal Law of 1967). Because we ask the police to put their lives on the line in our behalf, it follows that they should enjoy this slight advantage over the rest of us.

Yet many states also have codified some variant of the common-law "fleeing felon" rule, which authorizes use of deadly force as a means of apprehending persons fleeing from suspected felonies. The Tennessee statute that eventually became the focus of *Tennessee v. Garner* (1985) illustrates the broadest category of such laws:

Resistance to Officer—If after notice of the intention to arrest the [felony] defendant, he either flees or forcibly resists, the officer may use all the necessary means to effect the arrest. (Tennessee Code Annotated § 40-7108:55)

THE LAW AS A CONTROL ON PROFESSIONAL DISCRETION   Although *Garner* moots some of the arguments about the great breadth of deadly force statutes, it does little to ameliorate a second and more general limitation of law in describing police shooting discretion: in no field of human endeavor does the criminal law alone define adequately the parameters of acceptable occupational behavior. In the course of their work, doctors, lawyers, psychologists, professors, soldiers, nursing home operators, truck drivers, government officials, and journalists can do many outrageous, unacceptable, and hurtful things without violating criminal law. In exchange for the monopolies on the activities performed by those in their crafts, the most highly developed of these professions keep their members' behavior in check by developing and enforcing codes of conduct that are both more specific and more restrictive than are criminal definitions. Who would submit to treatment by a surgeon whose choices in deciding how to deal with patients were limited only by the laws of homicide and assault?

Apply that logic to use of police firearms. Even post-*Garner*, no state law tells officers whether it is advisable to fire warning shots into the air on streets lined by high-rise buildings. The law provides no direction to officers who must decide quickly whether to shoot at people in moving vehicles and thereby risk turning them into speeding unguided missiles. The law related to police use of force, in short, is simply too vague to be regarded as a comprehensive set of operational guidelines.

Resistance to Rule Making Regarding Deadly Force

Even so, many police administrators did not act on policy recommendations like Chapman's until their officers had become involved in shootings that (although noncriminal) generated community outcries and crises. Their sometimes vigorous resistance to change was rooted in many considerations. First, police authority to restrict shooting discretion more tightly than state law was uncertain. In addition, apparently on the theory that jurors were unlikely to find police behavior unreasonable unless officers had violated their own departments' formal rules and policies, some police officials refrained from committing deadly force policies to paper. Time also has shown that this rather self-serving attempt to avoid accountability and liability was counterproductive: jurors do not need a piece of paper to tell them whether an individual officer acted reasonably, but typically they do find that a police department's failure to provide officers with such paper is inexcusable. Finally, many police officers feared that restrictive deadly force policies would endanger the public and the police; by removing whatever deterrent value inhered in the fleeing-felon rule, such policies would result in an increase in crime and a decrease in police ability to apprehend fleeing criminals.

Explanations of Variations in Police Homicide Rates

In attempts to explain why officers in some police departments are more likely than those in others to use deadly force and to kill, researchers generally have identified two sets of variables as salient. One is environmental and lies beyond the direct control of police administrators; the other is internal and is subject to control by police chiefs. The former category includes such variables as the level of violence among the constituencies of the police and the extent of lawful police authority to use deadly force. Included in the second category are such variables as general police operating philosophies and specific policies, both formal and unstated.

ENVIRONMENTAL EXPLANATIONS Because police exposure to situations likely to precipitate shooting is presumably greatest where levels of general community violence are high, we would expect to find strong relationships between police homicide rates and measures of community violence and police contact with offenders. Perhaps the first researchers to explore such a hypothesis were Kania and Mackey, who reported strong associations between National Center for Health Statistics (NCHS) police homicide rates (however inaccurate) and rates of public homicide and violent crime across the states. In their intercity study, Sherman and Langworthy found the same kinds of associations between police homicide rates and such measures of potential police-citizen violence as gun density and rates of arrest for all offenses and for violent offenses. Finally, I found strong associations between rates of shooting by on-duty officers and rates of public homicide and arrests for violent crime across 20 police subjurisdictions within New York City.

INTERNAL ORGANIZATIONAL EXPLANATIONS Certainly, the police reflect the violence of the environments in which they work, and the police are duty bound to operate within the law. Yet the limits of the law have been discussed already, and it is apparent that other things also are at work here. Most specifically, as Uelman suggested in his research on variations in shooting rates among 50 police departments in Los Angeles County, it is clear that such internal organizational variables as the philosophies, policies, and practices of individual police chiefs and supervisors account for a considerable amount of variation in police homicide rates. Uelman's conclusion has been buttressed by studies which report, with varying degrees of rigor and certainty, that reductions in police shooting frequency and changes in police shooting patterns have followed implementation of restrictive administrative policies on deadly force and weapons use.

A CASE IN POINT Without detailed analysis of the context and content of police officials' utterances and policy statements, it is impossible in an essay of this type to sort out their effects in a manner that would satisfy methodological purists. Even so, the effect of police operating philosophy and policy on police deadly force has been most striking in Philadelphia. There the police commissioner in 1970 and 1971 was Frank Rizzo, the flamboyant hard-liner who went on to serve as mayor from 1972 through 1979. In 1973, when the Pennsylvania legislature modified its deadly force statute to prohibit shooting at fleeing persons who were not suspected of "forcible felonies" (Pennsylvania Statutes, annotated 1973), the Philadelphia Police Department (PPD) abolished its former restrictive policy on deadly force on the grounds that the legislature had not defined forcible felonies adequately. From that point until Rizzo left office, PPD adopted an operating style in which police were effectively free to do anything with their guns, as long as they did not use them to resolve their own personal disputes.

Some PPD officers took great advantage of this freedom. During 1972, the last full year in which PPD operated under a restrictive deadly force policy, the PPD homicide rate per 1,000 officers was 1.47 (with 12 deaths resulting); the rate jumped to 2.87 (23 deaths) in 1973 and peaked at 3.52 (29 deaths) in 1974. In 1976, when the city was cooperating in a federal court request to develop means of ending abuse of citizens, the police homicide rate dipped briefly to 1.35. In 1977, after the U.S. Supreme Court dismissed the case that had resulted in this agreement, the rate doubled (deaths rose from 11 to 21). In 1981, the first full year of a new restrictive deadly force policy, the rate decreased to 0.80 and remained relatively low during the next two years. Overall, the PPD police homicide rates were 2.09 while Rizzo was police commissioner, 2.29 while he was mayor, and 1.05 after he was out of office.

These are powerful numbers. Indeed, when I attempted to quantify Rizzo's influence over PPD operations (O = Rizzo out of office, policy in place 1980-1983; 1 = Rizzo as mayor or commissioner, policy in place 1970-1973; 2 = Rizzo as mayor, no policy 1974-1979), I found that the extent of his authority was a strong predictor of the annual PPD police homicide rate, and that adding the public homicide rate to this equation added only marginally to predictive ability. In short, except for the bizarre MOVE incident, knowing what Frank Rizzo was doing was far more valuable for estimating the PPD police homicide rate than were data on public homicides.

Elective and Nonelective Shootings

This analysis obviously suffers from the body count flaw; it includes only fatal shootings rather than all incidents of deadly force by PPD officers. Further, although I am convinced otherwise, many researchers will argue that my analyses of PPD homicides may have omitted some critical variable or set of variables. In addition, and if we assume for the moment that I am correct in asserting that Frank Rizzo was the critical variable in all Philadelphia police issues during the years in question, analysis of trends in police use of deadly force typically involves far more sophistication than when police or government administrators are as straightforward as Rizzo in espousing and executing their views.

In less extreme cases, examining in detail the circumstances of shootings is perhaps the most direct way to measure the relative effects of organizational and environmental variables on officers' use of deadly force. For these purposes, it is useful to conceive of police shootings as incidents on a continuum that runs from elective situations, in which officers may decide to shoot or to refrain from shooting at no risk to themselves or to others, to nonelective situations, in which officers have no choice but to shoot or to die.

By these standards, Edward Garner's death —the shot at the back of the fleeing, unarmed, nonthreatening, property-crime suspect who presented no apparent danger to anybody—was the prototypical elective shooting. Shootings such as this are influenced by internal police organizational variables; Garner and others in Memphis were shot in such circumstances because the police department encouraged or tolerated such action. Yet, as in the case of the Memphis Police Department in 1979, the police also can put an end to such shootings by simple administrative fiat. Shootings at the other end of the continuum are a different matter; no police department can direct officers to refrain from shooting when failure to do so may mean imminent death. Formal discretionary guidelines are of little relevance in such situations because, by any reasonable standard, the officers involved have only one choice.

Between these two extremes are more ambiguous police shootings that may be influenced to varying degrees by such variables as general organizational culture and the presence or absence of training in tactics. It is my experience, for example, that officers in some departments sometimes find themselves in harm's way because they respond to encouragement, both formal and from peers, to take charge of threatening situations quickly with as little assistance (and as little inconvenience to colleagues) as possible. In other departments, the operative norm encourages officers to use caution, to take cover, and to search for nonlethal means of resolving potential violence. These midrange shootings typically involve officers who, for whatever reasons, find themselves dangerously close to individuals who are armed with knives or other weapons, who attempt to run them down with vehicles, or who are determined to overpower them through mere physical force. There is reason to believe that there exist important differences among cities in the exercise and effects of police-use of deadly force. First, police departments that permit shooting in elective situations are likely to experience high percentages of missed shots. Just as nonelective shootings are extremely dangerous for the officers involved, they are also very dangerous for their opponents. It is far easier to hit someone who is standing eight or ten feet away with a shotgun in his hands than someone who is running away in the dark. Second, such departments also tend to experience high percentages of woundings in relation to fatalities. For example, the four-to-one ratio of nonfatal to fatal wounds in Philadelphia did not result from any extraordinary humaneness on the part of PPD officers. It came about because an extraordinary percentage of the people shot at by the Philadelphia police were running targets; the officers fired at ranges so great that they were unable to hit the center body mass at which they were trained to shoot.

Who Gets Shot?

SUBJECT'S RACE Regardless of the care employed in restricting officers' shooting, every study that has examined this issue found that blacks are represented disproportionately among those at the wrong end of police guns. Takagi found that among the 2,441 males reported by the NCHS to have been killed by American police officers from 1960 through 1968, 1,188 (48.7 percent) were black. Using more recent figures from the same data source, Harring and associates reported that blacks' death rates from police homicide nationwide were nine to ten times as high than those of

whites. Even though the data source used by both of these studies was shown subsequently to be inaccurate, the general trend of these findings is consistent with those drawn from data that probably are more reliable.

Only the ingenuous and the naive can conclude from these figures, and the many other studies that show pronounced racial differences in shootings, that racism is not involved in police use of deadly force. Still, we should not be quick to point accusingly at the police, either individually or as an institution. These racial disparities parallel those found in other social phenomena such as life expectancy, rates of incarceration, unemployment, infant mortality, levels of income, educational attainments, and socioeconomic status. Therefore, as in the issue of intercity variations in police shooting rates, we should ask whether and to what extent racially disparate police homicide rates may indicate that police are simply quicker to shoot blacks than whites, or whether these disparate rates may be consequences of racial variations in officers' exposure to situations likely to precipitate shooting.

John Goldkamp frames this question in terms of two conflicting "belief perspectives." The first asserts that

disproportionate minority deaths [result] from both irresponsible use of deadly force by a small minority of police officers and differential administration of law enforcement toward minority citizens (which in effect produces disproportionately high arrest and death rates for minorities in general).

According to Goldkamp, adherents of the second perspective hold that

the disproportionately high death rates of minorities at the hands of the police can be explained by the disproportionately high arrest rates of minorities for crimes of violence, or by assumptions concerning the suspect's responsibility for his/her own death in violent police-suspect interactions.

If the first of these two extreme positions is the more accurate, black overrepresentation among those shot at by police might be reduced by attempting to eliminate racism within policing through improved personnel screening, training, and controls on officers' shooting discretion. The implications of Goldkamp's second belief perspective, however, are far more complex. If racial disparities in police homicide statistics are largely only another manifestation of whatever forces have placed so many blacks on the low end of the American ladder generally, it follows that they can be eliminated only by major social change.

With one exception, empirical tests of these alternative theses generally support Goldkamp's second belief perspective and offer little evidence in support of assertions that police discriminate with their trigger fingers. Researchers have found close associations between racial distributions of police shooting subjects and measures of the risk of being shot at, such as arrests for murder, robbery, aggravated assault, weapons offenses, and burglary, arrests for FBI Crime Index offenses, and arrests for violent Crime Index offenses.

Adherents of Goldkamp's first belief perspective on deadly force are likely to interpret these data as a sign that the Los Angeles Police Department was consciously more tolerant toward shootings of unarmed blacks than of unarmed whites. This may be the case, but it is also plausible that such a conspiratorial interpretation oversimplifies more subtle and complex phenomena. In Los Angeles, as elsewhere, race and place are associated closely. Blacks generally live and spend their time in ghettos characterized by relatively high rates of crime; whites generally live in and frequent more affluent and less violent areas. In Los Angeles, as elsewhere, ghetto police quickly learn that they work in a violent environment. Their workload is heavier and more demanding than that of their colleagues in country club districts; in my experience, their expectations also differ. Ghetto police officers learn quickly that they can expect anything when they respond to reports of trouble and usually are very careful to make themselves immune from attack. Officers in outlying police districts, however, find more often that most reports of crimes turn out to be false alarms and that street fights involve verbal disputes over parking spaces more often than armed combat.

Consequently, officers in outlying districts typically employ far less often the defensive tactics that are part of the ghetto officer's regular modus operandi.

Who Does the Shooting?

OFFICER'S RACE   Race is the most hotly discussed officer characteristic related to deadly force. Champions of representativeness in policing have long argued that one of the most promising routes to reducing police-citizen violence is to increase the percentage of minority officers. Presumably, these officers are attuned more closely to the problems and folkways of the minority citizens who are disproportionately the subjects of police deadly force and police attention generally.

The relevant research, however, does not lead easily to such a simplistic conclusion because the role of officers' race in police shootings is confounded by many other variables. When I first reported that black New York Police Department officers were about twice as likely as white officers to have shot or shot at citizens, I received protest from black friends who were convinced that I was in error and congratulations from other people who were convinced that my findings demonstrated that black officers were quicker on the trigger than whites. Both sides were wrong. My finding demonstrated only that black NYPD officers—both on duty and off duty—typically worked and lived in environments that were far more violent than those frequented by white officers. Much of the disparity between black and white NYPD shooting rates was attributable to the fact that black officers were involved in off-duty shootings about six times as often as white officers, largely because black officers more often lived in and frequented the city's high-crime areas. In those areas, their chances of encountering situations leading to shooting, justifiable or otherwise, were far greater than those of their suburban-dwelling white colleagues.

Disparities in on-duty shooting rates were attributable largely to racial differences in rank and assignment. One in six white NYPD officers (16.5 percent) held a supervisory or administrative rank (sergeant or above) in which exposure to street-level violence was limited or nil; fewer than one in 20 black officers (4.6 percent) held such a position. Among the remaining police officers and detectives, blacks were posted to high-risk assignments far more often than whites; in the final analysis, the shooting rates of black and white patrol officers in New York's euphemistically labeled "high experience precincts," who account for most NYPD shootings, were virtually indistinguishable (white officers' rate over five years = 196.5 per 1,000 officers, with n of 1,265; black rate = 198.6, n = 204; Hispanic rate = 210.2, n = 70).

OFFICER'S AGE   Intuition suggests that older—and presumably less impulsive—officers may be more likely than younger officers to refrain from shooting. I, however, found that when the NYPD's 3,000 junior officers were laid off and replaced in the field by 2,200 older officers who had been transferred from nonstreet assignments, the rate of officers' shooting did not decline. Instead, the layoffs apparently served only to increase the mean age and length of service of officers involved in line-of-duty shootings. Binder and his colleagues, who found no significant differences between the age distributions of shooters and of nonshooters in the departments they studied, did report that shooters were overrepresented among younger officers, but this disparity may be an artifact of age-related variations in assignment and in exposure to potential shooting situations. Blumberg, in contrast, compared shooters with those who had not fired their guns among Atlanta and Kansas City officers. Even when attempting to control for exposure to risk of shooting, he found that younger officers were somewhat more likely than older officers to have fired their guns.

THE BEST AND THE BRIGHTEST   The research on officers' intellectual capacity and educational attainment is not much more informative than research on age. Binder and his colleagues found that shooters were less well educated than nonshooters, but again, their findings may be confounded by educationally related variations in risk. Police officers with college degrees are far more likely to be operating their departments' computers than are officers who hold only general equivalency diplomas, and shootings rarely occur inside police headquarters. My analyses of the relationship between officers' IQ scores and NYPD adjudications of shootings (previously unreported) confuse the picture further. I found that the percentage of shootings condemned by the department was about twice as high among "dull" officers (IQ scores below 90) as among "dull-normal," "normal," or "bright-normal" officers (IQ scores of 90 to 124), but that the percentage of shootings by "very bright" officers (who had scored 125 or higher on test with a score of 133) disapproved by the department also was twice as high as that among their normal and bright-normal colleagues. This finding, too, is related closely to assignment. During the period in question, NYPD's brightest officers typically enjoyed administrative assignments in which the risk of engaging in legitimate violence was minimal. Consequently, the percentage of their shootings that involved illegitimate violence (e.g., off-duty personal disputes) was far higher than among less intellectually gifted officers.

THE 24-HOUR COP   The issue of off-duty shootings is substantial. Milton and associates reported that 17 percent of the 320 shootings they studied in Birmingham, Detroit, Indianapolis, Kansas City, Oakland, Portland (Oregon), and Washington, D.C. involved off-duty officers. I found a similar percentage in New York City, and I reported that many of NYPD's off-duty shootings were "bad"; 41.5 percent resulted in administrative condemnations, 3.8 percent were suicide attempts, 12.6 percent were accidents, and even many of those found to be justifiable involved officers who made bad situations worse by resorting quickly to firearms when they found themselves suddenly in the middle of restaurant or bar robberies. Geller and Karales reported that 23 percent of Chicago shootings involved off-duty officers and that 38 percent (n = 71) of the Chicago officers who were shot during the period they studied were shot by themselves or by other officers, frequently in off-duty situations.

Perhaps the most stunning data on off-duty officers' use of firearms are included in a report that describes the 92 incidents in which Detroit police killed citizens from January 1, 1975 through June 30, 1979. Twenty (21.7 percent) of these incidents involved off-duty officers who killed 23 persons, excluding suicides. Among these were two burglars, one robber, and one murderer. One officer, however, killed his wife and himself; another killed his wife and their two children; two officers killed their husbands; another killed his estranged wife and himself; another killed his girlfriend; another killed his wife accidentally; another killed his ex-wife's husband and committed suicide two months later; three others killed four people (two of whom were armed) during barroom altercations; and three others killed three people (two of whom were armed) during street altercations.

CONCLUSIONS

On balance, and even though the available data are skimpier than we would like, it appears that the frequency of police use of deadly force is influenced heavily by organizational philosophies, expectations, and policies; that levels of community violence are marginal predictors, useful chiefly when organizational variables may be held constant (as in studying a single police jurisdiction); and that variations in law play a role in determining frequency of deadly force only when administrators abdicate their responsibility to see that propriety is not limited only by statutory definitions of assault and homicide.

Research regarding the people involved in incidents of deadly force by police generally shows that blacks and other minorities are overrepresented at both ends of police guns. Explanations for these disparities vary, but at least by my interpretation they typically involve embarrassing realities over which police have little control. Black citizens are overrepresented in the most violent and most criminogenic neighborhoods; individual black officers, who are still underrepresented in American policing generally, are far more likely than individual white officers to draw the most hazardous police duties in those same neighborhoods. Until these realities are altered, we can expect continuing minority disproportion in deadly force statistics no matter how stringently police officers' discretion is controlled.

This probability, I think, illustrates the central theme that may be drawn from all the research on deadly force reviewed in this essay. Police officers and the people at whom they shoot are simply actors in a much larger play. When police officers' roles in this play are defined carefully by their administrators and when the officers have been trained well to perform those roles, their individual characteristics mean little; the young cop, the old cop, the male cop, the female cop, the white cop, and the black cop all know what is expected of them, and they do it. When such clear expectations are not provided, officers improvise, and often we give their performances bad reviews. Yet because we put them on the stage in the first place, we also should criticize ourselves for failing to assure that they have been directed adequately. When black children's roles are defined so clearly by the conditions in which so many are raised, we should expect that some will end their lives at the wrong end of police guns. We should not blame the police for that; we should blame ourselves for creating the stages on which so many black lives are played out.

Demeanor or Crime?
Why "Hostile" Citizens Are
More Likely to Be Arrested

DAVID A. KLINGER

INITIAL evidence linking citizen demeanor with arrest emerged in the early 1960s, when researchers began to explore conflict and labeling theorists' claims that extralegal factors are critical determinants of the operation of the criminal justice system in the United States. Becker argued that police officers are more severe in sanctioning citizens whose demeanor indicates a lack of respect for police authority. Piliavin and Briar tested Becker's argument in a study of police encounters with juveniles. Consistent with Becker's assertion, they found that "uncooperative" youths were more likely to be arrested than their "cooperative" peers. Soon other scholars cited this finding as evidence that hostility increases the odds of arrest, albeit with some caution about generalizability.

Research published between 1970 and 1980 offered further support for the position that citizen demeanor affects the likelihood of arrest. Additional studies of police encounters with juveniles, as well as studies that included adults, considered the role of demeanor in police arrest decisions. All reported that police officers were more likely to arrest hostile citizens than those who deferred to police authority. With mounting evidence in hand, many scholars proclaimed as truth the proposition that displays of hostility by citizens independently increase the likelihood of arrest.

From "Demeanor or Crime: Why Hostile Citizens Are More Likely to Be Arrested" by D. A. Klinger, 1994, *Criminology, 32*, pp. 15-40. Copyright 1994 by the American Society of Criminology. Reprinted by permission.

A series of studies published after 1980 helped cement scholarly faith in the hostility thesis. Almost a dozen studies of police encounters with citizens of all ages considered the direct effect of demeanor on arrest. Once again, the findings were uniform: each study reported that the likelihood of an encounter resulting in an arrest rises with increasing hostility on the citizen's part. Today, the assertion that hostility directly increases the odds of arrest is part of the criminological canon. As Simpson puts it, "That police decisions to arrest can be influenced by . . . the demeanor of the offender has been established."

QUESTIONS ABOUT
THE RESEARCH

With this impressive body of evidence, it seems that the proposition that hostility independently increases the likelihood of arrest deserves its status as an axiom of criminology. Examination of previous research, however, identifies two limitations that call into question the validity of findings that demeanor exerts a *direct causal* effect on arrest and therefore casts doubt on the claim that hostility by itself increases the likelihood of arrest. First, although demeanor is conceptually defined as legally permissible behavior, measures of demeanor often include criminal conduct. Second, criminal conduct is not controlled adequately when the effects of demeanor on arrest are estimated.

Conceptualizing and Measuring Demeanor

In the literature on crime and social control, the construct "citizen demeanor" refers to *legally permissible* behavior of citizens during interactions with police officers that indicates the degree of deference or respect they extend to the involved officers. That citizen demeanor is not regulated by criminal statute is apparent in Becker's initial arguments about demeanor's shaping police action. Speaking of police officers as "rule enforcers," he writes:

A good deal of enforcement activity is devoted not to actual enforcement of rules, but to coercing respect from the people the enforcer deals with. This means that one may be labeled as deviant not because he has actually broken a rule, but because he has shown disrespect to the enforcer of the rule.

The extralegal status of demeanor is also plain in scholars' descriptions of research findings about the demeanor-crime link. Consider, for example, Black's comment that the early empirical inquiry indicated that "the police are especially likely to sanction suspects who fail to defer to police authority *whether legal grounds exist or not*" (my emphasis).

Because demeanor is conceptually defined as conduct that violates no laws, indicators of demeanor must measure only legally permissible citizen conduct if they are to be valid. Demeanor measures in several studies, however, apparently include physical attacks on police officers, physical violence between citizens in the presence of police officers, or both. The discrepancy between conceptual and operational definitions of demeanor when physical violence is counted as hostility is illustrated in a report that Black offers as an example of an encounter where citizens exhibit a high degree of disrespect toward the police.

The officers had responded to what was reported as "a woman screaming." . . . As their elevator approached the floor of the reported incident, they heard a woman shouting and crying, "Help! Help! He's going to kill my brother!" . . . someone [then] yelled, "Who let the motherfuckin' police in?" A man thereupon "charged" toward a

woman in the corridor, and the officers attempted to restrain both, holding them by the arms. Another man entered the fray at that point and "cursed and slugged" one of the officers. A second woman also attacked, striking an officer in the eye. . . . In the end, three of the four were arrested, including the "screaming woman" who tried to attack one of the men with a broken lamp. During all of this, the police incurred one broken hand, a kick to the groin, various other blows, and two bites.

Since the only researchers to provide clear information about the behaviors they take to indicate hostility are Black, Lundman, and Visher, and their studies, as noted above, report counting some crimes as hostile demeanor, it is not possible to ascertain how many of the 14 other studies confound crime with demeanor. Yet because 13 of those studies drew their encounter samples from one of the data sets used by Black, Lundman, or Visher, it is reasonable to suspect that the number may be quite high.

Controlling for Crime in Police-citizen Encounters

The fundamental empirical challenge facing any claim that some factor other than criminal behavior affects the operation of law is to demonstrate effects of that factor after relevant criminal conduct has explained as much as it can. Otherwise, it is possible that the measured extralegal effects are due to the effects of crime. As Tittle states,

It is important to remember that [reports of extralegal effects] are of evidentiary value only if relationships can be shown not to be due to some intervening variable such as the amount or seriousness of actual rule breaking.

Thus, we can have faith in reports that demeanor increases the likelihood of arrest only if they are based on research that controls satisfactorily for criminal conduct in police-citizen encounters. This is not the case, however.

Encounters between police officers and citizens entail two primary temporal phases: a "preintervention" phase, consisting of the circumstances that prompt police intervention in citizens' lives, and an "interaction" phase that begins when officers contact citizens and ends when officers and citizens go their separate ways. These two phases involve at least three distinct aspects of police-citizen encounters that may relate to violations of criminal law. Each of these constitutes a unique dimension of criminality: (1) the legal nature of what occurred in the circumstances leading to police intervention; (2) the legal nature of citizen behavior toward the police during interaction, citizens may commit crimes such as attacking officers or interfering with their duties; and (3) interaction-phase crimes not directed against the police, such as assaulting other citizens.

Thus, to control comprehensively for criminal conduct when considering the effects of demeanor on arrest, investigators must control in a sound fashion for each of the three dimensions of criminality in police-citizen encounters. None of the published research did this. The studies published before 1981 did not control satisfactorily for crime. The situation is less apparent in the research published after 1980 because each investigator estimated demeanor effects in models that included measures of crime as control variables. But none of the post-1980 studies specify what their crime indicators measure. Finally, because studies published after 1980 do not specify what their crime indicators measure, it is possible that some measures tap both preintervention criminality and crimes against citizens after the police intervened. If this is so, the nature of the control issue shifts somewhat. Research that measured both preintervention and interaction-phase crime in a single indicator would have three limitations. First, none of the crime against the police would be controlled. Second, because the crime measures that were used are imprecise, the above-mentioned limited control that results from attenuation of measured crime effects would remain. Finally, if the singular measures tap the two distinct dimensions of crimes against citizens, some of the effects of these crimes on arrest would be masked in analysis and therefore would not be controlled when the independent effect of demeanor on arrest was estimated.

Consequences of the Problems

The roughness of the fit between indicators of demeanor and their referent construct and the lack of adequate controls for crime introduce the possibility that reported hostility effects are due to criminal conduct rather than to demeanor. When indicators of demeanor measure crime as hostility, measured hostility effects include any effects that the crimes thus confounded might exert. The lack of comprehensive control for crime raises the possibility that reported hostility effects that are "true" (i.e., due to demeanor that is hostile but violates no laws) may be explained and/or mediated by crime. This could be so if (1) crimes occur more often in encounters with hostile citizens than in encounters with respectful citizens and (2) officers are less likely to jail law-abiding citizens than citizens who commit crimes. It is logical to suspect that this is the case.

DATA, ANALYSIS, AND RESULTS

The data used in this chapter are drawn from an observational study of police behavior conducted in Dade County, Florida during 1985 and 1986. Trained civilian observers accompanied randomly selected officers from three districts of the Metro-Dade Police Department on 877 eight-hour patrol shifts. The observers recorded selected aspects of traffic stops, crimes in progress, and interpersonal disputes in observation schedules designed specifically for each type of encounter and wrote brief narrative reports summarizing each interaction.

During the course of observation, study officers handled 245 disputes in which they contacted at least two involved parties on opposite sides of a conflict and in which observers recorded information about each of the several variables of interest (see below). This sample size lies in the middle of the range of the number of cases used in previous studies that employed disputes as the unit of analysis.

The dispute instrument contained separate items designed to measure three distinct aspects of citizen conduct that may relate to violations of criminal laws. One item measured whether a crime had occurred before the police arrived and, if so, asked for the type of offense (e.g., assault, burglary). A second item measured whether any disputants attacked other disputants after the police intervened and, if so, whether it was an armed or an unarmed attacked. A third item asked whether officers were attacked physically.

Most of the 245 cases did not involve any criminal activity; two-thirds included no crime during the preintervention phase, citizens attacked one another in 20 encounters, and officers were attacked in six. Because none of the previous research measures preintervention crime in the manner used here and because none includes indicators of the two interaction phase dimensions of crime, it is not possible to compare these crime counts with frequencies in the extant research.

The Demeanor-Arrest Link

Analyses of these cases yielded a modest bivariate demeanor-arrest association. To ascertain whether this association was related to other characteristics of the cases, the analyses also examined the relationship between arrest, demeanor, prior crime, intervention-phase violence between citizens, and the training dummy as predictors, based on the 239 cases in which no officers were assaulted. In this model, the effect of attacks on officers was controlled by paring from the sample the six cases in which officers were attacked, all of which ended in arrest. These analyses did not find demeanor to be a significant predictor of arrest. Thus, when criminal conduct is controlled, demeanor exerts no significant independent effect on arrest.

To more thoroughly assess the possibility that demeanor conditions the police response to crime, I considered two other kinds of possible conditional hostility effects. First, I examined whether demeanor affects arrest only in cases in which crimes have occurred, that is, whether officers take demeanor into account only when deciding whether to jail citizens who have committed some crime. The second possibility is the converse of the first: that hostility affects arrest decisions only in cases in which no crime has occurred. As Black notes, many arrests, some 30 percent in his study, take place in noncrimi-

nal encounters. In the current data, the rate is somewhat lower: eight of the 37 arrests (22 percent) occurred in encounters that involved neither a prior crime, interaction-phase violence between citizens, nor an attack on the police. Because such arrests cannot be explained by crime, it is possible that they are due to hostile demeanor.

I examined the matter of hostility affecting arrest in criminal encounters by analyzing the 90 cases involving a prior crime, violence between citizens, or both (exclusive of the six cases in which citizens attacked officers). Factors examined in these analyses were demeanor, violence between citizens, the training dummy, and a four-step prior crime measure. Also, to look for a hostility effect in noncriminal encounters, I examined the demeanor-arrest association in the 149 cases that involved no crime of any type. Demeanor did not exert a significant effect on arrest in either of these two analyses.

DISCUSSION AND CONCLUSION

In this essay, I examined the criminological axiom that citizen hostility independently increases the likelihood of arrest in police-citizen encounters. A review of the research on which this axiom rests raised questions about the validity of findings that citizen demeanor exerts a direct causal effect on arrest. I conducted a conservative test of this axiom; it disclosed that when demeanor is operationalized so as to conform with its original conceptual definition as legal conduct, it does not exert an independent effect on arrest, once crime has explained as much as it can. A moderate zero-order correlation between demeanor and arrest was shown to be spurious when one controls the effects of crimes that occur after the police initiate contact with citizens. Moreover, additional analysis showed that demeanor does not affect arrest by conditioning police response to crime. Thus, the current data suggest that hostile suspects are more likely to be arrested because they are more likely to commit crimes against and in the presence of the police, not because their demeanor connotes a lack of respect for police authority.

Additional analysis of the current data indicates that demeanor is very stable even in disputes, where, because of their inherent volatility, one might expect to find a good deal of variability in citizens' level of deference toward police officers. Recall that the dispute instrument included items to record citizens' demeanor both at the outset of encounters and later in the interactions.

The evident stability of demeanor and the predominant decline of hostility in the few cases where it changes suggest that if demeanor is measured at the outset of encounters, the results would not misrepresent the role of hostility in arrest decisions.

Finally, the present research has additional salience for current understanding of the determinants of arrest. In addition to reporting hostility effects, observational research reports that other extralegal factors also affect the likelihood of arrest. For example, numerous studies report that police arrest decisions are influenced substantially by citizens' preferences for police action; some research indicates that arrest depends on suspects' status characteristics, such as race and sex.

The current research suggests that such findings should be viewed with caution. As was the case with demeanor, we can have confidence in reports describing how complainants' preferences and the like affect arrest only if they are drawn from analyses in which criminal conduct is controlled comprehensively. For the reasons detailed above, however (estimation of bivariate associations and the absence of precise measures of the various dimensions of crime as controls in multivariate models), previous research has not controlled comprehensively for crime when estimating extralegal effects.

Thus, the manner in which previous observational police research controlled for crime may have consequences beyond the demeanor issue. It raises the prospect that all reports of independent extralegal effects may misrepresent the nature of the relationship between the particular factor and arrest. Therefore, despite strong theoretical grounds for believing that extralegal factors powerfully influence police arrest decisions, the current research suggests that it might be wise to view as tentative all current "knowledge" gleaned from empirical research about the link between such factors and arrest.

POLICING APPROACHES

Broken Windows: The Police and Neighborhood Safety

JAMES Q. WILSON
GEORGE L. KELLING

IN the mid-1970s, the state of New Jersey announced a Safe and Clean Neighborhoods Program designed to improve the quality of community life in twenty-eight cities. As part of that program, the state provided money to help cities take police officers out of their patrol cars and assign them to walking beats. The governor and other state officials were enthusiastic about using foot patrol as a way of cutting crime, but many police chiefs were skeptical. Foot patrol, in their eyes, had been pretty much discredited. It reduced the mobility of the police, who thus had difficulty responding to citizen calls for service, and it weakened headquarters control over patrol officers.

Many police officers also disliked foot patrol, but for different reasons: it was hard work, it kept them outside on cold, rainy nights, and it reduced their chances for making a "good pinch." In some departments, assigning officers to foot patrol had been used as a form of punishment. And academic experts on policing doubted that foot patrol would have any impact on crime rates; it was, in the opinion of most, little more than a sop to public opinion. But since the state was paying for it, the local authorities were willing to go along.

Five years after the program started, the Police Foundation, in Washington, D.C., published an evaluation of the foot-patrol project. Based

on its analysis of a carefully controlled experiment carried out chiefly in Newark, the foundation concluded, to the surprise of hardly anyone, that foot patrol had not reduced crime rates. But residents of the foot-patrolled neighborhoods seemed to feel more secure than persons in other areas, tended to believe that crime had been reduced, and seemed to take fewer steps to protect themselves from crime (e.g., staying at home with the doors locked). Moreover, citizens in the foot-patrol areas had a more favorable opinion of the police than did those living elsewhere. And officers walking beats had higher morale, greater job satisfaction, and a more favorable attitude toward citizens in their neighborhoods than did officers assigned to patrol cars.

These findings may be taken as evidence that the skeptics were right—foot patrol has no effect on crime; it merely fools the citizens into thinking that they are safer. But in our view, and in the view of the authors of the Police Foundation study (of whom Kelling was one), the citizens of Newark were not fooled at all. They knew what the foot-patrol officers were doing, they knew it was different from what motorized officers do, and they knew that having officers walk beats did in fact make their neighborhoods safer.

But how can a neighborhood be "safer" when the crime rate has not gone down—in fact, may have gone up? Finding the answer requires first that we understand what most often frightens people in public places. Many citizens, of course, are primarily frightened by crime, especially crime involving a sudden, violent attack by a stranger. This risk is very real, in Newark as in many large cities. But we tend to overlook or forget another source of fear—the fear of being bothered by disorderly people. Not violent people, or, necessarily, criminals, but disreputable or obstreperous or unpredictable people: panhandlers, drunks, addicts, rowdy teenagers, prostitutes, loiterers, the mentally disturbed.

What foot-patrol officers did was to elevate, to the extent they could, the level of public order in these neighborhoods. Although the neighborhoods were predominantly black and the foot patrolmen were mostly white, this "order maintenance" function of the police was performed to the general satisfaction of both parties.

One of us (Kelling) spent many hours walking with Newark foot-patrol officers to see how they defined "order" and what they did to maintain it. One beat was typical: a busy but dilapidated area in the heart of Newark, with many abandoned buildings, marginal shops (several of which prominently displayed knives and straight-edged razors in their windows), one large department store, and, most important, a train station and several major bus stops. Although the area was run-down, its streets were filled with people, because it was a major transportation center. The good order of this area was important not only to those who lived and worked there but also to many others, who had to move through it on their way home, to supermarkets, or to factories.

The people on the street were primarily black; the officer who walked the street was white. The people were made up of "regulars" and "strangers." Regulars included both "decent folk" and some drunks and derelicts who were always there but who "knew their place." Strangers were, well, strangers, and viewed suspiciously, sometimes apprehensively. The officer —call him Kelly—knew who the regulars were, and they knew him. As he saw his job, he was to keep an eye on strangers and make certain that the disreputable regulars observed some informal but widely understood rules. Drunks and addicts could sit on the stoops, but could not lie down. People could drink on side streets, but not at the main intersection. Bottles had to be in paper bags. Talking to, bothering, or begging

from people waiting at the bus stop was strictly forbidden. If a dispute erupted between a businessman and a customer, the businessman was assumed to be right, especially if the customer was a stranger. If a stranger loitered, Kelly would ask him if he had any means of support and what his business was; if he gave unsatisfactory answers, he was sent on his way. Persons who broke the informal rules, especially those who bothered people waiting at bus stops, were arrested for vagrancy. Noisy teenagers were told to keep quiet.

These rules were defined and enforced in collaboration with the "regulars" on the street. Another neighborhood might have different rules, but these, everybody understood, were the rules for *this* neighborhood. If someone violated them, the regulars not only turned to Kelly for help but also ridiculed the violator. Sometimes what Kelly did could be described as "enforcing the law," but just as often it involved taking informal or extralegal steps to help protect what the neighborhood had decided was the appropriate level of public order. Some of the things he did probably would not withstand a legal challenge.

A determined skeptic might acknowledge that a skilled foot-patrol officer can maintain order but still insist that this sort of "order" has little to do with the real sources of community fear—that is, with violent crime. To a degree, that is true. But two things must be borne in mind. First, outside observers should not assume that they know how much of the anxiety now endemic in many big-city neighborhoods stems from a fear of "real" crime and how much from a sense that the street is disorderly, a source of distasteful, worrisome encounters. The people of Newark, to judge from their behavior and their remarks to interviewers, apparently assign a high value to public order and feel relieved and reassured when the police help them maintain that order.

Second, at the community level, disorder and crime are usually inextricably linked, in a kind of developmental sequence. Social psychologists and police officers tend to agree that if a window in a building is broken *and is left unrepaired,* all the rest of the windows will soon be broken. This is as true in nice neighborhoods as in run-down ones. Window-breaking does not necessarily occur on a large scale because some areas are inhabited by determined window-breakers whereas others are populated by window-lovers; rather, one unrepaired broken window is a signal that no one cares, and so breaking more windows costs nothing. (It has always been fun.)

Philip Zimbardo, a Stanford psychologist, reported in 1969 on some experiments testing the broken-window theory. He arranged to have an automobile without license plates parked with its hood up on a street in the Bronx and a comparable automobile on a street in Palo Alto, California. The car in the Bronx was attacked by "vandals" within ten minutes of its "abandonment." The first to arrive were a family—father, mother, and young son—who removed the radiator and battery. Within twenty-four hours, virtually everything of value had been removed. Then random destruction began—windows were smashed, parts torn off, upholstery ripped. Children began to use the car as a playground. Most of the adult "vandals" were well-dressed, apparently clean-cut whites. The car in Palo Alto sat untouched for more than a week. Then Zimbardo smashed part of it with a sledgehammer. Soon, passersby were joining in. Within a few hours, the car had been turned upside down and utterly destroyed. Again, the "vandals" appeared to be primarily respectable whites.

Untended property becomes fair game for people out for fun or plunder, and even for people who ordinarily would not dream of doing such things and who probably consider themselves law abiding. Because of the nature of community life in the Bronx—its anonymity, the frequency with which cars are abandoned and things are stolen or broken, the past experience of "no one caring"—vandalism begins much more quickly than it does in staid Palo Alto, where people have come to believe that private possessions are cared for and that mischievous behavior is costly. But vandalism can occur anywhere once communal barriers—the sense of mutual regard and the obligations of civility—are lowered by actions that seem to signal that "no one cares."

We suggest that "untended" behavior also leads to the breakdown of community controls.

A stable neighborhood of families who care for their homes, mind each other's children, and confidently frown on unwanted intruders can change, in a few years or even a few months, to an inhospitable and frightening jungle. A piece of property is abandoned, weeds grow up, a window is smashed. Adults stop scolding rowdy children; the children, emboldened, become more rowdy. Families move out, unattached adults move in. Teenagers gather in front of the corner store. The merchant asks them to move; they refuse. Fights occur. Litter accumulates. People start drinking in front of the grocery; in time, an inebriate slumps to the sidewalk and is allowed to sleep it off. Pedestrians are approached by panhandlers.

At this point, it is not inevitable that serious crime will flourish or violent attacks on strangers will occur. But many residents will think that crime, especially violent crime, is on the rise, and they will modify their behavior accordingly. They will use the streets less often, and when on the streets will stay apart from their fellows, moving with averted eyes, silent lips, and hurried steps. "Don't get involved." For some residents, this growing atomization will matter little, because the neighborhood is not their "home" but "the place where they live." Their interests are elsewhere; they are cosmopolitans. But it will matter greatly to other people whose lives derive meaning and satisfaction from local attachments rather than worldly involvement; for them, the neighborhood will cease to exist except for a few reliable friends whom they arrange to meet.

Such an area is vulnerable to criminal invasion. Although it is not inevitable, it is more likely that here, rather than in places where people are confident they can regulate public behavior by informal controls, drugs will change hands, prostitutes will solicit, and cars will be stripped. That the drunks will be robbed by boys who do it as a lark, and the prostitutes' customers will be robbed by men who do it purposefully and perhaps violently. That muggings will occur.

Among those who often find it difficult to move away from this are the elderly. Surveys of citizens suggest that the elderly are much less likely to be the victims of crime than younger persons, and some have inferred from this that the well-known fear of crime voiced by the elderly is an exaggeration: perhaps we ought not to design special programs to protect older persons; perhaps we should even try to talk them out of their mistaken fears. This argument misses the point. The prospect of a confrontation with an obstreperous teenager or a drunken panhandler can be as fear inducing for defenseless persons as the prospect of meeting an actual robber; indeed, to a defenseless person, the two kinds of confrontation are often indistinguishable. Moreover, the lower rate at which the elderly are victimized is a measure of the steps they have already taken—chiefly, staying behind locked doors—to minimize the risks they face. Young men are more frequently attacked than older women, not because they are easier or more lucrative targets but because they are on the streets more.

Nor is the connection between disorderliness and fear made only by the elderly. Susan Estrich, of the Harvard Law School, has recently gathered together a number of surveys on the sources of public fear. One, done in Portland, Oregon indicated that three-fourths of the adults interviewed cross to the other side of a street when they see a gang of teenagers; another survey, in Baltimore, discovered that nearly half would cross the street to avoid even a single strange youth. When an interviewer asked people in a housing project where the most dangerous spot was, they mentioned a place where young persons gathered to drink and play music, despite the fact that not a single crime had occurred there. In Boston public housing projects, the greatest fear was expressed by persons living in the buildings where disorderliness and incivility, not crime, were the greatest. Knowing this helps one understand the significance of such otherwise harmless displays as subway graffiti. As Nathan Glazer has written, the proliferation of graffiti, even when not obscene, confronts the subway rider with the "inescapable knowledge that the environment he must endure for an hour or more a day is uncontrolled and uncontrollable, and that anyone can invade it to do whatever damage and mischief the mind suggests."

In response to fear, people avoid one another, weakening controls. Sometimes they call the police. Patrol cars arrive, an occasional arrest occurs, but crime continues and disorder is not abated. Citizens complain to the police chief, but he explains that his department is low on personnel and that the courts do not punish petty or first-time offenders. To the residents, the police who arrive in squad cars are either ineffective or uncaring; to the police, the residents are animals who deserve each other. The citizens may soon stop calling the police, because "they can't do anything."

The process we call urban decay has occurred for centuries in every city. But what is happening today is different in at least two important respects. First, in the period before, say, World War II, city dwellers—because of money costs, transportation difficulties, familial and church connections—could rarely move away from neighborhood problems. When movement did occur, it tended to be along public-transit routes. Now mobility has become exceptionally easy for all but the poorest or those who are blocked by racial prejudice. Earlier crime waves had a kind of built-in self-correcting mechanism: the determination of a neighborhood or community to reassert control over its turf. Areas in Chicago, New York, and Boston would experience crime and gang wars, and then normalcy would return, as the families for whom no alternative residences were possible reclaimed their authority over the streets.

Second, the police in this earlier period assisted in that reassertion of authority by acting, sometimes violently, on behalf of the community. Young toughs were roughed up, people were arrested "on suspicion" or for vagrancy, and prostitutes and petty thieves were routed. "Rights" were something enjoyed by decent folk, and perhaps also by the serious professional criminal, who avoided violence and could afford a lawyer.

This pattern of policing was not an aberration or the result of occasional excess. From the earliest days of the nation, the police function was seen primarily as that of a night watchman: to maintain order against the chief threats to order—fire, wild animals, and disreputable behavior. Solving crimes was viewed not as a police responsibility but as a private one. In the March, 1969, *Atlantic,* one of us (Wilson) wrote a brief account of how the police role had slowly changed from maintaining order to fighting crimes. The change began with the creation of private detectives (often ex-criminals), who worked on a contingency-fee basis for individuals who had suffered losses. In time, the detectives were absorbed into municipal police agencies and paid a regular salary; simultaneously, the responsibility for prosecuting thieves was shifted from the aggrieved private citizen to the professional prosecutor. This process was not complete in most places until the twentieth century.

In the 1960s, when urban riots were a major problem, social scientists began to explore carefully the order maintenance function of the police and to suggest ways of improving it—not to make streets safer (its original function) but to reduce the incidence of mass violence. Order maintenance became, to a degree, coterminous with "community relations." But as the crime wave that began in the early 1960s continued without abatement throughout the decade and into the 1970s, attention shifted to the role of the police as crime-fighters. Studies of police behavior ceased, by and large, to be accounts of the order maintenance function and became, instead, efforts to propose and test ways whereby the police could solve more crimes, make more arrests, and gather better evidence. If these things could be done, social scientists assumed, citizens would be less fearful.

A great deal was accomplished during this transition, as both police chiefs and outside experts emphasized the crime-fighting function in their plans, in the allocation of resources, and in deployment of personnel. The police may well have become better crime-fighters as a result. And doubtless they remained aware of their responsibility for order. But the link between order maintenance and crime prevention, so obvious to earlier generations, was forgotten.

That link is similar to the process whereby one broken window becomes many. The citizen who fears the ill-smelling drunk, the rowdy teenager, or the importuning beggar is not merely expressing his distaste for unseemly behavior; he is also giving voice to a bit of folk wisdom that happens to be a correct generalization—namely, that serious street crime flourishes in areas in which disorderly behavior goes unchecked. The unchecked panhandler is, in effect, the first broken window. Muggers and robbers, whether opportunistic or professional, believe they reduce their chances of being caught or even identified if they operate on streets where potential victims are already intimidated by prevailing conditions. If the neighborhood cannot keep a bothersome panhandler from annoying passersby, the thief may reason, it is even less likely to call the police to identify a potential mugger or to interfere if the mugging actually takes place.

Some police administrators concede that this process occurs, but argue that motorized-patrol officers can deal with it as effectively as foot-patrol officers. We are not so sure. In theory, an officer in a squad car can observe as much as an officer on foot; in theory, the former can talk to as many people as the latter. But the reality of police-citizen encounters is powerfully altered by the automobile. An officer on foot cannot separate himself from the street people; if he is approached, only his uniform and his personality can help him manage whatever is about to happen. And he can never be certain what that will be—a request for directions, a plea for help, an angry denunciation, a teasing remark, a confused babble, a threatening gesture.

In a car, an officer is more likely to deal with street people by rolling down the window and looking at them. The door and the window exclude the approaching citizen; they are a barrier. Some officers take advantage of this barrier, perhaps unconsciously, by acting differently if in the car than they would on foot. We have seen this countless times. The police car pulls up to a corner where teenagers are gathered. The window is rolled down. The officer stares at the youths. They stare back. The officer says to one, "C'mere." He saunters over, conveying to his friends by his elaborately casual style the idea that he is not intimidated by authority. "What's your name?" "Chuck." "Chuck who?" "Chuck Jones." "What'ya doing, Chuck?" "Nothin'." "Got a P.O. [parole officer]?" "Nah." "Sure?" "Yeah." "Stay out of trouble, Chuckie." Meanwhile, the other boys laugh and exchange comments among themselves, probably at the officer's expense. The officer stares harder. He cannot be certain what is being said, nor can he join in and, by displaying his own skill at street banter, prove that he cannot be "put down." In the process, the officer has learned almost nothing, and the boys have decided the officer is an alien force who can safely be disregarded, even mocked.

Our experience is that most citizens like to talk to a police officer. Such exchanges give them a sense of importance, provide them with the basis for gossip, and allow them to explain to the authorities what is worrying them (whereby they gain a modest but significant sense of having "done something" about the problem). You approach a person on foot more easily, and talk to him more readily, than you do a person in a car. Moreover, you can more easily retain some anonymity if you draw an officer aside for a private chat. Suppose you want to pass on a tip about who is stealing handbags, or who offered to sell you a stolen TV. In the inner city, the culprit, in all likelihood, lives nearby. To walk up to a marked patrol car and lean in the window is to convey a visible signal that you are a "fink."

The essence of the police role in maintaining order is to reinforce the informal control mechanisms of the community itself. The police cannot, without committing extraordinary resources, provide a substitute for that informal control. On the other hand, to reinforce those natural forces the police must accommodate them. And therein lies the problem.

Should police activity on the street be shaped, in important ways, by the standards of the neighborhood rather than by the rules of the state? Over the past two decades, the shift of police from order maintenance to law enforcement has brought them increasingly under the influence of legal restrictions, provoked by media complaints and enforced by court decisions and departmental orders. As a consequence, the order maintenance functions of the police are now governed by rules developed to control police relations with suspected criminals. This is, we think, an entirely new development. For centuries, the role of the police as watchmen was judged primarily not in terms of its compliance with appropriate procedures but rather in terms of its attaining a desired objective. The objective was order, an inherently ambiguous term but a condition that people in a given community recognized when they saw it. The means were the same as those the community itself would employ, if its members were sufficiently determined, courageous, and authoritative. Detecting and apprehending criminals, by contrast, was a means to an end, not an end in itself; a judicial determination of guilt or innocence was the hoped-for result of the law enforcement mode. From the first, the police were expected to follow rules defining that process, although states differed in how stringent the rules should be. The criminal-apprehension process was always understood to involve individual rights, the violation of which was unacceptable because it meant that the violating officer would be acting as a judge and jury—and that was not his job. Guilt or innocence was to be determined by universal standards under special procedures.

Ordinarily, no judge or jury ever sees the persons caught up in a dispute over the appropriate level of neighborhood order. That is true not only because most cases are handled informally on the street but also because no universal standards are available to settle arguments over disorder, and thus a judge may not be any wiser or more effective than a police officer. Until quite recently in many states, and even today in some places, the police make arrests on such charges as "suspicious person" or "vagrancy" or "public drunkenness"—charges with scarcely any legal meaning. These charges exist not because society wants judges to punish vagrants or drunks but because it wants an officer to have the legal tools to remove undesirable persons from a neighborhood when informal efforts to preserve order in the streets have failed.

Once we begin to think of all aspects of police work as involving the application of universal rules under special procedures, we inevitably ask what constitutes an "undesirable person" and why we should "criminalize" vagrancy or drunkenness. A strong and commendable desire to see that people are treated fairly makes us worry about allowing the police to rout persons who are undesirable by some vague or parochial standard. A growing and not-so-commendable utilitarianism leads us to doubt that any behavior that does not "hurt" another person should be made illegal. And thus many of us who watch over the police are reluctant to allow them to perform, in the only way they can, a function that every neighborhood desperately wants them to perform.

This wish to "decriminalize" disreputable behavior that "harms no one"—and thus remove the ultimate sanction the police can employ to maintain neighborhood order—is, we think, a mistake. Arresting a single drunk or a single vagrant who has harmed no identifiable person seems unjust, and in a sense it is. But failing to do anything about a score of drunks or a hundred vagrants may destroy an entire community. A particular rule that seems to make sense in the individual case makes no sense when it is made a universal rule and applied to all cases. It makes no sense because it fails to take into account the connection between one broken window left untended and a thousand broken windows. Of course, agencies other than the police could attend to the problems posed by drunks or the mentally ill, but in most communities—especially where the "deinstitutionalization" movement has been strong—they do not.

The concern about equity is more serious. We might agree that certain behavior makes one person more undesirable than another, but how do we ensure that age or skin color or national origin or harmless mannerisms will not also become the basis for distinguishing the undesirable from the desirable? How do we ensure, in short, that the police do not become the agents of neighborhood bigotry?

We can offer no wholly satisfactory answer to this important question. We are not confident that there *is* a satisfactory answer, except to hope that by their selection, training, and supervision, the police will be inculcated with a clear sense of the outer limit of their discretionary authority. That limit, roughly, is this—the police exist to help regulate behavior, not to maintain the racial or ethnic purity of a neighborhood.

Consider the case of the Robert Taylor Homes in Chicago, one of the largest public-housing projects in the country. It is home for nearly 20,000 people, all black, and extends over

ninety-two acres along South State Street. It was named after a distinguished black who had been, during the 1940s, chairman of the Chicago Housing Authority. Not long after it opened in 1962, relations between project residents and the police deteriorated badly. The citizens felt that the police were insensitive or brutal; the police, in turn, complained of unprovoked attacks on them. Some Chicago officers tell of times when they were afraid to enter the Homes. Crime rates soared.

Today, the atmosphere has changed. Police-citizen relations have improved—apparently, both sides learned something from the earlier experience. Recently, a boy stole a purse and ran off. Several young persons who saw the theft voluntarily passed along to the police information on the identity and residence of the thief, and they did this publicly, with friends and neighbors looking on. But problems persist, chief among them the presence of youth gangs that terrorize residents and recruit members in the project. The people expect the police to "do something" about this, and the police are determined to do just that.

But do what? Although the police can obviously make arrests whenever a gang member breaks the law, a gang can form, recruit, and congregate without breaking the law. And only a tiny fraction of gang-related crimes can be solved by an arrest; thus, if an arrest is the only recourse for the police, the residents' fears will go unassuaged. The police will soon feel helpless, and the residents will again believe that the police "do nothing." What the police in fact do is to chase known gang members out of the project. In the words of one officer, "We kick ass." Project residents both know and approve of this. The tacit police-citizen alliance in the project is reinforced by the police view that the cops and the gangs are the two rival sources of power in the area and that the gangs are not going to win.

None of this is easily reconciled with any conception of due process or fair treatment. Since both residents and gang members are black, race is not a factor. But it could be. Suppose a white project confronted a black gang, or vice versa. We would be apprehensive about the police taking sides. But the substantive problem remains the same: how can the police strengthen the informal social-control mechanisms of natural communities in order to minimize fear in public places? Law enforcement, per se, is no answer. A gang can weaken or destroy a community by standing about in a menacing fashion and speaking rudely to passersby without breaking the law.

We have difficulty thinking about such matters, not simply because the ethical and legal issues are so complex but because we have become accustomed to thinking of the law in essentially individualistic terms. The law defines *my* rights, punishes *his* behavior, and is applied by *that* officer because of *this* harm. We assume, in thinking this way, that what is good for the individual will be good for the community, and what does not matter when it happens to one person will not matter if it happens to many. Ordinarily, those are plausible assumptions. But in cases where behavior that is tolerable to one person is intolerable to many others, the reactions of the others—fear, withdrawal, flight—may ultimately make matters worse for everyone, including the individual who first professed his indifference.

It may be their greater sensitivity to communal as opposed to individual needs that helps explain why the residents of small communities are more satisfied with their police than are the residents of similar neighborhoods in big cities. Elinor Ostrom and her co-workers at Indiana University compared the perception of police services in two poor, all-black Illinois towns—Phoenix and East Chicago Heights—with those of three comparable all-black neighborhoods in Chicago. The level of criminal victimization and the quality of police-community relations appeared to be about the same in the towns and the Chicago neighborhoods. But the citizens living in their own villages were much more likely than those living in the Chicago neighborhoods to say that they do not stay at home for fear of crime, to agree that the local police have "the right to take any action necessary" to deal with problems, and to agree that the police "look out for the needs of the average citizen." It is possible that the residents and the police of the small towns saw themselves as engaged in a collaborative effort to maintain a certain standard of communal life, whereas those of the big city felt themselves to be simply requesting and supplying particular services on an individual basis.

If this is true, how should a wise police chief deploy his meager forces? The first answer is that nobody knows for certain, and the most prudent course of action would be to try further variations on the Newark experiment, to see more precisely what works in what kinds of neighborhoods. The second answer is also a hedge—many aspects of order maintenance in neighborhoods can probably best be handled in ways that involve the police minimally, if at all. A busy, bustling shopping center and a quiet, well-tended suburb may need almost no visible police presence. In both cases, the ratio of respectable to disreputable people is ordinarily so high as to make informal social control effective.

Even in areas that are in jeopardy from disorderly elements, citizen action without substantial police involvement may be sufficient. Meetings between teenagers who like to hang out on a particular corner and adults who want to use that corner might well lead to an amicable agreement on a set of rules about how many people can be allowed to congregate, where, and when.

Where no understanding is possible—or if possible, not observed—citizen patrols may be a sufficient response. There are two traditions of communal involvement in maintaining order. One, that of the "community watchmen," is as old as the first settlement of the New World. Until well into the nineteenth century, volunteer watchmen, not policemen, patrolled their communities to keep order. They did so, by and large, without taking the law into their own hands—without, that is, punishing persons or using force. Their presence deterred disorder or alerted the community to disorder that could not be deterred. There are hundreds of such efforts today in communities all across the nation. Perhaps the best known is that of the Guardian Angels, a group of unarmed young persons in distinctive berets and T-shirts, who first came to public attention when they began patrolling the New York City subways but who claim now to have chapters in more than thirty American cities. Unfortunately, we have little information about the effect of these groups on crime. It is possible, however, that whatever their effect on crime, citizens find their presence reassuring, and that they thus contribute to maintaining a sense of order and civility.

The second tradition is that of the "vigilante." Rarely a feature of the settled communities of the East, it was primarily to be found in those frontier towns that grew up in advance of the reach of government. More than 350 vigilante groups are known to have existed; their distinctive feature was that their members did take the law into their own hands, by acting as judge, jury, and often executioner as well as policeman. Today, the vigilante movement is conspicuous by its rarity, despite the great fear expressed by citizens that the older cities are becoming "urban frontiers." But some community-watchmen groups have skirted the line, and others may cross it in the future. An ambiguous case, reported in the *Wall Street Journal,* involved a citizens' patrol in the Silver Lake area of Belleville, New Jersey. A leader told the reporter, "We look for outsiders." If a few teenagers from outside the neighborhood enter it, "we ask them their business," he said. "If they say they're going down the street to see Mrs. Jones, fine, we let them pass. But then we follow them down the block to make sure they're really going to see Mrs. Jones."

Although citizens can do a great deal, the police are plainly the key to order maintenance. For one thing, many communities, such as the Robert Taylor Homes, cannot do the job by themselves. For another, no citizen in a neighborhood, even an organized one, is likely to feel the sense of responsibility that wearing a badge confers. Psychologists have done many studies on why people fail to go to the aid of persons being attacked or seeking help, and they have learned that the cause is not "apathy" or "selfishness" but the absence of some plausible grounds for feeling that one must personally accept responsibility. Ironically, avoiding responsibility is easier when a lot of people are standing about. On streets and in public places, where order is so important, many people are likely to be "around," a fact that reduces the chance of any one person acting as the agent of the community. The police officer's uniform

singles him out as a person who must accept responsibility if asked. In addition, officers, more easily than their fellow citizens, can be expected to distinguish between what is necessary to protect the safety of the street and what merely protects its ethnic purity.

But the police forces of America are losing, not gaining, members. Some cities have suffered substantial cuts in the number of officers available for duty. These cuts are not likely to be reversed in the near future. Therefore, each department must assign its existing officers with great care. Some neighborhoods are so demoralized and crime-ridden as to make foot patrol useless; the best the police can do with limited resources is respond to the enormous number of calls for service. Other neighborhoods are so stable and serene as to make foot patrol unnecessary. The key is to identify neighborhoods at the tipping point—where the public order is deteriorating but not unreclaimable, where the streets are used frequently but by apprehensive people, where a window is likely to be broken at any time, and must quickly be fixed if all are not to be shattered.

Most police departments do not have ways of systematically identifying such areas and assigning officers to them. Officers are assigned on the basis of crime rates (meaning that marginally threatened areas are often stripped so that police can investigate crimes in areas where the situation is hopeless) or on the basis of calls for service (despite the fact that most citizens do not call the police when they are merely frightened or annoyed). To allocate patrol wisely, the department must look at the neighborhoods and decide, from first-hand evidence, where an additional officer will make the greatest difference in promoting a sense of safety.

One way to stretch limited police resources is being tried in some public-housing projects. Tenant organizations hire off-duty police officers for patrol work in their buildings. The costs are not high (at least not per resident), the officer likes the additional income, and the residents feel safer. Such arrangements are probably more successful than hiring private watchmen, and the Newark experiment helps us understand why. A private security guard may deter crime or misconduct by his presence, and he may go to the aid of persons needing help, but he may well not intervene—that is, control or drive away—someone challenging community standards. Being a sworn officer—a "real cop"—seems to give one the confidence, the sense of duty, and the aura of authority necessary to perform this difficult task.

Patrol officers might be encouraged to go to and from duty stations on public transportation and, while on the bus or subway car, enforce rules about smoking, drinking, disorderly conduct, and the like. The enforcement need involve nothing more than ejecting the offender (the offense, after all, is not one with which a booking officer or a judge wishes to be bothered). Perhaps the random but relentless maintenance of standards on buses would lead to conditions on buses that approximate the level of civility we now take for granted on airplanes.

But the most important requirement is to think that to maintain order in precarious situations is a vital job. The police know this is one of their functions, and they also believe, correctly, that it cannot be done to the exclusion of criminal investigation and responding to calls. We may have encouraged them to suppose, however, on the basis of our oft-repeated concerns about serious, violent crime, that they will be judged exclusively on their capacity as crime-fighters. To the extent that this is the case, police administrators will continue to concentrate police personnel in the highest-crime areas (although not necessarily in the areas most vulnerable to criminal invasion), emphasize their training in the law and criminal apprehension (and not their training in managing street life), and join too quickly in campaigns to decriminalize "harmless" behavior (although public drunkenness, street prostitution, and pornographic displays can destroy a community more quickly than any team of professional burglars).

Above all, we must return to our long-abandoned view that the police ought to protect communities as well as individuals. Our crime statistics and victimization surveys measure individual losses, but they do not measure communal losses. Just as physicians now recognize the importance of fostering health rather than simply treating illness, so the police—and the rest of us—ought to recognize the importance of maintaining, intact, communities without broken windows.

Police Crackdowns

LAWRENCE W. SHERMAN

ONE of the most widespread developments in American policing in the 1980s has been the "crackdown." Drunk driving, domestic violence, public drug markets, streetwalking prostitutes, illegal parking, and even bicycle riders have all been targets for publicly announced police crackdowns. What all these target problems have in common is such a high volume of occurrence that police had previously ignored most individual transgressions. What the crackdowns had in common was a sharp increase in law enforcement resources applied to the previously underenforced laws, with a clear goal of enhancing general deterrence of the misconduct.

Police crackdowns increase enforcement resources in two basic ways that often overlap. One is an *offense-specific* policy change about how to handle specific cases, such as arresting wife beaters rather than counseling them or towing illegally parked cars rather than just ticketing them, wherever the problem is encountered. The other is a *geographically focused* increase in the dosage of police presence, which can approximate a temporary state of full enforcement of every law on the books. Both kinds of crackdowns attempt to communicate a far more powerful threat of apprehension and punishment than does "normal" policing.

Both kinds of crackdowns are highly controversial, although the geographically focused approach is probably more vulnerable to charges that police violate civil liberties. Much of the controversy centers on the effectiveness of crackdowns: are they worth the price in tax dollars

From *Crime and Justice, An Annual Review of Research* (pp. 49-84), M. Tonry and N. Morris, editors, 1990, Chicago: University of Chicago Press. Copyright 1990 by the University of Chicago Press. Reprinted by permission.

and public inconvenience? Vocal constituencies may strongly support crackdowns, but police critics often argue that crackdowns are undertaken cynically for political purposes or as an excuse for police to earn overtime pay. It is claimed that police know crackdowns are really ineffective, but cannot afford to admit that fact in public.

Similarly, academic observers have been skeptical about the effects of police crackdowns. The leading student of drunk driving enforcement has argued that such crackdowns fail to create lasting deterrence, while a leading police scholar has suggested that massive, sudden increases in police patrol can deter street crimes temporarily but not over the long run.

All of these debates fail to make important distinctions among the different kinds of deterrent effects crackdowns can produce. Among other distinctions, they fail to separate any *initial* deterrence in the immediate wake of a crackdown from the possible *residual* deterrence after the crackdown has been withdrawn and the speed with which any initial deterrence *decays* during or after the crackdown.

These distinctions suggest a new way to increase the effectiveness of police crackdowns. Rather than attempt to maintain crackdowns over long periods of time, as many departments have done, police might use their resources more effectively if crackdowns are seen as short-term efforts frequently shifted from area to area or problem to problem. By constantly changing crackdown targets, police may reduce crime more thorough residual deterrence than through initial deterrence. And by limiting the time period devoted to each target, police might also avoid wasting scarce resources on a decaying initial deterrent effect.

This essay examines the basic reasoning for this hypothesis. There is evidence that some crackdowns do create initial deterrence, or at least displacement, of some kinds of offending. However, it is hard to sustain many crackdowns over a long period, either because of decaying implementation or decaying offender perception of the crackdown as creating a high risk of apprehension. Several of the crackdowns reviewed in this essay, which were intentionally ended quite early, suggest that such risk perceptions may decay slowly, even when the actual police effort has been returned to normal. The slow decay constitutes a "free bonus" residue of deterrence. This residue fits the growing body of theory and evidence about how people make decisions under conditions of uncertainty, since intermittent, unpredictable crackdowns make risks of apprehension far more uncertain than could any system of fixed police priorities—including long-term crackdowns. But systematic empirical evidence for the residual deterrence hypothesis is still quite meager, and field experiments in police departments are needed to test it adequately.

The purpose of this essay is not to advocate crackdowns but rather to consider how they might be employed and evaluated more effectively. Section 1 begins with a description of the scarcity problem—a problem as old as the American police—that a rotating police crackdown policy could help to manage. Section 2 defines some concepts and theory for analyzing that problem and discusses its possible management by intermittent crackdowns. Section 3 presents a series of case studies on crackdowns on a variety of target problems that illustrate the extent and limits of our knowledge of the crackdowns. Varieties of crackdown effects are identified in Section 4.

1. MANAGING THE SCARCITY PROBLEM

The basic theory of criminal justice is that crime can be deterred through certain punishment. But in modern America, there is too much crime and too little law enforcement to make punishment very certain. Despite continuing debate, there have been few recent revenue increases devoted to increasing the certainty of police apprehension per offense. After 1978, in fact, the total number of police in big cities began to decline while reports of both serious and minor crimes increased substantially.

Triage

There are two ways for policymakers to adapt to this dilemma of scarce police resources. One is the constant shifting of priorities suggested in this essay but rarely used in practice. The more common method is simply to set permanent "triage" priorities: some kinds of offenses are ignored and others given very little attention, so that resources can be concentrated on more serious problems. In some cities, for example, police will not investigate burglaries unless the value of loss exceeds $5,000. In other cities, pot smoking and public drinking have been virtually legalized by police inattention. And until quite recently, police, prosecutors, and judges rarely took any action against minor domestic violence. These practical compromises were all seen as necessary ways to have enough personnel and prison space for armed robbers, narcotics pushers, rapists, and murderers.

One consequence of this triage approach is endless wrangling over what the priorities should be. Thus, an early 1986 *New York Times* editorial took New York's police commissioner to task for failing to enforce bicycle traffic laws after three deaths and many injuries to pedestrians. The commissioner's public response was that he could not spare the personnel from dealing with the "crack" epidemic. Nonetheless, by July of that year New York police had launched an unannounced crackdown on cyclists, issuing 3,633 summonses in two weeks, and prompting Buffalo, New York police to follow suit.

These sporadic pressures on police are nothing new. Like the exhausted parent, police fail to crack down out of sheer poverty of resources rather than poverty of desire. The "overreach" of the criminal law has long made it necessary for police to ignore many, and perhaps most, violations of the criminal law. But when political pressures or the news media focus attention on some offense pattern that has been subjected to little enforcement, police resources may be temporarily diverted from normal priorities to that long-ignored problem.

The effect is almost a change in the interpretation of the criminal law, a virtual admission that the offense had previously been too low a priority to command scarce enforcement resources. The crackdown communicates to the law-breaking public a statement that, in effect, the law is back on the books. Indeed, when Milwaukee police cracked down on misdemeanor domestic violence in 1986 with a new arrest policy, street officers often explained their actions to the arrestees as the result of a new law.

Historical Context

The very origins of the American police are tied to the permanent crackdown strategy. After watching public behavior patterns among recent immigrant groups become increasingly disorderly, or at least a threat to the status position of the earlier settlers, city after city in the nineteenth century created a full-time, uniformed police force. Research on the enforcement activity of these early police departments shows that they had little impact on the level of felony arrests, which continued to be made by independent marshals and constables. Instead, the new police bureaucracies produced a drastic increase in the number of arrests for public disorder, especially drinking and fighting. Some early police officers made over ten arrests a day, a rate unheard of by modern standards—even for disorder offenses. Thus, even at their birth, a primary function of American police was to crack down on an enormous (and probably overwhelming) volume of what Reiss has labeled "soft crime."

But the widespread and persistent patterns of that behavior created inertia against sustained police enforcement, so that the first century of American policing was a saga of repeated, failed attempts to achieve a permanent crackdown on public disorder. Lincoln Steffens describes the 1890s efforts of New York City's Protestant ministers and Police Commissioner Teddy Roosevelt to have the prostitution, gambling, and saloon-closing laws enforced, with sporadic success. William Whyte's *Street Corner Society* shows how even systematic police corruption in Boston, in the 1930s, and crackdowns on vice were a recurring political necessity but never an effective long-term policy:

While the system is organized to adjust itself to a certain quota of arrests, periodic crises of law enforcement involve serious dislocations to the racket organization. Crises arise when some spectacular event, such as an act of violence, draws public attention to conditions which have existed all the time. As an agent commented, "You remember that shooting in Maxton? After that the horse rooms and gambling places were closed up all over the county. And after that killing in Crighton, Crighton was all closed up for a few weeks." In such a time of crisis few places are actually raided, but the racketeers are told by their friends in the department that they must close their establishments, and they do—for the duration.

Punishment Risks
Are Too Predictable

The intermittent pressures for crackdowns in different areas may temporarily disrupt the normal triage solution to the police scarcity problem. But such pressures are rare enough, or can be handled with few enough officers, so that the triage is generally kept constant. Whether the triage priorities should be permanent is a major question of police strategy.

Permanent law enforcement priorities may make the risks of punishment all too predictable for criminals. They know that the risks of being punished for killing a police officer, for example, are enormous, and then will try to avoid that offense if they are at all rational. But they also know that the risks of being caught and punished for most stranger-to-stranger crime—residential burglary, purse snatching, car theft, and lesser crimes—are very low. What is more, the risks were low yesterday and they will be low tomorrow, next year, and the year after.

This means that we need to make Reuter's important distinction between the *risk* of getting caught and the *certainty* about what that risk is for any given offense on any given day. If potential criminals were very certain of a high risk that they would be caught and punished, we might create the greatest deterrent effect. What we offer them instead is high certainty of low risk of punishment for most offenses. But for the same dollar cost, we could offer them low certainty about whether the risk of punishment is high—or low at any given time and place—and perhaps reduce some kinds of crime substantially.

2. CRACKDOWN CONCEPTS AND THEORY

This section defines the key concepts in police crackdowns. It then integrates them to form a theoretical argument. The hypothesis is that, given a fixed level of resources, police can create more general deterrence through rotating crackdowns than through permanent priorities.

Concepts

Increases in either the certainty or severity of official police reaction to a specific type of crime or all crime in a specific area are called crackdowns. More precisely, police crackdowns can be defined as a sudden change in activity which is usually proactive, although it can include increased likelihood of arrest during encounters initiated by citizens, and intended drastically to increase either the communicated threat or actual certainty of apprehension for a specific type or types of offense that have been highly visible or widely committed in certain identifiable places or situations.

Crackdowns must be distinguished from normal police personnel allocation decisions. The distribution of officers around a city is normal, unequal per square mile since it is guided by such factors as the relative density of population, calls for service, and reported crime in each area. Simply adjusting the allocations as those factors change is not a crackdown but a fine-tuning of the permanent triage priorities. Crackdowns are focused on specific target problems, which provide the sole justification for reallocation of police resources outside the usual formula.

Police crackdowns have three possible tactical elements: *presence, sanctions,* and *media*
threats. Presence is simply an increased ratio of police officers per potential offender, either in places or in situations. Increased presence can be accomplished either through uniformed presence (which communicates a visible threat) or plainclothes surveillance (which enhances the potential offenders' uncertainty about the risks of apprehension). Sanctions denote any coercive police imposition on offenders or potential offenders: stopping cars or pedestrians for identification checks, issuing warnings, mounting roadblock check points, conducting breathalyzer tests, making arrests, and so on. Media threats are announced intentions to increase sanctioning certainty and are reported in newspapers, public service announcements on TV and radio, or even billboard campaigns.

The actual combinations of these tactical elements vary in practice. The interaction between presence and sanctions, for example, is ironically perverse: greater presence can produce more sanctions, but sanctions can reduce presence by taking police away to process arrests. In the Georgetown crackdown in 1985, Washington police avoided this dilemma by installing a booking center in a trailer parked on the street on weekend nights, saving the police a two-mile drive to the station for each arrest. Area crackdowns tend to emphasize presence, while offense-specific crackdowns emphasize sanctions. Whether a media campaign is added to the other elements of a crackdown may depend upon public interest in the problem as well as business interest in providing such advertising services free of charge.

A *backoff* is the usual sequel to a crackdown. For reasons of necessity (which may be a virtue), crackdowns rarely last forever. On rare occasions, some crackdowns may become part of the permanent triage, realigning the previous priority system. But most will eventually terminate in a backoff, which can be defined as a reduction in the visible threat or actual certainty of apprehension created by a crackdown. Backoffs occur suddenly or gradually, by policy decision or by uncorrected informal action of enforcement personnel, and by reduced presence or reduced sanctioning.

These concepts of enforcement activity and threats to take action require corresponding concepts of their effects on crime. The principal effect is some level of crime after a crackdown begins; crime either declines, remains unchanged, or increases, all to a greater or lesser degree. Any crime reduction is arguably a *general deterrent* effect, even though it fails to distinguish between the participation rate of offending in the population and the frequency rate of offending by active offenders. This distinction has never been addressed in crackdown research, although Sampson and Cohen have used it in cross-sectional deterrence analysis.

Interpreting any crime reduction as deterrence is problematic in other ways. A reduction could have been caused by incapacitation of a few active offenders early on in the crackdown. It could have been caused by other reasons, such as changing transportation patterns or declining area population. But over short-term periods with large enough numbers of offenses, it seems reasonably plausible for police to interpret a crime reduction as a deterrent effect.

The more important point is the distinction between initial and residual deterrence. If a crime reduction is achieved while the crackdown tactic—presence, sanctions, or publicity—is still in operation, then it is plausibly an initial deterrence effect. But if the crime reduction is sustained after the tactic is terminated or reduced, then it might plausibly be a residual deterrent effect. The "hangover" perceived risk of apprehension could influence decisions not to commit offenses after the risk (or the communicated threat) is actually reduced, at least until such time as other evidence shows the quasi-rational actors that the risk has returned to its prior level. Decay, or a gradual decline from initial changes, is therefore a central concept for crackdowns in at least three ways: crackdown decay, initial deterrence decay, and residual deterrence decay.

CRACKDOWN DECAY   Since a crackdown requires greater police effort, the usual bureaucratic regression to the mean level of effort may cause the implementation of the crackdown itself to decay. Fewer arrests are made, fewer people are stopped, more officers are diverted to other duties, all of which could be planned by

police commanders or just carried out by the lower ranks.

INITIAL DETERRENCE DECAY   With or without a decay of police effort, an initial crime reduction might decay through potential offenders' learning through trial and error that they had overestimated the certainty of getting caught at the beginning of the crackdown.

RESIDUAL DETERRENCE DECAY   The same learning process can take place gradually after the effort is actually reduced, with the residual deterrence slowly declining as word of mouth communication and personal experience show that it is once again "safe" to offend.

3. CASE STUDIES

This section reviews the case study evidence on the implementation of police crackdowns, with more limited evidence on their initial and residual deterrent effects. The section is organized by the target problems that recent crackdowns have addressed. It begins with a relatively detailed description of an *area-focused* crackdown in the Georgetown section of Washington, D.C., in the mid-1980s. It then considers both scholarly studies and press accounts of crackdowns on drugs, drunk driving, prostitution, residential calls to police, and various other targets. The drugs section includes a brief review of crackdowns by private citizens. Finally, the section interprets other police experiments in the crackdown framework.

An Area Crackdown: Georgetown, 1985

Crackdowns are often directed at a wide range of crime and disorder problems within a specific geographic area. One example of the operations and effects of area crackdowns is described in the case study of the 1985 crackdown on illegal parking and disorder in the Georgetown section of Washington, D.C. The crackdown was prompted by large numbers of high school-age youths drawn to Georgetown by the district's low minimum age (18) for legal beer and wine drinking, especially after the drinking age was gradually raised in Maryland and Virginia. The crackdown was intended not only to control illegal parking and public drinking on busy weekend nights but also, as Wilson and Kelling suggest, to control street crime attracted by such disorder.

In January of 1985, the second district commander and the Georgetown area commander announced a crackdown on disorderly behavior: "The public must see that in Georgetown no breach of the law is so trivial that it can be ignored." The police program implemented on April 5 focused on the weekend periods of large and disorderly crowds in ways designed to restore order rather than to make large numbers of arrests for violent crimes.

PUBLICITY   The Georgetown crackdown was aided by a massive amount of publicity. The publicity, in turn, was related to the most visible element of the crackdown: a ban on weekend evening parking on certain key streets near many restaurants and bars. The Washington area public of all ages now risked having their cars towed in Georgetown. Other elements included at least a 30 percent increase in installing a trailer at the key intersection for total weekend manpower; booking arrestees; military police, including at least four MPs on weekend foot patrol, to deal with the large numbers of military personnel from nearby bases; increased plainclothes patrol along the residential side streets; and extra tow trucks patrolling the area for parking enforcement. The publicity was almost instantly favorable in pronouncing the crackdown a success. The publicity kept up intermittently over the summer, in a generally favorable fashion, with continued stress on the parking enforcement. It was hard to live in the Washington area that year and not have some sense that the cops were being more vigilant in Georgetown.

PARKING ENFORCEMENT   The official statistics support the impression of increased vigilance. While no comparisons to prior years were available, police told the local paper that between March and September up to eighty police and an unknown number of traffic department employees had produced 60,487 parking tickets, 9,231 moving violations, 2,062 arrests, and 6,407 vehicle tows. The very high certainty of parking enforcement the crackdown created is supported by the results of a systematic poll of the street population of Georgetown done by Anne Roschelle in late 1985. Of 150 respondents interviewed at the corner of Wisconsin and M Streets at different times of day or night (with sixty-seven refusals, for a 69 percent response rate in a sample of 217), 41 percent said they had gotten a parking ticket and 11 percent said they had had their cars towed since the crackdown had begun the prior spring.

DISORDER ENFORCEMENT   There was a clear increase in arrests for public disorder. During the first three months of the six-month crackdown, disorder arrests numbered almost twice as many as during the same period in the preceding year. By the second three-month period, the increase had dropped to 10 percent. But for the entire six-month crackdown period, the average was a 40 percent increase.

Still, one is struck by how few arrests there were relative to the reported size of the crowds. Even at 500 arrests each week, that is still only some seventy per day. If even 400 arrests were made on weekends, that would be 200 per day out of 20,000 people or 1 percent of the population on the streets at peak periods. Given the descriptions of how badly behaved that population was, either police had to overlook many continued violations or their deterrent presence greatly reduced the number of disorder-arrest opportunities. There was little change in other types of arrest.

THE BACKOFF   The police Anne Roschelle interviewed clearly indicated the backoff had begun by Halloween. Not only were there fewer officers, but as the *Washington Post* reported, the officers who were there may have done less—a predictable example of crackdown decay. One officer said on November 15, "I haven't been looking as hard for illegally parked cars in recent months." Another said, on November 20, "I don't ticket as many cars as I did during April through August. Now that the summer is over the bulk of the crowds have gone."

EFFECT ON CRIME What effect did the crackdown have on crime? It is hard to answer that question scientifically. This case study illustrates many of the statistical problems involved in assessing deterrent effects in natural quasi-experiments, especially for very small geographic areas. Although such areas are very important for police policy, they are often too small to provide enough weekly reported crimes for an adequate statistical test. The weekly average number of street robberies in Georgetown, for example, declined by 10 percent. But because the absolute numbers dropped from only 2.6 to 2.3 per week, the reduction could easily have occurred by chance. Moreover, the Georgetown-area crime trends did not differ from the citywide trends or trends in a comparison area.

PERCEPTIONS OF THE CRACKDOWN Nonetheless, we found other evidence that the crackdown had both a short-term deterrent effect and longer-term residual deterrence. One opportunity sample of forty-nine people surveyed in local bars found that 100 percent of the respondents thought the area was less crowded, 92 percent thought it was safer, 80 percent thought there was less crime, and—a month after the crackdown ended—55 percent thought the crackdown was still in force with no backoff.

The other opportunity sample of 150 persons (at a 69 percent response rate) walking on the principal street corner (Wisconsin and M) found similar results: 87 percent were aware of the crackdown, 79 percent believed police were still enforcing the parking ban strictly (a month after the backoff), 72 percent thought the area was safer, 71 percent thought the area was less crowded, and 67 percent thought it was more orderly. Only 35 percent thought crime had gone down, but perhaps because 11 percent of the respondents said they had been towed and 41 percent had been ticketed, 47 percent had changed their parking habits since the crackdown—something which might have made residual deterrence of illegal parking by this six-month crackdown last for many months or years.

Drug Crackdowns

A more common police crackdown target in the 1980s has been open-air drug markets. They have been attacked with a variety of tactics: parking a police trailer in their midst, increasing uniformed police presence, surprising drug dealers with plainclothes officers in a "jump-out" squad, and even using citizen patrols. Both the anecdotal and the statistical evidence on the effectiveness of these tactics is mixed.

POLICE TRAILER CRACKDOWNS Unlike the police trailer in Georgetown, the parking of a trailer in a drug market is not a tool for making more arrests with less booking time. It is more like sending in the fleet, rattling the saber so there will be no arrests. The Washington police employed this tactic in the most publicized drug market in the city, Hanover Place, in early 1985 (Operation Avalanche). One *Post* reporter has found the constant presence of sixty police officers per day on the block to be an effective long-term initial deterrent, at least while this presence was maintained: "For years the city's busiest cocaine market, it had become one of the deadliest blocks in town, the few residents living like prisoners in their homes. . . . Today Hanover Place remains a transformed area where children play in their yards and adults sit comfortably on front steps."

The effects of such massive police presence may appear obvious, as well as prohibitively expensive. Yet a trailer with just two officers in it may be insufficient to deter drug dealing. An Albany, New York alderman—whose statements may not be without political bias—reported witnessing drug deals on two separate occasions right in front of a police trailer in the Pine Hills neighborhood of that city. The alderman, who was protesting a two-year-old decision to close the local neighborhood precinct station, described the police in the trailer as vulnerable to sniper fire and unaware of what was going on outside. Meanwhile, the mayor of nearby Schenectady was persuaded to replicate the Albany two-officer trailer in a drug market.

POLICE PRESENCE CRACKDOWNS The evidence on police presence crackdowns is far more detailed but equally mixed. On one side stands

Kleiman's generally favorable evaluations of intensified uniformed presence in drug markets in Lynn, Massachusetts. On the other stands the generally negative evaluations of such crackdowns in Lawrence, Massachusetts and a Washington, D.C. citywide crackdown on drug markets.

LYNN AND LAWRENCE Through interviews and crime statistics, Kleiman describes a crackdown, focused on a geographically small open-air heroin market in Lynn, beginning in September of 1983 and lasting at least four years. The crackdown began with six state police officers assigned for nine months (and then shifted to Lawrence) and one city officer. It was continued after nine months with four to six city officers. In its first ten months, the crackdown officers made 140 arrests aimed at disruption of the market. Arrests subsequently continued at a "much lower rate." Kleiman reports that heroin consumption apparently declined, with an 85 percent increase in local demand for drug treatment, which was unmatched statewide. Moreover, robberies and burglaries declined substantially citywide for two years after the beginning of the crackdown, without any apparent increase in those crimes nearby (local displacement).

The experience in Lawrence with the same state police unit was less encouraging. A larger market area was harder to control, except for the most flagrant public housing project. Unlike practices in Lynn, Lawrence's police tactics emphasized search warrants more than observation-of-sale arrests. The close proximity of alternative drug markets in nearby Lowell made it difficult to restrict drug supplies to street criminals. There was no apparent decline in drug use, and there was a substantial *increase* in violent crime.

WASHINGTON Perhaps the most dramatic example of a citywide police-presence drug crackdown is Washington's Operation Clean Sweep. Begun in August 1986, the crackdown allocated 100-200 officers to fifty-nine drug markets throughout the city. In its first seventeen months, it claimed 29,519 arrests, or about sixty a day. Tactics included roadblocks, observation

of the open-air markets, "reverse buy" sell-and-busts by undercover officers, and the seizure of cars. The program was conducted by officers on overtime, some of whom reportedly doubled their salaries but suffered extreme exhaustion. Local residents praised its efforts, but some made two key complaints: the resurgence of drug trade after police left a drug market (although with apparently some residual deterrent decay) and rapid displacement of drug markets to nearby locations. But an independent analysis found that the crackdown was "well-executed and coordinated," with high levels of prosecution, conviction, and sentencing resulting from the large numbers of arrests made.

The citywide impact of Clean Sweep on drug traffic was disappointing. While fewer drug markets operated openly, two indicators of drug use showed substantial increases from 1986 to 1987: urinalysis of arrestees and emergency room admissions. This failure to reduce measured drug abuse may be simply a result of the late arrival of "crack" to Washington in mid-1987, a major change in the nature of the drug market. Without the operation of a strong police crackdown, the rising tide of drug abuse might even have risen much faster. The absence of any control group observations makes it impossible to tell.

What is most disturbing about this massive crackdown followed by a "crack" explosion, however, is the record increase in Washington's homicides. Homicides rose from a total of 148 in 1985 to 287 by the end of October 1988, and the percentage of homicides "attributed" to drugs rose from 17 to 68. Many victims were killed in crossfire between rival drug dealers exchanging shots. Some were killed on the streets, while others (including children) were killed in apartments, where more drug dealing seemed to take place after the crackdown had been in effect for a while. This pattern leads some local observers to suggest that the crackdown helped cause the increase in murders in two ways. One is that "intensified enforcement has raised the violence of the drug trades, simply because the participants feel more threatened." Another cause is that crackdowns move drug conflicts indoors, where children and other innocent bystanders are closer at hand.

These possibilities are all the more troubling to the basic hypothesis of this essay, since the structure of Operation Clean Sweep was essentially the rotating target strategy we considered at the outset. The target rotation has been geographic rather than substantive, however, turning the local criminal justice system almost into a drug abuse control system. Perhaps rotating the substantive emphasis as well as the geographic locales of the drug markets would have produced different results; so might a greater emphasis on treatment and prevention, such as trailer-based drug treatment clinics in crackdown areas.

Drunk Driving Crackdowns

Perhaps the best studied target for police crackdowns has been drunk driving. The easily identifiable target (drivers) and relatively clear outcome measure (accidents) makes it ideal for such analysis. The major drawback of generalizing from drunk driving enforcement to other issues is the difference in the social class of the potential offenders.

Drunk drivers may include a far higher proportion of middle-class, educated offenders than do street drug dealers or robbers. This may alter the sensitivity to possible sanctions, since a drunk driving arrest can be far more devastating to a white-collar worker's career than a robbery arrest is to a marginally employed person. Class differences may also make drunk driving more sensitive than other offenses to publicity about police detection efforts since better-educated persons may be more likely than others to read newspapers or follow other news media reports closely.

Whether they are typical or not, drunk drivers have been found to be highly sensitive to communicated threats of apprehension. If anything, they seem more sensitive to the threat communication than to the actual differences in police sanctioning.

The clearest evidence of this pattern comes from the New Zealand drunk driving "blitz" evaluation. In two separate multiweek crackdowns aimed at intensifying police enforcement for higher certainty of apprehension per drunk driver trip, a several-week period of public announcements preceded the actual enforcement increase. The public was told that the principal tactic would be to give breath tests at every conceivable opportunity. They were even told when the blitz would begin. Measures, both of cars parked in tavern parking lots and patients admitted to hospitals for auto crash injuries, showed substantial reductions in the weeks preceding the actual crackdown. This also occurred before the second crackdown, which was implemented six months after the first.

If one assumes New Zealanders expect a threat from their police to be carried out, then the publicity effect before and after the first blitz is not surprising. But it is striking that the residual deterrence of accidents disappeared after the end of the postblitz publicity, rising from 140-odd per week back to the preblitz level of over 190. A publicity effect before the second blitz is perhaps more important, for it suggests that the first blitz provided a convincing demonstration of the crackdown threat and maintained its credibility. Even without publicity after the end of the second blitz, however, the residual deterrent effect lasted about as long as the blitz itself, taking as many weeks to return to the preblitz level of crashes.

This short-term drunk driving crackdown provides the best measured examples of residual deterrence after a sharply defined backoff. Longer-term drunk driving crackdowns, however, show the clear pattern of initial deterrence and decay (just as in Lynn), even with increases in police sanctioning levels. The Ross evaluation of the 1967 British Road Safety Act showed that after an initial 66 percent reduction in serious and fatal crashes in the first year of the law, the number of crashes doubled in the second year of the law and continued to rise quite steadily thereafter—despite steady increases in the number of breath tests actually administered.

4. VARIETIES OF CRACKDOWN EFFECTS

Taken together, these case studies suggest several varieties of crackdown effects among at least two varieties of crackdowns themselves: short term and long term. Other varieties of crackdowns, such as relative emphasis on presence, sanctions, and publicity, can also be distinguished. The varieties of effects concern five key questions: Was there an initial deterrent effect? Was there any crime increase? Was there apparent local displacement? Did any initial deterrence decay? Was there any residual deterrence?

Initial Deterrence Successes

Perhaps the most important, if expected, conclusion from previous studies is that most of the crackdowns produced initial deterrence. This evidence, even without reference to specific police dosage levels, contradicts the conclusion many have drawn from the Kansas City Preventive Patrol Experiment that variations in police presence do not affect crime. In general, increases in police presence, sanctioning, or media threats can be expected to produce at least brief reductions in the target crime problem. Discounting this finding because crackdowns rarely produce lasting deterrence may miss the important point that something *can* work, predictably, to fight crime in specific ways.

Backfire: Crime Increases

The initial successes must be tempered not only by failures but also by two that may have caused a crime increase (both drug crackdowns). The causal link between the crackdown and the crime increase is not strong, but it is about as strong as the causal link in the successful cases. There are plausible reasons for the Lawrence crackdown to have caused more robbery and for Washington's Clean Sweep to have caused more drug homicides. The point of these case studies should be that crackdowns on market-driven forces like drug markets can have complex results and that it is possible for well-intended efforts to make things worse.

Displacement

A more encouraging finding is that displacement was clearly indicated in only a few of the crackdowns, all but one of them focused on drug markets. Drug dealing may be the most resilient

and movable crime problem to which crackdowns are applied. None of the drunk driving crackdowns, for example, show any signs of displacement, perhaps because they affected such large geographic areas. The other cases all suffered from poor measurement of displacement, which poses a difficult task for any researcher. Some displacement will probably occur with most geographic police-presence crackdowns. But it is not yet known what proportion will be displaced and whether there will be a net reduction in offending. There are good theoretical reasons to suggest that changing the opportunity structure for crime through crackdowns can yield a net reduction in crime. Moreover, as Barr and Pease suggest, even total displacement can have good effects if the "deflected" crimes are less serious than they would have been otherwise.

Deterrence Decay

There are two important things about decaying deterrence across studies of crackdowns. One is that none of the five successful short-term crackdowns suffered deterrence decay, confirming the expectation that the decay problem may be limited to longer crackdowns. The other finding is that decay is not a universal pattern even in longer-term crackdowns. The two years of apparent continued deterrence of open drug dealing (but not robbery) in the Lower East Side, the two years of possible deterrence in New York's subways, and over six months of deterrence by Muslims and the police in Mayfair Mansions suggest that it may be possible to sustain the benefits of a crackdown under certain conditions. Nonetheless, most of the long-term crackdowns with initial deterrence saw at least some aspects of that effect decay, over time. The deterrence wore off after two years in Lynn and two years in the subways, despite constant levels of police presence.

Residual Deterrence Successes

Only six of the documented crackdowns measured crime during a backoff period. One of these had no initial deterrence. All of those that achieved initial deterrence and then backed off produced a residual effect. The combination of the short-term residual pattern with the long-term decay suggests that much of the deterrent effect of any crackdown may result from its initial shock to the potential offenders. We cannot know how many of the decay cases would have shown residual deterrence if the crackdowns had been stopped sooner, but we can speculate that the rebounding crime rates might have looked much the same without continued expenditure of police resources. Since the major obstacle to broader police use of crackdowns is limited numbers of personnel, aiming for residual (if decaying) deterrence could make wider use of crackdowns far more feasible than trying to achieve sustained deterrence over time. The only way to be sure would be to undertake far more systematic research than we have just reviewed. The research would require varying the nature of the crackdown tactics, the target crime problems, and the length of the efforts in a series of well-controlled experiments: preferring the tortoise of such an accumulation to the hare of multivariate analysis.

The Kansas City Preventive Patrol Experiment: A Summary Report

GEORGE L. KELLING
TONY PATE
DUANE DIECKMAN
CHARLES E. BROWN

EVER since the creation of a patrolling force in thirteenth-century Hangchow, preventive patrol by uniformed personnel has been a primary function of policing. In twentieth-century America, about $2 billion is spent each year for the maintenance and operation of uniformed and often superbly equipped patrol forces. Police themselves, the general public, and elected officials have always believed that the presence or potential presence of police officers on patrol severely inhibits criminal activity.

One of the principal police spokesmen for this view was the late O. W. Wilson, former chief of the Chicago Police Department and a prominent academic theorist on police issues. As Wilson once put it, "Patrol is an indispensable service that plays a leading role in the accomplishment of the police purpose. It is the only form of police service that directly attempts to eliminate opportunity for misconduct." Wilson believed that by creating the impression of police omnipresence, patrol convinced most potential offenders that opportunities for successful misconduct did not exist.

To the present day, Wilson's has been the prevailing view. While modern technology, through the creation of new methods of transportation, surveillance, and communications,

From *The Kansas City Preventive Patrol Experiment* (pp. 20-45) by G. L. Kelling, et al., 1974, Washington, DC: Police Foundation.

has added vastly to the tools of patrol, and while there have been refinements in patrol strategies based upon advanced probability formulas and other computerized methods, the general principle has remained the same. Today's police recruits, like virtually all those before them, learn from both teacher and textbook that patrol is the "backbone" of police work.

No less than the police themselves, the general public has been convinced that routine preventive patrol is an essential element of effective policing. As the International City Management Association has pointed out, "For the greatest number of persons, deterrence through ever-present police patrol, coupled with the prospect of speedy police action once a report is received, appears important to crime control." Thus, in the face of spiraling crime rates, the most common answer urged by public officials and citizens alike has been to increase patrol forces and get more police officers "on the street." The assumption is that increased displays of police presence are vitally necessary in the face of increased criminal activity. Recently, citizens in troubled neighborhoods have themselves resorted to civilian versions of patrol.

It was in this context that the Kansas City, Missouri, Police Department, under a grant from the Police Foundation, undertook in 1972 the most comprehensive experiment ever conducted to analyze the effectiveness of routine preventive patrol.

DESCRIPTION OF THE PREVENTIVE PATROL EXPERIMENT

The impetus for an experiment in preventive patrol came from within the Kansas City Police Department in 1971. While this may be surprising to some, the fact is that by that year the Kansas City department had already experienced more than a decade of innovation and improvement in its operations and working climate and had pined for a reputation as one of the nation's more progressive police departments.

Within the South Patrol Division's 24-beat area, nine beats were eliminated from consideration for the experiment as unrepresentative of the city's socioeconomic composition. The remaining 15-beat, 32-square mile experimental area encompassed a commercial-residential mixture, with a 1970 resident population of 148,395 persons and a density of 4,542 persons per square mile (significantly greater than that for Kansas City as a whole, which in 1970 with only 1,604 persons per square mile was 45th in the nation). Racially, the beats within this area ranged from 78 percent black to 99 percent white. Median family income of residents ranged from a low of $7,320 for one beat to a high of $15,964 for another. On the average, residents of the experimental area tended to have been in their homes from 6.6 to 10.9 years.

Police officers assigned to the experimental area were those who had been patrolling it prior to the experiment and tended to be white, relatively young, and somewhat new to the police department. In a sample of 101 officers in the experimental area taken across all three shifts, 9.9 percent of the officers were black, the average age of the officers was 27 years, and average time on the force was 3.2 years.

The 15 beats in the experimental area were computer matched on the basis of crime data, number of calls for service, ethnic composition, median income and transiency of population into five groups of three each. Within each group, one beat was designated reactive, one control, and one proactive. In the five reactive beats, there was no preventive patrol as such. Police vehicles assigned these beats entered them only in response to calls for service. Their noncommitted time (when not answering calls) was spent patrolling the boundaries of the reactive beats or patrolling in adjacent proactive beats. While police availability was closely maintained, police visibility was, in effect, withdrawn (except when police vehicles were seen while answering calls for service).

In the five control beats, the usual level of patrol was maintained at one car per beat. In the five proactive beats, the department increased police patrol visibility by two to three times its usual level both by the assignment of marked police vehicles to these beats and the presence of units from adjacent reactive beats.

Other than the restrictions placed upon officers in reactive beats (respond only to calls for service and patrol only the perimeter of the beat or in an adjacent proactive beat), no special instructions were given to police officers in the experimental area. Officers in control and proactive beats were to conduct preventive patrol as they normally would.

EXPERIMENTAL FINDINGS

The essential finding of the preventive patrol experiment is that decreasing or increasing routine preventive patrol within the range tested in this experiment had no effect on crime, citizen fear of crime, community attitudes toward the police on the delivery of police service, police response time, or traffic accidents.

EFFECTS ON CRIME, REPORTING, AND ARRESTS

Finding 1: Victimization

The Victimization Study found no statistically significant differences in crime in any of the 69 comparisons made between reactive, control, and proactive beats.

This finding would be expected for such categories as rape, homicide, and common or aggravated assault. For one thing, these are typically impulsive crimes, usually taking place between persons known to each other. Furthermore, they most often take place inside a building, out of sight of an officer on routine preventive patrol. The spontaneity and lack of high visibility of these crimes, therefore, make it unlikely that they would be much affected by variations in the level of preventive patrol.

Given traditional beliefs about patrol, however, it is surprising that statistically significant differences did not occur in such crimes as commercial burglaries, auto theft, and robberies.

Nonetheless, as measured by the victimization survey, these crimes were not significantly affected by changes in the level of routine preventive patrol.

Finding 2: Departmental Reported Crime

Departmental reported crimes showed only one statistically significant difference among 51 comparisons drawn between reactive, control, and proactive beats.

Statistical significance occurred only in the category of "other sex crimes." This category, separate from "rape," includes such offenses a molestation and exhibitionism. Since this category is not traditionally considered to be responsive to routine preventive patrol, however, it appears likely that this instance of significance was a statistically random occurrence.

Finding 3: Rates of Reporting Crime

Crimes that citizens and businessmen said they reported to the police showed statistical significant differences between reactive, control, and proactive beats in only five of 48 comparisons, and these differences showed no consistent pattern.

Of the five instances of statistical significance, three involved vandalism and two residence burglary. But where statistical significance was found, no consistent pattern emerged. On two occasions, the change was greater in the control beats, on two occasions greater in the proactive beats, and once it was greater in the reactive beats. Given the low number of statistically significant findings combined with a lack of consistent direction, the conclusion is that rates of reporting crimes by businessmen and citizens were unaffected by the experimental changes in levels of patrol.

Finding 4: Arrest Patterns

Police arrests showed no statistically significant differences in the 27 comparisons made between reactive, control, and proactive beats.

While arrest totals for 16 categories of crime were determined, it will be noted that in seven categories—common assault, larceny-purse snatch, homicide, nonresidence burglary, auto theft, larceny-auto accessory, and larceny-bicycle—either the number of arrests was too small to allow for statistical analysis or the preexperimental pattern of arrests was so distorted that statistical significance could not be determined. On the basis of the comparisons that could be made, however, the conclusion is that arrest rates were not significantly affected by changes in the level of patrol.

EFFECTS ON COMMUNITY ATTITUDES

CITIZEN FEAR OF CRIME The experiment measured community attitudes toward many aspects of crime and police performance to determine whether varying levels of routine preventive patrol—reactive, control, proactive—had any significant effect upon these attitudes. Previous investigators have shown that citizens can recognize, or at least sense, changes in levels of service or innovations in policing.

Thus, through the Community and Commercial Surveys which provided the victimization information used in the previous section of this summary, citizen attitudes toward crime and police were also measured before and after the experiment.

The first attitude measured was citizen fear of crime, determined by (1) a series of questions in the Community Survey designed to probe levels of fear; (2) a series of questions in the protective and security measures taken by citizens; and (3) questions in the Commercial Survey about protective and security measures used by businessmen at their place of business.

Finding 5: Citizen Fear of Crime

Citizen fear of crime was not significantly affected by changes in the level of routine preventive patrol.

In the Community Survey, citizen estimates of neighborhood safety and perceptions of violent crimes were obtained. Citizens were then asked what they thought the probability was that they might be involved in various types of crime, including robbery, assault, rape, burglary, and auto theft.

Of the 60 comparisons made between experimental areas, statistical significance was found in only five cases. Three involved the probability of being raped, one the probability of being robbed, and one the probability of being assaulted. The change in the level of fear was greater in reactive beats four times and greater in proactive beats once.

Yet when statistical significance is found, the patterns are inconsistent. For example, all cases in which the changes in the reactive beats are significantly higher than in other beats are found in the repeated sample. These findings are not confirmed by the nonrepeated sample, however. The one area in which control registered the higher change occurs in the nonrepeated sample, but this is not confirmed by the repeated sample.

The findings thus lead to the conclusion that citizen fear is not affected by differences in the level of routine preventive patrol.

Finding 6: Protective Measures (Citizens)

Protective and security measures taken by citizens against the possibility of being involved in crime were not significantly affected by variations in the level of routine preventive patrol.

The questions asked of citizens in the Community Survey on this subject dealt with the installation of such devices as bars, alarms, locks and lighting, the keeping of various types of weapons or dogs for protection, and the taking of certain actions, such as staying inside, as preventive measures.

Here, 84 comparisons were made between experimental areas, with statistical significance occurring 11 times. The significance occurred most often (six times) in those beats where pre-

ventive patrol had not changed, that is, in control beats. The change in the reactive beats showed significance three times, and in the proactive beats twice. There is no apparent explanation for the fact that the use of protective measures supposedly increased in the control beat relative to the other two conditions. For the most part, the findings are inconsistent and occur either in the nonrepeated sample or the repeated sample but never uniformly in both.

Thus, as measured by the use of protective and security measures, experimental preventive patrol conditions did not significantly affect citizen fear of crime.

Finding 7: Protective Measures (Businesses)

Protective and security measures taken by businesses in the experimental area to protect offices or other places of business did not show significant differences due to changes in the level of routine preventive patrol.

In the Commercial Survey, businessmen were asked such questions as whether they had installed alarm systems or reinforcing devices such as bars over windows, whether they had hired guards, or whether they kept watchdogs or firearms in their places of business.

All told, 21 comparisons were made and statistical significance was found once, where the change in the control beats was the greater as compared with the reactive beats.

Because this was a telephone survey, however, some problems with the findings were evident. Briefly, some businessmen were reluctant to talk about protective measures over the phone to persons unknown to them. This is discussed more fully in the technical report.

The conclusion remains, however, that preventive patrol variations seem to have little effect on fear of crime as indicated by protective measures taken by commercial establishments.

CITIZEN ATTITUDES TOWARD POLICE In addition to investigating citizen fear of crime and criminals, the preventive patrol experiment delved into citizen attitudes toward the police. Residents in the experimental area were asked, for instance, about the need for more police officers, about variations in patrol, police officer reputations and effectiveness, police treatment of citizens, and about their satisfaction with police service.

The attitudes of businessmen toward police were studied in the course of the preventive patrol experiment for a variety of reasons. One was simply that businessmen's attitudes have seldom been studied in the past, although these people are often affected by crime in ways more crucial to their survival than are citizens in general. It is not only the businessman's personal comfort and safety that may be involved, but also the ability to remain in business that may be affected by crime. At the same time, businessmen are often influential in their communities. For these reasons, assessing their attitudes is often crucial to the development of new policing programs. Therefore, businessmen were asked similar questions about police effectiveness, treatment of citizens, and so forth.

While the study of such attitudes is valuable in obtaining the impressions of a significant cross section of the community, most of the citizens and businessmen interviewed were unlikely to have experienced recent actual contact with the police. Thus, another part of the preventive patrol experiment focused on determining citizen responses to actual encounters with police officers. To determine such responses, citizens themselves, the police with whom they came in contact, and trained observers were all asked to complete reports on the encounter. Citizens were interviewed as soon as possible after the incident. Separate questionnaires were used, depending on whether the encounter was initiated by an officer or by a citizen.

Finally, a fourth measure was used to determine citizen attitudes. Here, in what has been given the title Police-Citizen Transactions, the trained observers focused on the outcome of police-citizen interactions in terms of the patrol assignment of the officer involved, that is, reactive, control, or proactive.

The next findings deal with citizen attitudes toward police, businessmen's attitudes toward police, police-citizen encounters initiated either by citizens (calls for service) or police (traffic arrests, suspect apprehension, etc.), and finally police-citizen transactions.

Finding 8: Citizen Attitudes Toward Police

Citizen attitudes toward police were not significantly affected by alterations in the level of preventive patrol.

A large number of questions in the Community Survey were designed to measure citizen attitudes toward the police. As a result, more comparisons were made here than in other cases and more instances of statistical significance were found. Altogether, 111 comparisons were made and statistical significance occurred 16 times. Items with significant differences included the need for more police officers in the city, the reputation of police officers, citizens' respect for police, police effectiveness, harassment, and change in neighborhood police officers.

Of the 16 instances of significance, the change in reactive beats was greater five times, in control beats ten times, and in proactive beats once, demonstrating no consistent pattern of statistical significance. The indication is that there was little correlation between level of patrol and citizen attitudes.

Finding 9: Businessmen's Attitudes Toward Police

Businessmen's attitudes toward police officers were not significantly affected by changes in the level of routine preventive patrol.

Like citizens in the Community Survey, businessmen in the Commercial Survey were asked about their attitudes toward police. Some of the questions in the Commercial Survey were similar to those in the Community Survey and some specially selected with regard to businessmen's interests.

In all, 48 comparisons were made to measure differences in businessmen's attitudes, but no statistically significant differences were found or even approached. The clear indication here is that variations in the level of preventive patrol have no effect on businessmen's attitudes.

Finding 10: Police-Citizen Encounters

Citizen attitudes toward police officers encountered through the initiative of either the citizen or the officer were not significantly affected by changes in patrol level.

Citizen attitudes were measured by both questions asked of citizens themselves and observations of trained observers. Citizens and observers alike were asked about such items as response time, characteristics of the encounter, the attitude and demeanor of officers in the encounter, and citizen satisfaction. Observers in officer-initiated encounters also recorded things not likely to be noted by citizens, including the number of officers and police vehicles present.

Including both citizen-initiated and officer-initiated encounters, a total of 63 comparisons were made and no statistically significant differences were found.

Finding 11: Police-Citizen Transactions

The behavior of police officers toward citizens was not significantly affected by the officers' assignment to a reactive, control, or proactive beat.

The finding is distinct from the previous finding in that the focus here is upon the police-citizen interaction in terms of the beat assignment of the officer rather than on the location of the contact. (Many police contacts with citizens take place outside of the officer's beat.) Data were recorded by participant observers riding with the officers. In all, 18 comparisons were made between experimental areas, and no statistically significant differences were found.

OTHER EFFECTS

EXPERIMENTAL FINDINGS IN REGARD TO POLICE RESPONSE TIME   The time it takes police officers to respond to a citizen call for assistance is usually considered an important measure of patrol effectiveness. The general principle is that the lower the response time, the more efficiently the police are doing their job.

Response time was studied to see if experimental conditions would have any effect on the amount of time taken by police in answering citizen calls for service. Before the experiment began, the hypothesis was that experimental

conditions would affect response time, particularly in the proactive beats. It was believed that since more officers were assigned to proactive beats, response time would be significantly reduced in those beats.

Finding 12: Response Time

The amount of time taken by police in answering calls for service was not significantly affected by variations in the level of routine preventive patrol.

To obtain this finding, data were gathered on such matters as distance from police car to scene of incident, mean time from receipt of calls to start of call, mean time from receipt of call to arrival at scene, and observer's estimate of patrol car speed. Citizen estimates of time and satisfaction were also measured.

In the area of response time, a total of 42 comparisons were made between patrol conditions. Statistical significance occurred only once: in the number of officers present at the scene of incidents in the reactive beats. The reason for this is unclear, but it can be theorized that police officers were exhibiting their concern for the safety of fellow officers and citizens in reactive beats.

While variations in the level of patrol did not significantly affect police response time, the Kansas City findings suggest that more research is necessary. It appears that response time is not only the result of rate of speed and distance, but also reflects the attitude of the officers involved and possibly other variables not investigated in this study.

CONCLUSIONS

The initial impetus behind the Kansas City preventive patrol experiment was the issue of time and staff resources. When the South Patrol Task Force began its deliberations, the concern was that any serious attempt to deal with priority problems would be confounded by the need to maintain established levels of routine patrol. Thus, in addition to testing the effect of various patrol strategies on such factors as crime, citizen fear and satisfaction, and response time, the experiment equally addressed the question of whether adequate time can be channeled to the development testing and evaluation of new approaches to patrol.

From the beginning phases of this experiment, the evaluators formed hypotheses based upon certain assumptions. One primary assumption was that the police, as an institutionalized mechanism of social control, are seriously limited in their ability to both prevent crime and apprehend offenders once crimes have been committed. The reasons for these limitations are many and complex. But they include the very nature of the crime problem itself, the limits a democratic society places upon its police, the limited amount of resources available for crime prevention, and complexities within the entire criminal justice system. As a result of these limitations, many have rightly suggested that we must now begin revising our expectations as to the police role in society.

Problem-Oriented Policing

HERMAN GOLDSTEIN

PROBLEM-ORIENTED policing grows out of a critique of the current state of policing. In a narrow sense, it focuses directly on the substance of policing—on the problems that constitute the business of the police and on how they handle them. This focus establishes a balance between the reactive and proactive aspects of policing. It also creates a vehicle for making more effective use of the community and rank-and-file officers in getting the police job done. In its broadest context, problem-oriented policing is a comprehensive plan for improving policing in which the high priority attached to addressing substantive problems shapes the police agency, influencing all changes in personnel, organization, and procedures. Thus, problem-oriented policing not only pushes policing beyond current improvement efforts, it calls for a major change in the direction of those efforts.

To initiate the exploration, I set forth, in this chapter, the fundamental elements of problem-oriented policing. Taken together, these constitute the core of the changes that are required in the way we think about the police job.

GROUPING INCIDENTS AS PROBLEMS

The primary work unit in a police agency today for the officer assigned to general patrol is the incident. In the course of a typical day, a police officer will usually handle several incidents, such as the theft of a car, a barking dog, a dispute among neighbors, a robbery, a request for infor-

mation, a report of suspicious circumstances, or a traffic accident.

The professional model of policing is designed to increase the efficiency with which incidents are handled. Much of the success of police officers is judged by how speedily and efficiently they handle the incidents to which they are assigned.

In handling incidents, police officers usually deal with the most obvious, superficial manifestations of a deeper problem—not the problem itself. They may stop a fight but not get involved in exploring the factors that contributed to it. They may disperse a group of unruly juveniles but not feel under any obligation to inquire into what brought the youths together in the first instance. They may investigate a crime but stop short of exploring the factors that may have contributed to its commission, except as these are relevant to identifying the offender. In handling incidents, police are generally expected to deal with the disruptive, intolerable effects of a problem. That requires a response quite different from what might be involved in dealing with the underlying conditions or problem. Clearly, some officers go further, dealing with the problem itself. But most policing is limited to ameliorating the overt, offensive symptoms of a problem.

It follows that incidents are usually handled as isolated, self-contained events. Connections are not systematically made among them, except when they suggest a common crime pattern leading to identifying the offender. This is so even though the incidents may involve the same behavior, the same address, or the same people and may recur frequently. One often gets the feeling that police, conditioned by the strong commitment to reactive policing, are resigned to dealing with incidents as isolated events—until some other force comes along that will treat the underlying problem. (The situation is perhaps best illustrated by an incident in which a police dispatcher assigned a newly hired officer to respond to a burglar alarm. The officer, unfamiliar with the area, asked for directions. His sergeant provided the directions and, aware of a long history of false alarms from this address, advised the officer: "Get used to it. It goes off all the time.")

The first step in problem-oriented policing is to move beyond just handling incidents. It calls for recognizing that incidents are often merely overt symptoms of problems. This pushes the police in two directions: (1) it requires that they recognize the relationships between incidents (similarities of behavior, location, persons involved, etc.), and (2) it requires that they take a more in-depth interest in incidents by acquainting themselves with some of the conditions and factors that give rise to them.

FOCUSING ON SUBSTANTIVE PROBLEMS AS THE HEART OF POLICING

The public expects the police to deal with such varied problems as the sexual abuse of children, widespread sales of drugs, robberies of store clerks, and destruction of public property. The public also expects the police to handle problems such as fights that break out in taverns, domestic disputes, missing children, complaints about unreasonable noise, disruptive gatherings of juveniles, and troublesome situations that involve the homeless, the mentally ill, and those incapacitated by alcohol. These are among the many substantive problems—that is, groups of frequently recurring incidents—that constitute police work.

These substantive problems can be defined at different levels and in different ways. Shoplifting, for example, can be viewed as a citywide problem, raising questions about how the entire police agency copes with it. Or it can be viewed as a problem within a specific shopping area or even within a specific store, raising questions about how the police and the merchants who are

directly involved deal with it. Likewise, one can profitably explore theft from residences as a city-wide problem, or one can examine theft from residences in a given precinct, neighborhood, or housing complex. It may even be profitable to zero in on a specific apartment house or even a single private residence if repeated thefts have been reported. The choice of the most appropriate level depends on an initial analysis of the problem.

But not all substantive problems need to be defined in behavioral terms descriptive of alleged wrongdoing. They may be defined more helpfully as troublesome areas (e.g., a park or housing complex), specific businesses (e.g., a tavern), specific people (e.g., a mentally ill person who harasses passersby), or groups of people (e.g., a juvenile gang) around which a variety of incidents might cluster. Thus, for example, if initial analysis led one to focus on a concentration of liquor-serving establishments and adult entertainment on a city block, one might bring together incidents that otherwise might be routinely classified as disorderly conduct, assaults, prostitution, drunkenness, runaways, parking violations, and liquor license violations.

Because the police—as "hired hands"—are available to deal with the aspects of life in the community, the citizenry tends to define substantive problems as *police* problems. But it would be more accurate to define substantive problems as *community* problems. The emphasis on community has two implications. It means looking to the community to define the problems that should be of concern to the police, rather than succumbing to the tendency of the police on their own to define the problems of concern to the community. And it means gaining an understanding of all of the dimensions of a problem in the total community. What the police are seeing is often but a part of the total problem. Thus, for example, in a study of the drinking driver, it was found helpful to consult with prosecutors, judges, alcohol-treatment personnel, insurance executives, tavern keepers, liquor-licensing authorities, victims, the survivors of victims, physicians, nurses, driver-education instructors, and driver-improvement personnel. The picture that emerged was radically different from the picture one gets of the drinking-driver problem by focusing exclusively on the arrest and prosecution of such drivers.

Typically, when police speak of problems in policing, they refer to problems in the internal management of the police agency: for example, lack of adequate personnel, limited promotional opportunities, nonfunctioning equipment, poor morale, or—reaching a little beyond—frustrations in the prosecution of alleged offenders. But even when police are instructed in the meaning of "substantive" problems and are then asked to focus on them, they are apparently so conditioned to thinking in terms of the problems of the organization that they frequently slip back to identifying concerns in the management of the agency. Thus, focusing on the substantive, community problems that the police must handle is a much more radical step than it initially appears to be, for it requires the police to go beyond taking satisfaction in the smooth operation of their organization; it requires that they extend their concern to dealing effectively with the problems that justify creating a police agency in the first instance.

Viewed in this manner, a "problem" becomes the unit of police work. This serves as a useful, constant reminder of the underlying premise that the job of policing consists of much more than dealing with crime and enforcing the criminal law. To describe police work as consisting of the handling of problems is a more accurate definition of the police function. It has the added value of avoiding the confusion that arises from using the manner in which the police may respond to a task to describe that task, as occurs when the job of the police is described as law enforcement. It is a more neutral way of describing the police work unit, helpful to further analysis because it avoids any implication of a premature judgment as to how the police may deal with it.

ANALYSIS OF THE MULTIPLE INTERESTS IN PROBLEMS

If the police were asked, in the past, why they were concerned about a particular problem, they would often explain that the conduct involved was against the law. That response would not have been unsatisfactory so long as one adhered to the old notions that the primary job of the police was to enforce the law and that the police had no discretion in deciding how the law was to be enforced. But with increased awareness that the job of the police is much broader and that police must, of necessity, exercise discretion in using the law to deal with community problems, one must examine more critically the nature of the police concern with each of the problems the police are expected to handle. More penetrating analysis of a problem requires examination of some of the interests served in making the conduct illegal. And even if the conduct is not legislatively proscribed, the same need exists to identify the various interests in controlling a problem. The nature of the community's concern and interest in a problem is of critical importance in deciding how best to respond to it.

This point is nicely illustrated by examining the multiple interests in a common problem such as street prostitution, which is clearly illegal. Narrowly, one could assert that police are in the business of dealing with street prostitution because it is against the law. But large numbers of street prostitutes—both male and female—can usually be found in our urban areas. Other problems compete for police time. Enforcement is difficult. Simply viewing the conduct as illegal is not helpful in formulating a response. The challenge to the police is to develop a program that will deal with the most troubling aspects of prostitution in the fairest and most effective manner. Development of a rational plan requires careful analysis and the answer to some specific questions: Why is the community concerned? What are the social costs? Who is being harmed and to what degree? In an effort to answer these questions, one might identify as many as 13 different and often competing interests:

1. The behavior constitutes an offense to the moral standards of some segments of the community.
2. It creates a nuisance to passersby and to adjacent residents and business establishments.

3. Uninvolved individuals who must frequent the area are offended if they are solicited.

4. Juveniles may become prostitutes.

5. A prostitute may be harmed by her or his customers.

6. Those who patronize a prostitute may be assaulted, robbed, or defrauded.

7. Prostitutes may be exploited financially and physically by their pimps.

8. Street prostitution may provide the seedbed for organized criminal interests in the community.

9. Prostitution is usually linked to drugs, with the possibility that the prostitutes make extensive use of drugs.

10. Prostitutes as citizens have rights that need to be protected.

11. Street prostitutes create parking and traffic problems in the area where they congregate.

12. The presence of prostitutes may have a deleterious effect on the economy of the area, reducing the value of buildings and limiting their use.

13. Prostitutes may spread sexually transmitted diseases such as syphilis, herpes, and AIDS.

PROBLEM-ORIENTED COMPONENTS IN THE COMMUNITY-ORIENTED POLICING PROJECTS OF SEVERAL OTHER CITIES

Systematically addressing substantive community problems is by no means limited to those jurisdictions that have implemented some form of problem-oriented policing. As previously noted, community-oriented policing has often led to intensive work on substantive community problems. Although these efforts may be less systematic and more influenced by a desire to improve relations with the community than by a commitment to solve the problems, they are no less relevant to this exploration. Unfortunately, these experiences have not been as fully monitored and documented. There are notable exceptions including programs in Flint, Michigan; New York City; Los Angeles; Houston; and Edmonton, Alberta.

Flint, Michigan

The Flint Neighborhood Foot Patrol Program began in 1979 and, at its height in 1982, placed a police officer in each of the 64 areas into which the city was divided. It incorporated a number of the basic elements of problem-oriented policing. Initially funded with a grant from the Mott Foundation, the project was eventually supported by a special tax levy approved by the voters. In the larger context of building a partnership between the police and the community, the project dealt with the problems the community identified, and the police officer developed into a neighborhood problem solver. Officers were relieved of most of the pressures of reactive patrol and were encouraged to work on a given problem from the beginning through to its solution. Both the initiative and the burden for dealing with community problems were left to the officer on the beat. No systematic process for the identification and analysis of problems was used, nor did the department identify and address problems that extended beyond the boundaries of a beat. Support for the Flint project has wavered since 1987, with changes in mayors and police chiefs, reflecting the fragile nature of such undertakings.

New York City

At the initiative of Commissioner Benjamin Ward and with the technical support of the Vera Institute of Justice, the New York City Police Department launched its Community Patrol Officer Program (CPOP) in 1984. The program has since been expanded to cover all of the city's 75 precincts. Under the program, each of 9 or 10 officers in a participating precinct is assigned responsibility for a specific beat. Every community patrol officer (CPO) is expected to provide the full range of police services within his or her beat (although relieved of responding to routine calls). This officer is also expected to work with community residents in identifying local problems and in designing solutions for them. In a critique of the program by the Vera Institute staff, the job of the CPO as a problem solver was identified as the most distinctive feature of the CPO's role. Urging that attention be given to developing this role, the report asserted: "To the extent that CPOs fail at the planning and problem-solving dimension of the role, their distinctive utility as a police resource is threatened. If that happens, their performance on the street will become much like that of the conventional foot patrol officer."

Los Angeles

The Los Angeles Police Department has started several programs aimed at achieving some of the goals of community policing, but each has suffered because of the continuing pressures to respond first to calls for police service. In the most recent initiative, however, the police leadership in the Wilshire area, in establishing its Community Mobilization Project (CMP), vowed to give highest priority to working with the community. In one of the earlier experiments in community policing, the rank of senior lead officer (SLO) had been created to head a team of officers who were given 24-hour responsibility for a given beat, with the understanding that the SLO would devote substantial time to relating to the needs of the community. But the function of the SLO has eroded since the position was first created in 1970, and most SLOs now police in traditional ways. In the Wilshire project, all eight SLOs were taken off routine patrol and assigned to dealing more intensively with recurring incidents by viewing them as related and giving sustained attention to the underlying problems. As a result of these efforts, the officers are credited with totally eliminating troublesome conditions that had long plagued the areas to which they are assigned.

Houston

The Houston Police Department has been undergoing rapid change since the appointment of Lee P. Brown as chief of police in 1982. The introduction of a wide range of innovations, reflecting extraordinary sensitivity to all of the new insights and research findings in policing, has contributed significantly to developments on the national scene. Not surprisingly, a common characteristic in these innovations has been the commitment to fashioning a partnership with each neighborhood. In implementing a concept of neighborhood-oriented policing, Houston officers will continue to respond to calls for service, but they will also be expected to initiate self-directed activities defined as actions taken by officers, in collaboration with their neighborhoods, to identify and address community problems. Management is urged to encourage officers to think about their work in more abstract ways and to examine conditions that cause and perpetuate problems. Community policing, as adopted in Houston, is defined as an interactive process in which the police and the community jointly define problems, determine the best ways of addressing them, and combine their resources for solving them. Numerous steps have been taken to create a working environment that supports individual officers in broadening their role. In addition, Houston has undertaken to study a number of substantive problems that cut across many neighborhoods, for example, in its comprehensive study of "crack houses" established for the sole purpose of selling the drug.

Edmonton, Alberta

A pilot program was initiated in 1988 in Edmonton that incorporated many of the elements commonly associated with community policing but places special emphasis on proactively solving problems. From among the 561 grids into which the city is divided by the police for administrative purposes, only 36 are included in the project. But the selected areas accounted for 28 percent of all of the calls received for police service in the previous year. These grids were assigned to 21 beats. Upon implementation of the project, a constable was permanently assigned to each of the beats, operating on foot out of a storefront office manned by citizen volunteers. Each officer is systematically provided with data that aid the officer in identifying problems. In one grid, it was found that 58 percent of all calls generated from the approximately 1,000 addresses in the grid came from only 21 locations. The constables are freed from many of the usual organizational constraints and are encouraged to make maximum use of their knowledge, skills, and creativity in solving problems within their beat.

. . . . .

Welcome as this added dimension may be to the overall concept of problem-oriented policing, it is important to recognize that engaging rank-and-file officers more directly in a street-level analysis of problems adds to the complexity of the concept. There is a world of difference between what is involved in critically examining, at the highest levels of the organization, problems of a citywide nature (e.g., spousal abuse) and in examining specific problems of a more local character at the operating level (problems relating, e.g., to an individual or an intersection). The first requires a major research effort, the second, a high-quality investigation but without the usual focus on establishing criminal intent. Yet these radically different undertakings mirror each other in that they reflect a common commitment to encouraging critical, creative thinking throughout the police agency—at the bottom as well as the top. Making effective use of these analyses requires developing a sense for the varying levels at which problems can be most effectively addressed and learning how inquiries initiated at different levels in the organization interrelate.

SUGGESTED READINGS

Banton, Michael. 1964. *The Policeman in the Community*. New York: Basic Books.

Bayley, David H. 1985. *Patterns of Policing: A Comparative International Analysis*. New Brunswick, NJ: Rutgers University Press.

Black, Donald. 1980. *Manners and Customs of the Police*. New York: Academic Press.

Ericson, Richard V. 1981. *Making Crime: A Study of Detective Work*. Toronto: Butterworths.

———. 1982. *Reproducing Order: A Study of Police Patrol Work*. Toronto: University of Toronto Press.

Goldstein, Herman. 1977. *Policing a Free Society*. Cambridge, MA: Ballinger.

Langworthy, Robert H. 1986. *The Structure of Police Organizations*. New York: Praeger.

Manning, Peter K. 1977. *Police Work*. Cambridge: MIT Press.

———. 1982. "Organisational Work: Enstructuration of the Environment." *British Journal of Sociology* 33:118-39.

———. 1988. *Symbolic Communication: Signifying Calls and the Police Response*. Cambridge: MIT Press.

Monkkonen, Eric H. 1975. *The Dangerous Class: Crime and Poverty in Columbus, Ohio, 1860-1885*. Cambridge, MA: Harvard University Press.

———. 1981. *Police in Urban America, 1860-1920*. New York: Cambridge University Press.

———. 1992. "History of the Urban Police." Pp. 547-80 in *Modern Policing*, edited by Michael H. Tonry and Norval Morris. Chicago: University of Chicago Press.

Oppenlander, N. 1982. "Coping or Copping Out: Police Service Delivery in Domestic Disputes." *Criminology* 20:449-65.

Reiss, Albert J., Jr. 1971. *The Police and the Public*. New Haven, CT: Yale University Press.

———. 1974. "Discretionary Justice." Pp. 679-99 in *Handbook of Criminology*, edited by Daniel Glaser. Chicago: Rand McNally.

———. 1992. "Police Organization in the Twentieth Century." Pp. 52-68 in *Modern Policing*, edited by Michael H. Tonry and Norval Morris. Chicago: University of Chicago Press.

Rubinstein, Jonathan. 1973. *City Police*. New York: Farrar, Straus and Giroux.

Skolnick, Jerome. 1966. *Justice Without Trial*. New York: John Wiley.

Skolnick, Jerome and James J. Fyfe. 1993. *Above the Law: Police and the Excessive Use of Force*. New York: Free Press.

Trojanowicz, Robert and Bonnie Bucqueroux. 1989. *Community Policing: A Contemporary Perspective*. Cincinnati, OH: Anderson.

van Maanen, John. 1974. "Working the Street." Pp. 83-130 in *The Potential for Reform of Criminal Justice*, edited by Herbert Jacob. Beverly Hills, CA: Sage.

Vera Institute of Justice. 1977. *Felony Arrests: Their Prosecution and Disposition in New York City's Courts.* New York: Vera Institute of Justice.

Westley, William. 1970. *Violence and the Police.* Cambridge: MIT Press.

Wilson, James Q. 1968. *Varieties of Police Behavior.* Cambridge, MA: Harvard University Press.

QUESTIONS FOR DISCUSSION AND WRITING

1. Contrast Black's characterization of factors influencing the likelihood of arrest with those identified in Klinger's research. What are the differences? What are the similarities?

2. According to Skolnick, how do officers' concerns about a "symbolic assailant" influence police work? What measures, if any, could be taken by police departments to reduce these concerns?

3. Compare Wilson's conceptions of order maintenance and law enforcement. How are these concepts similar to or different from Packer's due process and crime control models of criminal justice (see Part I)?

4. What is the significance of Fyfe's finding that many police shootings involve off-duty officers? How does this assist in explaining race differences among officers in patterns of shootings?

5. What does Fyfe argue is the most effective way of regulating inappropriate use of deadly force by police officers? Explain with examples.

6. The essays by Sherman and by Kelling and his colleagues suggest that many measures taken by police departments to reduce levels of crime may have little or no effect. Explain why this occurs.

7. How are Goldstein's ideas about the need for problem-oriented policing similar to Wilson and Kelling's ideas about community crime control in their chapter "Broken Windows"?

IV

WHAT ROLE DO COURTS PLAY IN CRIMINAL JUSTICE?

NEARLY thirty years ago, the President's Commission on Law Enforcement and Administration of Justice issued its report *The Challenge of Crime in a Free Society*. The authors of the report began the discussion of courts as follows:

> The criminal court is the central, crucial institution in the criminal justice system. . . . It is the institution around which the rest of the system has developed and to which the rest of the system is in large measure responsible. It regulates the flow of the criminal process under governance of the law. The activities of the police are limited or shaped by the rules and procedures of the court. The work of the correctional system is determined by the court's sentence.

The truth of this statement has not diminished. Courts remain a pivot point for much of the administration of criminal justice. The actions of prosecutors, defense attorneys, and judges influence how effective police actions are in enforcing the law and in punishing criminal offenders. Furthermore, those same actions determine the number and types of offenders who ultimately come under the control and supervision of our prisons and correctional agencies.

An inquiry into how courts work must of necessity examine each of the officiating roles in criminal courts: the prosecutor, the defense attorney, and the judge. Accordingly, Part IV of our book is divided into three sections, corresponding to these roles. The essays included in the section examine aspects of decision making for each role—for example, decisions to file charges by prosecutors, defense attorneys' working relations with clients, and judges' sentencing practices. Furthermore, the essays examine the important social and legal contexts affecting how the roles may vary. Recognizing that the actions and views of court officials vary significantly across time and place is essential to understanding the functions of courts in the administration of criminal justice.

THE PROSECUTOR

One of the least understood roles in the criminal court is that of the prosecutor. Decisions to file criminal charges or to negotiate pleas of guilt have not routinely been open to public scrutiny or to investigation by social scientists. Part IV includes four essays on the prosecutor. The first of these essays, William F. McDonald's "The Prosecutor's Domain," is an excerpt from McDonald's important book *The Prosecutor.* This essay offers an interesting overview of the domain of prosecutors' activities. McDonald argues, drawing on historical material and observations from contemporary prosecutors' offices, that the prosecutor's domain has increased dramatically in the U.S. legal system over the past two centuries, with much of the expansion occurring since the beginning of the twentieth century. The essay asserts that some aspects of contemporary criminal justice—for example, mandatory-sentencing legislation—have blurred the prosecutor's role with that of sentencing judges'. Under mandatory-sentencing laws, prosecutors can directly influence the types of sentences imposed in cases through the selective filing of criminal charges or negotiation of guilty pleas. From observations such as this, McDonald concludes that the office of the public prosecutor has grown from a nonexistent role in the eighteenth century to a position of central power in the system.

The second and third essays in this part of our book examine issues in the filing of criminal charges. Joan Jacoby's essay, "The Charging Policies of Prosecutors," explains how prosecutors may vary in their views and policies in the filing of criminal charges. Her essay develops a typology of charging policies that reveals how an individual prosecutor's views about the purposes of criminal prosecution will influence, along with other factors, both the approach to the filing of charges and the outcomes of many charging decisions.

George Cole's essay, "The Decision to Prosecute," offers a different perspective on criminal prosecution. In his classic story, Cole portrays the criminal court as a marketplace wherein legal officials (judges, prosecutors, police, and defense attorneys) routinely engage in "exchange" relationships. Cole uses information on the prosecutor in King County, Washington (Seattle) to illustrate the types of exchanges that influence how prosecutors make decisions to file charges in criminal cases. Whereas Jacoby's analysis explores the relationship between prosecutors' views of their work and their actions, Cole examines how the structure of court activity influences prosecutors' work and decision-making processes.

The final essay on prosecutors examines plea bargaining, and it does so using the voices of the prosecutors themselves. Milton Heumann's essay, "Prosecutorial Adaptation to Plea Bargaining," describes the results of a study of prosecutors that relies heavily on accounts of the plea negotiation process from interviews with prosecutors. Heumann's essay shows how prosecutors' views on plea bargaining change as their careers develops, with less experienced prosecutors holding views about plea bargaining that are less accommodating than the views of more experienced prosecutors. Furthermore, the comments from prosecutors reveal how the prosecutor's personal views about crime and criminals may influence the outcomes of plea bargains. The following statement by one of the prosecutors in Heumann's study illustrates this point:

> Each prosecutor has different feelings. Some people are very hard on some types of offenses, and others don't feel they're very serious at all. I've got a thing about purse snatchers, particularly ones who pick on the older women, the older women who they feel can't identify them or, even if they can, won't identify them because of their age and because they're afraid. A lot of these old women get knocked down and injured severely, and, you know, it's permanent injury at that age. I feel very tough about somebody like that who comes in. I won't bend a finger to help them.

THE DEFENSE ATTORNEY

Although our legal process is often described by lawyers and jurists as adversarial, with the prosecution and defense battling in court against each other over the outcomes of cases, most social science research on courts portrays the process quite differently. In particular, research on defense lawyers concludes that only very rarely are there adversarial exchanges between the prosecution and defense. Rather, studies routinely show that the defense lawyer is, as one of the essays included in this section maintains, a "double agent" who must simultaneously serve the client and protect the working relationships he or she has established with judges and prosecutors. This conflict in the defense attorney's roles complicates the practice of criminal law. The four essays included in this section of our book examine different aspects of the defense attorney's roles.

The first essay, "The Practice of Law as a Confidence Game" by Abraham Blumberg, introduces the idea of "organizational co-optation" into the analysis of defense lawyers. Blumberg suggests that the organizational goals and structure of criminal courts impose a set of demands on the defense lawyers that causes them to abandon "their ideological and professional commitments to the accused client, in the service of these higher claims of the court organization." Thus, Blumberg argues that the structure of court relations co-opts defense lawyers, requiring them to become agent-mediators who restructure their clients' perceptions so as to increase the likelihood that they will agree to a plea of guilty. The essay points to the structure of the fee-collecting process for private attorneys that partly encourages the development of this double-agent role.

Most criminal defendants rely on public defenders or court-appointed attorneys whose legal fees are paid not by the client but by the court or by the state. These types of defense attorneys often experience unique problems with their clients, many of which center around client/attorney relational difficulties or the attorney's own difficulties associated with defending individuals he or she knows have committed crimes. The second and third essays on defense attorneys address these issues. The essay by Roy Flemming, "Client Games: Defense Attorneys' Perspectives on Their Relations With Criminal Clients," includes interviews with defense attorneys in which they describe their most difficult clients. Lisa McIntyre's essay is an excerpt from her book *The Public Defender: The Practice of Law in the Shadows of Repute*. McIntyre's essay, also using interviews, reveals that lawyers find it difficult to focus only on the legal aspects of their cases because others often question the morality of the defense lawyer's job. The essay also shows how defense attorneys, who routinely lose criminal cases, must redefine the concept of "winning" in court to save face among other lawyers.

A final area of concern involves the decision-making processes defense attorneys engage in while handling criminal cases. Similar to the Flemming essay, David Sudnow's piece, "Normal Crimes: Sociological Features of the Penal Code in a Public Defender's Office," reveals the ways in which defense attorneys view clients. A very important part of the Sudnow essay is his discussion of the typifications or stereotypes that defense lawyers use to classify defendants. That defense attorneys distinguish "normal crimes" from others and use the distinction to assist in preparing cases and in negotiating with prosecutors their outcomes is one of the most provocative and interesting aspects of Sudnow's research.

THE JUDGE

Judges play a vital role in the criminal court process. They oversee all court proceedings and by their rulings influence many of the decisions of police, prosecutors, and defense counsel. Furthermore, their decisions on sentencing and the revocation of probation directly affect the operations of correctional agencies. Our collection of essays on judges includes four readings on courts and judicial decision making. Although not all of these focus on judges' decision-making practices, together they reveal much about judges, judicial discretion, and the factors influencing judges' behavior on the bench. The first two essays should be considered together. The essay by Malcolm Feeley, "The Process Is the Punishment: Handling Cases in a Lower Criminal Court," is an excerpt from his book *The Process Is the Punishment*. The second essay, "Adjudication and Sentencing in a Misdemeanor Court: The Outcome Is the Punishment" by John Paul Ryan, was written in response to Feeley's chapter. The two essays offer contrasting views of the criminal process in lower or misdemeanor courts.

Feeley's essay claims that the punishments imposed in misdemeanor courts are not necessarily reflected in the sentences meted out by judges. His essay reports the result of a study conducted in New Haven's (Connecticut) misdemeanor court showing that much of the punishment that occurs is associated with the criminal court process. Feeley offers a compelling account of the costs defendants in misdemeanor courts accrue and that often these and other costs are far more punitive than sentences imposed by judges. He argues that the costs associated with the need to make bail, to hire a defense attorney, and to be present at court appearances are extremely expensive in comparison with the punishments meted out to defendants on conviction. In misdemeanor crimes, few offenders are ever incarcerated, and the monetary fines are often trivial.

In contrast, John Paul Ryan's essay reports the results of a study of the misdemeanor court in Columbus (Ohio) revealing exactly the opposite. Ryan shows that in Columbus' court, the penalties that are imposed are severe compared to those imposed in New Haven for similar crimes and criminal offenders. Ryan explains the difference in terms of the political culture of Columbus as compared to New Haven and the political orientations of the judges. For example, at the time of Feeley's study four Democratic and three Republican judges sat in the New Haven lower court. At the time of Ryan's study, twelve Republican judges sat with a lone Democratic judge in the Columbus municipal court. Ryan suggests that differences such as these produced a much more formalistic and punitive legal process in the Columbus court.

Martin Levin's essay, "Urban Politics and Policy Outcomes: The Criminal Courts," suggests that debates such as that between Feeley and Ryan actually reflect major regional differences in judicial decision making and the factors influencing how judges reach adjudication and sentencing decisions. Because most judges at the state and county level are either elected by the public, appointed by political parties, or initially appointed and then elected, judges are products of an inherently political process and their actions cannot be understood apart from that process. Accordingly, Levin assesses how differing political systems (Minneapolis and Pittsburgh) and differing judicial selection systems may influence the outcomes of judicial decision making. His essay reports the results of this assessment, showing that judges in the two cities adopt decision-making styles that correspond to the cities' different social and political structures.

The final essay in this section examines the effects of mandatory-sentencing laws on judicial sentencing practices. John Kramer and Robin Lubitz's essay, "Pennsylvania's Sentencing Reform: The Impact of Commission-Established Guidelines," reviews the impact of laws that drastically reduced judicial discretion in sentencing. In the 1980s, sentencing guidelines attracted extensive attention at the state and federal levels as an approach to reduce sentencing disparity among judges and across regions. Kramer and Lubitz's findings suggest that the imposition of sentencing guidelines in Pennsylvania had an appreciable effect on sentencing practices, demonstrating a move toward sentencing uniformity and a corresponding reduction in sentencing variability. Racial differences in sentencing were also greatly lessened.

THE PROSECUTOR

The Prosecutor's Domain

WILLIAM F. McDONALD

> No good results can come from having the prosecutor's overlap the functions of the police at one end and those of the magistrates on the other.
>
> National Commission on Law Observance and Enforcement

The purpose of this chapter is to provide a framework for understanding the role of the prosecutor in the administration of justice. Instead of the concept of role, however, we will use the concept of domain. We will show that domain is not something that is fixed and final. Rather, it has evolved historically and is continuing to undergo change. It differs considerably among various jurisdictions. We will identify some of the factors that have influenced its development and show how changes in the prosecutor's domain have accompanied changes in the respective domains of other components of the criminal justice system. Finally, we will illustrate some of the conflicts involved in such changes.

THE CONCEPT OF DOMAIN

The concept of domain is used here as it has been developed in the literature on organizational behavior. The criminal justice system can be characterized as an "industry" with a "long-linked" technology. That is, it consists of a sequence of serially interdependent organizations whose combined efforts result in various products. As studies of other industries have shown, each organization in an industry must establish

From *The Prosecutor* (pp. 15-59), W. F. McDonald, editor, 1979, Newbury Park, CA: Sage Publications, Inc. Copyright 1979 Sage Publications, Inc. Reprinted by permission.

some niche, some boundaries around that total effort for which that organization takes initiative. For instance, in their study of relationships among health agencies in a community, Levine and White reported that among health agencies, domain consisted of claims which respective organizations staked out for themselves in terms of the diseases covered, the population served, and the services rendered.

In the criminal justice industry, the domains of the component organizations appear at first glance to be clearly defined and well established. Police do the policing, the prosecutors do the prosecuting, and the judges do the judging. But appearances can be deceptive. This image represents only the formal division of labor, the textbook description of how the system works. It is quite misleading. It exaggerates the extent to which these various functions can be and are in fact divided among different components of the system. It wrongly suggests that various roles in the system are hard, fast, and final. An alternative view is to see these roles as blurred, shared, evolving, and always open to negotiation. Typically, the answer to the question "What is the role of the prosecutor (or any other official) in the criminal justice system?" has been in terms of what that official usually does in some particular jurisdiction or in terms of some ideal of what he is supposed to do. However, a few field trips to some jurisdictions will show the discrepancies between both of these answers and what actually happens. In some places, prosecutors control the charging decision. In others, they do not. In some of those jurisdictions where prosecutors formally control the initial charging decision, the actual decision is made informally by the police and only rubber-stamped by the prosecutor. The variety of things which one can find prosecutors doing in at least some jurisdictions is amazing. Some prosecutors control the court calendar; some appoint defense counsel in indigent cases; some dominate the sentencing decision through plea bargaining; some do extensive investigative and police work; some operate special services for victims and witnesses; some play active roles in parole decisions; and some actively lobby at the state legislature.

One approach to the study of roles in organizations is to focus on domains. Prosecutors' offices are prosecutors' offices, but the range of their domains varies considerably. Some have laid claims to substantial parts of the total effort that goes into the criminal justice process. Others have made more modest claims. All differ to some extent in regard to the particular parts of the process that they claim. It is our purpose not to address this policy question directly but rather to provide a basis for future discussion of it by answering some of the factual questions we have posed above. Our overall thesis is that the role of the prosecutor has historically evolved from one virtually nonexistent role in the criminal justice process to one where the prosecutor claims substantial domain. Furthermore, the domain claimed is of such a strategic position in the criminal justice process that the prosecutor's overall influence in that process extends far beyond the particular boundaries of his domain.

Increases in the prosecutor's domain have come in two ways. On the one hand, the criminal justice process itself has become more complicated over time. As that process has become more elaborate, there has been more territory for organizations participating in the process to lay claim to. On the other hand, another major source of the increment in the prosecutor's domain has been at the expense of one or more other organizations participating in the process. As the prosecutor's domain has expanded, the domains of the police, the judiciary, the defense

bar, and even the correctional system have been correspondingly diminished. This has led to conflict between agencies and to some blurring of roles.

The expansion of the prosecutor's domain has occurred over the past two centuries as a result of increasing urbanization with its associated increases in crime and the simultaneous transformation of the Anglo-American criminal justice system from a small-scale, rurally based system of privately initiated criminal prosecutions with minimal formality—operated largely by amateurs or part-timers—to a sprawling, large-scale, urban bureaucracy in which criminal prosecutions are initiated on behalf of the state by full-time, publicly paid professionals who must dispose of large caseloads within the restrictions of an extensive legal procedure. Formerly, the criminal justice process was a trial-based procedure in which virtually all cases that entered the system were disposed of by jury trials. Today, the jury trial is a rarity. Most justice is dispensed administratively by the actions of the prosecutor who either terminates the prosecution or negotiates a guilty plea through plea bargaining. The gross outlines of this transformation had taken shape by the turn of the past century and were well documented by the crime commissions of the 1920s. But only recently have prosecutors begun to recognize and fully implement their potentially central role in the administration of justice. In jurisdictions where this realization has occurred, there have been significant further refinements upon this new system of justice through and by the public prosecutor. These recent changes are the direction of the future.

DEVELOPMENTS IN JUSTICE: EXPANDING THE PROSECUTOR'S DOMAIN

Plea Bargaining

The shift to a system of criminal justice in which 90 percent of the felony convictions were obtained by guilty pleas did not automatically and simultaneously bring about an expansion of the prosecutor's domain. Only where guilty pleas were the result of explicit bargains in which the prosecutor played a major negotiating role was the prosecutor's domain extended. We believe that that domain started small and expanded greatly over the course of the past century, especially in the past decade.

To clarify this point, it is useful to distinguish three major kinds of plea bargaining: explicit bargains involving charge bargaining, explicit bargains involving sentence bargaining, and implicit bargains (which always involve sentences). An implicit bargain refers to those situations in which the defendant does not negotiate a specific agreement with anyone but learns (somehow) that if he is found guilty at trial he will be punished more severely than he would have been if he had pled guilty. This kind of bargaining is controlled by the judge. It is up to him to decide whether as a personal policy he will punish defendants convicted at trial more severely than he would otherwise have done if they had pled guilty. In contrast, charge bargaining is within the exclusive control of the prosecutor (although judges may occasionally pressure prosecutors to engage in this type of bargaining).

A third type of bargaining, namely, sentence bargaining, is a mixed case. It is not in the exclusive control of the prosecutor or of the judge. Prosecutors can sentence bargain by agreeing to drop all charges in exchange for some consideration from the defendant. Judges can sentence bargain through open negotiation with the defense over the specific sentence that would be given in exchange for a guilty plea. A third possibility is that both the prosecutor and the judge cooperate in a system of sentence bargaining. This occurs in jurisdictions where judges have permitted prosecutors to make sentence recommendations as part of their plea negotiations and virtually always follow the prosecutors' recommendations.

Habitual Offender and Mandatory-Sentencing Legislation

Another important factor in the confusion of roles between prosecutor and judge has been the enactment of penal codes containing manda-

tory-sentencing provisions. This has been particularly relevant to the habitual offender laws. These laws transferred power from the judiciary to the prosecutor and established him in the sentencing business. This was immediately recognized and protested—but to no avail—by the judiciary when it happened in New York in the early 1900s.

Habitual offender laws provided for enhanced sentencing of repeat offenders. These sentence-enhancing provisions, however, were under the control not of the judge but rather of the prosecutor. From a formal legal point of view, this made sense. Initiating these habitual offender proceedings was simply a special kind of charging decision, that is, charging the defendant with being a habitual offender. Since in legal theory charging belongs to the prosecutor, he should be given this new charging power. But as the New York judges who protested Baume's law knew, such logic places form over substance. When mandatory sentences are involved, the charging decision becomes the sentencing decision.

Habitual offender legislation is just one illustration of how features in the penal code affect the prosecutor's domain. Several scholars have clarified this relationship. The prosecutor's domain and his general influence over the sentencing process tends to be greater when penal codes have the following characteristics either alone or in combination: (1) when they contain mandatory-sentencing provisions; (2) when they provide for indeterminate sentences with the final release decision determined not by the judge but by a separate sentencing authority; (3) when there is a presumption or requirement that sentences for multiple charges and/or offenses be served consecutively; and (4) when there is a graded system of punishment linked with a graded system of offenses and the differences among the grades entail substantial differences in the severity of the punishment. In short, when the penal code is such that the prosecutor's charging decision can make a major impact on the type of sentence that will be served and this cannot be substantially altered by the judge, the prosecutor's domain is expanded into the traditional judicial prerogative of sentencing.

The Initial Screening Decision

While the police may have dominated the front end of the criminal justice system in many jurisdictions, they did not dominate in all. The crime commissions of the 1920s revealed that in some urban jurisdictions the prosecutor was very much in control of the initial charging decision. In 1926, the Missouri Crime Survey reported that the prosecutor's office in St. Louis (city) was rejecting 40 percent of the arrests brought to it by the police. The Jackson County prosecutor was rejecting 18 percent of the arrests in his jurisdiction. But in other states, the initial screening decision was either fragmented among several agencies of justice or dominated by an agency other than the prosecutor. In Chicago, the police (not the prosecutor) presented cases at the preliminary hearing and the judge (not the prosecutor) performed the initial screening function. The Illinois Crime Survey of 1929 found that 56 percent of the incoming felony cases were eliminated at the preliminary examination. Judges continued to dominate the initial screening process in Chicago until the early 1970s, when because of unusual political circumstances, a Republican was elected state's attorney and altered the initial screening process. Under the new system, the prosecutor's office has taken over the initial screening function.

Aside from the long-standing concern about overcrowded court dockets, one of the major stimuli for the recent move by prosecutors to take real control over the initial screening process has been the concern over plea bargaining. Although explicit plea bargaining has been around for decades, it became a heated political and scholarly issue only in the late 1960s. Even though the American Bar Association and the U.S. Supreme Court had endorsed the practice of plea bargaining, prosecutors found themselves on the defensive with both the general public and the scholarly community. In 1972, the National Advisory Commission on Criminal Justice Standards and Goals recommended that plea bargaining be abolished by 1978. The movement to eliminate or minimize plea bargaining was well under way and took various forms. In Florida, legislation was proposed to make plea bargaining a crime. In numerous jurisdictions, total or partial no-plea-bargaining policies were established.

Plea bargaining, as it had developed, proved to have many benefits to the new system of justice administered by professional organizations. The police came to rely upon it to secure the services of informants (whose cases would be dismissed or reduced after they had performed satisfactorily); it assured the prosecutor of a politically beneficial high rate of conviction; and particularly important, it provided a way to obtain convictions in cases that might have been lost at trial because of inherently weak evidence, sloppy police work, incompetent prosecution, or biased or unpredictable juries. When plea bargaining came under attack in the 1960s, the propriety of the various "benefits" that plea bargaining provided were challenged. Plea bargaining had been justified as necessary to deal with overwhelming caseloads. But if this were so, than an alternative solution was to reduce the flow of cases entering the system. This could be done by making the threshold standards used for accepting a case into the system higher than they had traditionally been. The traditional standard was one of legal sufficiency. Did probable cause exist, and was the arrest lawful in other respects? But with the crush of massive caseloads, legal sufficiency was not enough. There were too many cases that could meet that standard. A higher standard would have to be used, but no one wanted this standard imposed by law. It could be imposed, however, as a matter of policy by prosecutors. But this meant that prosecutors would have to be in real control of the initial charging decision.

The other advantages of plea bargaining were also seen in a new light. When Attorney General Gross initiated the no-plea-bargaining policy in Alaska, his purpose was in part to force the criminal justice system to drop its reliance on plea bargaining as a substitute for competent professional work. He specifically disapproved of using plea bargaining to get convictions in cases that would not otherwise have resulted in convictions. He directed that "an effective screening of cases filed . . . will have to be instituted in order to avoid filing cases which might be 'bargains' under the existing system but which could not be won at trial."

One of the major criticisms of plea bargaining is the practice of "overcharging." Although there is not yet any adequate definition of this practice, it can be partially defined as the practice of charging a defendant with the highest number and degree of charges that can possibly be supported by the available evidence. This practice had become standard procedure in the criminal justice process. It is called overcharging, not to suggest anything illegal but to convey the notion of overkill. The charges are higher than anyone reasonably expects the defendant to be convicted of or punished for given the usual local practice for similarly situated offenders. Overcharging has the benefit of giving both the police and the prosecutor something to negotiate for guilty pleas or services of informants. Overcharging allows the prosecutor to reduce charges without really giving anything away. The defendant pleads to a sentence which is virtually the same he would have received had he been convicted at trial.

INTERORGANIZATIONAL
CONFLICTS OVER DOMAIN

The historical evolution of the office of public prosecutor had extended the boundaries of his domain into territories formerly held by the police, the grand jury, the petit jury, the defense bar, and the judiciary. The police and the judiciary have not allowed this to happen without a protest. The defense bar has also lost some territory but more importantly has been forced to change its method of operation as a result of the changes brought about by prosecutors in the extent of their domain and the way they are performing their function. The defense bar has also resisted the prosecutorial changes. As for the grand jury and the petit jury, there is no contest because no vested interests were at stake. Below, we illustrate some of the conflicts which have accompanied the growth of the prosecutor's domain.

The Police Versus the Prosecutor

As noted earlier, when prosecutors have taken real control in initial screening decisions, it has been accompanied by strong reaction from the police. In Alaska, the police loudly protested and resisted the no-plea-bargaining policy. This came as a surprise to Attorney General Gross, because the police there—as elsewhere—have long been critical of the prosecutor's use of plea bargaining. It should be noted, however, that where police have objected to no-plea-bargaining police policies their objection has not been so much focused on plea bargaining as on the new role the prosecutor is playing at the initial screening. Formerly, prosecutors' offices had been largely rubber stamps for the police at initial screening. But this was going to change. Attorney General Gross told his assistants, "Merely because you are brought a police file does not mean that you are required to file a criminal charge. . . . I am not interested in seeing the office file on Assault With a Deadly Weapon charges and then reduce them to Simple Assault with suspended impositions of sentence with no fine or jail time purely because we never had a case in the first place."

The American police have not been very discriminating in what they let into the criminal justice system. In their minds, if a fellow police officer felt the case was good enough to make an arrest then it was good enough to go to trial. Every case rejected is an implied criticism of the arresting officer. When the tough screening policy was established in New Orleans and the case rejection rate went up to 46 percent, the police response was that they refused to believe they were "wrong" in almost half the arrests they make.

In some jurisdictions, the police have come to rely on the initial charging policies of the prosecutor to protect them from civil suits for false arrests. Accommodating prosecutors have done one of two things to cooperate. They file charges in cases they might otherwise reject just to convince the defendant the arrest was lawful, or they require the defendant to sign a release waiving any claim of false arrest. The defendant's case is not dropped unless he signs a release. Tough screening policies would disrupt these informal arrangements.

Another concern is that the police like to be able to control the doing of substantive justice as they see it. This has two sides to it—both to reduce and increase the punishment that some offenders get. For instance, our ten-year veteran in the New Orleans police department complained that under the charging and no-plea-bargaining policies of Connick, he was not able to charge certain types of cases in the way he thought they deserved. He mentioned the "hypothetical" case where the police officer arrests a second-time offender for possession of a gun. The officer may want the man charged with the misdemeanor of possession of a weapon because the person has been "toeing the line for quite a while." Under Connick's policies, however, the police officer's wishes would not prevail. Instead, the offender would be charged with the felony and with being a habitual offender.

A final source of police dissatisfaction with the new charging policies is that the police have become committed to the old system of a little punishment for a lot of people. They believe at a visceral level that it is better than the alternative policy of a lot of punishment for a few people. They are unhappy at the thought that cases which formerly would have been accepted and resulted in conviction will now be rejected outright. They fear that certain classes of offenders or offenses will go unpunished altogether. One chief of police in Alaska complained that the no-bargaining policy there meant, in effect, that the prosecutor had declared "open season on misdemeanors." Other Alaskan police officers had the same complaint. The Alaska Judicial Council reported:

Police investigators often objected strongly to dismissal of charges by prosecutors. Investigators working with bad check cases cited several examples of cases in which charges had been dismissed, giving the reasons they believe that caused the dismissals. "If a guy pays up on a check case charges are dropped." "We had a recent forgery case involving numerous checks. The D.A. and defense attorney got together, the defendant pled guilty to two charges and the others were dropped." "In the old system [of plea bargaining], they pled guilty to three out of five charges. Now, no deals are made, but they still drop charges, without talking to defense counsel." "If there aren't enough judges to go around at calendar call or the D.A.s are busy, they only take more serious

cases and dismiss the others." "If they eliminated plea bargaining entirely, it would be O.K. but if we've got four counts, some shouldn't be dropped." Police were indignant that charges were dropped without any concessions in return by the defendant.

The Judiciary Versus the Prosecutor

The trend in the relationship between the prosecutor's domain and that of the judiciary has been steadily in the direction of increasing the former at the expense of the latter. Before the American Revolution, the judge interrogated the defendant and served as prosecutor at the trial. Thereafter, those functions were assumed by the police and the prosecutor. The judiciary once controlled the initiation of prosecutions through its control of the issuance of warrants. That function has since been steadily taken over by the prosecutor. In the heyday of the jury trial, the judiciary had a major influence in the process of determining guilt and innocence and the sentence. But that system was replaced by the system of administrative justice in which over 60 percent of the incoming cases are disposed of by the prosecutor without a finding of guilt or innocence, and in which 90 percent of the convictions are obtained by plea bargaining in which the prosecutor usually plays a key role. Even in the bail decision, the prosecutor now plays an influential role.

Some of these transfers of domain from the judiciary to the prosecutor have been accompanied by strong protests from the judiciary, and there are still some judges resisting this trend. But their efforts are in vain. Today's criminal justice industry is big business with large case volumes being processed through multijudge courts. As the Wickersham Commission realized, that kind of system must have a central executive officer if it is to achieve any degree of efficiency at all. Although the chief judge in a multijudge court system can perform this function to some extent, the officer in the best position to do it is the chief prosecutor.

Today many judges do not seem to be resisting the growth of the prosecutor's domain. In fact, with the decline of the grand jury and petit jury as institutions available to take the brunt of public criticisms for unpopular decisions, judges appear to be happy to have the prosecutor share in their decision making. It diffuses responsibility. Of particular interest in this regard is the experience in El Paso, Texas, where the prosecutor decided to stop plea bargaining. This left the judges with the responsibility of setting the appropriate (but unpopular) sentences. Within a short time, however, the judges got out of that sentencing function by establishing a no-plea-bargaining policy.

The Defense Bar Versus the Prosecutor

Inasmuch as the prosecutor and the defense attorney are adversaries, one might suppose that there is little opportunity for their domains to come into conflict. One would not expect to find prosecutors performing services for defendants that their attorneys might perform. But to some limited extent this has happened. One illustration will make the point.

Defense attorneys in many jurisdictions have reported that they sometimes are able to have prosecutors reject cases at initial screening or dismiss them at a later point as the result of new information brought to light by the defense attorney. This frequently is information that could have been discovered by a diligent prosecutor's office bent on careful case screening. For instance, a Greenville, South Carolina attorney with a long-established reputation of trust among the local prosecutors reported he was once able to telephone the prosecutor's office and have a case not charged. He told them that the defendant, his client, was out of town on the date in question and that he (the attorney) had the airline and hotel receipts to prove it. For getting this case dropped, this attorney received a fee.

In New Orleans, the prosecutor's office has placed a heavy emphasis on initial case screening. Assistant prosecutors are given financial and other incentives for being innovative and diligent in finding the kind of information that would show that a case should not be put through the system. If our Greenville attorney's case had occurred in New Orleans, there is a good chance the prosecutor's office might have established the defendant's alibi themselves and

dropped the case. Of course, this would have been at public expense. No attorney's fee would have been paid.

This example, however, is the exception. The expansion of the prosecutor's domain has not usually been at the expense of the domain held by the defense bar. The conflict that has occurred between the two components of the system has more often been the result of the fact that in expanding his domain the prosecutor has changed the way in which the functions he has taken over are performed. This has posed a threat to the interests of the defense bar. Vigorous initial screening is a threat because every case rejected from the prosecution is a potential client lost. Furthermore, the stronger and the more serious the cases are that are accepted for prosecution, the less the defense attorney is going to be able to do for his client, the more often he is likely to have to go to trial, the more often his client is going to be convicted at trial, the more often his client is going to be severely sentenced either after trial or at plea bargaining, the less outstanding the defense attorney's reputation will be, and the less pleased the attorney will feel about his ability to serve his clients.

The no-plea-bargaining policies are a threat because the defense attorney will no longer be able to function as he once did; he will have to go to trial more often; he will be less able to show his client that he has gotten something for him; he will be less able to maintain the image of manipulator, wheeler-dealer, or fixer; and (as with the police) he will be less able to ensure that substantive justice as he sees it will occur. Little wonder that in jurisdictions such as Alaska, New Orleans, and El Paso (Texas) where tough screening and/or no-plea-bargaining policies have been instituted, there have been strong protests from the defense bar. The prosecutors in these jurisdictions did not usurp domain but forced the defense bar to change the performance of its functions.

CONCLUSION

The traditional formal view of the division of labor among criminal justice agencies is misleading. Legal pronouncements about the clear distinction between the functions of these agencies obscure the reality of the overlapping and constantly changing roles they perform. It is more useful to regard each component of the criminal justice industry as having a domain, that is, a claim to control performance of certain parts of the process. Those claims are always open to negotiation. The domain of any particular component may be expanded either because the criminal justice process itself had been enlarged or because the existing domain of some other component of the process has been usurped. Furthermore, changes in the way one organization performs its part of the work will cause changes in the way other components perform. Encroachment on domain and the forcing of changes in performance of one's function will be resisted if vested interests are at stake.

Over the course of the past two centuries, the American criminal justice industry had been transformed from a small amateur operation into a sprawling bureaucratic machinery operated by full-time professionals. The old system consisted of three main components: the victim, the judge, and the jury; the major form of disposition was trial by jury. Today the main components in the system are the police, the public prosecutor, the judge, and the correctional agencies; the major form of disposition is by the prosecutor's decision to decline or dismiss cases. In addition, most convictions are obtained from negotiations in which prosecutors are usually involved.

In this transformation, the office of the public prosecutor has grown from virtually a nonexistent role to the position of central actor in the system. Much of this growth has been by displacing other components of the criminal justice system. In so doing, the prosecutor has displaced the police, the judiciary, and the defense bar from territory that was once theirs. The public prosecutor has also continued to displace the judge and jury as determiners of guilt and of sentence. The increase in the size and complexity of the criminal justice industry brought with it the need for a centralized chief executive to bring some efficiency and coordination to its operation. The public prosecutor was the only component in the system able to do this. Today's system is one of criminal law administration through and by the prosecutor, and it is likely to become even more so in the future.

The Charging Policies of Prosecutors

JOAN E. JACOBY

THE key to understanding the nature of prosecutorial policy is understanding the nature of the prosecutor himself. As the public official responsible for criminal prosecution in his political subdivision, his nature is shaped by three distinct and important roles. They are the legal, the bureaucratic, and the political. The prosecutor is the chief law enforcement official in his district having authority to prosecute violations of the law. He is a bureaucrat because he is responsible for supervising and managing the operations and resources allocated to him to carry out his legal functions. And he is a politician because, generally, he holds his office as a result of popular election.

All prosecutorial policy is made within the bounds created by these three considerations. In reality, prosecutorial policy is simply a microcosm of much larger considerations—the values that society itself places on controlling aberrant behavior among its citizens. The prosecutor's nature is discretionary. Within a general framework of state law and local economics, he is given the latitude to choose among alternative courses of actions. His policy is simply the course that he does choose. Those choices may be limited or constrained by various external influences over which he has little or no control. Some of the more important exogenous variables are the size of the jurisdiction, the type of court structure, and the amount of appropriated monies. Although they may account to some degree for his selection of policy, nevertheless, once a course of action has been chosen, the policy of the prosecutor has been defined and a

base upon which his performance must be evaluated has been created.

This chapter will discuss the connection between prosecutorial policy and the disposition of individual decisions which manifest that policy. The discussion assumes that policy implies the existence of a value system used in the decision-making process to produce observable outcomes. In attempting to compare the outcomes of different policies, the concept of policy as a discretionary choice is critical. More important, it points out the obvious necessity of identifying policy before undertaking any evaluation, since results can only be evaluated in terms of identifiable and rational goals.

A CONCEPTUAL MODEL FOR POLICY ANALYSIS

Prosecutorial policy is best examined through a conceptual frame which assumes that the local environment affects prosecutorial policy; that it shapes and colors the policy of the prosecutor and his perception of this role and restricts the extent to which he may select policies not acceptable to the community he represents.

It also assumes that the prosecutor's policy is implemented through an organizational structure that can be described by its resource allocation pattern, management, and operational procedures and controls to ensure the implementation of policy.

Various strategies may be used to achieve a policy's goals. Of those available to the prosecutor, there is generally little variation from one jurisdiction to another. Although statutes, the Constitution, or court rule may preclude the use of some of these strategies in certain states, it can

From *The Prosecutor* (pp. 15-59), W. F. McDonald, editor, 1979, Newbury Park, CA: Sage Publications, Inc. Copyright 1979 Sage Publications, Inc. Reprinted by permission.

be assumed that each will be selected or rejected on the basis of its consistency with the policy.

The dispositions that result from the implementation of a policy will, when aggregated, produce a dispositional pattern that is distinctive to the policy. Thus, if one knows the policy of the prosecutor, one should be able to predict an expected dispositional pattern.

Underlying all of these assumptions is a basic (although controversial) one. We assume that the prosecutive function is rational and that what may appear to be irrational behavior to the observer is only so because the purpose of an action is not clearly specified or placed in proper perspective.

A POLICY TYPOLOGY OF PROSECUTOR'S CHARGING DECISIONS

Prosecutorial policy is not circumscribed by the limits of the office. Its impact can be measured in other criminal justice agencies, particularly corrections. Depending upon the prosecution policy, the future size and characteristics of the correctional population can be anticipated. Where treatment programs are used, prosecutorial policy may well indicate the needs and requirements of such activity. This predictive power can be turned into a highly effective planning and management tool as well as a testing mechanism for attempted solutions to some of the problems confronted by the criminal justice system.

Because of their widespread ramifications, it is important to understand what types of policies exist and how they influence the distribution of justice in a community. Emphasis will be placed on prosecutorial policy as it is reflected by the charging decision. Since this decision acts as a gatekeeper for the office, it, more than any other subsequent ones, dictates the quality and tone of prosecution in a community. With this background, four "ideal" policies will be examined, representing the range of those that are likely to be found in one form or another in prosecutors' offices. The results of the policies will be discussed in terms of expected case disposition rates, and the strategies and resource allocation

patterns that support the policies will be briefly described.

Prosecutorial Policies

No matter what the external environment or a prosecutor's perception of his discretionary authority, the prosecutor operates with a policy (usually either the one for which he was elected or the one he inherited) and implements the policy by various strategies. One might expect the policies of the district attorney to vary as much as the characteristics of the approximately 3,400 prosecutors. However, experience and observation have shown that only a few generalized classifications need delineation. Of the four discussed here, all have been observed operating in almost "pure" form in offices throughout the United States. The differences between offices were so marked that the abstraction of their operations into policy models was not a difficult task. The examples presented below are therefore discussed as ideals or models.

For convenience, the policies have been given the abbreviated descriptive names of *legal sufficiency, system efficiency, defendant rehabilitation,* and *trial sufficiency*. Policy goals of each type are equated to outcomes which should be maximized or minimized. Once the goals are established, other outcomes are logically predictable. One can expect them to occur with high frequency; others with low frequency. A few outcomes appear to occur independent of the policy and goals in some instances.

LEGAL SUFFICIENCY POLICY   Some prosecutors believe that if any case is legally sufficient (i.e., if the elements of the crime are present) then it is their responsibility to accept the case for prosecution. For example, in a breaking-and-entering case, if there was evidence of forcible entry and if the person arrested was found to have in his possession items belonging to the victim, the case would be prosecuted because it was legally sufficient. The elements of the case are present. However, what may on the surface seem to be a prosecutable case might ultimately be lost because of constitutional questions, such as an illegal search and seizure.

Implementing this policy at the charging level requires only an examination for legal defects. If the basis for a charge is not legally sufficient, either additional investigation could be ordered or the case would be rejected. The legal sufficiency policy is prevalent in lower, misdemeanor courts processing large workloads or in offices giving little attention to screening either by choice or necessity. A routine but rapid examination for obvious defects prior to court appearance generally constitutes the extent of screening that a case receives. As a result, overloads occur, plea bargaining is encouraged to reduce the volume, and with scant case preparation time, dismissals and acquittals abound.

SYSTEM EFFICIENCY POLICY Another common policy is labeled system efficiency because it aims for the speedy and early disposition of cases by any means possible. The time to disposition and the place in the court process where disposition occurs are measures of success in addition to favorable dispositions. Under this policy, the breaking-and-entering case would have been rejected because emphasis is placed on screening as a primary technique for minimizing workload. The search-and-seizure issue would have been spotted and the case rejected at intake. If there were no search-and-seizure issue, after acceptance the case would have been charged as a felony and at the committing magistrate hearing the defendant might have pled to a reduced charge of unlawful trespassing or larceny (both misdemeanors). The system efficiency policy usually emerges when the trial court is overloaded or backlogged, or when the resources of the prosecutor are so limited that the early dispositions are a necessity if he is to move the caseload.

Under these conditions, in addition to the emphasis placed on pretrial screening, other methods of case disposal will be sought and used. The prosecutor himself may be an active searcher in the community for additional avenues of case disposition. Extensive use will be made of community resources, other agency resources, and diversion programs so that cases may be kept out of the criminal justice system. Cases will be examined for their ability to be plea bargained (to achieve this, overcharging

may occur). If possible, charges will be broken down for handling in the lower courts or modified and referred to another court with a different jurisdiction (e.g., a county court case referred to another court with a different jurisdiction, perhaps a municipal court). Full use of the court's resources and the charging authority will be made to dispose of cases as soon as possible. Particular emphasis will be placed on the disposal of the case before a bindover to the higher court or grand jury.

DEFENDANT REHABILITATION POLICY A third approach is a defendant-oriented policy. It incorporates some of the elements of the early and speedy disposition policy but should not be confused with it. Under this policy, the prosecutor believes that the most effective treatments for the vast majority of defendants who pass through his office can be found outside the formal criminal justice processing system. Citing the breaking-and-entering case again, if the defendant were a first offender or had a drug problem and if restitution were made to the victim, the defendant might very well be placed in a pretrial diversion program. If this option were not available, prosecution might be deferred or, with the court's concurrence, the defendant could be sentenced to probation without verdict. In a defendant-oriented policy, the charging and prosecution decision depends primarily on the circumstances of the defendant and secondarily on the offense that the defendant allegedly committed. Thus, the goal of a defendant rehabilitation policy is the early diversion of many defendants from the criminal justice system coupled with serious prosecution of those cases accepted. It is logical to expect vigorous prosecution of this latter category, especially if the defendant's history includes prior convictions with no evidence of rehabilitation. Offices using this policy tend to rely heavily on the resources in the community, as well as in the criminal justice system, to move eligible defendants out of the judicial and correctional systems. Close cooperation with the court often ensues, particularly in using the sentence recommendation power of the prosecutor to ensure consistency in the recommended treatment plan for the defendant.

TRIAL SUFFICIENCY POLICY The fourth policy is that of trial sufficiency. This policy states that a case will be accepted and charged at a level capable of being sustained at trial. Under these circumstances, the prosecutor views his responsibility stringently but not without leniency. The decisions to accept and to charge are crucial to the implementation of this policy. If a decision was made to charge the defendant of the hypothetical breaking-and-entering case and, again, if the constitutional questions of the search were overcome, the defendant would be charged with a felony and a conviction at this level would be expected. Since changing a charge is discouraged, implementation of trial sufficiency should be supported by either good police reporting or experienced investigative staff. It also requires alternatives to prosecution for the cases rejected. Most important, it requires court capacity because with plea bargaining minimized it is expected that the cases will go to trial. Finally, this policy must rely on extensive management controls to ensure the proper setting of the initial charge and to ensure that the charges, once made, will not be modified or changed.

The Decision to Prosecute

GEORGE F. COLE

THIS essay is based on an exploratory study of the Office of Prosecuting Attorney, King County (Seattle), Washington. The lack of social scientific knowledge about the prosecutor dictated the choice of this approach. An open-ended interview was administered to one-third of the former deputy prosecutors who had worked in the office during the ten-year period 1955-1965. In addition, interviews were conducted with court employees, members of the bench, law enforcement officials, and others having reputations for participation in legal decision making. Over fifty respondents were contacted during this phase. A final portion of the research placed the author in the role of observer in the prosecutor's office. This experience allowed for direct observation of all phases of the decision to prosecute so that the informal processes of the office could be noted. Discussions with the prosecutor's staff, judges, defendants' attorneys, and the police were held so that the interview data could be placed within an organizational context.

The primary goal of this investigation was to examine the role of the prosecuting attorney as an officer of the legal process within the context of the local political system. The analysis is therefore based on two assumptions. First, the legal process is best understood as a subsystem of the larger political system. Because of this choice, emphasis is placed upon the interaction and goals of the individuals involved in decision making. Second, and closely related to the first point, it is assumed that broadly conceived political considerations explained to a large extent "who gets or does not get—in what amount—

From "The Decision to Prosecute" by G. F. Cole, 1970, *Law and Society Review, 4*, pp. 313-343. Copyright 1970 by the Law and Society Association. Reprinted by permission.

and how, the good (justice) that is hopefully produced by the legal system." By focusing upon the political and social linkages between these systems, it is expected that decision making in the prosecutor's office will be viewed as a principal ingredient in the authoritative allocation of values.

THE PROSECUTOR'S OFFICE IN AN EXCHANGE SYSTEM

While observing the interrelated activities of the organizations in the legal process, one might ask, "Why do these agencies cooperate?" If the police refuse to transfer information to the prosecutor concerning the commission of a crime, what are the rewards or sanctions which might be brought against them? Is it possible that organizations maintain a form of "bureaucratic accounting," which, in a sense, keeps track of the resources allocated to an agency and the support returned? How are cues transmitted from one agency to another to influence decision making? These are some of the questions which must be asked when decisions are viewed as an output of an exchange system.

The major findings of this study are placed within the context of an exchange system. This serves the heuristic purpose of focusing attention upon the linkages found between actors in the decision-making process. In place of the traditional assumptions that the agency is supported solely by statutory authority, this view recognizes that an organization has many clients with which it interacts and upon whom it is dependent for certain resources. As interdependent subunits of a system, then, the organization and its clients are engaged in a set of exchanges across their boundaries. These will involve a transfer of resources between the organizations which will affect the mutual achievement of goals.

The legal system may be viewed as a set of interorganizational exchange relationships analogous to what Long has called a community game. The participants in the legal system (game) share a common territorial field and collaborate for different and particular ends. They interact on a continuing basis as their responsibilities demand contact with other participants in the process. Thus, the need for the cooperation of other participants can have a bearing on the decision to prosecute. A decision not to prosecute a narcotics offender may be a move to pressure the U.S. Attorney's office to cooperate on another case. It is obvious that bargaining occurs not only between the major actors in a case—the prosecutor and the defense attorney—but also between the clientele groups that are influential in structuring the actions of the prosecuting attorney.

Exchanges do not simply "sail" from one system to another, but take place in an institutionalized setting which may be compared to a market. In the market, decisions are made between individuals who occupy boundary-spanning roles and who set the conditions under which the exchange will occur. In the legal system, this may merely mean that a representative of the parole board agrees to forward a recommendation to the prosecutor, or it could mean that there is extended bargaining between a deputy prosecutor and a defense attorney. In the study of the King County prosecutor's office, it was found that most decisions resulted from some type of exchange relationship. The deputies interacted almost constantly with the police and criminal lawyers, while the prosecutor was more closely linked to exchange relations with the courts, community leaders, and the county commissioners.

THE PROSECUTOR'S CLIENTELE

In an exchange system, power is largely dependent upon the ability of an organization to create clientele relationships which will support and enhance the needs of the agency. For although interdependence is characteristic of the legal system, competition with other public agencies for support also exists. Since organizations operate in an economy of scarcity, the organization must exist in a favorable power position in relation to its clientele. Reciprocal and unique claims are made by the organization and its clients. Thus, rather than being oriented toward only one public, an organization is beholden to several publics, some visible and others seen clearly only from the pinnacle of leadership. As Gore notes, when these claims are "firmly anchored inside the organization and the lines drawn taut, the tensions between conflicting claims form a net serving as the institutional base for the organization."

An indication of the stresses within the judicial system may be obtained by analyzing its outputs. It has been suggested that the administration of justice is a selective process in which only those cases which do not create strains in the organization will ultimately reach the courtroom. As noted in Figure 1, the system operates so that only a small number of cases arrive for trial, the rest being disposed of through reduced charges, *nolle pros.*, and guilty pleas. Not indicated are those cases removed by the police and prosecutor prior to the filing of charges. As the focal organization in an exchange system, the Office of Prosecuting Attorney makes decisions which reflect the influence of its clientele. Because of the scarcity of resources, marketlike relationships, and the organizational needs of the system, prosecutorial decision making emphasizes the accommodations which are made to the needs of participants in the process.

Police

Although the prosecuting attorney has discretionary power to determine the disposition of cases, this power is limited by the fact that usually he is dependent upon the police for inputs to the system of cases and evidence. The prosecutor does not have the investigative resources necessary to exercise the kind of affirmative control over the types of cases that are brought to him. In this relationship, the prosecutor is not without countervailing power. His main check on the police is his ability to return cases to them

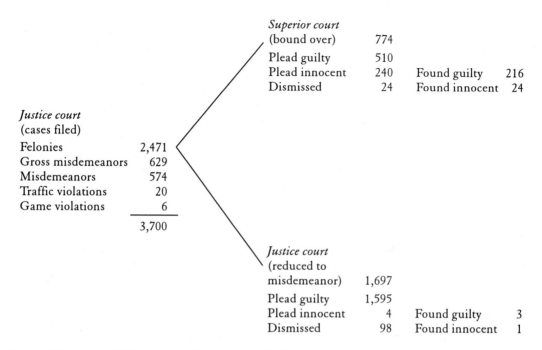

Figure 1 *Disposition of felony cases—King County, 1964.*

Superior court (bound over)	774			
Plead guilty	510			
Plead innocent	240	Found guilty	216	
Dismissed	24	Found innocent	24	

Justice court (cases filed)		
Felonies	2,471	
Gross misdemeanors	629	
Misdemeanors	574	
Traffic violations	20	
Game violations	6	
	3,700	

Justice court (reduced to misdemeanor)	1,697			
Plead guilty	1,595			
Plead innocent	4	Found guilty	3	
Dismissed	98	Found innocent	1	

for further investigation and to refuse to approve arrest warrants. By maintaining cordial relations with the press, a prosecutor is often able to focus attention on the police when the public becomes aroused by incidents of crime. As the King County prosecutor emphasized, "That [investigation] is the job for the sheriff and police. It's their job to bring me the charges." As noted by many respondents, the police, in turn, are dependent upon the prosecutor to accept the output of their system; rejection of too many cases can have serious repercussions affecting the morale, discipline, and workload of the force.

A request for prosecution may be rejected for a number of reasons relating to questions of evidence. Not only must the prosecutor believe that the evidence will secure a conviction, but he must also be aware of community norms relating to the type of acts that should be prosecuted. King County deputy prosecutors noted that charges were never filed when a case involved attempted suicide or fornication. In other actions, the heinous nature of the crime, together with the expected public reaction, may force

both the police and prosecutor to press for conviction when evidence is less than satisfactory. As one deputy noted, "In that case [molestation and murder of a 6-year-old girl] there was nothing that we could do. As you know the press was on our back and every parent was concerned. Politically, the prosecutor had to seek an information."

Factors other than those relating to evidence may require that the prosecutor refuse to accept a case from the police. First, the prosecuting attorney serves as a regulator of caseloads not only for his own office but for the rest of the legal system. Constitutional and statutory time limits prevent him and the courts from building a backlog of untried cases. In King County, when the system reached the "overload point," there was a tendency to be more selective in choosing the cases to be accepted. A second reason for rejecting prosecution requests may stem from the fact that the prosecutor is thinking of his public exposure in the courtroom. He does not want to take forward cases which will place him in an embarrassing position. Finally, the prosecutor may return cases to check the quality of police work. As a former chief criminal deputy said, "You have to keep them on their toes, otherwise they get lazy. If they aren't doing their job, send the case back and then leak the situation to the newspapers." Rather than spend the resources necessary to find additional evidence, the police may dispose of a case by sending it back to the prosecutor on a lesser charge, implement the "copping out" machinery leading to a guilty plea, drop the case, or in some instances send it to the city prosecutor for action in municipal court.

In most instances, a deputy prosecutor and the police officer assigned to the case occupy the boundary-spanning roles in this exchange relationship. Prosecutors reported that after repeated contacts they got to know the policemen whom they could trust. As one female deputy commented, "There are some you can trust, others you have to watch because they are trying to get rid of cases on you." Deputies may be influenced by the police officer's attitude on a case. One officer noted to a prosecutor that he knew he had a weak case, but mumbled, "I didn't want to bring it up here, but that's what they [his superiors] wanted." As might be expected, the deputy turned down prosecution.

Sometimes the police perform the ritual of "shopping around," seeking to find a deputy prosecutor who, on the basis of past experience, is liable to be sympathetic to their view on a case. At one time, deputies were given complete authority to make the crucial decisions without coordinating their activities with other staff members. In this way, the arresting officer would search the prosecutor's office to find a deputy he thought would be sympathetic to the police attitude. As a former deputy noted, "This meant that there were no departmental policies concerning the treatment to be accorded various types of cases. It pretty much depended upon the police and their luck in finding the deputy they wanted." Prosecutors are now instructed to ascertain from the police officer if he has seen another deputy on the case. Even under this more centralized system, it is still possible for the police to request a specific deputy or delay presentation of the case until the "correct" prosecutor is available. Often a prosecutor will gain a reputation for specializing in one type of case.

This may mean that the police will assume he will get the case anyway, so they skirt the formal procedure and bring it to him directly.

An exchange relationship between a deputy prosecutor and a police officer may be influenced by the type of crime committed by the defendant. The prototype of a criminal is one who violates person and property. However, a large number of cases involve "crimes without victims." This term refers to those crimes generally involving violations of moral codes, where the general public is theoretically the complainant. In violations of laws against bookmaking, prostitution, and narcotics, neither actor in the transaction is interested in having an arrest made. Hence, vice control men must drum up their own business. Without a civilian complainant, victimless crimes give the police and prosecutor greater leeway in determining the charges to be filed.

One area of exchange involving a victimless crime is that of narcotics control. As Skolnick notes, "The major organizational requirement of narcotics policing is the presence of an informational system." Without a network of informers, it is impossible to capture addicts and peddlers with evidence that can bring about convictions. One source of informers is among those arrested for narcotics violations. Through promises to reduce charges or even to *nolle pros.,* arrangements can be made so that the accused will return to the narcotics community and gather information for the police. Bargaining observed between the head of the narcotics squad of the Seattle Police and the deputy prosecutor who specialized in drug cases involved the question of charges, promises, and the release of an arrested narcotics pusher.

In the course of postarrest questioning by the police, a well-known drug peddler intimated that he could provide evidence against a pharmacist suspected by the police of illegally selling narcotics. Not only did the police representative want to transfer the case to the friendlier hands of this deputy, but he also wanted to arrange for a reduction of charges and bail. The police officer believed that it was important that the accused be let out in such a way that the narcotics community would not realize that he had become an informer. He also wanted to be sure that the reduced charges would be processed so that the informer could be kept on the string, thus allowing the narcotics squad to maintain control over him. The deputy prosecutor, on the other hand, said that he wanted to make sure that procedures were followed so that the action would not bring discredit on his office. He also suggested that the narcotics squad "work a little harder" on a pending case as a means of returning the favor.

Courts

The ways used by the court to dispose of cases is a vital influence in the system. The court's actions effect pressures upon the prison, the conviction rate of the prosecutor, and the work of probation agencies. The judge's decisions act as clues to other parts of the system, indicating the type of action likely to be taken in future cases. As noted by a King County judge, "When the number of prisoners gets to the 'riot point,' the warden puts pressure on us to slow down the flow. This often means that men are let out on parole and the number of people given probation and suspended sentences increases." Under such conditions, it would be expected that the prosecutor would respond to the judge's actions by reducing the inputs to the court either by not preferring charges or by increasing the pressure for guilty pleas through bargaining. The adjustments of other parts of the system could be expected to follow. For instance, the police might sense the lack of interest of the prosecutor in accepting charges, hence they will send only airtight cases to him for indictment.

The influence of the court on the decision to prosecute is very real. The sentencing history of each judge gives the prosecutor, as well as other law enforcement officials, an indication of the treatment a case may receive in the courtroom. The prosecutor's expectation as to whether the court will convict may limit his discretion over the decisions on whether to prosecute. "There is great concern as to whose court a case will be assigned. After Judge _____ threw out three cases in a row in which entrapment was involved, the police did not want us to take any cases to him." Since the prosecutor depends upon the plea-bargaining machinery to main-

tain the flow of cases from his office, the sentencing actions of judges must be predictable. If the defendant and his lawyer are to be influenced to accept a lesser charge or the promise of a lighter sentence in exchange for a plea of guilty, there must be some basis for belief that the judge will fulfill his part of the arrangement. Because judges are unable formally to announce their agreement with the details of the bargain, their past performance acts as a guide.

Within the limits imposed by law and the demands of the system, the prosecutor is able to regulate the flow of cases to the court. He may control the length of time between accusation and trial; hence he may hold cases until he has the evidence which will convict. Alternatively, he may seek repeated adjournment and continuances until the public's interest dies; problems such as witnesses becoming unavailable and similar difficulties make his request for dismissal of prosecution more justifiable. Further, he may determine the type of court to receive the case and the judge who will hear it. Many misdemeanors covered by state law are also violations of a city ordinance. It is a common practice for the prosecutor to send a misdemeanor case to the city prosecutor for processing in the municipal court when it is believed that a conviction may not be secured in justice court. As a deputy said, "If there is no case, send it over to the city court. Things are speedier, less formal, over there."

In the state of Washington, a person arrested on a felony charge must be given a preliminary hearing in a justice court within ten days. For the prosecutor, the preliminary hearing is an opportunity to evaluate the testimony of witnesses, assess the strength of the evidence, and try to predict the outcome of the case if it is sent to trial. On the basis of this evaluation, the prosecutor has several options: he may bind over the case for trial in superior court; he may reduce the charges to those of a misdemeanor for trial in justice court; or he may conclude that he has no case and drop the charges. The President Judge of the Justice Courts of King County estimated that about 70 percent of the felonies are reduced to misdemeanors after the preliminary hearing.

Besides having some leeway in determining the type of court in which to file a case, the prosecutor also has some flexibility in selecting the judge to receive the case. Until recently, the prosecutor could file a case with a specific judge. "The trouble was that Judge _____ was erratic and independent, [so] no one would file with him. The other judges objected that they were handling the entire workload, so a central filing system was devised." Under this procedure, cases are assigned to the judges in rotation. However, as the chief criminal deputy noted, "The prosecutor can hold a case until the correct judge came up."

Defense Attorneys

With the increased specialization and institutionalization of the bar, it would seem that those individuals engaged in the practice of criminal law have been relegated, both by their profession and by the community, to a low status. The urban bar appears to be divided into three parts. First, there is an inner circle which handles the work of banks, utilities, and commercial concerns; second, another circle includes plaintiffs' lawyers representing interests opposed to those of the inner circle; and finally, an outer group scrapes out an existence by "haunting the courts in hope of picking up crumbs from the judicial table." With the exception of a few highly proficient lawyers who have made a reputation by winning acquittal for their clients in difficult, highly publicized cases, most of the lawyers dealing with the King County prosecutor's office belong to this outer ring.

. . . . .

In a legal system where bargaining is a primary method of decision making, it is not surprising that criminal lawyers find it essential to maintain close personal ties with the prosecutor and his staff. Respondents were quite open in revealing their dependence upon this close relationship to successfully pursue their careers. The nature of the criminal lawyer's work is such that his saleable product or service appears to be influence rather than technical proficiency in the law. Respondents hold the belief that clients

are attracted partially on the basis of the attorney's reputation as a fixer, or as a shrewd bargainer.

There is a tendency for ex-deputy prosecutors in King County to enter the practice of criminal law. Because of his inside knowledge of the prosecutor's office and friendships made with court officials, the former deputy feels that he has an advantage over other criminal law practitioners. All of the former deputies interviewed said that they took criminal cases. Of the eight criminal law specialists, seven previously served as deputy prosecutors in King County, while the other was once prosecuting attorney in a rural county.

Because of the financial problems of the criminal lawyer's practice, it is necessary that he handle cases on an assembly-line basis, hoping to make a living from a large number of small fees. Referring to a fellow lawyer, one attorney said, "You should see _____. He goes up there to Carroll's office with a whole fist full of cases. He trades on some, bargains on others and never goes to court. It's amazing but it's the way he makes his living." There are incentives, therefore, to bargain with the prosecutor and other decision makers. The primary aim of the attorney in such circumstances is to reach an accommodation so that the time-consuming formal proceedings need not be implemented. As a Seattle attorney noted, "I can't make any money if I spend my time in a courtroom. I make mine on the telephone or in the prosecutor's office." One of the disturbing results of this arrangement is that instances were reported in which a bargain was reached between the attorney and deputy prosecutor on a "package deal." In this situation, an attorney's clients are treated as a group; the outcome of the bargaining is often an agreement whereby reduced charges will be achieved for some, in exchange for the unspoken assent by the lawyer that the prosecutor may proceed as he desires with the other cases. One member of the King County Bar has developed this practice to such a fine art that a deputy prosecutor said, "When you saw him coming into the office, you knew that he would be pleading guilty." At one time this situation was so widespread that the "prisoners up in the jail had a rating list which graded the attorneys as either 'good guys' or 'sellouts.' "

The exchange relationship between the defense attorney and the prosecutor is based on their need for cooperation in the discharge of their responsibilities. Most criminal lawyers are interested primarily in the speedy solution of cases because of their precarious financial situation. Since they must protect their professional reputations with their colleagues, judicial personnel, and potential clientele, however, they are not completely free to bargain solely with this objective. As one attorney noted, "You can't afford to let it get out that you are selling out your cases."

The prosecutor is also interested in the speedy processing of cases. This can only be achieved if the formal processes are not implemented. Not only does the pressure of his caseload influence bargaining, but also the legal process with its potential for delay and appeal creates a degree of uncertainty which is not present in an exchange relationship with an attorney with whom you have dealt for a number of years. As the Presiding Judge of the Seattle District Court said, "Lawyers are helpful to the system. They are able to put things together, work out a deal, keep the system moving."

Community Influentials

As part of the political system, the judicial process responds to the community environment. The King County study indicated that there are differential levels of influence within the community and that some people had a greater interest in the politics of prosecution than others. First, the general public is able to have its values translated into policies followed by law enforcement officers. The public's influence is particularly acute in those gray areas of the law where full enforcement is not expected. Statutes may be enacted by legislatures defining the outer limits of criminal conduct, but they do not necessarily mean that laws are to be fully enforced to these limits. There are some laws defining behavior which the community no longer considers criminal. It can be expected that a prosecutor's charging policies will reflect this attitude. He may not prosecute violations of laws regulating some forms of gambling, certain sexual practices, or violations of Sunday Blue Laws.

Because the general public is a potential threat to the prosecutor, staff members take measures to protect him from criticism. Respondents agreed that decision making occurs with the public in mind—"will a course of action arouse antipathy toward the prosecutor rather than the accused?" Several deputies mentioned what they called the "aggravation level" of a crime. This is a recognition that the commission of certain crimes, within a specific context, will bring about a vocal public reaction. "If a little girl, walking home from the grocery store, is pulled into the bushes and indecent liberties taken, this is more disturbing to the public's conscience than a case where the father of the girl takes indecent liberties with her at home." The Office of Prosecuting Attorney has a policy requiring that deputies file all cases involving sexual molestation in which the police believe the girl's story is credible. The office also prefers charges in all negligent homicide cases where there is the least possibility of guilt. In such types of cases, the public may respond to the emotional context of the case and demand prosecution. To cover the prosecutor from criticism, it is believed that the safest measure is to prosecute.

The bail system is also used to protect the prosecutor from criticism. Thus, it is the policy to set bail at a high level with the expectation that the court will reduce the amount. "This looks good for Prosecutor Carroll. Takes the heat off of him, especially in morals cases. If the accused doesn't appear in court the prosecutor can't be blamed. The public gets upset when they know these types are out free." This is an example of exchange where one actor is shifting the responsibility and potential onus onto another. In turn, the court is under pressure from county jail officials to keep the prison population down.

A second community group having contact with the prosecutor is composed of those leaders who have a continuing or potential interest in the politics of prosecution. This group, analogous to the players in one of Long's community games, are linked to the prosecutor because his actions affect their success in playing another game. Hence, community boosters want either a crackdown or a hands-off policy toward gambling, political leaders want the prosecutor to remember the interests of the party, and business leaders want policies which will not interfere with their own game.

Community leaders may receive special treatment by the prosecutor if they run afoul of the law. A policy of the King County office requires that cases involving prominent members of the community be referred immediately to the chief criminal deputy and the prosecutor for their disposition. As one deputy noted, "These cases can be pretty touchy. It's important that the boss knows immediately about this type of case so that he is not caught 'flat footed' when asked about it by the press."

Pressure by an interest group was evidenced during a strike by drug store employees in 1964. The striking unions urged Prosecutor Carroll to invoke a state law which requires the presence of a licensed pharmacist if the drug store is open. Not only did union representatives meet with Carroll, but picket lines were set up outside the courthouse protesting his refusal to act. The prosecutor resisted the union's pressure tactics.

In recent years, the prosecutor's tolerance policy toward minor forms of gambling led to a number of conflicts with Seattle's mayor, the sheriff, and church organizations. After a decision was made to prohibit all forms of public gaming, the prosecutor was criticized by groups representing the tourist industry and such affected groups as the bartenders union, which thought the decision would have an adverse economic effect. As Prosecutor Carroll said, "I am always getting pressures from different interests—business, the Chamber of Commerce, and labor. I have to try and maintain a balance between them." In exchange for these considerations, the prosecutor may gain prestige, political support, and admission into the leadership groups of the community.

SUMMARY

By viewing the Office of Prosecuting Attorney, King County as the focal organization in an exchange system, data from this exploratory study suggests the marketplace relationships which exist between actors in the system. Since prosecution operates in an environment of scarce resources and since the decisions have potential political ramifications, a variety of officials influence the allocation of justice. The decision to prosecute is not made at one point, but rather the prosecuting attorney has a number of options which he may employ during various stages of the proceedings. But the prosecutor is able to exercise his discretionary powers only within the network of exchange relationships. The police, court congestion, organizational strains, and community pressures are among the factors which influence prosecutorial behavior.

Prosecutorial Adaptation to Plea Bargaining

MILTON HEUMANN

PERHAPS the most important outcome of the prosecutor's adaptation is that he evidences a major shift in his own presumption about how to proceed with a case. As a newcomer, he feels it to be his responsibility to establish the defendant's guilt at trial, and he sees no need to justify a decision to go to trial. However, as he processes more and more cases, as he drifts into plea bargaining, and as he is taught the risks associated with trials, his own assumption about how to proceed with a case changes. He approaches every case with plea bargaining in mind; that is, he presumes that the case will be plea bargained. If it is a "nonserious" matter, he expects it to be quickly resolved; if it is "serious" he generally expects to negotiate time as part of the disposition. In both instances, he anticipates that the case will eventually be resolved by a negotiated disposition and not by a trial. When a plea bargain does not materialize, and the case goes to trial, the prosecutor feels compelled to justify his failure to reach an accord. He no longer is content to simply assert that it is the role of the prosecutor to establish the defendant's guilt at trial. This adversary component of the prosecutor's role has been replaced by a self-imposed burden to justify why he chose to go to trial, particularly if a certain conviction—and, for serious cases, a period of incarceration—could have been obtained by means of a negotiated disposition.

Elatedly, the prosecutor grows accustomed to the power he exercises in these plea-bargaining negotiations. As a newcomer, he argued that his job was to be an advocate for the state and that

From *Plea Bargaining: The Experiences of Prosecutors, Judges, and Defense Attorneys* (pp. 55-105) by M. Heumann, 1978, Chicago: University of Chicago Press. Copyright 1978 by the University of Chicago Press. Reprinted by permission.

it was the judge's responsibility to sentence defendants. But, having in fact "sentenced" most of the defendants whose files he plea bargained, the distinction between prosecutor and judge becomes blurred in his own mind. Although he did not set out to usurp judicial prerogatives—indeed, he resisted efforts to engage him in the plea-bargaining process—he gradually comes to expect that he will exercise sentencing powers. There is no fixed point in time when he makes a calculated choice to become adjudicator as well as adversary. In a sense, it simply happens; the more cases he resolves (either by charge reduction or sentence recommendations), the greater the likelihood that he will lose sight of the distinction between the roles of judge and prosecutor.

Contrary to suggestions in the literature that prosecutors develop a "mentality" that is biased toward harsh dispositions, my data reflect a consensus that prosecutors mellow over time. With two important exceptions that we will explore below, prosecutors generally become inclined to negotiate more lenient sentences as they gain experience in the criminal justice system.

Q. Would you [an experienced prosecutor] make a prediction as to how _____ [a relative newcomer to this court] would handle cases if I came back here in several years?

A. If he is still around, I'd say he'd mellow a lot, sure.

Q. Why?

A. Why, I don't know. You are aware of other factors and life itself. You know what I mean. You are not so conscious of what the book says. You know the book calls for a sentence of one year and a fine of up to five thousand dollars, but you're more willing to say, "Oh sure it does,

does, but . . ." You recognize that a good many arrests are lousy. You know a good many things like that, and a lot of people are really up against it, and the jails are overcrowded, and you can't be sending everybody to jail, anyway. A lot of crazy things come into it, you know _____ and I [two relative newcomers to the court] would be pretty even in nolles and jail time. _____ [a veteran] would be lower in jail time and higher in nolles. Maybe because we haven't been here that long and the system still hasn't sunk into our heads yet. We haven't mellowed, or whatever you want to call it. _____ has been here eight years, and from all we've heard, he has changed.

As best as could be determined, the answers to these questions appear to be qualified "no"s. I would not be surprised to learn that there have been isolated but ongoing instances of particular prosecutors' and particular defense attorneys' tradeoffs based exclusively on friendship ties; there certainly are occasional deals made in which these ties are an influencing factor. Also, I am sure that friendship has some bearing on marginal cases, cases in which a little bit of prosecutorial leniency can go a long way (e.g., no time in relatively minor "serious" cases). But for the most part, I do not think it accurate to explain prosecutorial mellowing (or plea bargaining) in these terms. Plea bargains are not consummated because of personal ties between the putative opposing sides.

I think the opportunity for defense attorneys to cite relatively mild dispositions in roughly comparable "precedent cases" and the susceptibility of prosecutors to "habits of disposition" contribute to the already-described mellowing of prosecutors. Prosecutors may simply not consider thoroughly the seriousness of a particular case when negotiating it with a familiar defense attorney who comes armed with ample "precedent cases." Thus, a good defense deal in one case can have a trickle-down effect in others and, to the extent that prosecutors are susceptible to claims of equity, can contribute to prosecutorial mellowing.

There are two exceptions to the "prosecutors mellow over time" hypothesis. The first reflects the propensity of some prosecutors to become "harder" on certain types of crime. Although the prosecutor mellows overall—that is, he becomes inclined to settle for lighter sentences than he would have as a newcomer to the court—he singles out one or more types of crime as being particularly heinous/dangerous, and for these he determines to hold firm. In the language of the prosecutors, he has "got a thing" for these crimes. When he is asked to negotiate one of these cases, he is less likely to be willing to go along with a no-time disposition if the defense attorney argues it is a minor matter, and less likely to grab certain time if it is discussed as a serious case. In these instances, the prosecutor is looking for substantial time, and although he probably will end up plea bargaining the case, he will hold out for a more severe disposition.

I like to see higher sentences in robbery, assault, but probably not burglary, than my associates do. I agree with most of them on drugs and sex cases. So in the robbery or assault case, I argue for greater sentences.

Each prosecutor has different feelings. Some people are very hard on some types of offenses, and others don't feel they're very serious at all. I've got a thing about purse snatchers, particularly ones who pick on the older women, the older women who they feel can't identify them or, even if they can, won't identify them because of their age and because they're afraid. A lot of these old women get knocked down and injured severely, and, you know, it's permanent injury at that age. I feel very tough about somebody like that who comes in. I won't bend a finger to help them. Others feel more seriously about alcoholic-related crimes, others about drug-related offenses. You know, everybody's got their own feelings. Some people feel very strongly on larceny, shoplifting, which I rate very low.

The second exception to the "mellowing hypothesis" relates to sanctions imposed by prosecutors on defense attorneys who raise motions and who take cases to trial. I argue that prosecutors have emerged as the central figures in the local criminal court, and they presume that a plea bargain will be expeditiously arrived at in every case. This expectation is predicated on their belief that most defendants are factually guilty and have little cause to challenge the state's case. Veteran prosecutors scoff at the notion that plea bargaining coerces innocent defendants to plead guilty.

Defendants would be the first ones not to want it [the elimination of plea bargaining]. They are always saying: "I don't want the trial, the jury. I want to plead guilty, and get a 'rec.'" And most defendants are guilty. One of the things that I have learned over the years is that I've rarely had a guy go to prison that wasn't guilty. Once in a rare while maybe. But, by and large, most of them are guilty, know that they are guilty, and plead because they are guilty. Most of the cases in this court are cases of guilty people.

What you are saying is that there is the possibility of an innocent person suffering a conviction and maybe even a short, or reduced, prison term. It's possible, depending on what you are dealing with, because they didn't want to take the chance of an increased prison sentence. Naturally, that is the danger that everybody hollers about in plea bargaining. I think it is a very artificial danger, a very uncommon danger. I've seen in the course of my prosecutorial career two cases where I felt the guy was innocent—the defendant was innocent—and one of those cases was not prosecuted, and in the other my judgment was overruled by somebody senior in the office. The person was prosecuted and acquitted. You never can be really sure whether somebody is guilty or innocent, but . . . I don't know what goes through the minds of many of these defendants, but every time that a plea is taken, they are asked in open court whether or not they committed the crime, and whether or not the facts and their involvement in the crime are as the state had stated. Now that's the moment of truth. If a person is so swayed by the possibility of a greater jail sentence or greater exposure that he'll lie at that point . . . I just don't believe that most of them do.

In the prosecutor's eyes, the guilty defendant without any substantial legal defense ought to plead guilty. If he so pleads, a reward can justifiably be attached to his decision. But if the defendant's attorney insists on pursuing what the prosecutor perceives as pointless legal motions, and/or a pointless trial, the prosecutor feels that the reward should be canceled or that a penalty should be attached to the sentence ultimately meted out. The attorney is wasting the court's time with "frivolous" pursuit of an acquittal, and he has to bear the costs of these dilatory actions. The prosecutor's initial willingness to negotiate a reasonable disposition (under the assumption of an expeditious resolution of the case) is replaced by a feeling that the attorney chose to raise these motions, chose to go trial, and now must suffer the consequences. The prosecutor does not believe that an innocent defendant will feel coerced into pleading because of the "here today, gone tomorrow" nature of the plea bargain offer. Though theoretically possible, the "coerced to plead" argument is undercut by his own observations that the defendant is guilty and that no innocent defendant is coerced into pleading.

The prosecutor has come a long way from his status as a novice eager to establish the defendant's guilt at trial, eager to leave sentencing to the judge after trial. He now believes that the issue of the defendant's guilt is generally a foregone conclusion and that prosecutor and defense attorney ought to direct their efforts to the nature of the final disposition. From the evidence examined thus far, it appears that the prosecutor is extraordinarily successful in realizing these new goals. Most cases are resolved in plea-bargaining sessions between prosecution and the defense.

THE DEFENSE ATTORNEY
The Practice of Law as a Confidence Game

ABRAHAM S. BLUMBERG

. . . . .

COURT STRUCTURE DEFINES THE ROLE OF DEFENSE LAWYER

The overwhelming majority of convictions in criminal cases (usually over 90 percent) are not the product of a combative, trial-by-jury process at all but instead merely involve the sentencing of the individual after a negotiated, bargained-for plea of guilty has been entered. Although more recently the overzealous role of police and prosecutors in producing pretrial confessions and admissions has achieved a good deal of notoriety, scant attention has been paid to the organizational structure and personnel of the criminal court itself. Indeed, the extremely high conviction rate produced without the features of an adversary trial in our courts would tend to suggest that the "trial" becomes a perfunctory reiteration and validation of the pretrial interrogation and investigation.

The institutional setting of the court defines a role for the defense counsel in a criminal case radically different from the one traditionally depicted. Sociologists and others have focused their attention on the deprivations and social disabilities of such variables as race, ethnicity, and social class as being the source of an accused person's defeat in a criminal court. Largely overlooked is the variable of the court organization

itself, which possesses a thrust, purpose, and direction of its own. It is grounded in pragmatic values, bureaucratic priorities, and administrative instruments. These exalt maximum production and the particularistic career designs of organizational incumbents, whose occupational and career commitments tend to generate a set of priorities. These priorities exert a higher claim than the stated ideological goals of "due process of law" and are often inconsistent with them.

Organizational goals and discipline impose a set of demands and conditions of practice on the respective professions in the criminal court, to which they respond by abandoning their ideological and professional commitments to the accused client, in the service of these higher claims of the court organization. All court personnel, including the accused's own lawyer, tend to be co-opted to become agent-mediators, who help the accused redefine his situation and restructure his perceptions concomitant with a plea of guilty.

Of all the occupational roles in the court, the only private individual who is officially recognized as having a special status and concomitant obligations is the lawyer. His legal status is that of "an officer of the court," and he is held to a standard of ethical performance and duty to his client as well as to the court. This obligation is thought to be far higher than that expected of ordinary individuals occupying the various occupational statuses in the court community. However, lawyers, whether privately retained or of the legal-aid, public defender variety, have close and continuing relations with the prose-

From "The Practice of Law as a Confidence Game" by A. S. Blumberg, 1967, *Law and Society Review, 1,* pp. 15-39. Copyright 1967 by the Law and Society Review. Reprinted by permission.

cuting office and the court itself through discreet relations with the judges via their law secretaries or "confidential" assistants. Indeed, lines of communication, influence, and contact with those offices, as well as with the Office of the Clerk of the court, Probation Division, and with the press, are essential to present and prospective requirements of criminal law practice. Similarly, the subtle involvement of the press and other mass media in the court's organizational network is not readily discernible to the casual observer. Accused persons come and go in the court system schema, but the structure and its occupational incumbents remain to carry on their respective career, occupational, and organizational enterprises. The individual stridencies, tensions, and conflicts a given accused person's case may present to all the participants are overcome, because the formal and informal relations of all the groups in the court setting require it. The probability of continued future relations and interaction must be preserved at all costs.

This is particularly true of the "lawyer regulars," that is, those defense lawyers, who by virtue of their continuous appearances in behalf of defendants, tend to represent the bulk of a criminal court's nonindigent case workload, and those lawyers who are not "regulars," who appear almost casually in behalf of an occasional client. Some of the "lawyer regulars" are highly visible as one moves about the major urban centers of the nation, their offices line the back streets of the courthouses, at times sharing space with bondsmen. Their political visibility in terms of local clubhouse ties, reaching into the judge's chambers and prosecutor's office, are also deemed essential to successful practitioners. Previous research has indicated that the "lawyer regulars" make no effort to conceal their dependence upon police, bondsmen, and jail personnel. Nor do they conceal the necessity for maintaining intimate relations with all levels of personnel in the court setting as a means of obtaining, maintaining, and building their practice. These informal relations are the sine qua non not only of retaining a practice but also in the negotiation of pleas and sentences.

The client, then, is a secondary figure in the court system as in certain other bureaucratic settings. He becomes a means to other ends of the organization's incumbents. He may present doubts, contingencies, and pressures which challenge existing informal arrangements or disrupt them, but these tend to be resolved in favor of the continuance of the organization and its relations as before. There is a greater community of interest among all the principal organizational structures and their incumbents than exists elsewhere in other settings. The accused's lawyer has far greater professional, economic, intellectual, and other ties to the various elements of the court system than he does to his own client. In short, the court is a closed community.

This is more than just the case of the usual "secrets" of bureaucracy which are fanatically defended from an outside view. Even all elements of the press are zealously determined to report on that which will not offend the board of judges, the prosecutor, probation, legal-aid, or other officials, in return for privileges and courtesies granted in the past and to be granted in the future. Rather than any view of the matter in terms of some variation of a "conspiracy" hypothesis, the simple explanation is one of an ongoing system handling delicate tensions, managing the trauma produced by law enforcement and administration, and requiring almost pathological distrust of "outsiders," bordering on group paranoia.

The hostile attitude toward "outsiders" is in large measure engendered by a defensiveness itself produced by the inherent deficiencies of assembly line justice, so characteristic of our major criminal courts. Intolerably large caseloads of defendants which must be disposed of in an organizational context of limited resources and personnel, potentially subject the participants in the court community to harsh scrutiny from appellate courts and from other public and private sources of condemnation. As a consequence, an almost irreconcilable conflict is posed in terms of intense pressures to process large numbers of cases, on the one hand, and the stringent ideological and legal requirements of "due process of law," on the other hand. A rather tenuous resolution of the dilemma has emerged in the shape of a large variety of bureaucratically ordained and controlled "work crimes," short cuts, deviations, and outright rule violations adopted as court practice in order to meet production norms. Fearfully anticipating criticism on ethical as well as legal grounds, all the significant participants in the court's social structure are bound into an organized system of complicity. This consists of a work arrangement in which the patterned, covert, informal breaches, and evasions of "due process" are institutionalized, but are, nevertheless, denied to exist.

These institutionalized evasions will be found to occur, to some degree, in all criminal courts. Their nature, scope, and complexity are largely determined by the size of the court and the character of the community in which it is located, for example, whether it is a large, urban institution or a relatively small, rural county court. In addition, idiosyncratic, local conditions may contribute to a unique flavor in the character and quality of the criminal law's administration in a particular community. However, in most instances a variety of stratagems are employed—some subtle, some crude—in effectively disposing of what are often too large caseloads. A wide variety of coercive devices are employed against an accused client, couched in a depersonalized, instrumental, bureaucratic version of due process of law, and which are in reality a perfunctory obeisance to the ideology of due process. These include some very explicit pressures which are exerted in some measure by all court personnel, including judges, to plead guilty and avoid trial. In many instances, the sanction of a potentially harsh sentence is used as the visible alternative to pleading guilty, in the case of recalcitrants. Probation and psychiatric reports are "tailored" to organizational needs or are at least responsive to the court organization's requirements for the refurbishment of a defendant's social biography, consonant with his new status. A resourceful judge can, through his subtle domination of the proceedings, impose his will on the final outcome of a trial. Stenographers and clerks, in their function as record keepers, are on occasion pressed into service in support of a judicial need to "rewrite" the record

of a courtroom event. Bail practices are usually employed for purposes other than simply assuring a defendant's presence on the date of a hearing in connection with his case. Too often, the discretionary power as to bail is part of the arsenal of weapons available to collapse the resistance of an accused person. The foregoing is a most cursory examination of some of the more prominent "short cuts" available to any court organization. There are numerous other procedural strategies constituting due process deviations, which tend to become the work style artifacts of a court's personnel. Thus, only court regulars who are "bound in" are really accepted; others are treated routinely and in almost a coldly correct manner.

The defense attorneys, therefore, whether of the legal-aid, public defender variety or privately retained, although operating in terms of pressures specific to their respective role and organizational obligations, ultimately are concerned with strategies which tend to lead to a plea. It is the rational, impersonal elements involving economies of time, labor, expense, and a superior commitment of the defense counsel to these rationalistic values of the maximum production of court organization that prevail in his relationship with a client. The lawyer regulars are frequently former staff members of the prosecutor's office and use the prestige, know-how, and contacts of their former affiliation as part of their stock in trade. Close and continuing relations between the lawyer regular and his former colleagues in the prosecutor's office generally overshadow the relationship between the regular and his client. The continuing colleagueship of supposedly adversary counsel rests on real professional and organizational needs of a quid pro quo, which goes beyond the limits of an accommodation or modus vivendi one might ordinarily expect under the circumstances of an otherwise seemingly adversary relationship. Indeed, the adversary features which are manifest are for the most part muted and exist even in their attenuated form largely for external consumption. The principals, lawyer and assistant district attorney, rely upon one another's cooperation for their continued professional existence, and so the bargaining between them tends usually to be "reasonable" rather than fierce.

FEE COLLECTION AND FIXING

The real key to understanding the role of defense counsel in a criminal case is to be found in the area of the fixing of the fee to be charged and its collection. The problem of fixing and collecting the fee tends to influence to a significant degree the criminal court process itself, and not just the relationship of the lawyer and his client. In essence, a lawyer-client "confidence game" is played. A true confidence game is unlike the case of the emperor's new clothes wherein that monarch's nakedness was a result of inordinate gullibility and credulity. In a genuine confidence game, the perpetrator manipulates the basic dishonesty of his partner, the victim or mark, toward his own (the confidence operator's) ends. Thus, "the victim of a con scheme must have some larceny in his heart."

Legal service lends itself particularly well to confidence games. Usually, a plumber will be able to demonstrate empirically that he has performed a service by clearing up the stuffed drain or repairing the leaky faucet or pipe and therefore merits his fee. He has rendered, when summoned, a visible, tangible boon for his client in return for the requested fee. A physician, who has not performed some visible surgery or otherwise engaged in some readily discernible procedure in connection with a patient, may be deemed by the patient to have "done nothing" for him. As a consequence, medical practitioners may simply prescribe or administer by injection a placebo to overcome a patient's potential reluctance or dissatisfaction in paying a requested fee "for nothing."

In the practice of law, there is a special problem in this regard, no matter what the level of the practitioner or his place in the hierarchy of prestige. Much legal work is intangible either because it is simply a few words of advice, some preventive action, a telephone call, negotiation of some kind, a form filled out and filed, a hurried conference with another attorney or an official of a government agency, a letter or opinion written, or a countless variety of seemingly innocuous, and even prosaic, procedures and actions. These are the basic activities, apart from any possible court appearance, of almost all lawyers, at all levels of practice. Much of the activity is not in the nature of the exercise of the traditional, precise professional skills of the attorney such as library research and oral argument in connection with appellate briefs; court motions; trial work; and drafting of opinions, memoranda, contracts, and other complex documents and agreements. Instead, much legal activity, whether it is at the lowest or highest "white shoe" law firm levels, is of the brokerage, agent, sales representative, lobbyist type of activity, in which the lawyer acts for someone else in pursuing the latter's interests and designs. The service is intangible.

The large-scale law firm may not speak as openly of their "contacts," their "fixing" abilities, as does the lower-level lawyer. They trade instead upon a facade of thick carpeting, walnut paneling, genteel low pressure, and superficialities of traditional legal professionalism. There are occasions when even the large firm is on the defensive in connection with the fees they charge because the services rendered or results obtained do not appear to merit the fee asked. Therefore, there is a recurrent problem in the legal profession in fixing the amount of fee and in justifying the basis for the requested fee.

Although the fee at times amounts to what the traffic and the conscience of the lawyer will bear, one further observation must be made with regard to the size of the fee and its collection. The defendant in a criminal case and the material gain he may have acquired during the course of his illicit activities are soon parted. Not infrequently, the ill-gotten fruits of the various modes of larceny are sequestered by a defense lawyer in payment of his fee. Inexorably, the amount of the fee is a function of the dollar value of the crime committed and is frequently set with meticulous precision at a sum which bears an uncanny relationship to that of the net proceeds of the particular offense involved. On occasion, defendants have been known to commit additional offenses while at liberty on bail, in order to secure the requisite funds with which to meet their obligations for payment of legal fees. Defense lawyers condition even the most obtuse clients to recognize that there is a firm interconnection between fee payment and the zealous exercise of professional expertise, secret knowledge, and organizational "connections" in their behalf. Lawyers, therefore, seek to keep their clients in a proper state of tension and to arouse in them the precise edge of anxiety which is calculated to encourage prompt fee payment. Consequently, the client attitude in the relationship between defense counsel and an accused is in many instances a precarious admixture of hostility, mistrust, dependence, and sycophancy. By keeping his client's anxieties aroused to the proper pitch, and establishing a seemingly causal relationship between a requested fee and the accused's ultimate extrication from his onerous difficulties, the lawyer will have established the necessary preliminary groundwork to assure a minimum of haggling over the fee and its eventual payment.

In varying degrees, as a consequence, all law practice involves a manipulation of the client and a stage management of the lawyer-client relationship so that at least an *appearance* of help and service will be forthcoming. This is accomplished in a variety of ways, often exercised in combination with each other. At the outset, the lawyer professional employs with suitable variation a measure of sales-puff, which may range from an air of unbounding self-confidence, adequacy, and dominion over events to that of complete arrogance. This will be supplemented by the affectation of a studied, faultless mode of personal attire. In the larger firms, the furnishings and office trappings will serve as the backdrop to help in impression management and client intimidation. In all firms, solo or large scale, an access to secret knowledge and to the seats of power and influence is inferred, or presumed to a varying degree, as the basic vendible commodity of the practitioners.

The lack of visible end product offers a special complication in the course of the professional life of the criminal court lawyer with respect to his fee and in his relations with his client. The plain fact is that an accused in a criminal case always "loses" even when he has been exonerated by an acquittal, discharge, or dismissal of his case. The hostility of an accused which follows as a consequence of his arrest, incarceration, possible loss of job, expense, and other traumas connected with his case is directed, by means of displacement, toward his lawyer. It is in this sense that it may be said that a criminal lawyer never really "wins" a case. The really

satisfied client is rare, since in the very nature of the situation even an accused's vindication leaves him with some degree of dissatisfaction and hostility. It is this state of affairs that makes for a lawyer-client relationship in the criminal court which tends to be a somewhat exaggerated version of the usual lawyer-client confidence game.

At the outset, because there are great risks of nonpayment of the fee, due to the impecuniousness of his clients and the fact that a man who is sentenced to jail may be a singularly unappreciative client, the criminal lawyer collects his fee in *advance*. Often, because the lawyer and the accused both have questionable designs of their own upon each other, the confidence game can be played. The criminal lawyer must serve three major functions, or stated another way, he must solve three problems. First, he must arrange for his fee; second, he must prepare and then, if necessary, "cool out" his client in case of defeat (a highly likely contingency); and third, he must satisfy the court organization that he has performed adequately in the process of negotiating the plea, so as to preclude the possibility of any sort of embarrassing incident which may serve to invite "outside" scrutiny.

In assuring the attainment of one of his primary objectives, his fee, the criminal lawyer will very often enter into negotiations with the accused's kin, including collateral relatives. In many instances, the accused himself is unable to pay any sort of fee or anything more than a token fee. It then becomes important to involve as many of the accused's kin as possible in the situation. This is especially so if the attorney hopes to collect a significant part of a proposed substantial fee. It is not uncommon for several relatives to contribute toward the fee. The larger the group, the greater the possibility that the lawyer will collect a sizable fee by getting contributions from each.

A fee for a felony case which ultimately results in a plea, rather than a trial, may ordinarily range anywhere from $500 to $1,500. Should the case go to trial, the fee will be proportionately larger, depending upon the length of the trial. But the larger the fee the lawyer wishes to exact, the more impressive his performance must be, in terms of his stage-managed image as a personage of great influence and power in the court organization. Court personnel are keenly aware of the extent to which a lawyer's stock in trade involves the precarious stage management of an image which goes beyond the usual professional flamboyance, and for this reason alone the lawyer is bound in to the authority system of the court's organizational discipline. Therefore, to some extent, court personnel will aid the lawyer in the creation and maintenance of that impression. There is a tacit commitment to the lawyer by the court organization, apart from formal etiquette, to aid him in this. Such augmentation of the lawyer's stage-managed image as this affords is the partial basis for the quid pro quo which exists between the lawyer and the court organization. It tends to serve as the continuing basis for the higher loyalty of the lawyer to the organization; his relationship with his client, in contrast, is transient, ephemeral, and often superficial.

DEFENSE LAWYER AS DOUBLE AGENT

The lawyer has often been accused of stirring up unnecessary litigation, especially in the field of negligence. He is said to acquire a vested interest in a cause of action or claim which was initially his client's. The strong incentive of possible fee motivates the lawyer to promote litigation which would otherwise never have developed. However, the criminal lawyer develops a vested interest of an entirely different nature in his client's case: to limit its scope and duration rather than do battle. Only in this way can a case be "profitable." Thus, he enlists the aid of relatives not only to assure payment of his fee, but he will also rely on these persons to help him in his agent-mediator role of convincing the accused to plead guilty and ultimately to help in cooling out the accused if necessary.

It is at this point that an accused defendant may experience his first sense of "betrayal." While he had perhaps perceived the police and prosecutor to be adversaries, or possibly even the judge, the accused is wholly unprepared for his counsel's role performance as an agent-mediator. In the same vein, it is even less likely to occur to an accused that members of his own family or other kin may become agents, albeit at the behest and urging of other agents or mediators, acting on the principle that they are in reality helping an accused negotiate the best possible plea arrangement under the circumstances. Usually, it will be the lawyer who will activate next of kin in this role, his ostensible motive being to arrange for his fee. But soon latent and unstated motives will assert themselves, with entreaties by counsel to the accused's next of kin, to appeal to the accused to "help himself" by pleading. Gemeinschaft sentiments are to this extent exploited by a defense lawyer (or even at times by a district attorney) to achieve specific secular ends, that is, of concluding a particular matter with all possible dispatch.

The fee is often collected in stages, each installment usually payable prior to a necessary court appearance required during the course of an accused's career journey. At each stage, in his interviews and communications with the accused, or in addition, with members of his family, if they are helping with the fee payment, the lawyer employs an air of professional confidence and "inside-dopesterism" in order to assuage anxieties on all sides. He makes the necessary bland assurances and in effect manipulates his client, who is usually willing to do and say the things, true or not, which will help his attorney extricate him. Since the dimensions of what he is essentially selling, organizational influence and expertise, are not technically and precisely measurable, the lawyer can make extravagant claims of influence and secret knowledge with impunity. Thus, lawyers frequently claim to have inside knowledge in connection with information in the hands of the district attorney, police, or probation officials or to have access to these functionaries. Factually, they often do, and need only to exaggerate the nature of their relationships with them to obtain the desired effective impression upon the client. But as in the genuine confidence game, the victim who has participated is loathe to do anything which will upset the lesser plea which his lawyer has "conned" him into accepting.

In effect, in his role as double agent, the criminal lawyer performs an extremely vital and delicate mission for the court organization and the accused. Both principals are anxious to terminate the litigation with a minimum of expense and damage to each other. There is no other personage or role incumbent in the total court structure more strategically located who, by training and in terms of his own requirements, is more ideally suited to do so than the lawyer. In recognition of this, judges will cooperate with attorneys in many important ways. For example, they will adjourn the case of an accused in jail awaiting plea or sentence if the attorney requests such action. While explicitly this may be done for some innocuous and seemingly valid reason, the tacit purpose is that pressure is being applied by the attorney for the collection of his fee, which he knows will probably not be forthcoming if the case is concluded. Judges are aware of this tactic on the part of lawyers, who, by requesting an adjournment, keep an accused incarcerated awhile longer as a not too subtle method of dunning a client for payment. However, the judges will go along with this, on the grounds that important ends are being served. Often, the only end served is to protect a lawyer's fee.

The judge will help an accused's lawyer in still another way. He will lend the official aura of his office and courtroom so that a lawyer can stage manage an impression of an "all out" performance for the accused in justification of his fee. The judge and other court personnel will serve as a backdrop for a scene charged with dramatic fire, in which the accused's lawyer makes a stirring appeal in his behalf. With a show of restrained passion, the lawyer will intone the virtues of the accused and recite the social deprivations which have reduced him to his present state. The speech varies somewhat, depending on whether the accused has been convicted after trial or has pleaded guilty. In the main, however, the incongruity, superficiality, and ritualistic character of the total performance is underscored by a visibly impassive, almost bored reaction on the part of the judge and other members of the court retinue.

Afterward, there is a hearty exchange of pleasantries between the lawyer and district attorney, wholly out of context in terms of the supposed adversary nature of the preceding events. The fiery passion in defense of his client is gone, and the lawyers for both sides resume their offstage relations, chatting amiably and perhaps including the judge in their restrained banter. No other aspect of their visible conduct so effectively serves to put even a casual observer on notice that these individuals have claims upon each other. These seemingly innocuous actions are indicative of continuing organizational and informal relations, which, in their intricacy and depth, range far beyond any priorities or claims a particular defendant may have.

Criminal law practice is a unique form of private law practice since it really only appears to be private practice. Actually, it is bureaucratic practice, because of the legal practitioner's enmeshment in the authority, discipline, and perspectives of the court organization. Private practice, supposedly, in a professional sense involves the maintenance of an organized, disciplined body of knowledge and leaning; the individual practitioners are imbued with a spirit of autonomy and service, the earning of a livelihood being incidental. In the sense that the lawyer in the criminal court serves as a double agent, serving higher organizational rather than professional ends, he may be deemed to be engaged in bureaucratic rather than private practice. To some extent, the lawyer-client confidence game, in addition to its other functions, serves to conceal this fact.

THE CLIENT'S PERCEPTION

The "cop-out" ceremony, in which the court process culminates, is not only invaluable for redefining the accused's perspectives of himself but also in reiterating publicly in a formally structured ritual the accused person's guilt for the benefit of significant "others" who are observing. The accused not only is made to assert publicly his guilt of a specific crime but also a complete recital of its details. He is further made to indicate that he is entering his plea of guilt freely, willingly, and voluntarily and that he is not doing so because of any promises or in consideration of any commitments that may have been made to him by anyone. This last is intended as a blanket statement to shield the participants from any possible charges of coercion or undue influence that may have been exerted in violation of due process requirements. Its function is to preclude any later review by an appellate court on these grounds and also to obviate any second thoughts an accused may develop in connection with his plea.

However, for the accused, the conception of self as a guilty person is in large measure a temporary role adaptation. His career socialization as an accused, if it is successful, eventuates in his acceptance and redefinition of himself as a guilty person. However, the transformation is ephemeral, in that be will, in private, quickly reassert his innocence. Of importance is that he accept his defeat, publicly proclaim it, and find some measure of pacification in it. Almost immediately after his plea, a defendant will generally be interviewed by a representative of the probation division in connection with a presentence report which is to be prepared. The very first question to be asked of him by the probation officer is: "Are you guilty of the crime to which you pleaded?" This is by way of double affirmation of the defendant's guilt. Should the defendant now begin to make bold assertions of his innocence, despite his plea of guilty, he will be asked to withdraw his plea and stand trial on the original charges. Such a threatened possibility is, in most instances, sufficient to cause an accused to let the plea stand and to request the probation officer to overlook his exclamations of innocence.

. . . . .

CONCLUSION

Recent decisions of the Supreme Court, in the area of criminal law administration and defendant's rights, fail to take into account three crucial aspects of social structure which may tend to render the more libertarian rules as nugatory. The decisions overlook (1) the nature of courts as formal organization; (2) the relationship that the lawyer regular actually has with the court organization; and (3) the character of the lawyer-client relationship in the criminal court (the routine relationships, not those unusual ones that are described in "heroic" terms in novels, movies, and TV).

Courts, like many other modern large-scale organizations, possess a monstrous appetite for the co-optation of entire professional groups as well as individuals. Almost all those who come within the ambit of organizational authority find that their definitions, perceptions, and values have been refurbished, largely in terms favorable to the particular organization and its goals. As a result, recent Supreme Court decisions may have a long-range effect which is radically different from that intended or anticipated. The more libertarian rules will tend to produce the rather ironic end result of augmenting the existing organizational arrangements, enriching court organizations with more personnel and elaborate structure, which in turn will maximize organizational goals of "efficiency" and production. Thus, many defendants will find that courts will possess an even more sophisticated apparatus for processing them toward a guilty plea!

Client Games: Defense Attorneys' Perspectives on Their Relations With Criminal Clients

ROY B. FLEMMING

LAWYER-CLIENT relations substantially define the reality of law in society. It is through these interactions and encounters that the legal system takes on form and substance for both parties. What clients learn of the reality of their rights, the operation of courts, and the inner workings of the law and whether they feel they are treated fairly or justly are all colored by their experiences with attorneys. By the same token, the satisfactions and disappointments, financial rewards, and social returns of lawyering strongly reflect the kinds of clients attorneys represent. Moreover, as professionals, lawyers presumably have considerable latitude in choosing how to relate to clients, raising concerns over their accountability to clients and equal treatment of them.

The social preconditions for traditional lawyer-client relationships that putatively foster accountability are often missing in the practice of criminal law, however. Criminal clients express deep misgivings about attorneys assigned to them by courts, reactions to a policy reform not anticipated at the time of its adoption. While attention to the client's or defendant's perspective on attorneys has not languished for this reason, the attorney's view of clients has been neglected. And yet a fuller understanding of this relationship obviously demands an exploration of the attorney's side. This study takes this tack

From "Client Games: Defense Attorney's Perspectives on Their Relations with Criminal Clients" by R. B. Flemming, 1986, *American Bar Foundation Research Journal* (Spring), pp. 253-277. Copyright 1986 by the University of Chicago Press. Reprinted by permission.

and looks at how attorneys feel they are seen by their clients and the implications of client reactions for how they practice criminal law. In this sense, it adds another dimension toward a more complete view of the professional behavior of criminal attorneys, a dimension that stresses the difference between public and private clients in affecting the accountability or, at least, responsiveness of attorneys to their clients.

Doubts about a lawyer's professional skills and fears of not being faithfully represented raise questions about the attorney's role as described in Blumberg's "confidence game." For what kind of game is it if clients do not trust their attorneys? And how do lawyers cope with this problem? Without the aura of professional legitimacy, do they dominate their clients to the degree found in civil cases? And how do they gain control of them? When faced with these problems plus the social, racial, and economic differences that usually separate them from criminal defendants, how can they function as "translators" of their needs as they apparently do in civil matters, where the social gap between lawyer and client is often narrower?

This study offers answers to these questions. Specifically, it reports how attorneys feel they are viewed by their clients, how they try to develop working relationships with them, and what roles they think are most useful in dealing with criminal clients. Interviews with 155 defense attorneys provide the data for this study, and excerpts are presented to establish their concerns and views. The study concludes by placing the defense attorneys' relations with criminal clients in a perspective that extends and revises Blumberg's notion of a confidence game between attorneys and their clients to show how attorney accountability arises in a situation characterized by mistrust.

PROBLEMATIC AUTHORITY AND PUBLIC CLIENTS

Attorneys with public clients labor in the shadow of the "public defender" stereotype. Whether they actually work as public defenders makes no difference; their clients give them little respect and distrust them. A sampling of the attorneys' comments illustrates their problem:

The standard joke around this county is, "Do you want a public defender or a real attorney?"

Well, I think the general impression is, "I don't have the money to hire a real attorney, so I have you." We get a lot of that.

They think because you're free, you're no good.

Public clients have doubts about the status of their lawyers, are skeptical about their skills as advocates, and are worried about whose side the lawyers are on. These attitudes complicate the attorneys' work. They cannot assume their clients respect them professionally, and they do not presume that they have their trust or confidence. Thus, perhaps even before procedural or substantive issues can be thrashed out, attorneys need to establish relationships with public clients that will quiet their qualms. Attorneys with private clients run into these problems less often:

Private clients accept that you are going to do a good job or you know what you're doing. Public defender clients have no idea where you come from; no idea of your background, no idea of whether you've ever done another criminal case in your life.

A guy that comes in here and pays $5,000 in cash wants to believe you're good, I guess. He handles you with a lot of respect and is less likely to call you every day with some bullshit question. He's more likely to treat you as you want to be treated as an attorney, that you're representing him as best as you can, and you have his interests in mind always.

A third attorney explained why he refused to take any further public defender cases after a client questioned his professional judgment.

Well, I like to be my own man, and I was assigned to represent this . . . man who was caught stone cold in a robbery. I filed a habeas corpus petition, and I took it over to him to show him.

He said, "Not good enough, man." It was fine. It was enough to get me where I wanted to go. It was fine. So I said, "Well, why don't you do this? Why don't you go to law school and learn? And then take my petition and stick it up your ass." I quit. That was the end of it.

I certainly believe you should take your client's interest to heart and do the best job you possibly can, but I'm not going to have some idiot tell me that my paperwork is wrong when it's not.

Client disrespect dismays and irritates attorneys; it sours associations with clients and makes the job less pleasant. A public defender complained, "It's frustrating to have to constantly sell yourself" to clients. Moreover, the etiquette of normal client-professional relations seems weaker to public attorneys who find that their clients or family and friends freely criticize them and treat them cavalierly. When asked what makes their work unsatisfying, attorneys often point to their public clients.

Distrust undermines the chances for cooperation. "Because they think you're part of the system, you end up doing all the worrying, you end up doing all the scrambling around, and your client could really care less," an attorney quoted earlier concluded. Another said a "prime frustration" in representing public clients was the feeling that "basically, you're out there by yourself because you don't have a client along with you." Finally, trust matters because disgruntled clients can make trouble for attorneys later on. The prospects of facing grievances or appeals loom too large for an attorney to shrug off a client's distrust.

Attorneys see client disrespect and mistrust as inherent to indigent defense systems. Few mentioned that racial or class differences impede empathy or communication. Still, one attorney confided, "I don't really identify with my clients. I'm not from that level of society." Two others also commented on this problem.

I'm an attorney, live in a nice neighborhood. I'm white. I don't know whether the black defendant in particular trusts me as much as he would a black lawyer.

In a lot of ways, our clientele is our worst enemy. . . . We get quite a few poverty cases in here. Guys come in, they're on welfare. You sit down and work with them. You say, "You're going to trial. I want you dressed like you're going to church." Because I've had guys come in for trial dressed in T-shirts. I say, "Hey, are you crazy?" It's really difficult for me to comprehend.

Attorneys' perceptions of public clients do not rest on vague, unsubstantiated notions that the grass is greener on the private side of the legal fence; many handled both kinds of clients, and their perceptions corresponded with those of attorneys who had never practiced privately. Attorneys' experience of day-to-day defense work, then, divides sharply according to this public-private dimension and may be underlined by racial or class differences. Attorneys find publicly assigned clients to be more skeptical, less deferential, and less trusting. These perceived qualities are more than mere irritations or inconveniences for attorneys, however, because when they perceive an absence of client respect and trust, they feel that their professional authority is weakened. Consequently, as long as clients question or reject this authority, "client control" remains problematic.

CLIENT CONTROL: GAINING THE CLIENT'S RESPECT AND TRUST

The attorney's craft rests on knowing how to persuade clients who have the most to lose from tactical miscues or strategic errors to listen to them. When considering the stakes involved, an attorney admitted, "I suppose it's natural to feel like you want to be in control of your own destiny." Nonetheless, attorneys try to disabuse clients of this desire as well as of other misconceptions of their role. As one attorney put it, "I'm not gonna let any guy [client] tell me how to try my case. . . . So I think client control is a key."

A lot of these defendants are very streetwise, and they will try to manipulate the system and their lawyer. And they look at the lawyer as someone who is going to get them off, as opposed to protect their rights. And that's a problem. You have got to establish yourself from the outset with them, so that they don't take advantage of you.

I've been through the system ten damn years, and I know the ins and outs. . . . And this schmuck doesn't know from nothing. He wants to run some bullshit by you. He didn't do it. Well, maybe he didn't. But in my experience there's damn few of them like that. When a dude just says, "I didn't do it," white or black, because they're too smart to admit to anything, you got problems.

Client control requires respect and trust for the lawyer. Without respect from the client, the attorney's advice or suggestions may be ignored. Without the client's trust, the attorney may not be believed; in turn, attorneys are not always sure if they can trust their clients. Once attorneys secure their clients' confidence, they can exercise their judgment and satisfy a desire for professional autonomy.

Spending time with clients, attorneys claim, can help win their confidence. Yet time, a limited resource, also carries opportunity costs. Time spent with clients favorably influences their reactions to attorneys, but its effects on case outcomes are questionable. Moreover, client demands are not always reasonable and, because attorneys have no way of knowing in advance which ones deserve attention, time spent with clients may be wasted. Attorneys grow weary of listening to clients if what they say has little bearing on their case; moreover, indigent clients are often detained, which means visiting the jail—an unpleasant chore. Finally, because actions usually speak louder than words, the exchange value of time when purchasing a client's confidence is weak compared with what is gained when the client actually sees the attorney at work in the courtroom.

"Being honest" also can settle client misgivings because, according to one attorney, "The biggest problem with court-appointed counsel is the credibility factor. . . . So you go out to the jail, and you try to be up front and candid with him right off the bat." By extending candor, attorneys hope to purchase their clients' trust, honesty, and cooperation. This overture counters their suspicions that they will not be dealt with squarely. Moreover, by telling them what they think of their stories, what their chances look like, and how the case will be handled in court, attorneys flourish their insider's knowledge, which bolsters efforts to win the clients' respect as well. During these encounters, attorneys who are skilled at impression management take the opportunity to portray themselves as competent, concerned, and not easily fooled or buffaloed.

Client control too bluntly describes the complex, often-subtle relationships attorneys try to arrange to gain their clients' confidence. Once it is established, they feel they are less likely to be surprised by a sudden balkiness or by unexpected revelations of something the client concealed from them. Again, this task is harder in public cases than in private ones, and it affects the manner in which attorneys approach clients when making decisions about the dispositions and handling of their cases.

STYLES OF CLIENT CONTROL: ADVISING AND RECOMMENDING

If attorneys prepare the ground well enough by giving clients time, frank assessments of their situations, and the impression they can be trusted, and if the clients respond by listening and offering to cooperate, the attorneys' authority takes root in the nascent relationship. This social exchange nurtures and, in effect, legitimates their status with public clients, while with private clients, professional legitimacy generally accompanies the retainer or fee. In either instance, legitimation forms the basis for client control and allows attorneys to moderate their

clients' demands and adjust their expectations to courthouse realities. The styles they use, however, range from a soft "advising" approach to a more forceful "recommending" posture, with finer gradations in between. Advising can consist of simply listing the options facing clients and leaving the decision in their hands, or it can mean providing much blunter appraisals that, even without explicit recommendations, make the attorneys' preferences clear. Similarly, recommendations can be made in ways that give clients room to disagree or that present little more than a "take it or leave it" proposition.

A public defender described a situation that approximates the latter extreme of the recommending approach. With the plea conditions set beforehand, the lawyer relies on four factors to convince the client to take the plea offer: a lenient sentence (11 1/2 to 23 months in the local jail), the favorable reactions and support of his client's detained colleagues, the client's doubts about the fairness of the court, and the odds against getting a better sentence.

Most times I've struck a deal before I even talk to my client. You know pretty well what the hell went on without talking to your guy. I think I've run across three people who I believe to be innocent since I've been here, and that's five years.

If I get a good deal, then I'll go over to the guy, and I'll say, "Look, here's the way it is. That's the best I could get from the D.A. I think you ought to take it." And then I go over the case, you know, what the strong points are, what the weak points are, etc., etc. . . . And then I say, "11 1/2 to 23." The guy says, "No, man, I'm not going to do any time. I want to go to court." You know, "I'm gonna take this up to the Supreme Court."

So, you say, "Fine, are you prepared to spend 10 months in jail asserting your rights?" They aren't completely stupid, you know. They come around. I'll say, "OK, I'll see you tomorrow. Talk to your guys in the joint because they know what's good and what isn't."

I never really pressure them per se, but I guess you could say that I use some influence upon them. Most of our people are black, and I think they realize they just really aren't going to get that great a shake out here. Either with the jury or with the judge. And most of our guys have street sense. They know what the hell is going on.

In contrast with this attorney, who exerts "some influence" and orchestrates his client's decision, others adopt a softer, more indirect "advising" style for reasons of effectiveness and professional ethics. As one of these lawyers explained,

I find that if they are actively involved at all points in the proceedings, they'll give you more help, you'll find out things about the case that you wouldn't have known. And it isn't so much that when they get into court that they're gonna balk at what happened or say, "I didn't expect this to happen," it's just keeping them involved at all times is vitally important to your own role as a defense attorney. Also, I don't think it's ethically proper for an attorney to make decisions for his client, especially in a criminal defense situation.

Attorneys generally prefer this lawyer's advising approach when representing public clients. An emphatic stance and urgent recommendations strain fragile relationships with wary clients and raise the possibility of problems farther down the road. As two lawyers quoted earlier mentioned, attorneys must "cover their rear end" and perhaps "swallow their pride" to avoid having public clients "turn on" them.

This short analysis is not definitive. Yet when viewed in light of systematic, comparative analyses of the impact of defense attorneys on other measures of case outcomes such as sentencing, the evidence indicates that public clients do not fare more poorly in court than their peers who retain private counsel. Although the sampling of attorney complaints about public clients clearly shows that their dealings with these clients are often contentious and at times disagreeable, with few notable exceptions in the nine counties, public clients are not treated in significantly different ways than are private clients. In this sense, attorney-client relations may be best viewed as part of procedural justice, in which style, approach, rapport, attitudes, and perception define "fairness." Thus, in games between attorneys and clients, clients perceive fairness if they trust their attorneys and believe

they have a say or voice in the handling of their cases.

CLIENT GAMES: CONCLUDING THOUGHTS, A PARADOX, AND POLICY QUESTIONS

This exploration of attorney-client relations in criminal cases relied on the comments of "regular" attorneys. The picture that emerges reflects their particular angle of vision and exposes only certain aspects of lawyer relationships with criminal clients. For example, in their eyes, public clients were skeptical and uncooperative, but by the same token, some frankly admitted they did not give these clients much of their time. Thus, they stressed the resistance of public clients while downplaying their own actions or inactions that may have played a part in their clients' negative responses.

Most also felt their difficulties with public clients were institutionally rooted in the fact that indigent defense systems rarely allow criminal defendants to choose their lawyers. This fact, when combined with the commonly held precept that "you get what you pay for," suggests that the public client's lack of trust and respect is neither peculiar to certain programs nor characteristic of particular kinds of clients. Instead, these responses are intrinsic to an involuntary relationship in which the client holds no readily available, easily employed, and culturally sanctioned lever to assure professional accountability.

The nature of the transaction between attorney and client provides a context *for interpreting* the behavior of the attorney. In part because the defendant (or his family) was paying the attorney, the whole tone of the relationship was altered.

Defense attorneys work in a social setting where expectations and interpretations of their behavior count as much as what they actually do. Their role, then, is symbolic as well as substantive because they need the respect and trust of clients before they enter the courtroom or do anything on a case. When combined with its intangible qualities, this inherently political side of lawyering produces, as Blumberg argued, a confidence game with clients.

But it is a confidence game in the literal sense, since attorneys must win the confidence of clients who do not initially recognize or accept their professional authority before they can gain their cooperation. Client control, therefore, is a confidence game in which cooperation between lawyers and mistrustful clients is at stake.

Clients refuse to cooperate in various ways. Some have mild consequences for attorneys, others do not. For instance, attorneys said that public clients were discourteous or that they refused to talk to them, which made their work unpleasant and more arduous. An attorney lamented earlier that some clients were so alienated that "you don't have a client along with you," while another complained that attorneys "end up doing all the worrying" and "doing all the scrambling around" because "your client could really care less." Clients may also spurn advice or balk at suggestions, which not only increases the lawyers' work but threatens their reputation for client control within the courthouse community.

By the same token, public clients hold serious reservations as to how vigorously attorneys will represent client interests if it means sacrificing their own longer-term interests within the court system, and the attorneys know the clients are thinking this. As one attorney put it, "You know, the scuttlebutt goes around the jail, 'Hey, the public defender, they get along well with the state's attorney. They're gonna send you down the river.' " And as another explained, "If you say to an indigent client, 'I think you should plead,' and he doesn't want to plead, he'll say, 'See, that proves it. They appointed him to lean on me.' "

Attorneys acknowledge how they are perceived. Thus, in their relations with clients, they are enmeshed in perceptions and expectations running along the lines of "If he thinks I am thinking of selling him out, he will not trust me even though I am not thinking of that, and if he knew this, he would go along with what I say." Attorneys fear their clients will not cooperate because they think they will be deceived. They fear deceit by clients just as much. Attorneys consequently fret over what kind of game their clients may be playing and whether they will find out soon enough to know if they should try to change their minds or take other precautions.

The decision to cooperate with attorneys depends lastly on its rewards and costs. If clients believe that confiding in their lawyers will not penalize them, they will be more likely to cooperate. Sentencing weighs heavily in this equation. Client concerns and uncertainties over this issue offer attorneys another opening to persuade them to cooperate, since they are the ones with knowledge of what is likely to occur and the ability to do something about it. The attorney's chore is lightened especially if the client is faced with a lenient sentence on the one hand and the specter of more severe punishment for going to trial on the other. For the nine courts taken as a whole, nearly two-thirds (65.8 percent) of the 4,100 sampled cases that ended in guilty pleas received probation. Defendants who went to trial and were convicted, however, fared worse—even after controlling for relevant sentencing variables. First offenders less often received probation after a jury trial, and repeat offenders were sentenced more severely than comparable defendants who plead guilty.

The mere threat of trial penalties probably eases the attorney's efforts. The prospect of more severe punishment, for whatever reason, usually chills a client's desire to go to trial rather than to plead guilty. Similarly, the price for deceiving an attorney may be a stiffer sentence if the client miscalculates and the deception is uncovered. The upshot is that if attorneys succeed in convincing their public clients to trust them and persuade them to listen to them, they successfully convert the public client confidence game into something more like the cooperative game attorneys perceive to exist with private clients.

A paradox may exist in this confidence game between suspicious public clients and wary attorneys who are involuntarily joined in an association from which they generally cannot exit until the case is over. Rosenthal distinguished between "traditional" and "participatory" models of lawyer-client relations. In the traditional model, "the client who is passive, follows instructions, and trusts the professional without criticism, with few questions or requests, is preferable, and will do better than the difficult client who is critical and questioning." Conversely, the participatory model stresses an active, skeptical client who shares the responsibility for making choices with an attorney who must be patient and earn the client's cooperation. Many criminal attorneys who handle public cases may prefer the traditional model, particularly younger or less experienced ones who are insecure about their professional status and react to questioning clients as though their self-esteem and pride were threatened; but with practice, others learn to adopt more participatory styles because of the suspiciousness of their public clients. The need to win their confidence means attorneys must persuade their clients that they can be trusted or else they may fail to gain control of them.

The paradox here is twofold. First, the mistrust public clients hold for their attorneys may force them to bow more to their clients' wishes than one might expect from folk wisdom or from arguments about "client expendability." Because of their clients' qualms, attorneys may find the advisory role more palatable, with the result that clients participate more actively in the progress of their cases. By including clients in decisions and restraining their own urge to make them alone, attorneys hope to prove that they are not trying to stampede their clients into decisions contrary to their interests. The second aspect involves the involuntary nature of their relationship. The public client's reluctance to recognize an attorney's professional authority denies the lawyer a major resource in gaining the client's compliance and acquiescence, yet the attorney cannot refuse to handle the case as easily as one who is privately retained. The lawyer's overtures and advice also can be shunned, which threatens his or her reputation for client control, and unless matters between

them get totally out of hand, little can be done but to try again. This involuntary relationship means the client gains a measure of power in dealings with the attorney, a certain equalization of positions buttressed further by the client's ability to file grievances or appeal cases. Together these add yet other incentives to adopt the participatory model—advising public clients about their options and letting them bear the responsibility for making decisions. The paradox, then, is that those things which irritate attorneys about public clients foster what many observers consider a more appropriate professional role, although clients evidently do not see it this way. They still prefer fee arrangements with private lawyers where, ironically, according to the lawyers in this study, more traditional lawyer-client relationships prevail because they have their clients' confidence.

In the eyes of criminal clients, professional accountability hinges on a market conception and fee-for-service definition of lawyer responsibility. They place little faith in the notion that ethical concerns and feelings of professional obligation by themselves are sufficient guarantees that a lawyer picked seemingly "out of the hat" will adequately represent their interests. Post-conviction proceedings offer them something of a retributive stick, but by that time they already have paid a price for what they feel was mistakenly listening to their lawyers; moreover, the prevalence of guilty pleas removes many grounds for appeal and grievances. Stuck with their attorneys, and their attorneys stuck with them, they are caught up in a confidence game in which competing interests and the need for accommodation are resolved in ways that are not as self-evidently effective as choosing and paying a lawyer to represent them.

The Work of the Public Defender: "But How Can You Sleep at Night?"

LISA J. McINTYRE

HARDLY anyone will take issue with the idea that everyone, guilty or innocent, is entitled to a fair trial. But beyond this, the views of lawyers and nonlawyers diverge. To the non-lawyer, a fair trial is one that results in convicting the defendant who is factually guilty and acquitting the defendant who is not. But it is the lawyer's job to do every possible thing that can be done for the defendant, even when that means getting a criminal off scot-free. Loop-holes and technicalities are defense attorneys' major weapons. Laypeople are inclined to feel that using legal tricks to gain acquittals for the guilty is at least morally objectionable, if not reprehensible. What many people want to know is how defense attorneys can live with themselves after they help a guilty person escape punishment.

It might be supposed that lawyers are unimpressed by what, to the rest of us, is the core dilemma of their profession—that is, how to justify defending a guilty person. It might be reasoned that lawyers escape this quandary because their legal training has taught them that it does not exist. In law school, everyone learns that a defendant is innocent until proved guilty. Lawyers believe this—and can act on it—because they have been taught to "think like lawyers." Legal reasoning, "although not synonymous with formal reasoning and logic . . . is closely tied to them. Promotion of these skills encourages abstracting legal issues out of their

social contexts to see issues narrowly and with precision."

Simply put, legal reasoning depends on a closed set of premises; some propositions are legal, others are not. The nonlawyer can scarcely be expected to appreciate or understand the difference, for it takes trained men to "winnow one from the other." But lawyers, by virtue of this training, are expected to cope with complex issues, to detach themselves from difficult moral questions and focus on legal ones, to take any side of an argument while remaining personally uninvolved, and to avoid making moral judgments about their clients or their clients' cases. Thus—and this is a surprise to nonlawyers—the factual guilt or innocence of the client is *supposed* to be irrelevant. A lawyer is expected to take a point of view and argue it; a criminal defense lawyer is expected to put on a vigorous defense even when the client is known to be guilty.

On the other hand, however much their training sets them apart, there are some attorneys who cannot detach themselves, cannot overlook the social and moral meanings and consequences of their jobs. There are lawyers who in fact see the issues very much as nonlawyers do. Ohio attorney Ronald L. Burdge explained to columnist Bob Greene why he had given up defending criminal cases:

If your client is guilty and you defend him successfully, then you have a criminal walking the streets because of your expertise. I have a couple of children. I just didn't like the idea of going home at night knowing that I was doing something so—unpalatable. I found it difficult to look

From *The Public Defender: The Practice of Law in the Shadows of Repute* (pp. 139-170) by L. J. McIntyre, 1987, Chicago: University of Chicago Press. Copyright 1987 by the University of Chicago Press. Reprinted by permission.

at my kids knowing that this was how I was making a living.

In spite of their training, lawyers may find it difficult to focus only on the narrow legal aspects of their cases because they are rarely isolated from others who question the morality of the defense lawyer's job. Seymour Wishman, in his book *Confessions of a Criminal Lawyer,* says a chance encounter with one of these "others" marked a turning point in his career, made him rethink how he was spending his life. It happened in a hospital emergency room:

Across the lobby, a heavy but not unattractive woman in a nurse's uniform suddenly shrieked, "Get that motherfucker out of here!" Two women rushed forward to restrain her. "That's the lawyer, that's the motherfucking lawyer!" she shouted.

I looked round me. No one else resembled a lawyer. Still screaming, she dragged her two restrainers toward me. I was baffled. As the only white face in a crowd of forty, I felt a growing sense of anxiety.

I didn't know what she was talking about.

"Kill him and that nigger Horton!"

Larry Horton . . . of course. Larry Horton was a client of mine. Six months before, I had represented him at his trial for sodomy and rape. At last I recognized the woman's face. She had testified as the "complaining" witness against Horton.

Wishman remembered how he had humiliated this woman when she testified against his client, how by cross-examination he had undone her claim that she had been raped and had made her seem to be little more than a prostitute. Seeing her rage started him thinking that society—and, more specifically, the victims of those whom he had defended—were "casualties" of his skill as a defense lawyer. After years spent preparing for and practicing criminal law, Wishman believed that he had to change: "I had never turned down a case because the crime or the criminal were despicable—but now that would change. I could no longer cope with the ugliness and brutality that had for so long, too long, been part of my life."

Given that the public defender's goal is to zealously defend and to work toward acquittal for his or her clients (even clients whom they themselves believe are guilty of heinous crimes), how do these lawyers justify their work? As I explain below, it is not as if public defenders harbor any illusions about the factual innocence of the usual client; on the contrary, most will openly admit that the majority of their clients are factually guilty. If conventional morality has it that defending guilty people is tantamount to an obstruction of justice, how do public defenders justify their rebellion? How *do* they defend those people?

How can you defend people who you know are guilty? Public defenders say that question is incredibly naive, that for the most part they have little patience with that question and little time for anyone who asks it. One suspects that they would like to answer with shock and outrage when asked how they do what they do—and sometimes they do answer like that. But usually they respond in a manner that is more weary than indignant:

Oh God, that question! How do you represent someone you know is guilty? So you go through all the things. You know, "he's not guilty until he's proven guilty, until a judge or a jury say he's guilty, until he's been proved guilty beyond a reasonable doubt." I think everyone deserves the best possible defense, the most fair trial he can get. It's a guarantee of the Constitution, no more, no less.

The sincerity of the public defenders' beliefs is compelling, but the persuasiveness of their arguments is less so. The litany of constitutional ideals rarely convinces the hearer any more (as I will suggest) than it emotionally empowers public defense lawyers to act zealously in the defense of their clients. Attorney Burdge, for example, states unequivocally that he *still believed* in the constitutional rights of defendants, that all he was abandoning was his personal protection of these rights: "I just think I'd let other lawyers defend them."

MAKING A CASE DEFENSIBLE

Under some circumstances, mere empathy with the client's situation permits lawyers to feel justified when defending someone who they know is factually guilty:

Especially when I was in misdemeanor courts, I could see myself as a defendant. Sometimes you get angry enough at somebody to take a swing at them—if you had a gun, to take a shot at them. I could see myself doing that. . . . Just because somebody was arrested and charged with a crime doesn't mean they are some kind of evil person.

Look, kids get into trouble, some kids get into serious trouble. I can understand that. In juvenile court our job isn't to punish, the result is supposed to be in the best interests of the minor. Here you've got to keep them with their family and give them all the services you can so they don't do this again.

Not unexpectedly, at some point the ability to empathize breaks down. This is especially true for public defenders who have passed through juvenile or misdemeanor assignments and into felony trial courts, where they are less able—or maybe less willing—to see themselves as being like their clients:

Your clients have no funds, they know witnesses who only have one name and not even an address because they all hang out on the streets. They don't have phones. They just don't have a life like the rest of us.

While the differences between attorney and client mean that the attorney sometimes has a hard time understanding his or her client (and especially the client's motive), *it does not mean* that the client cannot be defended:

A guy hits somebody over the head and takes a wallet—no problem. A guy that gets into a drunken brawl—no problem. I understand that. Somebody that goes out in the street and commits a rape—I still don't know what goes on [in] his mind. No, it doesn't make it harder to defend. There is *never* any excuse for a rape, but you don't have to understand what makes a rapist tick to defend him effectively.

Sometimes I would question their motive—if it [the crime] seemed senseless, if it seemed particularly brutal or something like that. Then I realized that those were really, for me, irrelevant questions. I still wonder, of course, but I don't ask anymore.

But the alien character especially of the crimes that their clients are alleged to have committed—and the sorts of attributions that they make about their clients because of their crimes—often mean that "you have to care more about your clients' rights than you can usually care about your clients."

The Moral Context of Public Defending

On the surface, what a defense lawyer does is simply protect the client's rights. But many lawyers transform the nature of the battle. They are not fighting for the freedom of their client per se but to keep the system honest: "It doesn't mean that I want to get everybody off. It means that I try to make sure the state's attorneys meet up to their obligations, which means that the only way they can prove someone guilty is beyond reasonable doubt, with competent evidence, and overcoming the presumption of innocence. If they can do that, then they get a guilty. If they can't do that, then my client deserves to go home."

The lawyers' way of "bracketing" their role, of focusing not on the guilt or innocence of their client but on the culpability of the state, transforms circumstances of low or questionable morality into something for which they can legitimately fight. They do not defend simply because their clients have rights but because they believe that those rights have been, are, or will be ignored by others in the criminal justice system. That their adversaries often cheat is taken for granted by public defenders. As one put it, "I expected a fairly corrupt system, and I found one. Here I am representing people who cheat, lie, and steal, and I find the same intellect represented in the police who arrest them, in some of the prosecutors and some of the judges as well." Even when not asked to provide examples, every public defender with whom I spoke offered examples of cheating. There was cheating by the police:

When I was [working] in the state's attorney's office, I would have cops walking up to me as I was preparing a case and I would say, "Officer, tell me what happened." And they would say, "Well, how do *you* want it to have happened?"

The biggest form of police dishonesty was this street files thing. They were hiding evidence that would get people off—or get the correct person. But they had decided in their own minds, "This guy is the guy I'm going after," instead of letting the court system decide who was right.

And there was cheating by state's attorneys:

Sometimes you know it; sometimes you just suspect that they are kinking the case. One guy, fairly high up in the state's attorney's office, described one of their lawyers as naive because he'd been shocked to find a state's attorney had kinked the case. He said of the lawyer, "He thinks this is for real?"
Q: Kinked the case?
R: You might call it supporting perjury; you might call it jogging the memory.
Q: Are you saying that state's attorneys are sometimes a little unprofessional?
R: Yes, yes, yes! Lying, having witnesses lie; they lie themselves on the record, they make inferences that I'm lying. It's just a basic matter of cheating, of not being professional. Because they feel they *must* win the case and will do anything to win the case. . . . Their obligation is *not* to win; it is to make sure the law is upheld—and to make sure that my client gets a fair trial. And to them, *that* is a fallacy.

On the one hand, they seem willing to trust the judges to do the right thing.

I think if you stand up there and talk like you know what you are talking about, judges who don't know the law tend to listen to you. If you can present it in a fair-minded way and not ranting and raving and saying, "You idiot, you can't do that and you can't do that!" Sometimes it

doesn't work, but, for the most part, it is better if you rationally and calmly explain why you are right.

On the other hand, one gets a definite impression that what public defenders trust about judges is not their fair-mindedness and good will, but rather, in many cases, the judges' desire not to get into trouble by being overturned by a higher court. In any case, many public defenders told me that they just do not trust the judges' "instincts":

Knowing legal theory is important, I guess, but it doesn't do any good in Cook County courts, because the question is not, Does the law apply? but, Can you get the judge to obey it, even though his instincts are to fuck you?

Oh, I wised up real quick and found that judges don't care about the law; they don't always follow the law.
Q: Do they know the law?
R: Sometimes . . .
Q: But there's always a public defender there to teach them?
R: Yeah [laugh], but they don't usually care.

There is good evidence that the things that public defenders cite when they complain about police, prosecutorial, and judicial misconduct do happen, but it would be difficult, of course, to determine just how widespread such behaviors actually are. Yet the real frequency of misconduct is beside the point. The point is that most public defenders *believe* that such things do happen "all the time. It's something you really have to watch for."

Whether or not public defenders are correct in their assumptions that police lie, that prosecutors will often do anything to win, and that judges do not really care or know enough to be fair, it is quite clear that the way in which the public defenders see the world not only excuses their work but makes it seem important. Their rationales are enabling mechanisms for the public defenders. But what ultimately pushes the lawyer to do the job is, I believe, something even more personal—the desire to win.

"Adversariness"

Perspectives on the criminal justice system sometimes make use of two ideal-type models: the classic adversarial model, which is "couched in constitutional-ideological terms of due process," and the "dispositional" or "bureaucratic" model, which serves only "bland obeisance to constitutional principles. It is characterized by the superficial ceremonies and formal niceties of traditional due process, but not its substance." The difference between the two models is the difference between the presumption of innocence and the presumption of guilt.

It is significant that social scientists who study public defenders tend to discuss their findings only in terms of the second model—the bureaucratic or plea-bargaining model. Never is the matter of how public defenders measure up as trial attorneys studied. The stereotype of the public defender as plea bargainer is, to put it mildly, firmly entrenched in the literature.

Public defenders do not deny the importance of plea bargaining in their work; they openly and easily acknowledge that the greatest majority of their cases are ultimately disposed of through pleas of guilty. But, they stress, plea bargaining is not their reason for being there but is just a tool:

Q: Now here you are telling me that you are a "trial attorney." How can you say that? To be fair, isn't most of your work really plea bargaining?

R: Plea bargaining is just part of procedure. Just like I wouldn't say, "I'm a procedural attorney." . . . It's part of what you go through, and it's one of the options available to my clients. You know, "If you in fact did this, and you want this deal, and you understand what you are offered, here is the deal."

THE ROLE OF TRIALS IN LOCAL JUSTICE

The majority of their clients do plead guilty, but trials are not unimportant in the world of the public defender. They are important, on the one hand, because what happens during trials helps determine the outcome of cases that are plea bargained. For example, prosecutors wish to maintain a strong record of conviction at trial or else defendants who might otherwise opt for a plea bargain will seek acquittal at a trial. Rulings on evidence made by judges during trials also have an impact on the negotiating process. Attorneys from both sides will evaluate the strength of their positions by the standards evolved through trial court and appellate hearings; these rulings made by trial judges, as well as the sentences given to defendants found guilty, help parties in a plea bargain to determine what their respective cases are "worth."

Public defenders often said that they like the trial work more than any other part of their job. Each one will admit, however, that there are some who do not feel that way. These were pointed out to me as examples of bad public defenders or "kickers."

Sometimes we get a public defender that does idiot work. He'll force his guy to take a plea, finally, on the last day before trial: "Listen, guy, you can take a plea, which is the best thing you could do, or you can go to trial. But I'm not prepared for trial and you're going to lose because you are *supposed* to lose this case—you know that too."

Some public defenders are labeled as bad lawyers because they cannot hack it in the courtroom; the reason that they cannot hack it (it is said) is that they are afraid. As many pointed out, being "on trial" is scary. One veteran lawyer told me: "We lose a lot of public defenders because they can't handle being on trial."

But all of them, even the lawyers who love trial work, are ambivalent about it. Trial work, or so most of them acknowledge (in words, if not by deed), is as terrifying as it is exhilarating.

Trials? *That's* when I can't sleep well at night; I'm too busy thinking. A trial is not one issue, it's many. It's win or lose; it's deadlines, organizing things, making sure your witnesses are ready, looking good in front of the jury, looking confident in front of the judge, watching everything you are doing, being alert, keeping a lot of things in your mind at once. And remembering that your client's freedom depends on your polish, how well you can bring it off.

Doing Trials

Public defenders are quick to admit that they usually *do not* ask their clients whether they are guilty or innocent. Why not ask? The lawyers claimed that it was simply not relevant, that it was something that they did not need to know.

I don't ask, "Did you do it?" anymore. I realized it was irrelevant.

I say to them first thing: "I don't care if you did it or not."

I say: "I don't give a damn whether you did it or not. I'm not your judge, I'm not your priest, I'm not your father. My job is to defend you, and I don't care whether you did it."

It might be that public defenders do not ask because they know that their client is probably guilty and because, as one said, "They will all lie anyway." But there seems to be more to it than that. Many said that, when it comes down to it, they do not ask because they are afraid that the client will tell them the truth!

Public defenders do not begin their relationship with a client by asking awkward questions (e.g., Did you do it?) because once the client admits guilt, it limits what the public defender can ethically do. Being honest, ethical, and "scrupled" in a system that many of them believe is corrupt is very important to the lawyers with whom I spoke. Although some (naive observers) may wonder at the fragility of this honesty, it is something in which the public defenders take pride:

There aren't many public defenders—if any—that I can point to and say, "That man is dishonest. He lied and distorted everything, just to get a client off." That just doesn't happen. The same cannot be said for lawyers in the state's attorney's office. You test the state's evidence, you doubt it, you put it into its worst light. But that is not dishonest. Quite the contrary, that is how you get at the truth!

Public defenders learn quickly that the tell-me-the-truth approach will only help defend an innocent person—the exceptional client. Defenders argue that it is not their job to decide who is guilty and not. Instead, it is the public defender's job to judge the quality of the case that the state has against the defendant. If the lawyer does decide that the state has a case that cannot be called into reasonable doubt, then the lawyer will probably try to get the defendant to admit guilt so that pleading is more palatable—but usually only then.

Losing

In his look at the legal profession, sociologist Talcott Parsons commented that adherence to procedure (i.e., doing everything that can be done when it ought to be done and as it ought to be done) protects lawyers from being devastated when they lose: "The fact that the case can be tried by a standard procedure relieves [the attorney] of some pressure of commitment to the case of his client. He can feel that, if he does his best, then having assured his client's case of a fair trial, he is relieved of the responsibility for an unfavorable verdict."

One of the attorneys with whom I spoke seemed to confirm Parsons's hypothesis, at least with respect to loser cases: "There is a certain consolation of going to trial with a loser case. If I lose, what the hell. I gave it my best shot. If I lose, *it was a loser.* If I win, it's amazing."

Most of the attorneys, however, were not so sanguine and could not detach themselves from the outcomes of their cases so easily. Even losing a loser case, most of them said, is incredibly hard on the attorney. The attorneys are not much comforted by the fact that the client was guilty—or probably guilty, anyway.

Q: When you feel bad about losing a case, doesn't it help to know that the client was probably guilty anyway?

R: Yeah [pause], maybe. But in the middle of the trial, it's you, you know? You are trying to make them believe what you are trying to sell them, and, if you don't win, it means that they don't believe *you.* That's probably one of the reasons that it doesn't help.

There was a case, not too long ago, that I really came to believe that they had no evidence on my man, and I fought very hard for him. We lost, and I felt very bad about that.

Afterward, he just fell apart, started screaming at me back in the lockup. We had this big fight. And I yelled at him: "You know, I really put myself on the line too, and I did everything I could for you, and what are you doing yelling at me?" Cause I really believed, and I worked hard.

And then I misspoke myself, because I said, "And I really believed that you didn't do this."

And he said, "Would it make you feel any better if I told you that I *did* do it?" [Laugh].

Q: How did you answer him?

R: [Laugh] I said, "I don't want to know; don't tell me!" I still don't want to know, and that's how it is.

Most telling is how these lawyers talk about doing trial work. They do not say, "I'm doing a trial now"; they do not ask, "Are you doing a trial this week?" They say, "*I'm* on trial": they ask, "Are *you* on trial?"

Lawyers hate to lose because, although reason tells them a case is a loser, sentiment says that justice favors not the stronger case but the better lawyer. What makes losing any case, even a loser, so bad is their belief that, in the hands of a *good* attorney, there is really no such thing as a dead-bang loser case. One attorney told me: "Fewer and fewer of my cases are losers. . . . Because I am a better and better lawyer."

None of the current public defenders with whom I spoke said they preferred innocent clients, and all but two said they actually preferred representing defendants whom they believed were guilty. Many of the attorneys did not want to talk about such cases, even hypothetically. Most of them just said something like, "In my own gut I know I have a harder time defending people I know are innocent than people I suspect are guilty—the pressure to win is so much greater then," or "it is just harder to defend an innocent person because there is so much pressure." Although no public defender said as much, given what they did say, I suspect that what makes defending an innocent client so

stressful is the fact that if one should fail to win an acquittal, it would be difficult to avoid the conclusion that it was the lawyer's fault (although in theory, this may not be true). In such cases, the weight of the client's sentence really hangs on the defender. One lawyer told me how he protected himself from the possibility of that kind of "incredible stress." He explained that he "tried not to think about having innocent clients [pause], but it's academic since they are all guilty anyway."

Lawyers are helped some by their ability to distinguish a loss from a defeat. Even when they lose, public defenders search for evidence that they did a better job, that they "out-tried" the state's attorneys. Out-trying one's adversaries can mean anything from simply acting more professional to forcing your opponent to commit reversible error. Sometimes it just means making him or her look silly in court.

During long or tough cases the level of exchange between defense and prosecuting attorneys can destroy all ideals that one might have about noble adversaries. Attorneys will sometimes bait each other, trying to force their opponents to do something regrettable. The following are snatches of dialogue from a death-penalty case. All these exchanges took place on the record (I have, however, changed the lawyers' names). Mr. Buford and Mr. Petrone speak for the prosecution; attorneys Carney, Stone, and Richert appeared for the defense:

[Time One]

Richert: [To the court] During Mr. Carney's remarks, Mr. Buford came to me personally and pointed to Mr. Stone and said, "Do you realize your partner looks like Lenin?" I would appreciate if the prosecutor would avoid interfering with my participation in proceedings such as these.

The Court: Which prosecutor? Who is he talking about? Who looks like Lenin?

[Later that day]

Carney: [To Buford] Oh, put your foot down [off the table]. Act like an attorney. What is wrong with you?

Buford: Come on.

Carney: Take your foot off the table!

Buford: You don't tell me what to do!

Carney: It insults me as an attorney.

Buford: I may do that, but you don't tell me what to do!

The Court: We will take a recess.

[Time Two]

Petrone: Let's go. We have been wasting seven months for it.

Stone: That's unprofessional.

Petrone: That's as unprofessional as you, Mr. Stone.

Stone: Wasn't it enough that we showed you how to pick a jury?

Petrone: You showed us how to pick a jury? You pleaded him right into the electric chair!

[Time Three]

Buford [in chambers]: I am at this time requesting that we go out in the court and requesting that—I just did—that we go on the record, because once again, I am not going to put up with any more of this state's attorney baiting or this other *bullshit* that's gone on here in chambers.

Carney: That's on the record!

Buford: Right, exactly. That has gone on here for eight weeks. I request that we go out in open court. Let the record reflect [pause]. [To judge] Look at Mr. Carney!

Carney: And I am looking at Mr. Buford, judge. And I have never heard that word said in a court of law in eight years, judge, by a state's attorney or any defense lawyer, and I am *really* shocked!

Buford: Look at these facts that they are making. I am asking that you to hold them in direct contempt!

The Court: All right, but I just wanted to know what witnesses are you calling?

The defense lost the case. They had hoped to "win" by getting a life sentence, but their client was sentenced to death. To any observer, it was a total loss. After listening to testimony for several weeks, the jury took less than an hour and only one vote to make the decision unanimous. Still, the attorneys (Mr. Carney, in particular) appeared to derive a great deal of satisfaction from their belief that they had not been "defeated," that they had caused their opponents (Mr. Buford, in particular) to "lose it" several times during the case. The night before the case ended, Mr. Carney recalled what for him had been a major highlight of the case. "Lisa, you know what Buford said to me that first day? He said, 'Carney, I heard you were a choker; I *collect* chokers, Carney.' When Buford said 'bullshit' in chambers, I leaned over and whispered to him: 'C-H-O-K-E.'" After the end of the last day in court, after hearing that their client would be sentenced to death, at a dinner that could more properly be called a wake a deeply depressed Carney repeated several times: "We sure got that bastard Buford; we sure beat their asses, didn't we?" "Yes," he was assured again and again, "we *sure did.*"

In retrospect, the attorneys seemed a bit childish, their bickering like juvenile acting-out. Yet when one is trying to salvage something that is a lost cause, anyway, every little bit seems to help.

Normal Crimes: Sociological Features of the Penal Code in a Public Defender's Office

DAVID SUDNOW

THE present report will examine the operations of a public defender system. It will address the question: what of import for the sociological analysis of legal administration can be learned by describing the actual way the penal code is employed in the daily activities of legal representation? First, [illegible] the guilty plea as a way of han[illegible] focusing on some features [illegible] a description of a popul[illegible] Then I shall describe the p[illegible] tion with special attention [illegible] are represented. The place [illegible] penal code in this represe[illegible] ined. Last, I shall briefly a[illegible] which the public defende[illegible] ducts a "defense." The latter sectio[illegible] to indicate the connection between certain prominent organizational features of the public defender system and the penal code's place in the routine operation of that system.

GUILTY PLEAS, INCLUSION, AND NORMAL CRIMES

It is a commonly noted fact about the criminal court system, generally, that the greatest proportion of cases are settled by a guilty plea. In the county from which the following material is drawn, over 80 percent of all cases never go to trial. To describe the method of obtaining a guilty-plea disposition, essential for the discussion to follow, I must distinguish between what shall be termed "necessarily included lesser offenses" and "situationally included lesser offenses." Of two offenses designated in the penal code, the lesser is considered to be that for which the length of required incarceration is the [illegible]er period of time. Inclusion refers to the [illegible]ion between two or more offenses. The [illegible]essarily included lesser offense" is a strictly [illegible]l notion:

> [illegible]ether a lesser offense is included in the crime [illegible]rged is a question of law to be determined [illegible]ly from the definition and corpus delicti of the [illegible]ense charged and of the lesser offense. . . . If all [illegible] elements of the corpus delicti of a lesser crime can be found in a list of all the elements of the offense charged, then only is the lesser included in the greater.

Stated alternatively:

> The test in this state of necessarily included offenses is simply that where an offense cannot be committed without necessarily committing another offense, the latter is a necessarily included offense.

The implied negative is put: could Smith have committed *A* and not *B*? If the answer is yes, then *B* is not necessarily included in *A*. If the answer is no, *B* is necessarily included. While in a given case a battery might be committed in the course of a robbery, battery is not necessarily included in robbery. Petty theft is necessarily included in robbery but not in burglary. Bur-

---

From "Normal Crimes: Sociological Features of the Penal Code in a Public Defender's Office" by D. Sudnow, 1978, *Social Problems, 12,* pp. 255-275. Copyright 1980-81 by the Law and Society Association. Reprinted by permission.

glary primarily involves the intent to acquire another's goods illegally (e.g., by breaking and entering); the consummation of the act need not occur for burglary to be committed. Theft, like robbery, requires that some item be stolen.

I shall call *lesser* offenses that are not necessarily but only *actually* included, "situationally included lesser offenses." By statutory definition, necessarily included offenses are actually included. By actual here, I refer to the "way it occurs as a course of action." In the instance of necessary inclusion, the way it occurs is irrelevant. With situational inclusion, the way it occurs is definitive. In the former case, no particular course of action is referred to. In the latter, the scene and progress of the criminal activity would be analyzed.

The issue of necessary inclusion has special relevance for two procedural matters:

> A. A man cannot be charged and/or convicted of two or more crimes any one of which is necessarily included in the others, unless the several crimes occur on separate occasions.

If a murder occurs, the defendant cannot be charged and/or convicted of both homicide and intent to commit a murder, the latter of which is necessarily included in first-degree murder. If, however, a defendant intends to commit a homicide against one person and commits a homicide against another, both offenses may be properly charged. While it is an extremely complex question as to the scope and definition of "in the course of," in most instances the rule is easily applied.

> B. The judge cannot instruct the jury to consider as alternative crimes of which to find a defendant guilty, crimes that are not necessarily included in the charged crime or crimes.

If a man is charged with statutory rape, the judge may instruct the jury to consider as a possible alternative conviction of contributing to the delinquency of a minor, as this offense is necessarily included in statutory rape. He cannot, however, suggest that the alternative of intent to commit murder be considered and the jury cannot find the defendant guilty of this

latter crime, unless it is charged as a distinct offense in the complaint.

It is crucial to note that these restrictions apply only to (a) the relation between several charged offenses in a formal allegation, and (b) the alternatives allowable in a jury instruction. At any time before a case goes to trial, alterations in the charging complaint may be made by the district attorney. The issue of necessary inclusion has no required bearing on (a) what offense(s) will be charged initially by the prosecutor, (b) what the relation is between the charge initially made and what happened, or (c) what modifications may be made after the initial charge and the relation between initially charged offenses and those charged in modified complaints. It is this latter operation, the modification of the complaint, that is central to the guilty-plea disposition.

Complaint alterations are made when a defendant agrees to plead guilty to an offense and thereby avoid a trial. The alteration occurs in the context of a deal consisting of an offer from the district attorney to alter the original charge in such a fashion that a lighter sentence will be incurred with a guilty plea than would be the case if the defendant were sentenced on the original charge. In return for this manipulation, the defendant agrees to plead guilty. The arrangement is proposed in the following format: "if you plead guilty to this new lesser offense, you will get less time in prison than if you plead not guilty to the original, greater charge and lose the trial." The decision must then be made whether or not the chances of obtaining complete acquittal at trial are great enough to warrant the risk of a loss and higher sentence if found guilty on the original charge. As we shall see below, it is a major job of the public defender, who mediates between the district attorney and the defendant, to convince his "client" that the chances of acquittal are too slight to warrant this risk.

If a man is charged with drunkenness and the public defender and public prosecutor (hereafter P.D. and D.A.) prefer not to have a trial, they seek to have the defendant agree to plead guilty. While it is occasionally possible, particularly with first offenders, for the P.D. to convince the defendant to plead guilty to the originally charged offense, most often it is felt that some exchange or consideration should be offered, that is, a lesser offense charged.

To what offense can drunkenness be reduced? There is no statutorily designated crime that is necessarily included in the crime of drunkenness. That is, if any of the statutorily required components of drunk behavior (its corpus delicti) are absent, there remains no offense of which the resultant description is a definition. For drunkenness, there is, however, an offense that while not necessarily included is "typically situationally included," that is, typically occurs as a feature of the way drunk persons are seen to behave—disturbing the peace. The range of possible sentences is such that, of the two offenses, disturbing the peace cannot call for as long a prison sentence as drunkenness. If, in the course of going on a binge, a person does so in such a fashion that disturbing the peace may be employed to describe some of his behavior, it would be considered as an alternative offense to offer in return for a guilty plea. A central question for the following analysis will be: in what fashion would he have to behave so that disturbing the peace would be considered a suitable reduction?

If a man is charged with molesting a minor, there are not any necessarily included lesser offenses with which to charge him. Yet an alternative charge—loitering around a schoolyard—is often used as a reduction. As above, and central to our analysis, the question is: what would the defendant's behavior be such that loitering around a schoolyard would constitute an appropriate alternative?

If a person is charged with burglary, petty theft is not necessarily included. Routinely, however, petty theft is employed for reducing the charge of burglary. Again, we shall ask: what is the relation between burglary and petty theft and the *manner in which the former occurs* that warrants this reduction?

NORMAL CRIMES

In the course of routinely encountering persons charged with petty theft, burglary, assault with a deadly weapon, rape, possession of marijuana,

and so on, the P.D. gains knowledge of the typical manner in which offenses of given classes are committed, the social characteristics of the persons who regularly commit them, the features of the settings in which they occur, the types of victims often involved, and the like. He learns to speak knowledgeably of "burglars," "petty thieves," "drunks," "rapists," "narcos," and so on and to attribute to them personal biographies, modes of usual criminal activity, criminal histories, psychological characteristics, and social backgrounds. The following characterizations are illustrative:

Most ADWs (assault with deadly weapon) start with fights over some girl.

These sex fiends (child molestation cases) usually hang around parks or schoolyards. But we often get fathers charged with these crimes. Usually the old man is out of work and stays at home when the wife goes to work and he plays around with his little daughter or something. A lot of these cases start when there is some marital trouble and the woman gets mad.

I don't know why most of them don't rob the big stores. They usually break into some cheap department store and steal some crummy item like a $9.95 record player you know.

Kids who start taking this stuff (narcotics) usually start out when some buddy gives them a cigarette and they smoke it for kicks. For some reason they always get caught in their cars, for speeding or something.

They can anticipate that point when persons are likely to get into trouble:

Dope addicts do O.K. until they lose a job or something and get back on the streets and, you know, meet the old boys. Someone tells them where to get some and there they are.

In the springtime, that's when we get all these sex crimes. You know, these kids play out in the schoolyard all day and these old men sit around and watch them jumping up and down. They get their ideas.

The P.D. learns that some kinds of offenders are likely to repeat the same offense while others are not repeat violators or, if they do commit crimes frequently, the crimes vary from occasion to occasion:

You almost never see a check man get caught for anything but checks—only an occasional drunk charge.

Burglars are usually multiple offenders, most times just burglaries or petty thefts.

Petty thefts get started for almost anything—joy riding, drinking, all kinds of little things.

These narcos are usually through after the second violation or so. After the first time some stop, but when they start on the heavy stuff, they've had it.

I shall call *normal crimes* those occurrences whose typical features, for example, the ways they usually occur and the characteristics of persons who commit them (as well as the typical victims and typical scenes), are known and attended to by the P.D. For any of a series of offense types, the P.D. can provide some form of proverbial characterization. For example, burglary is seen as involving regular violators, no weapons, low-priced items, little property damage, lower-class establishments, largely Negro defendants, independent operators, and a nonprofessional orientation to the crime. Child molesting is seen as typically entailing middle-aged strangers or lower-class middle-aged fathers (few women); no actual physical penetration or severe tissue damage; mild fondling, petting, and stimulation; bad marriage circumstances; multiple offenders with the same offense repeatedly committed; and a child complainant, via the mother. Narcotics defendants are usually Negroes, not syndicated, persons who start by using small stuff, hostile with police officers, and caught by some form of entrapment technique. Petty thefts are about 50-50 Negro-white, unplanned offenses, generally committed on lower-class persons and do not get much money, do not often employ weapons, do not make living from thievery, and usually younger defendants with long

juvenile assaultive records. Drunkenness offenders are lower-class white and Negro, get drunk on wine and beer, have long histories of repeated drunkenness, do not hold down jobs, are usually arrested on the streets, and seldom violate other penal code sections.

Some general features of the normal crime as a way of attending to a category of persons and events may be mentioned:

1. The focus, in these characterizations, is not on particular individuals, but offense types. If asked "What are burglars like?" or "How are burglaries usually committed?" the P.D. does not feel obliged to refer to particular burglars and burglaries as the material for his answer.

2. The features attributed to offenders and offenses are often not of import for the statutory conception. In burglary, it is "irrelevant" for the statutory determination whether or not much damage was done to the premises (e.g., except where explosives were employed and a new statute could be invoked). Whether a defendant breaks a window or not, destroys property within the house or not, and so on does not affect his statutory classification as a burglar. While for robbery the presence or absence of a weapon sets the degree, whether the weapon is a machine gun or pocket knife is "immaterial." Whether the residence or business establishment in a burglary is located in a higher-income area of the city is of no issue for the code requirements. And, generally, the defendant's race, class position, criminal history (in most offenses), personal attributes, and particular style of committing offenses are features specifically not definitive of crimes under the auspices of the penal code. For deciding "Is this a burglary case I have before me?" however, the P.D.'s reference to this range of nonstatutorily referable personal and social attributes, modes of operation, and so on is crucial for the arrangement of a guilty plea bargain.

3. The features attributed to offenders and offenses are, in their content, specific to the community in which the P.D. works. In other communities and historical periods, the lists would presumably differ. Narcotics violators in certain areas, for example, are syndicated in dope rackets or engage in systematic robbery as

professional criminals, features which are not commonly encountered (or, at least, evidence for which is not systematically sought) in this community. Burglary in some cities will more often occur at large industrial plants, banking establishments, warehouses, and so on. The P.D. refers to the population of defendants in the county as "our defendants" and qualifies his prototypical portrayals and knowledge of the typically operative social structures, "for our county." An older P.D., remembering the "old days," commented:

We used to have a lot more rapes than we do now, and they used to be much more violent. Things are duller now in _____.

4. Offenses whose normal features are readily attended to are those which are routinely encountered in the courtroom. This feature is related to the last point. For embezzlement, bank robbery, gambling, prostitution, murder, arson, and some other uncommon offenses, the P.D. cannot readily supply anecdotal and proverbial characterizations. While there is some change in the frequencies of offense-type convictions over time, certain offenses are continually more common and others remain stably infrequent. The troubles created for the P.D. when offenses whose features are not readily known occur, and whose typicality is not easily constructed, will be discussed in some detail below.

5. Offenses are ecologically specified and attended to as normal or not according to the locales within which they are committed. The P.D. learns that burglaries usually occur in such and such areas of the city, petty thefts around this or that park, ADWs in these bars. Ecological patterns are seen as related to socioeconomic variables, and these in turn to typical modes of criminal and noncriminal activities. Knowing where an offense took place is thus, for the P.D., knowledge of the likely persons involved, the kind of scene in which the offense occurred, and the pattern of activity characteristic of such a place:

Almost all of our ADWs are in the same half a dozen bars. These places are Negro bars where laborers come after hanging around the union halls trying to get some work. Nobody has any money and they drink too much. Tempers are high and almost anything can start happening.

6. One further important feature can be noted at this point. Its elaboration will be the task of a later section. As shall be seen, the P.D. office consists of a staff of twelve full-time attorneys. Knowledge of the properties of offense types of offenders, that is, their normal, typical, or familiar attributes, constitutes the mark of any given attorney's competence. A major task in socializing the new P.D. deputy attorney consists in teaching him to recognize these attributes and to come to do so naturally. The achievement of competence as a P.D. is signaled by the gradual acquisition of professional command not simply of local penal code peculiarities and courtroom folklore but, as important, of relevant features of the social structure and criminological wisdom. His grasp of that knowledge over the course of time is a key indication of his expertise.

PUBLIC "DEFENSE"

Recently, in many communities, the burden of securing counsel has been taken from the defendant. As the accused is, by law, entitled to the aid of counsel, and as his pocketbook is often empty, numerous cities have felt obliged to establish a public defender system. There has been little resistance to this development by private attorneys among whom it is widely felt that the less time they need spend in the criminal courts, where practice is least prestigeful and lucrative, the better.

Whatever the reasons for its development, we now find, in many urban places, a public defender occupying a place alongside judge and prosecutor as a regular court employee. In the county studied, the P.D. mans a daily station, like the public prosecutor, and defends all who come before him. He appears in court when court begins and his clientele, composed without regard for his preferences, consists of that residual category of persons who cannot afford to bring their own spokesmen to court. In this county, the "residual" category approximates 65 percent of the total number of criminal cases. In a given year, the twelve attorneys who comprise the P.D. office "represent" about 3,000 defendants in the municipal and superior courts of the county.

While the courtroom encounters of private attorneys are brief, businesslike, and circumscribed, interactionally and temporally, by the particular cases that bring them there, the P.D. attends to the courtroom as his regular workplace and conveys in his demeanor his place as a member of its core personnel.

While private attorneys come and leave court with their clients (who are generally "on bail"), the P.D. arrives in court each morning at nine, takes his station at the defense table, and deposits there the batch of files that he will refer to during the day. When, during morning "calendar," a private attorney's case is called, the P.D. steps back from the defense table, leaving his belongings in place there, and temporarily relinquishes his station. No private attorney has enough defendants in a given court on a given day to claim a right to make a desk of the defense table. If the P.D. needs some information from his central office, he uses the clerk's telephone, a privilege that few private lawyers feel at home enough to take. In the course of calendar work, a lawyer will often have occasion to request a delay or continuance of several days until the next stage of his client's proceedings. The private attorney addresses the prosecutor via the judge to request such an alteration; the P.D. talks directly over to the D.A.:

> Private attorney: If the prosecutor finds it convenient Your Honor, my client would prefer to have his preliminary hearing on Monday, the 24th.
> Judge: Is that date suitable to the district attorney?
> Prosecutor: Yes, Your Honor.
> Private attorney: Thank you, Your Honor.
> Public defender: Bob (D.A.), how about moving Smith's prelim up to the 16th?
> Prosecutor: Well, Jim, we've got Jones on that afternoon.

> Public defender: Let's see, how's the 22nd?
> Prosecutor: That's fine, Jim, the 22nd.

If, during the course of a proceeding, the P.D. has some minor matter to tend to with the D.A., he uses the time when a private attorney is addressing the bench to walk over to the prosecutor's table and whisper his requests, suggestions, or questions. The P.D. uses the prosecutor's master calendar to check on an upcoming court date; so does the D.A. with the P.D.'s. The D.A. and P.D. are on a first-name basis and throughout the course of a routine day interact as a team of co-workers.

While the central focus of the private attorney's attention is his client, the courtroom and affairs of court constitute the locus of involvements for the P.D. The public defender and public prosecutor, each representatives of their respective offices, jointly handle the greatest bulk of the court's daily activity.

The P.D. office, rather than assign its attorneys to clients, employs the arrangement of stationing attorneys in different courts to represent all those who come before that station. As defendants are moved about from courtroom to courtroom throughout the course of their proceedings (both from municipal to superior courtrooms for felony cases, and from one municipal courtroom to another when there is a specialization of courts, e.g., jury, nonjury, arraignment), the P.D. sees defendants only at those places in their paths when they appear in the court he is manning. A given defendant may be represented by one P.D. at arraignment, another at preliminary hearing, a third at trial, and a fourth when sentenced.

RECALCITRANT DEFENDANTS

Most of the P.D.'s cases that "have to go to trial" are those where the P.D. is not able to sell the defendant on the "bargain." These are cases for which reductions are available, reductions that are constructed on the basis of the typicality of the offense and allowable by the D.A. These are normal crimes committed by "stubborn" defendants.

So-called stubborn defendants will be distinguished from a second class of offenders, those who commit crimes which are atypical in their character (for this community, at this time, etc.) or who commit crimes which while typical (recurrent for this community, this time, etc.) are committed atypically. The manner in which the P.D. and D.A. must conduct the representation and prosecution of these defendants is radically different. To characterize the special problems the P.D. has with each class of defendants, it is first necessary to point out a general feature of the P.D.'s orientation to the work of the courts that has hitherto not been made explicit. This orientation will be merely sketched here.

As we noticed, the defendant's guilt is not attended to. That is to say, the presupposition of guilt, as a *presupposition,* does not say, "You are guilty" with a pointing accusatory finger, but "You are guilty, you know it, I know it, so let's get down to the business of deciding what to do with you." When a defendant agrees to plead guilty, he is not *admitting* his guilt; when asked to plead guilty, he is not being asked, "Come on, admit it, you know you were *wrong,*" but rather, "Why don't you be sensible about this thing?" What is sought is not a confession, but reasonableness.

The presupposition of guilt as a way of attending to the treatment of defendants has its counterpart in the way the P.D. attends to the entire court process, prosecuting machinery, law enforcement techniques, and the community.

For P.D. and D.A. it is a routinely encountered phenomenon that persons in the community regularly commit criminal offenses, are regularly brought before the courts, and are regularly transported to the state and county penal institutions. To confront a criminal is, for D.A. and P.D., no special experience, nothing to tell their wives about, nothing to record as outstanding in the happenings of the day. Before "their court" scores of criminals pass each day.

The morality of the courts is taken for granted. The P.D. assumes that the D.A., the police, the judge, the narcotics agents, and others all conduct their business as it must be conducted and in a proper fashion. That the police may hide out to deceive petty violators; that narcotics agents may regularly employ illicit en-trapment procedures to find suspects; that investigators may routinely arrest suspects before they have sufficient grounds and only later uncover warrantable evidence for a formal booking; that the police may beat suspects; that judges may be tough because they are looking to support for higher-office elections; that some laws may be specifically prejudicial against certain classes of persons—whatever may be the actual course of charging and convicting defendants—all of this is taken, as one P.D. put it, "as part of the system and the way it has to be." And the P.D. is part of the team.

While it is common to overhear private attorneys call judges "bastards," policemen "hoodlums," and prosecutors "sadists," the P.D., in the presence of such talk, remains silent. When the P.D. "loses" a case—and we shall see that losing is an adequate description only for some circumstances—he is likely to say, "I knew *he* couldn't win." Private attorneys, on the other hand, will not hesitate to remark, as one did in a recent case, "You haven't got a fucking chance in front of that son-of-a-bitch dictator." In the P.D. office, there is a total absence of such condemnation.

The P.D. takes it for granted and attends to the courts in accord with the view that "what goes on in this business is what goes on and what goes on is the way it should be." It is rare to hear a public defender voice protest against a particular law, procedure, or official. One of the attorneys mentioned that he felt the new narcotics law (which makes it mandatory that a high minimum sentence be served for possession or sale of narcotics) was not too severe "considering that they wanted to give them the chair." Another indicated that the more rigid statute "will probably cure a lot of them because they'll be in for so long." One P.D. feels that wire-tapping would be a useful adjunct to police procedure. It is generally said, by everyone in the office, that "_____ is one of the best cities in the state when it comes to police."

The routine trial, generated as it is by the defendant's refusal to make a lesser plea, is the "defendant's fault":

What the hell are we supposed to do with them. If they can't listen to good reason and take a bargain, then it's their tough luck. If they go to prison, well, they're the ones who are losing the trials, not us.

When the P.D. enters the courtroom, he takes it that he is going to lose, for example, the defendant is going to prison. When he prepares for trial, he does not prepare to "win." There is no attention given to "how am I going to construct a defense in order that I can get this defendant free of the changes against him?" In fact, he does not prepare for trial in any ordinary sense. (I use the term *ordinary* with hesitation; what *preparation for trial* might in fact involve with other than P.D. lawyers has not, to my knowledge, been investigated.)

For the P.D., preparation for trial involves, essentially, learning what "burglary cases" are like, what "rape cases" are like, what "assaults" are like. The P.D.'s main concern is to conduct his part of the proceedings in accord with complete respect for proper legal procedure. He raises objections to improper testimony; introduces motions whenever they seem called for; demands his "client's rights" to access to the prosecution's evidence before trial (through so-called discovery proceedings); cross-examines all witnesses; does not introduce evidence that he expects will not be allowable; asks all those questions of all those people that he must in order to have addressed himself to the task of ensuring that the corpus delicti has been established; and carefully summarizes the evidence that has been presented in making a closing argument. Throughout, at every point, he conducts his defense in such a manner that no one can say of him, "He has been negligent, there are grounds for appeal here." He systematically provides, in accord with the prescriptions of due process and the Fourteenth Amendment, a completely proper, "adequate legal representation."

At the same time, the district attorney, and the county which employs them both, can rely on the P.D. not to attempt to morally degrade police officers in cross-examination; not to impeach the state's witnesses by trickery; not to attempt an exposition of the entrapment methods of narcotics agents; not to condemn the community for the "racial prejudice that produces our criminals" (the phrase of a private attorney during closing argument); not to challenge the prosecution of "these women who are trying to raise a family without a husband" (the statement of another private attorney during closing argument on a welfare fraud case); in sum, not to make an issue of the moral character of the administrative machinery of the local courts, the community, or the police. He will not cause any serious trouble for the routine motion of the court conviction process. Laws will not be challenged, cases will not be tried to test the constitutionality of procedures and statutes, judges will not be personally degraded, police will be free from scrutiny to decide the legitimacy of their operations, and the community will not be condemned for its segregative practices against Negroes. The P.D.'s defense is completely proper, in accord with correct legal procedure, and specifically amoral in its import, manner of delivery, and perceived implications for the propriety of the prosecution enterprise.

In return for all this, the district attorney treats the defendant's guilt in a matter-of-fact fashion, does not get hostile in the course of the proceedings, and does not insist that the jury or judge "throws the book," but rather "puts on a trial" (in their way of referring to their daily tasks) in order to, with a minimum of strain, properly place the defendant behind bars. Both prosecutor and public defender thus protect the moral character of the other's charges from exposure. Should the P.D. attend to demonstrating the innocence of his client by attempting to undermine the legitimate character of police operations, the prosecutor might feel obliged in return to employ devices to degrade the moral character of the P.D.'s client. Should the D.A attack defendants in court, by pointing to the specifically immoral character of their activities, the P.D. might feel obligated, in response, to raise into relief the moral texture of the D.A.'s and police's and community's operations. Wherever possible, each holds the other in check. But the check need not be continuously held in place, or even attended to self-consciously, for both P.D. and D.A. trust one another implicitly. The D.A. knows, with certainty, that the P.D. will not make a closing argument that resembles the following by a private attorney, from which I have paraphrased key excerpts:

If it hadn't been for all the publicity that this case had in our wonderful local newspapers, you wouldn't want to throw the book at these men.

If you'd clear up your problems with the Negro in _____ maybe you wouldn't have cases like this in your courts.

(after sentence was pronounced) Your Honor, I just would like to say one thing—that I've never heard or seen such a display of injustice as I've seen here in this court today. It's a sad commentary on the state of our community if people like yourself pay more attention to the local political machines than to the lives of our defendants. I think you are guilty of that, Your Honor.

(At this last statement, one of the P.D.s who was in the courtroom turned to me and said, "He sure is looking for a contempt charge.")

The P.D. knows how to conduct his trials because he knows how to conduct "assault with deadly weapons" trials, "burglary" trials, "rape" trials, and the rest. The corpus delicti here provides him with a basis for asking "proper questions," making the "proper" cross-examinations, and pointing out the "proper" things to jurors about "reasonable doubt." He need not extensively gather information about the specific facts of the instant case. Whatever is needed in the way of "facts of the case" arise in the course of the D.A.'s presentation. He employs the strategy of directing the same questions to the witness as were put by the D.A. with added emphasis on the question mark, or an inserted, "Did you really see _____?" His defense consists of attempting to bring out slightly variant aspects of the D.A.'s story by questioning his own witnesses (whom he seldom interviews before beginning trial but who are interviewed by the office's two investigators) and the defendant.

With little variation, the same questions are put to all defendants charged with the same crimes. The P.D. learns with experience what to expect as the facts of the case. These facts, in their general structure, portray social circumstances that he can anticipate by virtue of his knowledge of the normal features of offense categories and types of offenders. The details of the instant case are discovered over the course of hearing them in court. In this regard, the information that comes out is often new to him as to the jury.

Employing a commonsense conception of what criminal lawyers behave like in cross-examination and argument, and the popular portrayal of their demeanor and style of addressing adversary witnesses, the onlooker comes away with the sense of having witnessed not a trial at all, but a set of motions, a perfunctorily carried-off event. A sociological analysis of this sense would require a systematic attempt to describe the features of adversary trial conduct.

SOME CONCLUSIONS

An examination of the use of the penal code by actually practicing attorneys has revealed that categories of crime, rather than being unsuited to sociological analysis, are so employed as to make their analysis crucial to empirical understanding. What categories of crime are, that is, who is assembled under this one or that, what constitute the behaviors inspected for deciding such matters, what "etiologically significant" matters are incorporated within their scope, is not, the present findings indicate, to be decided on the basis of an a priori inspection of their formally available definitions. The sociologist who regards the category "theft" with penal code in hand and proposes necessary, "theoretically relevant" revisions, is constructing an imagined use of the penal code as the basis for his criticism. For in their actual use, categories of crime, as we have reiterated continuously above, are, at least for this legal establishment, the shorthand reference terms for that knowledge of the social structure and its criminal events upon which the task of practically organizing the work of "representation" is premised. That knowledge includes, embodied within what burglary, petty theft, narcotics violations, child molestation, and the rest *actually stand for,* knowledge of modes of criminal activity, ecological characteristics of the community, patterns of daily slum life, psychological and social biographies of offenders, criminal histories and futures; in sum, practically tested criminological wisdom. The operations of the public defender system, and it is clear that upon comparative analysis with other legal firms it would be somewhat distinctive in character, are routinely maintained via the proper use of categories of crime for everyday decision making. The properties of that use are not described in the state criminal code, nor are the operations of reduction, detailed above.

THE JUDGE

The Process Is the Punishment: Handling Cases in a Lower Criminal Court

MALCOLM FEELEY

THIS essay develops the argument that in the lower criminal courts the process itself is the primary punishment. In this chapter, I identify the costs involved in the pretrial process and examine the ways they affect organization, as well as the way a defendant will proceed on his journeys through the court. This examination should help explain why lower courts do not fit their popular image, and why cases are processed so quickly in the New Haven (Connecticut) Court of Common Pleas.

The first set of factors I examine deals with the consequences of pretrial detention and the problems of securing pretrial release. The second explores the costs of securing an attorney. There are obvious financial outlays involved in retaining a private attorney, but there are also hidden costs associated with obtaining free counsel. A third set of factors deals with the problem of continuances. While delay often benefits the defendant, its importance for the defendant is often exaggerated, and it is crucial to distinguish defendant-induced delay from continuances which are arranged for the convenience of the court.

By themselves, these costs may appear to be minor or even trivial in a process formally structured to focus on the crucial questions of adjudication and sentencing. However, in the aggregate, and in comparison with the actual consequences of adjudication and sentencing, they

often loom large in the eyes of the criminally accused and emerge as central concerns in getting through the criminal justice system.

These pretrial costs account for a number of puzzling phenomena: why so many people waive their right to free appointed counsel; why so many people do not show up for court at all; and why people choose the available adversarial options so infrequently. Furthermore, pretrial costs are part of the reason why pretrial diversion programs designed to *benefit* defendants and provide alternatives to standard adjudication do not receive a more enthusiastic response. The accused often perceive these programs as cumbersome processes which simply increase their contact with the system.

The relative importance of the pretrial process hinges on one important set of considerations. Students of the criminal courts often overlook what many criminologists and students of social class do not, that the fear of arrest and conviction does not loom as large in the eyes of many people brought into court as it does in the eyes of middle-class researchers. While I did not systematically interview a sample of defendants, I had informal and often extended discussions with dozens of defendants who were waiting for their cases to be called, and I watched still more discuss their cases with attorneys and prosecutors. While there were obvious and numerous exceptions, I was nevertheless struck by the frequent lack of concern about the stigma of conviction and by the more practical and far more immediate concerns about what the sentence would be and how quickly they could get out of court.

There are several reasons for this. First, many arrestees already have criminal records, so that whatever stigma does attach to a conviction is already eroded, if not destroyed. Second, many arrestees, particularly young ones, are part of a subculture which spurns conventional values and for which arrest and conviction may even function as a celebratory ritual, reinforcing their own values and identity. In fact, they may even perceive it as part of the process of coming of age. Third, lower-class people tend to be more present oriented than middle-class people, and for obvious reasons. Many defendants are faced with an immediate concern for returning to work or their children, and these concerns often take precedence over the desire to avoid the remote consequences that a (or another) conviction might bring. This relative lack of concern about conviction is reinforced by the type of employment opportunities available to lower-class defendants. If an employee is reliable, it may make little difference whether or not he pleads guilty to a minor charge emerging from a "Saturday night escapade." Indeed, an employer is not likely to find out about the incident unless his employee has to arrange to miss work in order to appear in court.

If the stigma of the criminal sanction is not viewed as a significant sanction, the concrete costs of the pretrial process take on great significance. When this occurs, the process itself becomes the punishment.

PRETRIAL RELEASE:
AN OVERVIEW

A quick reading of relevant Connecticut statutes, case law, and administrative directives conveys the impression that the state has an unswerving commitment to prompt pretrial release. There is an elaborate multilayered system for decision and review, there are a variety of pretrial release alternatives, and assurance of appearance at trial is the sole criterion for establishing release conditions.

The police are empowered to make the initial release decision and can either release a suspect at the site of the arrest or take him to the central booking facility. Once the suspect is booked,

police retain the power to establish release conditions, and they may release suspects on a written promise to appear (PTA) or on bond, which they set. If they do not release the arrestee, at this point, the police are then required to notify a bail commissioner who in turn is supposed to "promptly conduct [an] interview and investigation as he deems necessary to reach an independent decision." If after this the accused is still not released, then the bail commissioner "shall set forth his reasons . . . in writing." The accused has a third opportunity to seek release at arraignment and all subsequent appearances, at which time he can request the judge to consider a bond reduction or release on PTA.

This liberal release policy is reflected in practice as well. Most of those arrested (89 percent) were released prior to the disposition of their cases, and 52 percent of them were released on nonfinancial conditions, by police field citation or PTA. Thirty-seven percent were released on bond, and only 11 percent were detained until disposition. Although the proportion of arrestees released pending trial is typically regarded as the most important measure of a jurisdiction's "liberality," it is far from a complete picture. Two additional questions must be answered. First, at what point in the process do people secure release? To identify as "released" only those who were free at the time their cases were disposed of is to overlook those who were held in detention for a while before eventually securing release. And if a person is released on bail, at what price was freedom purchased?

Length of Time in Pretrial Custody

Seventeen percent were released almost immediately on police citations. A much larger group—44 percent—was released within three hours after being taken to the "lockup," and a third group was released within a period of thirteen to twenty-four hours after arrest. Many of the people in this group were released in court the morning after their arrest, at which time they were able to secure reductions in the amount of bond or contact a bondsman or family member to post bond; some pleaded guilty and were discharged from custody. However, 6 percent of the sample remained in pretrial custody for a period of two days or longer, and a small number were held three weeks or more.

Other arrestees secure delayed release because the lockup facility becomes overcrowded. On Saturday evenings, police may "weed out" the lockup by granting PTAs to Friday evening's arrestees in order to make room for new arrivals. Women are housed in a separate facility in another location and are generally more likely to be released earlier on lower bond.

PRETRIAL RELEASE: PROCESS

The Role of the Police

Although most students of the pretrial process focus on judicial bail setting at arraignment, their observations may often miss the mark, since in many jurisdictions—including New Haven—the bulk of the pretrial release decisions is made by other people before the accused is ever presented in court. In New Haven, it is not the judge or the bail commissioner who dominates the release process, but rather the police. They are responsible not only for arresting and charging suspects but also for releasing them before a trial. A number of observers have commented that Connecticut in general, and New Haven in particular, has liberal policies on pretrial release. They attribute these to the multilayered system of decision and review and to the existence of bail commissioners. But, in fact, one cannot attribute these practices directly to this elaborate system. They probably have more to do with the intuitive judgments of the initial decision makers, the police.

Unless a suspect is released on a field citation at the site of an arrest, the arresting officer takes him to the central booking facility. After the booking, the officer is required by departmental order to complete a detailed bail interview form, which seeks information about the arrestee's ties to the community and other factors on which the release decision is to be based. The form also provides a space for reasons if the arrestee should not be released. Rarely is there anything that might be characterized as an "interview." Only occasionally is the bail interview form completed in detail, and whatever information it does record is likely to have been filled in *after*

a release decision has already been made. While different officers have different practices, most of them require little more than the accused's name, address, and the charges being pressed before making a decision to release on PTA or a small bond.

If the charges are more serious, or if the arrestee has a prior record of arrests or failure to appear (and well over 50 percent do), then the officer may insist on a bond. In setting its amount, he often consults a "bail schedule." This document, prepared by the Judicial Department and adopted by a resolution of all circuit court judges in 1967, specifies a monetary amount for each type of charge and provides for "discounts," depending upon the accused's ties to the community.

Although officers setting the conditions of release must complete a section of the bail interview form which calls for a statement of reasons if an arrestee is not released immediately, this section is rarely filled out. In my review of over 100 bail interview forms for people who were *not* immediately released, only a handful—15 or so—had this section completed. Only occasionally did they specify that the arrestee was a "poor risk" because he had no local address, or because he had a record of failures to appear. Most of the reasons related instead to the police officer's perception of the arrestee's condition, which was often characterized as "abusive," "threatening," or "wants to return to the incident," reasons which encouraged them to favor immediate situational justice or specific deterrence.

These officers are often in a dilemma. They are agents of the community, expected to enforce the law and make arrests. But then they must immediately turn around and release those very people whom they have just apprehended and arrested. It is not surprising that the tensions produced by these conflicting roles place a strain in the formal rules these people are charged with applying and that they have taken advantage of the lax enforcement of the law to pursue their own conceptions of rough justice. Occasionally, they use this detention power arbitrarily to administer their own system of punishment. Often they fear that an arrestee will return to a fight if he is released, so that they purposefully set bail beyond the arrestee's means in order to detain him until they think he has calmed down. The statutes on release make no provision for this latter concern, and the police can pursue it only by ignoring the literal letter of the law. But in bending the law in this "reasonable" direction, the door is opened for justifications to bend it for other, less benign reasons. Police may impose situational sanctions on arrestees whom they think deserve to "sit in jail for a time" because the courts will just "let them out."

SECURING AN ATTORNEY

A person accused of a criminal offense must decide whether or not to obtain an attorney. This seemingly simple choice in fact involves a complex set of decisions: whether or not to get a lawyer and who to get, a public defender or a private attorney; if a private attorney, then which one? The decision is confusing and costly in terms of both time and money.

Private Counsel

Unless an arrestee has had prior experience with a particular lawyer and has been satisfied, he is confused about what to do, whom to call, if anyone, how much it will cost him, and whether the amount is reasonable. He is overly suspicious and afraid of being taken advantage of. Some arrestees will call an attorney with whose name he or his friends are familiar. Others may turn to other inmates or their captors—the police—for advice, or perhaps to a bondsman. Still others, fearful of the expense, decide to do without representation.

If the arrestee telephones an attorney from the lockup, the attorney is likely to ask him a few questions about the charges, then ask to speak to the police officer in charge or contact a bail commissioner in an effort to get the bond lowered to an amount the arrestee can make. After this, he may contact a bondsman. If the arrestee secures his release before arraignment, the case is scheduled for a week or two later, and in the interim the attorney will arrange an appointment with his caller. If the arrestee is not released, the attorney will try to meet his prospective client just before arraignment in order to argue for bail reduction and afterward hold a brief conference to discuss financial terms and the case.

It is important that an attorney assess his would-be client's ability to pay early on; once he has begun to represent a defendant, he is bound by the canon of ethics to continue his representation until disposition. While it is possible to withdraw later from the case, it can be awkward and embarrassing. Most attorneys can relate instances of being "taken" by clients, and the result is a rather hard-nosed approach to fees, even among the more liberal "client-oriented" attorneys who are frequently young, not well established, and in particular need of the income.

Fees and billing practices vary widely from attorney to attorney and from case to case. Most private attorneys expect an initial retainer based on their own assessment of the "worth of the case."

Although most attorneys bill clients based on the amount of time they spend—or say they spend—on a case (and all things being equal, they feel that the type of charge provides a rough indication of this), they also adjust this amount according to their assessment of their client's ability to pay. Some attorneys are critical of such billing practices, but those who use them claim that they allow the better-off to subsidize the less fortunate.

Some attorneys have experimented with a flat fee for a case, which in one small firm is $300 for a case in the lower court and $1,000 for a case in upper court. But this means that those people whose cases are disposed of quickly after only one or two court appearances pay an extremely high per hour or per appearance cost, while those whose cases require considerable research, investigation, court appearances, or a trial get a real bargain.

Public Defenders

In order to obtain a public defender, a person must be poor. There are rather rigid guidelines for eligibility, but they are not strictly adhered to, and in fact most arrestees who apply for a public defender routinely obtain one. There are several reasons for this. Perhaps most important is the prevailing belief among prosecutors, public defenders, and most judges that the formal guidelines are overly restrictive, and that by denying a person *free* counsel they are in effect denying him *any* counsel. As a consequence they may overlook an income ceiling or an obvious undervaluing of personal assets. Although some judges occasionally suggest it, few in fact seriously expect an applicant to sell his 5-year-old automobile in order to raise an attorney's fee.

A second reason is the drive for administrative efficiency. The application form requires detailed information about the applicant's financial condition, and to verify all of it would require more effort than the public defender is willing to extend in most cases. The public defender's staff finds it far easier to take the partial information at face value and recommend assignment of a public defender knowing that errors will be made. They justified this by arguing that it might permit a few more people to have a public defender than deserve one, but at least it does not exclude those who do. In addition, public defenders are reluctant to question or challenge ambiguous or inconsistent answers about income and assets, feeling that to do so would create an atmosphere of suspicion and hostility and undercut their ability to gain the full confidence of their clients.

But it can still be difficult to obtain an attorney. In court, the prosecutor's first question to an unrepresented defendant is: "Do you want to get your own attorney, apply for a public defender, or get your case over with today?" The very way the question is phrased encourages people *not* to seek counsel and suggests preferential treatment if they plead guilty immediately. If someone asks for a public defender, then he is shunted off for an interview to determine his eligibility, and the interview itself can become a humiliating experience.

In light of the consistently lenient sentences and the casual way in which so many cases linger on, it is understandable why many defendants do not obtain attorneys—public or private—at all, and when they do, why so many of them desire little more than a quick and perfunctory meeting with their attorneys.

CONTINUANCES

Although defendants usually want to get their cases over with as quickly as possible, they are not always successful. The court has its own pace, which is often at odds with the defendant's self-interest. Defense attorneys and prosecutors usually turn (or return) their attentions to a case on the morning it is scheduled on the calendar, and if they are not able to resolve any differences before the calendar call, they will agree to a (or another) continuance. Problems which impede the resolution of a case can vary considerably, and a great many continuations stem from confusion and carelessness. A defense attorney may have overcommitted himself on that day, or in a more difficult case be unwilling to spend a few additional moments to track down a full-time prosecutor. Occasionally, a defendant may appear in court only to find that his case is not on the calendar. Or the defense attorney may forget to show up. A court-ordered report such as a laboratory report on drugs may not have been completed, or a defendant's file may simply be lost. Whatever the reasons for delay, it may be two or three hours after the defendant has first taken his seat in the gallery before he is informed that his case will be continued. Rarely is this decision made in consultation with him or even with an appreciation of the problems it might involve for him. Unable to comprehend the details of court operations, most defendants are overwhelmed by the details of the processes. Rarely can they distinguish reasonable from unreasonable, careful from careless decisions, and they are left with generalized discontent and haunting suspicions.

But delay is not always the result of bumbling, and it is often a highly effective defense strategy. As one attorney observed:

We can make life difficult for the prosecutors by filing a lot of motions. . . . So when I push a legalistic line I am not expecting to have a complicated legal discourse; rather it's part of my ammunition to secure my objectives. They know I'm serious and that I'll spend a lot of time to pursue it. I'll wear them down that way.

Motions may be filed one at a time, so that a case may be strung out over a long period. Strategic delay can also be secured by pleading not guilty and asking for a trial by jury. This request automatically provides a several-week (and at times a several-month) continuance, during which period the complainant may calm down or restitution can be arranged.

Because delay can be and often is an effective defense strategy, it can also be used successfully by a defense attorney to justify his own carelessness or actions performed for the sake of convenience. While public defenders may use it to cope with a pressing caseload, private attorneys may use it to boost their own fees or insure payment. In any case, all but the most knowledgeable of defendants will be unable to identify the *real* reasons for delay.

FAILURE TO APPEAR

The Causes of Nonappearance

For many arrestees, the central question is not how to maneuver to reduce the chances of conviction, a harsh sentence, or the number of court appearances but whether to show up in court at all. This consideration is not restricted to a small handful of "absconders" or would-be absconders; it concerns large numbers of arrestees. Roughly one-third of those in my sample missed one or more of their scheduled court appearances, and a substantial number (one person in five) never did return to court even after they received repeated letters of warning. While a number of these people had their cases terminated by a court action which called for a "bond forfeiture with no further action," about one in every eight or nine cases was never formally resolved by the court in any way, and are filed as outstanding, closed only if and when the accused is arrested on other, unrelated charges. Most of those who fail to appear (FTA) are charged with minor misdemeanors, but the problem is by no means restricted to them. A third of the FTAs were charged with the most serious class of misdemeanors, and fully 20 percent of them were charged with felonies. Both in terms of absolute numbers and the seriousness of the charges, failures to appear present a serious and continuing problem for the court.

Like other efforts, mine to identify predictors of appearance/nonappearance focused on characteristics of *individual* defendants. Yet the discussion above suggests that the label FTA itself is problematic because it depends in part on whether a bondsman is present in court to secure a continuance and whether a prosecutor is willing to make accommodations for those who step out of the courtroom momentarily. Furthermore, by focusing on the *personal* characteristics of the defendant we overlook the importance of *organizational* features in the court which may encourage nonappearance. People without attorneys may *show up* in court with the same frequency as those with attorneys, but because their cases are not called until late in the day some of them give up and go home, either because they are bored and irritated or because they think a recess is an adjournment. My observations of the court lead me to believe that nonappearance is more likely to be accounted for in terms of how well defendants understand the operations of the court (e.g., are they in the correct courtroom?), how much respect they have for the court, how seriously they take the proceedings, how aware they are of their scheduled court appearances, and what they believe the consequences will be if they fail to appear. In other words, the *interaction between the court organization and the accused* is likely to provide the best explanation for appearance or nonappearance.

PRETRIAL DIVERSION

One way for an accused person to reduce the chances of conviction and postconviction penalty is to make an advance effort to "rehabilitate" himself. There are a variety of ways in which the accused can demonstrate this effort to the court. One way is the Pretrial Diversion Program sponsored by the New Haven Pretrial Services Council. Representatives of this program approach new arrestees who meet its initial eligibility criteria and offer them an opportunity to participate in its in-house group counseling program or to take advantage of its job placement services. If those who are accepted faithfully participate in these activities for a period of ninety days, then the program will recommend to the prosecutor that the charges be nolled.

Despite the seeming benefits which flow from this program, very few of the eligible arrestees take advantage of it. Estimates constructed from my sample indicated that over three-quarters of all arrestees met the program's *initial* eligibility requirements, but of the 800 eligibles for whom data were available, only 19, or 2.3 percent of them, actually participated in the diversion program. Officials of the diversion program attempt to account for these low numbers by pointing to the prosecutor's discretion to veto prospective participants who are otherwise eligible and interested. While these factors certainly limit the program's size, there is another much more important reason for its limited effectiveness: arrestees consider participation in the program itself a penalty that is much more severe than the one they think they will receive if they do *not* participate.

One evaluation of the program attempted to estimate what might have happened to the program's participants if they had not been diverted. Identifying a control group and tracing its path through the court, the researchers found that one-fifth to one-third of the control group obtained nolles or dismissals; most of them pleaded guilty and received a small fine of $10 to $20. *None* of them went to jail. In short, they concluded tentatively, those people who are eligible but decline to enter the diversion program are not likely to be treated harshly by the court.

In contrast, people who do participate in the program must agree to participate in regularly scheduled meetings for a three-month period with no definite assurances that their cases will be nolled afterward. It is not surprising, then, that so many people pass up the diversion program.

CONCLUSION:
THE AGGREGATED EFFECTS
OF THE PRETRIAL PROCESS

The costs of lower court—the tangible, direct, and immediate penalties extracted from those accused of minor criminal offenses—are not those factors which have received the greatest attention from legal scholars, social scientists, or indeed court officials. Liberal legal theory directs attention to formal outcomes, to the conditions giving rise to the application of the criminal sanction at adjudication and sentence. Much social science research has followed this lead, searching for the causes of sanctioning at these stages. But this emphasis produces a distorted vision of the process and the sanctions it dispenses. The real punishment for many people is the pretrial process itself; that is why criminally accused invoke so few of the adversarial options available to them.

This inverted system of justice dramatizes the dilemma of lower courts. Expanded procedures designed to improve the criminal process are not invoked because they might be counterproductive. Efforts to slow the process down and make it truly deliberative might lead to still harsher treatment of defendants and still more time loss for complainants and victims. Devices designed to control official discretion do not perform their expected functions (the failure to litigate bail is a clear case-in-point). And whereas rapid and perfunctory practices foster error and caprice, they do reduce pretrial costs and in the aggregate may render rough justice.

In light of the pretrial costs and the actual penalties meted out in the lower court, one is tempted to scoff at the formal theory which so ineffectively governs official behavior in the lower court and to dismiss it as unworkable and overly elegant—as proceduralism run amok—for the types of petty problems presented to the court. Would not simple summary justice with a minimum of procedures provide a more appropriate and workable set of standards? Perhaps the police court magistrate meting out immediate kadi-like justice without reliance on defense counsel—but also without the need for bail, repeated court appearances, and the like—might be more satisfactory. Or perhaps community-based courts might be more adept at ferreting out the underlying causes of conflict and providing ameliorating responses.

In a great many cases, these alternatives might work more effectively, yet the impulse for formality, even with its manifest shortcomings, cannot be so quickly dismissed. While lower courts sentence very few people to terms in jail, in theory almost all of those appearing before them face a slim possibility of incarceration. While creating a record of petty criminal offenses may not significantly affect the future of most people who find themselves before the bench, it can have a long-lasting and unpredictable impact on some. Citizenship can be placed in jeopardy, careers destroyed, aspirations dampened, delinquent propensities reinforced. Such problems may be few in number, but they do occur. And it is impossible to tell in advance which cases may precipitate these more serious consequences, since the specific impact of a record may not make itself felt until much later in life.

As long as conviction for petty criminal offenses carries the possibility of a jail sentence or of jeopardizing one's future, the ideal of a formal, adversarial process will remain strong and attractive even to those who acknowledge that the process itself is the punishment for most people. However, there may be some alternatives which both facilitate the rapid handling of petty cases and protect the interests of the accused.

Adjudication and Sentencing in a Misdemeanor Court: The Outcome Is the Punishment

JOHN PAUL RYAN

A description and analysis of the Columbus (Ohio) Municipal Court is presented in the context of comparison with Malcolm Feeley's recent study of the New Haven lower court. The findings suggest that the Columbus court is much more severe in the sanctions imposed upon convicted defendants. These differences are attributed, in part, to contrasting local political cultures whose influence upon courts is mediated by police department orientations, police-prosecutor relationships, and methods of judicial assignment.

INTRODUCTION

A recently published work on misdemeanor courts concludes that the major punishment of defendants occurs during the processing of their cases. Feeley contends that the pretrial costs associated with arrests on misdemeanor charges typically outweigh any punishments imposed after conviction. The need to make bail, hire an attorney, be present at court appearances, and even help prepare one's defense drain the economic and psychological resources of many defendants, whether they are ultimately adjudicated guilty or innocent. By contrast, the punishments meted out to defendants upon

From "Adjudication and Sentencing in a Misdemeanor Court: The Outcome Is the Punishment" by J. P. Ryan, 1980-81, *Law and Society Review*, 15, pp. 79-108. Copyright 1980 by the Law and Society Association. Reprinted by permission.

conviction appear insubstantial. Few are incarcerated, and fines rarely exceed $50.

These findings and arguments have a distinct appeal. They provide a new and creative interpretation to case processing in the lower criminal courts, one at variance with our understanding of felony courts. Yet as Feeley himself acknowledges, his work is a case study. His data are drawn exclusively from the New Haven (Connecticut) Court of Common Pleas. What about other misdemeanor courts? Is it reasonable to believe that most lower courts are like New Haven's? Studies of criminal justice and political culture might suggest otherwise. Levin's study of the felony courts of Pittsburgh and Minneapolis indicates substantial differences in sentencing severity, attributable in part to the political culture or values of the two communities. Levin found that sentences were typically less severe in the highly partisan, ethnically diverse, working-class city (Pittsburgh) than in the reform-minded, socially homogeneous city (Minneapolis). Similarly, Eisenstein and Jacob found sentencing practices in Baltimore to be much more harsh than in either Detroit or Chicago, and they attributed the greater harshness to a heritage of conservatism and racism in that southern border city. Likewise, the working environments of courts differ. In short, the character of a community—its history, politics, and lifestyle—affects what takes place in its courts, both in terms of process and outcomes.

If the relationships between political culture and trial courts are viewed at all seriously, one must question not only the generalizability of

Feeley's data but also his primary argument. More data from different communities would help to show whether the process actually constitutes a substantial punishment in the lower courts. These data should speak to the processing of cases and defendants, because it can be expected that some courts minimize pretrial costs by expediting cases, liberalizing indigency requirements for counsel, and using cash bonds infrequently. Perhaps even more important, additional data should be collected on case outcomes, for likewise it can be expected that lower courts vary in the severity of sanctions imposed upon convicted defendants.

Data relating to process and outcomes in the Franklin County, Ohio, Municipal Court (Columbus) are reported below. This inquiry, like Feeley's, is a case study, but one that serves as a counterpoint. The findings suggest that New Haven may be among the least punitive lower courts in the nation. The Columbus court is sufficiently more severe in its sanctions and less demanding in its process costs—that the outcome is the primary punishment. Throughout the chapter, comparative reference is made with an eye toward dramatizing the very real differences between the two courts.

Columbus and New Haven: Contrasting Local Political Cultures

Columbus is a medium-sized American city, more populous and more sprawling than New Haven. Over half a million people live in the city of Columbus, a figure sharply on the rise in the 1960s and early 1970s, compared with a steadily declining population in New Haven of only 125,000. The citizenry of Columbus is better educated, more affluent, and of different ethnic origins than that of New Haven. Feeley aptly characterizes New Haven as a town "beset with the standard ills of many old urban areas— shrinking population, declining tax base, deteriorating housing, smog, poor schools, encroaching superhighways, and an increasing underemployed minority population." In a comparative vein, Feeley goes on to say:

It [New Haven] represents neither the worst nor the best of American urban centers. It does not

convey the sense of hopelessness and decay that observers report in such urban centers as Newark or Gary, nor . . . the same sense of optimism as do new and more culturally homogeneous and prosperous cities as Des Moines or Minneapolis . . . [or, one might add, Columbus].

These differences in the physical and cultural characteristics of the two cities predictably presage differences of political culture. New Haven is predominantly Democratic in partisanship; Columbus is heavily Republican, an "urban Republican stronghold." Differences in partisan orientation are evident in presidential votes, mayoralty elections, and congressional representation. Columbus has not had a Democratic mayor in the past decade; New Haven has not had a Republican mayor in two decades. Two conservative Republicans represent portions of Columbus and its surrounding suburbs in Washington; one liberal Democrat represents New Haven. The political affiliation of judges, too, parallels community orientations, although judges are formally appointed on a statewide basis in Connecticut and elected locally in Ohio. Feeley reported four Democratic and three Republican judges in the New Haven lower court. At the time of the study in Columbus, twelve Republican judges sat with a lone Democratic judge in that municipal court. Equally important, the significance of partisanship in the delivery of public services is much greater in New Haven than in the "good government" atmosphere of Columbus.

The political structure of the two communities also differs. Although both claim mayor-council forms of government, the similarity ends there. New Haven has been described as having a pluralistic leadership structure. More impressionistical, Columbus has been described as relatively monolithic, dominated economically by big banks and insurance companies and ideologically by the Wolfe family and their newspaper, and lacking New Haven's "vigorous group of residents involved in actively trying to cope with problems."

The courts also look quite different in their personnel, operations, and informal relationships. These differences are often traceable to the local political culture. Feeley reports a substantial patronage system surrounding the New Haven courthouse, even after reforms intended to alleviate political influence in the courts were enacted. For example, judgeships are viewed as rewards for faithful party service. Prosecutors and public defenders are likely to be drawn from families active in the local political organizations. Lower-level personnel (deputies, clerks, etc.) are likely to come from the ranks of "ward leaders and vote mobilizers." Columbus, by contrast, reflects little political influence of this kind in its courts. Judgeships come either from association with the governor or a popular local campaign, possibly aided by bar endorsement. Prosecutors and public defenders need not have political sponsors. Lower-level court personnel are recruited through an elaborate system of checks and balances designed to remove partisan politics and judicial whim.

The orientation of the police department and its relations with the prosecutor's office are also quite distinctive in the two communities. Feeley describes the New Haven police department as oriented to dispute resolution or, in Wilson's terminology, "order-maintenance." Accordingly, it is not surprising that the police appear to play a small role in the development of prosecution cases, having little communication with the prosecutor and rarely appearing as witnesses in court. Prosecutors seem dominant vis-à-vis the police in the New Haven court, albeit both share dispute-processing views of the role of the lower court. In Columbus, the police department is much better characterized as "law enforcement" oriented, accounting for the importance which police officers attach to successful prosecution of minor cases. Officers regularly appear as witnesses in brief trials and are ready to appear on other occasions when a plea is entered. Indeed, when police officers "hang around" the Columbus court waiting for their cases to be called, they often sit in other courtrooms watching outcomes (with occasional astonishment at the perceived leniency of some judges). In short, by custom the police in Columbus have been an important, perhaps dominant, force in the lower court, much to the chagrin of the local defense bar.

Finally, there are differences of court structure, rooted in political history, that affect relationships among courtroom actors, notably between judges and others. Connecticut, unlike Ohio, does statewide assignment of judges, which in practice means that lower-court judges are frequently rotated. Feeley argues that one important consequence of rotation is the gravitation of judicial responsibility toward prosecutors and others permanently assigned to one court. Judges in New Haven have been heard to ask prosecutors about the "going rate" for particular offenses, suggesting a desire to adhere to work-group norms. In Columbus, the judges— who are elected or appointed to that municipal court—are much more individualistic and autonomous in their approach to sentencing.

New Haven, in sum, is a criminal court system that reflects the "particularistic values of ethnic, religious, political, and family associations" in its rendering of "swift, substantive justice." Columbus, by contrast, is a system that reflects the universalistic values of professional competence and technical efficiency in its rendering of swift but formal justice through the mechanisms of an adversary system as applied to a misdemeanor court.

. . . . .

THE COLUMBUS COURTS CASELOAD: AN OVERVIEW

The Franklin County (Columbus) Municipal Court has jurisdiction over a variety of matters, including small claims, civil cases up to $10,000, and preliminary hearings in felony cases. As Table 1 indicates, the court's misdemeanor caseload is composed of almost equal proportions of traffic and criminal cases. Operating a motor vehicle under the influence of alcohol (OMVI) is the most frequent type of case, and it accounts for nearly two-thirds of all traffic cases. Other traffic cases include reckless operation of a motor vehicle (ROMV), driving without a valid license or with a suspended license, hit-and-run, speeding, and lesser violations. The dominance of OMVI cases is not unique to Columbus. Although arrests for drunk driving are more frequent in Columbus than elsewhere

TABLE 1

Distribution of the court's misdemeanor caseload (limited to cases scheduled for a pretrial).

	Percentage	N
Traffic		
OMVI[a]	30.2	834
Other traffic	17.8	492
Criminal		
Assault	17.1	472
Theft	10.8	300
Bad checks	7.1	196
Other criminal	17.0	470
	100.0	2,764

a. OMVI = operating a motor vehicle under the influence of alcohol.

in Ohio, other municipal courts also report a large percentage of drunk driving cases.

Assault is the most frequent type of criminal case, followed by theft and passing bad checks. Other criminal cases include trespass, carrying a concealed weapon, obstructing justice, disorderly conduct, soliciting, drug use, public indecency, housing code violations, fleeing from a police officer, and resisting arrest. The Columbus court's criminal caseload is presumably lightened by the operation of a night prosecutor program, which screens all citizen-initiated complaints and diverts interpersonal disputes and bad check cases, in substantial numbers, from the court.

Modes of Case Disposition

The court uses a number of ways to dispose of cases that proceed beyond arraignment. These include guilty plea to the original charge, guilty plea to a reduced charge, court trial, jury trial, bond forfeiture, dismissal, and—in multiple-charge cases—combinations of these. In addition, some defendants fail to appear, and these "no shows" are treated, for statistical purposes, as case terminations.

Almost half of the sample of cases in Columbus were disposed through a guilty plea, similar to the percentage in New Haven. The majority of these represent pleas to reduced charges, indicating a form of charge bargaining. Case type is the most important factor in determining whether a reduction of charges will occur. In OMVI cases in particular, a charge reduction is common. This reflects some uneasiness in imposing the required incarceration where a defendant is convicted of drunk driving.

· · · · ·

Prosecutors and defense counsel are the primary actors in the forging of guilty pleas, particularly in charge bargaining. But what about the role of the trial judge? Trial judges in misdemeanor courts do not always restrict their role to ratifying bargains struck by other parties. Observations in Columbus suggest that at least a few judges do actively engage in sentence bargaining from the bench. For example, Judge H, who has the reputation for making sentence commitments in advance as his normal practice, remarked to defense counsel in one case that was observed: "If the defendant wants to plead, I'll put on a fine and wrap it up today" (assault case). Judge D also encouraged guilty pleas, through a mixture of occasional sentence leniency and frequent gratuitous comments to defendants about the "break" they were getting. Furthermore, Judge D sometimes intimated that he would find a defendant guilty were the case to go to trial ("you gotta keep your eyes open" to a defendant charged with jaywalking, or "a driver has a responsibility, even under icy road conditions" to a defendant ticketed in an auto accident).

· · · · ·

Trials are very infrequent in Columbus, but they are by no means the extinct species which Feeley reports in New Haven. In the sample of 2,764 cases, 32 (1.1 percent) were resolved by jury trial and 46 (1.6 percent) by court trial. One gained the distinct impression from interviews and observations that trials are welcomed by many judges and attorneys, as an occasional relief from the monotony of calendar calls. Judge G remarked, "I enjoy trials when I get two good lawyers." The defender noted of Judge G, "He gives you a good trial." Not surprisingly then, trials proceeded in a thorough and unharried manner.

. . . . .

Conviction at trial is likely, but far from certain. Defendants fared better at jury trials, where the conviction rate was 56.3 percent (18 of 32 cases). In court trials, the conviction rate was 71.7 percent (33 of 46 cases). Likelihood of conviction varies by case type. Combining jury and court trials, the conviction rate was 5.5:1 in OMVI cases, 4:1 in theft cases, 3:1 in other traffic cases, 3:2 in other criminal cases, and a mere 2:3 in assault cases. The individual judge also makes some difference. Consider that two of the court's most active plea-bargaining judges, D and H, did not acquit a single defendant in the seven court trials which they heard. Their "inducements" to defendants to plead guilty, then, were reinforced by a reluctance to find for a defendant in a court trial.

. . . . .

Dismissals are a frequent occurrence in Columbus. One-third of the cases in the sample were dismissed (*nolle prosequi*). According to both the prosecutor and the defender, the most frequent cause of dismissal is the failure of the complaining witness to prosecute. These perceptions are supported by data collected and analyzed in the prosecutor's office. An examination of dismissals in January, 1979, revealed the lack of a prosecuting witness to be the most frequently noted reason. Most often it was a civilian witness, but occasionally it was the failure of a police witness to appear.

. . . . .

Defendants in Columbus who fail to appear for a pretrial session in the courtroom are not as lucky as some of the "no shows" in New Haven. It is one thing not to appear at arraignment in a petty case; these cases in Columbus typically result in a bond forfeiture and termination. Failure to appear at a pretrial invariably results in the issuing of a bench warrant by the judge, often with a substantial bond. No precise data are available on the percentage of these defendants who return to court for disposition, but court participants think the figure is quite high. For the sample period, 12 percent of all defendants scheduled to appear at a pretrial session failed to appear.

. . . . .

FORMS OF SENTENCE OR SANCTION

Misdemeanor courts inflict upon their convicted defendants a wider variety of less severe sanctions than do felony courts. The Columbus misdemeanor court is no exception. Fines, bond forfeitures, terms in the county jail or municipal workhouse, suspensions of a driver's license, attendance at programs for alcoholics and drunk drivers, and probation are among the primary sanctions available and employed by the court. Sometimes convicted defendants receive only one form of sentence, but quite often they face several sanctions.

Fines are routinely imposed upon convicted defendants in Columbus. Some judges frequently hand out stiff fines, then suspend a portion of the fine. The practice may be designed to enhance a judge's popularity, as a skeptical Judge G remarked, declaring that "a heavy fine makes the police happy . . . suspending part of it makes the defense happy." Alternatively, the suspension may help to "keep in line" a defendant placed on probation, as Judge E noted. Both of these judges occasionally suspend portions of fines. The motives of judges who frequently suspend large portions of stiff fines, like Judges C and M, are not always clear.

. . . . .

These fines represent a significant amount of money to most defendants, even in our presently inflated economy. This is particularly true for indigent defendants represented by the public

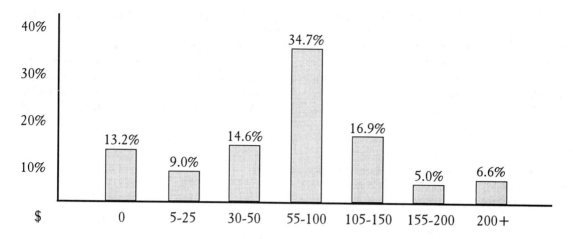

FIGURE 1 *Distribution of (net) fines (cumulates fines imposed upon a defendant convicted on more than one charge).*

Note: $N = 1,281$. $\overline{X} = \$111$. Statistics are based on a distribution excluding defendants not fined (0). $SD = 86$; median $= 100$; mode $= 100$.

defender's office. The severity of fines in Columbus is all the more striking when compared with New Haven. The two courts differ substantially in the amount of the fines they impose. In Columbus, nearly three-fourths of the net fines exceeded $50 (Figure 1), whereas only a handful of fines (4 percent) in New Haven were greater than $50. Furthermore, in Columbus 87 percent of all convicted defendants paid some fine, compared with only 45 percent in New Haven.

. . . . .

Jail terms are announced to a majority (52 percent) of convicted defendants. However, one-third of these terms are entirely suspended, and many others are suspended in part. The use of suspended sentences for jail terms is much more widespread among the court's judges; nine judges suspend, in part or whole, more than half of their jail terms. Nearly 35 percent of convicted defendants serve some jail time, most often in the city workhouse. About half of these defendants serve three or four days; most of the others serve either thirty days or a longer sentence. Defendants convicted in OMVI cases are most likely to be incarcerated (44 percent), but typically serve a short sentence (three or four days).

Comparisons with New Haven again are striking. Only 4.9 percent of convicted defendants in New Haven served a jail term, whereas almost *six times* as many defendants received a jail term in Columbus. Some mitigating factors should be considered in this comparison. Many defendants who do serve time in Columbus do not have their lives totally disrupted (e.g., by loss of job). It is common for shorter sentences, and even some longer sentences, to be served on weekends, a phenomenon growing in popularity elsewhere. Also, drunk driving cases contribute a moderately disproportionate number of jail terms in the Columbus court. Nevertheless, it appears that across a similar range of criminal cases (e.g., assault, theft) a defendant in Columbus stands a much higher likelihood of incarceration, if convicted.

. . . . .

Probation is extensively used as a sanction in this court. A supervising officer in the probation department reported that more than 2,000 defendants convicted on misdemeanor charges are currently on probation, and he noted that probation is more frequently used now than ever before. The bulk of the department's caseload stems from theft, bad check, and alcohol-related cases—areas where recidivism is high. Judges themselves vary in how often they use probation, some imposing it frequently, others selectively ("taking into account our caseload problems"), and one judge not at all. We have no further data on the use of probation, because the case files do not contain such information.

Finally, more than one type of sanction is often imposed. In criminal cases, about one defendant in five is incarcerated and fined. In traffic cases, fully half of all defendants face multiple sanctions involving some combination of fines, incarceration, suspension of the driver's license, and attendance at drunk-driver programs. Furthermore, the use of multiple sanctions is seemingly not considered in determining the severity of each sanction. For example, leniency in fines is generally not granted to defendants who are sentenced to serve time in jail. Indeed, defendants who are sentenced to serve jail time are fined more heavily ($121 on average) than those not incarcerated ($83 on average), differences mostly attributable to traffic cases. Similarly, defendants do not typically attend a drunk-driver's program in lieu of a (heavier) fine; it is usually in addition to the fine. The heaviest fines in OMVI and other traffic cases are levied against defendants who are incarcerated, lose their license for a period of time, and who must attend an alcohol-control program.

In sum, the Columbus misdemeanor court views the variety of sanctions available in a relatively punitive, rather than ameliorative, light. Instead of choosing which one sanction to employ against convicted defendants, this court often chooses *how much* of several sanctions. In this regard, the court is quite different from New Haven where fines are used much less frequently, and where combinations of probation and suspended sentence often serve as punishment. No wonder, perhaps, that Feeley viewed the process to be the primary punishment. In Columbus, the outcome is the punishment.

. . . . .

Urban Politics and Policy Outcomes: The Criminal Courts

MARTIN A. LEVIN

IN recent years, students of urban government have analyzed the ways in which conflict is managed in various cities. Some large cities (of over 300,000 in population) have a "traditional" political system with (typically) a formally partisan city government, with, to a varying degree, strong parties that (1) rely on material rewards rather than issues to attract members; (2) have a generally working-class orientation toward politics; (3) emphasize conferring material benefits upon individuals; (4) identify with local areas of the city, rather than the city "as a whole"; and (5) centralize influence. Other large cities have a "good government" or reform political system with (typically) a formally nonpartisan city government and weak parties which (1) rely on nonmaterial rewards (primarily issues or personalities); (2) have a generally middle-class orientation toward politics; (3) emphasize maximizing such values as efficiency, honesty, impartiality, professionalism, and an identification with the city "as a whole"; and (4) decentralize influence.

In, short, these studies sought to answer the question, "Who governs?" However, even more recently students of urban government have attempted to raise and answer a second and probably more important question: "What difference does it make who governs?" What difference does it make to *average citizens* whether they live in a city with a "traditional" political system or a "good government" political system? It is very likely, as James Q. Wilson has

argued, that the struggle for power in a city has little direct effect on the life of average citizens, but that the services provided by the government once in power (such as the administration of criminal justice, education, and welfare) are very likely to affect them directly and significantly. Moreover, it is possible that the policies followed in providing these services are closely related to, and indeed perhaps the product of, the city's political system. Thus, these policies can be viewed as the outputs of the city's political system, and the political processes of the city can be viewed as the inputs.

This chapter attempts to ascertain what consequences different political systems have for the sentencing decisions of the criminal court judges in Minneapolis and Pittsburgh and thus for the individuals that come into the courts. It also attempts to discover what happens when the selection of judges is taken "out of politics."

JUDICIAL AND POLITICAL REFORM, EVALUATION, AND THE APPROACH OF THIS STUDY

To evaluate empirically the consequences of differing political systems and differing judicial selection systems, comparative research was undertaken on the criminal courts and political systems of Pittsburgh and Minneapolis. These cities represent two more or less opposed types of political systems (the traditional and the good government, respectively) and both types of judicial selection systems (the political and the reform, respectively).

Pittsburgh has a formally partisan and highly centralized city government. In 1966, when this research was begun, the Democratic party organization was strong, hierarchical, disciplined, highly cohesive, and attracted workers with material incentives. It has dominated city politics since the early 1930s and has been influential in state and national politics. Public and party offices are filled by party professionals whose career patterns are hierarchical and regularized. They patiently "wait in line" because of the party's need to maintain ethnic and religious balance, even on a judicial ticket. There is a high degree of centralization of influence, and the citizens tend to accept pro-union and liberal social welfare policies. There is wide acceptance of partisanship and party activity in almost every sphere of Pittsburgh local government. Indeed, there has been little public enthusiasm for efforts to take the selection of judges out of politics, and parties view positions on the courts and their related agencies as primary sources of rewards for their workers.

There are nineteen judges on the Pittsburgh (Allegheny County) common pleas court (the trial court for both criminal and civil jurisdictions), and they are elected on a partisan basis for ten-year terms. Party designation appears on the ballot. In practice, the political parties, especially the Democratic party, dominate primaries and the general elections for judicial positions in Pittsburgh, and the local bar association usually plays a very limited role.

When a court vacancy occurs, the governor appoints a successor who must stand for reelection at the next general election. Ten of the nineteen incumbent judges in 1965 initially reached the bench in this manner. These interim appointments have also been controlled by the local parties. The Pittsburgh judges' career patterns also reflect the dominance of the parties and the limited role of the bar association in judicial selection. Almost all of the judges held a government position such as city solicitor, assistant prosecutor, city council member, state legislator, or even congressional representative prior to coming to the bench (all are partisan offices and are controlled by the parties). They were also active members of the party organization.

Minneapolis has a formally nonpartisan and structurally fragmented city government. The Democratic-Farmer-Labor (DFL) party and the Republican party play a significant but limited role in city politics. They are both formally (because of nonpartisan elections) and informally (because of the wide acceptance of nonpartisanship) limited. The parties are moderately weak, loosely organized, highly democratic, and undisciplined. They attract workers through nonmaterial incentives. Thus, the parties do not overcome the formal decentralization of authority in the city. Individuals, including "amateur" politicians with the ability and willingness to work but with little seniority in the party, can and do rise rapidly in the party and in city government. The citizens tend to be disposed toward conservative policies for city government. Nonpartisanship in city politics is accepted by the people and even by many party workers and some party leaders. Indeed, the electorate has had a strong negative response to candidates or incumbents who violate, or seem to violate, this ideal. This is especially true of the courts and their related agencies, and thus party leaders and workers tend not to regard them as a source of party rewards.

There are sixteen judges on the Minneapolis (Hennepin County) district court (the trial court for both criminal and civil jurisdictions), and they are formally elected for six-year terms on a nonpartisan basis. In practice, the political parties have almost no role in the selection of judges in Minneapolis, while the local bar association generally plays a major role. Prior to a judicial election, the Minneapolis Bar Association polls its members and publicizes the results. The "winner" of the poll (or the second or third highest candidate) almost always wins the election. The governor makes appointments to interim vacancies, and fourteen of the sixteen incumbent judges in 1965 initially reached the bench in this manner. When vacancies occur, the Minneapolis Bar Association conducts a poll, and the Minnesota governors have closely adhered to the bar's preferences. The two DFL governors who have served in the past ten years have been significant exceptions to this pattern, but they were strongly criticized for this (even by some of their own party members) and had to work carefully around the bar association. Moreover, during the administrations of these DFL governors, the party played almost no role in judicial selections because the governor's decisions were, at the most, influenced by "political" rather than "party" considerations (e.g., the appointees' relationships to these governors were personal rather than organizational).

The Minneapolis judges' career patterns also reflect the minor role of the parties and the major role of the bar association in judicial selection. Prior to coming to the bench, fourteen of the eighteen Minneapolis judges in this study had been exclusively or predominantly in private legal practice (usually business-oriented, and often corporate, practices). Those who held public positions before coming to the bench did not hold elective positions (with one exception) and were generally not active in either party.

To understand typical judicial behavior patterns in each city, sentencing decisions were compared statistically for the nine most common felony offenses. To understand the judges' attitudes, decision-making processes, and courtroom behavior, interviews were conducted with all but one of the judges in both cities, and courtroom trial proceedings were observed over a period of several months in 1966.

THE JUDGES'
SENTENCING DECISIONS

There are significant differences in the sentencing decisions of the judges in each city. On the whole, the decisions are more lenient in Pittsburgh than in Minneapolis. For example, white and black defendants receive both a greater percentage of probation and a shorter length of incarceration in Pittsburgh. Throughout every aspect of the data, the pattern runs almost entirely in one direction—greater leniency in Pittsburgh—and there are only some marginal variations in the degree of this greater leniency.

Although both white and black defendants receive more lenient sentences in Pittsburgh, in both cities whites receive a greater percentage of probation than blacks in most categories, and in Minneapolis whites receive a shorter length of incarceration than blacks in most categories. In

Pittsburgh, blacks receive a shorter length of incarceration than whites in almost all offenses. On the whole, sentencing decisions are more favorable for blacks in Pittsburgh than in Minneapolis, both in absolute terms and relative to whites.

In the comparison of sentencing decisions by type of plea, the Minneapolis judges penalize defendants who plead not guilty by giving them more severe sentences more frequently than do the Pittsburgh judges. On the whole, in Pittsburgh, decisions for such defendants are only slightly more severe than those for defendants who plead guilty; in Minneapolis much more severe.

There is also much more consistency in the length of the terms of incarceration in Minneapolis than in Pittsburgh. In Minneapolis, white and black defendants with the same type of prior record received the identical or nearly identical median term of incarceration in five of the seven offenses in which there is a sufficient number of cases for comparison. By contrast, there is almost none of this consistency in Pittsburgh. White and black defendants with the same type of prior record receive a nearly identical median term of incarceration in two of the nine offenses in which there are sufficient cases.

THE JUDGES' VIEWS AND
DECISION-MAKING PROCESSES

The Minneapolis judges typically tend to be more oriented toward "society" and its needs and protection than toward the defendant. They are also more oriented toward the goals of their professional peers. Their decision making is legalistic and universalistic. The Pittsburgh judges typically are oriented toward the defendant, and they tend to lack orientation toward punishment or deterrence. Their decision making is nonlegalistic in that it tends to be particularistic, pragmatic, and based on policy considerations.

There are also significant differences in the judges' courtroom behavior prior to sentencing. Most nonjury trials in Pittsburgh are informal (e.g., witnesses stand at the front bar) and abbreviated, and most of the judges prefer this arrangement. Most of the Pittsburgh judges also prefer informal procedures for obtaining information concerning defendants (the defense attorney's trial presentation, individuals intervening with the judge outside of court, the court staff's knowledge about the defendant) rather than the presentence investigations of the probation department. Trials in Minneapolis are formal, deliberate, and unabbreviated, and all of the judges prefer this arrangement. They also use presentence investigations in almost every case, and most of them dislike using any informal sources of information concerning the defendant. In both cities, plea bargaining is infrequent.

The Minneapolis and Pittsburgh judges' views, decision-making processes, and sentencing behavior very closely approximate two general models of decision making. The Minneapolis judges' views and behavior approximate a judicial decision-making model, and the Pittsburgh judges' approximate an administrative decision-making model. The judicial model has the following characteristics: (1) Decisions are made on the basis of the "best" evidence as defined under the laws of evidence. (2) Decisions are made on the basis of complete evidence as developed by the adversary system. (3) Judges feel that they must maintain an image of detached objectivity, because it is as important to appear just as to be just. (4) A judge's decisions have a dichotomous specificity (yes-no), and they must assign legal wrong to one of the two parties. (5) Judges deduce their decision by a formal line of reasoning from legal principles that exist independent of policy considerations. (6) Judges evaluate their success by the degree to which their decisions have followed these procedures and by their satisfaction of abstract notions of justice and law. They generally have greater concern for procedure than for substantive issues, and thus are more concerned with satisfying "the law" as an abstract doctrine than arriving at "just" settlements of individual cases. (7) Judges base their decisions on what they feel is best in objective terms—their criteria usually come from "the law" rather than what might be considered best from the perspective of the individual's self-interest, and they reach their decisions regardless of considerations of person.

The administrative model of decision making has the following characteristics: (1) Decisions are made on the basis of the kind of evidence on which reasonable people customarily make day-to-day decisions. (2) Decisions are made on the basis of sufficient evidence gathered by the administrator's own investigation, and the length and depth of the investigation is determined by the resources available. (3) Administrators feel that they must seek intimate contact with the real world to be able to administer effectively. They feel that this is more important than maintaining an image of detached objectivity (i.e., appearing just). (4) Administrators may adopt dichotomous (yes-no) or intermediate decisions (e.g., compromise decisions or delayed enforcement of a decision). (5) Administrators deduce their decisions by pragmatic methods from the policy goals incorporated in the programs they administer. They have greater concern for arriving at "just" settlements based on the particular merits of individual cases than for adherence to abstract notions of justice and the law. They seek to give their clients what they feel they "deserve" and they base their decisions in large part on the needs of their individual clients. (In some instances, administrators may perceive that one of their client needs is exemption from the treatment involved in their program.) (6) Administrators have greater concern for substantive issues than for procedure, and thus they evaluate their success by the way the programs they administer "fit" real-world demands and supports. Thirteen of the seventeen Minneapolis judges seem to have little empathy for the defendants whom they describe as "coming from low intelligence groups," "crummy people," "congenital criminals," "not learning from their mistakes," or "not able to consider the consequences before they act." They tend to be resigned to the "criminality" of most defendants and often seem inclined to "give up" on them. The Minneapolis judges' tendency to penalize with more severe sentences defendants who plead not guilty seems to be an indication of their greater concern for the needs of society than for the defendants.

Universal criteria dominate the Minneapolis judges' decision making. They rarely regard individual characteristics (age, whether only property is involved in the crime, a black defendant's environment, a favorable family or employment situation, or addiction to alcohol or narcotics) as a legitimate basis for making exceptions. They tend to follow a doctrine of equity rather formalistically: their consideration of individual and personal characteristics tends to be limited to highly unusual situations. Judge Slovak described such a situation:

There are only a few situations in which I will give a fellow extra consideration. I had one in here on burglary and his attorney made a very emotional plea about the fellow's wife going blind and that he had to raise some money to help her. So I gave him probation.

In short, their legalistic decision making is based on attributes of behavior rather than attributes of person. It tends to be based on the legal view of the act with little consideration of the context of the act—especially the personal context—or distinctions that might be made on this basis.

In Pittsburgh, judges' decision making is characterized by numerous exceptions, which tend to be made in the direction of lenient decisions. Sixteen of the eighteen judges describe their decision making as being exceptional and expedient. They speak of seeking bases for making an exception, giving defendants "breaks," and "helping" them. For example, Judge Guggliemi explained,

If I can find a way—if the evidence ameliorates in some way—I'll give [the defendant] a "break." I suppose that it's unfair, but I try to help as many as I can. . . . I'm not constrained in sentencing by viewing defendants in set categories; I'm just trying to help them out.

The basis of these exceptions are not distinctions defined by the law as being relevant; they are distinctions based on the policy considerations which the judges feel are relevant to their decision making. These judges seem to consider one of the following characteristics as bases for making exceptions and giving breaks: the absence of a prior record, youthfulness, the commission of "only" a crime against property, the

defendant's "nonprofessional criminal" status, the environmental background of a black defendant, or the defendant's "favorable" employment or family situation.

THE EXPLANATION OF THE JUDGES' VIEWS AND BEHAVIOR

The behavior of the Pittsburgh and Minneapolis judges appears to be the indirect product of the cities' political systems. These systems influence judicial selection, leading to differential patterns of socialization and recruitment that in turn influence the judges' views and decision-making processes. The prejudicial careers of most of the Pittsburgh judges in political parties and government and their minority ethnic and lower-income backgrounds seem to contribute to the development of the characteristic which many successful, local professional politicians possess—the ability to empathize and to grasp the motives of others by entering imaginatively into their feelings. This prejudicial experience (reinforced by the lack of highly legalistic experience) seems to have contributed to the nonlegalistic, particularistic character of the judges' decision making, their focus on police considerations, and their use of pragmatic criteria.

Their client relationships were usually characterized by expedient, exceptional, benevolent, and affirmative decisions which were the antithesis of legalistic behavior. Their decisions focused on interpersonal relationships and involved a great deal of discretion with little attention given to general rules. Indeed a primary task of local party workers is to view a situation in personal terms, to dispense favors, and to make exceptions rather than to apply legal rules. It is usually their job to say yes particularly to an individual who has a problem or who is in trouble. The Pittsburgh judges seem to have brought many of these patterns to the bench with them.

The predominantly legalistic prejudicial careers of most of the Minneapolis judges and their predominantly middle-class, northern-European, Protestant backgrounds seem to have contributed to the development of their greater orientation toward "society" than toward the defendant. In their careers, few had contact with individuals from lower-income backgrounds. Their experience in predominantly business-oriented private practice typically involved major societal institutions such as the law, corporations, and commercial transactions.

This prejudicial experience (reinforced by their lack of party policy-oriented experiences) seems to have contributed to the legalistic and universalistic character of their decision making and their eschewal of policy considerations. In this milieu, rules are generally emphasized, especially legalistic ones; these rules were used to maintain and protect these societal institutions. Learning to "get around" involved skill in operating in a context of rules. Their success seems to have depended more on their objective achievements and skills than on personal relationships. Furthermore, the predominantly middle-class background of these judges may in itself have contributed directly to the development of their universalistic decision making and their emphasis on the importance of laws.

Both the judges' social backgrounds and prejudicial career experiences seem to have influenced their decision making. However, in both cities the decision making of the judges with cross-cutting backgrounds and experiences in effect serves as a control, and it seems to indicate that prejudicial career experiences have been the more important influence. The decision making of the few Pittsburgh judges with middle-class, Protestant backgrounds who also had careers in party and government positions tends to be oriented toward the defendant, particularistic, and based on policy considerations. Unfortunately, all of the Pittsburgh judges with minority ethnic and lower-class backgrounds also had party and government careers, and thus this conclusion cannot be tested with both variables independently controlled, but it can be in Minneapolis. The decision making of the few Minneapolis judges with middle-class, northern-European, Protestant backgrounds who had less legalistic careers tend to be less oriented toward society and less legalistic and universalistic than that of most of the other Minneapolis judges.

EVALUATING THE COURTS AND SOME POLICY IMPLICATIONS

This analysis of the Pittsburgh and Minneapolis judges' decision making in criminal court indicates some of the consequences of these cities' political systems and methods of judicial selection. However, to more fully understand these consequences, some evaluation of these judges' decisions in themselves is necessary.

Ultimately, this evaluation must examine the Pittsburgh and Minneapolis criminal court judges directly in terms of their behavior—lenient decisions and informal procedures in Pittsburgh and more severe decisions and formal procedures in Minneapolis. It is possible to make a persuasive case for the Minneapolis criminal court in terms of the goals of equality and the "rule of law," all other things being equal. In actual policy situations, however, "all other things" are rarely equal. Realistic policy choices are never made in an ideal context, but in a real, and therefore imperfect, context. Most big-city criminal courts, including those in this study, operate in a context of a heterogeneous population which includes a large proportion of lower-class and minority-group individuals.

In this context, it is possible to make a persuasive case for the Pittsburgh criminal court whose judges often tend to base their decisions on the standards of conduct of the group in which the offense occurred. Indeed, the assumptions of the rule of law (that all men are equal or similar) seldom square with the realities of our urban context. Nevertheless, despite the benevolence of intention, criminal court decisions based on these extralegal standards may tend to have serious unintended consequences. John Dollard suggests this with respect to criminal justice in the South. He concludes that among the institutional features of southern life that sustain the high level of aggression among poor blacks is the double standard of justice—viewing "black crime" as less serious than "white crime." This tension between the style of criminal court which may be preferable in an ideal context and that which may be necessary because of the actual context and the difficulties inherent in the latter style seems to be a product of a more general tension in the larger cities of our society and in our theory of democracy. According to the rule of law and democratic theory, we ought to ignore class differences, but urban realities are such that it is difficult. "Two cultures" exist in our large cities—a large lower class as well as the dominant middle-class culture—but our theory of democracy assumes that we will be a society with one culture. It assumes that we will be able and willing to live together under a single set of rules or standards. The idea that two sets of rules may be necessary—one for the middle class and the other for the lower class—cannot be reconciled to our theory.

This tension indicates that any evaluation or policy prescription concerning the criminal courts in our large cities must consider the ex-istence of these two cultures. The Minneapolis judges tend to adhere to the rule of law, but they fail to consider these two cultures. On the other hand, the Pittsburgh judges, in part, often tend to base their decisions on the existence of these two cultures, but they usually fail to adhere to the rule of law. These shortcomings in both courts are thus largely a function of these two cultures—a factor *external* to these court systems. Any prescription for remedying these inadequacies should be primarily directed at this external factor and more basic cause. As long as these two cultures exist, there will be a tension in our theory of democracy, and the criminal courts will have to ignore either the rule of law or the realities of urban life.

Pennsylvania's Sentencing Reform: The Impact of Commission-Established Guidelines

JOHN H. KRAMER
ROBIN L. LUBITZ

E ARLY reform advocates who called for the replacement of indeterminate sentences with determinate sentences hoped to create more certain, more lenient, and less disparate sentences. These hopes have given way to the cautions of the 1980s. It is not necessary to recount here the debate regarding the potential of determinate sentencing except to point out that the advocates criticized judicial and parole board discretion under indeterminate sentencing and the level of punishment administered under the rehabilitative ideal.

These early critics proposed various mechanisms to replace the unfair, uncertain, harsh, and ineffective indeterminate sentence. They have been joined in the attack by conservatives who likewise view indeterminacy as too uncertain and disparate but see the result as excessive leniency rather than excessive harshness. The legislative accords struck between the liberals and conservatives are sentencing reforms that fall far short of the liberal goals.

The early failures of Maine, Illinois, Indiana, and, to a lesser degree, California to fulfill the aims of determinacy are attributed to the inability of the legislature to withstand the conservative arguments. In addition, legislatures are seen as incapable of developing sentencing reform that is adequate to cope with the complexity of the sentencing process. To withstand this trend, reformers began to propose that the mechanism best suited to developing a reasonable and coherent sentencing scheme was a commission. In 1978, Singer summarizes the arguments:

The debate over "just deserts" as a sentencing principle continues in this country. A common criticism of that principle is that legislatures will set unreasonably high sentences. This problem might be avoided if the responsibility for setting sentence guidelines were confined to a separate body—that is, a sentencing commission. Removed from the immediate political furor and composed of various representatives of the criminal justice community, as well as lay members, the sentencing commission would both establish and revise sentencing guidelines for judges on the basis of continuing collection of data.

Such a broad-based and somewhat insulated commission would be able to write comprehensive and rational sentencing guidelines and also be able to implement, monitor, and revise them.

Minnesota, Pennsylvania, and Washington have all adopted the sentencing commission approach to sentencing reform. The guidelines developed by each of these commissions are more complex and comprehensive than legislatively developed reform. Particularly important, each has established extensive training, monitoring, and evaluation mechanisms for their im-

From "Pennsylvania's Sentencing Reform: The Impact of Commission-Established Guidelines" by J. H. Kramer and R. L. Lubitz, 1985, *Crime and Delinquency, 31,* pp. 481-500. Copyright 1985 by Sage Publications, Inc. Reprinted by permission.

plementation. The unanswered question is whether or not commission-based guidelines will actually affect the sentences given. Because of the ability of courtroom work groups to subvert the enactments, it is possible that these reform efforts will not change sentencing. Rather, it might be hypothesized that guidelines will make no difference in sentencing decisions.

In this essay, we report on the impact of Pennsylvania's sentencing guidelines. However, prior to presenting the methodology and impact data, we think it important to describe the guidelines in some detail.

THE GUIDELINES IN PENNSYLVANIA

The Pennsylvania Commission on Sentencing was created by the legislature in 1978 and given the responsibility to promulgate sentencing guidelines that would specify (1) a range of sentences for crimes of a given degree of gravity; (2) an increased range of sentences for crimes involving use of a deadly weapon; (3) an increased range of sentences for defendants with prior felony convictions; and (4) variations from these ranges on account of aggravating or mitigating circumstances.

The legislation creating the commission differs from states that have adopted determinate sentencing in that it maintains the parole board and the indeterminate sentence. Thus, the commission's task was to author guidelines that structure judicial discretion regarding incarceration and length of confinement. The minimum sentence in Pennsylvania is the parole eligibility date for any sentence with a maximum equal to or greater than two years. Sentences with maximums less than two years are generally served in county institutions and under the parole discretion of the sentencing judge.

Under the guidelines, all defendants receive an offense gravity score based on the seriousness of the crime committed and a prior record score reflecting the extent and gravity of criminal history. These two scores allow the judge to locate the sentencing recommendations on a Sentence Range Chart (see Figure 1).

For each combination of offense gravity score and prior record score, three levels of recommended guideline ranges are prescribed: the standard range, the aggravated range (for use when aggravating circumstances are present), and the mitigated range (for use when mitigating circumstances are present). The ranges refer to the minimum sentence under Pennsylvania law.

An enhanced range of guideline sentences is prescribed when the defendant uses a deadly weapon during the commission of the offense. When the judge determines that none of these ranges are appropriate, he or she may sentence outside of the guidelines but must provide a contemporaneous written statement of the reasons for the departure. The enabling legislation provides both the district attorney and the defense attorney the right to appeal the sentence.

Fairness and Guideline Simplicity

The guidelines provide ranges of sentences for each combination of offense gravity score and prior record score. Although this scaling system is generally successful in grouping together similar offenders and offenses, the commission recognized the cautions of the Twentieth Century Fund Report and Singer that these categorizations are oversimplifications. There are many subtle and important variations in offense behavior and offender culpability not built into this system. The Twentieth Century Fund Report clearly points out the diversity of criminal behavior that falls under any particular statutory definition. Once presumptive sentences or ranges are attached to these statutory definitions, the risk is that the diversity of behaviors (and, most important, the differences in severity of criminal behavior) is lost in favor of simplicity. The loss is in terms of fairness and equitability.

WILL GUIDELINES MAKE A DIFFERENCE?

There are several factors that have been postulated to affect the impact of guidelines on sentencing practices. The earlier literature cited the need for guidelines to have the enforcement of

Offense Gravity Score	Prior Record Score	Standard Range*	Aggravated Range*	Mitigated Range*
10 Third-degree murder**	0	48-120	Statutory limit***	36-48
	1	54-120	Statutory limit***	40-54
	2	60-120	Statutory limit***	45-60
	3	72-120	Statutory limit***	54-72
	4	84-120	Statutory limit***	63-84
	5	96-120	Statutory limit***	72-96
	6	102-120	Statutory limit***	76-102
9 For example: rape; robbery inflicting serious bodily injury**	0	36-60	60-75	27-36
	1	42-66	66-82	31-42
	2	48-72	72-90	36-48
	3	54-78	78-97	40-54
	4	66-84	74-105	49-66
	5	72-90	90-112	54-72
	6	78-102	102-120	58-78
8 For example: kidnapping; arson (Felony I); voluntary manslaughter**	0	24-48	48-60	18-24
	1	30-54	54-68	22-30
	2	36-60	60-75	27-36
	3	42-66	66-82	32-42
	4	54-72	72-90	40-54
	5	60-78	78-98	45-60
	6	66-90	90-112	50-66
7 For example: aggravated assault causing serious bodily injury; robbery threatening serious bodily injury**	0	8-12	12-18	4-8
	1	12-29	29-36	9-12
	2	17-34	34-42	12-17
	3	22-39	39-49	16-22
	4	33-49	49-61	25-33
	5	38-54	54-68	28-38
	6	43-64	64-80	32-43
6 For example: robbery inflicting bodily injury; theft by extortion (Felony III)**	0	4-12	12-18	2-4
	1	6-12	12-18	3-6
	2	8-12	12-18	4-8
	3	12-29	29-36	9-12
	4	23-34	34-42	17-23
	5	28-44	44-55	21-28
	6	33-49	49-61	25-33

FIGURE 1 *Pennsylvania Sentence Range Chart.*

*Weapon enhancement: At least 12 months and up to 24 months of confinement must be added to the above lengths when a deadly weapon was used in the crime.

**These offenses are listed here for illustrative purposes only. Offense scores are given in § 303.7.

***Statutory limit is defined as the longest minimum sentence permitted by law.

law; to be developed by a broad-based, respected commission; and to be accompanied by extensive training and monitoring. Pennsylvania's guidelines meet each of these criteria; however, another issue that has implications for the impact of the guidelines on sentencing is the width of the guideline ranges.

Width of Guideline Ranges

The wider the ranges provided the judiciary, the less the impact of the guidelines on sentencing practices. This may appear obvious; however, it is too important to overlook. The wider the ranges provided under the guidelines, the greater the discretion left to the judge; therefore, the more likely that judges will be able to sentence as they have in the past. Pennsylvania has established ranges that are relatively wide when compared to those established in Minnesota and Washington. However, in comparison to the determinate sentencing laws in Illinois and Indiana, Pennsylvania's ranges are relatively narrow. Moreover, Pennsylvania establishes that incarceration is the appropriate sentence for certain crimes, whereas Illinois, Indiana, and California generally leave that decision to the judge. In this respect, Pennsylvania does, in fact, give more guidance to the judiciary. In addition, by looking at sentencing practices in 1980 and comparing them to the guideline sentences, we know that the guidelines are substantially different from past practice.

METHODOLOGY

The postguideline sentencing data are based on sentences reported to the commission as part of its Guideline Evaluation and Monitoring System. To date, 19,213 sentences imposed in 1983 have been reported to and processed by the commission for offenses that occurred on or after July 22, 1982 (the effective date of the guidelines). Some sentences imposed during November and December of 1983 are still being processed and are not included in the postguidelines database. Additionally, because the data are based on offenses occurring after a specific date, those offenses that are processed most expedi-

tiously through the court system are most likely to be included in the data. For these reasons, the data may underrepresent serious offenses that generally take longer to process through the courts.

The preguideline data are based on a study of 1980 sentences imposed in 23 representative Pennsylvania counties (Pennsylvania has 67 counties). These counties were selected according to their population and geographical placement in order to ensure that counties of all sizes in all regions of the state were represented in the data. Information was collected for sentences imposed for the crimes of aggravated assault, burglary, rape, and robbery. In most of the counties, information was collected on all appropriate sentences. However, in four of the larger counties, systematic samples were chosen. In Philadelphia and Allegheny counties, random samples of sentences were selected for each of the four crime categories.

IMPACT OF SENTENCING GUIDELINES

This section investigates the impact that sentencing guidelines have had on sentences imposed in Pennsylvania. First, current sentencing practices under the guidelines are examined and particular attention is paid to conformity to the guidelines and the role of race in judicial sentencing. Second, preguideline information is compared with postguideline data to analyze changes in rural/urban sentencing practices, in incarceration decisions, and on sentencing disparity.

Current Compliance to Guidelines

Approximately 88 percent of all sentences fell within the recommended guideline ranges in 1983; 81.9 percent fell within the standard range, 1.4 percent fell within the aggravated range, and 4.7 percent fell within the mitigated range. The remaining 12 percent of all sentences departed from the guideline recommendations. For the vast majority of these departures (90 percent), sentences were imposed that were less severe than those recommended by the guidelines. The overall compliance rate to the guidelines is deceptively high because it includes a large number of misdemeanors for which the guideline ranges are very wide relative to the statutory limits; therefore, they exhibit extremely high rates of compliance. In general, the more serious the offenses, the lower the conformity rates.

Clearly, overall compliance varies substantially depending on the crime. In particular, conformity levels for the crimes of aggravated assault, arson, escape, and involuntary deviate sexual intercourse are lower than most other offenses. The high departure rates for these offenses are not particularly surprising. The guideline recommendations for these offenses represent substantial increases over past sentencing patterns, and resistance to these changes is to be expected. In addition, it is possible that arson and aggravated assault may be overcharged by prosecutors and, thus, result in more frequent departures below the guidelines.

The Influence of Race in Current Sentencing Practices

In order for guidelines to fulfill their goal of promoting fairness and equity in sentencing, it is imperative that they be free of racial or ethnic bias. In order to test whether the guidelines are neutral with respect to the race of the defendant, sentences imposed under the guidelines are analyzed to see if there are detectable differences between sentences imposed for whites and nonwhites. Overall, nonwhites have slightly higher incarceration rates and longer average minimum sentences.

To test whether these differences are explained by differences in prior record or offenses gravity, the expected nonwhite incarceration rates and minimum incarceration lengths are calculated. This assumes that nonwhites were sentenced exactly the same as whites. To perform this calculation, the number of nonwhites in each cell of the guideline matrix was multiplied by the in-cell white incarceration rate and the in-cell white average minimum incarceration length. As a result of these calculations, overall incarceration rates and average incarceration lengths were computed. Again, this assumes that nonwhites were sentenced the same as whites. The results indicate that the expected incarceration rates and minimum incarceration lengths are very similar to the actual figures.

Based on this preliminary comparison, there do not appear to be any racial sentencing differences that are detectable by this analysis within the structure of the guidelines. This finding is of particular note in view of Knapp's findings in Minnesota that "after controlling for the severity levels and criminal history scores (guideline indices), minority offenders receive more severe sanctions than white offenders." Our results do not, of course, rule out racial bias in arrest, charging, plea-bargaining, or conviction practices.

Preguideline and Postguideline Sentencing Comparisons

In this section, 1983 (postguideline) compliance with the guidelines is compared to 1980 (preguideline) consistency with the guidelines. Blumstein and his colleagues distinguished between consistency and compliance as follows:

A sentence is compliant with the guidelines when a judge has consciously considered the sentences indicated by the applicable guideline sentence and elected to impose a sentence within the guideline range. A sentence may be consistent with guidelines even if a judge was unaware of their existence.

For our purposes, preguideline consistency with the guidelines was found by applying the guidelines retroactively to the 1980 sentences. In order for a sentence to be either consistent or compliant with the guidelines, it must have fallen within the standard, aggravated, or mitigated guideline range.

Overall consistency with the guidelines was extremely low in the 1980 data, whereas the postguideline data show a large increase in overall guideline compliance. Most of this increase is attributable to sentences previously below the guidelines that moved into the guideline ranges. These data show that the guidelines are recommending sentences that vary substantially from past practice and that the guidelines appear to have altered current sentencing practices.

One research question is whether consistency or compliance with the guidelines is dispositional (related to the in/out decision) or durational (related to length of confinement for "in" sentences). The current level of agreement to the guideline in/out recommendation shows a substantial increase over the preguideline data. Agreement with the durational recommendation (standard, aggravated, or mitigated range) has increased over the preguideline data.

Rural and Urban Sentencing Differences

Prior to the creation of the sentencing commission, there was widespread belief that sentences in urban areas of the state (especially Philadelphia and Pittsburgh) were generally less severe than those imposed elsewhere in the state. A study of 1977 sentences conducted by the commission found that overall county incarceration rates were related to overall county population density. The more urban counties, which included higher proportions of serious crimes and higher proportions of offenders with long prior records, exhibited the lowest incarceration rates.

With the promulgation of guidelines, it was anticipated that the sentencing differential between rural and urban counties would be reduced. In 1980, there were substantial differences in the levels of guideline consistency for the various groups of counties, ranging from 27 percent in Philadelphia to 62 percent in rural/unpopulated counties. In the postguideline data, the levels of guideline compliance increased (relative to 1980) in all counties. More important, the large differences in compliance levels among counties were greatly reduced.

Reductions in Judicial Sentencing Disparity

One of the primary reasons for establishing the sentencing commission was to address the problem of unjustified disparity in judicial sentencing. Although the concept of disparity is easily understood, it is difficult to operationalize. Commonly, sentencing disparity is defined as unlike punishment for like offenders. Difficulty arises, however, in identifying like offenders and in developing classification schemes for grouping like offenders into distinct categories. In many respects, disparity is in the eye of the beholder.

The commission elected to group like offenders based on their offense gravity and prior record scores. Accepting the premise that this classification scheme successfully identifies and groups similar offenders, it follows that all offenders in each group should receive similar sentences. The greater the variation of sentences within each classification category, the greater the disparity.

Impact of Guidelines on Incarceration

Much of the impetus for the guidelines stemmed from dissatisfaction with perceived leniency in judicial sentencing. Following legislative rejection of initial proposed guidelines, the general assembly instructed the commission to increase sentence severity for violent offenses. Given this background, it was expected that guidelines would increase overall sentencing severity for these serious crimes.

For all crimes, the rate of incarceration increased in the postguideline data as did the average minimum incarceration length for those incarcerated. These increases are most significant for aggravated assault and burglary and less substantial for rape and robbery. The net effect of these increases is an overall increase in the number of "months sentenced" (number incarcerated times average minimum incarceration length) for these target crimes.

Increases in sentence severity, however, are difficult to interpret because of the recent increase in sentencing severity that predates the sentencing guidelines. However, this problem does not affect the view that the guidelines have acted to reduce sentencing disparity.

DISCUSSION

The findings reported in this article strongly suggest that the imposition of sentencing guidelines has had an appreciable impact on sentencing practices in Pennsylvania. Sentencing patterns, which once showed wide variability, are now converging toward common guideline ranges. The extent of this change can be seen by contrasting the preguideline consistency figures with the postguideline compliance data. With this move toward sentencing uniformity, there has been a corresponding reduction in sentencing variability. Race appears to play no significant role in the imposition of sentences, and the influence of regional factors (urban vs. rural) has been greatly lessened. Furthermore, average incarceration rates and average sentence lengths have all moved toward the levels recommended by the guidelines. In concert, these findings imply a significant reduction in sentencing disparity as measured by the guidelines.

Why have the guidelines had such an impact? It has often been noted that organizations, and particularly courts, tend to reaffirm the status quo rather than adopt real change. The recent review of sentencing reform by Blumstein and his colleagues emphasizes that efforts to revise sentencing through mandatory sentences, presumptive sentences, or sentencing guidelines are often met with resistance and bureaucratic adjustments that serve to undermine the reform and to protect traditional authority. Pennsylvania's guidelines' apparent impact on sentencing may rest in large part on the commission's statutory power to write, promulgate, monitor, and revise guidelines. These powers are reinforced through a system of appellate review that grants either the defense or prosecution the right to appeal the sentence. With such formal authority, the commission exerts a powerful influence over judicial opinion and behavior. This legal authority is augmented by an aggressive program of guideline training, monitoring, and evaluation that keeps the commission highly visible within the courts.

SUGGESTED READINGS

Albonetti, Celesta A. 1987. "Prosecutorial Discretion: The Effects of Uncertainty." *Law & Society Review* 21:291-313.

―――. 1991. "An Analysis of Judicial Discretion: Toward a Reconceptualization of the Variables Affecting Sentence Severity." *Social Problems* 38:247-60.

Baldus, David C., Charles A. Pulaski, Jr., and George Woodworth. 1986. "Arbitrariness and Discrimination in the Administration of the Death Penalty: A Challenge to State Supreme Courts." *Stetson Law Review* 15:133-261.

Baldus, David C., George Woodworth, and Charles Pulaski. 1985. "Monitoring and Evaluating Contemporary Death Sentencing Systems: Lessons From Georgia." *U.C. Davis Law Review* 18:1375-1407.

Benson, Michael L. and Esteban Walker. 1988. "Sentencing the White-Collar Offender." *American Sociological Review* 53:294-302.

Bernstein, Ilene Nagel, William R. Kelly, and Patricia A. Doyle. 1977. "Societal Reaction to Deviants: The Case of Criminal Defendants." *American Sociological Review* 42:743-95.

Bowers, William J. and Glenn L. Pierce. 1980. "Arbitrariness and Discrimination Under Post-Furman Capital Statutes." *Crime & Delinquency* 26:563-635.

Eisenstein, James and Herbert Jacob. 1977. *Felony Justice: An Organizational Analysis of Criminal Courts.* Boston: Little, Brown.

Frankel, Marvin. 1972. *Criminal Sentences.* New York: Hill and Wang.

Greenberg, David and Drew Humphries. 1980. "The Cooptation of Fixed Sentencing Reform." *Crime & Delinquency* 26:206-23.

Heumann, Milton. 1977. *Plea Bargaining.* Chicago: University of Chicago Press.

Heumann, Milton and Colin Loftin. 1979. "Mandatory Sentencing and the Abolition of Plea Bargaining." *Law & Society Review* 13:393-430.

Katz, Jack. 1979. "Legality and Equality: Plea Bargaining in the Prosecution of White-Collar and Common Crimes." *Law & Society Review* 13:431-59.

Loftin, Colin, Milton Heumann, and David McDowall. 1983. "Mandatory Sentencing and Firearms Violence: Evaluating an Alternative to Gun Control." *Law & Society Review* 17:287-318.

Shapiro, Susan P. 1985. "The Road Not Taken: The Elusive Path to Criminal Prosecution for White-Collar Offenders." *Law & Society Review* 19:179-217.

Wolfgang, Marvin. 1974. "Racial Discrimination in the Death Sentence for Rape." Pp. 109-20 in *Executions in America,* edited by William J. Bowers. Lexington, MA: Lexington Books.

Wolfgang, Marvin and Marc Riedel. 1973. "Race, Judicial Discretion and the Death Penalty." *Annals of the American Academy of Political and Social Science* 407:119-33.

Zatz, Marjorie S. 1984. "Race, Ethnicity, and Determinate Sentencing: A New Dimension to an Old Controversy." *Criminology* 22:147-71.

―――. 1987. "The Changing Forms of Racial/Ethnic Biases in Sentencing." *Journal of Research in Crime and Delinquency* 24:69-92.

QUESTIONS FOR DISCUSSION AND WRITING

1. McDonald's essay maintains that the prosecutor's domain in the administration of justice has increased over time. Describe how this may have influenced the operating effectiveness and fairness of the courts in the handling of criminal cases?

2. Contrast the findings of Cole's study of the charging decision with Jacoby's analysis of charging styles. What conclusions do they share in common about factors influencing the decision to prosecute?

3. How would you characterize the changes that prosecutors experience over their careers in their views on plea bargaining?

4. A major concern of scholars who study the administration of criminal justice is whether structural aspects of the court—particularly, the informal norms and practices of the court as a social organization—influence the outcomes of cases. What evidence in the readings on defense attorneys supports the idea that informal norms and understandings among court officials may influence how defense attorneys handle their clients and caseloads? Explain.

5. Define and explain Blumberg's concept of defense lawyer as "double agent."

6. Sudnow concludes that defense attorneys use typifications of offenders to classify and process criminal cases. Is this appropriate, given that the typifications may influence how cases are ultimately decided?

7. The essays by Feeley, Ryan, and Levin reveal the importance of social and political context in understanding how judicial decisions are made. Basing your response on these essays, explain the process by which aspects of community political structure actually influences how judges reach decisions in criminal cases, either at adjudication or at sentencing.

8. The Kramer and Lubitz essay on sentencing guidelines argues that extensive judicial discretion in sentencing is problematic and warrants reform. Do you agree? Under what circumstances would it seem appropriate for judges to have extensive discretion in sentencing?

9. To what extent do you think the imposition of sentencing guidelines such as those described by Kramer and Lubitz can lessen the influence of factors such as community political structure, like that identified by Ryan and Levin, on the sentencing practices of judges? Explain.

V

WHAT ROLE DO THE CHARACTERISTICS OF INDIVIDUALS AND COMMUNITIES PLAY IN CRIMINAL JUSTICE?

THE administration of criminal justice relies heavily on symbolic representations of fairness to legitimate the power it exercises over individuals and groups in our society. No more salient among these symbols are the words *equal justice under the law* engraved in the stone facade of the U.S. Supreme Court building in Washington, D.C. These symbols are grounded in law—the U.S. Constitution and the laws and policies of virtually every federal and state court in the country espouse doctrines of equal protection and due process, equality of treatment by courts and court officials for those accused of crimes.

It should come as no surprise that social scientists who study the administration of criminal justice view the idea of equal treatment as complex and quite difficult to achieve. Many of the essays in earlier sections of this book reveal a system of justice that relies heavily on the individual judgment and discretion of legal officials. Further, officials' exercise of this discretion is often unequal and unfair. The essays by Skolnick and Fyfe on the police, Cole and Heumann on prosecutors, Blumberg and Sudnow on defense attorneys, and Ryan and Levin on judges portray decision making by officials as influenced as much by the social and political context in which decision making occurs as by the characteristics of defendants and criminal cases processed through the courts. The essays reveal decision-making practices that are more punitive toward some types of persons than toward others. Fyfe's research illustrates this idea most forcefully—persons of color are far more likely than are whites to be victims of shootings by police.

Part V of our book examines the characteristics of the accused and their communities. The five essays included in the section portray the administration of criminal justice quite differently. Whereas some of the essays maintain that individual and community characteristics play a limited role in legal decision making, others offer compelling evidence to the contrary. The first two essays examine different perspectives on the role of race in criminal sentencing. The first essay, Gary Kleck's "Racial Discrimination in Criminal Sentencing," provides an important review of previously published research on racial differences in sentencing. Kleck's essay asserts that many of the early studies showing pronounced racial differences in sentencing—with minority offenders typically receiving more severe penalties—ignored important differences among offenders in the crimes they committed and in their previous criminal records. Kleck believes that more recent studies taking these differences into account show very few unexplained race differences in sentencing. He concludes, based on a thorough review of the studies, that race by itself is not an important factor influencing the outcomes of sentencing decisions.

The second essay in this section, "Changing Conceptions of Race: Toward an Account of Anomalous Findings of Sentencing Research," summarizes the results of a sentencing study by Ruth Peterson and John Hagan. Peterson and Hagan's study is important for at least two reasons. First, their research suggests that whether race influences the outcomes of sentencing decisions depends in part on the temporal context in which sentencing takes place. During those periods when officials and the public perceive minority offenders as a particularly serious threat to communities, judges impose punishments that are more severe for minority offenders than for whites. The essay documents this pattern using information on drug dealing in New York in the 1970s. Second, Peterson and Hagan use very different types of evidence to support their claims. Drawing from court records and newspaper accounts of drug dealers, they show that black drug dealers were perceived as a very serious threat in New York during some periods of the 1970s and were punished much more severely than white dealers during the same period.

The third essay in the section examines gender differences in sentencing. Kathleen Daly's essay, "Discrimination in the Criminal Courts: Family, Gender, and the Problem of Equal Treatment," explores the gender/punishment relationship. Her essay reports the results of a study conducted in New York City showing that male and female defendants are treated differently on the basis of their ties to and responsibilities for others. Daly's study observed that men and women in families (with spouses and/or children) were less likely to be detained before trial and were less likely to receive the harsher types of nonjail sentences than the nonfamilied men and women. Furthermore, defendants who had dependents, whether in a marriage or not, were much more likely to receive lenient treatment at sentencing. According to Daly, much of the apparent gender disparity in processing occurs because women are more likely on average than men to benefit from the apparent advantage of having dependents.

The final two essays in this section examine the characteristics of communities and states that influence the administration of criminal justice. The first of these essays is by Martha Myers and Susette Talarico, titled "Urban Justice, Rural Injustice? Urbanization and Its Effect on Sentencing." Their essay examines whether there exist significant urban/rural differences in criminal sentencing practices. Drawing from many different perspectives, Myers and Talarico expect that urban courts are less likely to be arbitrary in sentencing than rural courts because they are often bound by burdensome bureaucratic rules and procedures reducing the discretion of sentencing judges. In contrast, they expect rural courts to operate on informal rules of thumb, affording judges more discretion in sentencing decisions. The findings of their research on Georgia courts show significant urban/rural differences exist in sentencing but not in the anticipted direction. If anything, urban rather than rural judges drew sharper distinctions between offenders based on background characteristics such as age, race, and sex.

In the final essay in this section, George Bridges and Gina Beretta examine the relationships between race and gender in a study of imprisonment and other institutions of social control. This essay, "Gender, Race, and Social Control: Toward an Understanding of Sex Disparities in Imprisonment," is primarily concerned with how gender and race are related to patterns of imprisonment across the United States. Among the more interesting findings of the study is the observation that differences in rates of imprisonment between men and women are greatest—other factors being equal—in those states where differences between men and women in labor force participation and hospitalization of the mentally ill are greatest. Evidence is presented that suggests that in some states hospitalization for mental illness is a form of social control applied primarily to women in lieu of processing through the administration of criminal justice.

Racial Discrimination in Criminal Sentencing

GARY KLECK

I T is widely believed, and frequently stated, that the criminal justice system has been in the past and remains racially discriminatory. The most frequently cited category of evidence for this assertion has been research indicating more severe sentencing of black criminal defendants than white defendants, especially in imposition of the death penalty. As there have been at least sixty empirical studies of adult criminal sentencing published which refer to race, it is not surprising that at least one critic of the criminal justice system has asserted that evidence on racial discrimination in sentencing is probably the strongest evidence of racial bias in the criminal justice system. Because the outcomes of sentencing decisions are among the most visible of legal processing, the legal system's claim to legitimacy is especially dependent on the public's perception of the pattern of such outcomes. Therefore, it seems particularly important to take a close look at evidence bearing on this issue.

The first part of this essay attempts a comprehensive assessment of the published scholarly empirical research on racial bias in criminal sentencing in the United States in connection with both capital punishment and noncapital sentencing. One of the principal sources of distortion regarding this issue in the past has been selective citation of studies supporting one position or another; therefore, great care has been taken to be as exhaustive as possible in finding relevant studies. The second part of the essay presents new evidence on race and capital punishment, consisting of an analysis of execution rates for blacks and whites over the period 1930 to 1967, for the United States as a whole and for the South, and of death-sentencing rates for the period from 1967 to 1978.

Varieties of Racial Bias: Some Conceptual Distinctions

At least five different practices can produce racial differentials in criminal sentences which are likely to be viewed as illegitimate or unjust.

1. *Overt racial discrimination against minority defendants.* This refers to the imposition of more severe dispositions on members of a subordinate racial group, independent of their legally relevant individual merits, and primarily as a direct result of the conscious or unconscious racial prejudice of the sentencing decision makers.

2. *Disregard for minority crime victims.* This would include the failure to sentence offenders (of any race) who victimize minority-group members as severely as those who victimize non-minority-group members.

3. *Class discrimination.* This refers to more severe treatment of lower-class defendants as a consequence of class prejudice. It may be due to hostility or indifference of middle-class decision makers toward culturally different defendants, or because lower-class defendants better fit popular stereotypes of serious or dangerous criminals. Because blacks in the United States are disproportionately members of the lower class, class discrimination would affect them

more heavily than whites, independent of any overt racial discrimination. This assumes that among the set of criminal defendants blacks are more likely to be lower class than whites, a debatable assumption considering the overwhelmingly lower-class character of criminal defendants of all races.

4. *Economic discrimination.* When a society's legal system is structured so that significant private economic resources are required in order to effectively obtain full legal protection, this constitutes economic discrimination, even where there is no class discrimination (as defined above). If low-income defendants receive more severe sentences than middle-income defendants because they cannot affo.d to hire an outside private attorney or cannot make bail, this constitutes economic discrimination and could produce racial differentials in sentencing outcomes.

5. *Institutional racism.* This refers to the application, possibly in a universalistic fashion, of decision-making standards which in themselves have considerable consensual support (possibly even among minority members) but which result in less favorable outcomes for minority defendants. As used in the past, the term seems to have referred to, among other things, practices 2 through 4, but institutional racism in sentencing can take other forms as well. For example, if racial-minority defendants are likelier to have prior criminal convictions, then the use of prior record as a criterion for sentence determination will tend to produce less favorable outcomes for minority defendants and would therefore be an instance of institutional racism. The establishment, by legislatures, of higher statutory penalties for crimes committed more frequently by racial minority members than by others (such as violent interpersonal crimes) would also constitute institutional racism, regardless of the behavior of judges, prosecutors, and others who influence sentencing outcomes.

For the sake of verbal and conceptual clarity, it is misleading to label either practice 3 or 4 "racial" bias or discrimination. Although clearly unjust and certainly related to race in the United States, these practices are not directly racial in themselves, since they affect whites as well as blacks and could occur in jurisdictions or socie-

ties where no racial distinctions of any sort were made. Therefore, although reference will be made to them in examining the evidence regarding overt racial discrimination, these practices are not themselves primary objects of the analysis.

The concept of institutional racism is highly problematical. It is so flexible that any practice producing unfavorable sentencing outcomes for racial-minority members can be characterized as racist, no matter how the outcomes were produced, whether they were intentionally sought, and regardless of what criteria were involved in the decisions producing the outcomes. Any pattern of sentencing involving the crimes commonly dealt with by U.S. criminal courts could be construed as institutional racism, since blacks commit a disproportionate share of such crimes relative to their share of the population and therefore are bound to receive a disproportionate share of the criminal punishment, no matter how fairly the sentencing process is administered. Only an alteration of the social conditions producing differentials in the racial distribution of criminal behavior or a radical redefinition of which crimes the courts focus on could eliminate institutional racism of this sort. For these reasons, neither this study nor any other study of sentencing per se could reject the hypothesis of institutional racism in sentencing. Consequently, attention in this analysis will be primarily focused on overt racial discrimination and secondarily on disregard for minority crime victims.

ASSESSMENT OF PRIOR RESEARCH

This review is intended to be an exhaustive assessment of all scholarly empirical studies of race and criminal sentencing of adults in the United States published through 1979. It does not cover the few studies relating ethnicity and sentencing, such as Castberg or Hall and Simkus, nor studies of conviction, as opposed to sentencing, such as Forslun. It does cover studies of the determination of degree of homicide of which defendants were convicted, such as Farrell and Swigert, since such a determination is tantamount to determination of sentence.

Also included are studies of commutations of death sentences, as these have commonly been cited as sentencing studies.

Probably the most serious shortcoming of death-penalty discrimination studies is that they nearly all fail to control for prior criminal record. In the one study which introduced such a control, Judson and his colleagues found no evidence of racial discrimination, suggesting that apparent racial differences in other studies may actually have been due to racial differences in prior criminal activity. This hypothesis is supported by Wolfgang's findings that black homicide offenders were significantly more likely to have previous criminal arrest records than white homicide offenders. It is further supported by Hagan's reanalysis of Nagel's research, which indicated that where crude controls for prior record (record/no record) were introduced, racial effects shrank. Where more adequate controls for prior record (number of prior convictions) were introduced, the racial difference disappeared altogether, suggesting that the dichotomous measure of prior record may be inadequate for control purposes.

All of the studies purporting to find racial bias in use of the death penalty for murder failed to control for income, class, or occupation of the defendants. However, the most methodologically sophisticated study of the subject, which did control for defendant's occupation, found no racial effect on whether or not a death sentence was imposed for murder by California penalty juries. Further, they found no relationship between the victim/offender racial relationship and sentence imposed, suggesting that the findings of Johnson and Garfinkel may have reflected regional and temporal peculiarities characteristic of North Carolina (or more generally, the South) in the 1930s and earlier.

Several points should be noted about the pattern of findings on discrimination in use of the death penalty for murder. First, every single study consistently indicating discrimination toward blacks was based on older data from Southern states, and three of these four studies were based on overlapping data from North Carolina. Second, all of the studies finding discrimination in administration of capital punishment for murder were not in fact studies of

sentencing, although most of them have been cited in the research literature as if they were. Third, all of these studies failed to control for prior criminal record of the defendant, for the defendant's class or income, or for the distinction between felony and nonfelony killings. Since studies which do introduce such controls find that they reduce the sentencing differentials between blacks and whites, even in the South the racial differential may have been due to differences in criminal record, income, or type of homicide committed rather than discrimination. The evidence considered as a whole indicates no racial discrimination in use of the death penalty for murder outside the South, and even for the South empirical support for the discrimination hypothesis is weak.

Noncapital Punishment Sentencing Studies

Studies were classified, in somewhat arbitrary fashion, according to what proportion of their findings were in favor of the discrimination hypothesis. They were characterized as mixed if from one-third to one-half (inclusive) of the findings favored the discrimination hypothesis and as favorable to the hypothesis if more than one-half of the findings favored it. For example, if a study examined eight different offenses, it would be labeled "yes" if evidence of bias against black defendants was found for four or more offenses, as "mixed" if such evidence was found for three of the offenses, and as "no" if two or fewer offenses showed such evidence. Since it could be argued that evidence of discrimination even for one crime or sentence-outcome measure out of many is evidence worth taking very seriously, readers must judge for themselves the significance of the mixed findings.

Of the forty studies examined, only eight consistently support the racial discrimination hypothesis, while twelve are mixed and the remaining twenty produced evidence consistently contrary to the hypothesis. Since a study's findings were characterized as mixed even if as few as a third of them favored the discrimination hypothesis, this means that a substantial majority of all of the findings of these forty studies contradicted the hypothesis. However, the evidence for the hypothesis is even weaker than these numbers suggest, since of the minority of studies which produced findings apparently in support of the hypothesis, most either failed completely to control for prior criminal record of the defendant, or did so using the crudest possible measure of prior record—a simple dichotomy distinguishing defendants with some record from those without one. This is probably the most important flaw in studies drawing a conclusion of racial discrimination, since the most methodologically sophisticated sentencing studies have consistently shown various measures of prior record to be either the strongest predictor, or among the strongest predictors, of sentences received. It appears to be the case that the more adequate the control for prior record, the less likely it is that a study will produce findings supporting a discrimination hypothesis.

Interracial Relationship of Offender and Victim

It has long been argued that racial bias in sentencing is not to be detected only by looking at the race of the defendant, but by noting the racial relationship of the offender and the victim. Specifically, it is asserted that crimes involving black offenders and white victims are punished more severely than crimes involving the other three racial combinations, either because crimes involving black victims are taken less seriously or because the crossing of racial lines in the commission of a crime is taken very seriously. While black offender-white victim crimes, especially homicides and rapes, are punished more severely than crimes with other racial combinations, it is unclear whether this is due to the racial character of the crime, or to related, confounding factors. Black offender-white victim killings are more likely than other killings to involve an offender and a victim who are strangers to each other, and such killings are much more severely punished regardless of the races involved. Such killings are also more likely to be committed in connection with some other felony, like robbery.

Finally, black-white killings are less likely than black-black killings to be victim precipitated, and victim-precipitated killings in turn

are less likely to be premeditated, leading one to expect less severe punishment of black-black killings for this reason, rather than the racial relationship per se. Eleven studies have examined sentencing outcomes by racial combination, and of these, seven found more severe punishment for black-white offenses. However, none of these studies controlled for the possibly confounding factors we have mentioned. The only four studies which did introduce such controls all found no evidence of such sentencing patterns. Thus, the interracial relationship itself may not affect the sentencing decision, except in connection with the punishment of rape in the South.

Examination of prior studies on the question of racial discrimination and use of the death penalty for murder has suggested that many of their conclusions may be seriously time bound and region bound. Their findings may not be generalizable to areas outside the South, considering the generally contrary findings of studies of non-Southern jurisdictions using more recent data. Given these considerations, it would seem reasonable to study national sentencing practices, making regional comparisons, using data covering as long a period of time as possible.

EXECUTION RATES AND DEATH SENTENCING BY RACE

It has been claimed that "racial discrimination is strongly suggested by the national execution figures." Clearly, blacks have been executed in numbers far out of proportion to their numbers in the population. Over the period 1930-1976, 53.6 percent of all legally executed persons in the United States were black, although blacks constituted only about 10-11 percent of the U.S. population during that period. This disproportion, however, cannot in itself be taken as evidence of racial discrimination, since blacks also commit a large proportion of U.S. homicides, the crime most frequently punished by death. A more meaningful measure of capital punishment sentencing outcome would be an indicator of execution risk, that is, an execution rate. A true rate compares a number of events (such as executions) with the number of times the event could have occurred. Therefore, the ideal base for the execution rate could be the number of persons convicted of a capital offense, that is, a crime for which, in a given jurisdiction, the offender could be sentenced to death. However, there are no national data on the number of such crimes committed or on persons arrested for the crimes. Therefore, a surrogate measure is needed.

In this analysis, execution risk by race is measured as the number of executions (for murder) of persons of a given race in a given year, divided by the number of homicide victims of that race who died in the previous year. The number of homicide victims of a given race is used as an approximation of the number of persons of that race who committed a homicide, whether a capital murder or a noncapital murder. Since 92-97 percent of all homicides involve killers and victims of the same race, the racial distribution of homicide victims can be used to describe the racial distribution of homicide offenders with very little error.

For the period 1930-1967, there were 1,663 executions of whites for murder and 1,638 executions of blacks, while for the period 1929-1966 there were 159,482 white homicide victims and 168,518 black homicide victims (and presumably roughly equal numbers of homicide offenders). Therefore, the white execution rate for the entire period was 10 executions per 1,000 homicides and the black rate was 9.720 executions per 1,000 homicides. Thus, over the entire period, blacks were subject to a lower execution risk than whites.

Given the regional pattern of discrimination findings of previous studies of capital punishment sentencing, it may be the case that execution rates are higher for blacks than for whites in the South and that this fact is obscured in national data. These data, in fact, indicate that the execution risk of black homicide offenders (actually nonwhites in this analysis) has indeed been greater than that of white homicide offenders in the South, while the opposite has been true in the rest of the United States. However, the excess of the black execution risk over the white execution risk in the South has declined over time, to the point where execution rates were roughly equal in the period since 1950.

The evidence, considered in combination with prior research on capital punishment sentencing outcomes, suggests that use of the death penalty is not inevitably or inherently discriminatory, but rather that racial discrimination in its administration has been highly variable over time and between regions. These data support the racial discrimination hypothesis in connection with death penalty sentencing only for the South. Of particular interest is the somewhat surprising finding that in the recent past, outside of the South, the white execution risk has been substantially higher than the nonwhite risk, a fact which apparently has gone unnoticed in the literature.

CONCLUSIONS

The conclusions which can be drawn from the available evidence on the racial patterning of sentencing may be briefly summarized as follows:

1. The death penalty has not generally been imposed for murder in a fashion discriminatory toward blacks, except in the South. Elsewhere, black homicide offenders have been less likely to receive a death sentence or be executed than whites.
2. Regarding noncapital sentencing, the evidence is largely contrary to a hypothesis of general or widespread overt discrimination against black defendants, although there is evidence of discrimination for a minority of specific jurisdictions, judges, crime types, and so on.
3. Although black offender-white victim crimes are generally punished more severely than crimes involving other racial combinations, the evidence indicates that this is due to legally relevant factors related to such offenses, not the racial combination itself.
4. There appears to be a general pattern of less severe punishment of crimes with black victims than those with white victims, especially in connection with imposition of the death penalty. In connection with noncapital sentencing, the evidence is too sparse to draw any firm conclusions.

None of these findings are inconsistent with the assertion of institutional racism or income discrimination in sentencing. It is quite possible that low income makes it more difficult to make bail, hire a private attorney genuinely independent of the court, and so on, for both blacks and whites, and that these factors in turn result in more severe sentencing outcomes, as Lizotte's research indicates. If black criminal defendants are poorer than white criminal defendants, then income discrimination would produce racial differentials in sentences received. Nor are the data inconsistent with a hypothesis of overt discrimination at earlier stages of the criminal justice process. We might expect violations of stated values such as equal protection and justice for all to occur most commonly in connection with the least visible decisions, such as the decision to arrest, charge, prosecute, or release a defendant on bail. However, these decisions are less well studied than the sentencing decision, so the evidence for discrimination is necessarily even weaker than that regarding sentencing, quite apart from the actual prevalence of discriminatory practice.

The findings of this study do not suggest a different explanation for a well-known phenomenon. Rather, they point to a phenomenon to be explained which differs from that conventionally addressed by American students of the legal reaction to crime and criminals. Students of the criminal justice system, concerned with the contemporary consequences of a historical pattern of racism, have sought to explain patterns of more severe treatment of blacks, while overlooking or downplaying the pattern of more lenient treatment of black defendants.

Blacks in the United States, both in the recent and more remote past, have been less likely than whites to receive a death sentence if they committed a homicide. Furthermore, this pattern is apparently not entirely limited to the sentencing of capital offenders. For a variety of specific crimes, jurisdictions, and judges, various researchers have produced data indicating more lenient treatment of black defendants than whites, although the admittedly scattered findings were usually de-emphasized or discounted as merely anomalous results attributable to some flaw in the analysis or research design.

The specification of phenomena to be explained is in a way a more fundamental scientific task than the development of explanations, since the former obviously must occur before the latter can even be imagined. The pattern of lenient treatment of black defendants in the South was recognized in the 1940s and before by observers such as Dollard and Myrdal, and various explanations were developed to account for it. Today, however, this phenomenon is largely disregarded.

Changing Conceptions of Race: Toward an Account of Anomalous Findings of Sentencing Research

RUTH D. PETERSON
JOHN HAGAN

CONCEPTIONS of race are closely linked to the settings in which they operate. Through time and across situations, then, conceptions of race change. Failure to consider fully this variability undermines our understanding of race relations, confusing debates over the "declining significance of race" and obscuring the "changing significance of race" in the determination of social and economic outcomes. For example, and as we illustrate further below, our tendency to treat the meaning of race as a constant has often made findings of sentencing research seem anomalous. Our premise is that the meaning of race must be understood in historical, contextual terms. With such an understanding, anomalous research findings come to make sense. Without such understanding, sociological theories of race relations are often as static as the genetic explanations they seek to replace.

Of course, scholars do not always fail to consider the specific social and historical context in examining the social significance of race. Contextual considerations are apparent in some works on racial inequality (in education, income, employment, occupations, etc.). In the criminal justice area, such considerations are

sometimes apparent in research on the social origins of law. These examples notwithstanding, in much social research race is treated as if the direction and level of its impact should always be the same.

THE ANOMALOUS FINDINGS OF SENTENCING STUDIES

Sentencing studies provide an example of an area of sociological research in which a static, simplistic understanding of race has impeded theoretical development. Thus, while the most popular theory of criminal sentencing, conflict theory, traditionally has predicted that non-white offenders would receive more severe sentences than whites, and while much of the American public has shared this expectation, recent reviews of sentencing research provide little support for this perspective. Indeed, Kleck goes so far as to call special attention to anomalous findings of differential lenience in the sentencing of black offenders.

For a variety of specific crimes, jurisdictions, and judges, various researchers have produced data indicating more lenient treatment of black defendants than whites, although the admittedly scattered findings were usually de-emphasized or discounted as merely anomalous results. For example, Bullock found that significantly shorter prison sentences were assigned to blacks convicted of murder; Levin's

From "Changing Conceptions of Race: Toward an Account of Anomalous Findings of Sentencing Research" by R. Peterson and J. Hagan, 1984, *American Sociological Review, 49,* pp. 56-70. Copyright 1984 by the American Sociological Association. Reprinted by permission.

Pittsburgh data indicate that blacks received more lenient dispositions than whites for eight of nine offense categories: and Bernstein and her colleagues found that blacks received significantly less severe sentences than whites. Gibson studied sentences given by individual judges and found that seven of eleven judges gave a higher percentage of severe sentences to whites than to blacks.

Making sense of such findings is the current challenge of sentencing research. One possibility is that they are simply random fluctuations from a trend toward equality. Such a trend may exist, but these findings are not random in appearance. We believe that a more convincing explanation of differential lenience and severity in sentencing is to be found in race-related conceptions of offender-victim relationships, conceptions that are specific to the contexts in which they operate.

For example, homicide and assault are characteristically intraracial offenses. When black offenders assault or kill black victims, the devalued status of the black victims and the paternalistic attitudes of white authorities can justify lenient treatment. Rape, on the other hand, is more frequently interracial. When blacks violate white victims, the high sexual property value attached to the white victims and the racial fears of authorities can justify severe treatment. Robbery is also becoming increasingly interracial. The higher value attached to white property and persons and the fears of white authorities may here also lead to more severe sentences for black offenders.

However, the above studies only consider crimes involving victims of interpersonal violence (homicide, assault, rape), or the threat of it (robbery). Such offenses constitute an important, but only a small part of the American crime problem. If race-related conceptions of offender-victim relationships like those highlighted above are to provide a more general explanation of sentencing disparities, they must be relevant to a broader range of offenses, including the so-called victimless crimes. Using drug law violations as an example, we argue below that a recent, historically specific tendency to see certain kinds of nonwhite offenders as victims may explain the anomaly of some nonwhite offenders receiving more lenient sentences than whites.

THE VICTIMS AND VILLAINS OF DRUGS

Through most of this century, the issue of race has been manifest in the American moral crusade against drugs. Multo observes that as early as "the nineteenth century addicts were identified with foreign groups and internal minorities who were already actively feared and the objects of elaborate and massive social and legal constraints." However, conceptions of deviant behavior are not static. Our interest is in demonstrating how such changes may have influenced the sanctioning of drug offenders. To do so, it is necessary to focus on a time and a setting that allow detailed analysis of changing conceptions of offenders and offenses. Temporally, we have chosen the period of the 1960s and 1970s because it includes the most recent and concerted national effort to mobilize criminal justice resources against drug crimes, a period which culminated with the Nixon administration's 1970 reform of federal drug laws. As a setting, we have selected the Southern Federal District of New York because it is widely recognized as the "premier" prosecution office in the country, among other reasons, for its pursuit of major drug cases.

An analysis of public opinion, media materials, and legislative activities summarized below suggests a subdivision of the time period we consider into three parts (1963-68, 1969-73, 1974-76), the most interesting of which is the middle interval. During this middle period, public interest in drugs seemed to peak. This point can be made first through a consideration of Gallup Poll data providing national opinion rankings of "the most important problem the country faces today." Drugs were not among ranked social problems in these data prior to 1970, and were not consistently ranked after 1973. However, from February 1971 to August 1973, through six Gallup pollings, drugs were never less than fifth in the national rankings and were usually ranked second or third in importance behind the Vietnam War and economic issues.

The treatment of an issue in the mass media is another index of shifts in public interest. Quantitative measures of such changes are presented elsewhere. Here we simply note that there was a rather dramatic increase in the coverage of drug problems in the New York print media that began in the late 1960s and declined dramatically by the mid-1970s: drug use, abuse, and trafficking were issues of much greater interest in the late 1960s and early 1970s than during either the early and mid-1960s or the mid- to late 1970s.

The qualitative changes in the nature of public opinion about drugs that accompanied these quantitative shifts are of even greater interest and importance. These changes are apparent in the content of drug-related editorials appearing in the *New York Times* between 1960 and 1978. The most important qualitative change over these eighteen years was the distinction increasingly made between dealers and users of drugs. This distinction became particularly salient during the Nixon administration, as the former group became the villains, and the latter victims, in the changing imagery of America's drug problems. The significance of this distinction lies in its origins and race-related nature and consequences. As we have seen, in the earlier part of this century it was sufficient to condemn drug offenders, who were presumed to be mostly of minority status, in an undifferentiated fashion. However, in the 1960s the composition of the drug-abusing population changed. Whether this change was linked to the growing popularity of the antiwar movement, or to a more general "morals revolution," its consequence was clear: "For the first time in the twentieth century, the objects of the drug control laws were persons from the dominant middle class whose value system served as the basis for the development and enforcement of the criminal code."

During the late 1960s and early 1970s, the legitimacy of the criminal justice system was threatened almost as much by the public's view that it was inappropriate to subject their children to criminal punishment as it was by youthful drug and protest behavior itself. A solution

to this problem seemed to lie in what Gusfield might refer to as altered deviance designations (i.e., in a redefinition of what constituted the "real" drug problem). Pushers, especially high-level dealers, became the designated villains in this new portrayal of the problem. Perceived as part of organized drug networks with ties to the underworld, professional traffickers were designated as the real source of the drug problem. They were assigned responsibility for the street crimes of addicts forced to steal to pay the high price of drugs and for the acts of violence committed by addicts under the influence of drugs so acquired. Their sins also included preying upon innocent victims, especially middle-class youth. "For material gain, he corrupted the young and introduced them to the joys and horrors of addiction. Thus the concept of the innocence of youth could be preserved and the source of corruption focused on the pusher."

These new deviance designations were reflected during 1969-73 in editorial coverage of drug-related events in the *New York Times,* as well as in the penalty provisions and intent of the Nixon Administration's Comprehensive Drug Abuse Prevention and Control Act of 1970. Beginning with the former, *Times* editors repeatedly called for a scaling down of penalties for "soft" drugs, users, and youthful offenders. Indeed, judges who imposed overly harsh penalties on these types of offenders were criticized openly. In sharp contrast to these liberal views, *Times* editors supported "throwing the book" at veteran pushers and dealers in hard drugs. As one editorial noted, "The penalties for those who prey on the innocent by peddling drugs can hardly be too severe."

We turn now to the relevant legislation. On October 27, 1970, President Nixon signed into law the Comprehensive Drug Abuse Prevention and Control Act. In the legislative debates leading to the 1970 act, Congress also focused on two target populations: young middle- and upper-class drug users, now seen as victims of drugs, and traffickers and professional drug criminals, now seen as the hardcore villains. Speaking of young middle- and upper-class drug users, Senator Dodd noted that "these people arrested for one drug offense or another are not hardened criminals . . . they are young people on the road to professional careers as lawyers and teachers." Dodd's concern was that the "cream of American youth" not be sent off to prison "where it is now obvious they will get worse rather than better." Representative Koch cogently summarized this commonly held view:

I believe that if we are to condemn and punish our young people, we ought to be sure that the cure is not worse than the disease . . . , it seems to me that the severe federal and state criminal penalties only exacerbate the problem.

On the other hand, severe penalties were widely seen as essential for the hardcore villains—the traffickers, pushers and big dealers. Representative Hunt asserted:

There is nothing wrong with imposing a mandatory sentence on a hard headed pusher. Mitigating circumstances should not apply to a person of this nature. The only way you can handle narcotics and get rid of the situation is to incarcerate those main pushers and help those who have unfortunately become addicted.

The penalties that emerged from congressional hearings and debates reflected compromises reached to "properly" deal with these two target populations. Reduction of first-offense possession and of distribution of small amounts of marijuana for no remuneration from felonies to misdemeanors, removal of mandatory minimum penalties, and a provision for special first-offender treatment served to minimize the possibility of subjecting middle- and upper-class youth to criminal penalties and their presumed negative consequences. On the other hand, the retention of a possession offense for the purpose of bargaining with informants, the relatively minor reductions in maximum penalties for trafficking offenses, the provision of mandatory special parole terms, the provision of extreme sanctions for two new offense categories of questionable constitutionality (Continuing Criminal Enterprise and Dangerous Special Drug Offender), and the passage of supplementary criminal enforcement provisions provided the coercive policies required for handling (and

warning) the second targeted population: major drug traffickers.

We suggest that the distinction drawn, by the public and lawmakers, between users as victims and dealers as villains could well account for the more lenient treatment of minorities. A factual premise that underwrites this suggestion is that the opportunity structure of the drug trade in America, like more conventional opportunity structures, is racially stratified. Most big dealers are white. Also, media sources (e.g., *New York Times*) and interviews with U.S. Attorneys from the Southern District confirm that operating assumptions of the public and criminal justice officials include the views that nonwhites (1) are more likely to be users than dealers, (2) are very unlikely to be big dealers, and (3) commit their drug crimes in part because of their victim status in society.

Our point then is not simply that minority offenders might be treated more leniently *because* they are in fact users, but rather that as an identifiable population, minority drug offenders may well have been "typed" or characterized as victims in a more *generalized* fashion. Coming as it did on the heels of the high point of the Civil Rights movement, our expectation is that this otherwise anomalous form of equity held sway in the formation of the new drug strategy. Indeed, we believe that it was this coalition of conservative purpose (i.e., a moral crusade against the big dealers of the drug trade) and liberal impulse (i.e., the recognition and treatment of youthful, better-educated, and minority offenders as victims of the world of drugs) that best accounts for the emergence of a new drug strategy. As indicated above, our expectation is that this strategy became most pronounced in the context represented by the years 1969-73: during these years we expect well-educated youth, minority offenders, and users of drugs to have received the most lenient treatment, while big drug dealers are expected to have experienced particularly harsh treatment.

One final point should be made. The lenience we expect for minority drug offenders is premised on their designation as victims. However, in those infrequent instances when minority offenders are clearly big dealers, it is unlikely that the designation as victim would apply. If the perspective we offer is correct, then we would not expect in these instances to encounter the anomaly of more lenient treatment for minority offenders. This implied interaction of race and dealer status is explored in the last part of our analysis.

THE MEASUREMENT OF CHANGE

The data considered in this study include crucial information on all drug offenders ($N = 4,371$) sentenced between 1963 and 1976 in the Southern Federal District of New York. The analysis considers sentencing decisions within the three contexts derived from the above discussion: 1963-68, 1969-73, and 1974-76.

Analyses of the data demonstrate that our most direct measures of villain and victims status influence imprisonment in expected ways. Users are *more* likely than others to go to jail between 1963 and 1968, but *less* likely to do so between 1969 and 1973. It is difficult to interpret these effects in any way other than the altered deviance designations of drug user that we have described. Although the effect of the big-dealer variable is not significant during any of the three periods, its influence is largest during the middle interval. And, while we were unable to find any significant status effects in the above analysis, we now find that middle-class status decreases significantly the likelihood of imprisonment in all time periods, and again as expected, this effect is strongest during 1969-73. Education and age also affect imprisonment, with education having the large impact, and with the likelihood of high school-educated offenders being jailed lowest for 1969-73. Nixon-appointed judges show a greater reluctance to imprison offenders than other judges during the last two periods, while judges with high severity scores for nondrug cases are more willing in drug cases to use imprisonment as a sanction. Pleading not guilty has a significant impact on the likelihood of imprisonment in all periods, with that impact being largest for 1969-73. Finally, although nonwhite offenders are less likely than white offenders to receive jail sentences in all three periods, counter to our expec-

tations, this effect is smallest and statistically nonsignificant for 1969-73.

SOME CONCLUSIONS

Explicit in our analysis is the premise that the meaning of race varies, and that, despite simplistic interpretations of conflict theory, both differential severity and leniency are possible. There are hints of such an understanding in prior sentencing studies of inter- and intraracial crimes with victims. However, we have suggested that race can influence societal reactions to the more frequent victimless crimes as well. The key, we have argued, is an understanding of changing race-related conceptions of offender-victim relationships.

For example, American drug prohibition began with the portrayal of minorities as the villains behind a growing drug menace. However, with the increasing nonmedical use of drugs by middle-class youth in the 1960s, this conception of the drug problem became problematic. A general shift occurred in the social image of the different types of parties involved, and a new strategy of control was required. Big dealers became the new villains, while middle-class youth and nonwhites (the latter insofar as they rarely were big dealers in a racially stratified drug trade) were reconceived as victims. We have argued that inclusion of nonwhites in the latter category was the product of a compromise between conservative and liberal impulses that facilitated a more specialized allocation of penal sanctions. The modern antidrug crusade reached its peak between 1969 and 1973, a period that included the passage of a new drug law spearheaded by the Nixon administration.

We were able to identify a series of outcomes consistent with the above perspective. The most dramatic of these effects included a peak in the punitive treatment of big dealers between 1969 and 1973. Lenient treatment of nonwhite offenders also peaked during these years. The latter ultimately was revealed to be a lenience restricted to *ordinary* nonwhite drug offenders, not big dealers. Indeed, there were signs that *nonwhite big dealers* received the most severe sentences of all.

These findings were reinforced by a series of follow-up interviews we conducted with three former heads of the drug enforcement division of the U.S. Attorney's Office of the Southern District of New York. When asked to explain the general pattern of leniency we found for nonwhite drug offenders, one former prosecutor answered with the immediate response, "Sure, three blacks equal one Italian, and three Italians equal one Corsican." Asked to elaborate, the former U.S. Attorney noted that the world of drugs is not only racially, but also ethnically, stratified. The remainder of this interview and the others we conducted are best characterized as reflecting a casual, jaded, and sometimes paternal indifference to nonwhite drug crime that is well captured in contemporary American films like "Prince of the City," which not coincidentally was set in the same time and place as the current study.

There is, however, a more ominous side to the new drug strategy that is reflected in the race/period/big-dealer interaction noted above. Indeed, there are dramatic examples of the extremely severe treatment of nonwhite big dealers. The case of Leroy "Nicky" Barnes offers a vivid illustration. On January 19, 1978, Barnes was sentenced to life imprisonment *without* parole on drug conspiracy charges *and* under the seldom used Continuing Criminal Enterprise provision of the 1970 Federal Drug Act. Regarded as possibly Harlem's biggest drug dealer, Barnes was listed in the New York Police Department's Blue Book of "Black Major Violators." In imposing such a severe sentence, the judge in the case explained that Barnes "is 'a great danger' to the community.... His narcot-

ics trafficking affected 'the lives of thousands of people.' And the saddest part of all . . . is that the great majority of people he is affecting are people in his own neighborhood [Harlem]" (*New York Times*). This latter comment is consistent with our suggestion that nonwhite big dealers are seen as more villainous and therefore as deserving more severe penalties, because they offend against an already victimized population. The following comment from a *Times Magazine* article (written prior to Barnes's 1978 conviction) is also noteworthy in light of our perspective.

Whatever the reasons, the failure to make an arrest stick has earned Barnes the street name "Mr. Untouchable." He is not a retiring man. Of medium height, he projects a presence larger than his size. He is muscular and recently shaved the beard he sported for years. He prefers luxurious motor cars and elaborate custom clothing. To the street people, he is a presence. To the police, this symbolic quality is as significant as the crimes they allege he has committed. To them he embodies the new trend in drug trafficking, in which blacks and Hispanics, the new ethnic successors in organized crime, have taken over from their predecessors, the Italian street gangsters.

More generally, we offer this study as an example of, and argument for, sociological research that takes context-specific conceptions of race into account. Our results suggest that there are patterns of advantage and disadvantage that only contextualized analyses can reveal. The role of race is more variable and more complicated than previously acknowledged.

Discrimination in the Criminal Courts: Family, Gender, and the Problem of Equal Treatment

KATHLEEN DALY

A common finding in statistical studies of criminal court outcomes is a persistent "sex effect," one showing that women receive more lenient treatment than men. Although some suggest this sex effect may be more apparent than real, that is, an artifact of inadequate control variables, reviews of multivariate studies that control for the defendant's prior record and the type/severity of the offense charged show a recurring pattern. Differences in the treatment of men and women are more often found in sentencing and pretrial release decisions than in those for case dismissal and conviction. Research to date shows that sex effects are real, but arise in particular decision-making contexts.

What explains the variability of the sex effect across differing court outcomes? And what explains the sex effect when it emerges? Interviews with court officials and observations of court practices suggest that pretrial release and sentencing decisions are shaped by defendants' familial relations and, in turn, are infused with concerns for maintaining family life. Drawing from this qualitative research, a social control/social costs framework is presented, and the hypotheses derived are subject to statistical test. The social control/social costs framework revises Kruttschnitt's and Kruttschnitt and Green's social control arguments and introduces the idea that there are social costs to pun-

From "Discrimination in the Criminal Courts: Family, Gender, and the Problem of Equal Treatment" by K. Daly, 1988, *Social Forces, 66,* pp. 152-175. Copyright 1988 by The University of North Carolina Press. Reprinted by permission.

ishment, these being the negative consequences to the state of imposing criminal justice sanctions, especially jail time, on defendants.

PREVIOUS THEORY

Gender differences in court outcomes have been explained by paternalism; gender-based variation in informal social control; gender "type-scripts" that allow men to exercise power by maintaining women's familial labor; and multifactor explanations that combine court chivalry, attributions of men's and women's criminality, and the practical problems of jailing women with children.

Chivalry, paternalism, and attributions of criminality are discussed elsewhere. Attention is given here to social control arguments and how they might be modified. The "practicality" problem and the maintenance of women's familial labor are theorized as constitutive of the social costs of punishment.

Social Control

In the most general terms, social control theory premises an inverse relation between informal (family/kin ties) and formal (state) control. So, for example, the more tied one is to the normative social order (via familial and work relations), the likelihood of "respectable" or law-abiding behavior is increased, and the application of formal social control is decreased. Hagan, Simpson, and Gillis consider gender-based variation in informal and formal social control for adolescents; however, Kruttschnitt first outlined the impact of gender-based variation in social control for the criminal court response to women and the differential treatment of men and women in the criminal courts.

Kruttschnitt argues that because women have more informal social control in their lives than men, they will be subject to a lower degree of formal social control. When this general proposition is operationalized and tested, however, two flaws are apparent: the locus of informal social control is misspecified, and gender differences in court outcomes cannot be adequately explained by it.

Locus of Social Control

Kruttschnitt suggests that women have a higher degree of informal social control in their lives than men because they are more likely than men to be economically dependent *on others* (e.g., a spouse or the state). This depiction of dependency relations in family life is partial and thus misleading. In comparison to men, women's lives may be characterized by a greater economic dependency on others. However, women are far more likely than men to have others dependent on their caretaking labor, and this latter dependency may be the more significant source of informal social control in women's lives. Thus, when theorizing about the impact of familial relations as informal social control, greater emphasis should be given to whether male and female defendants have dependents, not solely whether they are dependent on others.

Gender and Social Control

Although a social control formulation may explain variation in the treatment *among* men or women by the degree to which they are embedded in family life or have responsibilities for others, it cannot explain differences in the treatment *between* men and women. For example, when family variables are introduced in analyses of the pretrial release or sentencing outcomes, the magnitude of the sex effect is reduced, but it remains statistically significant. The reason for this residual sex effect, net of

family variables, is that gender divisions in work and family life have not been taken into account. More specifically, women's care for others and men's economic support for families are different types of dependencies in family life, and they elicit different concerns for the court.

SOCIAL CONTROL AND SOCIAL COSTS

Although the precise features of defendants' familial relations vary, court officials draw a major distinction between two groups of defendants—those with familial responsibilities and those without such responsibilities. These are termed "familied" and "nonfamilied" defendants, respectively. Interview and observational studies reveal that the familied defendants are thought to be more deserving of the court's leniency than the nonfamilied defendants. Among the nonfamilied defendants, however, judges may be more lenient in sentencing if the defendant has a "strong authority figure" in the household, has a good school or employment record, or in general has "strong family ties." The criminal court response to the nonfamilied defendant is identical to that in juvenile justice courts, that is, the more tied defendants are to the normative social order via familial and employment ties, the less formal social control may be applied.

Familied and Nonfamilied Men and Women

The distinctions drawn between familied and nonfamilied defendants and the justifications for treating them differently stem from two sources—social control and social costs. Court officials typify familied defendants as more anchored in the normative social order because their day-to-day lives are constrained by having responsibilities for the welfare of others. Interwoven with this characterization of greater social control in the lives of familied defendants is the court's concern with the *consequences* of decisions for separating defendants from families or jeopardizing the family unit. In contemplating jail time, judges say they do not want to "inflict a hurt on society" by jailing a familied defendant; or they ask, "Are you punishing a victim?" These "hurts to society" and the punishment of innocents are the social costs attached to sanctioning familied defendants—costs that are ideological and economic.

Ideologically, the court's reasoning is, first, in the interests of maintaining social order, one should not break up families; and second, in the interests of justice, one should punish the guilty (the defendant) but protect the innocent (family members dependent on a defendant). In some instances, "keeping families together" is also justified on economic grounds. When familied defendants are jailed, the state may incur added costs for replacing the defendants' economic support or care for others. Thus, the first hypothesis tested is whether familied men and women are treated more leniently than nonfamilied men and women.

Familied Men and Women

A mainstay of the research literature is that court officials find it impractical to impose jail sentences on women with children. Why, though, is it more impractical to jail a familied woman than a familied man? A social control formulation is mute on this issue, and to date, it has been assumed that the mitigating effect of "having dependents" should be the same for men and women. Interviews with court officials show that a different set of assumptions operates: they attach higher social costs to removing familied women than familied men from families. Given extant gender divisions of labor in work and family life, care for others—women's work—and providing for others—men's work—are not symmetrical types of dependency relations, nor are the consequences of removing familied men's and women's labor from families the same. The greater difficulty judges and other court officials have in removing parental care (rather than economic support) from families is couched in terms of the "psychological impact on the children," or "Who will care for the children?" From their viewpoint, caretaking labor is more indispensable to maintain the family unit than is economic support.

Extending on Harris, both men's and the state's interests are at stake in maintaining women's familial labor. State supports for families exist in the form of "father" but not "mother" surrogates; consequently, the loss of economic support can be more easily compensated by state supports than can the loss of care for others. Moreover, the court's concerns with "breaking up families" and "protecting the innocent" may more often apply to familied women than familied men. Thus, the second hypothesis tested is whether familied women are treated more leniently than familied men.

Summarizing the three elements contained in the social control/social costs formulation: (1) the more familied defendants are, that is, the more others are dependent on them, the less likely they will be subject to formal criminal justice control; (2) the effect of being familied will be stronger for women than for men; and (3) the mitigating impact of being familied will be most strong when decisions concern separating defendants from families.

RESULTS

Sex and Family Effects Across the Outcomes

Significant sex effects arise in two court outcomes, the pretrial release and sentencing decisions. Thus, in this jurisdiction sex effects are found in an in-out decision, as well as for nonjail sentences. As expected, sex effects are not found in the analysis dismissal decision or the conviction decision.

Based on the analysis, one would conclude that, net of the control variables, men are 8 percent more likely than women to be pretrial detained and 19 percent more likely than women to receive the harsher type of nonjail sentences. This pattern of discrimination, apparently favoring women, shifts dramatically when family variables and sex-family interaction terms are introduced.

The conclusions are that (1) non-familied men and women are treated the same (i.e., no sex effect); (2) familied men and women are treated more leniently than those who are non-familied; and (3) more favorable treatment is accorded familied women than familied men.

Put another way, differences in the response to men and women based on their familial situation, together with the stronger mitigating influence of being familied for women than men, explain the initial sex effect.

Pretrial Release and Sentencing Outcomes

For the pretrial release decision, men and women who are married and have dependents are significantly less likely to be pretrial detained than nonfamilied defendants, and analysis shows that the mitigating influence of being married and having dependents is stronger for women than men. The analysis reveals that married women without dependents may also be less likely subject to pretrial detention than nonfamilied women. This effect, which just neared statistical significance, suggests the marital tie alone (1) may differentiate treatment more among women than among men and (2) has a stronger mitigating influence on pretrial detention for women than men.

For the sentencing outcome, strong family and sex-family effects are seen. For this outcome, men and women with dependents receive the "real walk" of a conditional discharge more often than the nonfamilied men and women. Women with dependents—whether single or married—are more likely than nonfamilied women to receive the most lenient sentence. As the sex-family interaction terms show, the familied women are treated more leniently than the familied men. Familial status more strongly differentiates treatment among women than among men, and the "leniency return" from the marital tie, but more especially from having dependents, is higher for women than men.

For the sentencing outcome, single men with dependents are less likely to be jailed than nonfamilied men. If being single with dependents (rather than married with dependents) more significantly mitigates against jail sentences for men, it is possible that those men who care for others are treated like the familied women with dependents. That is to say, caretaking labor—whether carried out by men or women—is recognized by court officials as indispensable to the maintenance of families, and decisions are made accordingly.

Men, Work, and Family

The outcomes were also analyzed in more detail to determine potential joint effects of employment and familial status for men. If, for example, a male defendant is married and has dependents, but does not have a job, court officials may consider him an "irresponsible father" or not a "good family man." For each decision, the full equations were run separately for two groups of men, those currently employed and unemployed. The results of the analysis are mixed. For the pretrial release decision, the joint influence of employment and family is evident, but for the in-out sentencing decision it is not. Among employed men, those married with dependents are significantly less likely to be pretrial detained, but for unemployed men, the mitigating effects of family do not arise. For the sentencing outcome, family effects do not vary by employment status; they remain the same for single or married men with dependents, whether employed or unemployed.

Dismissal Decision

The results for the dismissal decision depart from all the other outcomes in several respects. First, the basis for the dismissal decision is poorly specified with little variation in dismissal explained by the independent variables. Evidentiary factors, such as the quality of the arrest and witness availability, together with the particular nature of victim-offender relations are most salient in this decision. Confirming patterns revealed in the Vera study on the deterioration of felony arrests, those charged with assault are more likely to be dismissed, a result which obtains for both men and women in separate analyses.

Unlike the other outcomes, case dismissal is unaffected by prior record, inversely related to charge severity, and does not evince family effects in the expected direction. Women with dependents—whether single or married—are less likely to be dismissed than nonfamilied women. Married men with dependents are, by contrast, more likely to be dismissed than non-familied men and familied women. These findings may be explained by the character of victim-offender relations in men's and women's cases subject to dismissal.

Type of Finding

Differences in the treatment of women, but not men, by familial status can be seen in the results of the analyses. Married women—with and without dependents—are significantly more likely to receive the lenient adjournment in contemplation of a dismissal (ACD) than are non-familied women. Because familial status for men does not affect the type of finding received, the sex-interaction effects reveal, not surprisingly, a stronger mitigating effect of being familied for women than men. Recalling the prosecutor's portrayal of who receives a break with an ACD—those whose "personal history and ties are good"—the results show that married women, both with and without dependents, are more likely accorded this break in comparison to other women and all other men.

If a larger view is taken of which defendants are more likely filtered out of the adjudication process, the results show that familied men and women are more likely to be tracked out of the system. Precisely why familied men are more likely accorded a straight dismissal in comparison to familied women, while familied women are more likely to receive the ACD finding in contrast to familied men, cannot be ascertained from the data. However, the net effect of the dismissal and type of finding outcomes is that familied men and women are less likely to be subject to any form of criminal court sanction in comparison to nonfamilied men and women.

SUMMARY AND DISCUSSION

Although the analysis revealed much complexity in the impact of gender and family on court outcomes, general patterns are revealed. Net of case severity, charge severity, the type of offense charged, prior record, and other defendant characteristics, male and female defendants are treated differently on the basis of their ties to and responsibilities for others. Familied men and women are less likely to be pretrial detained, they are less likely to receive the harsher types of nonjail sentences than the nonfamilied men and women, and the mitigating effect of being familied is stronger for women than men.

Having dependents, whether in a marital context or not, is generally the more determining feature of whether defendants receive lenient treatment. For men, being married without dependents confers no advantage at the pretrial release or the two sentencing decisions, but having dependents—whether single or married—does. For women, the situation is more mixed on the relative strength of the marital tie and having dependents. Married women, and especially those with dependents, are accorded greater leniency at the pretrial release decision, but women with dependents—whether married or single—receive the most lenient sentences. Family measures need to be developed which more accurately capture familial relations and dependencies than that presumed by the married/not-married dichotomy. What matters most for court personnel is whether defendants have day-to-day responsibilities for the welfare of others; such care or economic support can occur with or without a marital tie, and the specific form of care and economic support can vary by gender.

Familial status differentiates treatment among women to a greater extent than it does among men, a finding that can be interpreted in different ways. On one hand, in comparison to the nonfamilied women and familied men, familied women are least likely to be subject to criminal justice controls and sanctions. As such, of all familied groups, familied women benefit most by the importance the court places on the maintenance and protection of family life. On the other hand, such treatment can be seen to reinforce traditional conceptions of women's proper place in the family. These apparently competing interpretations may be reconciled by considering the ways in which gender interacts with familial relations.

First, nonfamilied men and women are, in a statistical sense, treated alike; thus, nonfamilied women are not penalized—any more than non-familied men are—for the lack of familial responsibilities. Traditional notions of women's *and* men's "proper place" in family life are operating, conferring advantage to both familied men and familied women. Second, the greater leniency accorded familied women than familied men stems from contemporary gender divisions in work and family life, specifically that women are more likely to care for others. In the criminal court, caretaking labor is privileged over economic support as being more indispensable for the maintenance of families. Familied men who care for others will be treated like familied women, as evidenced in the outcome and in interviews with court officials. Typically, though, what men and women do for families differs, and criminal court decision making acknowledges and reproduces this difference.

The mitigating effects of family were found in both the pretrial release and nonjail sentencing decisions. Thus, familied defendants may be accorded leniency even when decisions do not center on a defendant's loss of liberty. If, in these instances, court officials are not faced with the prospect of separating defendants from families, they may continue to use a social-costs logic in sanctioning familied defendants. That is to say, for families on the edge of economic survival, imposing a fine can jeopardize the welfare of family members, and probation sentences can entail time away from paid jobs or child care. This kind of social-costs logic merges with the notion that familied defendants require less formal social control to facilitate law-abiding behavior. Social control and social costs do not compete with one another in how court officials rationalize differences in the treatment of familied and nonfamilied defendants, and of familied men and women. Rather, the two are inseparable, each justifying the other.

IMPLICATIONS

Research in other jurisdictions is needed to determine whether the permeating effects of defendant's familial relations found in this jurisdiction obtain elsewhere. For this group of predominantly black and Hispanic men and women, gender differences are traced to the treatment of men and women with families.

Four implications are drawn from these findings. First, more research attention might be given to the salience of defendants' familial relations in the adjudication process, and the implications of these relations for the problem of equal treatment. Research has long focused on whether *individuals* are accorded equal treatment, overlooking the fact that many defendants come before the criminal court as indispensable members of familial social groups, not as individuals. By using the concept of the social costs of sanctioning, I explicated the different consequences of applying equal punishments (other factors equal) to familied and nonfamilied defendants and to familied men and women. By framing the problem of discrimination in this way, class, color, and gender differences can be seen to arise, in part, because the court is in a familial bind. If it is more difficult to punish groups (i.e., familied defendants with affective and/or economic dependents) than individuals (nonfamilied defendants), then questions of a legal, moral, and practical nature are raised for the legal ideal of "equal treatment."

Second, the assertion that women are treated more leniently than men in the criminal courts is misleading. It is more accurate to say that some women receive more lenient treatment than some men. Moreover, contrary to descriptions in the research literature that almost all women, but few men, have families, variation in fact exists in the familial situation of defendants. The defendant profile in this sample reveals that although higher proportions of women than men are familied, many women are nonfamilied (33 percent), and many men are familied (41 percent). Future research will benefit from a greater sensitivity to the fact that not only is familial variation apparent between men and women, but also among them.

A third implication is how familial status and gender are linked to the severity and type of offense charged and prior record in court decision making. Specifying the many interrelationships among these case and defendant attributes is beyond the scope of this chapter. However, future research should consider the joint influences of gender and familial status, not gender alone, as this interacts with the nature of offenses charged. Among other specification problems, for example, the "evil woman" thesis ignores variation among women in terms of their familial status. Other research suggests that familied defendants may more easily justify their wrongdoing by using need-based, rather than greed-based, explanations. In this regard, Steffensmeier's concern with gender differences in both the permanence and fear-evoking elements of illegal behavior could be joined with the familial status of defendants.

Finally, an important issue concerns whether there may be changes in the pattern of statistical sex effects in the future. Unlike those who predict that leniency toward women will decrease with changes in patterns of female criminality and with diminishing paternalistic attitudes toward women, I expect sex effects will persist in statistical analyses. For what the sex effect primarily reflects is differences in what men and women do for families, that is, it is a gender division of labor effect. Thus, as long as women have primary responsibility for child care and asymmetries remain in state supports for father and mother surrogates, we might expect that differences in the treatment of familied men and women will continue.

Urban Justice, Rural Injustice?
Urbanization and Its Effect on Sentencing

MARTHA A. MYERS
SUSETTE M. TALARICO

THE issue of unequal treatment provides the framework for most empirical examinations of criminal sentencing. Traditional approaches seek to estimate the magnitude and direction of differential treatment. More recent research approaches the issue differently and seeks to locate the *sources* of disparity and discrimination. It presumes that the magnitude and direction of unequal treatment can neither be predicted nor understood without identifying the social circumstances under which it is likely to occur. In short, research on sentencing has begun to demonstrate a growing awareness of broader contextual factors that determine the kind of treatment offenders receive.

Several studies have identified urbanization as an important contextual source of unequal treatment. This chapter refines and extends previous work. It distinguishes urbanization from its correlates, particularly court bureaucratization, and estimates its unique effect on sentencing. Further, the chapter broadens the scope of inquiry by considering differential treatment based not only on ascribed characteristics (e.g., race), but also on achieved and legally relevant attributes. Finally, it focuses on differences in setting both the type and duration of punishment.

PRIOR RESEARCH

The relationship between urbanization and crime has been well documented in the literature. Less well understood are its implications for social control responses to crime, in particular, punishment. Several theorists have defined a role for urbanization or its close correlate, bureaucratization. Implicit in this argument is the idea that in highly bureaucratized courts, punishment will not depend on factors that cannot be explicitly construed as legally relevant. By implication, in less bureaucratized courts, sentences will depend on "irrational"—that is, legally irrelevant—criteria.

Conflict theorists, particularly Chambliss and Seidman, also focus on the bureaucratized context within which sentences are imposed. However, they emphasize efficiency as an essential bureaucratic concern that fosters "policies and activities . . . [that] maximize the rewards and minimize the strains for the organization." In highly bureaucratized courts, the enforcement of the law will entail the use of power as an important criterion. To minimize organizational strain, "law enforcement agencies will process a disproportionately high number of the politically weak and powerless, while ignoring the violations of those with power." The specific conflict hypothesis is that in highly bureaucratized courts, sentences will depend on factors such as the relative power and status of the offender. In less bureaucratized courts, a reliance on offender status or power will be relatively less common or absent.

Despite long-standing theoretical interest in urbanization and bureaucratization, studies of their actual effects on sentencing have only recently been undertaken. Without exception, these studies document significant rural-urban differences in sentencing. This research conveys the impression that ostensibly similar offenders are treated differently, depending on whether they are sentenced in rural or in urban courts. Although there are exceptions, most findings support the idea that differential treatment appears to characterize rural courts. It declines with urbanization and subsequent court bureaucratization.

SAMPLE

Georgia's Department of Corrections maintains separate administrative and diagnostic files for offenders sentenced to probation and those sentenced to prison. For the period 1976 through June 1982, these files were combined and a random sample of offenders was drawn ($N = 17,217$). To represent all counties adequately (at least 100 cases per county), sampling was stratified by assigning different sampling percentages to each county. This data set was augmented by comparable samples ($n = 445$ and $n = 1,222$, respectively) collected in two counties (Fulton and DeKalb) that retain separate records on probationers. The total number of cases is 18,884, of which 61.4 percent ($n = 11,604$) received probation, 22.7 percent ($n = 4,285$) received only incarceration, and 15.9 percent ($n = 2,995$) received a split sentence—that is, incarceration followed by a specified term of probation.

FINDINGS

Table 1 presents the characteristics of the total sample. The first set of independent variables consists of offender and offense attributes. Because the probationer file lacked prior record and social class information, analyses for the first sentencing outcome, type of sentence, are particularly tentative. Preliminary analysis, based on two counties for which prior record

information was collected (Fulton and DeKalb), allows one to place some confidence in the findings. It indicated that prior record only slightly attenuates the effects of social background variables. However, because Fulton and DeKalb are urban counties, all findings for type of sentence must be cautiously interpreted.

To disentangle the effects of urbanization from those of court bureaucratization, three aspects of organization that vary markedly in Georgia's Superior Court are focused on workload, specialization, and size. Workload is indicated by the number of felony filings per judge. Specialization refers to the amount of assistance superior court judges receive from lower (e.g., probate, state) courts. It is operationalized as the percentage of other criminal cases (e.g., misdemeanor or traffic) heard by supporting state courts. Both workload and specialization data were available on a yearly basis and matched with the year the offender was sentenced. The final measure, court size, is indicated by the number of probation officers in the court, as of 1980.

The final set of factors included in the analyses were county attributes that are related to urbanization. Uniform Crime Report data allow sorting of the effects of urbanization from those of the county's crime problem. The choice of crime characteristics is based on two criteria: (1) their value as measures of the seriousness of the crime problem and (2) the degree to which they were related to urbanization. The first indicator, the index crime rate for 1980, provides a global measure of the volume of crime. The second measure, percentage of index crimes involving weapons, indicates the dangerousness of, or potential threat posed by, the most commonly occurring and serious crimes in the county.

DISCUSSION

The results presented above provide evidence that, net of selected correlates, urbanization independently affects sentencing outcomes. Importantly, however, the effects of urbanization provide an incomplete, at times misleading, picture of its role during sentencing. The more

TABLE 1

Means, standard deviations, and ranges for independent variables.

Variable	Mean	SD	Range
Offender characteristics			
Sex (female = 0; male = 1)	.89	.30	0-1
Race (black = 0; white = 1)	.57	.49	0-1
Age	26.31	7.35	14-97
Marital status (unmarried = 0; married = 1)	.27	44	0-1
Employment status (unemployed = 0; employed = 1)	.77	.42	0-1
Urban background (farm = 1; other rural = 2; small town = 3; urban = 4; SMSA = 5)	3.05	1.03	1-5
Type of crime			
Homicide = 1; other = 0	.04	.19	0-1
Aggravated assault = 1; other = 0	.08	.27	0-1
Rape = 1; other = 0	.05	.21	0-1
Robbery = 1; other = 0	.05	.22	0-1
Burglary = 1; other = 0	.28	.45	0-1
Property theft/damage = 1; other = 0	.33	.47	0-1
Drug = 1; other = 0	.17	.37	0-1
Offense seriousness	8.86	6.05	1.5-42
Conviction charges	1.61	1.31	1-6
Prior arrests	2.45	4.90	0-53
Prior incarceration (no = 0; yes = 1)	.20	.40	0-1
Urbanization	77,523.01	144,212.66	637-208,778
Court bureaucratization			
Felony filings per judge	267.14	94.38	88-576
Lower court assistance	91.78	11.92	15-100
Probation officers	7.12	2.65	2-14
Control variables			
Index crime rate	3,429.18	2,893.37	5-13,025
Percentage index crimes involving weapons	11.37	16.07	0-82
Income standard deviation	13,774.39	2,309.56	9,280-23,960
Racial income inequality	7,833.98	3,845.29	−1,828-18,082

Note: The following information was available only for prisoners (*n* = 4,285): marital status, employment status, urban background, Georgia native, conviction charges, prior arrests, and prior incarceration. Type of offense is dichotomized for presentation purposes only.

accurate conclusion is that the effect of urbanization on sentencing varies, depending upon the attributes and behavior of offenders.

Consistent with prior research, then, it was found that urbanization is a significant contextual determinant of differential treatment. Furthermore, it conditions differences based not only on ascribed statuses (e.g., race), the focus of most prior research. It also conditions differences based on selected achieved statuses and on the legally relevant variable of offense. Put differently, the effects of many case attributes depend in part on the extent to which the county where the offender was sentenced is urbanized. This is the case not only for decisions about the type of sentence but also for decisions involving the length of actual imprisonment.

In an important respect, however, these results diverge from those of previous research. Rather than diminish differences in treatment, urbanization usually increases them. Apart from regional variation in the conditioning role of urbanization, these findings could differ from previous work because court bureaucratization and other county attributes are controlled for. Thus, these estimates could be less biased than those reported in other analyses.

Whatever the source of these differences, there is consistent evidence that urbanization strongly conditions the relevance of both social background and offense factors. Consistent with conflict-based expectations, urbanization tends to further disadvantage offenders who are members of less powerful groups in society. It appears to increase the imprisonment risk for blacks while decreasing the probability of imprisonment for whites. Urbanization also increases the length of prison sentences imposed on female and unmarried offenders. In contrast, the prison sentences for male and married offenders tend to decline with urbanization. Finally, as counties become more urbanized, younger offenders receive less lenience than their older counterparts. Their prison sentences decline by only 5.7 years, while those of older offenders decline by nearly 10 years.

In sum, once rural-urban differences in crime, inequality, and bureaucratization are controlled, rural judges do *not* appear more particularistic than their urban counterparts. If anything, urban rather than rural judges draw sharper distinctions based on the social background factors of sex, race, and age. Clearly, one cannot exclude the possibility that rural judges discriminate on the basis of factors not included in this study. But at least for several attributes considered consequential in the literature, there is no evidence of greater particularism.

One possible explanation for this pattern lies in the anonymity that characterizes large urban courts. When questioned about their relationship with the public, several urban judges commented that the public generally had no idea of their job performances. They noted that the nature of the circuit helped diffuse responsibility among sentencing judges. The sheer size of the court, then, may foster particularistic judgments, whether well intended or ill intended. Rural judges, who are more visible and often do not share sentencing responsibility, may for these reasons take special pains to appear fair and just. Whatever the source for rural-urban differences in particularism, their existence cautions one against formulating simplistic notions of "urban justice" and "rural injustice."

Urbanization also intensifies differential treatment based on offense. For the initial decision to imprison, rural and urban counties differ in the sentencing of offenders convicted of rape, robbery, and burglary. As urbanization increases, the risk of being imprisoned increases for rape offenders and decreases for robbery and burglary offenders. Thus, urban counties appear particularly intolerant of rape. Their rural counterparts appear intolerant of certain property crimes (burglary and robbery). For the remaining offenses (homicide, assault, property theft/damage, and drug), no rural-urban differences in imprisonment probability exist.

Additional analyses show that the rural-urban differences found cannot be accounted for by rural-urban differences in the seriousness of offenses. Clearly, urban crime may differ from rural crime along dimensions incompletely captured by legal seriousness (e.g., race of victim, amount of property stolen). Unfortunately, the data set lacked more detailed information. Differences in treatment could also reflect rural-urban differences in the official incidence of specific offenses (e.g., homicide). Since only a global measure (index crime rate) was available, this possibility could not be examined. Finally, independent of the incidence of crime, rural counties may differ from urban counties in their fear of crime or in their tolerance level of certain types of criminality.

CONCLUSION

The complex and sometimes unexpected nature of the results contrasts sharply with the simplicity of theories that specify some role for urbanization during punishment. For example, urbanization's role in theories of punishment are largely indirect, being mediated by court bureaucratization. The analysis reported here indicates that bureaucratization does not appear to mediate the effects of urbanization. Instead, urbanization exerts an independent influence on sentencing and is itself a conditioner of differential treatment. Despite some support for conflict-based expectations, contradictory findings as well as differential treatment based on offense present a more complicated picture of sentencing than anticipated by theory. In general, then, the findings suggest the limitations of relying on any single social structural explanation of sentencing.

Finally, this research provides yet another illustration of the importance of placing punishment in its broader social context. It must be emphasized, however, that injunctions to contextualize punishment hardly imply that concern with factors at the individual level of analysis (e.g., race) be abandoned. Indeed, contextual and individual-level factors are inextricably linked. They must be considered simultaneously if one wishes to understand sentencing and, by implication, other social control responses to crime.

Gender, Race, and Social Control: Toward an Understanding of Sex Disparities in Imprisonment

GEORGE S. BRIDGES

GINA BERETTA

F EW features of criminal justice in the United States are more striking than the pronounced disparities in imprisonment between men and women. Whereas men make up slightly less than one-half of the general population of the United States, they make up nearly 95 percent of the prison inmates in the country. Such disparity continues to stir controversy over gender differences in the administration of justice. Courts espouse a doctrine of "equal treatment under the law." Yet gender disparities in imprisonment suggest the possibility of discrimination in the administration of justice— discrimination in the form of less severe punishments for women than men. One writer recently described the differential treatment of men and women by the legal system as a matter of "unequal justice," a legal and social concern demanding rigorous empirical study.

The present study is concerned with explaining gender disparities in imprisonment. The study focuses on whether characteristics of states such as state criminal laws, the administration of criminal justice and mental health services, the economic standing of women compared with men, and racial differences between men and women aid in explaining these disparities. Analyses presented in this chapter rest on the assumption that characteristics of states influence the likelihood of imprisonment for men and women above and beyond the characteristics of the individual defendants involved in criminal cases. The chapter examines the importance of these state characteristics to understanding disparity by comparing their differential influence on aggregate imprisonment rates for men and women. Further, the chapter examines the relationship between race and gender in contributing to disparities in imprisonment between men and women.

SCOPE OF PREVIOUS STUDIES

Almost all of the empirical research published in recent years on sex differences in punishment has focused on the differential treatment of individual criminal defendants processed within a single jurisdiction or court. Analyses done at this level are unable to identify the full effects of such factors as (1) statewide sentencing laws or mental health policies regarding the institutionalization of the mentally ill and (2) areal or regional levels of social inequality on imprisonment practices. Nevertheless, areal characteristics have significant effects on rates of imprisonment, above and beyond the characteristics of individual defendants. For example, state parole policies and laws governing the sentencing of chronic or "habitual" criminal offenders yield pronounced black/white disparities in imprisonment across states and regions of the country. Similarly, regional or state levels of social and economic inequality influence rates of imprisonment, independent of areal rates of serious and violent crime.

Although many of the more recent studies reveal pronounced differences in the treatment of men and women accused of crimes, there is confusion over the effects of major state characteristics on these differences. Factors such as state sentencing laws, practices of hospitalizing the mentally ill, and differences in the social standing of men and women may have differential effects on the imprisonment of men and women, causing excessively lenient dispositions for one group or excessively severe dispositions for another. Further, no studies known to the authors specify the process by which legal or social characteristics of states are associated with differences in male and female rates of imprisonment.

Laws

At least three aspects of state laws and legal policies governing the punishment of criminal offenders may influence sex disparities in imprisonment. The first is whether states have enacted mandatory or determinate sentencing. Typically, these types of laws establish sentences—in the form of prescribed terms for major categories of crime—that must expire before a prisoner may be released. Mandatory and determinate sentencing laws may have many possible effects on sex disparities in imprisonment. The laws tend to increase the length of prison terms, on average, for persons convicted of the most serious and violent offenses. To the extent that sex disparities in imprisonment involve persons convicted of serious and violent offenses and men are more heavily involved than women in these types of crime, mandatory sentencing laws may have the effect of increasing disparities by increasing the rate of imprisonment for men relative to women.

A different type of effect, however, is also possible. In practice, mandatory sentencing laws structure and limit the discretion afforded sentencing judges. With fixed sentence lengths for most classes of crime, judges have less freedom to be excessively lenient or excessively se-

vere in meting out criminal punishments. Sentencing judges who may otherwise be predisposed to treat women offenders more leniently than men will be less able to do so in states with mandatory sentencing. Thus, it is anticipated that the existence of these laws may actually decrease disparities by "equalizing" the treatment of men and women offenders. In this instance, the expected effect would be to increase the rate of imprisonment for women compared with men. Second, laws that impose additional sentences on persons classified as "career criminals" or "habitual offenders" may also influence sex disparities in imprisonment. Typically, "habitual offender" laws result in longer prison terms for those offenders with extensive histories of criminal behavior. To the extent that women defendants are less likely than men to have criminal histories, they will on the average serve shorter prison terms in those states with habitual offender statutes. Habitual offender laws may exacerbate sex disparities in imprisonment by increasing the rate of imprisonment for men relative to women.

Third, many states use individualized parole processes that release inmates from prison before the expiration of their prison terms. Typically, early release is contingent upon three factors: (1) cooperation with institutional programs and rules, (2) diminished threat of criminal recidivism upon release, and (3) compliance with the conditions of release while on parole. Policies such as these place women at an advantage over men because women may be more capable than men of meeting release conditions. Men may be more likely than women to commit infractions of institutional rules, particularly rules prohibiting fighting with other inmates. Further, they are more likely to constitute a threat of recidivism following release. Finally, women are less likely, following release, to have their parole revoked for violation of parole conditions.

It is anticipated that sex disparities in imprisonment will be greater in states that use parole heavily. Women may be more likely than men to obtain early release and avoid parole revocation in those states. As a result, they are more likely to serve shorter terms of imprisonment than men for similar types of offenses.

Hospitalization of the Mentally Ill

Typically, societies use formal mechanisms of control such as the administration of criminal justice only when other control mechanisms fail. Most sociologists agree that societies use imprisonment in inverse proportion to other governmental and social institutions that enforce important social norms. The greatest sex disparities in imprisonment would be expected in those areas where women who constitute problem populations are controlled or "taken care of" through other governmental agencies or institutions. One social institution that has been instrumental in the control of women, apart from prisons, is the psychiatric treatment of the mentally ill. Since the emergence of the mental asylum in the mid-eighteenth century, women have been much more vulnerable than men to being diagnosed or labeled as "mentally ill." And women continue to be more likely to define themselves and be defined by others as having serious mental problems.

Sex differences in imprisonment, particularly the low rates of imprisonment of women, may in part stem from pronounced sex differences in institutionalization in mental hospitals. In effect, hospitalization may serve as a substitute for imprisonment as a mechanism of social control. If state officials are more likely to view women offenders as "mentally ill" or "disturbed" than men, they may more frequently hospitalize them as psychiatric patients and thereby channel them away from prison. In those regions of the country and historical periods where deviant women are processed primarily through mental health facilities, sex disparities in imprisonment may be particularly high. Women will be imprisoned at disproportionately lower rates than men in those regions where women are hospitalized at particularly high rates. Conversely, women will be imprisoned at disproportionately higher rates in those regions where the rate of hospitalization for women is low.

Social Standing

Much of the recent writing on criminal punishment reasons that rates of imprisonment have integral ties to the broader economic and social order in society. For example, Marxist and feminist writers interpret sex differences in punishment in terms of the social standing of women relative to men. They reason that elites use mental health and legal institutions to subordinate women, particularly women who are not effectively regulated by informal or private mechanisms of control.

At least two aspects of the social standing of women are important to sex differences in crime and punishment. The first is the economic standing of women in society. Some writers argue that male elites are most likely to use the mental health system and the administration of criminal justice to enforce laws that preserve the existing economic order. However, in communities and regions characterized by rigid economic stratification of women and men—that is, communities where women occupy primarily marginalized economic roles with low levels of participation in the labor force—women may actually be regulated and controlled primarily through informal rather than formal mechanisms of control.

This line of reasoning suggests that women will experience higher rates of imprisonment in those states and regions of the country where they play active participatory roles in the labor force compared with men. Thus, sex differences in imprisonment in those areas would be expected to be particularly small. In contrast, relatively large sex differences would be expected in those states and regions of the country where women have relatively low rates of labor force participation relative to men.

A second aspect of social standing involves the role of women in the domestic division of labor and specifically in the provision of child care. Courts may impose less severe punishment on women because adult women typically are responsible for children and child raising. Imprisoning them creates a serious and complicated labor problem in the caring for adolescents and young children. Women, more than men, occupy caretaking roles in families that cannot easily be replaced or supplanted by other forms of social or economic support. Being lenient on women, particularly women with dependent children, ensures that parental care of the children continues. Such leniency is far less costly to the state. While "father surrogates exist in the form of welfare benefits and other state supports, ... mother surrogates in the form of foster or institutional care of children are more rare and expensive." Thus, sex disparities in imprisonment may be particularly large in those regions where the burden of dependent children is acute. Women will be imprisoned at disproportionately lower rates than men in those regions because of the heavy child-caring burden. Conversely, women will be imprisoned at disproportionately higher rates in those regions where the burden of dependent children is particularly low.

The Role of Race

In earlier historical periods, sex differences in punishment hinged in large part upon the race of the accused. Any leniency afforded women by courts was extended primarily to whites. Court officials in the nineteenth century viewed black women offenders much differently than white women, as "masculine and hence undeserving of protection." Thus, racial and ethnic differences directly influenced the gender/punishment relationship, conditioning how gender affected the actual outcomes of legal proceedings.

Some previous studies show that courts are more likely to punish minority women severely for crimes than white women. Others show that minority men receive more severe punishments for crimes than white men or minority or white women. Many studies, however, find few or no interactions between race and gender in the severity of punishments.

At least two alternative lines of reasoning suggest that race and gender may interact in relation to areal rates of imprisonment but in very different ways. First, courts may be more likely to imprison racial minorities than whites because minorities may be more heavily involved in serious and violent crime. Minority men, particularly black men, commit serious and violent crimes at significantly higher rates than white men and women and minority women. Further, minority women are more likely to commit serious crimes than white women and some white men. It follows that minority men in particular will be imprisoned at higher rates than white men and all women in areas where they have disproportionate involvement in serious crime. To a lesser extent, courts will also imprison minority women at higher rates than white women for the same reasons. Courts will imprison minority men and women at lower rates than whites in those areas where they have disproportionately low levels of criminal involvement.

A second argument offers an altogether different line of reasoning. Courts may actually be less likely to imprison minority women than white or minority men because they may process minority women offenders more frequently through mental health agencies and hospitals. Historically, minority women have been more vulnerable than white women or men to being labeled mentally ill. Perhaps as a result, minority women are processed and admitted as patients to mental hospitals with the most severe forms of chronic mental illness at rates significantly higher than white women, white men, or minority men. If minority women offenders are more likely to be viewed by justice and mental health officials as mentally ill than others, they may be much more likely to be hospitalized as psychiatric patients. Further, they may be imprisoned at lower rates than white women or men in those regions of the country where they are hospitalized in mental health facilities at particularly high rates.

METHODS OF THE PRESENT STUDY

The study collected data on crime patterns, the administration of criminal justice and mental health, the social standing of men and women, and the demographic composition of all states in the United States for 1980, in addition to data on sex- and race-specific rates of imprisonment for each state for 1982. Measures constructed from these data—aggregated to the state level—provided indicators of (1) male and female rates of imprisonment; (2) aspects of the social and legal structure of states; and (3) levels of crime and arrests for crime, prison capacity, and sex-specific rates of institutionalization for jails and mental hospitals.

The analysis of these data is based on the assumption that characteristics of states such as the laws and legal policies governing sentencing and parole have important effects on rates of imprisonment above and beyond the crime rate. We believe this to be a valid assumption for two reasons. First, laws and legal policies governing sentencing, for example, whether convicted defendants are sentenced under some form of determinate sentencing, typically have statewide jurisdiction. Thus, the effects of these laws on imprisonment, if any, will vary at the state level rather than across smaller jurisdictional areas. Second, states are the appropriate unit of analysis for analyzing disparities in imprisonment as they are operationalized in this chapter. The measure of disparity used in the analysis is as much a measure of length of stay as it is a measure of admission to prison. And because statewide sentencing laws and parole policies determine length of stay in prison, the appropriate unit of analysis is states, with a focus on differences across states in laws and legal policies.

RESULTS

The analyses explored the relationships between sex disparities in imprisonment and the other important characteristics of states. Four findings are particularly noteworthy. First, there is virtually no evidence supporting the assertion that differences in the levels of criminal involvement between men and women explain disparities in imprisonment. Sex differences in rates of arrest for violent crimes have almost no influence on differences in imprisonment, once other aspects of state law and social structure are taken into account.

Second, in sharp contrast is the relationship between the violent crime rate and imprisonment. States characterized by high rates of violent crime tend to have very high rates of imprisonment for both men and women. This finding is important, particularly when combined with the previous finding. It suggests that imprisonment is used in response to the threat of violent crime but not necessarily in direct relation to the rate of persons arrested for serious and violent crimes. Thus, rates of imprisonment may in-

crease or decrease in relation to broad social conditions such as the rate of reported crimes—the "violent crime climate"—rather than the actual volume of offenders arrested for serious and violent crimes.

Third, state parole-use policies and practices of hospitalizing the mentally ill significantly influence the imprisonment rates of men and women, but the effects do not differ significantly by sex. For example, rates of hospitalization of the mentally ill have the anticipated negative effect on imprisonment rates, serving as an alternative to imprisonment as a form of social control. However, there is no evidence that hospitalization rates have a pronounced effect on the imprisonment of women relative to men. Although the effect is greater for women than men, the difference is not statistically significant.

Finally, aspects of state social structure also influence rates of imprisonment. States characterized by relatively high rates of labor force participation by women have higher than average rates of imprisonment for women. Further, states with relatively high concentrations of blacks in the population have significantly higher than average rates of imprisonment for both men and women.

Among women, high rates of labor force participation may disadvantage women more than men. Women are imprisoned at rates significantly higher than average in states where their rates of labor force participation are particularly high. Although the difference between the effects of labor force participation for men and women is not statistically significant, its amount is consistent with the prediction that women's increased involvement in the labor force is likely to subject them to increased formal control. However, contrary to the arguments of some writers, increased participation in the labor force does not result in increased rates of imprisonment due to increased criminality by women. Criminal behavior plays no direct role in the labor force participation/imprisonment relationship.

Of particular concern to the present study is the role of race. Sex differences in punishment may hinge in large part upon the race of the accused, with any leniency afforded women by the administration of justice extended primarily to whites. Further, important racial differences in punishment persist even after controls are introduced for racial differences in involvement in crime. Blacks in urban areas may be more subject to attempts at formal social control and more vulnerable to those controls than whites. To determine whether the effects of state characteristics on sex differences in imprisonment vary by racial group—that is, analyses also explored whether their effects differed for whites and blacks.

Among whites, state characteristics influence men's and women's rates of imprisonment, but the effects do not differ significantly by sex. For example, rates of hospitalization of the mentally ill, as an alternative to imprisonment, advantages neither white men nor women. This finding contradicts the predictions of some scholars that hospitalization is more likely to serve as an alternative to imprisonment for women, particularly white women, as a form of social control. Similarly, rates of parole are associated with equally low rates of imprisonment for white men and women.

There are, however, two noteworthy differences between the equations for white men and women. The relationship between percentage black and imprisonment is substantially stronger for white women than white men, suggesting that white women are more disadvantaged in states characterized by large black populations than white men and more advantaged in areas characterized by extremely small black populations. White women may also be more advantaged than white men in states characterized by black populations disproportionately concentrated in urban areas. The relationship between imprisonment and the degree of urban concentration of the state's black population is stronger for white women than white men. In effect, white women's imprisonment rates are lower than the rates of white men—other factors being equal—in areas where the black population is heavily urbanized.

The evidence for blacks is similar, although the sex differences are more pronounced. Perhaps most striking is the differential influence of percentage black. Percentage black and imprisonment is more strongly related for black women than black men. Black women are sig-

nificantly more advantaged in states characterized by large black populations than black men and more disadvantaged in areas characterized by extremely small black populations. This finding is particularly important in light of the influence of percentage black on white imprisonment rates. Among states where percentage black is large, the imprisonment rates of white and black women are more likely to be equal. Black women's rates will be substantially lower and white women's rates will be substantially higher.

Among blacks, hospitalization for mental illness—as an alternative to imprisonment—may advantage women more than men. Black women are imprisoned at significantly lower rates in states where rates of hospitalization (for women) are particularly high. Although the difference between black men and women is not statistically significant, it sharply contrasts with the pattern observed among whites and is consistent with the prediction that hospitalization is more likely to serve as an alternative to imprisonment for women as a form of social control. It may also mean that hospitalization is rarely used as an alternative for imprisonment among black men.

SUMMARY AND CONCLUSIONS

This study has four noteworthy findings. First, sex differences in involvement in serious and violent crimes contribute substantially less to disparities in imprisonment than suggested or implied by many previous writers. Second, state laws, legal policies, and practices of hospitalizing the mentally ill have no differential influence on imprisonment disparity. And although there exist differences in the influence of rates of hospitalization between men and women, the differences are not pronounced. Third, minority men and women are no more likely than white men and women to be imprisoned at disproportionately high rates in states where they have disproportionate involvement in crime. Fourth, the concentration of blacks in the population has dramatically opposite effects on the imprisonment of white women and black women, significantly increasing the likelihood of imprisonment for white women while decreasing the likelihood of imprisonment for black women.

The study results imply that a common set of factors—more or less equally weighted for men and women—may be responsible for the patterns of imprisonment across states, including sex differences in imprisonment rates. Among these factors are sex-specific rates of labor force participation and hospitalization for mental illness. Sex differences in imprisonment rates will be greatest—other factors being equal—in those states where differences in sex-specific rates of labor force participation and hospitalization of the mentally ill are greatest.

These findings have clear implications for theories of gender, punishment, and social control. More general theories of punishment are needed that clearly specify the linkages between the structural relations of men and women in the larger society and the application of formal social controls in preserving those relations. For example, the results of the present study suggest that a theory of punishment is needed that recognizes the importance of work and specifically the role of gender differences in the labor force in explaining sex differences in rates of imprisonment. Quite clearly, this theory must not ignore the role of crime, particularly violent crime, in explaining variation in the severity of punishments imposed. However, it must view crime as a general property of areas—an element of the social climate—rather than a behavioral characteristic of specific groups giving rise to societal reactions. The theory must also not ignore the role of laws and legal policies in explaining variation in the imposition of punishments. But it must view specific laws as not necessarily mediating between structural relations in the larger society and the severity and types of punishments imposed. Laws and legal policies must play a central role in explanations of punishment. However, this role is extraneous to the relationship between structural relations and the actual punishments society or groups within society impose.

Explanations of disparities in punishment must, simultaneously, move toward perspectives that view criminal punishments in the broader context of other social controls used within the society. Theories of punishment are needed that clearly specify the linkages between the application of punishments and the application of other types of formal controls. For example, any theory must specify the conditions under which the state or courts use institutionalization in mental hospitals as an alternative to incarceration for regulating individuals and groups threatening social relations. Further, the theory must also specify the linkages between the application of punishments and the extensiveness and effects of other less formal controls. Of concern is the relationship between criminal punishments and other institutions within the society—for example, work. A theory of gender, punishment, and social control must explain the relationship between the informal controls placed upon men and women in a "gendered" division of labor and the pronounced sex differences associated with the application of criminal punishments.

SUGGESTED READINGS

Austin, Thomas L. 1981. "The Influence of Court Location on Type of Criminal Sentence: The Rural-Urban Factor." *Journal of Criminal Justice* 9:305-16.

Bickle, Gayle S. and Ruth D. Peterson. 1991. "The Impact of Gender-Based Family Roles in Criminal Sentencing." *Social Problems* 38:372-94.

Blumstein, Alfred. 1982. "On the Racial Disproportionality of United States' Prison Populations." *Journal of Criminal Law and Criminology* 73:1259-81.

Bridges, George S. and Robert D. Crutchfield. 1988. "Law, Social Standing and Racial Disparities in Imprisonment." *Social Forces* 66:601-18.

Bridges, George S., Robert D. Crutchfield, and Edith E. Simpson. 1987. "Crime, Social Structure and Criminal Punishment: White and Nonwhite Imprisonment Rates." *Social Problems* 34:345-65.

Carroll, Leo and Margaret E. Mondrick. 1976. "Racial Bias in the Decision to Grant Parole." *Law & Society Review* 11:93-107.

Curran, Debra. 1983. "Judicial Discretion and Defendant's Sex." *Criminology* 21:41-58.

Daly, Kathleen. 1987. "Discrimination in the Criminal Courts: Family, Gender and the Problem of Equal Treatment." *Social Forces* 66:152-75.

———. 1995. *Gender, Crime, and Punishment: Problems of Equality and Justice.* New Haven, CT: Yale University Press.

Frazier, Charles E., E. Wilbur Bock, and John C. Henretta. 1983. "The Role of Probation Officers in Determining Gender Differences in Sentencing Severity." *Sociological Quarterly* 24:305-18.

Gross, Samuel R. and Robert Mauro. 1989. *Death and Discrimination: Racial Disparities in Capital Sentencing.* Boston: Northeastern University Press.

Hagan, John. 1974. "Extra-Legal Attributes and Criminal Sentencing: An Assessment of a Sociological Viewpoint." *Law & Society Review* 8:357-83.

———. 1977. "Criminal Justice in Rural and Urban Communities: A Study of the Bureaucratization of Justice." *Social Forces* 55:597-612.

Kempf, Kimberly and Roy Austin. 1986. "Older and More Recent Evidence on Racial Discrimination on Sentencing." *Journal of Quantitative Criminology* 2:29-47.

Klepper, Steven, Daniel Nagin, and Luke-Jon Tierney. 1983. "Discrimination in the Criminal Justice System: A Critical Appraisal of the Literature." Pp. 55-128 in *Research on Sentencing: A Search for Reform,* edited by Alfred Blumstein, Jacqueline Cohen, Susan E. Martin, and Michael H. Tonry. Vol. 2. Washington, DC: National Academy Press.

Langan, Patrick. 1985. "Racism on Trial: New Evidence to Explain the Racial Composition of Prisons in the United States." *Journal of Criminal Law and Criminology* 76:666-83.

Myers, Martha A. and Susette M. Talarico. 1987. *The Social Contexts of Criminal Sentencing.* New York: Springer-Verlag.

Tittle, Charles R. and Debra A. Curran. 1988. "Contingencies for Dispositional Disparities in Juvenile Justice." *Social Forces* 67:23-58.

QUESTIONS FOR DISCUSSION AND WRITING

1. The essays by Kleck and by Peterson and Hagan offer contrasting information on the importance of race in sentencing decisions. Can their different findings and conclusions be reconciled? Explain why or why not.

2. Explain Daly's notion of defendants being "familied." Why should being familied make a differences to judges at pretrial release and sentencing decisions?

3. The Myers and Talarico essay and the Bridges and Beretta essay conclude that the social context of sentencing is extremely important in predicting sentencing decisions. Are these findings consistent with essays presented earlier in the book about judges and judicial behavior (e.g., the essays by John Paul Ryan and Martin Levin)?

4. The Bridges and Beretta essay suggests that for some groups of the population, the administration of criminal justice seems to work in tandem with the hospitalization of the mentally ill to control threats to public order or safety. What other social institutions might operate in the same way (i.e., managing or controlling persons in the society with problems who might otherwise end up in our prisons and jails)?

VI

WHAT ROLE DOES CORRECTIONS PLAY IN CRIMINAL JUSTICE?

ONE of the most important yet problematic aspects of the administration of criminal justice is corrections. Annually, state and federal correctional agencies confine and control nearly five million offenders with very diverse personal backgrounds, offense histories, and orientations to crime. Some are children as young as 10 years old; others are aging adults in the last years of their lives. Some offenders seem irrevocably committed to criminal careers; others are first-time offenders who have little experience or history of criminal behavior. Many have chronic drug and alcohol dependency problems, some have histories of extreme violence, and others have histories of acute mental problems and psychological disturbances. The diversity of offenders creates enormous challenges for correctional agencies. They are responsible for the safety and health of these inmates as they serve their sentences in prison, in jail, or on probation. At the same time, they must offer offenders meaningful programs of education, work, and therapy that reduce the likelihood of criminal recidivism.

Since the first penitentiaries in the United States were built at the beginning of the nineteenth century, the orientation and internal organization of American prisons have changed significantly. Whereas many of the earliest institutions stressed reformation of inmates through solitary confinement, religious conversion, and the completion of menial tasks, modern correctional facilities emphasize order and control of inmate populations through complex educational and work programs where inmates work with one another and with staff. Although this evolution has dramatically changed the structure and work of inmates, prison officials, and administrators, a continuing theme in writing and research on corrections has been the effect of imprisonment on inmate life. Much of the very important research on prisons has focused on the inmate social system—the culture and organization of inmate social roles. There is, however, disagreement about how this system develops. Whereas some scholars believe that the culture of inmate life is a direct response to the unique pains of imprisonment, others contend that it is an extension of the culture of poverty and crime in urban America that is imported by inmates into correctional institutions.

The ten essays included in this final section of our book examine the role of prisons and other correctional measures in the administration of justice. The first seven essays review the development and social organization of prisons. The opening essay, by Francis Cullen and Lawrence Travis, describes the historical development of the American prison. Their essay describes important changes in correctional ideologies associated with each major stage in the evolution of prisons.

The second essay is an excerpt from James Jacobs's very important book *Stateville*. The essay summarizes the results of his study of changes in an American prison in the period 1925-1975. Jacobs documents major shifts in correctional policy in Stateville (a maximum-security institution in Illinois) and how those influenced the structure of the prison's administration and social system. The essay is particularly important because the changes occurring at Stateville reflected shifts that occurred in many other states during the same period. Jacobs reveals an evolution of the prison from a state of anarchy to a state of bureaucratic restoration and control. The essay explains this evolution in terms of important changes in the types of power exercised by prison administrators and changes in the political environment external to the prison.

The third essay is an excerpt from Gresham Sykes's classic book on prisons, *The Society of Captives*. In this essay, "The Defects of Total Power," Sykes argues that despite the extreme imbalance of power between correctional staff and inmates, the actual behavior of the inmate population differs markedly from what is either expected or desired by correctional administrators. Violence, other crimes, and aberrant sexual conduct are ordinary occurrences in the institutional existence of a prisoner. The essay portrays correctional staff as constantly struggling to maintain order and control. Furthermore, the struggle is one in which staff often fail. Sykes explains this problem in terms of the types of power and control over inmates operating in prisons. It is, he argues, power without authority—the lack of a sense of duty among the captives. This, in conjunction with pressures toward the corruption of correctional officers, constitutes "structural defects in the prison's system of power" that complicate the management of inmate populations and that are not readily transformed or changed.

The fourth essay, Clarence Schrag's "Foundations for a Theory of Corrections," also discusses defects in the power relations within prisons. His essay is important for at least two reasons. First, the essay describes unique problems of prison administration that extend Sykes's ideas about institutional administration and control. For example, Schrag argues that the prison system operates on the erroneous assumption that correctional officers are fully committed to the objectives and policies of administrators. His essay observes, however, that in most prisons, symbiotic relationships tend to develop between inmates and staff such that the behavior of an inmate or a staff member in any given case is determined as much by the relationships between staff and inmates as by formal policies established by institutional administrators. A second reason the Schrag essay is important is the discussion of inmate social roles. Schrag was one of the first scholars to identify the different positions or "role configurations" inmates play as part of the prison social system.

The fifth and sixth essays, John Irwin's "The Prison Experience: The Convict World" and Hans Toch's "Prison Violence," offer compelling accounts of inmate life from the inmates themselves. Both essays rely heavily on inmate interviews in describing the frustrations of correctional confinement and inmate adaptations to those frustrations. Irwin's essay elaborates primarily on aspects of the inmate social roles identified by Schrag. Toch's essay examines violence within prison and how inmates adapt to the threat of violence in their daily routines. Their essays confirm many of Sykes's and Schrag's observations about the difficulty prison administrators and staff face in controlling inmate behavior.

The essay by Geoffrey Hunt and his colleagues, "Prison Gangs and the Case of the 'Pepsi Generation,'" examines recent changes in the inmate culture of contemporary prisons. Their essay documents greater turmoil in prisons than previous studies have shown. Among the most important causes of this turmoil are newly formed inmate gangs, changes in the demographic composition of inmate populations, and new developments in prison policy. Perhaps most surprising about this research is the fact that even experienced prisoners now seem "at a loss as to how to negotiate this new situation." The essay suggests that the activities of street gangs and prison gangs are inextricably intertwined and that the structure of the inmate social system is as much the result of life experiences external to the prison as it is to experiences within the prison itself.

The final set of essays examines alternatives to imprisonment. Although much of contemporary corrections focuses on prisons and their administration, there is increased interest among scholars, researchers, and political leaders in other methods of correctional control. The eighth essay, Joan Petersilia and Susan Turner's research titled "An Evaluation of Intensive Probation in California," examines the effects of an intensive probation program in the California correctional system. Their essay shows that the use of intensive probation yields no easy solutions to problems encountered in prison. If intensive probation is used with serious felons, recidivism rates will be high.

Kriss Drass and J. William Spencer's essay, "Accounting for Presentencing Recommendations: Typologies Probation Officers Use," describes the perceptual processes that probation officers use in assessing individual offenders' sentencing needs and risks. The essay addresses an important issue in the development and use of alternatives to imprisonment such as probation and intensive supervision. The issue is how individual offenders are selected for the sentencing alternatives. Drass and Spencer argue that probation officers, like police officers and defense attorneys (see essays by Skolnick and Sudnow in Parts III and IV, respectively) rely heavily on typifications of offenders as "low risk" or "high risk" in making their recommendations on sentencing alternatives to the court. Their research supports the idea that these recommendations, like police officers' decisions to arrest and defense attorneys' decisions to negotiate guilty pleas, are highly subjective and influenced by the probation officers' attitudes and beliefs about criminal offenders.

The final essay examines a relatively recent innovation in corrections, shock incarceration or "boot camps." The essay by Merry Morash and Lila Rucker titled "A Critical Look at the Idea of Boot Camp as a Correctional Reform" indicates that when the military boot camp model is combined with rehabilitative methods, the outcomes may not be altogether positive.

PRISONS

An American History of Corrections

FRANCIS T. CULLEN
LAWRENCE TRAVIS

"T HE concept of rehabilitation," Alan Dershowitz has observed, "would have been entirely alien to the early colonists. . . . Society's duty was simply to punish the offender swiftly, publicly and often quite harshly." The cultural baggage that the early settlers brought with them to America did not include the conception that criminal sanctions had the power to save the wayward. Informed by religious doctrines teaching the natural wickedness of the human spirit, they could envision little prospect of reforming those who pursued a sinful path. As historian Samuel Walker has noted, "The colonists took a pessimistic view of humankind: man was a depraved creature cursed by original sin. There was no hope of 'correcting' or 'rehabilitating' the offender. An inscrutable God controlled the fate of the individual." At best, the colonists believed, criminal punishments might scare offenders into mending their ways or convince those contemplating crime to resist such evil temptations. However, the more optimistic assumption that the lawless could be transformed into the law abiding through reformative measures imposed by the state would not arise for nearly two centuries after the Pilgrims and similar pioneers first came to America's shores. It would take this long for reformers to invent a new mechanism that promised to make even the most hardened criminals repent for their transgressions: the penitentiary would be born.

Colonial Americans invoked a wide array of punishments to enforce public safety. Property offenders were frequently sanctioned with fines and compelled to pay restitution for the goods that had been stolen or damaged. This was particularly true for community residents caught for their first violation of the law and fortunate enough to possess sufficient resources to cover the cost of their penalty. As those familiar with the workings of the current legal process are well aware, economic sanctions continue to be distributed with regularity in our courtrooms. Yet if the administration of justice in modern and colonial times shares this common thread, large differences in the two legal systems remain. In this light, three central and distinguishing features of the nature of criminal punishment in bygone days deserve special attention.

First, apart from financial penalties, the bulk of the sanctions used by the colonists intentionally inflicted physical pain by damaging or inconveniencing an offender's body. Perhaps the most favored corporal punishment of this era was whipping, which was often used in conjunction with or in place of fines. Its attractiveness lay in the fact that it held the capacity to subject a criminal to searing pain within moments, could be administered cheaply and easily, and could be imposed on those who lacked the property or means to pay economic sanctions. Yet other punitive measures, more curious by modern standards, were also available to the colonists.

Nearly every community, for instance, was equipped with stocks, a device that forced offenders to sit in a cramped position while their feet and usually their hands also were fastened in a locked wooden frame. A similar form of punishment was the pillory. Miscreants would stand upright and have their head and hands immobilized in openings cut out of a wooden frame. Those with the misfortune of being placed in this instrument could also expect that they might have their "ears nailed to the beams of the pillory and when released they would be compelled to tear their ears loose or have them carelessly cut away by the officer in charge." They could anticipate as well that they would be assaulted by the jeers of their fellow townspeople and, if especially unpopular, risked being pelted with vegetables or perhaps harder and more dangerous objects.

Many offenders, including some of the victims of the stocks and pillory, were branded on the hand and, for repeat or serious crimes, on the face. For example, the crime of blasphemy in Maryland called for imprinting a *B* on the offender's forehead, while thieves in New York had a *T* branded on their thumb. A milder form of identifying the lawless, one made famous in Hawthorne's novel *The Scarlet Letter,* was to force an offender to weave a letter onto his or her garment that symbolized the particular crime that had been committed (e.g., *A* for adultery). Any woman prone to "violence of the tongue" had an additional hazard to avoid: the ducking stool. "To cool her immoderate heat," a village scold or gossip would first be strapped into a chair attached to a lever resting on a post located on the bank of a stream or pond. Then, much to the delight of an onlooking crowd, she would be plunged repeatedly into the water until all were convinced that this bothersome woman would exercise more prudence in the future.

For those who failed to be discouraged by corporal punishment, the colonists displayed no reluctance to resort to surer means to deal with these sinful creatures and thereby preserve the social peace. Similar to the British practice of transporting criminals to America and later to Australia, the colonists simply banished many offenders from living in their community. In particular, strangers convicted of noncapital crimes could rarely avoid a court order mandating that they be flogged and then expelled. Those who were raised within the community yet persisted in recidivating would, if not banished first, inevitably earn a trip to the gallows. In Massachusetts, for instance, a thief convicted of a first offense would be fined or whipped, while the next crime would bring another fine, thirty lashes, and an hour's stay on the scaffold with a rope around one's neck. A further transgression would prove an offender incorrigible and lead to his or her execution.

A second feature of colonial punishments is that they were carried out in public. This tells us that the purpose of imposing sanctions was not simply to exact retributive justice but also to create a spectacle that would humiliate offenders and deter others who feared the prospect of undergoing a similar fate. Punishing the criminal was a truly collective experience in which community members would congregate around the whipping post, stocks, pillory, ducking stool, or gallows—usually located in the town square—to witness the ridicule and suffering of the criminally deviant. The identity of the wayward would be established for all to see and the offender would undergo complete social degradation. In the small, tightly knit colonial communities "where men ordered their behavior in fear of a neighbor's scorn," this public spectacle made for a rational and potent response to crime. Of interest is how drastically we have moved away from the concept of ceremoniously disciplining offenders before the public's eyes. With the exception of such oddities as road gangs working on highways, only rarely is today's citizen privy to the actual punishment offenders endure. Michel Foucault has captured the essence of this shift that has caused punishment to become "the hidden part of the penal process":

It is the conviction itself that marks the offender with the unequivocally negative sign: the publicity has shifted to the trial, and to the sentence; the execution itself is like an additional shame that justice is ashamed to impose on the condemned man; so it keeps its distance from the act, tending always to entrust it to others, under the seal of secrecy. It is ugly to be punishable, but there is no glory in punishing. . . . Those who carry out the penalty tend to become an autonomous sector; justice is relieved of responsibility for it by a bureaucratic concealment of the penalty itself.

A third and final distinguishing characteristic of colonial criminal justice is the sparse use of imprisonment as a punitive measure. Many counties did find the time and resources to erect a local jail. However, except under unusual circumstances, confinement to these structures was not employed as a means of punishing the convicted; nor was it anticipated that incarcerating offenders in an institutional environment could bring about their reform. Instead, jails were used almost exclusively to detain debtors and those awaiting either trial or the discharge of their penalty (e.g., hanging). As Harry Elmer Barnes observed, "They were rarely used for the incarceration of what were regarded as the criminal classes. At each session of the court, there occurred what was called a 'goal delivery,' when the jail was practically emptied of its inmates, only to be filled again during the interval between the delivery and the next session of the court."

It is thus of little surprise that the jail facilities built by the colonists were ill suited to deprive offenders of their liberty for more than a short period. Architecturally, they resembled a regular household; moreover, it was common practice for the keeper and his family to live on the premises. Inmates were free to roam unchained and uncuffed about the jail. Escapes were frequent, and only those held on the most serious charges such as murder would warrant a special guard. Prisoners were given no special clothes to wear and were often required to provide for their own food and living necessities. The prison as we are accustomed to visualizing it today was simply nonexistent. As David Rothman has remarked, "Even at the close of the colonial period, there was no reason to think that the prison would soon become central to criminal punishment."

ENLIGHTENED PUNISHMENT

In the years surrounding the American Revolution, the legitimacy and sensibleness of state-administered corporal punishment became increasingly difficult to sustain. Influenced by the advent of the Enlightenment and, more particularly, by the writings of British utilitarians and French philosophes, the citizens of the new nation began to develop revisionist conceptions of human nature, the social order, and the origins of criminality. Calvinist doctrines preaching the natural depravity of man and woman were largely cast aside and replaced by the more optimistic image of humans as rational beings in control of their own destinies. Political power could no longer be justified by appeals to traditional authority and to the "Divine Right of Kings." Instead, society's members were endowed with inalienable rights and the government's survival was made contingent on its ability to fulfill its part of the social contract. More generally, established institutional patterns and practices were now open to public scrutiny and became vulnerable to change if it could not be shown that they were grounded in principles of rationality.

In this context, it made little sense to trace the cause of crime to the natural sinfulness burdening all of God's human creations. Significantly, Americans in the last quarter of the eighteenth century did not have to search far to arrive at a new understanding of why illegality flourished. Even a cursory inspection of the colonists' legal system, they believed, revealed that criminal punishments were both brutalizing and irrationally administered. Such an archaic system had little hope of deterring humans who were at once free and calculating. It thus seemed urgent that steps be taken to sweep away the barbarous and ineffective sanctioning practices previously mandated by a repressive British monarchy. In the new nation, punishing criminals would finally become an enlightened enterprise. In the words of Harry Elmer Barnes, "The criminal jurisprudence and penal administration of the time could not long remain immune from the growing spirit of progress and enlightenment."

The design to be followed in renovating the legal system inherited from colonial days was supplied in the works of European writers, most notably in Cesare Beccaria's *On Crimes and Punishments* (1764; first published in America in 1777). Their message to American reformers was clear: (1) fashion a criminal code in which sanctions are commensurate with the level of social harm produced by each offense; (2) certainty of punishment is the most important ingredient in ensuring that the costs of crime outweigh the benefits; and (3) excessively severe penalties are both illegitimate and undermine the deterrent powers of the courts. Thus, Montesquieu, as Barnes has noted, "condemned the barbarous injustice of the French penal code and advocated reforms which would make punishments less severe and more nearly adapted to the specific crimes for which they were imposed." Similarly, Beccaria spoke of the need for "mildness of punishment." He asked, "Who, in reading history, can keep from cringing with horror before the spectacle of barbarous and useless torments, cold-bloodedly devised and carried through by men who called themselves wise?" He than asserted that "for punishment to attain its end, the evil which it inflicts has only to exceed the advantage derivable from the crime. . . . All beyond this is superfluous and for that reason tyrannical." Moreover, Beccaria warned that overly harsh sanctions lead only to inhumanity and pervasive lawlessness. "The severity of punishment of itself emboldens men to commit the very wrongs it is supposed to prevent; they are driven to commit additional crimes to avoid the punishment of a single one." Indeed, it is instructive that "the countries and times most notorious for severity of penalties have always been those in which the bloodiest and most inhumane deeds were committed, for the same spirit of ferocity that guided the hand of the legislator also ruled that of the parricide and assassin."

Inspired by the ideas of Beccaria and other Enlightenment thinkers, reformers enthusiastically set about the task of dismantling the colonial justice system and of constructing a correctional process that was to be both more rational and humane. Much effort was devoted to revising criminal codes so that they would better reflect the principle of certainty and to ensure that the punitiveness of sanctions would be proportionate to the harmfulness that any given crime engendered. However, an additional problem presented itself: what could be substituted for the brutal and unreasonably harsh corporal punishments that had been so wantonly imposed by their colonial predecessors? Post-Revolutionary reformers solved a portion

of this quandary by eliminating the use of the death penalty for all but the most serious offenses. But again, this still left open the question of how felons should be sanctioned now that public whippings, brandings, and similar sorts of state responses were deemed unacceptable.

It was not long, however, before an alternative was suggested that not only avoided the distasteful mutilation of an offender's body and the dehumanization of public humiliation but seemed eminently rational as well: criminals could be punished by being incarcerated. County jails, used for years as detention facilities for those awaiting trial, had become a permanent feature of the American landscape. It took only a short jump for reformers to imagine that such structures, if built to be sturdier and more secure, could be relied upon to perform the added function of confining those whom the court might wish to sentence to a more prolonged period of captivity. Further, imprisonment possessed the decided advantage of greatly facilitating the chore of devising a criminal code that made punishment commensurate with the gravity of each crime. Now a simple yet precise formula could be applied: the more serious the offense, the longer the deprivation of liberty.

What is important to remember is that however innovative a measure, the prison was viewed as an instrument of punishment and not one of rehabilitation. Scant consideration was given to how the internal workings of a jail might effect the correction of offenders. The reformers of this day, David Rothman has remarked, "hardly imagined that life inside the prison might rehabilitate the criminal. . . . A repulsion from the gallows rather than any faith in the penitentiary spurred the late eighteenth century [prison] construction." Instead, their major concern was how to resolve the exigency of developing and operating a custodial regime that did not resort to the cruelties of bygone punishments. Faced with this pressing yet quite unfamiliar task of administering an institutional order—after all, even Beccaria had offered no advice as to what the character of imprisonment should be—reformers enjoyed little success in their endeavors. Typically, they evolved facilities that were, in Ralph England's apt description, "dreadful." Perhaps the worst of these early experiments in incarceration was tried from 1776 to 1826 near East Granbury, Connecticut. Here, inmates were housed deep within the belly of a worked-out copper mine. These poor unfortunates found themselves

confined at night in little sheds erected in the mine tunnels, and making nails and shoes above ground during the day. The mine was entered by descending a nineteen-foot ladder into Stygian black and chilling damp. Fractious prisoners were flogged at a surface whipping-post or shackled to the wall of an unlighted chamber at the end of one of the tunnels, where the shackling-hasps are still in place.

Yet reformers in one state, Pennsylvania, proved to be more resourceful and progressive than this. Led by the Quakers and other liberal elements, they embarked on a project to build a prison that would be capable of more than merely punishing its charges. Their efforts eventually came to fruition in the Walnut Street Jail, a structure that Negley Teeters later called "the cradle of the penitentiary." It was here that the idea of using incarceration to reform the criminally deviant received its beginning test in the new nation.

A decade after the close of the Revolutionary War, the local jail situated on Walnut Street in Philadelphia could give the residents of the "City of Brotherly Love" little of which to be proud. Within this gloomy structure, the sexes intermingled freely, the young and naive sat side-by-side with the hardened criminal, jailers sold liquor to all takers, and inmates often stripped their more vulnerable counterparts of their clothes and sold the garments to purchase alcohol. Appalled by these deplorable conditions, Dr. Benjamin Rush asked a group of leading citizens to meet at Benjamin Franklin's home on March 9, 1787 to hear his ideas for criminal justice reform. Rush, a signer of the Declaration of Independence and considered by many to be the father of American psychiatry, urged that a prison be established that would bring about the cure rather than the degradation of its captives. Anticipating developments that would not blossom fully for another century, he called for a therapeutic program that included

the classification of inmates for housing, prison labor, indeterminate sentencing, and individualized treatment.

Rush's provocative presentation proved to be the stimulus for the creation two months later of the Philadelphia Society for Alleviating the Miseries of Public Prisons. In all, thirty-seven prominent Philadelphians banded together on May 8, 1787 to found this reform organization. Notably, the preamble to the society's constitution reflected not only the optimism and humanity inherent in Quakerism but also the conviction that the criminally wayward could be reclaimed.

When we consider that the obligations of benevolence, which are founded on the precepts and example of the author of Christianity, are not canceled by the follies or crimes of our fellow creatures . . . it becomes us to extend our compassion to that part of mankind, who are the subjects of these miseries. By the aids of humanity, their undue and illegal sufferings may be prevented . . . and such degrees and modes of punishment may be discovered and suggested, as may, instead of continuing habits of vice, become the means of restoring our fellow creatures to virtue and happiness.

One large question, however, remained for this nascent reform group to confront: how should the prison be altered to make it conducive to correction rather than to corruption? Evidence suggests that they gained an answer to this problem from their familiarity with the recommendations proposed by the famous British prison reformer, John Howard. Now Howard had become initiated into the pathologies of imprisonment when, at 47 years of age, he assumed the position of sheriff of Bedford, England. After inspecting the three local jails under his authority, he was thoroughly dismayed by the disease, filth, exploitation, and disorder that flourished within these structures. In search of a more adequate mode of prison organization, he set forth between 1773 and 1790 on several extensive tours of jails both in England and on the European continent. He was most impressed by the facility at Ghent in Flanders and by the St. Michele House of Correction for boys in Rome, both of which advocated the betterment of offenders through hard work, prayer, silence, and isolation in separate cells at night. In this light, Howard's own blueprint for prison reform championed the cause of rehabilitation over punishment as well as the curative potential of nightly solitude in a single cell: "if it be difficult to prevent their being together in the daytime, they should by all means be separated at night. Solitude and silence are favorable to reflection, and may possibly lead them to repentance."

The members of the reform society in Philadelphia had little reason to dispute the wisdom of Howard's faith in cellular incarceration. After all, their own observations of the Walnut Street Jail had amply demonstrated that it is pure folly to allow inmates to interact with one another and thereby reinforce their criminal inclinations. Further, Quakers could well remember the stories of their ancestors who were cast into British jails as part of their religious persecution. Here, these early Quakers endured vile living conditions and witnessed the tragedy of forcing offenders of all sorts to live within the same confines. Society members thus launched an enthusiastic campaign announcing the therapeutic advantages of single-cell imprisonment. "Solitary confinement to hard labor," they claimed, "will prove the means of reforming these unhappy creatures." Exercising substantial political influence, their labors proved productive shortly afterward. On April 5, 1790, they secured passage of a law mandating that a cell block be raised in the yard of the Walnut Street Jail. In all, sixteen individual cells were to be constructed, eight on each of two floors. These new domiciles were to be reserved to house the "more hardened and atrocious offenders" in solitary confinement. Further, reflecting a broader trend toward the centralization of governmental powers, the Walnut Street Jail was now given statewide responsibilities. Although still made to pay for the keep of all criminals sentenced in their local jurisdictions, counties were instructed to send their more confirmed offenders to do penance in the lonely solitude of the Walnut Street Jail. The notion of a state penitentiary had finally emerged in America.

The innovation at this Philadelphia prison quickly received substantial acclaim and attracted a stream of interested parties from both other states and foreign lands. Yet this initial optimism gradually turned into a profound despair. Beset by a flood of commitments, the core principle of solitary confinement no longer proved pragmatic and was violated repeatedly by those managing the institution. The Walnut Street Jail had been transformed into a den of idleness and criminal contamination. In the face of these disheartening circumstances, many stood poised "to throw the whole thing overboard and return to the simpler and swifter methods of dealing with criminals which had previously prevailed." However, this was not what was to occur in the years ahead.

THE INVENTION OF THE PENITENTIARY: THE GREAT AMERICAN EXPERIMENT

Today, the fact of imprisonment is deeply enmeshed within the taken-for-granted side of social life. For most of us, it strains the imagination to conceive of what could be done to serious felons if they were not incarcerated. Talk of abolishing prisons might provide some good argumentative fun, but "everyone knows" that in the end such ideas must be dismissed as merely utopian. Indeed, the conclusion that we must place offenders behind bars is such an accepted wisdom in our culture that one question on the Wechsler IQ Test for Children (Revised) is: why should criminals be locked up?

For Americans living in the first part of the nineteenth century, however, being able to supply an answer to this query would not necessarily have been looked upon as a sign of intelligence. The expanded use of jail sentences as a means of punishing criminals had accomplished little other than the creation of another social problem. Prison facilities were proving to be financial burdens, custodial nightmares, and incubators of crime and vice. Even the progressive reform at the Walnut Street Jail was wallowing in failure. The place of the social institution of imprisonment within society remained tenuous, and many could readily see the advantages of returning to earlier and less troublesome methods of inflicting punishment. "Our favorite scheme of substituting a state prison for the gallows," one New York lawyer remarked in 1818, "is a prolific mother of crime.... Our state prisons, as at present constituted, are grand demoralizers of our people." It seems unlikely that more than a few of his contemporaries would have found reason to voice any disagreement with this claim.

Further, when Americans glanced abroad, they could discover scant evidence that the sanction of imprisonment was either an efficacious or humane response to the problem of crime. European nations displayed a reluctance to embrace the prison sentence as the normative or preferred penalty to be imposed on adult felons, and no country had made offender reform the expressed goal of its criminal justice system. In Great Britain, for example, efforts to operationalize John Howard's design for a truly reformative institution had met with little success. While Englishmen committing minor property offenses did begin to receive short prison terms beginning in the 1770s, those convicted of more grievous felonies continued to be hanged or sent to Australia (which from 1787 to 1867 saw 163,000 convicts come to its shores). While awaiting transportation, many offenders were kept for much of each day within the dreary holes of "Hulks," decommissioned warships moored at dockyards. It was not until 1842 that the first real penitentiary appeared at Pentonville, and not until the 1850s that Britain would institute a national system of prisons and punish major crimes with long-term sentences.

Yet however bleak the future of the American prison appeared in the early portions of the 1800s, by the third decade of this century public opinion had experienced a remarkable reversal. Faith suddenly ran high that the errant could be restored to conformist ways if placed within an orderly prison that facilitated penitence through a regimen of discipline, religion, hard work, and separation from all criminal influences. The "penitentiaries" that emerged were now held up as sources of national pride. Foreign nations felt compelled to send emissaries—the most notable being the French observers Gustave de Beaumont and Alexis de Tocqueville—to study this "great American experiment" in penal reform. In this context, prison construction surged ahead, and Americans soon witnessed the invention of the first large-scale, state-administered penitentiary system that ostensibly had offender rehabilitation as its overriding concern.

What engendered this precipitous rise of prisons dedicated to the cure of its captives? One necessary condition was clearly the development of increasingly powerful and centralized state governments. Within an expanding capitalist economy, these new administrative structures possessed the authority and bureaucratic machinery to accumulate the huge sums of money required to construct and to operate large incarcerative institutions. Yet the special fervor that surrounded the notion that criminals should be saved and not simply punished through imprisonment can perhaps be traced more directly to another set of circumstances: changes in American society provided the populace with revised understandings of the origins of crime, which in turn enabled them to see the logic of pursuing an innovative control policy. The prospect of rehabilitating criminals in the prison was no longer to appear either futile or far fetched to Americans of the 1830s.

In his *The Discovery of the Asylum,* historian David Rothman has thus suggested that the fixed order and familiar ways of colonial days suffered a deep erosion as the new nation proceeded into the Jacksonian era. Americans found themselves residing in a more open and fluid society marked by geographical as well as socioeconomic mobility, urban growth, and the beginnings of modernization. With roots and memories extending back to an earlier and more stable era, many responded to these changes with considerable apprehension. It seemed that the social fabric was becoming unglued; disorder, not order, prevailed before them.

In this atmosphere, there was little mystery to Jacksonian Americans as to the origins of crime and deviance. Unlike their predecessors, they did not see these as resting in either the natural depravity of the human spirit or in the existence of an irrationally formulated and administered criminal law. Instead, the lawlessness threatening communal peace was now held to be symptomatic of a pervasive breakdown in the social order. With discipline attenuated and values in flux, the young and morally vulnerable were being readily exposed to the corrupting influences of an increasingly secular society.

Again, Americans in the 1820s and 1830s felt that they had good reason to be anxious about society's capacity to weather the severe strains it endured. Yet while they despaired at the passing of a life which was at once quieter and more cohesive than the one they now experienced, they nevertheless manifested a firm sense of optimism that criminal deviance could be eradicated from their midst. Notably, their conviction that the pressing problem of crime could be solved emanated directly from their understanding that social disorder was the root cause of all lawlessness. For this explanation immediately suggested what seemed a foolproof strategy for crime control: the casualties of the disorderly society should be placed within an orderly environment that would effect their reform by furnishing them with the strong moral fiber needed to resist the corrupting influences that were rampant in the wider community. As David Rothman has commented, Americans were convinced that the intimate connection between social chaos and criminality could be severed if only "a special setting for the deviant" could be fashioned. "Remove him from his family and community and place him in an artificially created and therefore corruption-free environment. Here he could learn all the vital lessons that others had ignored, while protected from the temptations of vice." The prison, of course, presented an ideal locale in which to pioneer this new reformative society.

The most urgent task confronting reformers was to restructure the internal routine of the penitentiary so that it would affirm the principles that had made for an orderly society in colonial times. It was clear that offenders would have to experience the discipline absent in their defective upbringing. Respect for authority would be mandated, and obedience to unbending rules demanded. Idleness, an inevitable occasion for vice and mischief, would be replaced by hard and steady labor aimed at instilling good habits that inmates could carry with them upon release. The value of religion would similarly be emphasized, with all offenders being amply educated in Christian doctrines. And above all, inmates would be totally separated from contacts that might result in their further contamination and commitment to criminal ways. The prison must not degenerate into a school for knavery and licentiousness.

Two competing reform movements emerged, each trumpeting a distinct program for how the core principles of an orderly society of captives could best be satisfied. As might be expected, the Quakers and other liberal elements in Pennsylvania combined to form one of the groups at the forefront of this quest to establish a truly rehabilitative institution. Learning from their dismal failure at the Walnut Street Jail, these reformers were adamant that freedom from debasing criminal interactions could only be attained through a system of total solitary confinement that was never to be compromised. They proposed that each inmate be housed in a separate cell, day and night, for the entire term of incarceration. No communication with either fellow captives or outside visitors would be permitted. Even contact with guards and prison authorities was to be kept to a bare minimum. Inmates would be compelled to work alone in their cells at such tasks as spinning or shoemaking. The Bible was to be the only reading material that would be made available, and it was anticipated that its teachings would facilitate the process of penitence as offenders reflected upon their errant ways in the loneliness of their cells.

The Pennsylvania plan was put into practice when the state legislature approved the construction of two prisons, one to be located in Pittsburgh and the other at Cherry Hill in Philadelphia. The latter institution, designed by John Haviland and completed in 1829, proved to be the more renowned of the two new "penitentiaries." Here, inmates resided in cells nearly twelve feet long, seven and one-half feet wide, and sixteen feet high. They were released from confinement for one hour each day to exercise in a yard adjoining their cells and enclosed by a high barrier that precluded sight in or out. The remainder of their tenure in captivity was spent working, eating, sleeping, Bible reading, and contemplating within the boundaries of their thick-walled rooms.

Meanwhile, a rival scheme of prison organization, the "silent" or "congregate" system, had evolved in New York. A new state prison had been erected in 1817 within the town of Auburn. Influenced by Quaker thinking, Auburn officials soon introduced the practice of total solitary confinement. Between 1821 and 1823, the "oldest and most heinous offenders" were held in a small seven by three and one-half by seven feet cell in complete seclusion and without the possibility of passing the time through labor. The results of this experiment were disastrous. Several inmates attempted suicide, and numerous others suffered mental collapse. The governor eventually intervened and pardoned those enduring the horrifying fate of idle solitude.

With the abandonment of solitary confinement at Auburn, an alternative mode of reformative discipline was desperately needed. Auburn warden Elam Lynds, assisted by his deputy John Cray, was quick to supply a prescription for tackling this exigent task. Inmates would now sleep alone in their cells, but congregate during the day for meals, hard labor, and Sunday worship. However, in Lynds's regime, inmates were not allowed

to utter a single word and were taught to march about the prison in a lock-step shuffle with eyes downcast. Where the Quakers sought to separate offenders from corrupting criminal conditions through secure and sturdy walls, Lynds and his fellow Auburn reformers relied upon the rule of silence, backed by a ready willingness to inflict the pain of the whip, to bring about this paramount end.

Advocates of the Quaker "solitary" model and of the Auburn "silent" system engaged in heated and at times vitriolic debate in their efforts to convince others—including foreign visitors—of the greater merits of their particular reform programs. The New Yorkers asserted that their plan was both more efficacious and economical and accused their competitors of building an apparatus certain to induce insanity. The proponents of the Pennsylvania design dismissed this latter charge and typically leveled one of their own: congregate living violates the sacred principle of absolute insulation from

criminal contamination and hence is doomed to failure. Yet whatever their disagreements over the specifics of what constitutes a preferred institutional routine, it must be remembered that both camps embraced the common vision that an orderly prison community would save the errant from a life of crime. They shared as well a belief that has persisted in varying degrees of intensity to this very day: the purpose of the criminal justice system should be to rehabilitate offenders and not merely to subject them to the irrationality of aimless punishment.

THE NEW PENOLOGY

By the time the maturing American republic advanced into the Civil War period, much of the penitentiary's initial glitter had badly waned. In stark contrast to the confident and ebullient atmosphere that had reigned just three decades before, few enthusiasts could now be located that would pronounce this "great" experiment in correctional reform a success. More common if not ubiquitous among social commentators was the conclusion reached by the noted penologists Enoch C. Wines and Theodore Dwight in their *Report on the Prisons and Reformatories of the United States and Canada*. After completing an extensive survey of existing penitentiaries, they declared that "there is not a state prison in America in which the reformation of the convicts is the one supreme object of the discipline, to which everything else must bend. . . . There is not a prison system in the United States, which . . . would not be found wanting. There is not one, we feel convinced . . . which seeks the reformation of its subjects as a primary object."

Several factors combined to leave the grand promise of reformers that penitentiaries will save the wayward substantially unfulfilled. Because congregate living was less expensive than unbroken solitary confinement and permitted the establishment of group work arrangements that proved to be more productive and hence profitable than the labors of single inmates, the Auburn design served as the blueprint for nearly all American prisons that were built in the middle portion of the 1800s. However, the wardens of these institutions were not always equal to the task of enforcing the regime of deafening silence prescribed by Elam Lynds and his fellow New York reformers. These wardens were often faced with the problem of severe overcrowding, which in turn undermined the pragmatics of providing nightly solitude for each of their charges and fostered idleness that gave inmates both the chance and need to communicate with their compatriots. Moreover, to effect the cure of the incarcerated, prison officials were equipped with an unproven theory of rehabilitation—isolation from social intercourse, which even if applied in good faith, few experts of today would see as enhancing the reintegration of convicts back into the eminently social world that prevails outside the penitentiary. This chore of changing the lawless into the law abiding was further complicated by the courts' reluctance to place the best candidates for reform—the young and beginning criminals—under the wardens' supervision. Rather, only the older and habitual offenders were to be the objects of their enlightened concern. To make matters still worse, these more refractory creatures were bereft of any incentive to strive for their betterment while in captivity. Since they all served flat or determinate sentences and thus their release from prison was not contingent on their showing signs of being cured, there was little a warden could do, short of physical abuse, to move inmates to undertake a concerted effort to forsake their sinful ways. Confronted with these diverse and seemingly insurmountable barriers to administering a reformative environment, officials soon abandoned therapeutic ends and instead concentrated their energies on the more pressing demand of maintaining peace and security within their prison communities.

It is notable as well that few in the more affluent and influential classes objected to this displacement of goals. For when they had occasion to scrutinize the composition of the penitentiary populace, they could see that only immigrants and the native poor were being held captive. There was some sentiment that these incarcerated souls suffered from hereditary defects that made them incurably treacherous, and considerable agreement that they were drawn from the worst element of the dangerous classes

mired at the bottom reaches of the social order. Many among the advantaged thus felt thankful that the high and impenetrable walls of society's fortress-like penitentiaries, once built to insulate inmates from corrupting influences, could now be used to ensure that these menacing criminals would remain securely caged and unable to prey upon the defenseless public. While "the promise of reform had built up the asylums," Rothman has remarked, "the functionalism of custody perpetuated them."

Yet just when it appeared that American corrections might discard the vision of doing good through rehabilitation and regress to the point of again espousing a purely punitive crime control ideology, a wave of fresh ideas holding out exciting possibilities burst upon the scene. In their attempt to reaffirm the viability of prison rehabilitation, the advocates of this "new penology" set forth an agenda that exalted an innovative reformative tool: the indeterminate sentence. They asserted that the founders of the initial penitentiaries had erred when they embraced the fallacious assumption that merely encapsulating offenders within the boundaries of an orderly and disciplined prison environment is sufficient to achieve their reformation. From their perspective, the flaw in this early theory of corrections is that it gave scant consideration to the problem of how the process of sentencing is intimately involved in the process of reform. The proponents of the Quaker and Auburn designs had thus accepted the Classical school's conception of criminal law shaped in the days of the Enlightenment. They simply had not perceived the need to be critical of a system that allowed judges, operating within the strictures of more or less specific criminal codes prescribed by legislators, to assign each offender a flat or determinate sentence. Those at the head of the movement for a new penology, however, were certain that fixed terms did little to make reform foremost in the minds of inmates. Knowing their exact release date prior to entering the penitentiary, convicts quickly learned that once they survived their sentence, they would be turned free, cured or not. As such, they could afford to be passive if not resistant actors in the process of reform as they shuffled in silence about the prison.

To rectify this counterproductive situation, post-Civil War reformers were clear that "the prisoner's destiny should be placed, measurably, in his own hands; he must be put into circumstances where he will be able, through his own exertions, to continually better his own conditions. A regulated self-interest must be brought into play, and made constantly operative."

This could be readily accomplished, they proposed, by making all sentences indeterminate and by investing powers of release in the hands of prison officials. In this way, inmates would be struck by the forceful reality that they would be deprived of their liberty until they were fully fit to resume their place in society. With the link between freedom and cure manifest, they would now have good reason to work diligently for their self-improvement. Meanwhile, prison officials would exercise their discretion to reward reformed inmates with release, while keeping their more incorrigible brethren safely incarcerated until the time when they too would bend to the therapeutic powers of the indeterminate sentence. A system that could promise both the reform of offenders and the protection of society was thus suddenly within reach.

The various threads of this new penology first coalesced into a coherent correctional philosophy at the National Congress on Penitentiary and Reformatory Discipline in October of 1870. Organized by Enoch C. Wines, this meeting attracted 130 delegates from 24 states, Canada, and South America. Over the course of a week, they listened to forty papers authored by the leading penologists of this era. Among the more influential were several papers, including one made available by Crofton himself, which described Sir Walter Crofton's famous "Irish Progressive System."

A Britisher by birth, Crofton had been appointed the director of the Irish prison administration in 1854. A short while later, he instituted a scheme that allowed inmates to gradually prove their reform and thereby win early release from their prison sentence. Upon arriving at the penitentiary, all offenders were immediately placed in solitary confinement for a period of eight to nine months. To appreciate the pains of idleness and, by comparison, the fruitfulness of labor, no work was allowed in the first three months of incarceration. After completing this initial stay in solitude, inmates were then advanced to a second stage. Here, each was allowed to be the "arbiter of his own fate." Similar to the token economies that modern-day behavior modifiers construct, inmates were rewarded with "marks" for industriousness and were penalized by having marks subtracted if they engaged in disruptive behavior or evidenced a defiant attitude. Once a sufficient number of marks had been accumulated, offenders would progress to an open prison in which guards were unarmed and few restrictions were imposed on the inmates' lives. Crofton conceptualized this "intermediate" institution as "a filter between the prisons and the community." Those who "misconduct themselves are at once reconsigned to more penal treatment," while those who continue to display self-discipline are "restored to liberty." The final stage was for inmates to be granted a conditional discharge on a "ticket-of-leave." These offenders were expected to register with the local police and could be returned to prison for a failure to adjust properly (e.g., unemployed, consort with bad companions, commit another offense) to their newly earned freedom. Since a total indeterminate structure of sentencing was not operative, inmates who were unable to progress through all of the stages were released once the maximum limit of their sentences had expired.

Significantly, Crofton drew many of the core features of his plan from the bold experiment in correctional reform previously undertaken by Alexander Maconochie. Yet he was not alone in borrowing from this pioneer in reformative penology. As John Barry recognized, many of the ideas promulgated at the 1870 Cincinnati Congress "were taken from Maconochie's writings, the language sometimes lifted bodily." Now Maconochie was granted the opportunity to embark on his innovative program of reform at the penal colony located on Norfolk Island, Australia. Appointed superintendent in 1840, a position he had sought, he welcomed the task of attempting to rehabilitate the criminal population that the English courts had seen necessary to transport to this distant continent. He promptly abolished the punitive and degrading practices that had been in use, and introduced in their place a "mark system" that would permit inmates to move incrementally toward a future of decreasing restrictions and, ultimately, of freedom. A firm believer in the indeterminate term, he commented that "when a man keeps the key to his own prison, he is soon persuaded to fit it to the lock." He voiced as well the conviction that we accomplish little by simply repressing the lawless. Using a medical metaphor that later writers would employ with regularity, he thus commented:

When a man breaks a leg, we have him into a hospital, and cure him as speedily as possible, without even thinking of modifying his treatment, so as to make his case a warning to others. We think of the individual, not of society. But when a poor fellow creature becomes morally dislocated, however imperious the circumstances to which he may have fallen victim, we abandon all thought of his welfare, and seek only to make "an example" of him. We think of society, not of the individual. I am persuaded that the more closely and critically we examine this principle, and whether abstractly, and logically, or above all Christianly and politically, the more doubtful it will appear, yet it lies at the root of nearly all our penal institutions, and reasoning on which they are founded.

By all accounts, Maconochie's experiment in the humanistic, rehabilitative treatment of offenders proved a resounding success. Yet despite such favorable results as low recidivism rates and a peaceful prison order, the controversy surrounding his "coddling" of criminals led to his dismissal in 1844. Within two years' time, floggings and then riots had returned to the penal colony at Norfolk Island.

It is clear, however, that the most discussed and energizing of all of the congress' presentations was the one delivered by Zebulon R. Brockway. As superintendent of the Detroit House of Correction, he had already succeeded in securing the passage of a variation of the indeterminate sentence. After much agitation, he had convinced the legislature to grant him the power to detain women over the age of 15 and convicted of prostitution for a period of up

to three years. The exact date of release for any individual inmate would then be regulated by her progress toward reform. Writing in 1868 on behalf of the law, Brockway had contended that "to commit these persons to the House of Corrections until they are reformed will be a strong inducement for them to enter immediately upon the work of self-improvement."

Now at the congress in 1870, Brockway was prepared to offer the delegates both a compelling defense of reformatory penology and a strategy for putting this hopeful theory into practice. Entitling his talk "The Ideal of a True Prison System for a State," he began by noting that if we are to believe that "punishment, suffering, degradation are . . . deterrent . . . then let prison reform go backward to the pillory, the whipping post, the gallows, the stake; to corporal punishment and extermination!" Brockway, however, was aware that we should be capable of much more than this. "But if the dawn of Christianity has reached us, if we have learned the lesson that evil is to be overcome with good, then let prisons and prison systems be lighted by this law of love." Indeed, to solve the crime problem we must abandon "the thought of inflicting punishment upon prisoners to satisfy so-called justice, and turn toward the real objects of the system: the protection of society by the prevention of crime and reformation of criminals." Yet Brockway followed up his appeal for the goal of inmate rehabilitation with the stern warning that efforts in this direction will inevitably founder until the time comes that prison stays are made indeterminate. "The remedy cannot be had," he argued, "so long as a determinate sentence is imposed at the time of trial. . . . The writer's experience of more than twenty years . . . forces the conviction that a reformatory system cannot exist without it, and that it is quite indispensable to the ideal of a true prison system."

Based in large part on Brockway's imaginative thinking and the pathbreaking experiments of Crofton and Maconochie, the congress concluded by setting forth a "Declaration of Principles." Thirty-seven in number, these principles elucidated the core parameters of the "new penology" that had crystallized during the fervor of the previous week's meetings. The delegates called for the creation of prison orders which embodied the Irish Progressive System and provided inmates with industrial labor and training as well as with academic and religious education. They asserted that offenders should live in sanitary and humane conditions while incarcerated and should be given assistance at finding employment and "regaining their lost position in society" when discharged. They felt also that separate institutions should be forged for women, juveniles, and the less hardened criminals. Further, they suggested that political influences be purged from the correctional system and that guards be supplied with more adequate training. But again, underlying these varied recommendations were two central doctrines: a firm belief in the curative powers of the indeterminate sentence and a fundamental conviction that the "supreme aim" of American criminal justice should be "the reformation of criminals, not the infliction of vindictive suffering."

The tenets of the new penology received their fullest expression in the reformatory that opened at Elmira, New York in 1876. None other than the eminent Zebulon Brockway was lured to supervise the establishment of this enterprising institution. By design, Elmira was to hold first-offenders from the ages of 16 to 30; in practice, much of the inmate population was composed of recidivists. Further, while Brockway would have preferred that all of his charges be given purely indeterminate sentences, he settled for a system of maximum terms prior to which cured inmates might be allowed to reenter the community. To facilitate inmate correction and following Crofton's lead, an elaborate mark scheme was developed. Brockway placed arriving offenders in the middle of three grades. Those exhibiting continued progress toward reform earned marks that advanced them to the first stage and eventually led to their conditional release. Alternatively, troublesome inmates were lowered one level, and then were faced with the tedious task of climbing their way back up to the higher stages where they could be considered for a ticket-of-leave or what Americans now termed "parole." Finally, all inmates were exposed to a strenuous daily schedule that included a combination of such diverse activities as industrial labor, vocational training, schoolwork, religious instruction and prayer, military drill, and methodical physical exercise. This regimen meshed nicely with Brockway's desire to ensure that offenders were left with not a "moment's idleness for either hand or head."

Despite the intense intellectual excitement that characterized the emergence of the new penology of the 1870s, this reform paradigm did not immediately spark a major renovation of the American system of crime control. Elmira did succeed in prompting a number of other states to erect reformatories for younger criminals. However, the principles drafted in Cincinnati found their way less quickly into the wider domain of adult corrections; life in the state penitentiaries remained much the same. Nevertheless, it must be recognized that the champions of the new penology played a large role in bolstering the legitimacy of rehabilitative ideology at a time when it appeared vulnerable to being discredited and swept aside. Moreover, they contributed a forceful therapeutic program that would constitute the starting point for a major reform movement which would arise in the very next generation ahead.

THE PROGRESSIVE ERA: INDIVIDUALIZED TREATMENT

The first two decades of the 1900s witnessed the ascendancy of a potent spirit of reform that reverberated throughout American society. It was a time, according to Richard Hofstadter, in which "the 'impulse' toward criticism and change . . . was everywhere so conspicuous." Those who pledged allegiance to what would become known as "Progressivism" were attracted to this movement from diverse backgrounds and for equally diverse motives. Nevertheless, they embraced the common vision that the social order was in desperate need of amelioration and shared as well the conviction that the maladies afflicting society were surmountable within the broad boundaries of existing institutional arrangements. Liberal though speedy reform, not revolutionary class warfare, would solve the difficulties facing the nation and bring forth the dawn of a new age of social progress.

For the Progressives, "big business" posed the gravest danger to the sanctity of American democratic ideals. The increasing concentration of corporate wealth and power now threatened both to make a mockery of the principle of free enterprise and to enable the "robber barons" to exert such inordinate influence on politicians as to fundamentally corrupt the cherished process of representative government. The corporate menace could only be diminished, the Progressives cautioned, if the public sector were fortified to the point where it could dominate the private sector. They thus argued that the state must be endowed with sufficient authority to regulate business practices and, when necessary, to bust perilous trusts.

The Progressives' faith in the state extended to other realms as well. The advent of a burgeoning and heartless capitalist industrialism had produced a variety of casualties, particularly among urban immigrants vulnerable to exploitation. "Insanitary [sic] housing, poisonous sewage, contaminated water, infant mortality, the spread of contagion, adulterated food, impure milk, smoke-laden air, ill-ventilated factories, dangerous occupations, juvenile crime, unwholesome overcrowding, prostitution, and drunkenness," Jane Addams zealously wrote, "are the enemies which the modern city must face and overcome would it survive." Christian charity might help to mitigate the harshness of these conditions, and social activists could uplift some unfortunates by manning settlement houses in the midst of slum neighborhoods. But the very enormity of the social problems besetting the urban environment demanded that larger measures be pursued that possessed the capacity to bring about more lasting and far-reaching improvements. In their crusade for social justice against entrenched interests, the Progressives had little choice but to turn to the government for support. They now billed the state as an "agency whose positive assistance is one of the indispensable conditions of human progress." Their strategy, successful in many instances, was to prompt legislators into passing laws that would give the injured worker compensation, ban child labor, supply financial aid to widows with children, provide for old-age pensions, and establish boards of community

hygiene. In their efforts to humanize the industrial society, they thus helped to launch the start of the welfare states.

For those disturbed by the plight of the criminal and delinquent within the correctional system, the coming of the Progressive era and its ethic of reform furnished a firm sense of optimism that meaningful changes could be won. In a presentation in 1911 titled "The Future Attitude Toward Crime," George W. Kirchwey commenced by telling his audience that "we are met at a fortunate time. The moral atmosphere . . . is electric with impulses toward a better understanding and a better ordering of the relations of society to the individual." But in this favorable context, what specifics should constitute the reform agenda to be followed? The beginning answer to this question, the Progressives felt, could be found in the "new" penology first espoused several decades before. It was clear that rehabilitation, not retributive punishment, should guide the sanctioning process. At the turn of the century, Charlton T. Lewis voiced sentiments that would be echoed repeatedly in the years to come when he asserted that "the method of apportioning penalties according to degrees of guilt implied by defined offenses is as completely discredited, and is as incapable of a part of any reasoned system of social organization, as is the practice of astrology or . . . witchcraft." He then continued, "The entire abandonment of retribution as a motive is the first condition of a civilized criminal jurisprudence." Further, there was a uniformly strong reaffirmation of the value of the indeterminate sentence. Again, Lewis's words prove a worthy example of Progressive thinking: "The time will come when the moral mutilations of fixed terms of imprisonment will seem as barbarous and antiquated as the ear-lopping, nose-slitting and head amputations of a century ago."

However, the Progressives were not content simply to apply the penological principles inherited from their predecessors, and hence they soon moved to embellish the new penology with the ideas of their own generation. In this regard, the incipient disciplines of psychology and sociology revealed how this earlier therapeutic paradigm could be fleshed out. Suggesting a Positivist school approach to crime and its control, the logic of these behavioral sciences instructed Progressives to begin by investigating the factors which precipitate criminal involvement. Since the life experiences of one offender will inevitably differ from the next, the source of crime in any given instance could be expected to vary. This meant that every lawbreaker would have to be processed on a case-by-case basis. It would be necessary to study an offender closely and then to diagnose the particular criminogenic condition—perhaps the sordid influences of a slum home, perhaps a mental conflict responsible for the person's waywardness. Once the cause of the problem was discovered, then the offender would be subjected to a treatment program specifically designed to eliminate the abnormality giving rise to the criminal inclinations in question. To administer this program of individualized treatment, correctional personnel would have to be invested with the unbridled discretion required to fit the "punishment" to the criminal rather than to the crime. Much like a physician exercises wide latitude in prescribing a cure for a patient, so too would the treaters of crime be given these powers to cure their "patients." Pursuing this medical analogy still further, many began to suggest that the very concept of prisons should be forfeited, and these institutions for criminals turned into hospitals. The flavor of the Progressives' perspective is well illustrated in these 1912 remarks by Warren F. Spaulding, secretary of the Massachusetts Prison Association:

Each criminal is an individual, and should be treated as such. . . . Character and not conduct is the only sound basis of treatment. Fundamental in the new scheme is . . . individualism. In the old system, the main question was, What did he do? The main question should be, What is he? There can be no intelligent treatment until more is known than the fact that a man did a certain thing. It is as important to know why he did it. Diagnosis is as necessary in the treatment of badness as it is in the treatment of illness.

Notably, the Progressives did not possess the overriding enthusiasm for incarceration that had been so characteristic of the Jacksonian reformers who initially built the penitentiary or

of the new penologists who had continued to popularize the stance that a well-ordered asylum was the most essential ingredient in the reform of the errant. While the Progressives agreed that many offenders required the strictures of the prison and the experience of the indeterminate sentence to be rehabilitated, they were equally adamant that many others could best be treated within the confines of the community. As a consequence, they called for the creation of parole boards, the increased use of parole-release from the penitentiary, and the establishment of supervision programs that would both facilitate an offender's reintegration into society and would ensure that the uncured would be returned to their cells. Similarly, they urged that the practice of probation be expanded drastically. As an alternative to imprisonment, offenders would now be placed under the guidance of a probation officer who was to act as a counselor and policeman—someone sensitive enough to understand an individual's problems but stern enough to lock offenders up if they persisted in criminal or profligate ways. However, probation officers were to perform an additional function as well. It was to be their duty to research the social and personal background of each convicted defendant, and then to provide judges with a detailed presentence report that would aid the court in assigning the correct treatment to each offender.

It should be recognized that the Progressives' commitment to the policy of individualized treatment was at the heart of their desire to give special life and legitimacy to "community corrections." Parole would permit the decarceration of the cured and the continued institutionalization of the incorrigible, while probation afforded judges a new sanctioning option and, through the officers attached to the court, access to the information required to make a sound sentencing decision. As William G. Hale commented in 1918, "As redemptive measures, our probation and parole laws have added vital wheels to our machinery of justice. They have gone far toward enabling us to deal with the individual as an individual and not as mere human grist, to be fed into an unthinking machine, and have thus made possible more ample provision for his reformation."

A final and significant feature of the Progressives' therapeutic agenda was an abiding belief that the state would carry out this agenda in good faith. Just as they trusted the state to bust corporate monopolies and to be an invaluable ally in the crusade for greater social justice, now they were convinced that the state and its agents could be trusted to bring about the humane and scientific cure of the criminally deviant. As such, they did not hesitate to grant court and correctional personnel the wide discretionary powers required for the individualized rehabilitation of offenders. In this same vein, they did not actively entertain the possibility that this discretion would be corrupted to serve organizational and class interests and not be used to do good as they had planned. Neither did it strike the Progressives that the practice of state-enforced therapy—where an inmate's cure is coerced and not volunteered—might suffer from any inherent theoretical defects or, still worse, that it might result in the physical and psychological abuse of the very people it intended to "save." As David Rothman has observed:

The most distinguishing characteristic of Progressivism was its fundamental trust in the power of the state to do good. The state was not the enemy of liberty, but the friend of equality—and to expand its domain and increase its power was to be in harmony with the spirit of the age. In criminal justice, the issue was not how to protect the offender from the arbitrariness of the state, but how to bring the state more effectively to the aid of the offender. The state was not a behemoth to be chained and fettered, but an agent capable of fulfilling an ambitious program. Thus, a policy that called for the state's exercise of discretionary authority in finely tuned responses was, at its core, Progressive.

In the context of America's "age of reform," to use Richard Hofstadter's designation, the Progressives' ideas for altering the correctional system did not fall idly by the wayside. By the end of this era, a flurry of legislative activity had transpired that instituted major portions of their reform program. In 1900, for instance, only five states allowed for indeterminate sentencing; a little over two decades later, the number had climbed to thirty-seven. The concept of parole, which had its origins in the ticket-of-leave systems of Maconochie and Crofton as well as in Brockway's reformatory system, had been adopted in only a handful of states at the turn of the century. By the middle part of the 1920s, forty-four states provided for parole and over half of the inmates in the nation were discharged in this manner. The beginnings of probation extend back to the 1840s when an affluent Boston shoemaker, John Augustus, voluntarily took errant youths under his care and supervision. In 1878, Massachusetts honored Augustus's pathbreaking work by becoming the first jurisdiction to pass a probation law. However, it was not until 1897 that another state followed suit. In contrast, by 1920 probation was permitted in two-thirds of the states for adults and in every state for juveniles.

It should be noted that the Progressives' therapeutic model received its most complete expression in the measures formulated to control delinquent behavior. Starting in 1899 in Cook County, Illinois, state after state created a separate legal system for processing youthful offenders. By the year 1920, all but three had established a special court for hearing juvenile cases. Now for the Progressives, rehabilitation was to be the exclusive concern in this newly created realm of juvenile justice. Under the guise of the concept of *parens patriae,* the Progressives wished to place the state in the role of a kindly parent that would nurture the wayward back to conformity. They felt as well that the task of "child saving" could best be accomplished if efforts were made to detect youths with such delinquent tendencies as truancy and illicit sexual activity prior to their falling into a life of more serious criminality.

In line with these assumptions, the Progressives were able to secure passage of legislation mandating that the state would no longer take an adversarial posture toward juvenile offenders. Since the state would now act in the best interests of delinquent youths, criminal trials, defense attorneys, rules of evidence, standards of guilt, and other due process protections were all stripped away in the daily rounds of the juvenile court. Judges were given the unfettered discretion to investigate what was wrong with a particular youth and then to prescribe the most corrective treatment available. This might involve supervision within the community or a stay in a special reformatory constructed just for juveniles where inmates could be kept until they achieved adulthood. Further, the powers of the state to intervene in the lives of troubled youths were greatly expanded. Unlike adults, juveniles could be brought before the court not only for violations of the criminal law, but also for engaging in a range of misbehaviors (known today as status offenses) which indicated that they were in a predelinquent stage and would soon be venturing into more nefarious activities. The court was also instructed to minister to those unfortunate youths who had been abandoned, neglected, or abused by their parents.

In sum, the Progressives succeeded in a major renovation of the criminal justice system. Within the space of two decades, their innovations reformulated sentencing practices in the direction of indeterminacy, established the new bureaucratic structures of probation and parole, created a separate system of juvenile justice, introduced wide discretionary powers throughout the legal process, and reaffirmed the vitality of the rehabilitative ideal. At the end of their era, nearly all of the elements of the criminal justice system familiar to today's students of crime control were securely in place. Of equal significance, the Progressives bequeathed a powerful rationale for the individualized treatment of offenders that would dominate American correctional policy until very recent times. As David Rothman has concluded, "The synthesis achieved in the 1900-1920 years dominated reform thinking and action down until yesterday."

THE LEGACY OF REFORM

The Progressives' version of a criminal justice system fully dedicated to the rehabilitation of criminal offenders was never achieved. While the framework of a therapeutic state had been erected, the substance in many instances was lacking. The Quakers' penitentiary did not become a modern hospital. Treatment programs in prisons frequently lacked integrity, and treatment personnel were often undertrained or sparse in number. In 1954, for example, there were only twenty-three full-time psychiatrists employed to run counseling sessions for the 161,587 inmates in state and federal prisons. Although California made advances in this direction, a pure system of indeterminate sentencing was not instituted in any state (all employed maximum limits for most prison terms handed out). Few offenders on probation or parole received intensive care. Moreover, it appears that the emergence of community corrections did not lessen the use of incarceration, but rather provided the state with the means to increase its surveillance of offenders who previously would have been either set totally free after serving their time in the penitentiary or given an unsupervised suspended sentence. Additionally, the problems within the arena of juvenile justice became so pervasive that the Supreme Court was eventually compelled to grant youthful delinquents an array of due process rights that would reduce the risk of their being abused by their "kindly parent," the state.

Yet if the reality of offender treatment only infrequently approximated the therapeutic design articulated by the Progressives, the philosophy of rehabilitation nevertheless continued to retain, if not expand, its appeal throughout much of the current century. Scarcely a decade ago, large proportions of both the general public and correctional workers believed that rehabilitation should be the primary goal of our prisons. One 1972 survey of juvenile correctional superintendents revealed that only 15 percent endorsed the abolition of the indeterminate sentence. Faith in treatment, although not absolute, was especially pronounced among liberal academics and similar leftist interest groups. For example, after reviewing ten of the leading criminology texts, Jackson Toby observed in 1964 that students reading these textbooks might infer that punishment is a vestigial carryover of a barbaric past and will disappear as humanitarianism and rationality spread.

As America pushed into the late 1960s, rehabilitation thus remained unchallenged as the dominant correctional ideology. There seemed to be little chance that there would be a call either to revert to the punitive principles of bygone days or to abandon the quest to build upon the foundation of the therapeutic state laid by the Quakers, new penologists, and Progressives. The long rise of rehabilitation seemed certain to proceed unabated in the immediate, if not into the distant, future. A decade later, however, the philosophy of rehabilitation had been substantially discredited, and concerted efforts were well under way to find a solution to the crisis in criminal justice policy precipitated by the demise of treatment ideology.

Stateville: The Penitentiary in Mass Society

JAMES B. JACOBS

> The position of all "democratic" currents, in the sense of currents that would minimize "authority," is necessarily ambiguous. "Equality" before the law and the demand for legal guarantees against arbitrariness demand a formal and rational "objectivity" of administration, as opposed to the personally free discretion flowing from the "grace" of the old patrimonial domination. If, however, an "ethos"—not to speak of instincts—takes hold of the masses on some individual question, it postulates substantive justice oriented toward some concrete instance and person: and such an "ethos" will unavoidably collide with the formalism and the rule-bound and cool "matter of factness" of bureaucratic administration.
>
> Max Weber, quoted in H. H. Gerth and C. W. Mills, *From Max Weber*

BETWEEN 1925 and 1975, Stateville passed through four distinct stages: anarchy, charismatic dominance, drift, and crisis. Beginning in 1975, a fifth stage is discernible: a period of restoration, in which the reforms of the past decade, as well as the redefinition of the prisoner's status, are integrated with aspects of authoritarian control. Before discussing the limits of this fifth stage it might be well to review the natural history of the prison.

Stateville Penitentiary was opened in 1925 as a reform era's effort to ameliorate the overcrowded, physically dilapidated, and scandal-ridden Joliet prison. In addition to the construction of the prison, attention of Progressive era reformers was directed toward several other aspects of prison reform. The Progressive Merit System was established in 1920. The position of sociologist-actuary was created upon the recommendations of the academically dominated Clabaugh commission in 1928. Another foothold for reformers in the prisons was the Office of the State Criminologist, which was estab-

lished in 1917. But the sum of these efforts by Progressive era reformers amounted to no more than segmental incursions into a system that was a tool of the state political organization.

Spoils politics penetrated the prison through both the staff and the inmates between 1925 and 1936. The warden and the bulk of the guard force owed their positions to political patronage. The existence of a staff without expertise in prison management or a career commitment to the job had fateful consequences for the prison's social organization. Rules and discipline vacillated according to who was exercising authority. Between 1925 and 1932, Stateville experienced one of the most violent and unstable periods in its history. Between 1932 and 1936, the deepening Depression in the larger society was paralleled inside the prison by idleness, deterioration of discipline, and complete collapse of a daily regimen. Authority passed from the hands of the state officials into the hands of powerful inmate gang leaders. Politics also penetrated the inmate social system as is indicated in Leopold's observation about the ties between the sizable number of Jewish inmates and one of Chicago's powerful political clubs. Favoritism, lack of uniform standards and rules, and particularistic relationships all characterized the organization during this early period.

During this first decade (1925-36), the prison pursued no consistent organizational goals and developed no stable internal equilibrium. The prisoners were beyond the concern of society's elite and out of touch with its central institutional and value systems.

The year 1936 was a watershed year in Stateville's history. The convergence of an aroused press, a highly critical blue ribbon commission, and a reform governor led to Joe Ragen's appointment as warden of the Stateville/Joliet complex. At the time Ragen's appointment seemed unexceptional. Like his predecessors, he was a political appointee and a former sheriff from downstate although he had also earned a good record in the several years that he had been warden of Menard.

Ragen's authoritarian system of personal dominance was first of all rooted in his ability to control the relationships between the prison and the outside. Between 1936 and 1961, he created his own independent political base by cultivating the press, the law enforcement community, and individual legislators. At the same time, it is likely that during and directly after World War II public attention was completely diverted from events within the state prisons. In addition, the full-employment economy during that period erased the importance of the prison as an instrument of political patronage.

Warden Ragen created a mystique about his own invincibility and omniscience. His daily inspection of the prison, accompanied only by his two dogs, symbolized his highly personalistic rule. He alone managed all contacts with the outside thereby reinforcing his personal power. From his staff he demanded absolute loyalty, identifying his own authority with the best interests of the prison. So great was his personal prestige, charisma, and resources that his system of dominance was not weakened by the forces of politicization and bureaucratization associated with the trend toward mass society in the decade after World War II.

Ragen exercised complete domination over the guard staff. His guards were exclusively recruited from southern Illinois. They lacked any ties to the Chicago or Joliet communities, identifying totally with the prison and the warden who personified its values. In addition, Ragen expanded the barracks and constructed a trailer court, reinforcing the staff's segregation from the surrounding community. The rigid and arbitrary discipline to which the guards were subjected generated high rates of turnover within the lower ranks. This diminished the probability that the line personnel would develop an effective counterforce. To the hand-picked elite who occupied top administrative posts, Ragen offered considerable fringe benefits: food allowance, state-owned homes, and inmate servants. Such "payment in kind" Weber considered a leading characteristic of the patrimonial regime.

The inmate social system during this period conforms to what has been described by scholars who studied other prison communities in the decades before and after World War II. Criminal identities imported from the street accounted for an inmate status system. Prison sentences were long and the inmate social system tended to remain stable. A viable reward system stimulated intense competition for the few luxuries that were attainable. Many of the natural leaders among the inmates were co-opted by good jobs and the legitimate and illegitimate opportunities which were attached.

Ragen's rule was that of a totalitarian. He would not be defied even on insignificant rules. He persistently emphasized to his staff that stress upon the smallest details would prevent authority from ever being openly and collectively challenged. An inmate who challenged the system and called attention to himself as a "no good son of a bitch" would find himself on the coal pile for years, in isolation on a stringent diet, or salted away in segregation for an indefinite term. Ragen's regime typified Weber's description of prebureaucratic forms of administration: "All non-bureaucratic forms of domination display a peculiar co-existence: on the one hand, there is a sphere of strict traditionalism, and, on the other, a sphere of free arbitrariness and lordly grace."

Particularly in the later years of Ragen's regime, the routine was systematized into a patriarchal system of administration based upon traditional authority. The latent charismatic content of the system only became explicit at infrequent moments of crisis. With Ragen's departure for Springfield, however, the charismatic aspect of the regime was greatly attenuated. Warden Pate's administration drifted into a collegial rule. Between 1961 and 1970, this system showed signs of extreme strain under pressures emanating from the outside.

The Civil Rights movement of the early 1960s served to politicize the prison's minority population, which emerged as a solid majority by 1960. The trend toward mass society redefined the status and value of marginal groups in the polity. The demand by prisoners for fuller participation in the core culture was reinforced by the greater sensitivity of the elites to the moral worth of marginal citizens.

It was the Black Muslims who first gave expression to the heightened aspirations and expectations of the black inmates. Alone among political and religious movements in the 1960s, the Muslims defined the prison as a legitimate arena for organizing a constituency. Later, political radicals, some of whom were themselves prisoners, also attempted to transform prisoners from a group in itself to a group for itself.

The Muslims carried out collective activities which challenged the authority of the patriarchal system. The Pate administration characteristically responded to the Muslims by adopting a policy of massive resistance. Every demand of the Muslims was rejected; their leaders were thrown in segregation. The system could not tolerate any challenge to its basis of control. If it were successfully challenged at any point, authority would be fatally undermined. In order to maintain the integrity of its authority, the Pate administration had no other choice than to repress the Muslims, but by doing so it made inevitable the complete collapse of authority after 1970.

The Muslims could not have sustained their challenge to the prison administration without the dramatic turn around in the orientation of the juridical system. Once again, the momentum of mass society was fateful. A wide-scale legal reform movement, beginning with the leadership of the Warren Court, extended substantive and procedural rights to the indigent, the illegitimate, minors, students, servicemen, and criminal defendants. A late aspect of this extension of the rights of citizenship to marginal groups was the abandonment of the "hands off" doctrine and the recognition that prisoners were not "slaves of the state." The limited but symbolic successes of the Muslims before the courts seemed to the prison authorities a total repudiation by the central institutional system of the larger society.

Law reform also penetrated the prison through the new penal code, which expedited parole eligibility. Indirectly, this reform had a powerful impact upon the social organization. By greatly increasing inmate turnover it had the effect of destabilizing the old con power structure which had subserved the authority of the system for decades and which was already undermined by rising inmate expectations and a shift from an individual to a group perspective on serving time. By 1970, the forces of bureaucratization and politicization and the penetration of juridical norms had undermined the traditional system of authority to the extent that control itself had become problematic. In the fall of 1970, Warden Pate resigned.

Between 1970 and 1975, the Stateville leadership struggled to regain its balance. The prison's boundaries had become permeable to the outside. Local control had been lost to centralized authority and the universalistic rule of law. The new emphasis on bureaucratization prescribed professional standards of preparation for a new administrative elite. Sharp conflict developed within the staff; the morale of the rank and file deteriorated. Given the weakened condition of organizational authority, politicized Chicago supergangs were able to penetrate the prison and broaden their organizational structures and prestige. Internally, the prison experienced a crisis in control that lasted until 1975.

In Springfield, a young, Yale-educated businessman became the first director of corrections in 1970. Eager to align himself with the liberal wing of American corrections, he imposed many reforms upon Stateville designed to "humanize" conditions and to extend "dignity" and "respect" to the "residents." A Unified Code of Corrections and comprehensive Administrative Regulations limited administrative discretion at the local level. The director sought the advice of reformers and academic specialists and opened the prison to representatives of minority groups.

The new Department of Corrections was far more centralized than its predecessor, the Department of Public Safety. The authority to formulate prison policy passed out of the hands of the local wardens and was exercised by a powerful, active central office in Springfield. The prison was no longer an autonomous institution.

At Stateville, Warden Pate's two immediate successors were well-educated professionals who adhered to the rehabilitative ideal and the human relations model of management. In place of the authoritarian system, they attempted to establish a regime based upon consensual authority. Captains and lieutenants were urged to counsel both rank-and-file guards and inmates before resorting to formal disciplinary mechanisms. Problems in the organization were attributed to problems in communication.

The first two reform regimes failed to establish a viable equilibrium. Inmate expectations increased far more rapidly than did material benefits or the amelioration of unsatisfactory living conditions. The reformers stressed a philosophical reinterpretation of the moral implications of imprisonment at the same time that concrete physical conditions were rapidly deteriorating. Indeed, increased organizational dysfunction meant fewer showers, worse food, dirtier cells, and less regular visiting procedures. The reform regime presided over a shrinking number of programmatic opportunities but, at the same time, encouraged inmate expectations.

Finally, the first two reform regimes failed to maintain control. The number of attacks upon guards and inmates greatly increased. In addition to individual acts of violence there were also many instances of collective violence, including strikes, riots, gang fights, and the seizure of hostages. Having no other strategy to maintain control, the reform regimes periodically reverted to measures even more repressive than those of previous decades. In the years 1970-75, the greatest percentage of inmates were placed in isolation and segregation in Stateville's history. Conditions in the maximum-security Special Program Unit deteriorated to a level of violence

and destruction beyond anything previously seen in Illinois.

Administrators attributed the crisis in control to the liberalized court decisions as well as to the power of the supergangs. I have argued that the substance of court decisions themselves did not *cause* the crisis in control, although they did heighten inmate expectations and stimulate protest.

The most important impact of the penetration of juridical norms was to bring to bear outside pressure upon the Stateville administration to bureaucratize. The tension between the rehabilitative ideal, which prescribed the individualization of treatment, and the rule of law, which demanded universalistic criteria of decision making, was decades ago observed by Weber. The transfer of power from the patriarchal regime of Warden Pate to the professional regimes of Wardens Twomey and Cannon did not automatically transform the administration into a rational-legal bureaucracy. The reform regimes never met the demands for rational and visible decision making which were made by the courts and the department's own central office.

The reform administrations failed to develop an organization capable of maintaining control or meeting basic demands for services. They also failed to meet the demands of the legal system for visible and rational decision making or to live up to their own reform rhetoric in the opinion of various outside interest groups. And they failed to meet the crucial challenge to order and security posed by the Chicago supergangs.

After 1970, the inmate social system was dominated by four Chicago street gangs which imported their organizational structures, ideologies, and symbol systems from the streets. The very emergence of these minority "supergangs" in Chicago can be accounted for by a new relationship between secular and religious institutions and traditional youth gangs. Beginning in the early 1960s, the federal government, private foundations, universities, and established churches redefined youth gangs and their leaders as legitimate indigenous grassroots organizations which spoke in the interest of the minority community. Through publicity, sizable grants, and technical assistance (as well as substantial police attention), these traditional youth gangs evolved into large proto-politicized supergangs. This transition of traditional gang boys into a potential political force was not acceptable to the political and law enforcement interests in Chicago (or to their spokesmen in Congress), and a concerted law enforcement drive against the gangs was pursued after 1968. One consequence was the massive infusion of members of the Black P Stone Nation, Disciples, Vice Lords, and Latin Kings into the state prisons.

The young gang members had assimilated a justificatory vocabulary as well as a set of rising expectations as they were growing up in the Chicago ghettos during the 1960s. The old prison reward system, which promised better jobs and the opportunity to score for "hooch," coffee, and extra food, was no longer compelling. Unlike the Muslims, the gang members had no specific issues and no concrete agenda. They brought to the prison diffuse goals and a general attitude of lawlessness and rebelliousness. The small minority of white inmates left at Stateville found themselves in grave danger, as did those blacks who were not affiliated with one of the gangs. Increasingly, inmates interrelated as blocks. For a while, the gang leaders were the organization's most stabilizing force as they struggled to reach an accommodation with one another and with the administration.

In exchange for using their services to keep things cool, the leaders continually demanded formal recognition and deference from the prison authorities. On this issue, the staff was divided sharply. Lower-ranking guards and civilians found it necessary to defer to the gang leadership in order to meet their goals. The top administrators remained far more reluctant to share their power with prisoner leaders although, to be sure, certain concessions were exacted. Finally, the gangs could not be controlled. General lockups occurred in 1971, 1972, and 1973, the third occasioned by an intergang melee between the Black P Stones and the Disciples. In September 1973, hostages were seized at Stateville and in April 1975 hostages were seized at the Joliet prison.

The rise of professionalism, the intrusion of the courts, and the emergence of unified blocks among the inmates all contributed to a crisis in morale among the custodial staff. Guards were afraid to come to work. Rumors of riots and killings reverberated through the shifts. Many guards followed a strategy of withdrawing from the disciplinary process altogether.

Afraid for their safety and no longer in "awe" of a charismatic leader, the guards began to turn toward the union to give voice to their interests. The union had earlier begun to organize, despite Pate's protestations, under the leadership of Ross Randolph, Ragen's successor as director of public safety. The crisis in control occasioned by the gangs, and the rise of professionals, from whom the guards were alienated, made the union all the more appealing. The small local affiliated with a national union, which provided professional expertise and assistance during a period when it was scoring great organizational successes statewide and nationally in agencies throughout the public sector. In 1973, the new Democratic governor (Walker) fulfilled his campaign pledge to support collective bargaining in the public sector; the union had become a major force in Illinois prisons.

At the local level, the union continually demanded more safety and security. After the first guard in thirty years was killed at Stateville in January 1973, the local staged a walkout, taking almost the entire rank and file with them. The spirit of the trade union movement necessarily is in conflict with the paramilitary organization and esprit de corps that had characterized the custody staff for decades. Guards objected to the arbitrary and capricious actions of their superiors and found institutional mechanisms to ensure that they were provided with due process in charges brought against them. These changes greatly weakened the authority of the higher-echelon custody staff.

The custody staff also became increasingly heterogeneous under the combined pressures of minority groups and government affirmative action. By 1975, almost 50 percent of the guard force was black or Latino. The minority guards were far more empathic with the plight of the minority inmates and often found themselves alienated from the southern Illinois white guards who occupied almost all the top positions. This tension represented one more strain in an organization that was highly fragmented, factionalized, and conflict-ridden.

The years 1925-70 demonstrated the historical limits of the authoritarian system of personal dominance that depended upon the peripheral position of the prison and its inmates vis-à-vis the central institutional and value systems of society. The years 1970-75 demonstrated the incompatibility of the rehabilitative ideal and the human relations model of management with the functional requisites of maintaining control in maximum-security prisons and with the demands of the courts for rational and visible decision making.

The Brierton regime suggests a fifth stage, one of restoration, in Stateville's history. The warden himself, a former chief guard of the Cook County Jail, is a physically imposing, charismatic figure. The early success of his leadership underscores the point that the maximum-security prison functionally requires an imperatively coordinated administration.

Brierton has strengthened security, improved services, and rebuilt the morale of the guard staff. In the first six months of his regime, he emphasized the physical reconstruction of the prison. He closed up tunnels, sealed the tiers with iron bars, placed television cameras along the cell house walls, hung tear gas canisters from the ceilings, and instituted serious riot training. He rejected the rehabilitative ideal and the human relations model of management in favor of a highly rational, problem-oriented "corporate" model of management which is characterized as professional, detached, and cost-conscious.

The new warden has stressed the need to provide basic services through regularized procedures and has de-emphasized the concern with redefinition of the inmate's status. On the other hand, Brierton has committed himself to justice; each prisoner should receive the treatment and opportunities commensurate with law and to which he is entitled. Each month, the warden personally speaks to every inmate in the prison on his "call line" and provides a prompt written reply to every inquiry or grievance. He demands the same formal responsiveness of his staff. Written records have proliferated. Each time an inmate showers, the event is documented, as is every contact between a counselor

and his client. Brierton has thus taken the initiative in attempting to fully bureaucratize the prison. If he is successful and can reestablish control at the same time as expanding basic services and programmatic opportunities, all without jeopardizing due process, Stateville is sure to reemerge in the next several years as a leading model of prison administration for the nation.

There are limits, however, to the degree to which the corporate model can implement a new equilibrium. The most important obstacle is resources. Will the legislature, in the face of fiscal crisis and an expanding prisoner population, provide the resources necessary to meet the needs of basic services, adequate staff, and increased security?

There may also be limits to a corporate bureaucracy's ability to be responsive to prisoner problems and needs. More prisoner complaints are being heard and "responded to," but merely because the rules have become concrete and impartial, there is no assurance that the prisoners' own conception of substantive justice will not collide with the "formalism" and "cool matter-of-factness" of bureaucratic administration. It is possible that the expectations engendered by the two previous reform administrations and by numerous interested parties on the outside, as well as by the courts, have created expectations that cannot be satisfied by the corporate model. Will the prisoners any longer accept a safe prison with regularized procedures, better food, regular yard time, and various (limited) programmatic opportunities? Both inmate material expectations and demands for representation in decision making may exceed the capacity of the system to provide solutions.

Third, there is potential for conflict with the media, private interest groups, and reformers. In developing the corporate model, Brierton has attempted to maintain a low profile but he has already met sporadic criticism. Some reformers completely reject such security techniques as television surveillance of the cells. There are sure to be claims that Brierton is creating an Orwellian nightmare. The rehabilitative ideal still has considerable vitality among representatives of the media, reformers, and academic specialists.

Related to potential criticism from reformers is a conflict over the guard's future role. Reformers cling to the idea that the guard's role can evolve into that of a quasi counselor. Brierton's system demands that the guard be a detached security specialist infused with an esprit de corps within a paramilitary regime. The union professional leadership is opposed to the paramilitary model. The Department of Corrections' central office itself does not seem to have moved to implement the security specialist guard role precisely because of ambivalence about completely abandoning the guard-as-counselor model.

There is the question of personnel. Can Brierton shape the kind of bureaucratic regime which he advocates with the staff he has inherited? It is true that there has been a wholesale shake-up of staff since he became warden, yet the professional skills, particularly of management and budget, are clearly lacking except for the few very top administrative positions. The rest of the Illinois maximum-security prisons are lagging far behind Stateville in becoming bureaucratized. At the Joliet prison (now under separate administration), a former guard captain without a college education and without sophisticated management skills has recently been elevated to warden. Will a change in political administrations or a reduced budget or the departure of Brierton mean that Stateville will slip back to where it was between 1970 and 1975 or earlier?

The restorational regime is also highly vulnerable to changes in the relationship of the prison to the political environment. The 1976 elections will see a change of governor in Illinois and perhaps a return to a more partisan style of administration. The Ragen legacy was a prison system well insulated from partisan politics, but that tradition is by no means immutable. It would be very difficult for any administration, no matter how partisan, to dismantle the many professional bureaucratic mechanisms built into the prison system at this point. The middle- and lower-level managers have civil service security and are in office to stay. But a partisan governor could choose to appoint a nonprofessional (like Peter Bensinger) as director of corrections, leaving it an open question whether political appointments would be made at the warden level. Even if they were not, a nonprofessional administrator could hardly provide the kind of centralized leadership that first began with Bensinger and was so substantially expanded under Sielaff.

What if the attempt to synthesize reform and control in the maximum-security prison fails? What if the prison reverts to arbitrary and capricious management in a situation marked by brutality, favoritism, and staff apathy? The danger is that, in that event, the larger effort to reform our bureaucracies and basic institutions will have been dealt a mortal blow. The failure to institutionalize prison reform could reinforce more general cynicism about the capacity of our society to reform itself.

The Defects of Total Power

GRESHAM SYKES

FOR the needs of mass administration today," said Max Weber, "bureaucratic administration is completely indispensable. The choice is between bureaucracy and dilettantism in the field of administration." To the officials of the New Jersey State Prison the choice is clear, as it is clear to the custodians of all maximum-security prisons in the United States today. They are organized into a bureaucratic administrative staff—characterized by limited and specific rules, well-defined areas of competence and responsibility, impersonal standards of performance and promotion, and so on—which is similar in many respects to that of any modern, large-scale enterprise, and it is this staff which must see to the effective execution of the prison's routine procedures.

Of the approximately 300 employees of the New Jersey State Prison, more than two-thirds are directly concerned with the supervision and control of the inmate population. These form the so-called custodian force which is broken into three eight-hour shifts, each shift being arranged in a typical pyramid of authority. The day shift, however, on duty from 6:20 a.m. to 2:20 p.m. is by far the largest. As in many organizations, the rhythm of life in the prison quickens with daybreak and trails off in the afternoon, and the period of greatest activity requires the largest number of administrative personnel.

In the bottom ranks are the Wing guards, the Tower guards, the guards assigned to the shops, and those with a miscellany of duties such as the guardianship of the receiving gate or the garage. Immediately above these men are a number of

From *The Society of Captives* (pp. 40-53) by G. Sykes, 1958, Princeton, NJ: Princeton University Press. Copyright 1958 by Princeton University Press. Reprinted by permission.

sergeants and lieutenants, and these in turn are responsible to the warden and his assistants.

The most striking fact about this bureaucracy of custodians is its unparalleled position of power—in formal terms, at least—vis-à-vis the body of men which it rules and from which it is supposed to extract compliance. The officials, after all, possess a monopoly on the legitimate means of coercion (or, as one prisoner has phrased it succinctly, "They have the guns and we don't"), and the officials can call on the armed might of the police and the National Guard in case of an overwhelming emergency. The 24-hour surveillance of the custodians represents the ultimate watchfulness and, presumably, noncompliance on the part of the inmates need not go long unchecked. The rulers of this society of captives nominally hold in their hands the sole right of granting rewards and inflicting punishments, and it would seem that no prisoner could afford to ignore their demands for conformity. Centers of opposition in the inmate population—in the form of men recognized as leaders by fellow prisoners—can be neutralized through the use of solitary confinement or exile to other state institutions. The custodians have the right not only to issue and administer the orders and regulations which are to guide the life of the prisoner but also the right to detain, try, and punish any individual accused of disobedience—a merging of legislative, executive, and judicial functions which has long been regarded as the earmark of complete domination. The officials of the prison, in short, appear to be the possessors of almost infinite power within their realm, and at least on the surface, the bureaucratic staff should experience no great difficulty in converting their rules and regulations—their blueprint for behavior—into a reality.

It is true, of course, that the power position of the custodial bureaucracy is not truly infinite. The objectives which the officials pursue are not completely of their own choosing and the means which they can use to achieve their objectives are far from limitless. The custodians are not total despots, able to exercise power at whim, and thus they lack the essential mark of infinite power, the unchallenged right of being capricious in their rule. It is this last which distinguishes terror from government, infinite power from almost infinite power, and the distinction is an important one. Neither by right nor by intention are the officials of the New Jersey State Prison free from a system of norms and laws which curb their actions. But within these limitations, the bureaucracy of the prison is organized around a grant of power which is without an equal in American society, and if the rulers of any social system could secure compliance with their rules and regulations—however sullen or unwilling—it might be expected that the officials of the maximum-security prison would be able to do so.

When we examine the New Jersey State Prison, however, we find that this expectation is not borne out in actuality. Indeed, the glaring conclusion is that despite the guns and the surveillance, the searches and the precautions of the custodians, the actual behavior of the inmate population differs markedly from that which is called for by official commands and decrees. Violence, fraud, theft, aberrant sexual behavior—all are commonplace occurrences in the daily round of institutional existence in spite of the fact that the maximum-security prison is conceived of by society as the ultimate weapon for the control of the criminal and his deviant actions. Far from being omnipotent rulers who have crushed all signs of rebellion against their regime, the custodians are engaged in a continuous struggle to maintain order—and it is a struggle in which the custodians frequently fail. Offenses committed by one inmate against another occur often, as do offenses committed by inmates against the officials and their rules. And the number of undetected offenses is, by universal agreement of both officials and inmates, far larger than the number of offenses which are discovered.

Most revealing are the so-called charge slips in which the guard is supposed to write out the derelictions of the prisoner in some detail. In the New Jersey State Prison, charge slips form an administrative residue of past conflicts between captors and captives and the following accounts are a fair sample:

This inmate threatened an officer's life. When I informed this inmate he was to stay in to see the Chief Deputy on his charge he told me if he did not go to the yard I would get a shiv in my back. Signed: Officer A

Inmate X cursing an officer. In mess hall inmate refused to put excess bread back on tray. Then he threw the tray on the floor. In the Center, inmate cursed both Officer Y and myself. Signed: Officer B

This inmate has been condemning everyone about him for going to work. The Center gave orders for him to go to work this a.m. which he refused to do. While searching his cell I found drawings of picks and locks. Signed: Officer C

Fighting. As this inmate came to I Wing entrance to go to yard this a.m. he struck Inmate G in the face. Signed: Officer D

Having fermented beverage in his cell. Found while inmate was in yard. Signed: Officer E

Attempting to instigate wing disturbance. When I asked him why he discarded [*sic*] my order to quiet down he said he was going to talk any time he wanted to and _____ me, do whatever I wanted in regards to it. Signed: Officer F

Possession of homemade shiv sharpened to razor edge on his person and possession of 2 more shivs in cell. When inmate was sent to 4 Wing, Officer H found 3" steel blade in pocket. I ordered Officer M to search his cell and he found 2 more shivs in process of being sharpened. Signed: Officer G

Insolence. Inmate objected to my looking at papers he was carrying in pockets while going to the yard. He snatched them violently from my hand and gave me some very abusive talk. This man told me to _____ myself, and raised his hands as if to strike me. I grabbed him by the shirt and took him to the Center. Signed: Officer H

Assault with knife on Inmate K. During Idle Men's mess at approximately 11:10 a.m. this man assaulted Inmate K with a homemade knife. Inmate K was receiving his rations at the counter when Inmate B rushed up to him and plunged a knife in his chest, arm, and back. I grappled with him and with the assistance of Officers S and V, we disarmed the inmate and took him to the Center. Inmate K was immediately taken to the hospital. Signed: Officer I

Sodomy. Found Inmate W in cell with no clothing on and Inmate Z on top of him with no clothing. Inmate W told me he was going to lie like a _____ _____ _____ _____ to get out of it. Signed: Officer J

Attempted escape on night of 4/15/53. This inmate along with Inmates L and T succeeded in getting on roof of 6 Wing and having homemade bombs in their possession. Signed: Officer K

Fighting and possession of homemade shiv. Struck first blow to Inmate P. He struck blow with a roll of black rubber rolled up in his fist. He then produced a knife made out of wire tied to a toothbrush. Signed: Officer L

Refusing medication prescribed by Doctor W. Said, "What do you think I am, a damn fool, taking that _____ for a headache, give it to the doctor." Signed: Officer M

Inmate loitering on tier. There is a clique of several men, who lock on top tier, who ignore rule of returning directly to their cells and attempt to hang out on the tier in a group. Signed: Officer N

It is hardly surprising that when the guards at the New Jersey State Prison were asked what topics should be of first importance in a proposed in-service training program, 98 percent picked "what to do in event of trouble." The critical issue for the moment, however, is that the dominant position of the custodial staff is more fiction than reality, if we think of domination as something more than the outward forms and symbols of power. If power is viewed as the probability that orders and regulations will be obeyed by a given group of individuals, as Max Weber has suggested, the New Jersey State Prison is perhaps more notable for the doubtfulness of obedience than its certainty. The weekly records of the disciplinary court and charge slips provide an admittedly poor index of offenses or acts of noncompliance committed within the walls, for these form only a small, visible segment of an iceberg whose greatest bulk lies beneath the surface of official recognition. The public is periodically made aware of the officials' battle to enforce their regime within the prison, commonly in the form of allegations in the newspapers concerning homosexuality, illegal use of drugs, assaults, and so on. But the ebb and flow of public attention given to these matters does not match the constancy of these problems for the prison officials who are all too well aware that "incidents"—the very thing they try to minimize—are not isolated or rare events but are instead a commonplace. The number of incidents in the New Jersey State Prison is probably no greater than that to be found in most maximum-security institutions in the United States and may, indeed, be smaller, although it is difficult to make comparisons. In any event, it seems clear that the custodians are bound to their captives in a relationship of conflict rather than compelled acquiescence, despite the custodians' theoretical supremacy, and we now need to see why this should be so.

I

In our examination of the forces which undermine the power position of the New Jersey State Prison's custodial bureaucracy, the most important fact is, perhaps, that the power of the custodians is not based on authority. Now power based on authority is actually a complex social relationship in which an individual or a group of individuals is recognized as possessing a right to issue commands or regulations and those who receive these commands or regulations feel compelled to obey by a sense of duty. In its pure form, then, or as an ideal-type, power based on authority has two essential elements: a rightful or legitimate effort to exercise control, on the one hand, and an inner, moral compulsion to obey, by those who are to be controlled, on the other. In reality, of course, the recognition of the legitimacy of efforts to exercise control may be qualified or partial, and the sense of duty, as a motive for compliance, may be mixed with motives of fear or self-interest. But it is possible for theoretical purposes to think of power based on authority in its pure form and to use this as a baseline in describing the empirical case.

It is the second element of authority—the sense of duty as a motive for compliance—which supplies the secret strength of most social organizations. Orders and rules can be issued with the expectation that they will be obeyed without the necessity of demonstrating in each case that compliance will advance the subordinate's interests. Obedience or conformity springs from an internalized morality which transcends the personal feelings of the individual; the fact that an order or a rule is an order or a rule becomes the basis for modifying one's behavior, rather than a rational calculation of the advantages which might be gained.

In the prison, however, it is precisely this sense of duty which is lacking in the general inmate population. The regime of the custodians is expressed as a mass of commands and regulations passing down a hierarchy of power. In general, these efforts at control are regarded as legitimate by individuals in the hierarchy, and individuals tend to respond because they feel they "should," down to the level of the guard in the cellblock, the industrial shop, or the recreation yard. But now these commands and regulations must jump a gap which separates the captors from the captives. And it is at this point that a sense of duty tends to disappear and with it goes that easily won obedience which many organizations take for granted in the naïveté of their unrecognized strength. In the prison, power must be based on something other than internalized morality, and the custodians find themselves confronting men who must be forced, bribed, or cajoled into compliance. This is not to say that inmates feel that the efforts of prison officials to exercise control are wrongful or illegitimate; in general, prisoners do not feel that the prison officials have usurped positions of power which are not rightfully theirs, nor do prisoners feel that the orders and regulations which descend upon them from above represent an illegal extension of their rulers' grant of government. Rather, the noteworthy fact about the social system of the New Jersey State Prison is that the bond between recognition of the legitimacy of control and the sense of duty has been torn apart. In these terms, the social system of the prison is very similar to a *Gebietsverband,* a territorial group living under a regime imposed by a ruling few. Like a province which has been conquered by force of arms, the community of prisoners has come to accept the validity of the regime constructed by their rulers but the subjugation is not complete. Whether he sees himself as caught by his own stupidity, the workings of chance, his inability to "fix" the case, or the superior skill of the police, the criminal in prison seldom denies the legitimacy of confinement. At the same time, the recognition of the legitimacy of society's surrogates and their body of rules is not accompanied by an internalized obligation to obey, and the prisoner thus accepts the fact of his captivity at one level and rejects it at another. If for no other reason, then, the custodial institution is valuable for a theory of human behavior because it makes us realize that men need not be motivated to conform to a regime which they define as rightful. It is in this apparent contradiction that we can see the first flaw in the custodial bureaucracy's assumed supremacy.

II

Since the officials of prison possess a monopoly on the means of coercion, as we have pointed out earlier, it might be thought that the inmate population could simply be forced into conformity and that the lack of an inner moral compulsion to obey on the part of the inmates could be ignored. Yet the combination of a bureaucratic staff—that most modern rational form of mobilizing effort to exercise control—and the use of physical violence—that most ancient device to channel man's conduct—

must strike us as an anomaly and with good reason. The use of force is actually grossly inefficient as a means for securing obedience, particularly when those who are to be controlled are called on to perform a task of any complexity. A blow with a club may check an immediate revolt, it is true, but it cannot assure effective performance on a punch-press. A "come-along," a straitjacket, or a pair of handcuffs may serve to curb one rebellious prisoner in a crisis, but they will be of little aid in moving more than 1,200 inmates through the mess hall in a routine and orderly fashion. Furthermore, the custodians are well aware that violence once unleashed is not easily brought to heel, and it is this awareness that lies behind the standing order that no guard should ever strike an inmate with his hand—he should always use a night stick. This rule is not an open invitation to brutality but an attempt to set a high threshold on the use of force in order to eliminate the casual cuffing which might explode into extensive and violent retaliation. Similarly, guards are under orders to throw their night sticks over the wall if they are on duty in the recreation yard when a riot develops. A guard without weapons, it is argued, is safer than a guard who tries to hold on to his symbol of office, for a mass of rebellious inmates may find a single night stick a goad rather than a restraint and the guard may find himself beaten to death with his own means of compelling order.

In short, the ability of the officials to physically coerce their captives into the paths of compliance is something of an illusion as far as the day-to-day activities of the prison are concerned and may be of doubtful value in moments of crisis. Intrinsically inefficient as a method of making men carry out a complex task, diminished in effectiveness by the realities of the guard-inmate ratio, and always accompanied by the danger of touching off further violence, the use of physical force by the custodians has many limitations as a basis on which to found the routine operation of the prison. Coercive tactics may have some utility in checking blatant disobedience if only a few men disobey. But if the great mass of criminals in prison are to be brought into the habit of conformity, it must be on other grounds. Unable to count on a sense of

duty to motivate their captives to obey and unable to depend on the direct and immediate use of violence to ensure a step-by-step submission to the rules, the custodians must fall back on a system of rewards and punishments.

Now if men are to be controlled by the use of rewards and punishments—by promises and threats—at least one point is patent: the rewards and punishments dangled in front of the individual must indeed be rewards and punishments from the point of view of the individual who is to be controlled. It is precisely on this point, however, that the custodians' system of rewards and punishments founders. In our discussion of the problems encountered in securing conscientious performance at work, we suggested that both the penalties and the incentives available to the officials were inadequate. This is also largely true, at a more general level, with regard to rewards and punishments for securing compliance with the wishes of the custodians in all areas of prison life.

In the first place, the punishments which the officials can inflict—for theft, assaults, escape attempts, gambling, insolence, homosexuality, and all the other deviations from the pattern of behavior called for by the regime of the custodians—do not represent a profound difference from the prisoner's usual status. It may be that when men are chronically deprived of liberty, material goods and services, recreational opportunities, and so on, the few pleasures that are granted take on a new importance and the threat of their withdrawal is a more powerful motive for conformity than those of us in the free community can realize. To be locked up in the solitary confinement wing, that prison within a prison; to move from the monotonous, often badly prepared meals in the mess hall to a diet of bread and water; to be dropped from a dull, unsatisfying job and forced to remain in idleness—all, perhaps, may mean the difference between an existence which can be borne, painful though it may be, and one which cannot. But the officials of the New Jersey State Prison are dangerously close to the point where the stock of legitimate punishments has been exhausted, and it would appear that for many prisoners the few punishments which are left have lost their potency. To this, we must couple the important fact that such punishments as the custodians can inflict may lead to an increased prestige for the punished inmate in the eyes of his fellow prisoners. He may become a hero, a martyr, a man who has confronted his captors and dared them to do their worst. In the dialectics of the inmate population, punishments and rewards have, then, been reversed and the control measures of the officials may support disobedience rather than decrease it.

In the second place, the system of rewards and punishments in the prison is defective because the reward side of the picture has been largely stripped away. Mail and visiting privileges, recreational privileges, the supply of personal possessions—all are given to the inmate at the time of his arrival in one fixed sum. Even the so-called good time—the portion of the prisoner's sentence deducted for good behavior—is automatically subtracted from the prisoner's sentence when he begins his period of imprisonment. Thus, the officials have placed themselves in the peculiar position of granting the prisoner all available benefits or rewards at the time of his entrance into the system. The prisoner, then, finds himself unable to win any significant gains by means of compliance, for there are no gains left to be won.

From the viewpoint of the officials, of course, the privileges of the prison social system are regarded as rewards, as something to be achieved. That is to say, the custodians hold that recreation, access to the inmate store, good time, or visits from individuals in the free community are conditional upon conformity or good behavior. But the evidence suggests that from the viewpoint of the inmates, the variety of benefits granted by the custodians is not defined as something to be earned but as an inalienable right—as the just due of the inmate which should not turn on the question of obedience or disobedience within the walls. After all, the inmate population claims, these benefits have belonged to the prisoner from the time when he first came to the institution.

In short, the New Jersey State Prison makes an initial grant of all its rewards and then threatens to withdraw them if the prisoner does not conform. It does not start the prisoner from scratch and promise to grant its available rewards one by one as the prisoner proves himself through continued submission to the institutional regulations. As a result, a subtle alchemy is set in motion whereby the inmates cease to see the rewards of the system as rewards, that is, as benefits contingent upon performance; instead, rewards are apt to be defined as obligations. Whatever justification might be offered for such a policy, it would appear to have a number of drawbacks as a method of motivating prisoners to fall into the posture of obedience. In effect, rewards and punishments of the officials have been collapsed into one and the prisoner moves in a world where there is no hope of progress but only the possibility of further punishments. Since the prisoner is already suffering from most of the punishments permitted by society, the threat of imposing those few remaining is all too likely to be a gesture of futility.

III

Unable to depend on that inner moral compulsion or sense of duty which eases the problem of control in most social organizations, acutely aware that brute force is inadequate, and lacking an effective system of legitimate rewards and punishments which might induce prisoners to conform to institutional regulations on the grounds of self-interest, the custodians of the New Jersey State Prison are considerably weakened in their attempts to impose their regime on their captive population. The result, in fact, is, as we have already indicated, a good deal of deviant behavior or noncompliance in a social system where the rulers at first glance seem to possess almost infinite power.

Yet systems of power may be defective for reasons other than the fact that those who are ruled do not feel the need to obey the orders and regulations descending on them from above. Systems of power may also fail because those who are supposed to rule are unwilling to do so. The unissued order, the deliberately ignored disobedience, the duty left unperformed—these are cracks in the monolith just as surely as are acts of defiance in the subject population. The "corruption" of the rulers may be far less dramatic than the insurrection of the ruled, for power unexercised is seldom as visible as power which is challenged, but the system of power still falters.

Now the official in the lowest ranks of the custodial bureaucracy—the guard in the cell-block, the industrial shop, or the recreation yard—is the pivotal figure on which the custodial bureaucracy turns. It is he who must supervise and control the inmate population in concrete and detailed terms. It is he who must see to the translation of the custodial regime from blueprint to reality and engage in the specific battles for conformity. Counting prisoners, periodically reporting to the center of communications, signing passes, checking groups of inmates as they come and go, searching for contraband or signs of attempts to escape—these make up the minutiae of his eight-hour shift. In addition, he is supposed to be alert for violations of the prison rules which fall outside his routine sphere of surveillance. Not only must he detect and report deviant behavior after it occurs, but he must curb deviant behavior before it arises as well as when he is called on to prevent a minor quarrel among prisoners from flaring into a more dangerous situation. And he must make sure that the inmates in his charge perform their assigned tasks with a reasonable degree of efficiency.

The expected role of the guard, then, is a complicated compound of policeman and foreman, of cadi, counselor, and boss all rolled into one. But as the guard goes about his duties, piling one day on top of another (and the guard too, in a certain sense, is serving time in confinement), we find that the system of power in the prison is defective not only because the means of motivating the inmates to conform are largely lacking but also because the guard is frequently reluctant to enforce the full range of the institution's regulations. The guard frequently fails to report infractions of the rules which have occurred before his eyes. The guard often transmits forbidden information to inmates, such as plans for searching particular cells in a surprise raid for contraband. The guard often neglects elementary security requirements, and on numerous occasions he will be found joining his prisoners in outspoken criticisms of the warden and his assistants. In short, the guard frequently shows evidence of having been "corrupted" by the captive criminals over whom he stands in theoretical dominance. This failure within the ranks of the rulers is seldom to be attributed to outright bribery—bribery, indeed, is usually unnecessary, for far more effective influences are at work to bridge the gap supposedly separating captors and captives.

In the first place, the guard is in close and intimate association with his prisoners throughout the course of the working day. He can remain aloof only with great difficulty, for he possesses few of those devices which normally serve to maintain social distance between the rulers and the ruled. He cannot withdraw physically in symbolic affirmation of his superior position; he has no intermediaries to bear the brunt of resentment springing from orders which are disliked; and he cannot fall back on a dignity adhering to his office—he is a *hack* or a *screw* in the eyes of those he controls and an unwelcome display of officiousness evokes that great destroyer of unquestioned power, the ribald humor of the dispossessed.

There are many pressures in American culture to "be nice," to be a "good Joe," and the guard in the maximum-security prison is not immune. The guard is constantly exposed to a sort of moral blackmail in which the first signs of condemnation, estrangement, or rigid adherence to the rules is countered by the inmate with the threat of ridicule or hostility. And in this complex interplay, the guard does not always start from a position of determined opposition to "being friendly." He holds an intermediate post in a bureaucratic structure between top prison officials—his captains, lieutenants, and sergeants—and the prisoners in his charge. Like many such figures, the guard is caught in a conflict of loyalties. He often has reason to resent the actions of his superior officers—the reprimands, the lack of ready appreciation, the incomprehensible order—and in the inmates he finds willing sympathizers: they too claim to suffer from the unreasonable irritants of power. Furthermore, the guard in many cases is marked by a basic ambivalence toward the criminals under his supervision and control. It is true that the inmates of the prison have been condemned by society through the agency of the courts, but some of these prisoners must be viewed as a success in terms of a worldly system of the values which accords high prestige to wealth and influence even though they may have been won by devious means, and the poorly paid guard may be gratified to associate with a famous racketeer. Moreover, this ambivalence in the guard's attitudes toward the criminals nominally under his thumb may be based on something more than a *sub rosa* respect for the notorious. There may also be a discrepancy between the judgments of society and the guard's own opinions as far as the "criminality" of the prisoner is concerned. It is difficult to define the man convicted of deserting his wife, gambling, or embezzlement as a desperate criminal to be suppressed at all costs, and the crimes of even the most serious offenders lose their significance with the passage of time. In the eyes of the custodian, the inmate tends to become a man in prison rather than a criminal in prison and the relationship between captor and captive is subtly transformed in the process.

In the second place, the guard's position as a strict enforcer of the rules is undermined by the fact that he finds it almost impossible to avoid the claims of reciprocity. To a large extent, the guard is dependent on inmates for the satisfactory performance of his duties, and like many individuals in positions of power, the guard is evaluated in terms of the conduct of the men he controls. A troublesome, noisy, dirty cellblock reflects on the guard's ability to "handle" prisoners and this ability forms an important component of the merit rating which is used as the basis for pay raises and promotions. As we have pointed out above, a guard cannot rely on the direct application of force to achieve compliance nor can he easily depend on threats of punishment. And if the guard does insist on constantly using the last few negative sanctions available to the institution—if the guard turns in charge slip after charge slip for every violation of the rules which he encounters—he becomes burdensome to the top officials of the prison bureaucratic staff who realize only too well that their apparent dominance rests on some degree of cooperation. A system of power which can enforce its rules only by bringing its formal machinery of accusation, trial, and punishment

into play at every turn will soon be lost in a haze of pettifogging detail.

The guard, then, is under pressure to achieve a smoothly running tour of duty not with the stick but with the carrot, but here again his legitimate stock is limited. Facing demands from above that he achieve compliance and stalemated from below, he finds that one of the most meaningful rewards he can offer is to ignore certain offenses or make sure that he never places himself in a position where he will discover them. Thus the guard—backed by all the power of the state, close to armed men who will run to his aid, and aware that any prisoner who disobeys him can be punished if he presses charges against him—often discovers that his best path of action is to make "deals" or "trades" with the captives in his power. In effect, the guard buys compliance or obedience in certain areas at the cost of tolerating disobedience elsewhere.

Aside from winning compliance "where it counts" in the course of the normal day, the guard has another favor to be secured from the inmates which makes him willing to forego strict enforcement of all prison regulations. Many custodial institutions have experienced a riot in which the tables are turned momentarily and the captives hold sway over their quondam captors; the rebellions of 1952 loom large in the memories of the officials of the New Jersey State Prison. The guard knows that he may some day be a hostage and that his life may turn on a settling of old accounts. A fund of good will becomes a valuable form of insurance, and this fund is almost sure to be lacking if he has continually played the part of a martinet. In the folklore of the prison, there are enough tales about strict guards who have had the misfortune of being captured and savagely beaten during a riot to raise doubts about the wisdom of demanding complete conformity.

In the third place, the theoretical dominance of the guard is undermined in actuality by the innocuous encroachment of the prisoner on the guard's duties. Making out reports, checking cells at the periodic count, locking and unlocking doors—in short, all the minor chores which the guard is called on to perform—may gradually be transferred into the hands of inmates whom the guard has come to trust. The cell-block runner, formally assigned the tasks of delivering mail, housekeeping duties, and so on, is of particular importance in this respect. Inmates in this position function in a manner analogous to that of the company clerk in the armed forces and like such figures they may wield power and influence far beyond the nominal definition of their role. For reasons of indifference, laziness, or naïveté, the guard may find that much of the power which he is supposed to exercise has slipped from his grasp.

Now power, like a woman's virtue, once lost is hard to regain. The measures to rectify an established pattern of abdication need to be much more severe than those required to stop the first steps in the transfer of control from the guard to his prisoner. A guard assigned to a cellblock in which a large portion of power has been shifted in the past from the officials to the inmates is faced with the weight of precedent; it requires a good deal of moral courage on his part to withstand the aggressive tactics of prisoners who fiercely defend the patterns of corruption established by custom. And if the guard himself has allowed his control to be subverted, he may find that any attempts to undo his error are checked by a threat from the inmate to send a *snitch-kite*—an anonymous note—to the guard's superior officers explaining his past derelictions in detail. This simple form of blackmail may be quite sufficient to maintain the relationships established by friendship, reciprocity, or encroachment.

It is apparent, then, that the power of the custodians is defective, not simply in the sense that the rules are rebellious but also in the sense that the rulers are reluctant. We must attach a new meaning to Lord Acton's aphorism that power tends to corrupt and absolute power corrupts absolutely. The custodians of the New Jersey State Prison, far from being converted into brutal tyrants, are under strong pressure to compromise with their captives, for it is a paradox that they can ensure their dominance only by allowing it to be corrupted. Only by tolerating violations of "minor" rules and regulations can the guard secure compliance in the "major" areas of the custodial regime. Ill equipped to maintain the social distance which in theory separates the world of the officials and the world of the inmates, their suspicions eroded by long familiarity, the custodians are led into a modus vivendi with their captives which bears little resemblance to the stereotypical picture of guards and their prisoners.

IV

The fact that the officials of the prison experience serious difficulties in imposing their regime on the society of prisoners is sometimes attributed to inadequacies of the custodial staff's personnel. The fact that the job of the guard is often depressing and dangerous and possesses relatively low prestige adds further difficulties. When combined with the job's low salary, there is also little doubt that the ensuing high turnover rate carries numerous evils in its train. Yet even if higher salaries could counterbalance the many dissatisfying features of the guard's job—to a point where the custodial force consisted of men with long service rather than a group of transients—there remains a question of whether or not the problems of administration in the New Jersey State Prison would be eased to a significant extent. This, of course, is heresy from the viewpoint of those who trace the failure of social organizations to the personal failings of the individuals who man the organizational structure. Perhaps, indeed, there is some comfort in the idea that if the budget of the prison were larger, if the higher salaries could be paid to entice "better" personnel within the walls, if guards could be persuaded to remain for longer periods, then the many difficulties of the prison bureaucracy would disappear. From this point of view, the problems of custodial institution are rooted in the niggardliness of the free community and the consequent inadequacies of the institution's personnel rather than flaws in the social system of the prison itself. But to suppose that higher salaries are an answer to the plight of the custodians is to suppose, first, that there are men who by reason of their particular skills and personal characteristics are better qualified to serve as guards if they could be recruited; and second, that experience and training within the institution itself will better prepare the guard for his role, if greater financial rewards could convince him to make a career of his prison employment. Both of these suppositions, however, are open to some doubt. There are few jobs in the free community which are comparable to that of the guard in the maximum-security prison and which, presumably, could equip the guard-to-be with the needed skills. If the job requirements of the guard's position are not technical skills but turn on matters of character such as courage, honesty, and so on, there is no assurance that men with these traits will flock to the prison if the salary of the guard is increased. And while higher salaries may decrease the turnover rate—thus making an in-service training program feasible and providing a custodial force with greater experience—it is not certain if such a change can lead to marked improvement. A brief period of schooling can familiarize the new guard with the routines of the institution, but to prepare the guard for the realities of his assigned role with lectures and discussions is quite another matter. And it seems entirely possible that prolonged experience in the prison may enmesh the guard deeper and deeper in patterns of compromise and misplaced trust rather than sharpening his drive toward a rigorous enforcement of institutional regulations.

We are not arguing, of course, that the quality of the personnel in the prison is irrelevant to the successful performance of the bureaucracy's tasks nor are we arguing that it would be impossible to improve the quality of the personnel by increasing salaries. We are arguing, however, that the problems of the custodians far transcend the size of the guard's paycheck or the length of his employment and that better personnel is at best a palliative rather than a final cure. The lack of a sense of duty among those who are held captive, the obvious fallacies of coercion, the pathetic collection of rewards and punishments to induce compliance, the strong pressures toward the corruption of the guard in the form of friendship, reciprocity, and the transfer of duties into the hands of trusted inmates—all are structural defects in the prison's system of power rather than individual inadequacies.

The question of whether these defects are inevitable in the custodial institution—or in any system of total power—must be deferred to a later essay. For the moment it is enough to point out that in the New Jersey State Prison the custodians are unable or unwilling to prevent their captives from committing numerous violations of the rules which make up the theoretical blueprint for behavior, and this failure is not a temporary, personal aberration but a built-in feature of the prison social system. It is only by understanding this fact that we can understand the world of the prisoners, since so many significant aspects of the inmate behavior—such as coercion of fellow prisoners, fraud, gambling, homosexuality, sharing stolen supplies, and so on—are in clear contravention to institutional regulations. It is the nature of this world which must now claim our attention.

Foundations for a Theory of Corrections

CLARENCE SCHRAG

PROBLEMS of criminality and activities of criminals have attained such prominence in contemporary social life that nearly all persons have some conception of the methods or techniques of crime, the supposed causes of crime, and tactics of crime control. Common conceptions of criminality exert an important influence on the activities of correctional administrators because administrators regard themselves as representatives of the broader community in their dealings with criminals. Moreover, they are so regarded by the members of the broader community. Correctional officials, in other words, carry a public trust, and their duties and responsibilities are defined for them in terms of conventional beliefs concerning criminal behavior. Thus, the objectives and policies of correctional institutions are largely reflections of beliefs and values that are indigenous to the broader community.

If their objectives deviate very far from those of the broader community, correctional officials encounter various forms of public opposition. Consequently, the assessment of changes or trends in public expectations is an inevitable and important task for the correctional official. To the extent that social conventions are supportive of confused or contradictory correctional objectives, it may be expected that prison policies will reflect these confusions and contradictions.

According to available evidence, the foremost responsibilities assigned to prison officials are maintenance of custodial security and protection of society against convicted offenders. Therapy comes next. "You can't treat the prisoners if you can't keep them" and similar mottoes

indicate the relative values ordinarily attached to treatment and custody. Among the goals that receive weaker public endorsements, although they are strongly invoked in special cases and in times of crisis, are deterrence of potential offenders and reinforcement of cultural norms and values.

While the relative importance attached to different correctional objectives may vary somewhat in different segments of the community, the protective functions of correctional institutions are usually given the highest rankings, followed by the therapeutic or restorative functions, and finally the integrative functions. Moreover, staff members of correctional institutions, in general, follow the same order of rankings, the primary exception being that top-level administrative officials who have been indoctrinated in modern treatment philosophy tend to place a higher premium on therapy.

Like the goals and objectives of correctional institutions, the policies of such organizations are greatly influenced by conventional assumptions concerning criminal behavior. Correctional programs are founded on a public conception of the criminal as a person who habitually engages in deliberative misconduct. In fact, the conception of malicious intent is an essential ingredient of criminal conduct as defined by statute. Furthermore, persons who are regarded as being incapable of willful wrongdoing, namely, children and the insane, do not ordinarily come under the purview of criminal law or under the correctional policies that are presumably designed for deliberative offenders.

Although the above conception of criminal behavior may be gradually changing under the impact of contemporary explanations of human conduct, it seems clear that the bulk of opinion and the weight of official and legal doctrine are still largely in support of the traditional notion that the criminal knows the difference between right and wrong, that he makes a rational and considered decision against the moral order, and that his choice is subject to voluntary control. Criminals and prisoners, in other words, are believed to be capable of conformity but disposed to play the role of the rebel. Prisoners consequently are expected to exhibit antisocial attitudes and to be resistive and unruly in their contacts with correctional authorities. To the degree that prisoner roles are conditioned by the traditional assumptions mentioned, these assumptions may be expected to strengthen the staff-inmate conflicts and the negativistic attitudes of prisoners that have been so frequently noted in correctional research.

The role of the prison official, as perceived in the broader community, also reflects the influence of the assumptions mentioned above. In effect, inmates are absolved of any responsibility for prison programs and policies, and officials are held fully accountable for the attainment of correctional objectives, the maintenance of plant and equipment, the protection of inmate health and welfare, and the enforcement of inmate conformity and obedience.

The focus of traditional prison policies is the enforcement of compliance and obedience despite the expected opposition of the inmates. Strict surveillance and punitive actions are deemed necessary to show the prisoner that society is stronger than he is. Force and restraints, according to the view that seems dominant in the broader community, should only be used when necessary to maintain control, but they should always be available in sufficient degree to ensure the maintenance of control. Thus, correctional institutions are frequently viewed as autonomous societies having police powers sufficient for the prompt detection of any rule violations and for rigorous enforcement of official rules and regulations.

The prison world, as seen from a conventional perspective, is a world of conflict between forces of good and of evil. Prisoners are expected to exercise their antisocial propensities if they can get away with it. Officers are, or are expected to be, the sentinels of the good society who carry the full authority of the official community in their relations with the inmate caste. Their first objective is to obtain by means of external constraints the compliance that prisoners are disinclined to display voluntarily.

Significantly, the traditional view of the prison is also the view of most staff members and inmates. Striking similarities can be noted in the previously mentioned assumptions and in the way staff members and inmates perceive their own social roles and the roles of each other.

To illustrate, staff members and inmates were questioned concerning various possible solutions to problematic situations that frequently arise in correctional institutions. In addition to stating their own preferred solutions to the problems, officers and inmates indicated the solutions that they thought would be adopted by most officers and by most inmates. Then the observed preferences of the two groups were compared with their anticipated preferences.

Responses to the questionnaires clearly show that the role of the inmate is quite uniformly perceived as an "antisocial" role, whereas the role of the officer is just as consistently perceived as an "authoritarian" role. That is, both staff members and inmates regularly overestimate the number of antisocial solutions to prison problems that are actually chosen by the inmates. Likewise, both staff members and inmates, in attempting to anticipate the solutions that are chosen with greatest frequency by staff members, consistently assign to prison officials a higher degree of authoritarianism than is warranted by their actual choices. Moreover, differences in the role of the inmate as perceived by officers and by the inmates themselves are relatively minor. The same thing holds for the role of the officer.

The conclusion suggested is that staff members and inmates share perceptual distortions in such a manner that they see the differences in their assigned roles as being greatly exaggerated. These distortions tend to reinforce the traditions of conflict between the two groups. Furthermore, the distortions are in complete accord with the conventional view of the prison as a world of conflict. It may consequently be assumed that the distortions reflect the influence of cultural factors upon the cognitive behavior of staff members and inmates. The cultural expectation of staff-inmate conflict impregnates the perceptions of the members of the prison community, and in this way it may function as a self-fulfilling prophecy.

Administrative Organization of the Prison

The structure of prison administration is organized around conventional definitions of correctional objectives and conventional assumptions concerning criminal behavior. More specifically, the administrative structure of the prison is comprised of a hierarchy of offices or staff positions, each of which implies certain duties and responsibilities, and a chain of command linking the various offices in a rationally predetermined manner. The immediate objective of this structure is the attainment of uniform compliance to a set of official rules and regulations that designates the behavior expected of staff members and inmates.

The articulation of authority patterns and staff positions provides a powerful and intricately balanced mechanism for manufacturing policy decisions. Everyday observations of inmate behavior are reported from the lower levels of command up the ladder to higher levels, where the numerous reports are collated and official decisions are made. Then directives and supportive information, sanctioned by top-level administrators, flow back down the ladder in a unilateral sequence, from division chief to supervisor to officer and, in turn, to the inmates. Hence, the typical communication pattern in the close-custody prison is for reports of a first-hand factual nature to move upward in the chain of command and for policies, directives, and interpretations of factual materials to move down the ranks of employees.

Despite the clear logic of its structure, there may be significant defects in the system of unilateral authority relations. First, the system assumes that officers are fully committed to the objectives and policies announced by the chief administrator. Second, it assumes that the administrative machinery of the prison embodies the power and authority of the broader community in dealing with the inmates. Third, it assumes that inmates occupy a castelike status that

deprives them of any influence in the determination of policy. None of these assumptions is very realistic if judged in terms of social activities that are normally observed in the prison community. Let us briefly examine these assumptions in the order mentioned.

ALIENATION OF THE OFFICER   Instead of ensuring agreement between rank-and-file officers and top-level administrators, the unilateral flow of authority and communication may tend to produce a considerable barrier between the low-ranking officer's world of everyday experience and the picture of that world as it is viewed from the top levels of command.

Frequently, persons in highest authority are far removed from the scene of contact between staff members and inmates where the relative worthiness of alternative policies is most clearly revealed. Administrative decisions regarding specific situations are based chiefly on facts reported by subordinates. Therefore, administrative judgments are sometimes jeopardized by the distortions of fact that tend to occur when reports are repeatedly reviewed, digested, and passed upward through the ranks of the administrative hierarchy. In addition, the highest authorities may be among the last persons to learn about the impact of their decisions upon the relations between staff members and inmates. Generally, the higher the rank of the administrative officer, the greater his dependence on reports of the observations of others and the less direct the sources of his information.

Again, the officers who are most immediately affected by correctional policies are the ones who play the least part in policy formation. The task of low-ranking officers is to carry out orders, not to evaluate them. Feedback, such as criticism of directives received, is minimized, and in some institutions no official procedure for such reverse flow of communication is available. When reverse flow of critical comment is tolerated, it is often restricted to informal relations among trusted associates and is not treated as a matter of policy. Failure of unilateral communication to exploit the possibilities of feedback encourages the development of unofficial channels for the diffusion of messages. This may seriously interfere with the operation of the formal machinery of administration.

Official communication, based on the unilateral design, seems to be at a distinct disadvantage when competing with the mutual give-and-take that characterizes unofficial relations among officers or between officers and inmates. Two factors are of special significance in this connection. First, official directives generally assume the form of unqualified and universal imperatives. This results from the tendency for rationalizations, justifications, and elaborations to get lost or misinterpreted as the directives filter down the ranks of the administrative hierarchy. Second, for every official directive that is issued there is likely to be an unofficial interpretation which results from comments and discussions occurring outside the official channels of communication. For subordinate officials, it is perhaps the unofficial version that has the more comprehensible meaning and fits the directive into the overall plan of prison administration. If this is the case, the unilateral system of communication, instead of eliminating the influence of hearsay and rumor, may tend to make unofficial messages an essential part of the officer's conception of prison policy.

Allegiance to the official administration may be less important to the subordinate officer than are his many involvements in the unofficial conventions of the prison community. His knowledge of the official program is sometimes limited to the specific rules and regulations that are his immediate concern. His information about prison affairs comes primarily from sources other than those that are officially prescribed. For example, over half of the subordinate officers in a state prison were unaware of the existence of a certain group therapy program that had been in operation for more than nine months. And the majority of those officers who knew about the program stated that they had learned of it from inmates or fellow officers rather than from their superiors.

In many institutions, the status of subordinate officers is essentially connected with their lack of official information, their limited influence, and their minimal participation in matters of administrative policy. Attitudes of detachment and feelings of powerlessness or meaninglessness with respect to the official program are also commonly noted. Objective factors related to the status of subordinate officers tend to reinforce their feelings of powerlessness, and vice versa. The result is that officers of the lower ranks frequently are alienated from the official program. This is reflected, for example, in the negative correlation that is observed between the length of service of low-ranking officers and the degree of their confidence in prison treatment programs.

THE ILLUSION OF UNLIMITED AUTHORITY
Because of the primacy of custodial functions, the greatest concern of prison administrators is the constant threat of prisoner escapes and uprisings. Major techniques for the control of inmate rebellions are, first, the show of force and, second, appeals to the inmates based on the notion that the prison's administration embodies the power and authority of the political state.

However, neither technique seems to be nearly as effective in organizing the routine activities of the prison community as are the unofficial alliances between staff members and inmates. Routine activities of the prison are largely governed by a system of symbiotic social relations that is designed to eliminate the necessity of force except in emergencies. This symbiotic system is based on certain fundamental weaknesses in the official structure of prison administration.

First of all, the repeated use of force is often self-defeating. Its cost is excessive in terms of manpower and material resources. It is detrimental to inmate morale and interest in staff-inmate harmony. Force begets force in the sense that officers who are employed in the continued use of force are thereby deprived of the major social means for obtaining voluntary inmate cooperation. This is largely the reason for the traditional separation of custodial and therapeutic functions in the close-custody prison.

A more crucial reason for restraint in the employment of force is that public opinion generally denies the necessity of its continued use in correctional institutions. Withdrawal of public support from correctional administrations that are founded on repetitious displays of official violence has occurred with increasing frequency during the course of our penal history. For example, the use of force in the recent wave of prison riots almost always resulted in public inquiries into the complaints of the rioting prisoners. These inquiries clearly revealed that public opinion was by no means unanimous in its support of prison policies, a situation that was apparently anticipated by the riot leaders and may have contributed to their rebellions.

While social conventions hold administrators responsible for the conduct of prison inmates, they also assume that strict surveillance and rigorous enforcement of appropriate penalties should make major displays of violence a rare occurrence. Consequently, most prison administrators, in order to maintain their official positions, must use devices other than violence in gaining inmate conformity and obedience. Force, then, is increasingly regarded as a device to be used as a last resort in case of emergency. Its public justification is sometimes threatened by the conventional belief that efficient prison administration should make its use unnecessary.

For the above reasons, the appeal to authority is a far more prevalent mechanism of official control. However, the functions of authority in the prison community are also subject to common misunderstanding. Authority is based on the assumption that persons in subordinate positions will voluntarily submit to the dictates of their superiors. But authority is effective only if subordinates share the social perspectives of their superiors. Our discussion of alienation has already suggested that officers occupying different ranks in the administrative hierarchy do not necessarily share similar views of the official program.

It is sometimes naively assumed that an officer's instruction to an inmate carries the full sanction of the prison's administration and that the officer's failure to enforce his order is evidence of the "corruption" of his authority. This is not necessarily the case. It would be far more realistic frankly to admit that the officer's control over an inmate depends primarily on his skills of persuasion and leadership.

Consider, for example, the alternative procedures that are available to an officer in the event that an inmate refuses to obey his command. First, he might resort to physical force. Gener-

ally, there are official regulations that restrict the use of force except in cases of attempted escape or threatened bodily injury. These regulations are designed to prevent unnecessary use of force. Therefore, if the officer uses force, he must justify his actions to his superiors in the same way that his superiors need to justify violence in the face of public opinion. His superiors are likely to hold the common opinion that effective leadership and preventive methods should make force unnecessary. Repeated involvement in violence against inmates is consequently likely to result in termination of the officer's employment by the institution.

Again, the officer may use the more common procedure of reporting inmate misconduct to his superiors. Penalties against the inmate may then be determined by a disciplinary committee. However, should the committee receive an extraordinary number of complaints or reports from a given officer, this too may be interpreted as evidence of incompetence on the part of the officer. Inmates, of course, are fully aware of the role they play in the official evaluation of an officer's services. Thus, continued employment of a given officer depends largely upon the degree of voluntary cooperation that he can win from the inmates. Skill in interpersonal relations is more important in this situation than is the "corruption" of highly restricted authority, and the idea that officials have unlimited authority is simply not consistent with the essential evidence.

THE FICTION OF OFFICIAL AUTONOMY Another defect of the unilateral system of communication and authority is the assumption that prison policies are autonomous and uninfluenced by inmate pressures. Official policy views the prisoner as being habitually antisocial and inclined to violate regulations if he can get away with it. Further, policy holds that the only defensible role for the officer to play is to enforce all rules to the letter and "let the chips fall where they may." Since the inmates are not involved in the formulation of policy, their only opportunity for influencing the administration of the institution is in the area of policy enforcement. Therefore, if the rules are enforced without deviation, complete domination over the inmates presumably can be gained.

For instance, rules aimed at curbing food pilferage may define as contraband all items of prison fare that are found in any place other than the mess hall. As a consequence, any inmate found in possession of unauthorized food is officially presumed to be guilty of theft or somehow involved in the food racket. Excuses do not count.

Similar presumptions of guilt operate with respect to other rules and regulations. The apparent purpose of the presumptions is to base the decision of guilt upon objective factors and to eliminate problems of judgment concerning extenuating circumstances. In this way, it is believed that the possibility of inmate influence in the dispensation of prison justice will be minimized.

However, undeviating enforcement of all rules can involve an officer in the repeated employment of force and/or the issuance of innumerable rule-infraction reports. The practical effect, in either case, may be to create official doubts concerning the officer's competence, as has already been mentioned. Furthermore, the officer may have full knowledge of extenuating circumstances in certain cases and may therefore disagree with the official presumption of guilt. If the officer takes into consideration the alleviating conditions and gives the inmate a "break," he is in danger of official reprimand. In addition, toleration of rule infractions in the face of a policy of complete enforcement makes the officer vulnerable to charges of collusion with the inmates. This is precisely the point at which conniving inmates seek to "get something on" the officer, to be held against him later in more important situations and progressively to bring him under inmate domination.

The traditional policy of complete rule enforcement breaks down because it does not allow room for individual judgment concerning the circumstances related to rule violations. It places the officer in a fine dilemma. As a practical matter, the officer can neither enforce all rules to the letter nor can he admit that he tolerates certain rule violations. This is why many correctional institutions, including some close-custody prisons, are developing mecha-

nisms for taking into account the circumstances related to rule violations. However, all of these mechanisms, so far as can be ascertained, involve distinctive modifications of the unilateral system of communication; they either give the officer considerable discretion in reporting violations, a procedure that is euphemistically called "counseling," or they provide for the inmate an official opportunity to defend his actions.

Nevertheless, insistence upon unilateral relations among staff members and between staff members and inmates, rather than paucity of treatment facilities, is the feature most characteristic of the traditional close-custody prison. Restrictions against feedback and participation in policy formation, of course, are extended to the inmate population. However, such restrictions apparently run counter to some of the assumptions underlying modern therapeutic techniques. Modern methods of group therapy and guided participation in programming activities, for example, encourage the inmate to evaluate and perhaps initially to criticize the behavior standards that he is expected eventually to adopt as his own. Frank expression of skepticism and freedom of discussion, instead of ensuring rejection of social norms, are believed to improve the inmate's understanding of social controls and to further the development of self-imposed discipline.

If the above analysis of defects in traditional prison policies is valid, then it seems clear that the unilateral organization of the close-custody prison may place severe limitations upon the treatment potential of our prisons and may provide a greater barrier against the resocialization of the offender than do the bars and walls that attract such adverse comment. How to modify traditional policy so as to integrate the roles of inmates and officers within a more efficient official organization continues to be one of the most difficult problems of prison administration.

Some Aspects of Prisoner Society

Juxtaposed with the official organization of the prison is an unofficial social system originating within the institution and regulating inmate conduct with respect to focal issues, such as length of sentence, relations among prisoners, contacts with staff members and other civilians, food, sex, and health. The unofficial system, contrary to administrative rules and regulations, does not demand uniformity of behavior. Rather, it recognizes alternative roles that inmates may play with respect to each of the focal issues.

In various subtle ways, the unofficial social system encourages reciprocal, complementary, or symbiotic relationships among inmates and between inmates and officers. Behavior prescriptions are based on interlocking role alternatives that are organized around the focal issues. Alternative roles are allocated among the inmates so as to maintain a fairly stable social equilibrium within the society of prisoners. To illustrate, consider some of the alternative roles that are organized around the procurement of illicit foods. Codes of conduct pertaining to food pilferage differ for "scores" (spontaneous or unplanned thefts) and "routes" (highly organized thefts). An inmate who "scores for food" may consume it or share it with friends, perhaps for past or expected favors, but he is not expected to sell it. Food obtained through organized theft is ordinarily sold in the illicit food racket.

Sale of pilfered food is regulated by an intricate division of labor and responsibility based on a network of symbiotic roles. Designated inmates are assigned the job of obtaining the food and delivering it to distributors. Distributors, in turn, may sell on credit to trusted inmate customers. Or the food may be sold on a cash basis to inmates from whom knowledge of procurement techniques is carefully concealed. Roles affiliated with the food racket are further delineated in terms of the kinds and quantities of foods stolen; in terms of the food sources, such as the officer's mess or the inmate's mess, for example; and, finally, in terms of the methods of distribution and exchange.

Only those inmates who are involved in the food racket, of course, need to know the details of the system. Designation of role incumbents is handled informally, chiefly by mutual agreement among the persons concerned. But once a role has been assumed, it places upon the incumbent fairly precise requirements regarding his relations with others who participate in the racket, and with nonparticipating inmates and staff members as well. Furthermore, the amount of knowledge and skill required of an inmate depends upon the degree of his involvement in the racket. The food racket may be so well organized, however, that if all persons involved in it know and fulfill their assignments, the pilferage system can operate with an efficiency that is alarming and costly to the prison's administration.

Maintenance of a sub rosa organization such as the food racket requires that inmates be capable of assessing the probable behavior and the loyalty attachments of their fellows. Roles and statuses must generally be appropriate to the skills and interests of the persons involved. Errors made by the inmates in the assignment of roles ordinarily work to the advantage of the prison's administration and its officials. In order to minimize such errors, a fairly elaborate system of role allocations is set into operation not only with respect to food pilferage but in all areas of behavior related to the focal issues.

Allocation of roles is based on evidence regarding the affective orientations of the inmates, the accuracy and consistency of their perceptions of role requirements, and the degree of agreement between their perceived role requirements and their performance. Role allocations not only reflect the assessments and expectations of fellow inmates relative to the person in question, but they also in a large measure determine this person's opportunities for future social contacts and his access to information and to other social resources.

Evidence relevant to role assignments is obtained from observations made during initiation ceremonies and from a variety of contrived testing situations that accompany the introduction of an inmate into the prisoner community. The process of role allocation commonly proceeds in a standardized sequence of events. First, a degree of consensus is attained regarding the inmate's relative loyalties to the administration and to his fellow prisoners. Attempts are made to determine whether a given inmate generally evaluates situations according to the codes of prisoner society or according to the dictates of the officials. Then, the inmate's knowledge of prisoner roles and his skill in dealing with problematic situations are carefully examined. Knowledge of prisoner society indicates a given inmate's potential for aiding or obstructing the goals and strategies of his fellow prisoners. Finally, the consistency, reliability, and integrity of the inmate's behavior are investigated in a variety of contrived situations. Within six months, or so, after the inmate's admission into the institution, his major roles in the prisoner community seem to have been pretty well established. Role assignments, of course, are sometimes modified through a continuous re-evaluation of the inmate's performance, but the frequency of such modifications is usually not great enough to disturb the social equilibrium.

In addition to exercising great care in the allocation of roles, especially in areas involving high risk of detection by the officials, inmate society sets up expectations of mutual care and protection among the prisoners. These expectations, of course, conflict with the official suggestion to "do your own time," and they provide a basis for strong inmate morale in the face of persistent staff opposition. Roles played by prisoners with respect to forbidden activities create sets of mutual obligations that define conceptions of loyalty and protect organized rackets from interference by nonparticipating inmates or staff members. The rule that an inmate should not do anything to interfere with another's participation in forbidden activities is apparently the strongest commandment in the prisoner's code of conduct.

For example, inmates engaged in the food racket, in order to maintain a climate favorable to the continuation of this enterprise, may be expected to support and protect various other forbidden activities. Inmates who profit from such support or nonintervention are required to reciprocate in like manner. A system of largely unspoken but finely graded reciprocities of this kind tends to integrate prisoner society in its opposition to the prison's official administration.

But the system of inmate reciprocities, like the official system of unilateral communications, is vulnerable in crucial ways to outside interference. Deviations from the system, although they may be largely concealed from many of the inmates, are as much the rule as the exception. One problem is competition among inmates who are striving for higher status and authority within the society of prisoners. Again, the system is far less autonomous than the inmates would like to believe, and whenever it is disrupted by official intervention, there is great difficulty in determining exactly what went wrong. Finally, many of the inmates refrain from full involvement in the system; they may feel an allegiance to the official codes or they may be greatly influenced by official rewards and punishments. All of this lessens the effectiveness of the social controls that are primarily accessible to the prisoners.

The result is that neither the official system nor the society of prisoners can long retain dominance in the prison community. Symbiotic relationships tend to develop in such a way that although the integrity of the two systems may be retained on the surface, the behavior of an inmate or a staff member in almost any given case is determined by intersecting influences that cannot be realistically accredited solely to either system. It is to this topic that we now turn our attention.

PATTERNS OF INMATE ADAPTATION

Sets of role alternatives, as previously indicated, reflect the organization of inmate behavior with regard to given focal issues. The conception of a social system, however, signifies a higher level of organization than that dealing with specific issues. Society, as an abstract concept, implies that the role alternatives assumed by given individuals with respect to various issues are interrelated in a more or less systematic manner. Thus, the pragmatic problem related to the concept of the social system is for research to determine the empirical regularities, if any, among sets of role alternatives. We call such regularities role configurations.

Major Role Configurations

Several configurations of inmate roles were found that cut across a number of issues within the prison community. Most important, in our opinion, is a set of configurations that deals primarily with issues involving social relations among inmates, contacts with staff members, and access to the civilian world. The set includes four major configurations, to which are attached the prison labels "square John," "right guy," "con politician," and "outlaw."

Briefly, inmates who fall within the "square John" configuration consistently define role requirements in terms of the prison's official social system. By contrast, "right guys" just as regularly perceive requirements according to the norms of prisoner society. "Con politicians" shift their frame of reference from staff norms to inmate norms with great alacrity. "Outlaws," deficient in aptitude for identification, are in a perpetual anarchistic rebellion against both normative systems and against affective involvements in general.

Whereas the above argot labels refer to specific sets of interconnected role alternatives, our interest is in developing a typological system relating these role configurations to other social or cultural aspects of the prison community. In order to emphasize this distinction, a shift from argot labels to a more neutral terminology seems advisable. Consequently, the terms *prosocial, antisocial, pseudosocial,* and *asocial* will hereafter be used in lieu of the argot labels in the respective order in which they have appeared. These role configurations, in the interest of brevity, will be called, collectively, social types.

Career Variables

To investigate the assumption that there are distinctive variations in the careers of the various social types, groups of inmates belonging to different types were interviewed and their case histories were carefully examined. Clear distinctions were noted in the criminal records of the social types, their family and community experiences, and their attitudes towards crime and society. Major findings are summarized below.

Prosocial inmates are most frequently convicted of violent crimes against the person, such as homicide and assault, or naive property offenses, chiefly forgery. Few have prior arrests, and their criminal careers are initiated relatively late in life. Their offenses are situational. That is, the offenses reflect extraordinary social pressures frequently involving real or imagined misbehavior on the part of a spouse or of close friends.

While in prison, prosocial inmates maintain strong ties with family and civilian associates, and they are sympathetic and cooperative toward prison officials. Generally supportive of established authority, they believe in the efficacy of punishment, show strong guilt for their offenses, and expect to pay for their crimes in order to renew civilian life with a clean slate. Naive about illegal techniques and strategies, they have little knowledge of, or contact with, organized crime.

Antisocial inmates are highly recidivistic, their careers frequently progressing through stages of truancy, expressive theft with other gang members, instrumental theft involving contacts with "fences" and other organized criminals, and culminating in patterns of unsophisticated crimes such as robbery, assault, and burglary.

Coming chiefly from families having other delinquent members and living in underprivileged urban areas, antisocial inmates frequently earn a livelihood via contacts with organized crime, but do not often rise to positions of power in this field. Rebellion against conventional norms has continuity in their careers and is noted in their educational, occupational, and marital adjustments. Close ties with the parental family were commonly seen, however.

In prison, the antisocial offenders continue their close association with criminalistic elements and their rebellion against civil authorities. Their philosophy of life, as reflected in the slogans "only suckers work," "politicians are crooks," and "big shots and real criminals never get caught," alleviates their sense of guilt and solidifies inmate opposition against the prison's administration.

Pseudosocial inmates are involved primarily in subtle, sophisticated, profit-motivated offenses, such as embezzlement, fraud, and forgery. Relatively few have juvenile records, and onset of criminality often occurs after a position of respectability has already been attained in the civilian community.

Family and community backgrounds are frequently middle class, but evidence of inconsistent parental discipline and other family disharmony is the most striking feature of their preinstitutional careers. Apparently, pseudosocial offenders acquire their facility in role-playing at an early age, and they are frequently described as having a pleasant, ingratiating manner. Educational and occupational records are far superior to those of antisocial offenders.

In prison, pseudosocial inmates display chameleonic skill in shifting their allegiances from staff members to inmates, and vice versa, according to the exigencies of the moment. Pragmatic and instrumentally oriented, they exploit to their own advantage the conflicts and inconsistencies inherent in the prison's social structure. Although they are recognized to be unreliable, their strategic position between the two social systems makes them the mediators in staff-inmate conflicts and results in rewards, such as relatively short sentences, desirable prison assignments, and reduced custody.

Asocial inmates commit a variety of offenses against persons and property, frequently using bizarre methods without clear motive or reason. Recidivism is extremely high, and there is early evidence of severe behavior disorders, although age at first arrest varies considerably.

Paramount among findings regarding social backgrounds is the seemingly universal evidence of early rejection. Asocial offenders are frequently reared in institutions, shifted around various foster homes or are otherwise lacking reasonable care and attention from their parents. Social abilities and skills in the use of social symbols are greatly retarded. The careers of asocial offenders are marked by high egocentrism and an inability to profit from past mistakes or to plan for the future. These persons often exhibit an apparent distrust and fear of personal ties of any kind. Their problems are solved by direct and immediate aggression.

In prison, asocial inmates are the undisciplined troublemakers who are chiefly involved in riots, escape plots, and assaults on both inmates and officers. Nevertheless, their lack of capacity for cooperative enterprise means that most of their rebellions are destined for failure.

Several tentative conclusions can be drawn from the above findings. Generally, antisocial offenders are reared in an environment consis-

tently oriented toward illegitimate social norms. Asocial and pseudosocial offenders exhibit defective normative perceptions growing out of early parental rejection and patterns of inconsistent discipline, respectively. They suffer severe personal frustrations at an early age and acquire distinctive adaptation techniques. Prosocial offenders, although using legitimate normative standards, seem unable to cope with intense social pressures or unique personal problems. That persons with such varied problems of adjustment should play distinctively different roles in the prison community does not seem surprising,

Cognitive and Affective Orientations

Prosocial offenders appear to evaluate problematic situations with reference to legitimate norms, to have greater cognitive understanding of legitimate role requirements than of illegitimate requirements, and generally to apply legitimate norms in specific situations regardless of the personal discomfiture that might result. Conversely, it is expected that antisocial offenders will consistently employ deviant or illegitimate norms as standards of reference, to exhibit detailed cognitive knowledge of illegitimate role requirements, and likewise to display their allegiance to these norms irrespective of the impact on personal goals or objectives. Their general opposition to legitimate means of achievement is expressed figuratively in the motto, "only suckers work." The two types, then, are alike in emphasizing collective values, such as loyalty, mutual aid, and group solidarity, but they differ in the normative systems used as standards of judgment.

Pseudosocial offenders, by contrast, are capable of shifting their normative perspectives according to the availability of instrumental rewards. They stress personal achievements rather than collective goals, exploitative strategies rather than conventional procedures, and affective neutrality rather than strong identifications with persons or social conventions. Their cognitive knowledge and role-playing skills extend to the deviant realm as well as to the conventional one. Above all, to be bound by social conventions or moral commitments is for them a sign of weakness.

Asocial offenders are similarly detached from social conventions and moral commitments. However, in their case detachment reflects ignorance of role requirements and deficiency in role-playing ability rather than emancipation. Moreover, their conceptions of the illegitimate system appear to be as much distorted as their conceptions of legitimate norms. They are generally incapable of developing affective ties either with prisoners or with officials. Thus, their behavior is ordinarily impulsive and motivated by expressive functions; only rarely does it reveal the deliberative and instrumental characteristics so commonly noted among the pseudosocial inmates.

Information obtained by presenting to staff members and inmates alternative solutions to common prison problems has already been mentioned. The solutions chosen by members of the different social types seem to agree with the above arguments. For example, staff members and prosocial inmates tend to choose the same solutions, while pseudosocial offenders choose solutions representative of both conventional and deviant prescriptions. Antisocial offenders are fairly consistent in following the choice-pattern dictated by the illegitimate normative system. Asocial offenders make the greatest number of irregular choices.

Evidence regarding cognitive knowledge possessed by the social types has been difficult to obtain. However, tests of argot vocabularies suggest that, at the time of admission to the institution, antisocial offenders have the best knowledge of prison lingo. Pseudosocial offenders, though, appear to learn more rapidly, and they may eventually attain a higher degree of proficiency. Asocial inmates, perhaps surprisingly, have a less adequate vocabulary, so far as labels for prisoner roles are concerned, than do the prosocial inmates, and both of these groups, of course, have vocabularies inferior to those of the antisocial or pseudosocial inmates. Further empirical investigation is needed, however, to demonstrate important anticipated differences in cognitive knowledge among the social types.

In summary, the social types reveal systematic differences in their cognitive and affective orientations toward the normative systems that are found in the close-custody prison, especially with respect to their attitudes regarding expressive (group integrating) and instrumental (goal-achievement) norms.

The Prison Experience:
The Convict World

JOHN IRWIN

THE convict population in California tends to be splintered. A few convicts orient themselves to the prison social system and assume roles in regard to the prison, and a few others withdraw completely, but the majority confine their association to one or two groups of convicts and attempt to disassociate themselves from the bulk of the population. These groups vary from small, close-knit, primary groups to large, casual groups. They also vary greatly in the basis of formation or focus. Many are formed on the basis of neighborhood and/or racial ties, others on the basis of shared criminal identities, especially in the case of thieves, dope fiends, heads, and hustlers, but the great majority of the groups are formed on a rather random basis. Many convicts who cell together or close to each other, who work or attend school together, maintain friendship ties which vary greatly in strength and duration.

The type of group affiliations the convict forms, the impact of this group participation, and the general impact of the prison experience upon his extended career are related to a wide range of factors, some systematic, some relatively random. Presently, four of these factors seem to stand out. These are (1) his preprison identity, (2) his prison adaptive mode, (3) his race-ethnicity, and finally (4) his relationship to perspective and identity of the "convict." The following paragraphs will focus primarily on the prison-adaptive modes, but the relationship between these modes and criminal identi-

From *The Felon* (pp. 67-85) by J. Irwin, 1970, Englewood Cliffs, NJ: Prentice Hall. Copyright 1980 by John Irwin. Reprinted by permission.

ties will be considered. Race-ethnicity and the convict perspective will be treated later in the chapter.

PRISON-ADAPTIVE MODES

Many studies of prison behavior have approached the task of explaining the convict social organization by posing the hypothetical question, How do convicts adapt to prison? It was felt that this was a relevant question because the prison is a situation of deprivation and degradation and, therefore, presents extraordinary adaptive problems. Two adaptive styles were recognized: (1) an individual style—withdrawal and/or isolation, and (2) a collective style—participation in a convict social system which, through its solidarity, regulation of activities, distribution of goods and prestige, and apparent opposition to the world of the administration, helps the individual withstand the "pains of imprisonment."

I would like to suggest that these studies have overlooked important alternate styles. First, let us return to the question that theoretically every convict must ask himself: How shall I do my time? or, What shall I do in prison? First, we assume by this question that the convict is able to cope with the situation. This is not always true; some fail to cope with prison and commit suicide or sink into psychosis. Those who do cope can be divided into those who identify with and therefore adapt to a broader world than that of the prison, and those who orient themselves primarily to the prison world. This difference in orientation is often quite subtle but always important. In some instances, it is the basis for forming very important choices, choices which may have important consequences for the felon's long-term career. For example, Piri Thomas, a convict, was forced to make up his mind whether to participate in a riot or refrain:

I stood there watching and weighing, trying to decide whether or not I was a con first and an outsider second. I had been doing time inside yet living every mental minute I could outside; now I had to choose one or the other. I stood there in the middle of the yard. Cons passed me by, some going west to join the boppers, others going east to neutral ground. The call of rep tore within me, while the feeling of being a punk washed over me like a yellow banner. I had to make a decision. *I am a con. These damn cons are my people. . . . What do you mean, your people? Your people are outside the cells, home, in the streets. No! That ain't so. . . . Look at them go toward the west wall. Why in hell am I taking so long in making up my mind? Man, there goes Papo and Zu-Zu, and Mick the Boxer; even Ruben is there.*

This identification also influences the criteria for assigning and earning prestige—criteria relative to things in the outside world or things which tend to exist only in the prison world, such as status in a prison social system or success with prison homosexuals. Furthermore, it will influence the long-term strategies he forms and attempts to follow during his prison sentence.

It is useful to further divide those who maintain their basic orientation to the outside into (1) those who for the most part wish to maintain their life patterns and their identities—even if they intend to refrain from most law-breaking activities—and (2) those who desire to make significant changes in life patterns and identities and see prison as a chance to do this.

The mode of adaptation of those convicts who tend to make a world out of prison will be called "jailing." To "jail" is to cut yourself off from the outside world and to attempt to construct a life within prison. The adaptation of those who still keep their commitment to the outside life and see prison as a suspension of that life but who do not want to make any significant changes in their life patterns will be called "do-

ing time." One "does time" by trying to maximize his comfort and luxuries and minimize his discomfort and conflict and to get out as soon as possible. The adaptation made by those who, looking to their future life on the outside, try to effect changes in their life patterns and identities will be called "gleaning." In "gleaning," one sets out to "better himself" or "improve himself" and takes advantage of the resources that exist in prison to do this.

Not all convicts can be classified neatly by these three adaptive styles. Some vacillate from one to another, and others appear to be following two or three of them simultaneously. Still others, for instance the noncopers mentioned above, cannot be characterized by any of the three. However, many prison careers fit very closely into one of these patterns, and the great majority can be classified roughly by one of the styles.

Doing Time

When you go in, now your trial is over, you got your time and everything and now you head for the joint. They furnish your clothing, your toothbrush, your toothpaste, they give you a package of tobacco, they put you up in the morning to get breakfast. In other words, everything is furnished. Now you stay in there two years, five years, ten years, whatever you stay in there, what difference does it make? After a year or so you've been . . . after six months, you've become accustomed to the general routine. Everything is furnished. If you get a stomachache, you go to the doctor; if you can't see out of your cheaters, you go to the optician. It don't cost you nothing.

As the above statement by a thief indicates, many convicts conceive of the prison experience as a temporary break in their outside career, one which they take in their stride. They come to prison and "do their time." They attempt to pass through this experience with the least amount of suffering and the greatest amount of comfort. They (1) avoid trouble, (2) find activities which occupy their time, (3) secure a few luxuries, (4) with the exception of a few complete isolates, form friendships with small groups of other convics, and (5) do what they think is necessary to get out as soon as possible.

To avoid trouble, the convict adheres to the convict code—especially the maxims of "do your own time" and "don't snitch," and stays away from "lowriders"—those convicts engaged in hijacking and violent disputes. In some prisons which have a high incidence of violence—knifings, assaults, and murders—this can appear to be very difficult even to the convicts themselves. One convict reported his first impression of Soledad:

The first day I got to Soledad I was walking from the fish tank to the mess hall and this guy comes running down the hall past me, yelling, with a knife sticking out of his back. Man, I was petrified. I thought, what the fuck kind of place is this?

To occupy their time, "time-doers" work, read, work on hobbies, play cards, chess, and dominoes; engage in sports, go to movies, watch TV, participate in some group activities, such as drama groups, gavel clubs, and slot car clubs; and while away hours "tripping" with friends. They seek extra luxuries through their job. Certain jobs in prison, such as jobs in the kitchen, in the officers' and guards' dining room, in the boiler room, the officers' and guards' barber shop, and the fire house, offer various extra luxuries—extra things to eat, a radio, privacy, additional shows, and more freedom. Or time-doers purchase luxuries legally or illegally available in the prison market. If they have money on the books, if they have a job which pays a small salary, or if they earn money at a hobby, they can draw up to twenty dollars a month which may be spent for foodstuffs, coffee, cocoa, stationery, toiletries, tobacco, and cigarettes. Or using cigarettes as currency, they may purchase food from the kitchen, drugs, books, cell furnishings, clothes, hot plates, stingers, and other contraband items. If they do not have legal access to funds, they may "scuffle," that is, sell some commodity which they produce—such as belt buckles or other handicraft items—or some commodity which is accessible to them through their job—such as food items from the kitchen. "Scuffling," however, necessitates becoming enmeshed in the convict social system and in-

creases the chances of "trouble," such as conflicts over unpaid debts, hijacking by others, and "beefs"—disciplinary actions for rule infractions. Getting into trouble is contrary to the basic tenets of "doing time," so time-doers usually avoid scuffling.

All convicts are more apt to choose "doing time," but some approach this style in a slightly different manner. For instance, doing time is characteristic of the thief in prison. He shapes this mode of adaptation and establishes it as a major mode of adaptation in prison. The convict code, which is fashioned from the criminal code, is the foundation for this style. The thief has learned how to do his time long before he comes to prison. Prison, he learns when he takes on the dimensions of the criminal subculture, is part of criminal life, a calculated risk, and when it comes he is ready for it.

Long before the thief has come to prison, his subculture has defined proper prison conduct as behavior rationally calculated to "do time" in the easiest possible way. This means that he wants a prison life containing the best possible combination of a maximum amount of leisure time and maximum number of privileges. Accordingly, the privileges sought by the thief are different from the privileges sought by the man oriented to prison itself. The thief wants things that will make prison life a little easier—extra food, a maximum amount of recreation time, a good radio, a little peace.

The thief knows how to avoid trouble; he keeps away from "dingbats," "lowriders," "hoosiers," "square Johns," and "stool pigeons" and obeys the convict code. He also knows not to buck the authorities; he keeps his record clean and does what is necessary to get out—even programs.

He occasionally forms friendships with other criminals, such as dope fiends, heads, and possibly disorganized criminals, but less often with square Johns. Formerly, he confined his friendship to other thieves with whom he formed very tight-knit groups. For example, Jack Black, a thief in the last century, describes his assimilation into the "Johnson family" in prison:

Shorty was one of the patricians of the prison, a "box man," doing time for bank burglary. "I'll put you in with the right people, kid. You're folks yourself or you wouldn't have been with Smiler."

I had no friends in the place. But the fact that I had been with Smiler, that I had kept my mouth shut, and that Shorty had come forward to help me, gave me a certain fixed status in the prison that nothing could shake but some act of my own. I was naturally pleased to find myself taken up by the "best people," as Shorty and his friends called themselves, and accepted as one of them.

Clemmer described two *primary* groups out of the fourteen groups he located, and both of these were groups of thieves. Presently in California prisons, thieves' numbers have diminished. This and the general loosening of the convict solidarity have tended to drive the thief into the background of prison life. He generally confines his friendships to one or two others, usually other thieves or criminals who are "all right"; otherwise he withdraws from participation with others. He often feels out of place amid the changes that have come about. One thief looking back upon fifteen years in California prisons states:

As far as I'm concerned their main purpose has been in taking the convict code away from him. But what they fail to do is when they strip him from these rules is replace it with something. They turn these guys into a bunch of snivelers and they write letters on each other and they don't have any rules to live by.

Another thief interviewed also indicated his dislocation in the present prison social world:

The new kinds in prison are wild. They have no respect for rules or other persons. I just want to get out of here and give it all up. I can't take coming back to prison again, not with the kind of convicts they are getting now.

Like the majority of convicts, the dope fiend and the head usually just "do time." When they do, they do not vary greatly from the thief, except that they tend to associate with other dope fiends or heads, although they too will associate with other criminals. They tend to form very close

bonds with one, two, or three other dope fiends or heads and maintain a casual friendship with a large circle of dope fiends, heads, and other criminals. Like the thief, the dope fiend and the head tend not to establish ties with squares.

The hustler in doing time differs from the other criminals in that he does not show a propensity to form very tight-knit groups. Hustling values, which emphasize manipulation and invidiousness, seem to prevent this. The hustler maintains a very large group of casual friends. Although this group does not show strong bonds of loyalty and mutual aid, they share many activities such as cards, sports, dominoes, and "jiving"—casual talk.

Square Johns do their time quite differently than the criminals. The square John finds life in prison repugnant and tries to isolate himself as much as possible from the convict world. He does not believe in the convict code, but he usually learns to display a token commitment to it for his own safety. A square John indicated his forced obedience to the convict code:

Several times I saw things going on that I didn't like. One time a couple of guys were working over another guy and I wanted to step in, but I couldn't. Had to just keep moving as if I didn't see it.

Jailing

Some convicts who do not retain or who never acquired any commitment to outside social worlds tend to make a world out of prison. These are the men who seek positions of power, influence, and sources of information, whether these men are called "shots," "politicians," "merchants," "hoods," "toughs," "gorillas," or something else. A job as secretary to the captain or warden, for example, gives an aspiring prisoner information and consequent power and enables him to influence the assignment or regulation of other inmates. In the same way, a job which allows the incumbent to participate in a racket, such as clerk in the kitchen storeroom where he can steal and sell food, is highly desirable to a man oriented to the convict subculture. With a steady income of cigarettes, ordinarily the prisoner's medium of exchange, he may assert a great deal of influence and purchase those things which are symbols of status among persons oriented to the convict subculture. Even if there is not a well-developed medium of exchange, he can barter goods acquired in his position for equally desirable goods possessed by other convicts. These include information and such things as specially starched, pressed, and tailored prison clothing; fancy belts, belt buckles or billfolds; special shoes; or any other type of dress which will set him apart and will indicate that he has both the influence to get the goods and the influence necessary to keep them and display them despite prison rules which outlaw doing so. In California, special items of clothing, and clothing that is neatly laundered, are called "bonaroos" (a corruption of *bonnet rouge,* by means of which French prison trustees were once distinguished from the common run of prisoners), and to a lesser degree even the persons who wear such clothing are called "bonaroos."

Just as doing time is the characteristic style of the thief, so "jailing" is the characteristic style of the state-raised youth. This identity terminates on the first or second prison term, or certainly by the time the youth reaches 30. The state-raised youth must assume a new identity, and the one he most often chooses, the one which his experience has prepared him for, is that of the "convict." The prison world is the only world with which he is familiar. He was raised in a world where "punks" and "dogqueens" have replaced women, "bonaroos" are the only fashionable clothing, and cigarettes are money. This is a world where disputes are settled with a pipe or a knife, and the individual must form tight cliques for protection. His senses are attuned to iron doors banging, locks turning, shakedowns, and long lines of blue-clad convicts. He knows how to survive, in fact prosper, in this world, how to get a cell change and a good work assignment, how to score for nutmeg, cough syrup, or other narcotics. More important, he knows hundreds of youths like himself who grew up in the youth prisons and are now in the adult prisons. For example, Claude Brown describes a friend who fell into the patterns of jailing:

"Yeah, Sonny. The time I did in Woodburn, the times I did on the Rock, that was college, man. Believe me, it was college. I did four years in Woodburn. And I guess I've done a total of about two years on the Rock in about the last six years. Every time I went there, I learned a little more. When I go to jail now, Sonny, I live, man. I'm right at home. That's the good part about it. If you look at it, Sonny, a cat like me is just cut out to be in jail.

"It could never hurt me, 'cause I never had what the good folks call a home and all that kind of shit to begin with. So when I went to jail, the first time I went away, when I went to Warwick, I made my own home. It was all right. Shit, I learned how to live. Now when I go back to the joint, anywhere I go, I know some people. If I go to any of the jails in New York, or if I go to a slam in Jersey, even, I still run into a lot of cats I know. It's almost like a family."

I said, "Yeah, Reno, it's good that a cat can be so happy in jail. I guess all it takes to be happy in anything is knowin' how to walk with your lot, whatever it is, in life."

The state-raised youth often assumes a role in the prison social system, the system of roles, values, and norms described by Schrag, Sykes, and others. This does not mean that he immediately rises to power in the prison system. Some of the convicts have occupied their positions for many years and cannot tolerate the threat of every new bunch of reform school graduates. The state-raised youth who has just graduated to adult prison must start at the bottom, but he knows the routine, and in a year or so he occupies a key position himself. One reason he can readily rise is that in youth prison he very often develops skills, such as clerical and maintenance skills, that are valuable to the prison administration.

Many state-raised youths, however, do not tolerate the slow ascent in the prison social system and become "lowriders." They form small cliques and rob cells, hijack other convicts, carry on feuds with other cliques, and engage in various rackets. Although these "outlaws" are feared and hated by all other convicts, their orientation is to the convict world, and they are definitely part of the convict social system.

Dope fiends and hustlers slip into jailing more often than thieves, due mainly to the congruities between their old activities and some of the patterns of jailing. For instance, a central activity of jailing is "wheeling and dealing," the major economic activity of prison. All prison resources—dope, food, books, money, sexual favors, bonaroos, cell changes, jobs, dental and hospital care, hot plates, stingers, cell furnishings, rings, and buckles—are always available for purchase with cigarettes. It is possible to live in varying degrees of luxury, and luxury has a double reward in prison as it does in the outside society: first, there is the reward of consumption itself, and second there is the reward of increased prestige in the prison social system because of the display of opulence.

This prison lifestyle requires more cigarettes than can be obtained legally; consequently, one wheels and deals. There are three main forms of wheeling and dealing for cigarettes: (1) gambling (cards, dice, and betting on sporting events); (2) selling some commodity or service, which is usually made possible by a particular job assignment; and (3) lending cigarettes for interest—two for three. These activities have a familiar ring to both the hustler and the dope fiend, who have hustled money or dope on the outside. They very often become intricately involved in the prison economic life and in this way necessarily involved in the prison social system. The hustler does this because he feels at home in this routine, because he wants to keep in practice, or because he must present a good front—even in prison. To present a good front one must be a success at wheeling and dealing.

The dope fiend, in addition to having an affinity for wheeling and dealing, may become involved in the prison economic life in securing drugs. There are a variety of drugs available for purchase with cigarettes or money (and money can be purchased with cigarettes). Drugs are expensive, however, and to purchase them with any regularity one either has money smuggled in from the outside or he wheels and deals. And to wheel and deal one must maintain connections for securing drugs, for earning money, and for protection. This enmeshes the individual in

the system of prison roles, values, and norms. Although he maintains a basic commitment to his drug subculture which supersedes his commitment to the prison culture and although he tends to form close ties only with other dope fiends, through his wheeling and dealing for drugs he becomes an intricate part of the prison social system.

The head jails more often than the thief. One reason for this is that the head, especially the "weed head," tends to worship luxuries and comforts and is fastidious in his dress. Obtaining small luxuries, comforts, and "bonaroo" clothing usually necessitates enmeshing himself in the "convict" system. Furthermore, the head is often vulnerable to the dynamics of narrow, cliquish, and invidious social systems, such as the "convict" system, because many of the outside head social systems are of this type.

The thief, or any identity for that matter, may slowly lose his orientation to the outside community, take on the convict categories, and thereby fall into jailing. This occurs when the individual has spent a great deal of time in prison and/or returned to the outside community and discovered that he no longer fits in the outside world. It is difficult to maintain a real commitment to a social world without firsthand experience with it for long periods of time.

The square John and the lower-class man find the activities of the convicts petty, repugnant, or dangerous, and virtually never jail.

Gleaning

With the rapidly growing educational, vocational training, and treatment opportunities, and with the erosion of convict solidarity, an increasing number of convicts choose to radically change their lifestyles and follow a sometimes carefully devised plan to "better themselves," "improve their mind," or "find themselves" while in prison. One convict describes his motives and plans for changing his lifestyle:

I got tired of losing. I had been losing all my life. I decided that I wanted to win for a while. So I got on a different kick. I knew that I had to learn something so I went to school, got my high school diploma. I cut myself off from my old YA buddies and started hanging around with some intelligent guys who minded their own business. We read a lot, a couple of us paint. We play a little bridge and talk, a lot of time about what we are going to do when we get out.

Gleaning may start on a small scale, perhaps as an attempt to overcome educational or intellectual inferiorities. For instance, Malcolm X, feeling inadequate in talking to certain convicts, starts to read:

It had really begun back in the Charlestown Prison, when Bimbi first made me feel envy of his stock of knowledge. Bimbi had always taken charge of any conversation he was in, and I had tried to emulate him. But every book I picked up had few sentences which didn't contain anywhere from one to nearly all of the words that might as well have been in Chinese. When I just skipped those words, of course, I really ended up with little idea of what the book said. So I have come to the Norfolk Prison Colony still going through only book-reading motions. Pretty soon, I would have quit even these motions, unless I had received the motivation that I did.

The initial, perfunctory steps into gleaning often spring the trap. Gleaning activities have an intrinsic attraction and often instill motivation which was originally lacking. Malcolm X reports how once he began to read, the world of knowledge opened up to him:

No university would ask any student to devour literature as I did when this new world opened to me, of being able to read and *understand*.

In trying to "improve himself," "improve his mind," or "find himself," the convict gleans from every source available in prison. The chief source is books: he reads philosophy, history, art, science, and fiction. Often after getting started, he devours a sizable portion of world literature. Malcolm X describes his voracious reading habits:

I read more in my room than in the library itself. An inmate who was known to read a lot could check out more than the permitted maximum number of books. I preferred reading in the total isolation of my own room.

When I had progressed to really serious reading, every night at about ten P.M. I would be outraged with the "lights out." It always seemed to catch me right in the middle of something engrossing.

Fortunately, right outside my door was a corridor light that cast a glow into my room. The glow was enough to read by, once my eyes adjusted to it. So when "lights out" came, I would sit on the floor where I could continue reading in that glow.

Besides this informal education, he often pursues formal education. The convict may complete grammar school and high school in the prison educational facilities. He may enroll in college courses through University of California (which will be paid for by the Department of Corrections), or through other correspondence schools (which he must pay for himself). More recently, he may take courses in various prison college programs.

He learns trades through the vocational training programs or prison job assignments. Sometimes he augments these by studying trade books, correspondence courses, or journals. He studies painting, writing, music, acting, and other creative arts. There are some facilities for these pursuits sponsored by the prison administration, but these are limited. This type of gleaning is done mostly through correspondence, through reading, or through individual efforts in the cell.

He tries to improve himself in other ways. He works on his social skills and his physical appearance—has his tattoos removed, has surgery on physical defects, has dental work done, and builds up his body "pushing iron."

He shies away from former friends or persons with his criminal identity who are not gleaners and forms new associations with other gleaners. These are usually gleaners who have chosen a similar style of gleaning, and with whom he shares many interests and activities, but they may also be those who are generally trying to improve themselves, although they are doing so in different ways.

DISORGANIZED CRIMINAL

In the preceding discussion of prison adaptive modes, the "disorganized criminal" was purposely omitted. It is felt that his prison adaptation must be considered separately from the other identities.

The disorganized criminal is human putty in the prison social world. He may be shaped to fit any category. He has weaker commitments to values or conceptions of self that would prevent him from organizing any course of action in prison. He is the most responsive to prison programs, to differential association, and to other forces which are out of his control. He may become part of the prison social system, do his time, or glean. If they will tolerate him, he may associate with thieves, dope fiends, convicts, squares, heads, or other disorganized criminals. To some extent these associations are formed in a random fashion. He befriends persons with whom he works, cells next to, and encounters regularly through the prison routine. He tends not to seek out particular categories, as is the case with the other identities. He does not feel any restraints in initiating associations, however, as do the square John and the lower-class man.

The friendships he forms are very important to any changes that occur in this person. Since he tends to have a cleaner slate in terms of identity, he is more susceptible to differential association. He often takes on the identity and the prison adaptive mode of the group with which he comes into contact. If he does acquire a new identity, however, such as one of the deviant identities that exist in prison, his commitment to it is still tentative at most. The deviant identities, except for that of the convict, exist in the context of an exterior world, and the more subtle cues, the responses, the meanings which are essential parts of this world cannot be experienced in prison. It is doubtful, therefore, that any durable commitment could be acquired in prison. In the meantime, he may be shaken from this identity, and he may continue to vacillate from social world to social world, or to wander bewildered in a maze of conflicting worldviews as he has done in the past.

RACE AND ETHNICITY

Another variable which is becoming increasingly important in the formation of cleavages and identity changes in the convict world is that of race and ethnicity. For quite some time in California prisons, hostility and distance between three segments of the populations—white, Negroes, and Mexicans—have increased. For several years, the Negroes have assumed a more militant and ethnocentric posture, and recently, the Mexicans—already ethnocentric and aggressive—have followed with a more organized, militant stance. Correspondingly, there is a growing trend among these two segments to establish, reestablish, or enhance racial-ethnic pride and identity. Many "Blacks" and "Chicanos" are supplanting their criminal identity with a racial-ethnic one. This movement started with the Blacks. A Black California convict gives his recently acquired views toward whites:

All these years, man, I been stealing and coming to the joint. I never stopped to think why I was doing it. I thought that all I wanted was money and stuff. Ya know, man, now I can see why I thought the way I did. I been getting fucked all my life and never realized it. The white man has been telling me that I should want his stuff. But he didn't give me no way to get it. Now I ain't going for his shit anymore. I'm a Black man. I'm going to get out of here and see what I can do for my people. I'm going to do what I have to do to get those white motherfuckers off my people's back.

Chicanos in prison have maintained considerable insulation from both whites and Blacks—especially Blacks—toward whom they have harbored considerable hostility. They possess a strong ethnic-racial identity which underpins their more specialized felonious one—which has usually been that of a dope fiend or lower-class man. This subcultural identity and actual group unity in prison has been based on their Mexican culture—especially two important dimensions of Mexican culture. The first is their strong commitment to the concept of *machismo,* which is roughly translated as manhood.

The second is their use of Spanish and *Calo* (Spanish slang), which has separated them from other segments. Besides these two traits, there are many other ethnic subcultural characteristics which promote unity among Chicanos. For instance, they tend to be stoic and intolerant of "snitches" and "snivelers" and feel that Anglos and Blacks are more often snitches and snivelers. Furthermore, they respect friendship to the extreme, in fact to the extreme of killing or dying for friendship.

Until recently, this has meant that Chicanos constituted the most cohesive segment in California prisons. In prison, where they intermingle with whites and Negroes, they have felt considerable distance from these segments and have maintained their identification with Mexican culture. However, there have been and still are some divisions in this broad category. For instance, various neighborhood cliques of Chicanos often carry on violent disputes with each other, which last for years. Furthermore, Los Angeles or California cliques wage disputes with El Paso or Texas cliques. Many stabbings and killings have resulted from confrontations between different Chicano groups. Nevertheless, underpinning these different group affiliations and the various criminal identities there has been a strong identification with Mexican culture.

Recently, the Chicanos, following the footsteps of the Negroes in prison and the footsteps of certain militant Mexican-American groups outside (e.g., MAPA and the Delano strikers) have started organizing cultural-activist groups in prison (such as Empleo) and shaping a new identity built upon their Mexican ancestry and their position of disadvantage in the white society. As they move in this direction, they are cultivating some friendship with the Negroes, toward whom they now feel more affinity.

This racial-ethnic militance and identification will more than likely become increasingly important in the prison social world. There is already some indication that the identity of the Black National and that of the Chicano is becoming superordinate to the criminal identities of many Negroes and Mexican-Americans or at least is having an impact on their criminal identities.

A dude don't necessarily have to become a Muslim or a Black National now to get with Black Power. He may still be laying to get out there and do some pimping or shoot some dope. But he knows he's a brother and when the shit is down we can count on him. And maybe he is going to carry himself a little differently, you know, like now you see more and more dude—oh, they're still pimps, but they got naturals now.

The reassertion or discovery of the racial-ethnic identity is sometimes related to gleaning in prison. Frequently, the leaders of Blacks or Chicanos, for example, Malcolm X and Eldridge Cleaver, have arrived at their subcultural activism and militant stance through gleaning. Often, becoming identified with this movement will precipitate a gleaning course. However, this is not necessarily the case. These two phenomena are not completely overlapping among the Negro and Chicano.

The nationalistic movement is beginning to have a general impact on the total prison world—especially at San Quentin. The Blacks and Chicanos, as they focus on the whites as their oppressors, seem to be excluding white prisoners from this category and are, in fact, developing some sympathy for them as a minority group which itself is being oppressed by the white establishment and the white police. As an indication of this recent change, one convict comments on the present food-serving practices of Muslim convicts:

It used to be that whenever a Muslim was serving something (and this was a lot of the time man, because there's a lot of those dudes in the kitchen), well, you know, you wouldn't expect to get much of a serving. Now, the cats just pile it on to whites and Blacks. Like he is giving all the state's stuff away to show his contempt. So I think it is getting better between the suedes and us.

THE CONVICT IDENTITY

Over and beyond the particular criminal identity or the racial-ethnic identity he acquires or maintains in prison and over and beyond the changes in his direction which are produced by his prison strategy, to some degree the felon acquires the perspective of the "convict."

There are several gradations and levels of this perspective and attendant identity. First is the taken-for-granted perspective, which he acquires in spite of any conscious efforts to avoid it. This perspective is acquired simply by being in prison and engaging in prison routines for months or years. Even square Johns, who consciously attempt to pass through the prison experience without acquiring any of the beliefs and values of the criminals, do to some extent acquire certain meanings, certain taken-for-granted interpretations and responses which will shape, influence, or distort reality for them after release.

Beyond the taken-for-granted perspective which all convicts acquire, most convicts are influenced by a pervasive but rather uncohesive convict "code." To some extent, most of them, especially those who identify with a criminal system, are consciously committed to the major dictum of this code, "do your own time." As was pointed out earlier, the basic meaning of this precept is the obligation to tolerate the behavior of others unless it is directly affecting your physical self or your possessions. If another's behavior surpasses these limits, then the problem must be solved by the person himself, that is, not by calling for help from the officials.

The convict code isn't any different than stuff we all learned as kids. You know, nobody likes a stool pigeon. Well, here in the joint you got all kinds of guys living jammed together, two to a cell. You got nuts walking the yard, you got every kind of dingbat in the world here. Well, we got to have some rules among ourselves. The rule is "do your own number." In other words, keep off your neighbors' toes. Like if a guy next to me is making brew in his cell, well, this is none of my business. I got no business running to the man and telling him that Joe Blow is making brew in his cell. Unless Joe Blow is fucking over me, then I can't say nothing. And when he is fucking over me, then I got to stop him myself. If I can't then I deserve to get fucked over.

Commitment to the convict code or the identity of the convict is to a high degree a lifetime commitment to do your own time, that is, to live and let live, and when you feel that someone is not letting you live, to either take it, leave, or stop him yourself, but never call for help from official agencies of control.

At another level, the convict perspective consists of a more cohesive and sophisticated value and belief system. This is the perspective of the elite of the convict world—the "regular." A "regular" (or, as he has been variously called, "people," "folks," "solid," a "right guy," or "all right") possesses many of the traits of the thief's culture. He can be counted on when needed by other regulars. He is also not a "hoosier"; that is, he has some finesse, is capable, is levelheaded, has "guts" and "timing." The following description of a simple bungled transaction exemplifies this trait:

Man, you should have seen the hoosier when the play came down. I thought that that motherfucker was all right. He surprised me. He had the stuff and was about to hand it to me when a sergeant and another bull came through the door from the outside. Well, there wasn't nothing to worry about. Is all he had to do was go on like there was nothin' unusual and hand me the stuff and they would have never suspected nothing. But he got so fucking nervous and started fumbling around. You know, he handed me the sack and then pulled it back until they got hip that some play was taking place. Well you know what happened. The play was ranked and we both ended up in the slammer.

The final level of the perspective of the convict is that of the "old con." This is a degree of identification reached after serving a great deal of time, so much time that all outside-based identities have dissipated and the only meaningful world is that of the prison. The old con has become totally immersed in the prison world. This identification is often the result of years of jailing, but it can result from merely serving too much time. It was mentioned previously that even thieves after spending many years may fall into jailing, even though time-doing is their usual pattern. After serving a very long sentence or several long sentences with no extended period between, any criminal will tend to take on the identity of the "old con."

The old con tends to carve out a narrow but orderly existence in prison. He has learned to secure many luxuries and learned to be satisfied with the prison forms of pleasure—for example, homosexual activities, cards, dominoes, handball, hobbies, and reading. He usually obtains jobs which afford him considerable privileges and leisure time. He often knows many of the prison administrators—the warden, the associate wardens, the captain, and the lieutenants, whom he has known since they were officers and lesser officials.

Often he becomes less active in the prison social world. He retires and becomes relatively docile or apathetic. At times he grows petty and treacherous. There is some feeling that old cons cannot be trusted because their "head has become soft" or they have "lost their guts," and are potential "stool pigeons."

The convict identity is very important to the future career of the felon. In the first instance, the acquiring of the taken-for-granted perspective will at least obstruct the releasee's attempts to reorient himself on the outside. More important, the other levels of the identity, if they have been acquired, will continue to influence choices for years afterward. The convict perspective, although it may become submerged after extended outside experiences, will remain operative in its latency state and will often obtrude into civilian life contexts.

The identity of the old con—the perspective, the values and beliefs, and other personality attributes which are acquired after the years of doing time, such as advanced age, adjustment to prison routines, and complete loss of skills required to carry on the normal activities of civilians—will usually make living on the outside impossible. The old con is very often suited for nothing except dereliction on the outside or death in prison.

Prison Violence

HANS TOCH

WHAT people need around them often depends on what goes on inside them. We prize conditions that help us to control our feelings, to govern our thoughts, and to achieve our aims. Requisites for our external environment relate to pressures in our internal environment.

The search for safety is, in some respects, the extreme version of the pursuit of privacy. In both cases, the person's equilibrium hinges on finding sanctuary from others. With the high-privacy person the issue is overstimulation, and the stimulus content is crowding. The issue with safety is violence. The content of the safety concern is that of danger and fear. The aim of high-safety persons is to escape conflict. Their external threat is violence from others, and their internal press is violence from within. The threat to safety is external danger and the impact it makes on the person who experiences it. In prisons, the danger and its impact are both sources of discomfort. The combined source is sometimes referred to as "tension" of the environment:

It's the general atmosphere in here. It's like an explosive atmosphere, you know what I mean? It seems like everybody is at everybody else's throat, and it's not easy to live with. You walk up and down the hall, and everybody's shooting daggers at everybody. It's hard to hold a civil conversation with anybody. . . . It's more visible here, it's more visible here than in another institution that I've been in. . . . Tense at all times. And you don't know how to make your next move. If you should make it.

From *Living in Prison* (pp. 80-100) by H. Toch, 1977, New York: The Free Press. Copyright 1993 by the American Psychological Association. Reprinted by permission.

Sure, there's always tension. You can walk down the corridor and see static electricity in the hall from the tension. It's only a figure of speech, but you know what I mean.

There is also a lot of tension there, not only between the officers and the inmates, but also among the inmates too. There is a lot of static jumping off down there. And a lot of the things that they did that I saw there got me emotionally involved, things that are terrible.

Tension must be controlled or discharged; if it is not monitored it accumulates and explodes. High-safety persons tend to see environments as not having enough checks on explosiveness and violence. Inmates in widely different prisons thus often make the point that their respective institutions are excessively "loose" or "lax":

You take a young kid coming in a penitentiary, as loose as Auburn is here, he's pretty certain to be taken off pretty fast. Because these kind of people, they'll take you off in a minute. . . . There are animals running around this place. This is not one of these seminars where you got a highly educated bunch of people. You got a bunch of animals in here. And it's too lax.

Where lack of control is not a pervasive feature, it is seen as a feature of particular people within the environment. In this view, there are groups of people whose self-control is manifestly negligible or weak. Such people are feared because they are apt to explode promiscuously. They may attack or victimize upon slight and unpredictable provocation. They may be mentally ill or emotionally unbalanced:

I'll tell you the truth, this is the only institution that I've seen in my life, how people that they are sick mentally, walking around with other people that are in the right state of mind. They have these people over here that they's sick, I mean they're supposed to be in the hospital, not in an institution like this. . . . They've got them walking around here. You can see, like, let's say lifting weights, right? You got to be watching your back. You don't know when this man might break out and you got three hundred or some pounds on top of you, and he might kick your head off or throw something. You got to be looking for these people, looking out for these people.

I had to get off the tier because a guy that sets fire to a book for nothing, there must be something wrong, and I can't figure out what's in his mind, so I had to get off. . . . I said, "Captain, this was where I was before, and I had trouble here, you know, and I wanted to go to another jail, man, because this other guy, he must think it's a joke to him to burn things." Guy comes down and sets everything on fire, and everybody starts laughing, and stuff like that. So I told him, "I got to get off here, man." . . . I told another shift that I didn't like this tier either, because I don't like it . . . it was a homicide tier, you know what I mean?

Emotional disequilibrium or loss of control in others may sometimes be ascribed to stress. In this model, the environment acts on dangerous people, and it subjects them to pressure that makes them dangerous:

Well, the lifers make it difficult, because you can never tell when they are going to be tired of doing their time, and they don't go nowhere, because this institution keeps them here. . . . They either escape as you see they have done before, or they turn against another inmate.

See, but something may jump off, and your wife may die, and you may not receive the letter, and you will turn on me, and I wouldn't understand that. You would be grouchy one day, and I feel good, and why should you be grouchy? Or we are both in grouchy moods, then you may have static.

A double control issue is posed where the environment contains controllers who may (as the fearful person sees it) run out of control themselves. A prison or hospital inmate can begin to see his keepers as potential sources of violence. This view is harrowing, because it (1) removes the most prominent source of institutional stability and control, (2) makes for an environment that has a person totally at its mercy, and (3) places danger at the doors of men who are potentially effective threats:

You always have the impression that any time of the night they might hit your cell for some reason, and something might happen to you. You never know. That makes you very uncomfortable also. That existed in Comstock and it existed in Clinton. You never know when they're going to hit your door and for what.

There was a guy in a cell with blood all over the place. They took him out of his cell and put him in the hospital, and when he got out of the hospital they put him in the box. And they had the audacity to say that he had done it to himself. There aren't too many inmates that'll take a razor blade to their face.

THE IMPACT OF PERCEIVED THREAT

The high-safety person lives in a world of low trust, high vigilance, uncertainty, and discomfort. Danger occupies his mind, circumscribes his actions, and governs his awareness. The anticipation of cues to danger makes the environment a map of open areas one must traverse between precarious and very temporary sanctuaries. It makes life a matter of being tensely and continuously on guard against dangers one cannot hope to locate, to anticipate, or to guard against:

Here if you go in your cell, you got to think about the next day, how's it going to go? If you go in a shop, is some guy going to be waiting for you with a pipe, is something going to happen? When you come back to your cell, is your stuff going to be in your cell?

In a place like this you don't know who to trust. The main thing is you don't know who to trust, and with the small population you know everybody, you get to know everybody, and you know who to stay away from, but every day I see faces that I never seen before, and I have been here for two months.

With accumulating tension, the link between external and internal violence may become explicit or manifest. The individual finds himself harboring violent thoughts and feelings or may sense himself nearing an explosion point. He may feel a need to seek protection from himself or may become concerned about harm he might do:

This is when all the tension just builds up in you over the months, and one day you feel tense, and you put the earphones on, and bam, too late though, you break down, and bam, you beat on the wall. It be all that tension, you know. . . . Well, it's just tension. The tension builds. You know, if too much tension builds up in you, and you get tired of beating your walls, and it still don't come out, then sometimes you might get that urge to do something devilish then. To relieve that tension, regardless of what it is. So you might get in that keep lock, so you don't get in no trouble. That's the safe way. When it comes down you're ready to do something, you say, "Give me a keep lock." And relax.

Just like the riot, that's what messed me up. When I got out on the street I started having nightmares from when I seen the dudes get killed and stuff like that, and I started drinking. I tried to avoid drinking, but, see, when I drink I forget about the problems. . . . Take a guy here, you come here—right?—when you're young. You come here, and there's older people here. He listens, and he don't never hear nothing good. He only hears that they killed somebody, they're going to rob this here, they're going to do this here, they call a woman a bitch. And a guy, subconsciously, he inherits all of this in his mind. And he starts acting like this too. Not that he wants to, but he be around day and night, around people like this here, and he start acting like this too. Acting like an uncivilized people. And when he gets out, the impression that

he had built up in here, and when he gets out it explodes. Especially if he drinks, and all the problems that was in here, whether people knows it or not, all the problems that a dude gets in here, when they get in the streets, see, they freak.

A more immediate issue is posed by the option of responding or not responding with violence to violence. Safety is very often seen in fight-flight terms. Fight, however, may entail (1) the threat of retaliation from one's victim, (2) a potential loss of self-control, and (3) a response of the larger environment, with a loss of status or safety:

The man has never really threatened me, but to avoid a problem for him and I—see, that's why I did ten years before, a lot of problems like hitting guys. I knew if the man approached me it would be a serious thing. I'm not running out of fear from him. I'm just running, I'm afraid if he does approach me somebody's going to be hurt very bad, in this crowd or the crowd that I'm in. Put it like this, I don't want to do anything because I still have eight and a half years to be in jail. . . . See, my brother, he's with organized crime, I'll put it to you that way. . . . You're not by yourself. So I know if I go out there it's going to be a war. And I know, whether I get hurt or not, it's going to jam me up bad, where I'm going to wind up CR, and I'm trying to avoid this.

EXERCISE THE FLIGHT OPTION

Despite its perceived liabilities, the flight option may be exercised by the high-safety inmate. He may seek physical sanctuary in a subenvironment (should it exist) in which he is protected, or where the peer group is low-pressure and nonthreatening:

I wouldn't leave this place if they offered me a thousand dollars, or a million dollars. It wouldn't pay to leave. Because there is a sense of security here.

I'm away from the population and I have peace of mind. I'm not always looking over my shoulder.

In here you never know what is going to happen next.

So you feel that your job assignment is beneficial?

Yes, very beneficial.

Another flight option is to withdraw from social intercourse or to restrict contact to a subgroup who is nondangerous:

Just mind my business, man. . . . You know, avoid unnecessary static. . . . If you mind your own business and don't fuck with nobody, you won't have no trouble. . . . Me, personally, I don't have no trouble.

If you're stupid enough to get involved with it, and knowing that you can get in trouble doing this and doing that there. If you're that dumb enough to go ahead and do it, then you deserve— if you stick your hand in the fire that's hot, you're going to get burned.

A third retreat option is psychological and involves restricting the range or intimacy of communication. While maintaining himself in physical circulation, a man may insist on superficiality and reserve in all of his contacts with others:

I am out in the streets, and the people that I hang around with, I trust them. I am not used to this, you know—like wanting to know who you talk to, you know, and all that. I have to change now, and I have to be careful what I tell someone, and most things I can't even tell to people, because I might be in a spot, you know.

Any retreat option has two liabilities. One is that a person may find it hard to reconcile a flight strategy with a self-image of autonomy or potency. The second liability revolves around the person's public image.

A person with high-safety concerns may be stigmatized to begin with, because victimization tends to go hand in hand with a reputation for weakness, cowardice, or explosiveness. In this connection, flight can ameliorate physical danger, but it can also exacerbate a man's stigma. Where a sanctuary protects, it also poses the question of how a man is to view himself when he leaves or when he rejoins the outside world:

I've always had a good name for myself, what they consider in jails and everything. And it's hard. . . . Maybe my mistake was the way I was brought up, with so-called wise guys. And I always got stuck in prison with them. Maybe if I got stuck with the so-called creeps, who I think are the best guys, maybe I would have never come back to jail again. . . . Well, what they consider like a creep is a guy that's not with the so-called guinea mob, a guy that's not pushing dope or who thinks like that. A guy that just came in for a jive crime, he ain't with nobody in the street, so he's supposed to be a creep. . . . It's hard, because, when you come to protection, right away everybody puts you down you're a stool pigeon. And it's uncomfortable, and you really can't talk when people know—it's hard to explain, it's just that you get a name. "I don't know why he's up in protection, but I think he's a stool pigeon, he ratted on somebody." It's not easy, especially when, like I said, you been a good guy all your life, with the so-called good people. People start saying, "I can't believe Denny—." . . . They'll make you feel it, because a lot of times you'll walk into a room or something, and guys will be talking in a corner, and right away everybody will stop. And right away you feel like a weasel. If you feel, like I said, like me, I'm right from the old school, where I say it was tough. If a guy was a rat, he was hurt.

THE SAFETY CYCLE

A review of one individual case may help us better to understand the safety concern of the obsessed inmate. The case is relevant here, because it highlights the relationship of environmental "threats" to individual "concerns" and environmental "solutions."

Our victim is a 21-year-old white property offender serving a four-year sentence at Auburn Prison. He is a parole violator with a juvenile record, whose institutional experience includes three years in an orphanage. He is tall (6 feet), of normal build (153 pounds), with some education and normal intelligence.

Auburn is an institution with a substantial client age range, and it can make a young inmate conscious of his youth. "Here I am, like, younger than everybody out there," our man tells us, "and I just got to watch myself more, you know. I just can't slip. I just can't say the wrong thing."

Constant vigilance reaps its perceptual result in the shape of repeated "evidence" of danger:

Well, see, the first day I came in here—I walked in the reception area, and I was standing down there, and I seen this guy, you know. This black guy just staring at me—just staring at me from about 6 feet away. And he started smiling. And I knew—I have been around, you know, and I have been through all of this before. And he started smiling, and I see him go away and talk to somebody else, and he was whispering, and I knew right off what was going on.

No one actually approached me, but I heard things running around, like so and so would say something, and they would come back and tell me, but a few instances like that—nothing that I would really worry about, but I had to watch out for it.

Like my hair was long and everything, and I looked about 16 years old, so I used to go to the mess hall and everybody would stare at me. I don't have no complex, but, gee—when everybody is staring at you, how can you miss it, you know? So I figured that the best thing would be to do was to cut my hair, so the next morning I got up and cut it. . . . It eased up after a while, and I realized that there are certain people that stare at you all the time.

You try to be calm if you can, but you can't, because it really bothers you. Like, I will see some people out there talking, and they look my way, and right away—they are talking about me, and I don't know what to think.

As fear builds up, the young man has thoughts of trying to escape into a segregation setting, possibly permanently. He holds this gambit in reserve, but rejects it as an immediate option. His reasoning here follows lines similar to those we have already discussed:

When I first came, I wanted to go to protection, and then I started to think, and I found that if I do that, you know, once they transfer you out it will be on your record that you were in protection . . . and then you have a bad name, and they make you look like a punk or something, so I figured that I had just better stick it out. So that is why I didn't go to protection.

Like, I have been taking chances all my life— like going out there and steal and petty stuff, you know, and I am in jail—just by taking chances. So that I am taking a chance being in the population, you know. And, like, if I hear today—if my friend comes up and tells me that he heard that they are going to jump on me—I will go and lock right in. I won't come out. Why take a chance, you know? I have been taking chances all my life.

To be sure, there are some saving factors in the picture. For one, the presence of guards is reassuring because it reduces the chances of a physical attack. There is also the fear-reducing counsel of friends, who raise questions about the seriousness of actual danger:

Like, I will go and call up my friend, and I will go and tell him, and he will say, "Don't worry about it—they ain't going to bother you." I guess that I am paranoid. I tell everybody that I am not, but I guess that I am, you know.

On the other hand, the help one gets is not all equally helpful. There are those who increase one's distrust by raising questions about the credibility of other men. And there are those (both among staff and peers) who stipulate the inevitability of violence, and who advocate a "fight-fire-with-fire" approach to the problem:

Like, this one guy that I was talking to out there, he seemed like he was all right. He was an Italian dude like me. A little bit older, but we are both Italians and we should look out for each other. So he looked out for me. And then I had this other guy come up and say, "What is happening? Don't turn your back on him, because he might do something to you, you know." I don't know what to think, because here this guy is going and being nice to me, and this guy is telling me to watch out for him. Like, I don't know what to think.

So you have had an opportunity to discuss this with one of the officers? And he understands the problems?

Yes. He told me—I told him that, like, when I came I had a knife and all that, and he told me that I had better put it up or better use it. "Just don't pull it out, you know, because if you pull it out and scare somebody—it will make them leave, but the next time they come up on you they will have something, and you might not have yours, and that is that. So if you are going to pull it out—use it.

PATTERNS OF INMATE VICTIMIZATION

We know that victimization is prevalent in male prisons, but it is hard to assign a number to the proportion of victims that become involved. Davis tells us that "virtually every person having the characteristics of a potential victim is approached by aggressors." The statement may hold true for settings such as East Coast youth prisons and reformatories, and for urban detention centers. But even in those institutions, the victimization rate is hard to establish, although we know the proportion of "inmates with victim characteristics" in the population. This is so because "approaches by aggressors" sometimes have negligible impact, sometimes fizzle out, and occasionally boomerang. If violence results, the aggressor may sometimes catch the brunt of it and thus turn "victim."

Inmates in two New York institutions, when we asked them about their experience with victimization, supplied us with a 28 percent victimization rate. Although our samples were random, this proportion is at worst meaningless, and at best suggestive. One of the two institutions involved was a youth prison, which increases the chances of finding victims and aggressors. Both prisons are New York State settings and contain the sort of contrasting populations (urban sophisticates and rural inmates) that make victimization likely. On the other hand, (1) some respondents were probably reluctant to talk about victimization experiences, and (2) the population contained relatively high proportions of serious offenders, which may depress the victimization rate.

At the most stressful end of the spectrum, the new arrival is confronted—preferably without warning—with a strange world that firmly sufficiently challenges his most basic assumptions. Such experiences are sufficiently disequilibrating to be "used" by some settings (such as concentration camps) to make people dazed, helpless, and malleable. An unscheduled transition trauma of this kind faces some young male inmates entering jails or prisons in which other young inmates are housed. This trauma can start at the earliest point of entry into the setting with the discovery that one has become a target for what appears to be homosexual attention:

Any new person, they hollered obscenities at them and all sorts of names, and throwing things down from the gallery and everything. They told me to walk down the middle of this line like I was on exhibition, and everybody started to throw things and everything, and I was shaking in my boots. . . . They were screaming things like, "That is for me" and "This one won't take long—he will be easy." And, "Look at his eyes" and "her eyes" or whatever, and making all kinds of remarks.

The experience of being targeted challenges a number of basic premises of the average young male. One such assumption is that of his own sex role, which he has taken for granted himself, and has assumed that other people will stipulate:

When you get in your cell sometimes, you get in there and you look at yourself and you say, "Why is this guy saying these things?" I had never thought of that myself. I always thought I was a good-looking man and I never thought about myself being a girl. . . . I've sat around a guy a lot of times, I've had my arm around a guy, somebody. We really got wrecked with each other, and then we went out the door and we had a good feeling, a friendship thing, and here I could never put my arm next to somebody. The person would think that I was either trying to make advances or he would turn around and say, "This is a freaky thing, baby." . . . Out there you wouldn't even think about it. You would pick up this *Midnight* magazine or some crazy thing like that, some crazy newspaper or something like that. And you read about a man being sodomized or something. And in here it's something that happens every day, and you have to watch out. . . . When they first start saying to me like, "Hey baby," I would expect to see a secretary walking by or something. I just could not believe that a male would be saying those kind of things to me. And I thought that the guy must be goofing on me or something, playing jokes. And I knew then after a while that, if the guy had a chance, he would want to kiss me and have sex with me. That is something you say to yourself, "This can't be true." And it's a freaky thing in the head, man. It's really hard to tell you the feeling that you get. It's like threatening your life, only instead he is threatening your manhood.

The experience also raises the question of one's status as an autonomous human being. As a person, one usually deals reciprocally with other persons. One's fate always hinges partly, or largely, on one's own actions. One is not prepared to encounter junctures where one is matter-of-factly regarded as an object available for the asking. Yet in prison the way one is defined and verbally addressed may make it clear that one is seen by other men as impotent, that others feel free to question one's capacity to keep oneself from being used or exploited:

Sometimes there is twenty or thirty people in the showers, and they're always making remarks to you, and you don't feel free. I'm used to on the streets, where you don't have any paranoia. Taking a shower is a beautiful thing. Here it's a paranoia thing, where they have you back against the wall. And if you turn around and wash your legs and you're bent over, besides getting remarks you might really get hurt. . . . And you take your shower in thirty seconds, and you feel really stupid, and you just pull your pants down, and there is all these guys waiting for you to pull your pants down. It's a sick thing. Even though the physical pressure is there for a short time, the mental pressure is there permanently. And if you're on the toilet and everybody is just walking by, then it's really an intense thing. I've been to the bathroom in front of people on the streets, and it's just nothing at all like it is in here. You just want to say,

"Jesus, leave me alone." But you can't close the door, and it's a cell, and people are looking at you. . . . Sometimes I have some heavy thoughts in my cell, thinking about why all this happened. Is this pressure going to build up to the point where I say I'm actually going to be a fag? I really wonder where and why all this is happening. What I was into. I never dreamed that I was going to be in this condition and in this kind of place and around these kind of people and around this kind of environment, where I would want to leave and couldn't.

THE FIGHT-FLIGHT PREMISE

The prevailing myth in prison is that there are two ways, and only two ways, of dealing with aggression. One way is to admit defeat and to ask for help or retreat to a protective setting. The other option is to publicly attack the aggressor. Most vulnerable men who interact with other inmates are advised to counter aggression with aggression. The prevailing norm calls for displays of weapons or preemptive strikes:

I had a friend come in about two months ago, and they put him in D block, and that is the worst block in the institution for homosexuality, for smaller guys and then some other guys that are homos. And I gave him a shank and told him that it would be better if he didn't use it. I said he would do better if he would crack them in the mess hall. Then he wouldn't have any trouble. And then he would be carrying his own weight. I said that, if he mess with the shank, then he would have to use it for all his fights, because everybody that approached him would know that he had one.

And so when this guy cut in front of me again, I hit him in the head with a tray as hard as I could. And when he went to the ground I hit him several more times before the guard could reach me, and that was the only way. It is regrettable, but it is the only way that you can handle it. And I didn't want to do it, but I did what I had to do to protect myself. It was self-preservation, the first law of nature. I had to do it. . . . You don't even have to do it. Your mind snaps and you do it anyway. And in that second you know that it is either that or you know that it is all over again. And you do it. You don't think about it, and you don't do it with malice in your heart, you do it out of self-preservation and for no other reason.

I even had a way of eating. I make it look like I was almost an animal. You know, I'd take the bread and just gouge out a piece of it with my teeth, and just look mean, you know? Or sit there with a fork and look like you're a caveman type. And it really was a game, you know? But nothing stopped this guy, he just couldn't be put off. And he came over, and he came around the table behind me, I knew he was coming, but, like I say, I just kept eating. And when he sat down, he had a cup of coffee in his left hand and he put his right arm around my whole shoulders. . . . I realized that this was it. I had come to the end of my rope and put up with this crap for long enough. And either they were going to lock me up for stabbing him or something. It all happened so fast. I had just come to the end of my rope. And when I jumped off then he stood up immediately. But he still had his coffee in his left hand and I poked at him with that fork, and he backed up, because he really thought that I was going to stab him. I was so angry, but I really wasn't going to stab him. I just wanted to make him realize that I could become violent. And, like, I said, "Back up, and if you ever touch me I'll kill you." And I was just ready to enact it. I was at the end. And there was no guards apparently there at the time, because if there was they would have said something to me. But he backed up and spilled coffee on his hand, and I know he carries a knife. And it wasn't bad enough that he was big, but he carried a knife, and I was glad that he didn't decide to take some violence. And it really upset me so much that I wasn't finished with my meal. And I got up and left.

The confrontation of aggressors and victims is a poker game in which the chips are indices of courage. The fight-flight perspective holds that violence is instrumental behavior and that it acts as a deterrent to aggression. But if violence works (and it does work), the reasons why it works are usually different from those presumed by the myth. Targets of victimization are chosen because they are deemed unmanly, and they are viewed as unmanly because they show fear or resourcelessness. A man loses his target attributes if he provides demonstrations of fearlessness, or if he sports stigmata of manliness. Violence works because it points to a misdiagnosis of the target. Violence also works because aggressors are not as sure of themselves as they pretend. A victim who reacts nonfearfully becomes an uninviting arena for proving one's manliness. He is uninviting because the confrontation can misfire into a demonstration of unmanliness. It is safer to seek other fish in the sea whose reactions are dependably fearful.

The dynamics of victimization account for the success of verbal communication which suggests that the victim is prepared to stand fast and is unwilling to act intimidated:

Every once in a while I would hear a remark, "Hi, cutie," or anything of this nature. And then he would smack with his lips. . . . And so I finally laid my cards down and went over to him and said, "You're disgusting," and, "Do you get any enjoyment out of that?" And his exact words were, "I'm going to get into your ass." And I told him right out, "It's going to be a cold day in hell before you ever think about it." He said, "If I have to I'll hit you over the head and take it that way." And I said right then and there, "That's the only way you're ever going to get anything like that from me." And since that there has been no recurrence, and he has never come back, and we have talks, like discussing a problem of the prison or something like that. . . . I believe that to my understanding that my boldness, which really I consider something to be beyond what I want to do. I'm usually shy and tend to stay away from people. I don't bother with people. And this was one of the few times in my life that I had to stand up and say something about what I disapproved of.

Unscheduled explosions can be disconcerting to aggressors, because they disrupt his script and compromise his game. The prospective aggressor may run away, not because he is outgunned, but because his modus operandi is demonstrably inapplicable. He is in the position of a Shakespearian director whose Lady Macbeth embarks on a striptease:

And he came down and sat down next to me, and he put his entire arm on my shoulder. And I just blew my top off. And I jumped up and I had my fork in my hand, and I told him that I would kill him. And I didn't intend to kill him. It was just a show to back him off. And I looked so outraged apparently that I must have looked like I was off my rocker, and then he spilled his coffee in his other hand and he backed off. And I told him that if he ever came near me again I would kill him. Either you or me. The hell with the consequences. And that was it. Apparently from then on that was the answer. He realized that I didn't want him touching me. . . . You know, he was a giant of a man. And that's what really had me almost intimidated. Because I didn't know what the hell to do. But as I say, I was lucky enough that when I jammed at him with a fork, he got off my back and then he got on somebody else's. He had backed off that way.

THE IMPACT OF VICTIMIZATION

Transactions involve both men and settings. Safety transactions, like other transactions, are joint man-milieu products. Threats can help us feel unsafe, and locks may help to reassure us. But there are men who laugh at odds; there are others who panic in seclusion.

Inmates are threatened in prison. More vulnerable inmates are more intensely threatened. Some inmates are harmed, and most are not harmed. Most inmate victims escape, explode, or find friends or sanctuaries. Threats do cease. Fear may wane as pressure eases. But the pressure may not ease. For some men, past danger lives in vivid recollection. For others, no bars or walls seem thick enough, no peers are ever friends. Assaulted sensibilities and exploited vulnerabilities may be wounds serious enough to heal slowly, or not to heal at all. An individual may feel chronically unsafe or may relive unassimilated traumas time and time again. He may feel unsettled, tense, unsure, and hurt. He may be unable to face tasks in the present. His hurtful past encroaches, charging him with being weak or reminding him of the undependability of the environment:

When I say it is a problem, I mean when I lay in my room and with the earphones on, and no matter what song comes on this always pops into my mind. It pops into my mind all the time. . . . I see it as a problem, because if someone asks me a question my mind is not in the right place, but I tell him something, and I don't even remember what I told the guy. They have, like, messed up my life. . . . The more I think of it the worse it comes to my mind. Regardless of what I am doing, once in a while this will pop into my head, and I wish that there was some way that I could get it out of my head. Like, if I am talking to someone maybe it will come off my mind sometime. . . . Because all I have got to do, I will be down and reading a book in my room and stuff, and this will go through my mind, and it will blow my mind apart. I will say, "Damn, I have to start thinking about this fucking shit again." I want to forget it and say past is past.

The only time that you feel free from it is when you're locked in your cell, and then you're free from the physical attack but there's still the mental thing, which is really heavy. . . . In Elmira I got ulcers from it. You know, I would be throwing up blood, and then out of frustrations I would eat a lot, and I came in weighing 125 pounds, and I don't know if it was psychologically or not, but I just kept on eating, and I wanted to be big. I got to be 180 pounds. . . . I know that personally I would like to get a few exhales out and sort of calm down a bit. It's gotten so bad that about a month and a half ago I started talking to the shrink, and I said that I'm really feeling a lot of tension, so he's got me on a drug at night and another drug during the day. And I'm in my cell, and I'm fine now. I'm a zombie. I walk around really loaded, and it's all right.

Like the flight stance, the fight stance lingers. Other men sense fear, and they exploit it. To cover fear, one reacts angrily and explosively. There are inmates who claim that they entered prison as trusting and gentle youths and have left prison as irritable, ungovernable men. The point may hold, and if it does, it is tragic. For it is one thing for prisons to fail to regenerate wolves. It is another thing for prisons to make beasts of lambs.

Prison Gangs and the Case of the "Pepsi Generation"

GEOFFREY HUNT
STEPHANIE RIEGEL
TOMAS MORALES
DAN WALDORF

S INCE Clemmer published the *Prison Com-munity* in 1940, sociologists and criminologists have sought to explain the culture of prisons. A key debate in this literature centers on the extent to which inmate culture is either a product of the prison environment or an extension of external subcultures. Those in the former camp, such as Sykes and Messinger, Cloward, and Goffman, have argued that the inmate social system is formed "as a reaction to various 'pains of imprisonment' and deprivation inmates suffer in captivity." These writers saw the prison as a total institution in which the individual, through a series of "status degradation ceremonies," gradually became socialized into prison life. Analysts such as Irwin and Cressey challenged this view of prison life, arguing that it tended to underestimate the importance of the culture that convicts brought with them from the outside. They identified two dominant subcultures within the prison—that of the thief and the convict—both of which had their origins in the outside world.

This research describes extensive interviews conducted with former inmates. Our interviews did not clearly support one or the other of these opposing views and instead suggested that other dynamics of prison life were key to understanding inmates' experiences. Salient in inmate interviews was a greater degree of turmoil than was common to prison life in the past. The reasons for this turmoil were complex and included newly formed gangs, changes in prison population demographics, and new developments in prison policy, especially in relation to gangs. All these elements coalesced to create an increasingly unpredictable world in which prior loyalties, allegiances, and friendships were disrupted. Even some of the experienced prisoners from the "old school" were at a loss as to how to negotiate this new situation. Existing theories were not helpful in explaining our findings for the current dynamics could not be attributed solely to forces emanating from inside the prison or outside it.

THE SAMPLE

The sample was designed to include offenders who had been released from prison. Respondents lived in the Oakland and San Francisco area and, during 1991 and 1992, were located through contacts with ex-convict organizations, education programs, and respondents in a street gang study. We eventually contacted 39 men, of whom 46 percent (18) identified themselves as gang members, and 38 percent (6) said they were members of street gangs prior to entering prison. The ethnic backgrounds of respondents were as follows: 16 Chicanos, 14 African Americans, 5 whites, 2 Native Americans, 1 French Creole, and 1 Chilean. The youngest was 19 and the oldest 60.

The vast majority of respondents had long criminal histories and had served several prison sentences in many different California state prisons. However, within the interviews we concentrated on obtaining information about their last major prison term, which we stipulated had to have lasted for at least one year. In addition, we asked questions about ethnicity, age, arrest history, and the different prisons where they served time. The bulk of our interviews concentrated on knowledge of prison gangs and their perceptions of changes in prison life.

Because the sample was relatively small, results cannot be considered definitive. Nevertheless, they provide insight not only into contemporary prison life but also into the role of gangs. The available literature on gangs, with a few notable exceptions, takes a correctional and institutional perspective and consequently has made little or no attempt to examine the prisoners' point of view.

THE ESTABLISHED CALIFORNIA PRISON GANGS

According to various accounts, the first California prison gang was the Mexican Mafia—a Chicano gang believed to have originated in 1957 in the Dueul Vocational Institution prison. This Chicano group began to intimidate other Chicanos from the northern part of the state. The nonaligned, predominantly rural Chicanos organized themselves together for protection. They initially called themselves "Blooming Flower," but soon changed their name to La Nuestra Familia. Like the Mexican Mafia, La Nuestra Familia adopted a military style structure, with a general, captains, lieutenants, and soldiers. However, unlike the Mexican Mafia, La Nuestra Familia had a written constitution consisting of rules of discipline and conduct.

The Texas Syndicate, a third Chicano gang, followed the model of the Mexican Mafia and La Nuestra Familia and used a paramilitary system with a president at its head. Its members are mainly Mexican American inmates, origi-

nally from Texas, who see themselves in opposition to the other Chicano groups, especially those from Los Angeles, whom they perceive as being soft and too "Americanized."

Both black and white prisoners are also organized. The general view on the origins of the Black Guerilla Family (B.G.F.)—the leading black gang—is that it developed as a splinter group of the Black Family, an organization reportedly created by George Jackson. The authorities were particularly wary of this group, both because of its revolutionary language and reports that its members, unlike those of other gangs, regularly assaulted prison guards.

The Aryan Brotherhood—the only white gang identified in California prisons—originated in the late 1960s. It is said to be governed by a three-man commission and a nine-man council who recruit from white supremacist and outlawed motorcycle groups. According to prison authorities, it is a "Nazi-oriented gang, anti-black [which] adheres to violence to gain prestige and compliance to their creed."

The available sociological literature on older prison gangs is divided on the issue of their relationship to street gangs. On the one hand, Moore in discussing Chicano gangs argues that they were started by "state-raised youths and 'psychos' " inside the prisons, while Jacobson sees them as an extension of street gangs. Although Moore sees the gangs as initially prison inspired, she describes a strong symbiotic relationship between the street and the prison. In fact, she notes that once the gangs were established inside the prisons, they attempted to influence the street scene. "The Mafia attempted to use its prison-based organization to move into the narcotics market in East Los Angeles, and also, reputedly, into some legitimate pinto-serving community agencies."

INSTITUTIONAL ATTEMPTS TO CONTROL THE GANGS

Prison authorities see gangs as highly undesirable and have argued that an increase in extortion, intimidation, violence, and drug trafficking can be directly attributed to their rise. In responding to prison gangs, the California Department of Corrections (CDC) introduced a number of strategies and policies, for example, using "confidential informants," segregating gang members in different buildings and prisons, intercepting gang communications, setting up task forces to monitor and track gang members, locking up gang leaders in high-security prisons, and "locking down" entire institutions. These changes were perceived by our respondents who saw the CDC as increasingly tightening its control over the prison system and the gangs.

Prison Guards

In spite of the "official" view that gangs should be eradicated, many prison authorities hold a more pragmatic view and feel that the gangs have "had little negative impact on the regular running of prison operations." Moreover, as Cummins has noted, there is often a considerable discrepancy between the official stance and what takes place within particular prisons. This point was emphasized by our respondents, who portrayed guards' attitudes toward the gangs as complex and devious and saw the guards as often accepting prison gangs and in some cases even encouraging them. In supporting this view, they gave three reasons why guards would allow gangs to develop or continue.

First, some noted guards' financial incentive to encourage gang behavior. They suggested that guards are keen to create "threats to security" which necessitate increased surveillance and, consequently, lead to overtime work.

They have a financial interest in getting overtime. . . . Anything that was "security" meant that there were no restrictions in the budget. So if there are gangs, and there are associations, if there is some threat in that focus of security, they make more money.

Others went even further and told us that some guards benefited from gangs' illegal activities.

Well, you know the guards, aren't . . . you'd be surprised who the guards affiliated with. Guards have friends that's in there. They have their friends outside, you know. Guards'll bring drugs

in. Sell 'em. Guards will bring knives in, weapons, food. The guards play a major role.

Not only were guards involved in illegal activities, but the practice was often overlooked by other guards. For example, as one respondent philosophically replied in answer to our question: "Were individual guards involved in illegal gang activities?"

Well, I think you have guards that are human beings that . . . don't really want to do more than they have to. So if they see a guard doing something a little shady, it's easy to turn a blind eye because of the hassle it would take to pursue it.

Finally, in addition to these financial incentives, some believed that guards encouraged gang activities and conflict in order to control the prison inmates more effectively and "keep the peace out of prisons."

They perpetuated the friction because, for instance, what they would do is . . . give false information to different groups. . . . Something to put the fear so that then the Latino would prepare himself for a conflict. . . . And so everybody's on point and the next thing you know a fight would break out and the shit would come down. So it was to their interest to perpetuate division amongst the inmates so that they would be able to better control the institution. Because if you are spending your time fighting each other you have no time . . . to fight the establishment.

This divide-and-rule policy was emphasized by many of our respondents and was seen as a major contributory factor in prisoner conflicts.

Jacketing and the Use of Confidential Informants

According to our respondents, another prison administration tactic was "jacketing"—officially noting in a prisoner's file that he was a suspected gang member. Once identified as a gang member, a prisoner could be transferred to a high-security prison or placed in a special housing unit. "Jacketing," which is similar to the "dirty jacket" procedure outlined by Davidson, was seen by our respondents as a particularly arbitrary process and one in which the prisoner had little or no recourse.

Like I said, if you're a sympathizer you could be easily jacketed as a gang member. You hang around with 'em. You might not do nothing. But hang out with 'em. Drive iron with 'em. Go to lunch with 'em.

Many respondents felt the process was particularly unfair because it meant that a prisoner could be identified as a gang member and "jacketed" purely on the basis of information from a confidential informant. Confidential informants or "snitches" supplied intelligence information to prison authorities about inmate activities, especially gang-related activities.

Now let's say you and I are both inmates at San Quentin. And your cellie gets in a fight and gets stabbed. So all of a sudden, the Chicano who is a friend of your cellie says that he'll get the boys and deal with this. They talk about it but nothing happens. All of a sudden one of the snitches or rats, says I think something is cooking, and people are going to make a move to the administration. What will happen is that they [the administration] will gather up you and me and whoever else you associate with and put us all on a bus straight to Pelican Bay. They will say we have confidential reliable information that you guys are planning an assault on Billy Bob or his gang. . . . And you're wondering, you've never received a disciplinary infraction. But by God now, information is in your central file that you are gang affiliated, that you're involved in gang violence.

Our respondents distinguished between two types of snitching—dry and hard.

Dry snitching is a guy who will have a conversation with a guard and the guard is just smart enough. He'll say you talk to Joe, don't ya? You say, oh, yeah, Joe's a pretty good ol' boy, I heard he's doing drugs but don't believe it. He might smoke a few joints on the yard, but nothing hard. He just dry snitched. He indirectly dropped a lug on Joe. And then you got the guy who gets himself in a jam and goes out and points out other inmates.

Dry snitching could also refer to a prisoner supplying general information to guards without implicating anyone by name. This allowed the prisoner to develop a "juice card" or a form of credit with the guard.

A "juice card" is that you have juice [credit] with a particular guard, a lieutenant, a sergeant or somebody that is part of staff. . . . Let's say that somebody is dry snitching. By dry snitching I mean that they might come up to their juice man that has a "juice card," let's just say it is a sergeant of the yard, and they might go up there and say, "Hey I hear that there is a rumble coming down. I can't tell you more than that but some shit is going to come down tonight." So they alert the sergeant right. The sergeant tells him, "I owe you one." Now the guy might come up to the sergeant and say, "Hey remember you owe me one, hey I got this 115 [infraction] squash it." "Okay I will squash it." That is the "juice card."

Many of our respondents felt there was a growing number of snitches. A key factor promoting this growth was the pressure exerted by the guards—a point denied by the prison authorities in Stojkovic's research.

Pressure could be applied in a number of ways. First, if for example a prisoner was in a high-security unit, he often found himself unable to get out unless he "debriefed," that is, provided information on other gang members. Many respondents felt that this was an impossible situation because if they did not snitch their chances of getting out were minimal. As one respondent remarked:

They [the guards] wanted some information on other people. . . . So I was put between a rock and a hard place. So I decided I would rather do extra time, than ending up saying something I would later regret.

Second, if the guards knew that a prisoner was an ex-gang member, they might threaten to send him to a particular prison, where he would be attacked by his own ex-gang.

See there is a lot of guys in there that are drop outs from whatever gang they were in, and they are afraid to be sent to a joint where some other tip might be. They even get threatened by staff that if they don't cooperate with them they will be sent to either Tracy, or Soledad and they are liable to get hit by their own ex-gang, so they cooperate.

However, it would be inaccurate to suggest respondents accused only the prison authorities, since many also pointed out other developments within the prison system, and especially within the prison population, to explain what they described as a deteriorating situation.

PRISON CROWDING, THE NEW GANGS, AND THE "PEPSI GENERATION"

Since 1980, the California prison population has increased dramatically. The net effect of this expansion has been severe overcrowding in the prisons. In 1970, prison institutions and camps were slightly underused and the occupancy rate stood at 98 percent. By 1980, they were full, and in 1990, the rate had risen dramatically to 180 percent of capacity. In order to cope with this overcrowding, institutions have been obliged to use all available space, including gymnasiums and dayrooms.

Many respondents graphically described the problems created by this situation and complained about the deterioration in prison services. However, in talking about prison overcrowding, they tended to concentrate more on the changes in the characteristics of the inmates currently arriving. Specifically, they focused on the growth of new gangs, the immaturity of new inmates, and the problems they caused within the prison. Respondents felt this change in prison population characteristics had a major effect on day-to-day activities and contributed to the fragmentary nature of prison life.

The New Gangs

According to our respondents, although all five of the older gangs still exist, their importance has diminished. The reasons for this appear to be twofold. First, many of the older gang members have either dropped out, gone undercover,

or have been segregated from the rest of the prison population. Second, a new crop of gangs has taken center stage. In other words, prison authorities' efforts to contain the spread of gangs led, unintentionally, to a vacuum within the prison population within which new prison groupings developed.

Information on these new gangs is relatively limited in comparison with information on the older gangs. Thus, it is difficult to be precise about their structure and composition. Moreover, a further complication is whether or not these groups fit current definitions of what constitutes a gang. For instance, if we adapt Klein and Maxson's definition of a street gang—community recognition as a group or collectivity, recognition by the group itself as a distinct group, and activities which consistently result in negative responses from law enforcement—then these new groupings constitute gangs if the prison is considered the community. However, if we compare them with the Mexican Mafia, La Nuestra Familia, or the Black Guerilla Family, which have developed hierarchies or clearly articulated constitutions, they constitute instead territorial alliances which demand loyalties and provide security and protection. Regardless of whether these groups fit traditional definitions, respondents made it clear they had a significant impact on the traditional prison loyalties and allegiances and contributed to conflicts among the prisoners.

CHICANO AND LATINO GANGS   Among Chicanos, the Nortenos and the Surenos are the most important groupings or gangs. These two groups are divided regionally between the north and south of California, with Fresno as the dividing line. Although regional loyalties were also important for the Mexican Mafia and La Nuestra Familia, the regional separation between north and south was not as rigid as it is today for Surenos and Nortenos.

In addition to the Nortenos and the Surenos, two other groups were mentioned—the New Structure and the Border Brothers. Our respondents provided differing interpretations of the New Structure. For instance, some noted it was a new Chicano group made up of Nortenos which started in San Francisco, while others implied it was an offshoot of La Nuestra Familia. Opinions differed as to its precise relationship to La Nuestra Familia.

The Border Brothers are surrounded by less controversy. Their members are from Mexico, they speak only Spanish and, consequently, keep to themselves. Most of our respondents agreed this was a large group constantly increasing in size and that most members had been arrested for trafficking heroin or cocaine. Although there was little disagreement as to the Border Brothers' increasing importance, which was partly attributed to their not "claiming territory," there was, nevertheless, some dispute as to their impact on the north/south issue. Some respondents saw the Border Brothers as keeping strictly to themselves.

The Border Brothers don't want to have anything to do with the Surenos-Nortenos—they keep out of that 'cause it's not our fighting and all of that is stupid. . . . Either you are a Chicano or you're not. There is no sense of being separated.

Others predicted that in the future, the Border Brothers will become involved in the conflict and will align themselves with the Surenos against the Nortenos.

It used to be Border Brothers over there and Sureno and Norteno, stay apart from each other. . . . But now what I see that's coming out is that the Border Brothers are starting to claim Trece now. What I think is going to happen, to the best of my knowledge, is that the Surenos instead of them knockin' ass with the Nortenos, they're going to have the Border Brothers lock ass with the Nortenos due to the fact that they're south and all that. Maybe in a few years we will see if my prediction is true or not.

BLACK GANGS The Crips, originally a street gang from South Central Los Angeles, is the largest of the new black gangs. It is basically a neighborhood group.

    I.: So the Crips is more a neighborhood thing than a racial thing?

    R.: Oh yeah. That's what it stems from. It stems from a neighborhood thing. There's one

thing about the Crips collectively, their neighborhoods are important factors in their gang structures.

The Bloods are the traditional rivals of the Crips. Although, like the Crips, they are a neighborhood group, they do not attribute the same importance to the neighborhood.

They're structured geographically in the neighborhood but it's not as important as it is for the Crips. Only in LA is it that important. Bloods from LA, it's important for them but they don't have as many neighborhoods as the Crips. But anywhere else in Southern California the neighborhoods are not that important. Only in LA.

The 415s is a third black prison gang emerging recently. The group is made up of individuals living within the 415 San Francisco Bay area telephone code. Although the group's visibility is high, especially in the Bay area, the organization appears to be loosely structured, so much so that one of our respondents suggested that the 415s were more an affiliation rather than a gang.

All of these gangs are said to be producing a significant impact on prison life. Whereas previously there were four or five major gangs, today there are nine or ten new groupings, each with its own network of alliances and loyalties. These crosscutting and often conflicting allegiances have a significant impact on prison life. They produce a confusing, disruptive situation for many prisoners and can even produce problems for existing friendships. As one Puerto Rican respondent noted, "When I first started going to the joints . . . it wasn't as bad to associate a guy from the north and the south. It wasn't that big of a deal." But as the fragmentation increased and dividing lines became more rigid, this type of friendship was much less acceptable. According to many of our respondents, another consequence of fragmentation was an increase in intraethnic conflict, especially among the black population.

Back then there was no Crips, there was no Bloods, or 415s. It is a lot different now. The blacks hit the blacks. When the blacks at one time were like the B.G.F. where the blacks would stick together, now they are hitting each other, from the Crips, to the Bloods, to the 415, are pretty much all enemies.

The picture provided by our respondents is one of an increasing splintering of prison groupings. Allegiances to particular groups, which had previously seemed relatively entrenched, are now questioned. Friendships developed over long prison terms are now disrupted, and where previously prisoners made choices about joining a gang, membership has now become more automatic, especially for Chicanos. Today, what counts is the region of the state where the prisoner comes from; if he comes from south of Fresno, he is automatically a Sureno, if he is from north of Fresno, he becomes a Norteno.

Pepsi Generation

Respondents not only described the conflict arising from the new divisions within the prison population but also attributed this conflict to new prison inmates. They emphasized that the new generation of prisoners differed from their generation—in their dress, attitudes, and behavior toward other prisoners and the prison authorities. Respondents described themselves as convicts who represented the "old school."

In my point of view there is what is called the old school. . . . And the old school goes back to where there is traditions and customs, there is this whole thing of holding your mud, and there is something you don't violate. For instance, you don't snitch, you are a convict in the sense that you go in and you know that you are there to do time. And there is two sides. There is the Department of Corrections and there is you as the convict.

A convict, in this sense, was very different from the present-day "inmate" who they described as not having

a juvenile record or anything like that, and so that when they come in they have no sense of what it is to do time. . . . The inmate goes in there and he goes in not realizing that, so that they are doing everybody else's number or expect somebody else to do their number. Which means for instance,

that if they can get out of something they will go ahead and give somebody up or they will go against the code. Say for instance, the food is real bad and the convict would say, look we have to do something about this so let's make up a protest about the food and present it to the warden. And the convict will go along with it because it is for the betterment of the convicts. The inmate will go and go against it because he wants to be a good inmate and, therefore, he is thinking about himself and not the whole population.

The prisons were full of younger prisoners who were described disparagingly by our respondents as "boys trying to become men," and the "Pepsi Generation," defined as

the young shuck and jive energized generation. The CYA [California Youth Authority] mentality guys in a man's body and muscles can really go out and bang if they want. They are the youngsters that want to prove something—how tough and macho and strong they are. This is their whole attitude. Very extreme power trip and machismo. The youngsters want to prove something. How tough they are. And there is really very little remorse.

According to our respondents, the Pepsi Generation went around wearing "their pants down below their ass" and showing little or no respect for the older inmates, many of whom had long histories of prison life which normally would have provided them with a high degree of status. Disrespect was exhibited even in such seemingly small things as the way that the younger prisoners approached the older inmates.

They'll come up and ask you where you are from. I had problems with that. They come with total disrespect. It seems like they send the smallest, youngest punk around and he comes and tries to jam you. You know, you've been around for a long time, you know, you've got your respect already established and you have no business with this bullshit. . . . And here you have some youngster coming in your face, talking about, "Hey man, where you from?"

This view was graphically corroborated by a 38-year-old Familia member who described the young inmates in the following way:

They're actors. Put it this way, they're gangsters until their fuckin' wheels fall off. . . . I'm a gangster too. But there is a limitation to everything. See I can be a gangster with class and style and finesse and respect. Get respect and get it back. That's my motto, my principle in life. Do unto another as you would like to have done to you. These kids don't have respect for the old timers. They disrespect the old men now.

The "younger generation" was not only criticized for its disrespect but for its general behavior as well. They were seen as needlessly violent and erratic and not "TBYAS"—thinking before you act and speak.

I think they're more violent. They are more spontaneous. I think they are very spontaneous. They certainly don't use TBYAS. I think their motivation is shallower than it was years ago.

Their behavior had the effect of making prison life, in general, more unpredictable, a feature many of our respondents disliked.

They have nothing but younger guys in prison now. And ah, it has just changed. I don't even consider it prison now anymore. I think it is just a punishment. It is just a place to go to do time. Which now since there are so many children and kids in prison it is hard to do time now. It is not like it used to be where you can wake up one morning and know what to expect. But now you wake up and you don't know what to expect, anything might happen.

INMATE CULTURE REASSESSED

The inmate's picture of prison life is of increasing uncertainty and unpredictability; more traditional groupings and loyalties are called into question as new groups come to the fore. Whereas previously, prisoners believed a clear dividing line existed between convicts and authorities, today they see this simple division

disintegrating. This occurs because, in their attempt to control the spread of prison gangs, authorities introduced a series of measures which contained the gangs, but also unexpectedly created a vacuum within the organizational structure of the prison populations—a vacuum soon filled by new groups. Group membership was taken from newer inmates, who, according to our respondents, had not been socialized into the convict culture. The dominance of these groups soon led to an environment where the rules and codes of behavior were no longer adhered to and even the more experienced prisoners felt like newcomers. Moreover, the ability of prisoners to remain nonaligned was hampered both by developments among the prisoners and by the actions of the authorities. For example, a Norteno arrested in the south and sentenced to a southern prison would find himself in a very difficult and potentially dangerous situation.

You'll see some poor northern dude land in a southern pen, they ride on [harass] him. Five, six, seven, ten deep. You know, vice versa—some poor southern kid comes to a northern spot and these northern kids will do the same thing. They ride deep on them.

Study respondents portrayed prison culture as changing, but the change elements they identified were both inside and outside the institution. The available theoretical approaches, which have tended to dichotomize the source of change, fail to capture the complexity and the interconnectedness of the current situation. Furthermore, the information we received produced no conclusive evidence to prove whether or not the street scene determined the structure of gangs inside the prison or vice versa. For example, in the case of the Crips and the Bloods, at first glance we have a development which supports the approaches of Jacobs and Irwin and Cressey. The Crips and the Bloods originated in the neighborhoods of Los Angeles and transferred their conflicts into the prison environment. In fact, according to one respondent, once in prison, they bury their intragang conflicts in order to strengthen their identities as Crips and Bloods.

Even when they are "out there" they may fight amongst themselves, just over their territory. . . . But when they get to prison they are wise enough to know, we gotta join collectively to fend off everyone else.

However, although the Crips and Bloods fit neatly into Jacobs's perspective, when we consider the case of the 415s and the Nortenos and the Surenos, we find their origins fit more easily into Cloward's alternative perspective. According to two accounts, the 415s began in prison as a defense group against the threatening behavior of the Bloods and the Crips.

It [the 415s] got started back in prison. In prison there is a lot of prison gangs . . . and they were put together a lot. They got LA gangs like the Bloods and the Crips, and they are putting a lot of pressure on the people from the Bay area. And we all got together, we got together and organized our own group.

Originally, the Nortenos and Surenos existed neither on the streets nor in the adult prisons but within the California Youth Authority institutions. Gradually, this division spread to the adult prisons and soon became powerful enough to disrupt the traditional loyalties of more established gangs. Furthermore, in-prison conflicts soon spread to the outside and, according to information from our San Francisco study, Norteno/Sureno conflicts are beginning to have a significant impact on the streets.

CONCLUSION

As Irwin noted, prisons today are in a turmoil. From both the Department of Corrections' perspective and the interview material, it is clear that the prison system is under immense pressures. As the prison population expands and the Department of Corrections attempts to find more bed space, the problems within the prisons multiply. The impact of this situation on the inmates is clear from the interviews—they complain about the increased fragmentation and disorganization that they now experience. Life in prison is no longer organized but instead is viewed as both capricious and dangerous.

For many, returning to prison after spending time outside means being confronted by a world which they do not understand even though they have been in prison many times before. Where once they experienced an orderly culture, today they find a world which operates around arbitrary and ad hoc events, and decisions seem to arise not merely from the behavior of their fellow prisoners but also from prison authorities' official and unofficial decisions. Where before they understood the dominant prison division—prisoners versus guards and black versus white inmates—today they find new clefts and competing allegiances. The Chicanos are split not only between the Mexican Mafia and La Nuestra Familia but also north versus south. A relatively unified black population is divided into different warring camps of Crips, Bloods, and 415s.

The world portrayed by our respondents is an important corrective both to the criminal justice literature, which portrays prison life in very simplistic terms, and to those theoretical approaches which attempt to explain prison culture solely in terms of internal or external influences. Our interviews have shown that the linkages between street activities and prison activities are complex and are the result of developments in both arenas. Therefore, instead of attributing primacy to one set of factors as opposed to the other, it may be more useful and more accurate to see the culture and organization of prison and street life as inextricably intertwined, with lines of influence flowing in both directions.

ALTERNATIVES TO IMPRISONMENT

An Evaluation of Intensive Probation in California

JOAN PETERSILIA
SUSAN TURNER

PROBATION is no longer a sentencing alternative reserved primarily for first-time misdemeanant and petty offenders. In 1988, 40 percent of the 114,000 adults placed on probation in California had been convicted of felonies in superior court. Of those adults, 15 percent were convicted of violent crimes. The probation population has not only changed to include more serious offenders, it has also increased substantially in size. Over the past decade, the number of probationers has increased by 50 percent, yet the number of probation officers has declined by 20 percent. Probation caseloads have grown so large (400 persons per officer in some locations) that several departments can provide active supervision to less than one-third of their probationers. Thus, it is not surprising that probationers typically receive minimal supervision and that enforcement of probation conditions is spotty.

Most Californians agree that something must be done to decrease the threat to the public posed by felony probationers. But what correctional alternatives are available other than routine probation or prison? There is a growing consensus that the best hope for both relieving prison crowding and ensuring public safety may be intensive supervision probation (ISP), a type of sanction that is more stringent and punitive

than traditional probation but less expensive and coercive than incarceration. ISP is designed to hold the middle ground between traditional routine probation and incarceration, in terms of punitiveness, the degree of safety afforded the public, and cost. Furthermore, depending on local needs, ISP programs can be targeted to provide enhanced supervision for high-risk probationers or to serve as an alternative to incarceration for prisonbound offenders.

There is no generic ISP program. So many programs call themselves ISP that the acronym alone reveals little about any program's particular character. The only common characteristic of ISP programs is that they involve more supervision than routine probation programs. Most ISP programs call for some combination of multiple weekly contacts with a probation officer, unscheduled drug testing, strict enforcement of probation conditions, and community service. Significantly, in ISP programs, caseloads of probation officers typically consist of thirty to fifty probationers—far fewer than in typical routine probation programs.

By 1990, jurisdictions in every state had instituted ISP programs, and the published evaluations of ISP programs have been encouraging. Reported recidivism rates are generally quite low—fewer than 10 percent of program participants have been rearrested while on ISP, and nearly all of those arrests have been for technical violations rather than for new crimes. Fewer than 5 percent of participants in ISP programs in Georgia and New Jersey have been convicted of new offenses. Moreover, many ISP programs claim to save at least $10,000 per year for each probationer who would otherwise have been sentenced to prison.

But despite the apparent promise of ISP programs, it is premature to claim that they are responsible for the observed outcomes. The low recidivism rates may actually reflect systematic differences between the types of offenders who are sentenced to ISP programs and the types who are sentenced to routine probation or to prison.

Because ISP programs are still experimental, judges exercise great caution in sentencing offenders to them. Most of the programs limit participation to property offenders with insubstantial criminal records, which undoubtedly helps explain the low recidivism rates. Further, although judges may be asked to certify that offenders who are directly sentenced to ISP would have gone to prison if the ISP alternative were not available, such certification can hardly be considered proof that the offenders were truly prison-bound. Unless the participants actually would have been imprisoned, the claims of cost savings are exaggerated.

This article focuses on the outcomes of the three California ISP programs, located in Los Angeles, Ventura, and Contra Costa Counties. These three programs were selected for separate analysis for a number of reasons. The most important reason was that, because the California sites were among the first to begin the random assignment experiment, by 1989 they had collected sufficient case data for an evaluation covering a full year's operation (the follow-up period). Also, the California ISP programs were probation-enhancement ISP programs rather than prison-diversion ISP programs. A probation-enhancement ISP program complements routine probation by providing increased and stricter supervision for those assessed to be "high-risk" probationers, whereas a prison-diversion ISP program uses ISP as an alternative sanction for offenders who would otherwise go to prison. At each of the California sites, the probationers who were selected to participate in the experiment had already been granted probation; under the demonstration's protocol, they were randomly assigned to ISP or routine pro-

bation. Thus, these three programs had similar purposes and dealt with rather similar probationer populations.

CALIFORNIA'S ISP AND ROUTINE PROBATION PROGRAMS

All three programs chose to identify eligible offenders by use of the National Institute of Corrections' (NIC) risk-needs instrument, an objective scoring system that categorizes offenders by risk of recidivism and need for services. The NIC instrument was already being used by the sites to decide what level of supervision should be given to offenders in their routine probation programs. Male and female adult probationers who were rated "high-risk" (i.e., those who scored a total of more than eleven points on the NIC scale) were initially targeted as potential ISP participants.

Los Angeles and Ventura Counties increased the number of potential participants by also allowing offenders to become eligible for ISP if the probation officer indicated a "serious offense override." This discretion was allowed so that offenders having serious current conviction crimes (e.g., homicide, rape, assault) could become eligible, even if their prior criminal records did not classify them as "high risk."

In contrast, Contra Costa County limited its pool of eligibles to offenders convicted of drug crimes or drug-related felonies who were sentenced to probation for at least one year. Los Angeles and Contra Costa eliminated offenders with any sex-offense history.

The ISP programs emphasized different techniques for monitoring compliance with probation conditions. Los Angeles implemented two ISP programs, one of which used an electronic monitoring system and is labeled ESP in this article. Contra Costa relied heavily on unannounced urinalysis testing, whereas Ventura coordinated extensively with the police in making unannounced home visits.

All of the programs called for reduced caseloads and for supervision phases under which "successful" probationers were gradually transferred to routine probation. The major features of the experimental ISP programs and the con-

TABLE 1

Characteristics of ISP and routine probation programs, Contra Costa County.

Characteristic	ISP[a]	Routine Probation
Target population	Adults convicted of drug offenses	Same
Selection criteria	Felony or misdemeanor drug conviction, or drug-related conviction; no sex-offense history	Same
Months in ISP program	12	
Contact levels	1. 1 face-to-face/week 2 phone calls/week 1 drug test/week 1 monitoring/week 2. 1 face-to-face/week 1 phone call/week 1 drug test/2 weeks 1 monitoring/week 3. 1 face-to-face/month discretionary drug test(s) 2 monitorings/month	Officers' discretion (contact standards by classification level, but difficult to enforce because of large caseloads)
Caseload size	40:1	150-200:1
Additional components		
Electronic monitoring		
Employment	X	
Counseling/referrals	X	
Random drug tests	X	
Probation fees		
Victim restitution/other		
Community service		
Police notification	X	
Job training/remedial education		

a. ISP = intensive supervision probation.

trol programs, which employed either routine probation or the Ventura Community Resource Management Team (CRMT, an existing inten-

sive supervision program but with less supervision than ISP; see Table 2), are summarized in Tables 1, 2, and 3.

TABLE 2

Characteristics of ISP and routine probation programs, Ventura County.

Characteristic	ISP[a]	CRMT[b]
Target population	Adults convicted of felonies	Same
Selection criteria	High-risk score (11+) on NIC scale, or serious offense override, or probation revocation for felony plus high-risk score	Same
Months in ISP program	A minimum of 9	

Contact levels	1. 4 face-to-faces/week
	   2 phone calls/week
	   1 drug test/week
	   2.5 monitorings/week
	2. 2 face-to-faces/week
	   1 phone call/week
	   1 drug test/2 weeks
	   2.5 monitorings/week
	3. 1 face-to-face/week
	   discretionary drug tests
	   2.5 monitorings/week
		Only one level
		1 face-to-face/2 weeks
		1 phone call/month

Caseload size	19:1	50:1
Additional components		
Electronic monitoring		
Employment	X	X
Counseling/referrals	X	X
Random drug tests	X	X
Probation fees		
Victim restitution/other	X	
Community service		
Police notification	X	
Job training/remedial education	X	X

a. ISP = intensive supervision probation.
b. CRMT = Community Resources Management Team, an existing intensive supervision program but with less supervision than ISP, chosen by Ventura as its control program.

TABLE 3

Characteristics of ISP and routine probation programs, Los Angeles County.

Characteristic	ISP and ESP[a]	Routine Probation
Target population	Adults convicted of felonies	Same
Selection criteria	High-risk score (11+) on NIC scale, or serious offense override, or probation revocation for felony plus high-risk score; no sex-offense history	Same
Months in ISP program	12	
Contact levels	1. 3-5 face-to-faces/week 2 phone calls/week 90+ days of electronic monitoring (ESP only) 2. 2-3 face-to-faces/week 2 phone calls/week 3. 1-2 face-to-faces/week 1 phone call/month	1 nonspecific/month
Caseload size	33:1	150-200:1
Additional components Electronic monitoring Employment Counseling/referrals Random drug tests Probation fees Victim restitution/other Community service Police notification Job training/remedial education	X (ESP only)	

a. ISP = intensive supervision probation augmented by electronic monitoring.

EFFECTS OF ISP PARTICIPATION ON OFFENDERS' FUTURE CRIMINALITY AND SOCIAL ADJUSTMENT

One of the goals of ISP programs is to reduce recidivism, that is, to reduce offenders' return to crime. It is very difficult to measure recidivism, because there is no uniformly accepted definition for the term. Indeed, the literature is replete with suggestions regarding correct definitions, optimal methods of counting, and the most valid sources of information.

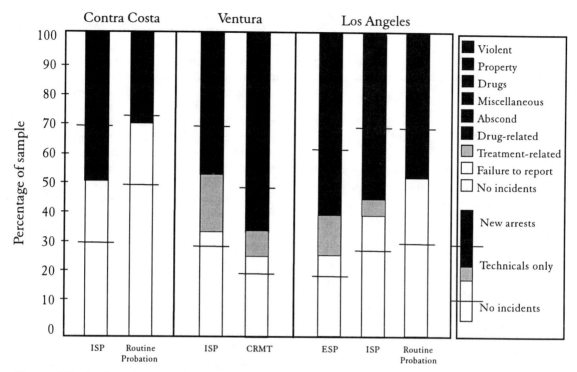

FIGURE 1 *Probationer's most serious recidivism outcome during one-year follow-up.*

To make the present study as comprehensive as possible, we used multiple indicators of recidivism. All of these indicators are derived from official records, not from probationer self-reports. Unfortunately, official records under-estimate criminality, since only a fraction of all crimes committed result in arrest.

Extent of Recidivism

Overall, between 41 percent and 73 percent of the studied probationers had new technical violations, primarily failures to appear for scheduled probation appointments, not participating in treatment programs, or violating drug-related conditions (usually drug use, as detected through urinalysis).

The extent of new arrests is slightly more encouraging. Across the ISP programs, about one-third of the participants had a new arrest, but fewer than 10 percent had new arrests for violent crimes.

Seriousness of Recidivism

Another way to examine recidivism is to investigate the seriousness of the recidivism events. Figure 1 categorizes individuals according to the most serious recidivism event they experienced during the one-year follow-up period.

In Contra Costa, 40 percent of the ISP probationers had technical violations as their most serious event, compared with 26 percent of those on routine probation. The figures are similar for Ventura, where 43 percent of the ISP and 29 percent of the CRMT probationers had technical violations as their most serious recidivism event. In Los Angeles, 42 percent of the ISP and 46 percent of the ESP participants had technical violations, in contrast to 40 percent of those on routine probation. Figure 1 also shows that between 2 percent and 9 percent of the various samples were arrested for a new violent crime (virtually all for robbery or assault).

For probationers with an arrest, we examined whether ISP probationers had less serious arrest offenses than control probationers. Arrests for violent offenses were considered the most serious, followed by property, drugs, and "other" crimes. Each arrested probationer was ranked by the most serious arrest he or she incurred during the one-year follow-up period.

COST COMPARISON OF ISP AND ROUTINE PROBATION

One goal of this study was to estimate the total criminal justice dollars spent on each probationer during the one-year follow-up period, including both corrections and court costs. We did this by

1. Estimating the costs of each type of local sanction or service "used" by the probationers.
2. Using information from the Status Calendars and Six-Month and Twelve-Month Review forms on each probationer's whereabouts (e.g., in jail, on ISP) on each day in the follow-up period to "bill" each probationer for each service used.
3. Averaging across all probationers, within a given site, in the ISP and control programs.

Information on the daily costs of supervision and incarceration was collected from each of the three California counties. The site-specific information was quite similar across sites, so the estimates were averaged, and the averages were used in the cost calculations. The average costs of processing an arrest or a technical violation were adapted from Haynes and Larsen. The daily costs of prison were taken from the California Commission on Inmate Population Management.

The cost totals show that placing felons on routine probation is much more costly than the currently estimated $300 to $2,000. The estimated corrections costs of the California routine probation programs studied here range from $4,024 to $6,122, simply because so many offenders on routine probation have violations and are sent to jail or prison.

In terms of correctional costs alone, ISP as implemented in Contra Costa and Los Angeles Counties costs about $1,500 to $1,900 more than routine probation. Ventura's ISP and CRMT

programs cost about the same, $6,957 versus $7,654. Court costs of between $900 and $1,950 in addition to the correctional costs result in yearly costs expended per routine or CRMT probationer that are between $4,923 and $9,606. It is also worth noting that the costs of ESP (the electronic monitoring ISP program) in Los Angeles were not greater than the costs of the Los Angeles ISP program, which had no electronic monitoring; persons assigned to either of the two programs cost the corrections system about $7,500 during the one-year follow-up period. The actual costs of a fully implemented ESP program may be higher than the costs reported here because only 44 percent of the ESP probationers were actually placed on ESP during the study period.

CONCLUDING REMARKS

Two conclusions emerge from this study's findings and implications: first, jurisdictions must judge the potential of ISP on the basis of their own candidate pools, their own resources, and their own political situations. Second, more research is needed on ISP, especially research involving random assignment of various kinds of offenders to routine probation, ISP, and prison.

The importance of the candidate pool has been discussed above at length. The importance of resources has been succinctly stated by two officials in California:

As anticipated, ISP without adequate resources in the community is only half a program. We're convinced that the proper role for probation and especially ISP includes holding probationers accountable and taking sure and swift actions on violations, but probation must also provide the offenders with opportunity to change. We found our probationers would not or could not wait months on a waiting list in order to get into a drug treatment program. This resulted in continuing drug use and a high violation rate.

Without drug treatment programs, and with our commitment to public safety, we ended up violating a lot of probationers who might have succeeded if we had effective treatments. Philosophically, we assume that drug offenders are often in states of social and emotional instability, and that our role is to move these probationers towards community stability and responsibility by control, counseling, drug testing and treatment. . . . Unfortunately, the lack of available treatment programs was a missed opportunity for these persons and the community.

It is particularly important for jurisdictions to understand how the public perceives the objectives of ISP. If the public expects and demands deterrence and the jurisdiction has a high-risk candidate pool, public support for ISP is not likely to be strong. However, a number of recent studies of public attitudes about crime and punishment have discovered that Americans strongly favor increasing the use of alternatives to incarceration, except for violent offenders. And support for alternative sanctions increases further as the public learns about the costs of incarceration.

Accounting for Presentencing Recommendations: Typologies Probation Officers Use

KRISS A. DRASS

J. WILLIAM SPENCER

ENTRAL to the processing of cases of deviance by social control agents are the formal and informal bureaucratic protocols which help define how such processing is to be accomplished. A relatively undeveloped, although useful, concept regarding these protocols is *theory of office*. According to Rubington and Weinberg, a theory of office refers to a "set of simple working categories for defining and responding to so-called deviants with which [agents] must deal." In other words, a theory of office is a "working ideology" which consists of typologies of deviant actors and appropriate processing outcomes, as well as rules which link the two. While this concept is an interesting one, its use has been restricted to deviance texts, and it has not been employed in empirical research. However, this concept is potentially useful for drawing together various other concepts and research findings regarding formal social reactions to deviance.

Research has established that social control agents "process and respond to cases with relation to, or as part of some larger, organizationally determined whole." Thus, one aspect of social reactions is the typing work by which agents "fit" an individual case into some larger category of cases. Agents accomplish this typing of individual cases by linking or articulating characteristics of a particular case with the characteristics of one or more general types of cases. Cicourel has conceived of this process as involving abductive reasoning whereby agents gather information about a case, apply this information to a typology, and then search for further information to confirm or disconfirm the initial typing. This typing work by agents of social control has received considerable attention in the interactionist literature. Since the typologies which agents use are provided by the organizations within which they work, the typologies are heavily influenced by the organization. In particular, typologies reflect and are sensitive to organizational goals and functions, particularly in the organization's place in some larger social structure. They also reflect the goals and viewpoints of the agents themselves within these organizational arrangements. For example, in his study of public defenders, Sudnow found that the public defenders' use of recipes for reaching plea agreements with district attorneys was greatly influenced by their presumption of their clients' guilt, concern with efficient use of time, and concern for maintaining relationship with the district attorney. Similarly, Scheff found that the use of psychiatric categories by screening boards reflected board members' concern for not disrupting ongoing procedures as well as their sensitivity to public pressure on judges who appoint the boards.

From "Accounting for Presentencing Recommendations: Typologies and Probation Officer's Theory of Office" by K. A. Drass and J. W. Spencer, 1987, *Social Problems, 34,* 277-293. Copyright 1987 by the Society for the Study of Social Problems. Reprinted by permission.

Finally, an important aspect of agents' decisions is that they are conveyed to others working within the same or related organizations. However, such decisions are not simply conveyed per se. Since these decisions are open to scrutiny, agents must justify their decisions by providing accounts which render their decisions reasonable and rational. These "accounting practices" have been documented by Garfinkel and others. In many instances, such accounting by social control agents takes the form of referencing "what everyone knows." Since these are directed to other agents who presumably share the same theory of office, "what everyone knows" will include the typologies of deviants which agents share, which presumably guided the decisions in the first place, and which therefore serve as evaluative criteria.

Our research addresses two questions. First, are there recognizable typologies or configurations of information which agents use to account for their decisions? Second, to the extent that such typologies are identifiable, do they influence agents' perspectives on their work? Our approach to these questions differs from previous work on accounting practices in that we use a combination of quantitative and qualitative analytic techniques. However, as we argue below, these techniques complement one another and together provide insights that neither alone could provide.

DATA AND VARIABLES

The data for this study are 126 presentence investigation reports (PSIs) prepared for felony offenders supervised by probation officers working in a county probation office in Dallas, Texas. The office that we studied serves a largely white, middle-class section of the city. The PSIs were part of a pool of approximately 270 felony cases active during the period October 1984 to January 1985. We selected PSIs for analysis if they contained an *explicit* evaluation of the defendant's risk of failure on probation.

A PSI is a written summary of the information obtained by a probation officer through interviews with a defendant and through investigation of a defendant's background. PSIs are largely structured documents with probation officers "filling in" standard information about the characteristics of the defendant and the circumstances surrounding his or her arrest. However, PSIs also contain a summary section in which the probation officer, in narrative form, highlights information about the defendant and presents an evaluation of the defendant's chance for successful completion of probation. We treated this summary as an "account" and operationalized our variables based upon the information presented in it.

ANALYSES AND RESULTS

Six factors are significantly related to reported risk of failure on probation. The most influential is prior record of arrests. Defendants with a prior record, on the average, are reported to be riskier than defendants with no prior record. Reporting that a defendant displayed a negative attitude toward the consequences of his or her offense also tends to increase the assigned level of risk of failure on probation. In contrast, risk of failure tends to be lower if the probation officer's account indicates that the defendant was convicted of a standard, less serious offense; the defendant is currently employed; the defendant displayed a positive attitude toward the consequences of his or her offense; the defendant displayed a positive attitude toward his or her future behavior.

However, when a probation officer mentions a positive attitude toward future behavior, he or she also tends to report a positive attitude toward the consequences of the offense and to assign a lower than average risk of failure. Since we are analyzing *accounts* of interviews, we cannot determine whether defendants actually display these two attitudes together or whether probation officers simply *perceive* them as fitting together (and report them together) for less risky defendants. However, we do tentatively conclude that probation officers do display leniency toward female defendants in their accounts of risk of failure on probation.

Race is not related to reported risk of failure on probation; that is, the average risk for black defendants is not significantly different from the average risk for white defendants. While this finding may indicate a true lack of bias in the accounting practices of probation officers, it may also be a function of our sample. The probation agency that we studied supervises a relatively small number of black defendants. Those who are clients live in the predominantly white, middle-class neighborhoods served by the agency. Therefore, the black defendants in our sample may not be the best comparison group for assessing a racial difference in reported risk of failure on probation.

The significant effects for prior record, employment status, and seriousness of offense are important, although not surprising. These findings parallel much of the input-outcome literature on social control decision making. According to the theory of office, the information used *in making* decisions should also be used in *accounting* for these decisions; both actions should reflect the same typologies regarding the attributes of deviant actors. These findings allow for such an interpretation.

The significant effects we find for negative attitude toward the consequences of the offense and positive attitude toward the future are important for two reasons. First, since Spencer found that probation officers cited these factors as important for making decisions, we once again have evidence of a correspondence in the typologies used to make and account for decisions. Second, we believe that these attitudinal variables may be related to the general concepts of "deference" and "demeanor." While we are not arguing that deference and demeanor can be completely reduced to three attitudes, our findings suggest that these attitudes may at least operationalize important dimensions of deference and demeanor.

These analyses, in conjunction with others performed, present a "classic" picture of a high-risk deviant: male, older, not married, a history of deviance, and a negative attitude toward the consequences of his deviance. While race does not have a significant effect as a variable, it is used in combination with other variables for distinguishing accounts of high-risk defendants. The remaining configurations are more of a "mixed bag" of positive and negative elements and convey a less consistent, although interesting, image of high-risk defendants.

A second major observation concerning these configurations is that probation officers are accounting for their high-risk assessments by constructing pictures of defendants which emphasize the relatively more *objective* background and offense variable. Generally, information about attitudes is notable by its *absence*. This is particularly true for positive attitude toward future behavior. The fact that "attitude toward the future not mentioned" occurs in several of the configurations means that this absence of information is unique to high-risk defendants. The only attitudinal information that is used to any extent is negative—specifically, negative attitude toward the consequences. Of the background and offense variables, probation officers generally use information about defendants' *behavior* to justify high-risk assessments. Most of the configurations contain information about either the presence of a prior record, a serious current offense, or both. Thus, probation officers typically justify their predictions about defendants' future behavior by highlighting information about defendants' present and past criminal behavior.

DISCUSSION AND CONCLUSION

We began our analysis by posing two general questions. First, we proposed that social control agents would use typologies of deviants to account for their decisions. Therefore, we asked: what typologies are reflected in probation officers' written accounts for their assessments of risk in PSIs? Combining insights from the input-outcome literature and the interactionist literature, we analyzed the patterning of information in probation officers' reports about defendants. At the level of individual variables, the indication is that prior record, seriousness of offense, negative attitude toward the consequences of the offense, positive attitude toward the future, and (possibly) gender are significantly and independently related to reported risk for probation. Additional analyses show how the individual pieces are joined together in coherent and theoretically meaningful patterns.

Based on the results of the analyses, it appears as though information about prior record, seriousness of offense, and negative attitude toward the consequences of the offense are central dimensions around which more complex typologies of high-risk defendants are constructed. The types include additional pieces of information (e.g., race, gender, age, marital status) that fill out the portraits of deviant actors in use by probation officers.

Our second research question was whether control agents' theory of office would lead them to account for their decisions in ways which would reflect their perspectives on work. Others have found that probation officers tend to use either a legalistic, social control perspective or a casework, counseling perspective in their work. We found evidence of *both* of these perspectives in the accounts produced by the probation officers in our study. The importance they placed on prior record and seriousness of current offense is consistent with a legalistic focus on offense-related factors. However, their use of negative attitude toward the consequences and, particularly, positive attitude toward future behavior is consistent with a casework focus on motivational factors related to reforming defendants. Rosecrance argues that in writing PSIs, probation officers want to establish and maintain credibility before an audience composed of the probation administration, prosecutors, and judges. Given the diversity of this audience, then, the mixture of elements that we found may represent an attempt to make decisions appear reasonable to all concerned parties. Unfortunately, lacking comparative data about the typologies of these other agents, we do not know if this mixture of perspectives is unique to probation officers. Clearly, comparative research will be necessary to identify the variety and the nature of typologies employed by agents in different positions within the criminal justice system.

Finally, although our concern here was with how agents account for decisions, our findings parallel studies of the factors that affect the outcome of social control decision making. Early ethnomethodological research argued that knowledge of the formal structure of a bureaucracy is of little help in understanding the routine activities of its agents. However, we have found that the records produced as part of these routine activities can be used to investigate this formal structure. Although accounts of decisions are separate from the actual decisions they document, both are products of the organizational typologies shared by members of rate-producing agencies as part of their theory of office. These typologies themselves are influenced by factors related to the structure of the rate-producing agencies as well as factors related to the training backgrounds of social control agents. This suggests that typologies may actually mediate the influence of macrolevel variables on social control decision making and accounts of those decisions.

Our use of the concept of theory of office provides an opportunity for comparative work on social reactions. As mentioned above, additional research needs to be done to identify the variety of typologies used by the different agents within the criminal justice system. In addition, it would also be informative to compare typologies *across* deviant processing systems. By systematically comparing the typologies used to account for decisions in these diverse settings, we can gain valuable insights about the operation and structure of the various social control agencies and the perspectives of their agents. Such data provide the opportunity to develop a general model of social reactions based on typologies, accounts, and the theory of office.

A Critical Look at the Idea of Boot Camp as a Correctional Reform

MERRY MORASH

LILA RUCKER

IN several states, correctional boot camps have been used as an alternative to prison in order to deal with the problem of prison overcrowding and public demands for severe treatment. Correctional boot camps are styled after the military model for basic training, and similar to basic training, the participants are primarily young males. However, the "recruits" are offenders, although usually nonviolent and first-time ones. Boot camps vary in their purpose, but even when they are instituted primarily to reduce overcrowding, the implicit assumption is that their programs are of equal or greater deterrent or rehabilitative value than a longer prison sentence.

By the end of 1988, boot camps were operating in one county (Orleans Parish, Louisiana) and in eight states (Georgia, Oklahoma, Mississippi, Louisiana, South Carolina, New York, Florida, and Michigan), they were planned in three states (North Carolina, Kansas, and New Hampshire), and they were being considered in at least nine other states. The model was also being considered for a large number of youthful Detroit offenders. And in the summer of 1989, the boot camp model was put forth by the House Crime Subcommittee chairman as a potential national strategy for treating drug abusers.

The popular image of military boot camp stresses strict and even cruel discipline, hard work, and authoritarian decision making and control by a drill sergeant. It should be noted that this image does not necessarily conform to either current practices in the U.S. military or to all adaptations of boot camp in correctional settings. However, in a survey of existing correctional boot camp programs, Parent found commonality in the use of strict discipline, physical training, drill and ceremony, military bearing and courtesy, physical labor, and summary punishment for minor misconduct. Some programs have combined selected elements of the military boot camp model with more traditional forms of rehabilitation. In Oklahoma, for example, the paramilitary structure, including the use of regimentation, has been only one aspect of an otherwise "helping, supportive environment" that is considered by the administration to be a prerequisite if "change is to last or have any carry over." In Michigan, the major emphasis has been on developing the "work ethic" by using various motivational tactics (e.g., chants), strong discipline, and rehabilitation. All participants work from 8:00 a.m. to 3:30 p.m. daily; evenings involve educational and therapeutic programs. When more traditional methods of rehabilitation are included, a consideration of the boot camp idea is more complex, requiring an analysis of both the costs and benefits of mixing the imagery or the reality of a boot camp approach with other measures.

Regardless of the actual degree to which a militaristic, basic training model has been emphasized, the press has taken this emphasis as primary and usually has portrayed it in a positive light. Numerous stories have been printed under titles such as "Boot Camp—In Prison: An

From "A Critical Look at the Idea of Boot Camp as a Correctional Reform" by M. Morash and L. Rucker, 1990, *Crime and Delinquency*, 36, pp. 204-222. Copyright 1990 by Sage Publications, Inc. Reprinted by permission.

Experiment Worth Watching," "New York Tests a Boot Camp for Inmates," " 'Squeeze You Like a Grape': In Georgia, a Prison Boot Camp Sets Kids Straight," and "Some Young U.S. Offenders Go to 'Boot Camp'—Others Are Put in Adult Jails." The text similarly has reflected a positive evaluation of the approach. For example, Raspberry wrote of the Louisiana boot camp that "the idea [is] to turn a score of law-breakers into disciplined, authority-respecting men." He quoted the warden: "We're giving an inmate a chance to get out of prison in 90 days instead of seven years. But you're making him work for it. . . . We keep them busy from the time they wake up until they fall asleep with chores that include such sillinesses as cleaning latrines with a toothbrush." The warden concluded that the approach "teaches them self-discipline and self-control, something many of these men have never had." Similarly, Martin wrote about the New York program:

Days are 16 hours long, and two-mile runs and calisthenics on cold asphalt are daily staples. Work is chopping down trees or worse. The discipline recalls Parris Island. . . . Those who err may be given what is genteelly termed "a learning experience," something like carrying large logs around with them everywhere they go or, perhaps, wearing baby bottles around their necks.

Life's coverage of the Georgia program included the following statement by one of the sergeants: "[Here] being scared is the point. You have to hit a mule between the eyes with a two-by-four to get his attention . . . and that's exactly what we're doing with this program."

The imagery of the people that we send to boot camp as deserving of dehumanizing treatment is in itself troubling, but even more so in light of the fact that the inmates are disproportionately minorities and underclass members. The boot camp idea also raises the disturbing question: Why would a method that has been developed to prepare people to go into war, and as a tool to manage legal violence, be considered as having such potential in deterring or rehabilitating offenders? Wamsley concluded from a review of officers' manuals and prior research that military basic training is designed to pro-

mote fundamental values of military subculture, including

(1) acceptance of all-pervasive hierarchy and deference patterns; (2) extreme emphasis on dress, bearing, and grooming; (3) specialized vocabulary; (4) emphasis on honor, integrity, and professional responsibility; (5) emphasis on brotherhood; (6) fighter spirit marked by aggressive enthusiasm; and (7) special reverence for history and traditions.

WHAT HAS BEEN TRIED AND WHAT WORKS IN CORRECTIONS?

The correctional boot camp model has been touted as a new idea. However, militarism, the use of hard labor, and efforts to frighten offenders—most recently surfacing in the "Scared Straight" programs—have a long history in prison settings. We will focus first on militarism. In 1821, John Cray, the deputy keeper of the newly constructed Auburn Prison, moved away from the use of solitary confinement when suicides and mental breakdowns increased. As an alternative, he instituted a military regime to maintain order in overcrowded prisons. The regime, which was based in part on his experiences as a Canadian army officer, required downcast eyes, lockstep marching, no talking or other communication among prisoners, and constant activity under close supervision. The issue for Cray and his contemporaries was the prevention of crime "through fear of punishment; the reformation of offenders being of minor consideration."

Neither Cray's attempts nor those of his Pennsylvania cohorts, however, achieved either deterrence or reform. During the Progressive era, there was a shift away from the sole emphasis on punishment. At Elmira Reformatory, Zebulon Brockway added a new twist to Cray's militaristic regulations, certain of which (lockstep marching and rules of silence) had fallen into disrepute because they were now seen as debasing, humiliating, and destructive of initiative. By 1896, the industrial reformatory at Elmira had "well-coordinated discipline which centered around the grading and marking system, an honest application of the indeterminate sentence, trade and academic schools, military organization and calisthenic exercises." Similar to many of the contemporary boot camps, at Elmira the philosophy was to combine both rehabilitation approaches and work with military discipline and physical activity to, among other things, improve self-esteem. However, the legacy of Brockway's Elmira Reformatory was not a move toward rehabilitation. Instead, the militaristic atmosphere set the stage for abusive punishment, and the contradiction between military discipline and rehabilitation was apparent.

Some might counter the argument that the militaristic approach opens the door for abusive punishment by pointing out that in contemporary correctional settings, physical punishment and harm are eliminated. However, as Johnson noted, nonphysical abuse can be viewed as a "civilized" substitute. Also, in some cases physical abuse is a matter of definition, as is seen in the accounts of dropouts from one contemporary boot camp. They reported being treated like "scum," working 18-hour days, being refused permission to use the bathroom, being provoked to aggression by drill instructors, being forced to push a bar of soap along the floor with their noses, and being forced to participate in an exercise called "air raids" in which trainees run and dive face down, landing on their chests with arms stretched out to their sides. At least in some settings, the military model has provided a legitimization of severe punishment. It has opened the door for psychological and even physical abuse that would be rejected as cruel and unusual punishment in other correctional settings.

Turning now to work in correctional settings, its persistent use has been supported by its congruence with alternative objectives, including punishment, incapacitation, rehabilitation, and control inside the institution. However, the form of work at a particular time has not been influenced just by ideals and objectives but by basic economic forces. For example, in order to protect private enterprise, the treadmill was used to occupy offenders following prohibitions against the use of prison labor. Also, in the nineteenth century, a major purpose of imprisonment was to teach the regular work habits demanded by employers. In contemporary discussions of correctional boot camp programs, work has been justified as both punitive and rehabilitative, as both exemplifying the harsh result of breaking the law and teaching the "work ethic." However, the economic constraints imposed by limited budgeting for rehabilitation efforts and the shrinking number of jobs for unskilled workers have shaped the form of work. Thus, hard physical labor, which has no transfer to the contemporary job market, has been the choice in correctional boot camps.

Further criticism of the form of work used in the boot camp settings rests on empirical research. The literature on work programs in general has not supported the conclusion that they produce a decrease in recidivism. Especially pertinent to the present analysis, in a recent article Maguire, Flanagan, and Thornberry showed that labor in a correctional institution was unrelated to recidivism after prisoner differences were taken into account. The exception was work programs that actually provided employment. Based on an extensive review of the literature, Gendreau and Ross further specified the characteristics of correctional work programs that were related to lower recidivism: "Work programs must enhance practical skills, develop interpersonal skills, minimize prisonization, and ensure that work is not punishment alone." Clearly, the evaluation literature contradicts the idea that hard, often meaningless, labor in the boot camp setting has some positive effect.

Moreover, although negative attitudes and lack of the work ethic might be one influence on the choice of economic crime instead of a job, structural arguments have provided alternative explanations. For example, Wilson documented that low-skilled minorities have been hardest hit by deindustrialization of the national labor force and changes in the geographic location of industries. The labor surplus in low-technology fields, and the strength of general social and psychological factors thought to cause criminal behavior, have been found to counteract most offender work programs. In a supporting ethnography, Sullivan showed that the slightly greater availability of jobs in white, working-class neighborhoods explained residents' lesser criminality; in black, lower-class neighborhoods where there were no work opportunities, males in their late teens used robbery as a regular source of income. Altering men's attitudes toward work does nothing to combat these structural deficiencies.

The "Scared Straight" programs, a contemporary version of correctional efforts intended to deter offenders through fright, also are not supported by empirical research. In a San Quentin program of this type, older adolescent participants were arrested less often but for more serious crimes than a comparison group. An evaluation of a similar New Jersey program showed that participants were more seriously delinquent than a control group. On the surface, an evaluation of a "tough" detention regime in British detention centers suggests that although there were no increases in recidivism, there also were no decreases. However, although the British detention center programs incorporated such "military" approaches as strict discipline, drill, and parades, a primary focus was on staff being personally helpful to the youth. Also, humiliating and punitive staff reactions were prohibited by general guidelines. Thus, the British detention center model departed markedly from many of the U.S. models. In general, then, the program elements of militarism, hard labor, and fear engendered by severe conditions do not hold much promise, and they appear to set the stage for abuse of authority.

MILITARY BOOT CAMPS

The idea of boot camp as applied in correctional settings is often a simplification and exaggeration of an outdated system of military training that has been examined and rejected as unsatisfactory by many experts and scholars and by the military establishment itself. The difficulties that the military has discovered with the traditional boot camp model, and the resulting implications for reforms, could be instructive to people in search of positive correctional measures.

A number of difficulties with what will be referred to as the "traditional" military boot camp approach that is now mimicked in correctional settings were uncovered by a task force appointed in the 1970s. The first difficulty with the traditional boot camp approach involved inconsistent philosophies, policies, and procedures. Ten years after the task force report was published, a follow-up study provided further insight into the problem of inconsistency and the related patterns of unreasonable leadership and contrived stressful situations. The study documented the "severe effects" of lack of predictability in such areas as standards for cleanliness and how cadence was called. According to the study, "predictability and reasonableness contribute to trainee self-esteem, sense of being valued by the unit and commitment to the organization." Further, "when authority is arbitrarily imposed, or when leaders lead strictly by virtue of their power or authority, the result is often anger and disrespect." Also, "dysfunctional stress [which results when work is irrelevant or contrived], heightens tensions, shortens tempers, and increases the probability of abuse while generally degrading the effectiveness of training." By contrast, "functional" stress is legitimate and work related, resulting from such instances as "the mental and physical stress of a tactical road march."

The second difficulty that the task force identified with traditional boot camp training was a widespread "we-versus-they" attitude and the related view that trainees were deserving of degrading treatment. The we-versus-they attitude was manifested by different behavioral and/or dress standards for trainees and for other personnel. Specifically, trainees were given "skinhead" haircuts and were prohibited from swearing and shouting, and physical training was used as punishment.

Aside from the investigative reports sponsored by the military, empirical studies of the effects of military boot camps, the effects of physical training (which is a major component of many correctional boot camp programs), and learning in general have provided relevant findings. Empirical evidence regarding the psychological impact of traditional military basic training on young recruits between the ages of 18 and 22 has demonstrated that "there was no increase in scores on ego-strength, or any other evidence of beneficial psychological effects accruing from basic training." Administration of the MMPI to recruits revealed that "the change in the shape of the [MMPI] profiles suggests that aggressive, impulsive, and energetic features became slightly more prominent." The authors concluded that the changes on the subscales imply that

more callous attitudes, a tendency to ignore the needs of others, and feelings of self-importance increase slightly during basic training. The recruits appear less prone to examine their own responsibility for conflicts, and more ready to react aggressively.

The importance of this finding is heightened by the conclusion of Gendreau, Grant, and Leipciger that components of self-esteem that were good predictors of recidivism include the very same characteristics, namely, "self-centered, exploitive of others, easily led, and anxious to please." Sonkin and Walker also speculated that basic training in the military can result in the transfer of violent solutions to family settings. Eisenberg and Micklow therefore proposed that military basic training be modified to include classes on "communication skills, stress reduction, and anger management." Although correctional boot camps do not provide training in the use of weapons or physical assault, they promote an aggressive model of leadership and a conflict-dominated style of interaction that could exacerbate tendencies toward aggression.

In another empirical study of military basic training, Wamsley contrasted the effects of Air Force Aviation Cadet Pre-Flight Training School with Air Force Officer's Training School. The Cadet School employed harsh techniques—including such activities as head shaving, marching miles in stiff shoes, and impromptu exercises as physical punishment—to inculcate basic values and eliminate the "unfit." After one week, 33 percent of recruits left. Wamsley wrote that "those with low capacities for anxiety, insufficient self-esteem to withstand and discredit abuse, inability to control or suppress anger, or those with latent neuroses or psychoses literally 'cracked' under the stress, and attempted suicides and psychiatric referrals were not uncommon." The purpose of constant exhortations to "get eager, mister" or "get proud,

Raunch" was to promote an aggressive fighter spirit, and the "common misery and despair created a bond" among the trainees.

Increased aggression and a bond among inmates are not desired outcomes of correctional boot camps, so again the efficacy of using the military boot camp model is in question. Moreover, it is unlikely that the offenders in correctional boot camps are more mentally healthy than Air Force recruits. What is the effect of using such techniques when there is no escape valve through dropping out of the program? And, if only the best-adjusted stay, what is accomplished by the program? The contrast of the Cadet School with the Officer's Training School, which did not use humiliation and severe physical conditions and punishment, provides convincing evidence of the ineffectiveness of such an approach to training people. Wamsley concluded that there was a "lack of a clear utility for Pre-Flight's intense socialization" and that the "socialization process was brutally expensive in human terms and produced exaggerated forms of behavior which were not clearly related to effective task accomplishments."

Additional research has shown that positive improvements in self-esteem result from physical training primarily when the environment is supportive. For example, Hilyer and Mitchell demonstrated that college students with low self-concepts who received physical fitness training in a helpful, facilitative, supportive environment demonstrated an increase in self-concept scores. The improvement was two and one-half times as great as that of low-concept peers who received physical fitness training and no support.

Also contradicting the negatively oriented training strategy that is characteristic of the old-style military boot camp model, virtually no empirically supported criminological theories have suggested that aggressive and unpredictable reactions by authority figures encourage prosocial behavior. The opposite has been promulgated by most learning theorists. For instance, Satir concluded that learning happens only when a person feels valued and is valued, when he or she feels like a connected part of the human race. Feelings of self-worth can only flourish in an atmosphere in which individual differences are appreciated and mistakes are tolerated; communication is direct, clear, specific, and honest; rules are flexible, human, appropriate, and subject to change; and links to society are open. Finally, there has been considerable theory and research showing that antisocial behavior is increased when authority figures provide aggressive models for behavior. Research in the sociology of sport has provided further evidence that physical training under the direction of an authoritarian trainer increases aggression.

There is no systematic evidence of the degree to which the problems in traditional-style military boot camps are manifested in correctional settings, but there is evidence that they do occur. The introductory descriptions of the correctional boot camp model clearly reveal a tendency for some of the "drill sergeants" to use negative leadership. Telephone interviews with representatives of nine correctional boot camps show a tendency to focus on "tearing down the individuals and then building them back up." Reflective of this philosophy are negative strategies alluded to earlier, such as the use of debasing "welcoming speeches," the "chair position," and "learning experiences" that require men to wear baby bottles around their necks or to carry tree limbs with them all day.

Correctional boot camps also provide settings conductive to high levels of unpredictability and contrived stress. In one program, dropouts, current trainees, and parolees who had completed the program all reported that "differences between DI [drill instructor] styles made it tough to avoid trouble. Trainees' beds may be made to satisfy DI A, but at shift change, if DI B doesn't approve of that particular style, trainees are punished." As further illustration, another inmate reported that on the first day of participation in the boot camp, he was told that he had quit and could not participate. When the inmate sat down for the rest of the day, he was reportedly "kicked out for sitting down," and his having left the program was listed as voluntary. The inmate reported that he had tried to participate but that the drill instructor kept telling him that he had quit. The interviewer reported that at the time of the interview, the offender was "still confused as to what actually had happened that day."

It is true that, as proponents of correctional boot camps claim, many military recruits feel that their survival of basic training is evidence of maturity and a major achievement in their lives. However, the sense of achievement is linked to the notion that the experience is the first step in preparing them for the unique role of a soldier. Moreover, military boot camp is intended as just a prelude to acquaint the recruits with their new environment, in which they will take more control of their lives. It is not obvious that the boot camp experience alone, including elements of capricious and dehumanizing treatment, would be seen in such a positive light by inmate participants.

Clearly, the view that boot camp is just the first step in a socialization process has not been carried over into the correctional setting. While nearly all programs reported either regular or intensive probation or parole periods following release, none of the postrelease programs have had the capability to provide the continuous and multifaceted support network inherent in being a member of the military "family" or process. Postrelease programs are not designed to provide either the tightly knit structure or the guaranteed work that characterize military life.

It could be argued that the purpose of correctional boot camp is not to bind soldiers to their leaders or to develop group solidarity. Thus, the failure of the outmoded military boot camp model to achieve these results may not be a serious concern. Even if we accept this argument, the research on military basic training raises serious questions about the potential for undesirable outcomes, including increased aggression.

STEREOTYPES OF MASCULINITY AND CORRECTIONAL MEASURES

The very idea of using physically and verbally aggressive tactics in an effort to "train" people to act in a prosocial manner is fraught with contradiction. The idea rests on the assumption that forceful control is to be valued. The other unstated assumption is that alternative methods for promoting prosocial behavior, such as the development of empathy or a stake in conformity (e.g., through employment), are not equally valued. Feminist theorists have noted the societywide valuation of the stereotypically masculine characteristics of forcefulness and aggression and of the related devaluation of the stereotypically feminine characteristics of empathy and cooperative group behavior. Heidensohn specifically wrote that programs like boot camp have been "designed to reinforce conventional male behavior" and that they range from "quasi-militaristic short, sharp shocks to adventure training."

There is little doubt that the military is a male-dominated institution and that there is a military ideology that rejects both women and stereotypically female characteristics. As Enloe wrote, there is a common assumption that "the military . . . is a *male* preserve, run by men and for men according to masculine ideas and relying solely on *man* power." In some military settings, terms such as "little girl," "woman," and "wife" have been routinely used to negatively label a trainee who is viewed as having failed in some way. Traditional marching chants have included degrading comments about women, and sexist terms for women and their body parts have been common in military settings. Stiehm concluded from her research that even after the mandated inclusion of women in the U.S. Military Academy, considerable derogatory name-calling and ridicule of women were common. The implication is that to fail is to be female, or, conversely, to succeed is to be aggressive, dominant, and therefore unquestionably "male."

One might argue that name-calling is not used in correctional settings. Given the military background of many correctional staff involved in the reforms and the popular image of boot camp experiences, the degree to which such an antiwoman attitude exists is an important empirical question. Aside from overt rejection of women and femaleness, the boot camp model, with its emphasis on unquestioned authority and aggressive interactions and its de-emphasis on group cooperation and empathy, promotes a limited image of the "true man."

It is not surprising that few have questioned the distorted image of masculinity embodied in the idea of boot camp, for this imagery is im-plicit in the assumptions of many criminological theories, and it is shared by many offenders. Focusing on criminologists, Naffine showed how several major theories have presented male offenders' aggression and assertiveness in a positive light while they have devalued characteristics associated with women. To be more specific, major theories have accepted the stereotypical characteristics of men as normal and have presented women as dependent, noncompetitive, and passive. Naffine's analysis revealed the "curious result of extolling the virtues of the male, as a good criminal, and treating conforming women as if they were the socially deviant group." This result has been echoed in the use of a military model that similarly extols the virtues that are often associated with both masculinity and aggression in our society.

Writing about images of masculinity among economically marginalized men, who are overrepresented in the offender population, Messerschmidt built on the notion that in our society "both masculinity and power are linked with aggression/violence while femininity and powerlessness are linked with nonviolence." He went on to note that as a result of the unavailability of jobs that are not degrading, powerless men seek out alternative avenues through which to exercise their masculinity. Other supports of criminality include an orientation toward "exploitative individualism," as opposed to any caring ties to group members, and male bonding, which is the ritual rejection of "weakness" associated with femininity. This rejection is demonstrated through activities like gang fights. Again, there is a parallel with the stereotype of masculinity embodied in the boot camp model. Specifically, Eisenhart has described military training's emphasis on self-sufficiency and the avoidance of attachment to others.

The irony in emphasizing an aggressive model of masculinity in a correctional setting is that these very characteristics may explain criminality. Theorists working in the area of crime causation have focused on both the identification with male stereotypical traits and roles, which are consistent with illegal behavior, and the frustration that males feel when they cannot achieve these stereotypes because of low social status. The empirical support to link stereotypical masculinity with criminality has been inconsistent. There is some evidence, however, that female stereotypical characteristics predict prosocial behavior.

An additional irony is found in the inclusion of women in correctional boot camps. Holm observed that in the military, "women . . . suffered from role identification problems when put through military training programs designed traditionally 'to make men out of boys,' " programs that had "more to do with the rites of manhood than the requirements of service jobs." There is serious doubt about the efficacy of placing women in a militaristic environment that emphasizes masculinity and aggressiveness and that in some cases rejects essentially prosocial images and related patterns of interaction associated with the stereotype of femininity.

ALTERNATIVE MODELS IN CORRECTIONS

Correctional policymakers and program staff are not alone in their application of the traditional boot camp model as an approach for training people outside of military settings. Looking again at news reports, we see that the boot camp type of training has been accepted in a variety of organizations as a means to increase the productivity, skill levels, efficiency, and effectiveness of participants. Such enterprises are as diverse as the Electronic Data Systems Corporation, the Nick Bollettieri Tennis Academy, and Japan's Managers' Training School. In keeping with the boot camp model, participants are made to endure humiliation so that a bond can develop with the teacher. There appear to be social forces supporting acceptance of the general idea that the boot camp model is appropriate as a method for promoting training and human development. In spite of the societal pressures to use such a model, our assessment has a number of negative implications for the application of boot camps in correctional settings.

The first implication is based on the research on boot camp and the development of human potential in a military setting. At certain times and in certain geographic locations, military personnel have been charged with training and employing populations that are not markedly dissimilar from the economically marginalized young men and women that populate the prisons. They also have been engaged in the imprisonment of people for the violation of criminal laws. A continued examination of their techniques and outcomes could provide further instruction. As a starting point, it might be noted that in the military, the version of boot camp used in correctional settings is not commonly viewed as an effective correctional measure. Furthermore, through Project 10,000, the military has been successful in integrating poorly educated recruits into their own workforce, although often in relatively low-skill positions that restricted transfer to the civilian workforce. Contrary to critics' anticipation of disciplinary problems with poorly educated recruits, less than 5 percent of the participants failed to conform to military rules and regulations. The approach to integration involved traditional methods of literacy training coupled with individualized teaching geared to a specific job assignment. This approach is consistent with the findings that we have reviewed on effective work programs in correctional settings.

A second implication of our analysis of the idea of boot camp is that we need to reconsider correctional alternatives. Harris wrote that the "development of a more humane, caring and benevolent society involves a continuing quest for higher standards of decency and good will and an ever decreasing resort to . . . degrading sanctions." For her, the continued and fundamental interdependence of self and other is primary, and she thinks in terms of "persuasion, nonviolent action, positive reinforcement, personal example, peer support and the provision of life-sustaining and life-enhancing services and opportunities." It is noteworthy that the rehabilitation models of corrections that many experts have publicly rejected reflect a de-emphasis on the questionable stereotypes of "how to be a man" that are promoted by the boot camp model.

A third implication has to do with the evaluation of existing and planned boot camp programs. A number of potential, negative outcomes of a boot camp environment have been identified. One of these is increased aggression, including physical and nonphysical punishment, directed against offenders by prison staff. Also included are increased offender aggression, a devaluation of women and so-called feminine traits (e.g., sensitivity), and other negative effects of an unpredictable, authoritarian atmosphere. In addition to considering these effects directly, program evaluation should monitor the degree to which the environment is characterized by inconsistent standards and expectations, dysfunctional stress, a we-versus-they attitude, and negative leadership styles. Furthermore, because correctional boot camp programs mix the elements of a military model with less coercive methods of human change, it is important to design research that reveals the actual program elements that produce both desired and undesired program outcomes.

SUGGESTED READINGS

Berk, Richard A., Sheldon L. Messinger, David Rauma, and J. E. Bercochea. 1983. "Prisons as Self-Regulating Systems: A Comparison of Historical Patterns in California for Male and Female Offenders." *Law & Society Review* 17:547-86.

Carlen, Pat. 1983. *Women's Imprisonment*. London: Routledge & Kegan Paul.

Clemmer, Donald. 1940. *The Prison Community*. New York: Holt, Rinehart and Winston.

Giallombardo, Rose. 1966. *Society of Women: A Study of Women's Prison*. New York: John Wiley.

Glaser, Daniel. 1969. *The Effectiveness of a Prison and Parole System*. Indianapolis, IN: Bobbs-Merrill.

Hawkins, Gordon. 1977. *The Prison: Policy and Practice*. Chicago: University of Chicago Press.

Ignatieff, Michael. 1978. *A Just Measure of Pain: The Penitentiary in the Industrial Revolution, 1750-1850*. New York: Columbia University Press.

————. 1981. "State, Civil Society and Total Institution: A Critique of Recent Social Histories of Punishment." Pp. 153-92 in *Crime and Justice: An Annual Review of Research,* edited by Michael Tonry and Norval Morris. Vol. 3. Chicago: University of Chicago Press.

Irwin, John. 1980. *Prisons in Turmoil*. Boston: Little, Brown.

Johnson, Richard. 1981. *Condemned to Die: Life Under the Sentence of Death*. New York: Elsevier.

Morris, Norval. 1974. *The Future of Imprisonment*. Chicago: University of Chicago Press.

Newman, Graeme. 1978. *The Punishment Response*. Philadelphia: J. B. Lippincott.

Rafter, Nicole Hahn. 1985. *Partial Justice: Women in State Prisons, 1800-1935*. Boston: Northeastern University Press.

Rothman, David J. 1971. *The Discovery of the Asylum*. Boston: Little, Brown.

————. 1980. *Conscience and Convenience*. Boston: Little, Brown.

Sherman, M. E. and Gordon Hawkins. 1981. *Imprisonment in America: Choosing the Future*. Chicago: University of Chicago Press.

Ward, David and Gene Kassebaum. 1965. *Women's Prison: Sex and Social Structure*. Chicago: Aldine.

Wright, Erik Olin. 1973. *The Politics of Punishment: A Critical Analysis of Prisons in America*. New York: Routledge.

Zimring, Franklin E. and Gordon Hawkins. 1991. *The Scale of Imprisonment*. Chicago: University of Chicago Press.

QUESTIONS FOR DISCUSSION AND WRITING

1. Contrast the histories of American corrections presented in the essays by Cullen and Travis and by Jacobs. Contrast the major themes in corrections in the nineteenth century with those in the twentieth century.

2. What do the two histories suggest about the future of American corrections? Do you think our society will turn to a more rehabilitative approach in the twenty-first century? Explain why or why not.

3. What feature of prisons does Sykes identify as critical to understanding why prisons have problems with crime, violence, and sexual deviance among prisoners? Would Sykes maintain that these problems can be eradicated?

4. What is the significance of Schrag's inmate role configurations? How could information on the development of role configurations assist the administration of prisons?

5. Based on the Irwin and Toch essays, describe any evidence that supports the idea that the pains of imprisonment are severe. Is there any evidence to the contrary?

6. The essay by Hunt and his colleagues indicates that the inmate social structure in many prisons has changed in recent years. How would you describe these changes? What influence might the changes have on prison security or the difficulty of "doing time"?

7. Does the Petersilia and Turner study suggest that intensive probation will be a major solution to corrections in the future? Explain why or why not.

8. The Drass and Spencer essay documents decision-making processes by probation officers. What does this study suggest about factors influencing their exercise of discretion?

9. The article by Morash and Rucker describes boot camps. What evidence does the essay offer in support of the boot camp idea?

10. If correctional agencies in the United States increasingly adopt measures like intensive probation (Petersilia and Turner) and boot camps (Morash and Rucker), what will be the likely benefits for offenders and for the society? What will be the likely costs (monetary and nonmonetary)?

Index

Rehabilitation;
Retribution (desert)

Q

Quakers, 287, 383-384, 386, 388

R

Race:
  assault and, 346
  bail system and, 344
  boot camps and, 467
  capital punishment and, 339,
    341, 342-343, 344
  drug law enforcement and,
    346-350
  gender and, 366, 368
  historical and social context
    and, 345-350
  homicide and, 342, 346
  institutional racism, 340
  judges and juries and, 279-280,
    318
  leniency and, 327, 339, 343,
    344, 345-346, 348-350
  mental illness and, 366
  number of crimes committed
    and, 340
  parole and, habitual offenders
    and, 363-364
  plea bargaining and, 294
  police and:
    arrest, 172, 174-175, 344
    deadly force usage, 191-193
    foot patrols, 201
    ghetto patrolmen, 178-179,
      192
  prisons and:
    gangs and, 445-446, 449-453
    inmate identity and, 432-433
    reform of, 399
    staff of, 401-402
  probation and, 318, 463-464
  public defenders and, 278, 298
  rape and, 346
  robbery and, 346
  rural vs. urban areas and, 361,
    368
  sentencing and. *See* Sentencing,
    race and

  social costs of sanctions and,
    356
  southern courts and, 321-322
  victimless crimes and, 346-350
  See also Black ghettos
Rackets, in prisons, 420-421, 427,
  428-429
Radicalism, 17
RAND Corporation study, 102,
  104
Rape:
  police and, 182, 223
  public defender's view of, 295
  public punitiveness felt toward,
    154
  race and, 346
  sentencing and, 325, 328, 361
  See also Sex offenders
Reactive law enforcement, 34-35,
  70, 222-224, 228-229, 230
Recidivism:
  assault and, 100
  boot camps and, 468-469, 470
  criminal sanctions and, 135-
    136, 137-138, 145, 157
  custody duration and, 78
  domestic violence and, 70,
    75-76, 80-81, 82, 83
  gender and, 364
  individual crime rates of
    recidivists, 99
  inmate climate and, 158
  misdemeanor, 315
  offender characteristics and,
    422, 423
  predicting, 98-100, 142-143.
    See also Identification
    (sociological)
  property crimes and, 100
  rehabilitation and, 113-123
    counseling/therapy, 115-
      116, 119-120, 137, 139
    educational and vocational
      training, 114-115
    Maconochie's experiment,
      390
    medical treatment, 118
    milieu therapy, 117-118,
      119, 137
    minimum- vs. maximum-
      security confinement,
      118

    overview of, 122-123, 124-125,
      129, 131-145
    parole (intensive), 120, 122
    parole vs. prison, 120
    probation (intensive),
      120-121, 454-455,
      458-460
    probation vs. prison, 120
    sentencing length, 118-119
  security levels and, 118
  sentence length and, 118-119
  sources of variation in, 135
  treatment in prison and, 97
  work programs and, 468-469
Records, alteration of, 270
Reformatories, positivism and, 15
Rehabilitation, 108-145, 157-158
  appropriateness of type of,
    136-137, 138-139, 140,
    143-145
  bureaucratization vs., 400
  by boot camps, 467-468
  by casework, 115, 116, 119
  by counseling/therapy. *See*
    Counseling/therapy
  by educational training,
    114-115, 129, 430-431
  by milieu therapy, 116-118,
    119, 129, 137
  by military service, 115
  by moral therapy, 129-130
  by operant conditioning, 119,
    138, 389, 391
  by parole, 120, 122, 129
  by probation, 120-121, 129
  by punishment, 129, 130-131
  by vocational training, 114-115,
    129, 430-431
  colonists and, 379
  conservative ideology and, 124,
    134
  costs of, 122
  criminal justice sanctions and
    setting and, 135-136,
    137-138, 141-142, 145
  decline of ideal of, 124, 134-135
  defendant rehabilitation
    charging policy, 255-256
  defined, 126-128
  deterrence (specific) vs., 127,
    128, 130
  effectiveness of:

negative view, 122-123,
124-125, 129, 131-135,
141-145, 157
positive view, 126, 135-140
*See also specific types of
rehabilitation*
empirical knowledge about,
113, 125-131
history of prisons and:
colonial period, 379
Enlightenment, 382, 383-384
modern era, 395-396
nineteenth century, 385-391
Progressivism, 392-395
incapacitative effect and, 97
incarceration and, 129, 130-131,
414, 417, 419
just deserts vs., 152
juvenile offenders and. *See*
Juvenile offenders,
rehabilitation and
liberal ideology and, 16-17,
134-135
manliness stereotype and,
472-473
Martinson Report, The,
113-123, 131-133
maturation vs., 127, 128
medical model and, 108-112,
118, 123, 124-125, 129
multiple-treatment approach,
129, 130
need principle and, 136, 138,
141, 142, 143-144, 145
outpatient principle for, 111-112
overview of, 46-47, 124, 126,
157-158
politics and, 16-17, 124, 134-135
positivism and, 15
pretrial diversion by, 306-307
punishment vs., 50, 157-158
recidivism and. *See* Recidivism,
rehabilitation and
responsivity principle and,
136-137, 138, 141, 142,
143-144, 145
risk principle and, 136, 138,
140, 141, 142-144, 145
theories of crime and, 128-129
theory of, 126-128
therapeutic attitude and, 110-111
types of, 111, 129-131

welfare and, 115
Relational distance, arrest and,
172, 174
Release costs, 102
Religion, history of punishment
and, 379, 380, 381, 383-388,
391
Republicans. *See* Conservatism
Research methodology, 39
Residential programming, 137, 139
Respect. *See* Disrespect
Responsibility, criminal, 26
Responsivity principle, rehabilitation and, 136-137, 138, 141,
142, 143-144, 145
Restitution, 136, 379
Retribution (desert), 146-159
as fundamental to human
interaction, 153-154
classicism and, 13
commensurate (just) deserts
principle, 149-152
decision-making models and,
319
defined, 146
deterrence and, 147-149
deterrence vs., 152
domestic violence and, 71
effectiveness of, 135
equilibrium restored by,
147-148, 155-157
identification with victim and,
153-154
incapacitation vs., 152
overview of, 47-48, 146-147
priority of, 152
Progressivism and, 392
rehabilitation vs., 152
sentencing and, 149-152, 323
social control functions of
punishment and, 154-158
unscaled penalties vs., 149-150
Rights:
of defendants, 19, 27-29, 275
of prisoners, 399, 409
Riots:
in prisons. *See* Prisons, violence/
uprisings in
"normal" court operations and,
33-34
police order-maintenance
function and, 204

police use of deadly force and,
187
Risk principle:
criminal behavior and, 212-213
rehabilitation and, 136, 138,
140, 141, 142-144, 145
Robbery:
bank, 295
disordered communities and,
204
identifying high-rate offenders,
94-95
offender characteristics, 422
police patrol and, 223
public defender's view of, 293,
294, 295
race and, 346
rate of, 92, 93, 95
recidivist, 100
sentencing and, 325, 328, 361
Rural areas, urban vs., sentencing
and, 328, 358-362, 368
Rush, Benjamin, 383

S

Safe and Clean Neighborhoods
Program, 200
"Scared Straight" programs, 137,
467, 469
Scientific method, positivist
school and, 14
Screening function, 22-23, 24-25,
244, 248-250, 251
Scuffling, 427
Searches, unreasonable, 20, 27
Securities violations, 37
Security, private, 105, 208-209, 224
Security guards, 208-209, 224
Security levels (incarceration),
recidivism and, 118
Selective incapacitation. *See*
Incapacitation, selective
Sentence bargaining, 35, 36-37,
39, 247, 312
Sentencing:
aggregate-offense-based, 85, 88
commission-established
guidelines for, 323-329
conflict theory and, 358, 362
criminal careers and, 88